Consuming Canada
Canada

READINGS IN ENVIRONMENTAL HISTORY

20080

NeW
CANADIAN
READINGS

SERIES EDITOR
J. L. GRANATSTEIN

Titles currently available

CONSUMING CANADA

READINGS IN ENVIRONMENTAL HISTORY

Edited by

CHAD GAFFIELD

University of Ottawa

PAM GAFFIELD

COPP CLARK LTD.
Toronto

ISBN: 0-7730-5449-9

executive editor: Jeff Miller
editor: Barbara Tessman
proofreaders: Pamela Erlichman and Sarah Robertson
design: Susan Hedley, Liz Nyman
cover design: Kyle Gell
cover illustration: A.J. Casson 1898–1992
  October, North Shore 1929
  oil on canvas
  76.4 x 91.8 cm
  McMichael Canadian Art Collection
  Purchase 1985
  1985.15
typesetting: April Haisell
printing and binding: Metropole Litho Inc.

Canadian Cataloguing in Publication Data

Main entry under title:

Consuming Canada

Includes bibliographical references.
ISBN 0-7730-5449-9

1. Canada – Environmental conditions – History.
2. Human ecology – Canada – History.   I. Gaffield,
Chad, 1951–   II. Gaffield, Pam.

GE160.C3C6   1995   333.7'0971   C95-930330-8

Copp Clark Ltd.
2775 Matheson Blvd. East
Mississauga, Ontario
L4W 4P7

Printed and bound in Canada

1 2 3 4 5   5449-9   99 98 97 96 95

FOREWORD

○

Canadians ought to be interested in the environment. We live in a huge land that has cities existing cheek by jowl with wilderness, and generations of families have trundled off to cottages beside pristine lakes summer after summer. And yet, Canadian companies have clear cut forests or strip mined huge tracts of land, while fishermen have all but eliminated the stocks of cod and salmon that once seemed limitless. Meanwhile, scientists warn of the greenhouse effect and the perils of global warming, something to which Canadians, wastefully burning their fossil fuels, contribute each and every day. How have we put ourselves into this mess? How can we get out of it?

This volume, not surprisingly, is better at answering the first question than the second. In this the first reader on Canadian environmental history, Chad and Pam Gaffield have brought together a collection of controversial articles that outlines the reactions of First Nations and white explorers to the astonishing bounty of North America and that traces the apparently inevitable cycles of ruthless exploitation and degradation of resources that followed. Here we can learn what governments did—and did not do—to regulate matters. Here we can discover how Native understanding of various species might have led to wiser choices. Here we can find feminist perspectives, the views of animal rights activists, the approaches of scientists and others in a veritable stew of conflicting approaches. If there is a way out of the environmental difficulties that beset us, it may well lie in these new approaches or in some combination of them. Certainly the old methods have not worked.

Environmental history is a new field of study in Canada (and elsewhere, too), and the articles collected here open up doors that have remained closed far too long. No one who reads this volume in the New Canadian Readings series will have any doubt that Canadian environmental history is well worth study, and is full of possibilities for innovative research.

J.L. Granatstein
General Editor

CONTENTS

○

INTRODUCTION

o

Consuming Canada provides an introduction to the exciting and innovative field of environmental history. The book has three goals: to offer history students a new perspective on the past; to illustrate for students in other programs the value of historical perspectives on current environmental concerns; and to provide an overview for general readers.

In one sense, the ambitions of this book should not require explanation; indeed, Canadians hardly need to be reminded of the importance of the environment. Many observers have even linked the formation of Canada's identity to the need to come to terms with an inhospitable setting. Margaret Atwood's emphasis on "survival" or Northrop Frye's perception of our "deep terror in regard to Nature" are only two of the well-known environmental interpretations of the Canadian psyche.[1]

Canadian historians have traditionally supported these interpretations by connecting our history to the non-human environment. Classic examples include Harold Innis's studies of beaver and cod in his analyses of the staples trade, Arthur Lower's focus on trees in his studies of the forest economy, and Donald Creighton's emphasis on rivers in his influential depiction of the St Lawrence "empire."[2] Revealingly, attention to the environment inspired the title of the book that was the most widely used introductory text between the 1960s and mid-1980s, J.M.S. Careless's *Canada: A Story of Challenge*.[3] The central theme of this book was "the emergence of a Canadian nation out of scattered colonies, in response to the challenge of the vast Canadian land and the forces that have played on its inhabitants."[4]

Only recently, however, have historians in Canada actually begun to undertake serious research in the field of environmental history. Despite their widespread recognition of the importance of the environment in defining the Canadian experience, historians in past decades did not systematically study the characteristics of this importance or how the relationships between humans and the rest of the environment changed over time. For example, in his two books on the cod fishery and the fur trade, Harold Innis devoted a chapter to the cod and one to the beaver but he never demonstrated the relevance of these chapters in his larger interpretations. Similarly, Maurice Careless began his survey text with a chapter on Canada's physical geography but, within his historical analysis, he never went beyond the observation that it was a "challenge" for Canadians to create a nation in this geographic setting. In fact, Careless offers a static and passive image of geography as a stage upon which (human) actors have made Canadian history.

The novelty of this Canadian interest in environmental history may seem surprising given the traditional recognition of the importance of the environment to Canada's past. However, until quite recently, historians emphasized the roles of French and British ideologies and institutions rather than "New World" influences in shaping Canadian history. Unlike their counterparts in the United States, Canadian scholars have tended to reject the idea that the North American environment helped to produce a society quite unlike those in France and Britain. For example, historians have traditionally concluded that Frederick Jackson Turner's classic frontier thesis in American history is inapplicable in Canada; rather than protraying the development of a new democratic and individualistic society in the rugged wilderness, historians stressed the role of large companies and the state in organizing Canadian society even in remote areas. In this view, Canada is best understood in European terms despite its vastly different environment. For example, William Eccles entitled his study of the seventeenth and eighteenth centuries *France in America*, while Carl Berger argued that a sense of Canadian identity emerged in the decades after Confederation within, rather than distinct from, identification with the British empire.[5]

Even the substantial rewriting of Canadian history that began in the early 1970s did not initially challenge the assumption that the environment was largely irrelevant to understanding our past. Early studies of social structure and working-class experience paid little attention to the specificity of the Canadian context. The emergence of cities such as Hamilton and Toronto was compared to the development of cities like Manchester in England and Philadelphia in the United States. Similarly, the "new social histories" of New France situated the origins of Canada within the successsful implantation of French institutions in the St Lawrence Valley. The most widely acclaimed book of the 1970s, Louise Dechêne's *Habitants et marchands de Montréal au XVIIe siècle* argued that imperial authorities completely overcame the New World environment and effectively established Old World forms of religious, social, and political organization that affected everyday family life.[6]

Nonetheless, the new questions and approaches of historians in the 1970s did encourage a rethinking of Canada's past, which opened the way (unintentionally, it should be noted) for research from an environmental perspective. The origins of this development can be traced to the redefinition of the makers of history as including all people rather than simply a dominant minority of the population. In their studies of the working class, women, and ethnic minorities, historians showed that although elites held a disproportionate share of power, they could not completely determine the course of history or even their own destinies. An extension of this conclusion is that the non-human environment (including both the organic and inorganic) has also made history in active ways that go well beyond previous acknowledgements of the roles of animals and geography.[7]

At the same time, historians also began focusing on relationships rather than on isolated people and events. The conviction that social class was not a "thing" but rather a "relationship" was characteristic of a new attempt to study the historical process in terms of interactions that included both conflicts and convergences. Initially, historians limited their studies to the relationships between individuals and groups, but in recent years they have increasingly insisted on the need to analyse the interconnectedness of humans and all other components of the biosphere. Just as scholars became convinced that individuals and groups must be defined in relationship to other individuals and groups, environmental historians in Canada have begun to insist that humans can be understood only by examining their connections to animals, plants, land, water, and the atmosphere.

After redefining the makers of history and then focusing on relationships in the research of the 1970s, historians developed during the next decade a renewed appreciation of the importance of context. Unlike the earlier studies of the "new social history" that examined specific times and places as representative of general patterns, more recent work assumes great complexity and diversity in the local articulations of large historical processes. For example, the experience of industrialization in the nineteenth century has been found to vary widely as specific circumstances affected the meaning of trends such as mechanization. In this sense, no one place can adequately represent the multiple paths of historical experience, and thus historians need to study the specific environments within which general processes took place.[8]

The emphasis on contextual importance has encouraged historians to focus on environmental questions as a way of explaining the relative distinctiveness of time and place. As so effectively shown in recent years by the publication of the three volumes of the *Historical Atlas of Canada*, communities and regions across the country have experienced our national history in diverse and complex ways in keeping with their specific environmental differences and similarities.[9] The goal now is to propose interpretations of our national history that do justice to the complexity and diversity of experience across Canada. This goal differs substantially from the earlier work that considered the Canadian environment simply as a "challenge" for humans to overcome. Historians are now defining the environment as an integrated human and non-human context within which all thought and activity must be situated.

In the same way, scholars are now pursuing the claim that the interplay of Canadians and their specific environment helps explain why Canada's history can be distinguished from that of other countries despite economic, political, social, and cultural similarities. The renewed emphasis on context is apparent in the claim that Canadians have developed a particular ecological sensitivity that differentiates them from other societies; for example, Canadians often argue that their historical experience has given them a "greater respect for nature" than their counterparts in the United States.[10] Whether or not such claims hold up under further historical investigation, it is likely that historians will increasingly study the environment as a way of coming to grips with the importance of context in specifying and explaining the complexity and diversity of historical experience.

The emergence of environmental history as a research field is also associated with the increased prominence of feminist scholars, some of whom have developed theories of ecofeminism in which men and women are perceived to have very different relationships with the environment. Ecofeminism is only now beginning to influence Canadian historical debate, which heretofore has been focused on the relationship between the environment and the actions and ideas of men. It seems likely that the influence of feminist scholarship on environmental history will increase significantly as it has in other fields of historical research since the late 1970s. Similarly, the emergence of gender history and the new history of masculinity should contribute to research on Canada's ecological past, examining, for example, the extent to which the construction of gender identities in various regions of Canada can be linked to the specific environmental relationships of men and women to the woods, the land, or the sea.

In emphasizing the contextualized diversity and complexity of experience, Canadian historians have played an important role in the larger intellectual retreat from linear analyses of change. Across the humanities and sciences, the assumption that scientific certainty can be gained through a step-by-step analysis of isolated, sequentially linked causal events has given way to a new organic, holistic appreciation of the biosphere as illustrated by "fuzzy" thinking among engineers, "chaos" theory among natural scientists, and the different concepts of complexity in many disciplines. Along with other scholars, historians now see the value of distinct "ways of knowing," ranging from the study of quantitative and qualitative evidence to the articulation of "intuition," as discussed in Milton Freeman's article in this volume. This new appreciation of the historical process has led in recent years to a renewed interest in oral history as a way to study many topics in social, economic, cultural, and political history. In the same way, traditional ecological knowledge has become increasingly valued and employed by Canadian researchers in their attempts to understand the environment.

Along with the new concepts and methods used within history and other disciplines, the development of interdisciplinary studies has also been closely associated with the growth of environmental research. Indeed, many scholars define the study of the environment as inherently interdisciplinary, in keeping with the need to examine connections and relationships within any setting. Since the 1970s, historians in Canada have borrowed and adapted theories and methods from the social sciences (especially sociology and anthropology) in their study of social change, but their new environmental interest is inspiring even more extensive co-operation, which includes the sciences. Similarly, the importance of a historical perspective has become clearer to researchers such as geographers and biologists as well as to policy makers.[11] These interdisciplinary trends are evident in colleges and universities both in the history curriculum, where environmental courses are now being established, and in environmental studies programs, where historical perspectives are increasingly included. Not surprisingly, the information highway is now also being used to promote access to information about environmental issues and to facilitate communication among all interested parties.[12]

During the years when scholars began asking new questions and using new approaches that helped prepare the way for the emergence of environmental history as a research field, a series of public debates also encouraged research on environmental issues. Since the 1960s, Canadians have expressed increasing anxiety about the ability to continue natural resource exploitation in the face of factors such as deforestation, fossil fuel exhaustion, and species extinction. At the same time, media attention to environmental degradation increased substantially concerning questions such as acid rain, toxic waste, and ozone depletion. As public debate continued, the hope that improved technology could always provide effective solutions became less and less reassuring; indeed, new technologies led to additional (and often unexpected) forms of degradation. Rural and urban areas, reflecting the not-in-my-backyard syndrome, became increasingly reluctant to deal with society's garbage. Taken together, these trends helped bring to the forefront our relationship to the non-human environment and, by implication, how this relationship has changed over time.

The key role that Native peoples have played in many recent environmental controversies in Canada has also focused attention on human/non-human interactions in particular settings. Initially, environmentalists tended to view very favourably the relationships between indigenous peoples and the flora and fauna. Unlike the depiction of an exploitative assault on nature by European-origin societies, Native groups were described as seeking to live in idyllic harmony with other members of the biosphere. Although subsequent historical research has questioned the extent and basis of Native environmental harmony,[13] this research has also made clear that indigenous peoples have had very different relationships with wildlife, the land, and the sea. These differences are attracting considerable scholarly attention since they point to the complex roles of culture and economy in determining the ways in which various societies perceive and relate to their surroundings.[14] The increased role that Native peoples have been playing in public debate in Canada was first reflected during the 1970s in the development of Native history as a research field, and it is now further stimulating the historical study of environmental issues.

Most recently, historians have turned to environmental history in their search for an overall coherence in historical understanding. From this perspective, an environmental approach offers a constructive response to the criticism that the "new social history" of recent decades has misrepresented the seamlessness of the historical process by "fragmenting" research into the thematic study of discrete individuals and groups and narrowly defined times and places. Because environmental history calls for analyses that integrate processes such as class, gender, ethnicity, and setting, this approach has the limitless ambition of an all-encompassing historical understanding. Although such an ambition obviously cannot be completely fulfilled, the theory and method of environmental history may offer a way to construct new "national histories" that do justice to the powerful and persuasive research findings of the new social history.

The readings in this book do not attempt to offer a comprehensive overview of Canadian history from an environmental perspective. Rather, they have the more modest ambition of illustrating some of the key themes scholars have identified thus far, as well as indicating how an environmental approach changes our way of seeing Canada's past. Most of the authors did not think of themselves as environmental historians when they were undertaking their research; indeed, some would not even define themselves as historians. This is not surprising given both the newness of environmental history as a research field and its interdisciplinary nature. *Consuming Canada* brings together selections from a wide range of periodicals and books, thus giving non-specialists access to research findings that have not yet attracted the wider attention they deserve. In addition, a selected bibliography is included for those who wish to pursue specific topics in greater depth.

Considered as a whole, the articles in this volume suggest that one key theme that may provide a coherent way of analysing Canada's national history involves the growing pressure placed on the rest of the environment as a result of a dominant economy and culture based on ever-increasing levels of production and consumption. Greater population densities and more powerful technologies have made the environmental impact of this economy and culture more starkly apparent with each passing decade. While historians have often emphasized the rise of the "consumer society" during the later nineteenth and twentieth centuries, the values and attitudes that underpin the desire to "consume" Canada appear to extend back to the origins of our history.

In this sense, the title *Consuming Canada* emphasizes the interconnections of ecology, economy, and culture. At the same time, the various articles demonstrate that the dominant economy and culture have never been static or all-pervasive. Rather, these readings suggest that Canada's environmental history has not only been diverse at all times but also ever-changing with the emergence of new ideas and behaviour among different individuals, groups, and institutions across a vast country in a dynamic biosphere. This complexity makes clear that the new research agenda for historians in Canada is challenging indeed.

NOTES

1. Margaret Atwood, *Survival: A Thematic Guide to Canadian Literature* (Toronto: Anansi, 1972), and Northrop Frye, "Conclusion" in *Literary History of Canada*, ed. Carl F. Klinck (Toronto: University of Toronto Press, 1965), as quoted in George Altmeyer, "Three Ideas of Nature in Canada, 1893–1914," *Journal of Canadian Studies* 11 (Aug. 1976): 21.

2. Harold A. Innis, *The Cod Fisheries: The History of an International Economy* (Toronto: University of Toronto Press, 1954) and *The Fur Trade in Canada: An Introduction to Canadian Economic History* (Toronto: University of Toronto Press, 1930);

A.R.M. Lower, *Great Britain's Woodyard: British America and the Timber Trade, 1963–1867* (Montreal: McGill-Queen's University Press, 1973) and *The North American Assault on the Canadian Forest: A History of the Lumber Industry Between Canada and the United States* (Toronto: Ryerson Press, 1938); and D.G. Creighton, *The Empire of the St. Lawrence* (Toronto: Macmillan, 1956).

3. J.M.S. Careless, *Canada: A Story of Challenge* (Toronto: Macmillan, 1953).

4. Ibid., v.

5. W.J. Eccles, *France in America* (Vancouver: Fitzhenry and Whiteside,

1973), and Carl Berger, *The Sense of Power: Studies in the Ideas of Canadian Imperialism, 1867–1914* (Toronto: University of Toronto Press, 1970).

6. Louise Dechêne, *Habitants et marchands de Montréal au XVIIe siècle* (Montreal: Plon, 1974).

7. See, for example, Lorne Hammond, "Marketing Wildlife: The Hudson's Bay Company and the Pacific Northwest, 1821–1849," *Forest and Conservation History* 37 (Jan. 1993): 14–25.

8. It is interesting to note that this approach helps explain the renewed interest in the work of Harold A. Innis who rejected universal economic models at a time when they were much in favour among mainstream scholars.

9. The three volumes have been published by the University of Toronto Press with the titles *From the Beginning to 1800, The Land Transformed, 1800–1891,* and *Addressing the Twentieth Century*. The French-language versions have been published by Les Presses de l'Université de Montréal.

10. For an illustration of this popular view, see Michael D. Judge, "America the Beautiful? Not from sea to shining sea," *Globe and Mail*, 28 Nov. 1994, A14.

11. Conferences on the environment that bring together historians with many other disciplines have been frequently held in recent years including, for example, Social Sciences and the Environment: An Interdisciplinary Conference, organized by the Social Science Federation of Canada and held in Ottawa on 17–19 February 1994.

12. For a description of Environmental Inter-Network, see "Computer network focuses on environment," *Ottawa Citizen*, 22 July 1994, A12.

13. See, for example, Martin W. Lewis, *Green Delusions: An Environmentalist Critique of Radical Environmentalism* (Durham, NC: Duke University Press, 1992).

14. This issue has also begun attracting considerable media attention. See, for example, "The myth of the noble savage shattered in the Amazon," *Ottawa Citizen*, 26 Sept. 1993, A3.

THEORY AND METHOD

○

T he theories and methods of environmental history challenge many of the presuppositions of conventional historical thinking. In the opening article of this section, John Wadland calls for a new perspective for Canadians by pointing to the contradictory ways in which the dominant culture interacts with the wilderness. On the one hand, the land is our birthright; on the other hand, the land is alien to our culture. In Wadland's view, Canadians have never really adapted to their environment, and thus have never really found "home." He argues for a new organic perception of the environment in which individuals, society, and nature interact and change in often unpredictable ways.

Donald Worster shows how historians who share Wadland's emphasis on the wholeness of the environment have begun studying the ways in which humans have affected, and been affected by, nature throughout history. Worster identifies three levels of analysis in environmental history: the study of both the organic and inorganic aspects of nature itself, the examination of how socioeconomic change interacts with the environment, and research on a culture's "dialogue with nature." Worster is in an excellent position to explain how historians have been taking an environmental approach since he has, in fact, played a pioneering role in the development of these approaches. Although his own research focuses on the United States, Worster has contributed significantly to the growing interest in Canada's environmental past.

The next article in this section not only calls for the study of reproduction as a fourth level of analysis in environmental history but also insists on the need to view all environmental questions from the perspective of gender. In enlarging Worster's ambition for the field, Carolyn Merchant is drawing upon insights gained in her research on the ways in which women have had distinct environmental relationships both in a cultural and material sense. Merchant's argument is twofold: that the process of reproduction is intimately related to the three levels of analysis identified by Worster; and that a gender perspective is needed to reveal the extent to which the roles of men and women have been distinct in the "global ecodrama."

The insistence on a gender perspective in environmental history raises substantial questions about research method since almost all of the evidence conventionally used by historians has been created by men. Moreover, virtually all of this evidence has been created and saved in official archives by the leaders of dominant cultures. The result is that historians who wish to go beyond the study of privileged men have had to rethink the accepted definition of historical evidence. In the case of environmental research, considerable attention has come to be focused on the ways in which ecological knowledge is possessed by tradition-based, non-industrial societies. In the final reading in this section, Milton M.R. Freeman discusses how scholars have recognized the inappropriateness of conventional, "scientific," linear thinking for analysing the multidimensional, interrelated processes of environmental change. Just as Merchant argues that, characteristically, women have a unique ecological knowledge as a result of a more "immediate and direct" connection to nature, Freeman emphasizes the comprehensive and complex ecological understandings of systems that are based on traditional knowledge.

The readings in this section show clearly that the starting point for an understanding of Canada's environmental history involves fundamental new concepts and approaches to the past. As Wadland concludes, we can no longer "treat nature simply as the stage upon which the human play is enacted."

WILDERNESS AND CULTURE *

JOHN WADLAND

o

The ultimate and the comprehensive meaning of Canadian history is to be found where there has been no Canadian history, in the North.[1]

W.L. Morton

... Although modern Canadians tend to consider wilderness and culture antithetical notions, as consumers they unite in identifying both with their leisure time—with their recreation. Traditionally, culture has been perceived as the product of civilization; the growth of civilization has, in turn, been equated with the rise of the metropolis. The linear historical imagination to which we are heirs has also established and reinforced the assumption that the metropolis spawns and contains our realities. In this context, the wilderness is regarded as an ambiguous, detached, and ultimately romantic space to which we "escape" from the metropolitan reality— whether on skis, in canoes, or comfortably seated in the family car.

Yet the metropolis and the wilderness really embody different perceptions of order, the former anthropocentric, the latter ecological. Historically, Canadians have demonstrated a particular passion for order of the first kind. Our pastoral landscapes, subdivided geometrically "into chessboards of square-mile sections and concession line roads," mirror the grid-ironed city and betray, in the words of Northrop Frye, "the conquest of nature by an intelligence that does not love it."[2] Even the wilderness must be catego-

---

* From Bruce W. Hodgins and M. Hobbs, eds., *Nastawgan: The Canadian North by Canoe and Snowshoe* (Weston, ON: Betelgeuse Books, 1987), 223–26. A slightly different version of this article first appeared in *Park News* 19, 2 (Summer 1982): 12–13. Reprinted with permission.

rized and coralled within park boundaries to create what Wayland Drew has called another form of "managerial unit" with a specialized function.[3] The tentacles of the progressive, ordered metropolitan culture reach everywhere, grasp everything.

Cultural questions in Canada are seldom (except by some artists) understood in organic, ecological terms. The land has seemed forever condemned both to receive and to perpetuate the compelling urban logic. At no time in our past have we wondered, even fleetingly, whether the wilderness contains rules—an order—to which we owe an allegiance. The very word "recreation," in some contexts, suggests that nature requires human intervention in order to achieve true meaning, that everything in nature automatically benefits from human alterations of it. Clearly one of the greatest deterrents to a serious criticism of this assumption has been the *amount* of wilderness (however defined) by which our metropolitan centres appear to be surrounded. Only very recently have we begun to take the most tentative steps toward an acceptance of the limitations implicit in a now visibly dwindling non-human nature.

The issue, then, becomes one of ascertaining whether culture can exist solely within extensions of the metropolitan order and as a parasite on wilderness, or whether wilderness, protesting its own diminishment by limiting our material culture, is demanding a voice which we ignore at our peril.

George F. Kennan once described totalitarianism as "a neurotic sense of tidiness." Several chilling controversies unearthed by the McDonald Commission[4] provided Canadians with ample evidence to question national tendencies in this direction—and certainly our fastidious manner of organizing space and time reflects and reinforces a profound sense of discomfort in the face of the unknown. Aspiring to make the unknown knowable, we attempt to render wilderness human, selectively picking off bits and pieces of the whole, reconstituting them as artifacts to serve preordained cultural values. Our culture, like the historical traditions of which it is both expression and culmination, creates and responds to its creations, almost invariably in metropolitan terms. The paradox, of course, is that the very immensity of land to which we are wedded, and which constitutes our geographical birthright, is at once alienated and alienating. We have never really learned the true meaning of adaptation to place, and despite our fascination with exploration, we have never found home.

The benchmarks by which we most often measure superior cultural achievement—grandiose architecture, Shakespearean theatre, classical ballet, the opera—are moulded by an aesthetic which mirrors what Brian Stock has labelled "The Great Tradition." This may have a marginal bearing on the lived experience of Canadians, but it is praised essentially for its "universality" and for its ability to win acceptance in the established cultural markets of the world. The spontaneously bred creativity of the "invisible culture" is demeaned and belittled by adjectives, like "primitive," "parochial," and "folkloric"—yet it is this dimension of our collective life which speaks most profoundly of our pluralism, of our regionalism, and ultimately of our quest for home.[5] The creativity of the true artist emerges from a felt experience of the known and the unknown. But although the capacity for artistry exists within us all, we have unwittingly permitted the alienating norms of the metropolitan reality to repress its expression. Perceiving ourselves mere consumers of creation, receivers of communicated culture, we have become dependent upon its interpreters (notably its critics) who, in our own age, seem intent upon assessing its meaning in the context of "The Great Tradition"—a tradition which, in all other respects, has failed us miserably.

Before issuing its final report, the Applebaum-Hébert Cultural Policy Review Committee released a preliminary *Summary of Briefs and Hearings*.[6] Running through many of the submissions is the predictable theme of inadequate funding. Appeals for increased subsidization of the arts are directed at the public and private sectors. In common these apparently disparate funding sources, filtered through an exotic web of forward and backward linkages, have at their root the profits derived from the extraction of natural resources in the wilderness. Indeed, many of our most powerful and influential citizens come closest to wilderness while perusing daily stock quotations in the local newspaper. Columns of mining, pulp and paper and oil exploration companies, neatly itemized in numerical format, help to underline the fundamental absurdity of the wilderness/culture dichotomy. As David, Margaret Atwood's myopic macho-man in *Surfacing*, says (in a rare moment of insight): "this country is founded on the bodies of dead animals. Dead fish, dead seals and historically dead beavers, the beaver is to this country what the black man is to the United States."[7]

The continued consumption of commodities blast-furnaced from staples is, we tell ourselves, essential if the occupations, by and through which we produce the taxes and disposable income to sustain creativity, are to prevail. Yet in the process of manufacturing and consuming the material goods which constitute our artifactual heritage—and which, at least in theory, generate our ordered sense of well being and security—we are individually responsible for eroding wilderness. The silent smoke permeating our atmosphere, which is rained upon and which acidifies our northern lakes and rivers with far-reaching ecological consequences, is born of a deep-seated metropolitan alienation that treats culture as a bought, rather than as a lived thing. What is to become of this culture when extinct species, exhausted strip mines and clear-cut forests formally proclaim the non-renewability of wilderness?

Culture cannot be relegated to a class of industry without itself becoming an uncritical defender of industrialism. Viewed organically, culture threads the fabric of our existence. It demands a cyclical perception of life that guarantees the roles of the individual, society, and nature, all of which act upon, and are reacted upon, in a perpetually evolving, unpredictable manner.[8] Such an integrated culture will grow and mature through the ecological changes it effects (and by which it is affected) only if human reason can acknowledge and address its own limitation by nature. The *sine qua non* of what we have chosen to identify as Canadian culture is the wilderness. And on a symbolic level wilderness is the closest we shall ever come to absolute nature. In the end, the question of basic survival—whether of man or of all living things—is centred on culture, and therefore on nature. Our history, which has been preoccupied by the measurement of individual and societal concerns, must, along lines suggested by Fernard Braudel and the French *Annales* school,[9] expand its analytical framework to include wilderness/nature as a functioning participant in the cyclical drama of experience. To treat nature simply as the stage upon which the human play is enacted is to betray our ignorance of its ultimate power over us. "Nature will certainly triumph," observes Wayland Drew, "Whether it will triumph over us or in us and through us remains to be seen."[10]

NOTES

1. W.L. Morton, "The 'North' in Canadian Historiography," *Transactions of the Royal Society of Canada*, Series IV, 8 (1970), 40.

2. Northrop Frye, *The Bush Garden: Essays on the Canadian Imagination* (Toronto 1971), 224.

3. Wayland Drew, "Killing Wilderness," *Ontario Naturalist*, 12 (September 1972), 23.

4. Canada. Commission of Inquiry Concerning Certain Activities of the Royal Canadian Mounted Police, *Reports* (Ottawa 1979–1981).

5. Brian Stock, "English Canada: The Visible and Invisible Cultures," *Canadian Forum*, 52 (March 1973), 29–33; "English Canada: Culture Versus Experience," *Canadian Forum*, 56 (April 1976), 5–9.

6. Canada. Federal Cultural Policy Review Committee, *Summary of Briefs and Hearings* (Ottawa: Ministry of Supply and Services, 1982). See also Francis Fox, *Culture and Communications: Key Elements of Canada's Economic Future* (Ottawa 1983).

7. Margaret Atwood, *Surfacing* (Toronto 1972), 40.

8. See Gregory Bateson, *Steps to an Ecology of Mind* (New York 1972).

9. *Mediterranean World in the Age of Philip II*, trans. by Sian Reynolds (New York 1972), 2 volumes.

10. Wayland Drew, "Wilderness and Limitation," *Canadian Forum*, 52 (February 1973), 19. For a splendid fictional rendering of all the points raised in this essay, see Wayland Drew, *The Wabeno Feast* (Toronto 1973).

DOING ENVIRONMENTAL HISTORY*

DONALD WORSTER

o

In the old days, the discipline of history had an altogether easier task. Everyone knew that the only important subject was politics and the only important terrain was the nation-state. One was supposed to investigate the connivings of presidents and prime ministers, the passing of laws, the struggles between courts and legislatures, and the negotiations of diplomats. That old, self-assured history was actually not so old after all—a mere century or two at most. It emerged with the power and influence of the nation-state, reaching a peak of acceptance in the nineteenth and early twentieth centuries. Often its practitioners were men of intensely nationalistic feelings, who were patriotically moved to trace the rise of their individual countries, the formation of political leadership in them, and their rivalries with other states for wealth and power. They knew what mattered, or thought they did.

But some time back that history as "past politics" began to lose ground, as the world evolved toward a more global point of view and, some would say, toward a more democratic one. Historians lost some of their confidence that the past had been so thoroughly controlled or summed up by a few great men acting in positions of national power. Scholars began uncovering long submerged layers, the lives and thoughts of ordinary people, and tried to reconceive history "from the bottom up." Down, down we must go, they maintained, down to the hidden layers of class, gender, race, and caste. There we will find what truly has shaped the surface layers of politics. Now enter still another group of reformers, the environmental historians, who

---

* Reprinted with permission from Donald Worster, ed., *The Ends of the Earth: Perspectives on Modern Environmental History* (Cambridge: Cambridge University Press, 1985), 289–307.

insist that we have got to go still deeper yet, down to the earth itself as an agent and presence in history. Here we will discover even more fundamental forces at work over time. And to appreciate those forces we must now and then get out of parliamentary chambers, out of birthing rooms and factories, get out of doors altogether, and ramble into fields, woods, and the open air. It is time we bought a good set of walking shoes, and we cannot avoid getting some mud on them.

So far this extending of the scope of history to include a deeper and broader range of subjects has not challenged the primacy of the nation-state as the proper territory of the historian. Social, economic, and cultural history are all still commonly pursued within national boundaries. Thus, to an extent that is quite extraordinary among the disciplines of learning, history (at least for the modern period) has tended to remain the insular study of the United States, Brazil, France, and the rest. Such a way of organizing the past has the undeniable virtue of preserving some semblance of order in the face of a threatening chaos—some way of synthesizing all the layers and forces. But at the same time it may set up obstacles to new inquiries that do not neatly fit within national borders, environmental history among them. Many of the issues in this new field defy a narrow nationality: the wanderings of Tuareg nomads in the African Sahel, for instance, or the pursuit of the great whales through all the world's oceans. Other environmental themes, to be sure, have developed strictly within the framework of single-nation politics, as a few of the essays in this book illustrate. But not all have done so, and in the history that will be written tomorrow, fewer and fewer will be.

Environmental history is, in sum, part of a revisionist effort to make the discipline far more inclusive in its narratives than it has traditionally been. Above all, it rejects the conventional assumption that human experience has been exempt from natural constraints, that people are a separate and "supernatural" species, that the ecological consequences of their past deeds can be ignored. The old history could hardly deny that we have been living for a long while on this planet, but it assumed by its general disregard of that fact that we have not been and are not truly part of the planet. Environmental historians, on the other hand, realize that we can no longer afford to be so naive.

The idea of environmental history first appeared in the 1970s as conferences on the global predicament were taking place and popular environmentalist movements were gathering momentum in several countries. It was launched, in other words, in a time of worldwide cultural reassessment and reform. History was hardly alone in being touched by that rising mood of public concern; scholarship in law, philosophy, economics, sociology, and other areas was similarly responsive. Long after popular interest in environmental issues crested and ebbed, as the issues themselves came to appear more and more complicated, without easy resolution, the scholarly interest continued to expand and take on greater and greater sophistication. Environmental history was, therefore, born out of a moral purpose, with strong political commitments behind it, but also became, as it matured, a scholarly enterprise that had neither any simple, nor any single, moral or political agenda to promote. Its principal goal became one of deepening our understanding of how humans have been affected by their natural environment through time and, conversely, how they have affected that environment and with what results.

One of the liveliest centers of the new history has been the United States, a fact that undoubtedly stems from the strength of American leadership in environmental matters. The earliest attempt to define the field was Roderick Nash's essay, "The State of Environmental History." Nash recommended looking at our entire surroundings as a kind of historical document on which Americans had been writing about themselves and their ideals. More recently, a comprehensive effort by Richard White to trace the development of the field credits the pioneering work of Nash and that of the conservation historian Samuel Hays, but also suggests that there were anticipations before them in the frontier and western school of American historiography (among such land-minded figures as Frederick Jackson Turner, Walter Prescott Webb, and James Malin). Those older roots became increasingly recalled as the field moved beyond Hays's politics of conservation and Nash's intellectual history to focus on changes in the environment itself and consider, once more, the environment's role in the making of American society.

Another center of innovation has been France, particularly the historians associated with the journal *Annales*, who have been drawing attention to the environment for several decades now. That journal was founded in 1929 by two professors at the University of Strasbourg, Marc Bloch and Lucien Febvre. Both of them were interested in the environmental basis of society, Bloch through his studies of French peasant life and Febvre as a social geographer. The latter's protégé, Fernand Braudel, would also make the environment a prominent part of his historical studies, notably in his great work on the Mediterranean. For Braudel, the environment was the shape of the land—mountains, plains, seas—as an almost timeless element shaping human life over the long duration (*la longue durée*). There was, he insisted, more to history than the succession of events in individual lives; on the grandest scale, there was history seen from the vantage of nature, a history "in which all change is slow, a history of constant repetition, ever-recurring cycles."

Like the frontier historians in the United States, the *Annalistes* in France found their environmental interests reanimated by the popular movements of the sixties and early seventies. In 1974, the journal devoted a special issue to "Histoire et Environnement." In a short preface Emmanuel Le Roy Ladurie, himself one of the leading lights in the field, gave this description (my translation) of the field's program:

> Environmental history unites the oldest themes with the newest in contemporary historiography: the evolution of epidemics and climate, those two factors being integral parts of the human ecosystem; the series of natural calamities aggravated by a lack of foresight, or even by an absurd "willingness" on the part of the simpletons of col-

onization; the destruction of Nature, caused by soaring population and/or by the predators of industrial overconsumption; nuisances of urban and manufacturing origin, which lead to air or water pollution; human congestion or noise levels in urban areas, in a period of galloping urbanization.

Denying that this new history was merely a passing fashion, Le Roy Ladurie insisted that the inquiry had in truth been going on for a long time as part of a movement toward "histoire écologique."

Much of the material for environmental history has indeed been around for generations, if not for centuries, and is only being reorganized in the light of recent experience. It includes data on tides and winds, on ocean currents, on the position of continents in relation to each other, on the geological and hydrological forces creating our land and water base. It includes the history of climate and weather, as these have made for good or bad harvests, sent prices up or down, ended or promoted epidemics, led to population increase or decline. All these have been powerful influences over the course of history, and continue to be so, as when massive earthquakes destroy cities or starvation follows in the wake of drought or rivers determine the flow of settlement. The fact that such influences continue in the late twentieth century is evidence of how far we are yet from controlling the environment to our complete satisfaction. In a somewhat different category are those living resources of the earth, which the ecologist George Woodwell calls the most important of all: the plants and animals (and one might add the soil as a collective organism) that, in Woodwell's phrase, "maintain the biosphere as a habitat suitable for life." These resources have been far more susceptible to human manipulation than the abiotic ones, and at no point more so than today. But pathogens are also a part of that living realm, and they continue, despite the effectiveness of medicine, to be a decisive agency in our fate.

Put in the vernacular then, environmental history is about the role and place of nature in human life. By common understanding we mean by "nature" the nonhuman world, the world we have not in any primary sense created. The "social environment," the scene of humans interacting only with each other in the absence of nature, is therefore excluded. Likewise is the built or artifactual environment, the cluster of things that people have made and which can be so pervasive as to constitute a kind of "second nature" around them. That latter exclusion may seem especially arbitrary, and to an extent it is. Increasingly, as human will makes its imprint on the forest, on gene pools, on the polar ice cap, it may seem that there is no practical difference between "nature" and "artifact." The distinction, nonetheless, is worth keeping, for it reminds us that there are different forces at work in the world and not all of them emanate from humans; some remain spontaneous and self-generating. The built environment is wholly expressive of culture; its study is already well advanced in the history of architecture, technology, and the city. But with such phenomena as the forest and the water cycle, we encounter autonomous energies that do not derive from us. Those forces impinge on human life, stimulating some reaction, some defense, some ambition. Thus, when we step beyond the self-reflecting world of humankind to encounter the nonhuman sphere, environmental history finds its main theme of study.

There are three levels on which the new history proceeds, three clusters of issues it addresses, though not necessarily all in the same project, three sets of questions it seeks to answer, each drawing on a range of outside disciplines and employing special methods of analysis. The first deals with understanding nature itself, as organized and functioning in past times; we include both organic and inorganic aspects of nature, and not least the human organism as it has been a link in nature's food chains, now functioning as womb, now belly, now eater, now eaten, now a host for microorganisms, now a kind of parasite. The second level in this history brings in the socioeconomic realm as it interacts with the environment. Here we are concerned with tools and work, with the social relations that grow out of that work, with the various modes people have devised of producing goods from natural resources. A community organized to catch fish at sea may have very different institutions, gender roles, or seasonal rhythms than one raising sheep in high mountain pastures. Power to make decisions, environmental or other, is seldom distributed through a society with perfect equality, so locating the configurations of power is part of this level of analysis. Then, forming a third level for the historian is that more intangible and uniquely human type of encounter—the purely mental or intellectual, in which perceptions, ethics, laws, myths, and other structures of meaning become part of an individual's or group's dialogue with nature. People are constantly engaged in constructing maps of the world around them, in defining what a resource is, in determining which sorts of behavior may be environmentally degrading and ought to be prohibited, and generally in choosing the ends of their lives. Though for the purposes of clarification, we may try to distinguish between these three levels of environmental study, in fact they constitute a single dynamic inquiry in which nature, social and economic organization, thought and desire are treated as one whole. And this whole changes as nature changes, as people change, forming a dialectic that runs through all of the past down to the present.

This in general is the program of the new environmental history. It brings together a wide array of subjects, familiar and unfamiliar, rather than setting up some new, esoteric specialty. From that synthesis, we hope, new questions and answers will come.

NATURAL ENVIRONMENTS OF THE PAST

The environmental historian must learn to speak some new languages as well as ask some new questions. Undoubtedly, the most outlandish language that must be learned is the natural scientist's. So full of numbers, laws, terms, and experiments, it is as foreign to the historian as Chinese was to Marco Polo. Yet, with even a smattering of vocabulary, what treasures are here to be understood and taken back home! Concepts from geology, pushing our notions of history back into the Pleistocene, the Silurian, the

Precambrian. Graphs from climatology, on which temperatures and precipitation oscillate up and down through the centuries, with no regard for the security of kings or empires. The chemistry of the soil with its cycles of carbon and nitrogen, its pH balances wavering with the presences of salts and acids, setting the terms of agriculture. Any one of these might add a powerful tool to the study of the rise of civilizations. Together, the natural sciences are indispensable aids for the environmental historian, who must begin by reconstructing past landscapes, learning what they were and how they functioned before human societies entered and rearranged them.

But above all it is ecology, which examines the interactions among organisms and between them and their physical environments, that offers the environmental historian the greatest help. This is so in part because, ever since Charles Darwin, ecology has been concerned with past as well as present interactions; it has been integral to the study of evolution. Equally significant, ecology is at heart concerned with the origins, dispersal, and organization of all plant life. Plants form by far the major portion of the earth's biomass. All through history people have depended critically on them for food, medicine, building materials, hunting habitat, and a buffer against the rest of nature. Far more often than not, plants have been humans' allies in the struggle to survive and thrive. Therefore, where people and vegetation come together more issues in environmental history cluster than anywhere else. Take away plant ecology and environmental history loses its foundation, its coherence, its first step.

So impressed are they with this fact that some scholars speak of doing, not environmental, but "ecological history" or "historical ecology." They mean to insist on a tighter alliance with the science. Some years back the scientist and conservationist Aldo Leopold projected such an alliance when he spoke of "an ecological interpretation of history." His own illustration of how that might work had to do with the competition among native Indians, French and English traders, and American settlers for the land of Kentucky, pivotal in the westward movement. The canebrakes growing along Kentucky bottomlands were a formidable barrier to any agricultural settlement, but as luck would have it for the Americans, when the cane was burned and grazed and chopped out, bluegrass sprouted in its place. And bluegrass was all that any farmer, looking for a homestead and a pasture for his livestock, could want. American farmers entered Kentucky by the thousands, and the struggle was soon over. "What if," Leopold wondered, "the plant succession inherent in this dark and bloody ground had, under the impact of these forces, given us some worthless sedge, shrub, or weed?" Would Kentucky have become American property as and when it did?

Shortly after Leopold called for that merging of history and ecology, the Kansas historian James Malin brought out a series of essays leading to what he termed "an ecological reexamination of the history of the United States." He specially had in mind examining his native grasslands and the problem in adaptation they had set for Americans, as they had for the Indians before them. From the late nineteenth century on, white settlers, coming out of a more humid, wooded country, had tried to create a stable agriculture on the dry, treeless plains, but with only mixed results. Malin was impressed that they had succeeded in turning the land into prosperous wheat farms, but not before they had had to unlearn many of their old agricultural techniques. Dissatisfied with traditional history, which did not give such matters any prominence, Malin found himself reading ecologists to find the right questions to ask. He read them with a certain freedom, as a source of inspiration rather than a set of rigid models. "The ecological point of view," he believed, "is valuable to the study of history; not under any illusion that history may thus be converted into a science, but merely as a way of looking at the subject matter and processes of history."

Those were alliances sought some thirty or forty years back. Since then, as ecology has developed into a more rigorously mathematical science, with more elaborate models of natural processes, neither Malin's nor Leopold's casual sort of alliance has seemed adequate. Environmental historians have had to learn to read at a more advanced level, though they are still faced with Malin's problem of deciding just how scientific their history needs to be and which ideas in science can or ought to be adopted.

Today's ecology offers a number of angles for understanding organisms in their environment, and they all have their limits as well as uses in history. One might, for example, examine the single organism and its response to external conditions; in other words, study adaptation in individual physiological terms. Or one might track the fluctuations in size of some plant or animal population in an area, its rates of reproduction, its evolutionary success or failure, its economic ramifications. Although both sorts of inquiry may have considerable practical significance for human society, there is a third strategy that holds the most promise for historians needing to understand humans and nature in the composite.

When organisms of many species come together, they form communities, usually highly diverse in makeup, or as they are more commonly called now, ecosystems. An ecosystem is the largest generalization made in the science, encompassing both the organic and inorganic elements of nature bound together in a single place, all in active, reciprocating relationship.[1] Some ecosystems are fairly small and readily demarcated, like a pond in New England, while others are sprawling and ill-defined, as large as the Amazonian rain forest or the Serengeti plain or even the whole earth. All are commonly described, in language derived heavily from physical mechanics and cybernetics, as self-equilibrating, like a machine that runs on and on automatically, checking itself when it gets too hot, speeding up when it slows and begins to sputter. Outside disturbances may affect that equilibrium, throwing the machine temporarily off its regular rhythm, but always (or almost always) it returns to some steady state condition. The numbers of species constituting an ecosystem fluctuate around some determinable point; the flow of energy through the machine stays constant. The ecologist is interested in how such systems go on functioning in the midst of continual perturbations, and how and why they break down.

But right there occurs a difficult issue on which the science of ecology has reached no clear consensus. How stable are those natural systems and how susceptible to upset? Is it accurate to describe them as balanced and stable until humans arrive? And if so, then at what point does a change in their equilibrium become excessive, damaging or destroying them? Damage to the individual organism is easy enough to define: It is an impairment of health or, ultimately, it is death. Likewise, damage to a population is not very hard to determine, simply, when its numbers decline. But damage to whole ecosystems is a more controversial matter. No one would dispute that the death of all its trees, birds, and insects would mean the death of a rain-forest ecosystem, or that the draining of a pond would spell the end of that system. But most changes are less catastrophic, and the degree of damage has no easy method of measurement.

The difficulty of determining ecosystem damage applies to changes worked by people as well as nonhuman forces. A South American tribe, for instance, may clear a small patch in the forest with its machetes, raise a few crops, and then let the field revert to forest. Such so-called swidden, or slash-and-burn, farming has usually been regarded as harmless to the whole ecosystem; eventually, its natural equilibrium is restored. But at some point, as this farming intensifies, the capacity of the forest to regenerate itself must be permanently impaired and the ecosystem damaged. What is that point? Ecologists are not sure and cannot give precise answers. For that reason the ecological historian more often than not ends up talking about people inducing "change" in the environment—"change" being a neutral and indisputable term—rather than doing "damage," a far more problematical concept.

Until recently the ruling authority in ecosystem science has been Eugene Odum, through the various editions of his popular textbook, *Fundamentals of Ecology*. Odum is a system man nonpareil, one who sees the entire realm of nature as hierarchically organized into systems and subsystems, all made up of parts that function harmoniously and homeostatically, the rhythm of each system rather resembling the eighteenth-century's watchlike nature that never missed a tick. That earlier version was supposed to reveal the contriving hand of its divine maker; Odum's, in contrast, is the spontaneous work of nature. But increasingly, ecologists are retreating from his picture of order. Led by paleoecologists, especially paleobotanists, who collect core samples from peat bogs and, through pollen analysis, try to reconstruct ancient environments, they are finding Odum's blueprint a bit static. Looking backward in time to the Ice Age and before, they are discovering plenty of disorder and upheaval in nature. Abstracted from time, the critics say, ecosystems may have a reassuring look of permanence; but out there in the real, the historical, world, they are more perturbed than imperturbable, more changing than not.

This scientific difference of opinion is partly over evidence, partly over perspective, like disputing whether a glass is half empty or half full. Stand back far enough, stand off in outer space as the British scientist James Lovelock has tried imaginatively to do, and the earth still looks like a remarkably stable place, with organisms maintaining conditions highly suitable for life for over a billion years: all the gases in the atmosphere properly adjusted, fresh water and rich soil preserved in abundance, though evolution rages on and on, ice sheets come and go, and continents go drifting off in all directions. That may be how things look to the cosmic eyeball. Seen up close, however, the organic world may have a very different aspect. Stand on any given acre in North America and contemplate its past thousand years or so, even a single decade, and the conclusion ecologists are coming to these days is change, change, change.

There is a further unresolved problem in translating ecology into history. Few scientists have perceived people or human societies as being integral parts of their ecosystems. They leave them out as distractions, imponderables. But people are what the historian mainly studies; consequently, his or her job is to join together what scientists have put asunder.

Human beings participate in ecosystems either as biological organisms akin to other organisms or as culture bearers, though the distinction between the two roles is seldom clear-cut. Suffice it here to say that, as organisms, people have never been able to live in splendid, invulnerable isolation. They breed, of course, like other species, and their offspring must survive or perish by the quality of food, air, and water and by the number of microorganisms that are constantly invading their bodies. In these ways and more, humans have inextricably been part of the earth's ecological order. Therefore, any reconstruction of past environments must include not only forests and deserts, boas and rattlesnakes, but also the human animal and its success or failure in reproducing itself.

HUMAN MODES OF PRODUCTION

Nothing distinguishes people from other creatures more sharply than the fact that it is people who create culture. Precisely what culture really is however, is anybody's guess. There are literally scores of definitions. For preliminary purposes it can be said that the definitions tend to divide between those including both mental and material activities and those emphasizing mental activities exclusively, and that these distinctions between the mental and material correspond to the second and third levels of analysis in our environmental history. In this section we are concerned with the material culture of a society, its implications for social organization, and its interplay with the natural environment.

In any particular place nature offers the humans dwelling there a flexible but limited set of possibilities for getting a living. The Eskimos of the northern polar regions, to take an extreme case of limits, cannot expect to become farmers. Instead, they have ingeniously derived a sustenance, not by marshaling seed, plows, and draft animals of other, warmer latitudes, but through hunting. Their food choices have focused on stalking caribou over the tundra and pursuing bowhead whales among floating cakes of ice, on gathering blueberries in season and gaffing fish. Narrow though those possibilities are, they are the gift of technology as much as nature. Technology is the application of skills and knowledge to exploiting the environment. Among the Eskimos technology has traditionally amounted to fish hooks, harpoons, sled runners, and the like. Though constrained by nature, that technology has nonetheless opened up for them a nutritional field otherwise out of reach, as when a sealskin boat allowed them to venture farther out to sea in pursuit of prey. Today's Eskimos, invaded as they are by the instruments of more materially advanced cultures, have still more choices laid before them; they can, if they desire, import a supply of wheat and oranges by cargo plane from California. And they can forget how their old choices were made, surrender their uniqueness, their independence of spirit, their intimacy with the icy world. Much of environmental history involves examining just such changes, voluntary or imposed, in subsistence modes and their ramifications for people and the earth.

As historians address these elemental issues of tools and sustenance, they soon become aware that there have been other disciplines at work here too, and for a long time. Among them is the discipline of anthropologists, and environmental historians have been reading their work with great interest. They have begun to search for clues from anthropologists to critical pieces of the ecological puzzle: What is the best way to understand the relation of human material cultures to nature? Is technology to be viewed as an integral part of the natural world, akin to the fur coat of the polar bear, the sharp teeth of the tiger, the fleet agility of the gazelle, all adaptive mechanisms functioning within ecosystems? Or should cultures be viewed as setting people apart from and outside of nature? Everything in the ecosystem, we are told by natural scientists, has a role and therefore an influence on the workings of the whole; conversely, everything is shaped by its presence in the ecosystem. Are cultures and the societies that create them also to be seen in that double position, both acting on and being acted on? Or are they better described as forming their own kind of "cultural systems" that mesh with ecosystems only in rare, isolated cases? Or, to make the puzzle more complicated still, do humans create with their technology a series of new, artificial ecosystems—a rice paddy in Indonesia or a carefully managed German forest—that require constant human supervision? There is, of course, no single or consistent set of answers to be given to such questions; but anthropologists, who are among the most wide-ranging and theory-conscious observers of human behavior, can offer some provocative insights.

Anthropological thinking on such questions goes back well into the nineteenth century, but it has been particularly the last three or four decades that have seen the emergence of an ecological school (one with no settled curriculum, bearing such contending labels as cultural ecology, human ecology, ecological anthropology, and cultural materialism). The best guide to this literature is probably John Bennett's *The Ecological Transition*, though there are other useful surveys by Emilio Moran, Roy Ellen, Robert Netting, and others. Bennett defines the ecology school as the study of "how and why humans use Nature, how they incorporate Nature into Society, and what they do to themselves, Nature, and Society in the process." Some of these anthropologists have maintained that culture is an entirely autonomous and superorganic phenomenon, emerging apart from nature and understandable only in its own terms—or at least, as Bennett himself would have it, modern culture is trying to become so. Others, in contrast, have argued that all culture is, to some important degree, expressive of nature and ought not be rigidly set off in its own, self-contained sphere. Both positions are illuminating to the environmental historian, though for the historical era that is the main focus of this book, Bennett's is surely the more plausible one.

No one did more to found the ecological study of culture than Julian Steward, who published in 1955 his influential work, *Theory of Culture Change*, from which comes the idea of "cultural ecology." Steward began by examining the relationship between a people's system of economic production and their physical environment. He asked what resources they chose to exploit and what technology they devised for that work. This set of subsistence activities he called the "cultural core." Then he asked how such a system affected the behavior of people toward one another, that is, how they organized themselves to produce their living. Social relations in turn shaped other aspects of culture. Some of the most interesting case studies for him were the great irrigation empires of the ancient world, in which large-scale control of water in arid environments led again and again to parallels in sociopolitical organization. Such regularities, he hoped, would suggest a general law of human evolution: not the old Victorian scheme that had all cultures moving along a single, fixed line of progress from hunting and gathering to industrial civilization, but rather one that explained the multilinear evolution of cultures, now diverging, now converging, now colliding with one another, with no end point in sight.

Steward's leadership in the new ecological approach inspired, directly or indirectly, a younger generation of field researchers who fanned out to all parts of the globe. John Bennett went to the Canadian prairies, Harold Conklin to the Philippines, Richard Lee to the !Kung Bushmen of Africa, Marshall Sahlins to Polynesia, Robert Netting to Nigeria to observe the hillside farmers there, Betty Meggers was off to the Amazon basin, Clifford Geertz to Indonesia, and there were still others. But above all, it has been Marvin Harris who has taken Steward's ideas and transformed them into a comprehensive and, some would complain, a highly reductive theory of the relationship between nature and culture. Like Steward, he has identified the "techno-environment" (i.e., the application of technology to environment) as providing the core of any culture, the main influence over how a people live with one another and think about the world. He has been even more rigidly deterministic than Steward was about that core. He has also been more interested in its dynamics. The techno-environmental system is not at all stable, he insists, certainly not forever. There is always the tendency to intensify production. It may come from population increase, climate change, or competition between states. Whatever the cause, the effect is always the same: depletion of the environment, declining efficiency, worsening living standards, pressures to move on—or if there is no new place to go, then pressure to find new tools, techniques, and resources locally, creating thereby another techno-environment. In other words, the degradation of the environment can be tragic, unhappy, or if people rise successfully to the challenge, it can mean the triumphant birth of a new culture. Harris calls this theory "cultural materialism." Clearly, it draws not only on Steward but on recent energy shortages, the present decline of a techno-environment based on the fossil fuels, and the revival of Malthusian anxieties about world resource scarcity, though Harris would argue that a time of scarcity can also be a time of opportunity and revolution.

Marvin Harris has explicitly compared his theory of cultural material-ism to that of Karl Marx, who gave the world "dialectical materialism," a view of history impelled forever forward by the struggle of one economic class to dominate another. The contrast between the two theories is emphatic: One sees change coming from the struggle of whole societies to exploit nature, with diminishing returns; the other points to internal con-flicts within societies as the prime historical agency, with nature serving as a passive background. Perhaps, however, the distance between the two men is not hopelessly unbridgeable. One might put a little more Marxism into Harris by arguing that, among the factors leading to depletion and ecologi-cal disequilibrium, is competition between classes as well as states. Capitalists devise a social and technological order that makes them rich and elevates them to power. They set up factories for mass production. They drive the earth to the point of breakdown with their technology, their man-agement of the laboring class, and their appetites. Subsistence gets rede-fined as endless want, endless consumption, endless competing for status. The system eventually self-destructs, and a new one takes its place. Similarly, we might improve Marxism by adding Harris's ecological factors to help explain the rise of classes and class conflict. Neither theory, taken alone, adequately accounts for the past. Together, they might work more effectively, each supplying the other's shortcomings. In so far as the course of history has been shaped by material forces, and hardly anyone would deny that they have indeed been important, we will undoubtedly need something like that merger of the two theories.

The modes of production are an endless parade of strategies, as com-plex in their taxonomies as the myriad species of insects thriving in the canopy of a rain forest or the brightly colored fish in a coral reef. In broad terms, we may speak of such modes as hunting and gathering, agriculture, and modern industrial capitalism. But that is only the bare outline of any full taxonomy. We must also include, as modes, submodes, or variations on them, the history of cowboys herding cattle across a Montana grassland, of dark-skinned fishermen casting their nets on the Malabar coast, of Laplanders trailing after their reindeer, of Tokyo factory workers buying bags of rice and seaweed in a supermarket. In all these instances and more, the environmental historian wants to know what role nature had in shaping the productive methods and, conversely, what impact those methods had on nature.

This is the age-old dialogue between ecology and economy. Though deriving from the same etymological roots, the two words have come to denote two separate spheres, and for good reason: Not all economic modes are ecologically sustainable. Some last for centuries, even millennia, while others appear only briefly and then fade away, failures in adaptation. And ultimately, over the long stretch of time, no modes have ever been perfectly adapted to their environment, or there would be little history.

PERCEPTION, IDEOLOGY, AND VALUE

Humans are animals with ideas as well as tools, and one of the largest, most consequential of those ideas bears the name "nature." More accurately, "nature" is not one idea but many ideas, meanings, thoughts, feelings, all piled on top of one another, often in the most unsystematic fashion. Every individual and every culture has created such agglomerations. We may think we know what we are saying when we use the word, but frequently we mean several things at once and listeners may have to work at getting our meaning. We may suppose too that nature refers to something radically separate from ourselves, that it is "out there" someplace, sitting solidly, concretely, unambiguously. In a sense, that is so. Nature is an order and a process that we did not create, and in our absence it will continue to exist; only the most strident solipsist would argue to the contrary. All the same, nature is a creation of our minds, too, and no matter how hard we may try to see what it is objectively, in and by and for itself, we are to a considerable extent trapped in the prison of our own consciousness and web of meanings.

Environmental historians have done some of their best work on this level of cultural analysis, studying the perceptions and values people have held about the nonhuman world. They have, that is, put people thinking about nature under scrutiny. So impressed have they been by the enduring, pervasive power of ideas that sometimes they have blamed present environmental abuse on attitudes that go far back into the recesses of time: as far back as the book of Genesis and the ancient Hebraic ethos of asserting dominion over the earth; or the Greco-Roman determination to master the environment through reason; or the still more archaic drive among patriarchal males to lord it over nature (the "feminine" principle) as well as women. The actual effects of such ideas, in the past or in the present, are extremely difficult to trace empirically, but that has not deterred scholars from making some very large claims here. Nor should it altogether. Perhaps we have too wildly exaggerated a notion of our mental prowess and its impact on the rest of nature. Perhaps we spend too much time talking about our ideas, neglecting to examine our behavior. But however overblown some of these claims may be, it is certainly true that our ideas have been interesting to contemplate, and nothing among them has been more interesting than our reflections on other animals, plants, soils, and the entire biosphere that gave birth to us. So, for good reason, environmental history must include in its program the study of aspects of esthetics and ethics, myth and folklore, literature and landscape gardening, science and religion—must go wherever the human mind has grappled with the meaning of nature.

For the historian, the main object must be to discover how a whole culture, rather than exceptional individuals in it, perceived and valued nature. Even the most materially primitive society may have had quite sophisticated, complex views. Complexity, of course, may come from unresolved ambiguities and contradictions as well as from profundity. People in industrial countries especially seem to abound in these contradictions: They may chew up the land wholesale and at a frightful speed through real estate development, mining, and deforestation but then turn around and pass laws to protect a handful of fish swimming in a desert spring. Some of this is simply confusion, some of it may be quite reasonable. Given the protean qualities of nature, the fact that the environment presents real dangers as well as benefits to people, this contradictoriness is inescapable. It has everywhere been true of the human reaction. Yet not a few scholars have fallen into the trap of speaking of "the Buddhist view of nature" or "the Christian view" or "the American Indian view," as though people in those cultures were all simple-minded, uncomplicated, unanimous, and totally lacking in ambivalence. Every culture, we should assume, has within it a range of perceptions and values, and no culture has ever really wanted to live in total harmony with its surroundings.

But ideas should not be left floating in some empyrean realm, free from the dust and sweat of the material world. They should be studied in their relations with those modes of subsistence discussed in the preceding section. Without reducing all thought and value to some material base, as though the human imagination was a mere rationalization of the belly's needs, the historian must understand that mental culture does not spring up all on its own. One way to put this relationship is to say that ideas are socially constructed and, therefore, reflect the organization of those societies, their techno-environments and hierarchies of power. Ideas differ from person to person within societies according to gender, class, race, and region. Men and women, set apart almost everywhere into more or less distinctive spheres, have arrived at different ways of regarding nature, sometimes radically so. So too have slaves and their masters, factory owners and workers, agrarian and industrial peoples. They may live together or in close proximity but still see and value the natural world differently. The historian must be alert to these differences and resist easy generalizations about the "mind" of a people or of an age.

Sometimes it is maintained that modern science has enabled us to rise above these material conditions to achieve for the first time in history an impersonal, transcultural, unbiased understanding of how nature works. The scientific method of collecting and verifying facts is supposed to deliver truth pure and impartial. Such confidence is naive. Few scholars writing the history of science today would accept it uncritically. Science, they would caution, has never been free of its material circumstances. Though it may indeed be a superior way of arriving at the truth, certainly superior in its capacity to deliver power over nature, it has nonetheless been shaped by the techno-environment and social relations of its time. According to historian Thomas Kuhn, science is not simply the accumulating of facts but involves fitting those facts into some kind of "paradigm," or model, of how nature works. Old paradigms lose their appeal, and new ones rise to take their place. Although Kuhn does not himself derive those paradigm shifts from material conditions, other historians have insisted that there is a connection. Scientists, they say, do not work in complete isolation from their societies but reflect, in their models of nature, their societies, their modes of production, their human relations, their culture's needs and values.

Precisely because of this fact, as well as the fact that modern science has had a critical impact on the natural world, the history of science has a part in the new environmental history.

Finally, the historian must confront the formidable challenge of examining ideas as ecological agents. We return to the matter of choices that people make in specific environments. What logic, what passion, what unconscious longing, what empirical understanding goes into those choices? And how are choices expressed in rituals, techniques, and legislation? Sometimes choices are made in the halls of national governments. Sometimes they are made in that mysterious realm of the zeitgeist that sweeps across whole eras and continents. But some are also made, even in this day of powerful centralized institutions, by scattered households and farmsteads, by lumberjacks and fishing crews. We have not studied often or well enough the implementation of ideas in those microcosms.

Once again, it is anthropologists who have a lot to offer the historian seeking insight and method. One of the most intriguing pieces of fieldwork that comes from them bears directly on this question of ideas at work in the small setting. It comes out of a mountain valley in New Guinea, where the Tsembaga people subsist on taro, yams, and pigs. Published by Roy Rappaport under the title *Pigs for the Ancestors*, it exemplifies brilliantly how one might conceive of humans and their mental cultures functioning within a single ecosystem.

The Tsembaga appear in Rappaport's study as a population engaged in material relations with other components of their environment. Unlike their plant and animal congeners, however, they create symbols, values, purposes, and meanings, above all, religious meanings, out of the world around them. And that culture performs, though at points obscurely and indirectly, an important function: It encourages the Tsembaga to restrain their use of the land and avoid its degradation. For long periods of time, up to twenty years, these people busy themselves raising pigs, which they accumulate as payment to their ancestral spirits for help in battles with their neighboring enemies. Then at last, when they feel they have enough pigs to satisfy the spirits, a ritualistic slaughter ensues. Hundreds of the animals die and are consumed on behalf of the ancestors. Now, the debt paid, the Tsembaga are ready to go back to war, confident that they will have divine power on their side again. So their lives go round, year after year, decade after decade, in a ritualistic cycle of pig-raising, pig-slaughtering, dancing, feasting, and warring. The local explanation for this cycle is wholly religious, but the outside observer sees something else going on: an elaborate ecological mechanism at work, keeping the number of pigs under control and the people living in equilibrium with their surroundings.

In this forested valley Rappaport has found an example, assuming the validity of the study, of how a culture can take shape through addressing the problems of living within a peculiar ecosystem. The harmony between the two realms of nature and culture seems in this case to be nearly perfect. But the historian wants to know whether human populations are always as successfully adaptive as the Tsembaga. Moreover, are the people that the historian is most likely to study—people organized in advanced, complex societies, relating to nature through modern rituals, religions, and other structures of meaning and value—quite so successful? Rappaport ventures to suggest that the "ecological wisdom" embodied unconsciously in the New Guinea ritual cycle is by no means common. It is most likely to be found where the household is the primary unit of production, where people produce for immediate use rather than for sale and profit, and where "signs of environmental degradation are likely to be apparent quickly to those who can do something about them." Modern industrial societies, on the other hand, he finds culturally maladaptive. In them an economic and technological rationality has replaced the Tsembaga's ecological rationality. Rappaport's case is therefore of limited application elsewhere. Nor does it explain why a change in rationality has occurred, why cultures have drifted away from ecosystem harmony, why modern religion fails to restrain our environmental impact. Generally, anthropology bows out as those issues arise, retiring to its remote green valleys and leaving the historian to face the grinding, shrieking disharmonies of modernity alone.

As it tries to redefine the search into the human past, environmental history has, as indicated above, been drawing on a number of other disciplines, ranging from the natural sciences to anthropology to theology. It has resisted any attempt to put strict disciplinary fences around its work, which would force it to devise all its own methods of analysis, or to require all these overlapping disciplines to stay within their own discrete spheres. Each may have its tradition, to be sure, its unique way of approaching questions. But if this is an age of global interdependence, it is surely also the moment for some cross-disciplinary cooperation. Scholars need it, environmental history needs it, and so does the earth.

One discipline not so far explicitly discussed is geography. Environmental historians have leaned on many geographers for insight, on names like Michael Williams and Donald Meinig among presently active scholars, and from the recent past, names like Carl Sauer, H.C. Darby, and Lucien Febvre. Over the last century scholars from the two disciplines have crossed into one another's territory often and found that they share much in temperament. Geographers, like historians, have tended to be more descriptive than analytical. Taking place rather than time as their focus, they have mapped the distribution of things, just as historians have narrated the sequence of events. Geographers have liked a good landscape just as historians have liked a good story. Both have shown a love of the particular and a resistance to easy generalizing—a quality that may be their common virtue and strength. But they also bear a neighborly resemblance in their weaknesses, above all in their recurring tendency to lose sight of the elemental human-nature connection: historians when they have measured time only by elections and dynasties, geographers when they have tried to reduce the earth and its complexities to the abstract idea of "space." Nature, the land, climate, ecosystems, these are the entities that have relevance. When and where geographers have talked about such forces, they have offered much in the way of information to the new history. More, it has preeminently been geographers who have helped us all see that our situation is no longer one of being shaped by environment; rather, increasingly we are doing the shaping, and often disastrously so. Now the common responsibility of both disciplines is to discover why modern people have been so determined to escape the restraints of nature and what the ecological effects of that desire have been.

Put so comprehensively, with so many lines of investigation possible, it may seem that environmental history has no coherence, that it includes virtually all that has been and is to be. It may appear so wide, so complex, so demanding as to be impossible to pursue except in the most restricted of places and times: say, on a small, scarcely populated island well isolated from the rest of the world and then only for a period of six weeks. Historians of every sort will recognize that feeling of being engulfed by one's subject. No matter how inclusive or specialized one's perspective, the past seems these days like a vast buzzing confusion of voices, forces, events, structures, and relationships defying any coherent understanding. The French speak bravely of doing "total history." History is everything, they say, and everything has a history. True and noble that realization may be, but it does not give much ease of mind. Even delimiting some part of the totality as "environment" may seem to leave us with the still unmanageable burden of trying to write the history of "almost everything." Unfortunately, there is no feasible alternative open to us any longer. We did not make nature or the past; otherwise, we might have made them simpler. Now we are challenged to make some sense of them—and in this case, to make sense of their working intricately together.

NOTES

1. "Systems" talk can be rather mystifying and jargonized. The *American Heritage Dictionary* defines a system as "a group of interacting, interrelated, or interdependent elements forming or regarded as forming a collective entity." One may then speak of systems in nature, in technology and economics, or in thought and culture. And all these, in turn, may be described as interacting systematically, until the mind reels before the complexity.

GENDER AND
ENVIRONMENTAL HISTORY◇

CAROLYN MERCHANT

○

"As it was the intuitive foresight of [Isabella of Spain] which brought the light of civilization to a great continent, so in great measure, will it fall to woman in her power to educate public sentiment to save from rapacious waste and complete exhaustion the resources upon which depend the welfare of the home, the children, and the children's children." So wrote Lydia Adams-Williams, self-styled feminist conservation writer, in 1908. Her compatriot Mrs. Lovell White of California argued that reversing the destruction of the earth brought about by "men whose souls are gang-saws" was a project that required the best efforts of women. These women of the Progressive conservation crusade of the early twentieth century exemplify an overtly feminist perspective of the environment.[1]

Donald Worster's "Transformations of the Earth," while a rich and provocative approach to the field of environmental history, lacks a gender analysis. His conceptual levels of ecology (natural history), production (technology and its socioeconomic relations), and cognition (the mental realm of ideas, ethics, myths, and so on) are a significant framework for research and writing in this emerging field. His use of the mode-of-production concept in differing ecological and cultural contexts and his account of the changing history of ecological ideas in his major books have propelled environmental history to new levels of sophistication.

A gender perspective can add to his conceptual framework in two important ways. First, each of his three categories can be further illuminated through a gender analysis; second, in my view, environmental history needs a fourth analytical level, that of reproduction, which interacts with the other three levels.[2] What could such a perspective contribute to the framework Worster has outlined?

◇ *Journal of American History* 76, 4 (March 1990): 117–21.

Women and men have historically had different roles in production relative to the environment. In subsistence modes of production such as those of native peoples, women's impact on nature is immediate and direct. In gathering-hunting-fishing economies, women collect and process plants, small animals, bird eggs, and shellfish and fabricate tools, baskets, mats, slings, and clothing, while men hunt larger animals, fish, construct weirs and hut frames, and burn forests and brush. Because water and fuelwood availability affect cooking and food preservation, decisions over environmental degradation that dictate when to move camp and village sites may lie in the hands of women. In horticultural communities, women are often the primary producers of crops and fabricators of hoes, planters, and digging sticks, but when such economies are transformed by markets, the cash economies and environmental impacts that ensue are often controlled by men. Women's access to resources to fulfill basic needs may come into direct conflict with male roles in the market economy, as in Seneca women's loss of control over horticulture to make agriculture and male access to cash through greater mobility in nineteenth-century America or in India's chipco (tree-hugging) movement of the past decade, wherein women literally hugged trees to protest declining access to fuelwood for cooking as male-dominated lumbering expanded.[3]

In the agrarian economy of colonial and frontier America, women's outdoor production, like men's, had immediate impact on the environment. While men's work in cutting forests, planting and fertilizing fields, and hunting or fishing affected the larger homestead environment, women's dairying activities, free-ranging barnyard fowl, and vegetable, flower, and herbal gardens all affected the quality of the nearby soils and waters and the level of insect pests, altering the effects of the microenvironment on human health. In the nineteenth century, however, as agriculture became more specialized and oriented toward market production, men took over dairying, poultry-raising, and truck farming, resulting in a decline in women's outdoor production. Although the traditional contributions of women to the farm economy continued in many rural areas and some women assisted in farm as well as home management, the general trend toward capitalist agribusiness increasingly turned chickens, cows, and vegetables into efficient components of factories within fields managed for profits by male farmers.[4]

In the industrial era, as middle-class women turned more of their energies to deliberate child rearing and domesticity, they defined a new but still distinctly female relation to the natural world. In their socially constructed roles as moral mothers, they often taught children about nature and science at home and in the elementary schools. By the Progressive era, women's focus on maintaining a home for husbands and children led many women such as those quoted above to spearhead a nationwide conservation movement to save forest and waters and to create national and local parks. Although the gains of the movement have been attributed by historians to men such as President Theodore Roosevelt, forester Gifford Pinchot, and preservationist John Muir, the efforts of thousands of women were directly responsible for many of the country's most significant conservation achievements. Women writers on nature such as Isabella Bird, Mary Austin, and Rachel Carson have been among the most influential commentators on the American response to nature.[5]

Worster's conceptual framework for environmental history can thus be made more complete by including a gender analysis of the differential effects of women and men on ecology and their differential roles in production. At the level of cognition as well, a sensitivity to gender enriches environmental history. Native Americans, for example, construed the natural world as animated and created by spirits and gods. Origin myths included tales of mother earth and father sky, grandmother woodchucks and coyote tricksters, corn mothers and tree spirits. Such deities mediated between nature and humans, inspiring rituals and behaviors that helped to regulate environmental use and exploitation. Similar myths focused planting, harvesting, and first fruit rituals among native Americans and in such Old World cultures as those in ancient Mesopotamia, Egypt, and Greece, which symbolized nature as a mother goddess. In Renaissance Europe the earth was conceptualized as a nurturing mother (God's vice-regent in the mundane world) and the cosmos as an organism having a body, soul, and spirit. An animate earth and an I/thou relationship between humans and the world does not prevent the exploitation of resources for human use, but it entails an ethic of restraint and propitiation by setting up religious rituals to be followed before mining ores, damming brooks, or planting and harvesting crops. The human relationship to the land is intimately connected to daily survival.[6]

When mercantile capitalism, industrialization, and urbanization began to distance increasing numbers of male elites from the land in seventeenth-century England and in nineteenth-century America, the mechanistic framework created by the "fathers" of modern science legitimated the use of nature for human profit making. The conception that nature was dead, made up of inert atoms moved by external forces, that God was an engineer and mathematician, and that human perception was the result of particles of light bouncing off objects and conveyed to the brain as discrete sensations meant that nature responded to human interventions, not as active participant, but as passive instrument. Thus the way in which world views, myths, and perceptions are constructed by gender at the cognitive level can be made an integral part of environmental history.[7]

While Worster's analytical levels of ecology, production, and cognition may be made more sophisticated by including a gender analysis, ideas drawn from feminist theory suggest the usefulness of a fourth level of analysis—reproduction—that is dialectically related to the other three. First, all species reproduce themselves generationally and their population levels have impacts on the local ecology. But for humans, the numbers that can be sustained are related to the mode of production: More people can occupy a given ecosystem under a horticultural than a gathering-hunting-fishing mode, and still more under an industrial mode. Humans reproduce themselves biologically in accordance with the social and ethical norms of the culture into which they are born. Native peoples adopted an array of benign and malign population control techniques such as long lactation, abstention, coitus interruptus, the use of native plants to induce abortion, infanticide, and senilicide. Carrying capacity, nutritional factors, and tribally accepted customs dictated the numbers of infants that survived to adulthood in order to reproduce the tribal whole. Colonial Americans, by contrast, encouraged high numbers of births owing to the scarcity of labour in the new lands. With the onset of industrialization in the nineteenth century, a demographic transition resulted in fewer births per female. Intergenerational reproduction, therefore, mediated through production, has impact on the local ecology.[8]

Second, people (as well as other living things) must reproduce their own energy on a daily basis through food and must conserve that energy through clothing (skins, furs, or other methods of bodily temperature control) and shelter. Gathering or planting food crops, fabricating clothing, and constructing houses are directed toward the reproduction of daily life.

In addition to these biological aspects of reproduction, human communities reproduce themselves socially in two additional ways. People pass on skills and behavioral norms to the next generation of producers, and that allows a culture to reproduce itself over time. They also structure systems of governance and laws that maintain the social order of the tribe, town, or nation. Many such laws and policies deal with the allocation and regulation of natural resources, land, and property rights. They are passed by legislative bodies and administered through government agencies and a system of justice. Law in this interpretation is a means of maintaining and modifying a particular social order. These four aspects of reproduction (two biological and two social) interact with ecology as mediated by a particular mode of production.[9]

Such an analysis of production and reproduction in relation to ecology helps to delineate changes in forms of patriarchy in different societies. Although in most societies governance may have been vested in the hands of men (hence patriarchy), the balance of power between the sexes differed. In gatherer-hunter and horticultural communities, extraction and production of food may have been either equally shared by or dominated by women, so that male (or female) power in tribal reproduction (chiefs and shamans) was balanced by female power in production. In subsistence-oriented communities in colonial and frontier America, men and women shared power in production, although men played dominant roles in legal-political reproduction of the social whole. Under industrial capitalism in the nineteenth century, women's loss of power in outdoor farm production was compensated by a gain of power in the reproduction of daily life (domesticity) and in the socialization of children and husbands (the moral mother) in the sphere of reproduction. Thus the shifts of power that Worster argues occurs in different environments are not only those between indigenous and invading cultures but also those between men and women.[10]

A gender perspective on environmental history therefore both offers a more balanced and complete picture of past human interactions with nature and advances its theoretical frameworks. The ways in which female and male contributions to production, reproduction, and cognition are actually played out in relation to ecology depends on the particular stage and the actors involved. Yet within the various acts of what Timothy Weiskel has called the global ecodrama should be included scenes in which men's and women's roles come to center stage and scenes in which nature "herself" is an actress. In this way gender in environmental history can contribute to a more holistic history of various regions and eras.[11]

NOTES

1. Carolyn Merchant, "Women of the Progressive Conservation Movement, 1900–1916," *Environmental Review*, 8 (Spring 1984), 57–85, esp. 65, 59.

2. For a more detailed discussion, see Carolyn Merchant, "The Theoretical Structure of Ecological Revolutions," *ibid.*, 11 (Winter 1987), 251–74. For a discussion of theoretical frameworks for environmental history, see Barbara Leibhardt, "Interpretations and Causal Analysis: Theories in Environmental History," *ibid.*, 12 (Spring 1988), 23–36.

3. Sandra Marburg, "Women and Environment: Subsistence Paradigms, 1850–1950," *ibid.*, 8 (Spring 1984), 7–22; Diane Rothenberg, "Erosion of Power: An Economic Basis for the Selective Conservativism of Seneca Women in the Nineteenth Century," *Western Canadian Journal of Anthropology*, 6 (1976), 106–22; Vandana Shiva, *Staying Alive: Women, Ecology, and Development* (London, 1988); Mona Etienne and Eleanor Leacock, eds., *Women and Colonization: Anthropological Perspectives* (New York, 1980).

4. Carolyn Merchant, *Ecological Revolutions: Nature, Gender, and Science in New England* (Chapel Hill, 1989); Corlann Gee Bush, "The Barn Is His, the House Is Mine," in *Energy and Transport*, ed. George Daniels and Mark Rose (Beverly Hills, 1982), 235–59; Carolyn E. Sachs, *The Invisible Farmers: Women in Agricultural Production* (Totowa, 1983).

5. Merchant, "Women of the Progressive Conservation Movement"; Vera Norwood, "Heroines of Nature: Four Women Respond to the American Landscape," *Environmental Review*, 8 (Spring 1984), 34–56.

6. Paula Gunn Allen, *The Sacred Hoop: Recovering the Feminine in American Indian Traditions* (Boston, 1984); Riane Eisler, *The Chalice and the Blade* (San Francisco, 1988); Pamela Berger, *The Goddess Obscured: Transformation of the Grain Protectress from Goddess to Saint* (Boston, 1985); Janet Bord and Colin Bord, *Earth Rites: Fertility Practices in Pre-Industrial Britain* (London, 1982); Carolyn Merchant, *The Death of Nature: Women, Ecology, and the Scientific Revolution* (San Francisco, 1980).

7. Merchant, *Death of Nature*. See also Evelyn Fox Keller, *Reflections on Gender and Science* (New Haven, 1985), 33–65. On gender in American perceptions of nature, see Annette Kolodny, *The Lay of the Land: Metaphor as Experience and History in American Life and Letters* (Chapel Hill, 1975); and Annette Kolodny, *The Land before Her: Fantasy and Experience of the American Frontier, 1630–1860* (Chapel Hill, 1984).

8. Ester Boserup, *The Conditions of Agricultural Growth: The Economics of Agrarian Change under Population Pressure* (Chicago, 1965); Ester Boserup, *Women's Role in Economic Development* (New York, 1970); Marvin Harris, *Cultural Materialism: The Struggle for a Science of Culture* (New York, 1979); Carolyn Merchant, "The Realm of Social Relations: Production, Reproduction, and Gender in Environmental Transfor-

mations," in *The Earth as Transformed by Human Action*, ed. B.L. Turner II (New York, forthcoming); Robert Wells, *Uncle Sam's Family: Issues and Perspectives in American Demographic History* (Albany, 1985), 28–56.

9. For a more detailed elaboration of reproduction as an organizing category see Merchant, *Ecological Revolutions*.

10. *Ibid.*, Nancy F. Cott, *The Bonds of Womanhood: "Woman's Sphere" in New England, 1780–1835* (New Haven, 1977); Barbara Leslie Epstein, *The Politics of Domesticity: Women,* *Evangelism, and Temperance in Nineteenth Century America* (Middletown, 1981); Ruth Bloch, "American Feminine Ideals in Transition: The Rise of the Moral Mother, 1785–1815," *Feminist Studies*, 4 (June 1978), 101–26; Barbara Welter, "The Cult of True Womanhood, 1820–1860," *American Quarterly*, 18 (Summer 1966), 151–74.

11. On environmental history as an eco-drama, see Timothy Weiskel, "Agents of Empire: Steps toward an Ecology of Imperialism," *Environmental Review*, 11 (Winter 1987), 275–88.

THE NATURE AND UTILITY OF TRADITIONAL ECOLOGICAL KNOWLEDGE◇

MILTON M.R. FREEMAN

o

Increasingly, the published scientific literature and the convening of conferences and workshops reflects the growing awareness that there is a legiti-
mate field of environmental expertise known as traditional ecological
knowledge. For about a half century anthropologists and some animal and
plant taxonomists[1] have recognized the accuracy with which various non-
western peoples have identified different species; indeed, such "folk-
taxonomies" include more than just those food or medicinal species having
obvious practical utility. The comprehensiveness of the taxonomic system
suggests that the extent of traditional knowledge may be quite profound,
and that, indeed, taxonomy is important (as in the biological sciences) as the
basis for building extensive systems of knowing about nature.

More recently, many scientists have begun to understand that such traditional knowledge extends far beyond what in western science would be
called descriptive biology, beyond knowing how to identify different species
of animals, or describe their feeding, reproduction, or migratory behaviour.
The knowledge possessed by such tradition-based, non-industrial societies is
essentially of an "ecological" nature, that is to say, it seeks to understand
and explain the workings of ecosystems, or at the very least biological communities, containing many interacting species of animals and often plants,
and the determinative role played by certain key biological and physical
parameters in influencing the behaviour of the total biological community.

In the recent social science literature this aspect of traditional knowledge has to a large extent been documented, more especially, for a large

number of so-called foraging (i.e., hunter-fisher-gatherer) peoples, from the tropics to the Arctic.[2] It is important to note that such traditional ecological knowledge has been found to have management relevance, especially in regard to sustainable use of renewable resources.[3] It is also important in such endeavours as Environmental Impact Assessment.[4]

Expressed another way, traditional ecological knowledge is more than merely esoteric; it is directed toward gaining a useful understanding of how ecological systems generally work, to how many of the key components of the total ecosystem interrelate, and how predictive outcomes in respect to matters of practical concern can best be effected. This is precisely what ecological scientists or wildlife and fisheries biologists attempt to do; however, the question remains: How successful are both groups (the scientists and the traditional resource users) in their efforts to understand these complex realities?

WHY QUESTION SCIENTISTS' ENVIRONMENTAL KNOWLEDGE?

First, it must be stated that even attempting to define the task at hand in relation to such dynamic complexity (as ecosystems represent) is a daunting task. Not only do such biophysical systems contain innumerable interacting components, or sub-systems, but most basic parts (e.g., the micro-organismic component that accounts for the greatest proportion of the biological activity of the ecosystem) are largely unknown to science and for the most part ignored in the analysis. Most ecologists have little understanding or even interest in microbial taxonomy, physiology, or ecology, yet the classical approach to analysing ecosystem structure and function is largely built upon the presumption that such knowledge is controlled.

Then it must be remembered that ecosystems are subject to purely stochastic (or random) variation from place to place, season to season, and year to year. Of course, variability can be allowed for, but it cannot be predicted. Lastly, we might consider the problem of comprehending the ecosystem-as-a-whole, when the methods of science are essentially reductionist, that is to say, they seek to understand organisms or nature by studying the smallest or simplest manageable part or sub-system in essential isolation.

How good, one may ask, is a methodology that takes the exceedingly complex whole apart, and essentially destroys its components? Is the whole really only the sum of all its disassociated parts? Can we ever come close to understanding so complex and interactive a system by studying each part in isolation, by treating it as if it were a non-living machine?

Perhaps we can gain such an understanding through the above methods of study. However, the task would seem to require that immense quantities of research be conducted so that each part is in fact adequately understood under an almost infinite variety of variable and constantly refigured conditions; and then it would require the very careful reintegration of all these disarticulated pieces of useful knowledge in order to reconstruct the system as a whole.

CAN WE MAKE ECOLOGICAL COMPLEXITY MORE UNDERSTANDABLE?

Some might suggest that there are more practical and reasonable ways of trying to understand complex systems as wholes than by taking them apart and then laboriously reassembling all the once-integrated bits and pieces to reconstruct a semblance of the former system-as-a-whole.

Traditional knowledge seeks to comprehend such complexity by operating from a different epistemological basis. It eschews reductionism, placing little emphasis on studying small parts of the ecological system in isolation from the dependent interacting biophysical milieu. It also recognizes that the reductionist approach is impractical in the extreme: even if one were to know everything there was to know about everything of importance under all possible combinations and permutations of variability, such an immense data base would be impossible to work with in practice.

Given such apparent limitations of the scientific method and its inherent appetite, scientists are always calling for more research data, in fact, for more and more knowledge about less and less. Why not, by way of contrast, approach the problem from a purely practical, as opposed to eminently impractical, standpoint? Fishery scientists are among those making such pleas for a simplified, intuitively generated analytic approach, remarkably similar to the tradition-based system of knowing.[5]

The traditional ecological knowledge (TEK) approach recognizes that a supercomputer of extraordinary sophistication does exist, and that it can work for all practical purposes with incomplete data sets. Indeed, it is able to creatively fill in many of the knowledge blanks, an absolutely essential characteristic in those cases where knowledge is not just unknown but, in fact, may be unknowable.

This supercomputer, the human brain, is programmed to collect and systematize knowledge, to intuitively filter out background noise and discern chaos, and to draw normative conclusions from various disparate data sets (via group experience extending through preceding generations) pertaining to the same general ecological system in all its varying states. The programs which run the computations in this supercomputer may be old, quite traditional in fact, but the data base is constantly updated as new data pertaining to changing environmental circumstances alter the behaviour of the biological communities which provide the empirically derived data which the brain receives, stores, and analyses.

Why should one believe that this old-style intuitive approach to knowing is relevant to assessing environmental circumstances? First, it operates on a rational basis that underlies much scientific research carried out today. For example, it employs critical comparative analysis: comparing what is happening now with what is known to have happened in the past. Scientists also do this: they study variability in data sets and attempt to account for it.

However, scientists rarely have comprehensive data sets that take note of a variety of co-varying environmental features over long periods of time.

Scientists continually warn of the need to accumulate "base-line" data, data against which future changes can be compared. Traditional knowledge-based systems already possess such data sets, often of sufficient length to cover several population "cycles" where periodicity may be measured in 70- or 80-year spans.

THE PROBLEM OF ACQUIRING "BASE-LINE DATA"

Even if scientists were fortunate enough to have such extensive year-round, somewhat standardized observations, annually repeated for those particular species, it is most unlikely that they would have concomitant data pertaining to such all-season environmental conditions as temperature, precipitation, parasite levels, or any of a very large number of seemingly pertinent ecological changes occurring in the system-as-a-whole at the same time. These are just the data sets that accumulate in TEK systems, or at least tend to be recorded when deviations take place from normative expectations.

The essential difference between the scientist's approach to knowing what is happening and that of the tradition-based resource user is not the difference existing between the attenuated data base available to the scientist compared to the more extensive data set of the local user. Nor is it the reductionism of the scientist versus the holism of the local resource user, important as these particular differences may be.

Perhaps the principal difference is again epistemological: the scientist is concerned with causality, with understanding an essentially linear process of cause and effect. If causes of observed effects can be measured and understood, then predictive statements about future outcomes can be made and the natural world can be managed. But the non-western forager lives in a world not of linear causal events but of constantly reforming multidimensional interacting cycles, where nothing is simply a cause or an effect, but all factors are influences impacting other elements of the system-as-a-whole.

Linear approaches to analysis cannot be applied to cyclical systems, and, as everyone now realizes, ecosystems are in fact complex cycles of recirculating energy matter, and relationships. Nowhere does the Cartesian model of modern science fail so completely and utterly as in trying to explain the workings of natural ecosystems.

THE CURRENT SCIENTIFIC REVOLUTION AND UNDERSTANDING NATURE

Physicists, as the leaders in the scientific revolution now underway, increasingly utilize words such as organic, holistic, systemic, and ecological in their understanding of the workings of natural events.[6] The recent findings of modern physicists are becoming similar to views held in many ancient mystical traditions, even though these traditional systems of thought are not necessarily known to the scientists who make these recent rediscoveries.[7]

In relation to scientists increasingly appreciating the inherent limitations of the classical scientific way of analysing nature, or ecological systems, reference was earlier made to the traditional ecological knowledge-based approach that denies the usefulness of a reductionist approach to seeking cause and effect as an operational principle for serious enquiry. In this regard, it is as well to consider that scientists now also understand that, at a fundamental level, certain phenomena are best understood not as being composed of isolated entities that can be studied as such, but rather they can better be understood by means of the influence they have on other phenomena. In other words, by means of their systemic relationships, outside of which they in fact cease to be definable.

So fundamental is this realization to some leading thinkers, that one such, Gregory Bateson, has argued "that relationships should be used as a basis for all definitions, and this should be taught to our children in elementary school. Anything . . . should be defined not by what it is in itself, but by its relations to other things."[8] It appears then, that in some important respects, the leading edge of scientific thinking is coming into remarkable alignment with the TEK-based system of understanding what is the appropriate way of comprehending nature.

The question posed earlier, and that still needs to be asked (as modern science appears to be without a workable methodology in relation to ecological understanding) is: "but does the alternative (i.e., TEK) work?" That depends on the criteria to be applied in assessing the "success" of TEK. How does one assess its degree of "rightness" or "truth"?

DOES TEK ADD ANYTHING USEFUL TO MODERN UNDERSTANDING?

Some might argue that, as TEK has provided the basis for whole groups of people surviving as food-gatherers, often in seemingly inhospitable environments, then the long-term persistence of these particular human societies should be evidence enough that it does work, at least most of the time. This "most of the time" rider would accommodate the obvious fact that sometimes people did not succeed, and either died of starvation or periodically suffered from serious food shortages.

However, such a means of assessing TEK has obvious shortcomings. For example, people (and in fact all predators) are obviously "smarter" than the prey species they hunt or fish, so for purely biologically determined reasons it can be assumed that people (as other predators) will naturally survive. If this were not so, the human population in question would not be present to be studied and assessed.

Perhaps the best way of trying to assess the efficacy of the TEK approach to understanding nature, is to look at some recent examples where it has been contrasted with scientific understanding of the same event. Here, I merely contrast a few examples that I have personal knowledge of, relating to events having taken place over the past several decades in the North American arctic regions.

CASE 1

This relates to Inuit knowledge that survival of Peary caribou in the High Arctic depends upon the social structure of the small herds in winter. Therefore, the management of these caribou for sustained harvesting requires, in addition to an overall quota system, the non-selective hunting of all animals encountered opportunistically rather than through the management system instituted by scientists where selective hunting of large males is advocated with a prohibition on hunting females and immature animals. The TEK view holds that only hunting large males will quickly result in the accelerated death of the remaining population, a view that has been borne out by subsequent monitoring of the south Ellesmere Island regional population.[9]

CASE 2

Inuit TEK of the social structure and behaviour of musk-oxen (an animal not at the time hunted due to a 50-year-old management restriction) argued that scientists' ideas of "solitary and surplus" males were incorrect, and that such animals play an important role in enhancing musk-oxen population survival. Therefore, instituting a program to harvest such "surplus" animals would prove unwise. Such views, contradicting scientists' conventional wisdom, were nevertheless independently corroborated.[10]

CASE 3

Scientific surveys indicated the Beaufort Sea bowhead whale population was very depleted, with only about 800 whales surviving in 1977. Local hunters stated the whale population was about 7000. They also took issue with assumptions underlying scientists' population estimates (e.g., that whales only migrated in open water leads, and were incapable of swimming under the ice offshore and did not feed during migration). On the other hand, Inuit hunters believe whales migrate hundreds of miles offshore under the ice and therefore cannot be censured by visual means alone. On the basis of these methodological criticisms, a sophisticated survey technique was developed, incorporating Inuit assumptions (later verified). Using the new census methods the 1991 bowhead population was conservatively estimated to be in excess of 8000 whales, despite an annual harvest of between 20 and 40 whales over the past decade. The findings tended to confirm the Inuit 1977 population assessment of about 7000 animals.[11]

CASE 4

In 1979 biologists warned, from the results of aerial censuses, that the barren-ground caribou west of Hudson Bay were seriously depleted and over-hunted. The Inuit hunters disputed these findings and the prognosis that the herds were about to become extinct. Scientists claimed a decrease of approximately 100 000 animals had occurred in just a few years. Inuit countered that the census techniques were deficient and that recent changes in seasonal caribou distribution also contributed to the low census figures. To resolve the conflict, surveys were carried out by census techniques suggested by Inuit hunters. The result was that population estimates increased by approximately 100 000 caribou, thus confirming that the herds were not threatened by "overhunting" and extinction.[12]

CONCLUSION

This paper suggests that a large quantity of information now exists in the published scientific literature to suggest that traditional ecological knowledge and its application to enlightened environmental assessment and management should be taken seriously. No one group of observers has a monopoly on truth, and the history of western science makes it quite clear that the scientific truths of today will, in ever-decreasing intervals of time, constitute the bulk of tomorrow's discarded hypotheses and superseded knowledge.

As scientists and philosophers working at the frontiers of knowledge increasingly find, the world view and technologies of many ancient cultures have a great deal to offer, whether in "new" health, or in ways of conserving ground water or increasing crop and time-tested understandings and approaches existing in regard to sustainable use of wild natural resources. The future will likely increasingly benefit by the critical assessment, and where appropriate application, of such efficacious means of managing our embattled environment.

NOTES

1. E. Mayr, E.G. Linsley, and R.L. Usinger, *Methods and Principles of Systematic Zoology* (New York: McGraw-Hill, 1953), 5.

2. See, for example, N.M. Williams and E.S. Hunn, eds., *Resource Managers: North American and Australian Hunter-gatherers* (Boulder, CO: Westview Press, 1982); M.M.R. Freeman and L.N. Carbyn, eds., *Traditional Knowledge and Renewable Resources Management in Northern Regions* (Occasional Paper no. 20, Boreal Institute for Northern Studies, Edmonton, 1988); and K. Ruddle and R. Johannes, eds., *The Traditional Knowledge and Management of Coastal Systems in Asia and the Pacific*, 2nd ed. (Jakarta: UNESCO, 1990).

3. B.J. McCay and J. Acheson, *The Question of the Commons* (Tucson:

University of Arizona Press, 1987); F. Berkes, ed., *Common Property Resources: Ecology and Community-based Sustainable Development* (London: Belhaven Press, 1989); and M.M.R. Freeman, Y. Matsuda, and K. Ruddle, eds., *Adaptive Marine Resource Management Systems in the Pacific* (Philadelphia: Harwood Academic Publishers, 1991).

4. For example, M.M.R. Freeman, "Assessing Movement in an Arctic Caribou Population," *Journal of Environmental Management* 3 (1975): 251–57; D. Craig, *Resolution of Conflict in Australian Water Management: Aboriginal Interests and Perspectives* (Centre for Resource and Environmental Studies, Australian National University, Canberra, 1989); and D.J. Nakashima, *Application of Native Knowledge in EIA: Inuit, Eiders and Hudson Bay Oil* (Report prepared for

the Canadian Environmental Assessment Research Council, Hull, 1990).

5. For example, S. Tanaka, *On a Practical Method for Stock Assessment* (Document SC/A86/CA5, International Whaling Commission, Cambridge, 1986).

6. See, for example, F. Capra, *The Turning Point: Science, Society and the Rising Culture* (London: Fontana, Collins, 1982), 66.

7. Ibid., 66–67.

8. Ibid., 70.

9. M.M.R. Freeman, "Appeal to Tradition: Different Perspectives on Wildlife Management" in *Native Power: The Quest for Autonomy and Nationhood of Aboriginal Peoples*, ed. J. Brosted, J. Dahl, et al. (Oslo: Universitetsforlaget, 1985), 265–81.

10. Ibid.; M.M.R. Freeman, "Population Characteristics of Musk-ox in the Jones Sound Region of the Northwest Territories," *Journal of Wildlife Management* 35 (1971): 105–10.

11. M.M.R. Freeman, "The Alaska Eskimo Whaling Commission: Successful Co-management Under Extreme Conditions" in *Co-operative Management of Local Fisheries*, ed. E. Pinkerton (Vancouver: University of British Columbia Press, 1989), 137–53.

12. M.M.R. Freeman, "Graphs and Gaffs: A Cautionary Tale in the Common Property Resource Debate" in *Common Property Resources: Ecology and Community-based Sustainable Development*, ed. F. Berkes (London: Belhaven Press, 1989), 92–109.

BIOLOGY, CULTURE,
AND IMPERIALISM

F rom an environmental perspective, the contact between Natives and newcomers at the origins of Canada was vastly more complex than suggested by the familiar images of indigenous groups interacting with fur traders, missionaries, settlers, and soldiers. As Alfred W. Crosby explains in the opening article of this section, this contact did not simply involve humans; rather, Europeans were only one of a diverse array of immigrant organisms that included animals, plants, and bacteria. Moreover, Crosby argues that the demographic takeover of the "New World" could not have been accomplished by humans alone, despite the power of their guns. Rather, the takeover resulted from the immigration of an "aggressive and opportunistic" ecosystem in which capitalism and Christianity were only part of a larger ecological imperialism.

In the next reading, Ramsay Cook builds on Crosby's interpretation by focusing on the intellectual component of this ecological imperialism. Cook's analysis is founded on his extensive research on French writings from the time of Jacques Cartier. These writings show how the metaphor of a garden underlay the establishment of New France. Rather than coming to grips with the North American environment on its own terms, French imperialists maintained the equation of civilization with European-style land cultivation.

Underlying the ambition to create a "garden" in New France during the seventeenth and eighteenth centuries was the general belief that humans should own and dominate the rest of the environment. In her article on the Great Plains, Irene M. Spry shows that this belief was similarly characteristic of the continued takeover by European-origin immigrants in nineteenth-century British North America and early Canada. However, Spry emphasizes that the Native peoples had an entirely different environmental perspective. She examines how Natives prized personal qualities such as skill, courage, and endurance, and did not judge individuals by their material possessions. Spry emphasizes the complex relationships between aboriginal peoples and the rest of the environment, and how the European invasion forced indigenous groups to reconfigure these relationships, often in ways that undermined their societies. Spry's use of concepts such as "paleolithic bliss" would not be supported by those scholars who have attacked the idea that any society has lived in harmony with nature, but her description of the Great Plains shows clearly how the longstanding European ambition of making a garden led to "dismal boredom, subordination, and dependence" for Native peoples.

Taken together, the articles in this section indicate some of the ways in which an environmental approach changes our understanding of the origins of Canada. Rather than assuming that human thought and action can be understood in isolation from the rest of the environment, historians are now recognizing the diverse contextual relationships at the heart of the Old World's encounter with the New World.

ECOLOGICAL IMPERIALISM: THE OVERSEAS MIGRATION OF WESTERN EUROPEANS AS A BIOLOGICAL PHENOMENON[*]

ALFRED W. CROSBY

o

Industrial man may in many respects be considered an aggressive and successful weed strangling other species and even the weaker members of its own.

Stafford Lightman,
"The Responsibilities of Intervention in Isolated Societies,"
Health and Disease in Tribal Societies

Europeans in North America, especially those with an interest in gardening and botany, are often stricken with fits of homesickness at the sight of certain plants which, like themselves, have somehow strayed thousands of miles eastward across the Atlantic. Vladimir Nabokov, the Russian exile, had such an experience on the mountain slopes of Oregon:

Do you recognize that clover?
Dandelions, *l'or du pauvre?*
(Europe, nonetheless, is over.)

A century earlier the success of European weeds in America inspired Charles Darwin to goad the American botanist Asa Gray: "Does it not hurt your Yankee pride that we thrash you so confoundly? I am sure Mrs. Gray will stick up for your own weeds. Ask her whether they are not more honest, downright good sort of weeds."[1]

---

[*] Reprinted with permission from Donald Worster, ed., *The Ends of the Earth: Perspectives on Modern Environmental History* (Cambridge: Cambridge University Press, 1985), 103–17.

The common dandelion, *l'or du pauvre*, despite its ubiquity and its bright yellow flower, is not at all the most visible of the Old World immigrants in North America. Vladimir Nabokov was a prime example of the most visible kind: the *Homo sapiens* of European origin. Europeans and their descendants, who comprise the majority of human beings in North America and in a number of other lands outside of Europe, are the most spectacularly successful overseas migrants of all time. How strange it is to find Englishmen, Germans, Frenchmen, Italians, and Spaniards comfortably ensconced in places with names like Wollongong (Australia), Rotorua (New Zealand), and Saskatoon (Canada), where obviously other peoples should dominate, as they must have at one time.

None of the major genetic groupings of humankind is as oddly distributed about the world as European, especially western European, whites. Almost all the peoples we call Mongoloids live in the single contiguous land mass of Asia. Black Africans are divided between three continents— their homeland and North and South America—but most of them are concentrated in their original latitudes, the tropics, facing each other across one ocean. European whites were all recently concentrated in Europe, but in the last few centuries have burst out, as energetically as if from a burning building, and have created vast settlements of their kind in the South Temperate Zone and North Temperate Zone (excepting Asia, a continent already thoroughly and irreversibly tenanted). In Canada and the United States together they amount to nearly 90 percent of the population; in Argentina and Uruguay together to over 95 percent; in Australia to 98 percent; and in New Zealand to 90 percent. The only nations in the Temperate Zones outside of Asia which do not have enormous majorities of European whites are Chile, with a population of two-thirds mixed Spanish and Indian stock, and South Africa, where blacks outnumber whites six to one. How odd that these two, so many thousands of miles from Europe, should be exceptions in not being predominantly pure European.[2]

Europeans have conquered Canada, the United States, Argentina, Uruguay, Australia, and New Zealand not just militarily and economically and technologically—as they did India, Nigeria, Mexico, Peru, and other tropical lands, whose native people have long since expelled or interbred with and even absorbed the invaders. In the Temperate Zone lands listed above Europeans conquered and triumphed demographically. These, for the sake of convenience, we will call the Lands of the Demographic Takeover.

There is a long tradition of emphasizing the contrasts between Europeans and Americans—a tradition honored by such names as Henry James and Frederick Jackson Turner—but the vital question is really why Americans are so European. And why the Argentinians, the Uruguayans, the Australians, and the New Zealanders are so European in the obvious genetic sense.

The reasons for the relative failure of the European demographic takeover in the tropics are clear. In tropical Africa, until recently, Europeans died in droves of the fevers; in tropical America they died almost as fast of the same diseases, plus a few native American additions. Furthermore, in neither region did European agricultural techniques, crops, and animals prosper. Europeans did try to found colonies for settlement, rather than merely exploitation, but they failed or achieved only partial success in the hot lands. The Scots left their bones as monument to their short-lived colony at Darien at the turn of the eighteenth century. The English Puritans who skipped Massachusetts Bay Colony to go to Providence Island in the Caribbean Sea did not even achieve a permanent settlement, much less a Commonwealth of God. The Portuguese who went to northeastern Brazil created viable settlements, but only by perching themselves on top of first a population of native Indian laborers and then, when these faded away, a population of laborers imported from Africa. They did achieve a demographic takeover, but only by interbreeding with their servants. The Portuguese in Angola, who helped supply those servants, never had a breath of a chance to achieve a demographic takeover.[3] There was much to repel and little to attract the mass of Europeans to the tropics, and so they stayed home or went to the lands where life was healthier, labor more rewarding, and where white immigrants, by their very number, encouraged more immigration.

In the cooler lands, the colonies of the Demographic Takeover, Europeans achieved very rapid population growth by means of immigration, by increased life span, and by maintaining very high birthrates. Rarely has population expanded more rapidly than it did in the eighteenth and nineteenth centuries in these lands. It is these lands, especially the United States, that enabled Europeans and their overseas offspring to expand from something like 18 percent of the human species in 1650 to well over 30 percent in 1900. Today 670 million Europeans live in Europe, and 250 million or so other Europeans—genetically as European as any left behind in the Old World—live in the Lands of the Demographic Takeover, an ocean or so from home.[4] What the Europeans have done with unprecedented success in the past few centuries can accurately be described by a term from apiculture: They have swarmed.

They swarmed to lands which were populated at the time of European arrival by peoples as physically capable of rapid increase as the Europeans, and yet who are now small minorities in their homelands and sometimes no more than relict populations. These population explosions among colonial Europeans of the past few centuries coincided with population crashes among the aborigines. If overseas Europeans have historically been less fatalistic and grim than their relatives in Europe, it is because they have viewed the histories of their nations very selectively. When he returned from his world voyage on the *Beagle* in the 1830s, Charles Darwin, as a biologist rather than a historian, wrote, "Wherever the European has trod, death seems to pursue the aboriginal."[5]

Any respectable theory which attempts to explain the Europeans' demographic triumphs has to provide explanations for at least two phenomena. The first is the decimation and demoralization of the aboriginal populations of Canada, the United States, Argentina, and others. The obliterating defeat of these populations was not simply due to European technological superiority. The Europeans who settled in temperate South Africa seemingly had the same advantages as those who settled in Virginia and

New South Wales, and yet how different was their fate. The Bantu-speaking peoples, who now overwhelmingly outnumber the whites in South Africa, were superior to their American, Australian, and New Zealand counterparts in that they possessed iron weapons, but how much more inferior to a musket or a rifle is a stone-pointed spear than an iron-pointed spear? The Bantu have prospered demographically not because of their numbers at the time of first contact with whites, which were probably not greater per square mile than those of the Indians east of the Mississippi River. Rather, the Bantu have prospered because they survived military conquest, avoided the conquerors, or became their indispensable servants—and in the long run because they reproduced faster than the whites. In contrast, why did so few of the natives of the Lands of the Demographic Takeover survive?

Second, we must explain the stunning, even awesome success of European agriculture, that is, the European way of manipulating the environment in the Lands of the Demographic Takeover. The difficult progress of the European frontier in the Siberian *taiga* or the Brazilian *sertão* or the South African *veldt* contrasts sharply with its easy, almost fluid advance in North America. Of course, the pioneers of North America would never have characterized their progress as easy: Their lives were filled with danger, deprivation, and unremitting labor; but as a group they always succeeded in taming whatever portion of North America they wanted within a few decades and usually a good deal less time. Many individuals among them failed—they were driven mad by blizzards and dust storms, lost their crops to locusts and their flocks to cougars and wolves, or lost their scalps to understandably inhospitable Indians—but as a group they always succeeded—and in terms of human generations, very quickly.

In attempting to explain these two phenomena, let us examine four categories of organisms deeply involved in European expansion: (1) human beings; (2) animals closely associated with human beings—both the desirable animals like horses and cattle and undesirable varmints like rats and mice; (3) pathogens or microorganisms that cause disease in humans; and (4) weeds. Is there a pattern in the histories of these groups which suggests an overall explanation for the phenomenon of the Demographic Takeover or which at least suggests fresh paths of inquiry?

Europe has exported something in excess of sixty million people in the past few hundred years. Great Britain alone exported over twenty million. The great mass of these white emigrants went to the United States, Argentina, Canada, Australia, Uruguay, and New Zealand. (Other areas to absorb comparable quantities of Europeans were Brazil and Russia east of the Urals. These would qualify as Lands of the Demographic Takeover except that large fractions of their populations are non-European.)[6]

In stark contrast, very few aborigines of the Americas, Australia, or New Zealand ever went to Europe. Those who did often died not long after arrival.[7] The fact that the flow of human migration was almost entirely from Europe to her colonies and not vice versa is not startling—or very enlightening. Europeans controlled overseas migration, and Europe needed to export, not import, labor. But this pattern of one-way migration is significant in that it reappears in other connections.

The vast expanses of forests, savannas, and steppes in the Lands of the Demographic Takeover were inundated by animals from the Old World, chiefly from Europe. Horses, cattle, sheep, goats, and pigs have for hundreds of years been among the most numerous of the quadrupeds of these lands, which were completely lacking in these species at the time of first contact with the Europeans. By 1600 enormous feral herds of horses and cattle surged over the pampas of the Rio de la Plata (today's Argentina and Uruguay) and over the plains of northern Mexico. By the beginning of the seventeenth century packs of Old World dogs gone wild were among the predators of these herds.[8]

In the forested country of British North America population explosions among imported animals were also spectacular, but only by European standards, not by those of Spanish America. In 1700 in Virginia feral hogs, said one witness, "swarm like vermaine upon the Earth," and young gentlemen were entertaining themselves by hunting wild horses of the inland counties. In Carolina the herds of cattle were "incredible, being from one to two thousand head in one Man's Possession." In the eighteenth and early nineteenth centuries the advancing European frontier from New England to the Gulf of Mexico was preceded into Indian territory by an avant-garde of semiwild herds of hogs and cattle tended, now and again, by semiwild herdsmen, white and black.[9]

The first English settlers landed in Botany Bay, Australia, in January of 1788 with livestock, most of it from the Cape of Good Hope. The pigs and poultry thrived; the cattle did well enough; the sheep, the future source of the colony's good fortune, died fast. Within a few months two bulls and four cows strayed away. By 1804 the wild herds they founded numbered from three to five thousand head and were in possession of much of the best land between the settlements and the Blue Mountains. If they had ever found their way through the mountains to the grasslands beyond, the history of Australia in the first decades of the nineteenth century might have been one dominated by cattle rather than sheep. As it is, the colonial government wanted the land the wild bulls so ferociously defended, and considered the growing practice of convicts running away to live off the herds as a threat to the whole colony; so the adult cattle were shot and salted down and the calves captured and tamed. The English settlers imported woolly sheep from Europe and sought out the interior pastures for them. The animals multiplied rapidly, and when Darwin made his visit to New South Wales in 1836, there were about a million sheep there for him to see.[10]

The arrival of Old World livestock probably affected New Zealand more radically than any other of the Lands of the Demographic Takeover. Cattle, horses, goats, pigs and—in this land of few or no large predators—even the usually timid sheep went wild. In New Zealand herds of feral farm animals were practicing the ways of their remote ancestors as late as the 1940s and no doubt still run free. Most of the sheep, though, stayed under human control, and within a decade of Great Britain's annexation of New Zealand in 1840, her new acquisition was home to a quarter million sheep. In 1974 New Zealand had over fifty five million sheep, about twenty times more sheep than people.[11]

In the Lands of the Demographic Takeover the European pioneers were accompanied and often preceded by their domesticated animals, walking sources of food, leather, fiber, power, and wealth, and these animals often adapted more rapidly to the new surroundings and reproduced much more rapidly than their masters. To a certain extent, the success of Europeans as colonists was automatic as soon as they put their tough, fast, fertile, and intelligent animals ashore. The latter were sources of capital that sought out their own sustenance, improvised their own protection against the weather, fought their own battles against predators and, if their masters were smart enough to allow calves, colts, and lambs to accumulate, could and often did show the world the amazing possibilities of compound interest.

The honey bee is the one insect of worldwide importance which human beings have domesticated, if we may use the word in a broad sense. Many species of bees and other insects produce honey, but the one which does so in greatest quantity and which is easiest to control is a native of the Mediterranean area and the Middle East, the honey bee (*Apis mellifera*). The European has probably taken this sweet and short-tempered servant to every colony he ever established, from Arctic to Antarctic Circle, and the honey bee has always been one of the first immigrants to set off on its own. Sometimes the advance of the bee frontier could be very rapid: The first hive in Tasmania swarmed sixteen times in the summer of 1832.[12]

Thomas Jefferson tells us that the Indians of North America called the honey bees "English flies," and St. John de Crèvecoeur, his contemporary, wrote that "The Indians look upon them with an evil eye, and consider their progress into the interior of the continent as an omen of the white man's approach: thus, as they discover the bees, the news of the event, passing from mouth to mouth, spreads sadness and consternation on all sides."[13]

Domesticated creatures that traveled from the Lands of the Demographic Takeover to Europe are few. Australian aborigines and New Zealand Maoris had a few tame dogs, unimpressive by Old World standards and unwanted by the whites. Europe happily accepted the American Indians' turkeys and guinea pigs, but had no need for their dogs, llamas, and alpacas. Again the explanation is simple: Europeans, who controlled the passage of large animals across the oceans, had no need to reverse the process.

It is interesting and perhaps significant, though, that the exchange was just as one-sided for varmints, the small mammals whose migrations Europeans often tried to stop. None of the American or Australian or New Zealand equivalents of rats have become established in Europe, but Old World varmints, especially rats, have colonized right alongside the Europeans in the Temperate Zones. Rats of assorted sizes, some of them almost surely European immigrants, were tormenting Spanish Americans by at least the end of the sixteenth century. European rats established a beachhead in Jamestown, Virginia, as early as 1609, when they almost starved out the colonists by eating their food stores. In Buenos Aires the increase in rats kept pace with that of cattle, according to an early nineteenth-century witness. European rats proved as aggressive as the Europeans in New Zealand, where they completely replaced the local rats in the North Islands as early as the 1840s. Those poor creatures are probably completely extinct today or exist only in tiny relict populations.[14]

The European rabbits are not usually thought of as varmints, but where there are neither diseases nor predators to hold down their numbers they can become the worst of pests. In 1859 a few members of the species *Orytolagus cuniculus* (the scientific name for the protagonists of all the Peter Rabbits of literature) were released in southeast Australia. Despite massive efforts to stop them, they reproduced—true to their reputation—and spread rapidly all the way across Australia's southern half to the Indian Ocean. In 1950 the rabbit population of Australia was estimated at 500 million, and they were outcompeting the nation's most important domesticated animals, sheep, for the grasses and herbs. They have been brought under control, but only by means of artificially fomenting an epidemic of myxomatosis, a lethal American rabbit disease. The story of rabbits and myxomatosis in New Zealand is similar.[15]

Europe, in return for her varmints, has received muskrats and gray squirrels and little else from America, and nothing at all of significance from Australia or New Zealand, and we might well wonder if muskrats and squirrels really qualify as varmints.[16] As with other classes of organisms, the exchange has been a one-way street.

None of Europe's emigrants were as immediately and colossally successful as its pathogens, the microorganisms that make human beings ill, cripple them, and kill them. Whenever and wherever Europeans crossed the oceans and settled, the pathogens they carried created prodigious epidemics of smallpox, measles, tuberculosis, influenza, and a number of other diseases. It was this factor, more than any other, that Darwin had in mind as he wrote of the Europeans' deadly tread.

The pathogens transmitted by the Europeans, unlike the Europeans themselves or most of their domesticated animals, did at least as well in the tropics as in the temperate Lands of the Demographic Takeover. Epidemics devastated Mexico, Peru, Brazil, Hawaii, and Tahiti soon after the Europeans made the first contact with aboriginal populations. Some of these populations were able to escape demographic defeat because their initial numbers were so large that a small fraction was still sufficient to maintain occupation of, if not title to, the land, and also because the mass of Europeans were never attracted to the tropical lands, not even if they were partially vacated. In the Lands of the Demographic Takeover the aboriginal populations were too sparse to rebound from the onslaught of disease or were inundated by European immigrants before they could recover.

The First Strike Force of the white immigrants to the Lands of the Demographic Takeover were epidemics. A few examples from scores of possible examples follow. Smallpox first arrived in the Rio de la Plata region in 1558 or 1560 and killed, according to one chronicler possibly more interested in effect than accuracy, "more than a hundred thousand Indians" of the heavy riverine population there. An epidemic of plague or typhus decimated the Indians of the New England coast immediately before the founding of Plymouth. Smallpox or something similar struck the aborigines of Australia's Botany Bay in 1789, killed half, and rolled on into the interior. Some unidentified disease or diseases spread through the Maori tribes of the North Island of New Zealand in the 1790s, killing so many in a number of villages that the survivors were not able to bury the dead.[17] After a series of such lethal and rapidly moving epidemics, then came the slow, unspectacular but thorough cripplers and killers like venereal disease and tuberculosis. In conjunction with the large numbers of white settlers these diseases were enough to smother aboriginal chances of recovery. First the blitzkrieg, then the mopping up.

The greatest of the killers in these lands was probably smallpox. The exception is New Zealand, the last of these lands to attract permanent European settlers. They came to New Zealand after the spread of vaccination in Europe, and so were poor carriers. As of the 1850s smallpox still had not come ashore, and by that time two-thirds of the Maori had been vaccinated.[18] The tardy arrival of smallpox in these islands may have much to do with the fact that the Maori today comprise a larger percentage (9 percent) of their country's population than that of any other aboriginal people in any European colony or former European colony in either Temperate Zone, save only South Africa.

American Indians bore the full brunt of smallpox, and its mark is on their history and folklore. The Kiowa of the southern plains of the United States have a legend in which a Kiowa man meets Smallpox on the plain, riding a horse. The man asks, "Where do you come from and what do you do and why are you here?" Smallpox answers, "I am one with the white men—they are my people as the Kiowas are yours. Sometimes I travel ahead of them and sometimes behind. But I am always their companion and you will find me in their camps and their houses." "What can you do," the Kiowa asks. "I bring death," Smallpox replies. "My breath causes children to wither like young plants in spring snow. I bring destruction. No matter how beautiful a woman is, once she has looked at me she becomes as ugly as death. And to men I bring not death alone, but the destruction of their children and the blighting of their wives. The strongest of warriors go down before me. No people who have looked on me will ever be the same."[19]

In return for the barrage of diseases that Europeans directed overseas, they received little in return. Australia and New Zealand provided no new strains of pathogens to Europe—or none that attracted attention. And of America's native diseases none had any real influence on the Old World— with the likely exception of venereal syphilis, which almost certainly existed in the New World before 1492 and probably did not occur in its present form in the Old World.[20]

Weeds are rarely history makers, for they are not as spectacular in their effects as pathogens. But they, too, influence our lives and migrate over the world despite human wishes. As such, like varmints and germs, they are better indicators of certain realities than human beings or domesticated animals.

The term "weed" in modern botanical usage refers to any type of plant which—because of especially large numbers of seeds produced per plant, or especially effective means of distributing those seeds, or especially tough roots and rhizomes from which new plants can grow, or especially tough seeds that survive the alimentary canals of animals to be planted with their droppings—spreads rapidly and outcompetes others on disturbed, bare soil. Weeds are plants that tempt the botanist to use such anthropomorphic words as "aggressive" and "opportunistic."

Many of the most successful weeds in the well-watered regions of the Lands of the Demographic Takeover are of European or Eurasian origin. French and Dutch and English farmers brought with them to North America their worst enemies, weeds, "to exhaust the land, hinder and damnify the Crop.[21] By the last third of the seventeenth century at least twenty different types were widespread enough in New England to attract the attention of the English visitor, John Josselyn, who identified couch grass, dandelion, nettles, mallowes, knot grass, shepherd's purse, sow thistle, and clot burr and others. One of the most aggressive was plantain, which the Indians called "English-Man's Foot."[22]

European weeds rolled west with the pioneers, in some cases spreading almost explosively. As of 1823 corn chamomile and maywood had spread up to but not across the Muskingum River in Ohio. Eight years later they were over the river.[23] The most prodigiously imperialistic of the weeds in the eastern half of the United States and Canada were probably Kentucky bluegrass and white clover. They spread so fast after the entrance of Europeans into a given area that there is some suspicion that they may have been present in pre-Colombian America, although the earliest European accounts do not mention them. Probably brought to the Appalachian area by the French, these two kinds of weeds preceded the English settlers there and kept up with the movement westward until reaching the plains across the Mississippi.[24]

Old World plants set up business on their own on the Pacific coast of North America just as soon as the Spaniards and Russians did. The climate of coastal southern California is much the same as that of the Mediterranean, and the Spaniards who came to California in the eighteenth century brought their own Mediterranean weeds with them via Mexico: wild oats, fennel, wild radishes. These plants, plus those brought in later by the Forty-niners, muscled their way to dominance in the coastal grasslands. These immigrant weeds followed Old World horses, cattle, and sheep into California's interior prairies and took over there as well.[25]

The region of Argentina and Uruguay was almost as radically altered in its flora as in its fauna by the coming of the Europeans. The ancient Indian practice, taken up immediately by the whites, of burning off the old grass of the pampa every year, as well as the trampling and cropping to the ground of indigenous grasses and forbs by the thousands of imported quadrupeds who also changed the nature of the soil with their droppings, opened the whole countryside to European plants. In the 1780s Félix de Azara observed that the pampa, already radically altered, was changing as he watched. European weeds sprang up around every cabin, grew up along roads, and pressed into the open steppe. Today only a quarter of the plants growing wild in the pampa are native, and in the well-watered eastern portions, the "natural" ground cover consists almost entirely of Old World grasses and clovers.[26]

The invaders were not, of course, always desirable. When Darwin visited Uruguay in 1832, he found large expanses, perhaps as much as hundreds of square miles, monopolized by the immigrant wild artichoke and transformed into a prickly wilderness fit neither for man nor his animals.[27]

The onslaught of foreign and specifically European plants on Australia began abruptly in 1778 because the first expedition that sailed from Britain to Botany Bay carried some livestock and considerable quantities of seed. By May of 1803 over two hundred foreign plants, most of them European, had been purposely introduced and planted in New South Wales, undoubtedly along with a number of weeds.[28] Even today so-called clean seed characteristically contains some weed seeds, and this was much more so two hundred years ago. By and large, Australia's north has been too tropical and her interior too hot and dry for European weeds and grasses, but much of her southern coasts and Tasmania have been hospitable indeed to Europe's willful flora.

Thus, many—often a majority—of the most aggressive plants in the temperate humid regions of North America, South America, Australia, and New Zealand are of European origin. It may be true that in every broad expanse of the world today where there are dense populations, with whites in the majority, there are also dense populations of European weeds. Thirty-five of eighty-nine weeds listed in 1953 as common in the state of New York are European. Approximately 60 percent of Canada's worst weeds are introductions from Europe. Most of New Zealand's weeds are from the same source, as are many, perhaps most, of the weeds of southern Australia's well-watered coasts. Most of the European plants that Josselyn listed as naturalized in New England in the seventeenth century are growing wild today in Argentina and Uruguay, and are among the most widespread and troublesome of all weeds in those countries.[29]

In return for this largesse of pestiferous plants, the Lands of the Demographic Takeover have provided Europe with only a few equivalents. The Canadian water weed jammed Britain's nineteenth-century waterways, and North America's horseweed and burnweed have spread in Europe's empty lots, and South America's flowered galinsoga has thrived in her gardens. But the migratory flow of a whole group of organisms between Europe and the Lands of the Demographic Takeover has been almost entirely in one direction.[30] Englishman's foot still marches in seven league jackboots across every European colony of settlement, but very few American or Australian or New Zealand invaders stride the waste lands and unkempt backyards of Europe.

European and Old World human beings, domesticated animals, varmints, pathogens, and weeds all accomplished demographic takeovers of their own in the temperate, well-watered regions of North and South America, Australia, and New Zealand. They crossed oceans and Europeanized vast territories, often in informal cooperation with each other—the farmer and his animals destroying native plant cover, making way for imported grasses and forbs, many of which proved more nourishing to domesticated animals than the native equivalents; Old World pathogens, sometimes carried by Old World varmints, wiping out vast numbers of aborigines, opening the way for the advance of the European frontier, exposing more and more native peoples to more and more pathogens. The classic example of symbiosis between European colonists, their animals, and plants comes from New Zealand. Red clover, a good forage for sheep, could not seed itself and did not spread without being annually sown until the Europeans imported the bumblebee. Then the plant and insect spread widely, the first providing the second with food, the second carrying pollen from blossom to blossom for the first, and the sheep eating the clover and compensating the human beings for their effort with mutton and wool.[31]

There have been few such stories of the success in Europe of organisms from the Lands of the Demographic Takeover, despite the obvious fact that for every ship that went from Europe to those lands, another traveled in the opposite direction.

The demographic triumph of Europeans in the temperate colonies is one part of a biological and ecological takeover which could not have been accomplished by human beings alone, gunpowder notwithstanding. We must at least try to analyze the impact and success of all the immigrant organisms together—the European portmanteau of often mutually supportive plants, animals, and microlife which in its entirety can be accurately described as aggressive and opportunistic, an ecosystem simplified by ocean crossings and honed by thousands of years of competition in the unique environment created by the Old World Neolithic Revolution.

The human invaders and their descendants have consulted their egos, rather than ecologists, for explanations of their triumphs. But the human victims, the aborigines of the Lands of the Demographic Takeover, knew better, knew they were only one of many species being displaced and replaced; knew they were victims of something more irresistible and awesome than the spread of capitalism or Christianity. One Maori, at the nadir of the history of his race, knew these things when he said, "As the clover killed off the fern, and the European dog the Maori dog—as the Maori rat was destroyed by the Pakeha (European) rat—so our people, also, will be gradually supplanted and exterminated by the Europeans."[32] The future was not quite so grim as he prophesied, but we must admire his grasp of the complexity and magnitude of the threat looming over his people and over the ecosystem of which they were part.

NOTES

1. Page Stegner, ed., *The Portable Nabokov* (New York: Viking, 1968), p. 527; Francis Darwin, ed., *Life and Letters of Charles Darwin* (London: Murray, 1887), vol. 2, p. 391.

2. *The World Almanac and Book of Facts 1978* (New York: Newspaper Enterprise Association, 1978), passim.

3. Philip D. Curtin, "Epidemiology and the Slave Trade," *Political Science Quarterly* 83 (June 1968), 190–216 passim; John Prebble, *The Darien Disaster* (New York: Holt, Rinehart & Winston, 1968), pp. 296, 300; Charles M. Andrews, *The Colonial Period of American History* (New Haven, Conn.: Yale University Press, 1934),

vol. 1, n. 497; Gilberto Freyre, *The Masters and the Slaves*, trans. Samuel Putnam (New York: Knopf, 1946), passim; Donald L. Wiedner, *A History of Africa South of the Sahara* (New York: Vintage Books, 1964), 49–51; Stuart B. Schwartz, "Indian Labor and New World Plantations: European Demands and Indian Responses in Northeastern Brazil," *American Historical Review* 83 (February 1978): 43–79 passim.

4. Marcel R. Reinhard, *Histoire de la population modiale de 1700 à 1948* (n.p.: Editions Domat-Montchrestien, n.d.), pp. 339–411, 428–31; G.F. McCleary, *Peopling the British Commonwealth* (London: Farber and Farber, n.d.), pp. 83, 94, 109–10; R.R. Palmer and Joel Colton, *A History of the Modern World* (New York: Knopf, 1965), p. 560; *World Almanac 1978*, pp. 34, 439, 497, 513, 590.

5. Charles Darwin, *The Voyage of the Beagle* (Garden City, N.Y.: Doubleday Anchor Books, 1962), pp. 433–4.

6. William Woodruff, *Impact of Western Man* (New York: St. Martin's, 1967), 106–8.

7. Carolyn T. Foreman, *Indians Abroad* (Norman: University of Oklahoma Press, 1943), passim.

8. Alfred W. Crosby, *The Columbian Exchange* (Westport, Conn.: Greenwood, 1972), pp. 82–88; Alexander Gillespie, *Gleanings and Remarks Collected during Many Months of Residence at Buenos Aires* (Leeds: B. DeWhirst, 1818), p. 136; Oscar Schmieder, "Alteration of the Argentine Pampa in the Colonial Period," *University of California Publications in Geography* 2 (27 September 1927): n. 311.

9. Robert Beverley, *The History and Present State of Virginia* (Chapel Hill: University of North Carolina Press, 1947), pp. 153, 312, 318; John Lawson, *A New Voyage to Carolina* (n.p.: Readex Microprint Corp., 1966), p. 4; Frank L. Owsley, "The Pattern of Migration and Settlement of the Southern Frontier," *Journal of Southern History* 11 (May 1945): 147–75.

10. Commonwealth of Australia, *Historical Records of Australia* (Sydney: Library Committee of the Commonwealth Parliament, 1914), ser. 1, vol. 1, p. 550; vol. 7, pp. 379–80; vol. 8, pp. 150–1; vol. 9, pp. 349, 714, 831; vol. 10, pp. 92, 280, 682; vol. 20, p. 839.

11. Andrew H. Clark, *The Invasion of New Zealand by People, Plants, and Animals* (New Brunswick, N.J.: Rutgers University Press, 1949), p. 190; David Wallechinsky, Irving Wallace, and A. Wallace, *The Book of Lists* (New York: Bantam, 1978), pp. 129–30.

12. Remy Chauvin, *Traité de biologie de l'abellie* (Paris: Masson et Cie, 1968), vol. 1, pp. 38–9; James Backhouse, *A Narrative of a Visit to the Australian Colonies* (London: Hamilton, Adams and Co., 1834), p. 23.`

13. Merrill D. Peterson, ed., *The Portable Thomas Jefferson* (New York: Viking, 1975), p. 111; Michel-Guillaume St. Jean de Crèvecoeur, *Journey into Northern Pennsylvania and the State of New York*, trans. Clarissa S. Bostelmann (Ann Arbor: University of Michigan Press, 1964), p. 166.

14. Bernabé Cobo, *Obras* (Madrid: Atlas Ediciones, 1964), vol. 1, pp. 350–1; Edward Arber, ed., *Travels and Works of Captain John Smith* (New York: Burt Franklin, n. d.), vol. 2, p. xcv; K.A. Wodzicki, *Introduced Mammals of New Zealand* (Wellington: Department of Scientific and Industrial Research, 1950), pp. 89–92.

15. Frank Fenner and F.N. Ratcliffe, *Myxomatosis* (Cambridge: Cambridge University Press, 1965), pp. 9, 11, 17, 22–23; Frank Fenner, "The Rabbit Plague," *Scientific American* 190 (February 1954): 30–5; Wodzicki, *Introduced Mammals*, pp. 107–141.

16. Charles S. Elton, *The Ecology of Invasions* (Trowbridge and London: English Language Book Society, 1972), pp. 24–5, 28, 73, 123.

17. Juan López de Velasco, *Geografía y descripción universal de las Indias* (Madrid: Establecimiento Topográfico de Fortanet, 1894), p. 552; Oscar

Schmieder, "The Pampa—A Natural and Culturally Induced Grassland?" *University of California, Publications in Geography* (27 September 1927): 266; Sherburne F. Cook, "The Significance of Disease in the Extinction of the New England Indians," *Human Biology* 14 (September 1975): 486–91; J.H.L. Cumpston, *The History of Smallpox in Australia, 1788–1908* (Melbourne: Albert J. Mullet, Government Printer, 1914), pp. 147–9; Harrison M. Wright, *New Zealand, 1769–1840* (Cambridge, Mass.: Harvard University Press, 1959), p. 62. For further discussion of this topic, see Crosby, *Columbia Exchange*, chaps. 1 and 2, and Henry F. Dobyns, *Native American Historical Demography: A Critical Bibliography* (Bloomington: Indiana University Press/Newberry Library, 1976).

18. Arthur C. Thomson, *The Story of New Zealand* (London: Murray, 1859), vol. 1, p. 212.

19. Alice Marriott and Carol K. Rachlin, *American Indian Mythology* (New York: New American Library, 1968), pp. 174–5.

20. Crosby, *Columbian Exchange*, pp. 122–64, passim.

21. Jared Eliot, "The Tilling of the Land, 1760," in *Agriculture in the United States: A Documentary History*, ed. Wayne D. Rasmussen (New York: Random House, 1975), vol. 1, p. 192.

22. John Josselyn, *New England's Rarities Discovered* (London: G. Widdowes at the Green Dragon in St. Paul's Church-yard, 1672), pp. 85, 86; Edmund Berkeley and Dorothy S. Berkeley, eds., *The Reverend John Clayton* (Charlottesville: University of Virginia Press, 1965), p. 24.

23. Lewis D. de Schweinitz, "Remarks on the Plants of Europe Which Have Become Naturalized in a More or Less Degree, in the United States," *Annals Lyceum of Natural History of New York*, vol. 3 *(1832) 1828–1836*, 155.

24. Lyman Carrier and Katherine S. Bort, "The History of Kentucky Bluegrass and White Clover in the United States," *Journal of the American Society of Agronomy* 8 (1916): 256–66; Robert W. Schery, "The Migration of a Plant: Kentucky Bluegrass Followed Settlers to the New World," *Natural History* 74 (December 1965): 43–4; G.W. Dunbar, ed., "Henry Clay on Kentucky Bluegrass," *Agricultural History* 51 (July 1977): 522.

25. Edgar Anderson, *Plants, Man, and Life* (Berkeley and Los Angeles: University of California Press, 1967), pp. 12–15; Elna S. Bakker, *An Island Called California* (Berkeley and Los Angeles: University of California Press, 1971), pp. 150–2; R.W. Allard, "Genetic Systems Associated with Colonizing Ability in Predominantly Self-Pollinated Species," in *The Genetics of Colonizing Species*, ed. H.G. Baker and G. Ledyard Stebbins (New York: Academic Press, 1965), p. 50; M.W. Talbot, H.M. Biswell, and A.L. Hormay, "Fluctuations in the Annual Vegetation of California," *Ecology* 20 (July 1939): 396–7.

26. Félix de Azara, *Descripción é historia del Paraguay y del Río de la Plata* (Madrid: Imprenta de Sanchez, 1847), vol. 1, 57–8; Schmieder, "Alteration of the Argentine Pampa," pp. 310–11.

27. Darwin, *Voyage of the Beagle*, pp. 119–20.

28. *Historical Records of Australia*, ser. 1, vol. 4, pp. 234–41.

29. Edward Salisbury, *Weeds and Aliens* (London: Collins, 1961), p. 87; Angel Julio Cabrera, *Manual de la flora de los alrededores de Buenos Aires* (Buenos Aires: Editorial Acme S.A., 1953), passim.

30. Elton, *Ecology of Invasions*, p. 115; Hugo Ilitis, "The Story of Wild Garlic," *Scientific Monthly* 68 (February 1949): 122–4.

31. Otto E. Plath, *Bumblebees and Their Ways* (New York: Macmillan, 1934), p. 115.

32. James Bonwick, *The Last of the Tasmanians* (New York: Johnson Reprint Co., 1970), p. 380.

1492 AND ALL THAT:
MAKING A GARDEN
OUT OF WILDERNESS[◇]

RAMSAY COOK

o

"Is not America," Fernand Braudel asks in *The Perspective of the World*, the third volume of his magisterial *Civilization and Capitalism*, "perhaps the true explanation of Europe's greatness? Did not Europe discover or indeed 'invent' America, and has Europe not always celebrated Columbus's voyages as the greatest event in history 'since the creation'?" And then the great French historian concludes that "America was . . . the achievement by which Europe most truly revealed her own nature."[1] Braudel wrote without any intended irony, but that final remark about Europe truly revealing "her own nature" is perhaps what is really at issue in the current reassessment of the implications of Columbus's landfall at Guanahari, or San Salvador, as he named it in his first act of semiotic imperialism. ("Each received a new name from me,"[2] he recorded.)

That "nature" is captured by Marc Lescarbot in a sentence from his remarkable *History of New France*, published in 1609, which goes right to the heart of what we have apparently decided to call the "encounter" between the Old World and the New that Columbus symbolizes. Acadia, he wrote "having two kinds of soil that God has given unto man as his possession, who can doubt that when it shall be cultivated it will be a land of promise?"[3] I hardly need to explain why I think that sentence is so revealing of the European "nature," but I will. It forthrightly articulates the renaissance European's conviction that man was chosen by the Creator to possess and dominate the rest of creation. And it further assumes that, for the land to be fully possessed, it must be cultivated: tilled, improved, devel-

---

◇ From *Canada, Quebec, and the Uses of Nationalism* by Ramsay Cook. Used by permission of the Canadian Publishers, McClelland & Stewart, Toronto.

oped. The result: a promised land, a paradise, a garden of delights. Lescarbot's observations seemed so axiomatic then, and for nearly five centuries afterward, that almost no one questioned his vision of a promised land—at least almost no European. But that has begun to change. Contemporary Europe, as much in its western as in its eastern portions, struggles to redefine itself. Consequently Europe overseas, as J.G.A. Pocock recently argued in a brilliant essay,[4] is being forced to look again at the meaning of what Gomera in his *General History of the Indies* (1552) called "the greatest event since the creation of the world"[5]—the meaning of the "discovery of America."

The general shape of that reassessment has been emerging for more than a decade. Indeed the seminal work, Alfred W. Crosby's powerful study, *The Columbia Exchange: Biological and Cultural Consequences of 1492*, is two decades old. In that book Crosby argued that most of the histories of European expansion had missed the real point. It was not principalities and powers but rather organisms, seeds and animals that wrought the most fundamental changes in post-Columbian America. "Pandemic disease and biological revolution," not European technology and Christian culture, allowed Europeans "to transform as much of the New World as possible into the Old World."[6]

If Crosby offered a startling new explanation for the ease with which Europeans conquered the Americas, it remained for a Bulgarian cultural critic, living in Paris, to dissect the language and ideology of Columbian imperialism. In his brilliant, if sometimes infuriatingly undocumented *Conquest of America*, Tzvetan Todorov argued that sixteenth-century Europeans adopted two equally destructive attitudes towards the inhabitants of the New World. On the one hand, Amerindians were viewed as "savages," radically different and inferior to Europeans. Consequently they could be enslaved. On the other hand, the native peoples were seen "not only as equal but as identical." Consequently they could be assimilated. Whether "noble savage" or just "savage" Amerindians were never accepted on their own terms—different but equal. "Difference," Todorov wrote, "is corrupted into inequality, equality into identity."[7] *The Conquest of America* is, in essence, a subtle questioning of Eurocentricity, an assertion that the conventional story of 1492 had for too long been a monologue in which only European voices and values had been heard. Together, Crosby and Todorov—not just them, though they have been essential—have argued that to understand the coming together of Europe and America the ecological and intellectual worlds of both sides of the encounter must be brought into dialogue. If Europe discovered America in the centuries following 1492, it is equally true that America discovered Europe—and each revealed its "own nature."

What began as a trickle with Crosby and Todorov has since become a near flood. Its most extreme and popularized form is found in Kirkpatrick Sale's recent *Conquest of Paradise*, a book which has received far more attention, even from serious reviewers, than it warranted. Sale is not just critical of the Admiral of the Ocean Sea, though he certainly is that, but his principal point is an indictment of "the essential unsuitability of European culture for the task on which it was embarking."[8] In Sale's view, pre-Columbian America was a continent whose people lived in such harmony with each other, and with nature, as to approximate paradise. The European quest for gold, inspired by greed and God, destroyed that Edenic life. Exaggerated as his claims are, and driven as they are by a kind of moral certainty unbecoming to an historian, Sale's book nevertheless does raise some matters which will increasingly be part of the historian's agenda in examining the early period of the European entry into the Americas.

And that brings me back to Marc Lescarbot and the issues that might be considered in an ecological approach to the early history of Acadia. The history of the environment and the people who lived in pre-contact and especially proto-historical Acadia is not a new subject. Though his name is rarely mentioned in books about Canadian historical writing, the pioneer in environmental history in the maritime region was an extraordinary scholar named William Francis Ganong. A graduate of the University of New Brunswick, Harvard and Munich, Ganong taught natural science—botany was his specialty—at Smith College, Massachusetts, throughout his scholarly life. But he devoted most of his research to the natural history, geography, and general history of Acadia. His maps of early explorations, his editions of Nicolas Denys's *Description and Natural History of Acadia* and Chrestien Le Clercq's *New Relation of Gaspesia*, and his hundreds of articles in a variety of journals represent a contribution to early Canadian history that has yet to be properly recognized—at least by historians. When I set out on my current research work on the natural and anthropological history of early Canada one of my ambitions was to compile an historical bird watcher's guide—a chronology of the discovery of the birds of Canada. I quickly found that Ganong had been there well before me: in 1909 he published in the *Transactions of the Royal Society of Canada* "The Identity of Plants and Animals mentioned by the Early Voyages to Eastern Canada and Newfoundland."

The second maritime scholar for whom the environment was a necessary component of history was Alfred G. Bailey. His work is more generally known because of the reissue in 1969 of his seminal *Conflict of European and Eastern Algonkian Cultures 1504–1700*, which had first appeared in a small edition in 1937 and then dropped from sight. Professor Bruce Trigger has argued persuasively that Bailey was the first practitioner of what has come to be known as ethnohistory, the synthesis of historical and anthropological techniques. It is also true that Bailey had a profound sense of that symbiosis of environment and culture that made North American societies what they were, and an understanding that, when European social, religious and economic practices altered that environment, Native culture could hardly remain unchanged.

Finally, there is the well-known work of the historical geographer Andrew Hill Clark. His *Acadia*, published in 1968, is a model of environmental history, though his emphasis is upon the impact of the newcomers on "the face of the earth," and the modification of European culture in the face of the demands of a new environment.

rally a constant preoccupation. "The entire country is covered with very dense forests," Champlain wrote of the site that would become Annapolis Royal, " . . . except a point a league and a half up the river, where there are some oaks which are very scattered and a number of wild vines. These could be easily cleared and the place brought under cultivation." Nor did Champlain miss the minerals and metals—silver at Mink Cove, iron further north on Digby Neck.[15]

Moreover, it is from these writers that at least a partial sketch of the lives and customs of the Northeastern Algonquian peoples can be reconstructed. Champlain recorded the practice of swidden agriculture among the Abenaki—corn, beans and squash—and even noted the use of horseshoe crab shells, probably as fertilizer.[16] Hunting and fishing methods were remarked upon, though the lack of detail is somewhat surprising particularly when contrasted with the lengthy accounts of religious beliefs—or supposed lack of them—of the various inhabitants of Acadia. "Jugglery" or shamanism, and also medical practices, were of particular interest—indeed, Dièreville even convinced himself of the efficacy of some shamanistic cures. So, too, dress, hairstyles, courtship and marriage customs, and ceremonies surrounding childbirth and death were carefully recorded and sometimes compared to classical and contemporary European practices. Lescarbot, for example, concluded that the Jesuits were quite mistaken in attempting to force Christian monogamy on the Micmacs, arguing that indigenous marriage customs would best be "left in the state in which they were found." In contrast to some Jesuit writers—and Brian Moore—Lescarbot judged the aboriginal people very modest in sexual matters. This he attributed partly to their familiarity with nakedness but chiefly "to their keeping bare the head, where lies the fountain of the spirits which excite to procreation, partly to the lack of salt, of hot spices, of wine, of meats which provoke desire, and partly to their frequent use of tobacco, the smoke of which dulls the senses, and mounting up to the brain hinders the functions of Venus." On the other hand, he believed that one romantic innovation introduced by the French actually contributed to the improvement of aboriginal life: the kiss. Though Professor Karen Anderson has followed up Lescarbot's insight about the impact of the missionaries on marriage among the Native people of New France, no one, as far as I know, has advanced our knowledge of the relationship between civilization and osculation.[17]

Virtually all male European visitors to Acadia were struck by the division of labour in aboriginal communities. Women, it was agreed, "work harder than the men, who play the gentleman, and care only for hunting or for war." Despite this, Lescarbot wrote approvingly, "they love their husbands more than women of our parts." It is interesting that in his discussion of the ease with which Micmac marriages could be dissolved Father Le Clercq remained detached and uncensorious. "In a word," he remarked laconically, "they hold it as a maxim that each one is free; that one can do whatever he wishes: and that it is not sensible to put constraint upon men." And the priest understood that the maxim applied to both men and women.[18]

Games and the Native peoples' apparent penchant for gambling were described though not always understood. Then there was science and technology. Father Le Clercq, perhaps the most ethnologically astute of seventeenth-century observers, provided an intriguing account of the ways the Gaspesians read the natural world: their interpretation of the stars and the winds, how they reckoned distance and recognized the changing seasons. The usefulness and limitations of indigenous technology was also commented upon. The efficiency of the birchbark canoe won widespread admiration. "The Savages of Port Royal can go to Kebec in ten or twelve days by means of the rivers which they navigate almost up to their sources," Lescarbot discovered, "and thence carrying their little bark canoes through the woods they reach another stream which flows into the river of Canada and thus greatly expedite their long voyages." While household utensils, manufactured from bark, roots and stumps were ingenious, the French realized that the aboriginals were happy to replace them with metal wares. War and its weaponry drew the somewhat surprised comment that "neither profit nor the desire to extend boundaries, but rather vengeance, caused fairly frequent hostilities between native groups." Torture was graphically described, and condemned, though it was recognized—and judged a sign of savagery—that "to die in this manner is, among the savages, to die as a great captain and as a man of great courage."[19]

Much else also caught the attention of these ethnologists: the commonality of property, the importance of gift exchange, the practice of setting aside weapons before entering into discussion with strangers, and the expectation that strangers should do the same. And even though "crafty, thievish and treacherous," Lescarbot admitted somewhat superciliously that "they do not lack wit, and might come to something if they were civilized, and knew the various trades."[20]

Though observations and judgements were made with great confidence, indeed often rather cavalierly, these Europeans were aware that there often existed an unbridgeable communications chasm between the observers and the observed. Like every explorer before them, the French in Acadia attempted to resolve the problem in two ways. The first was to take young Natives back to France for an immersion course in French. ("We had on board a savage," Lescarbot noted in 1608, "who was much astonished to see the buildings, spires and windmills of France, but more the women, whom he had never seen dressed after our manner.") While these interpreters were doubtless helpful in breaking down the "effects of the confusion of Babel," it was hardly a permanent resolution to what Father Biard realized was a fundamental problem. Yet for the French to learn the local languages was time-consuming and the results often frustrating. Learning words was not the same as learning to communicate. "As these Savages have no formulated Religion, government, towns, nor trade," Biard recorded in exasperation, "so the words and proper phrases for all of these things are lacking." The confusion of words with things, of the sign with the referent was, as Todorov has brilliantly shown, endemic to the European attempt to comprehend America. Acadia was no exception though I have, unfortunately, not found any example quite so delicious as the linguistic dilemma encountered by Protestant missionaries in Hawaii. There the Islanders reportedly practised some twenty forms of sexual activity judged illicit—perhaps better, non-missionary. Each had a separate name in the Native language, thus making translation of the Seventh Commandment virtually impossible without condoning the other nineteen forms of the joy of sex! The Native peoples of Acadia were apparently much less resourceful— or the celibate Jesuits less well trained as participant-observators.[21]

The natural, ethnographic and linguistic accounts were not, of course, the work of biological scientists, or cultural anthropologists—even taking into account our contemporary scepticism about the objectivity of anthropologists. Rather they were the observations of seventeenth-century Frenchmen taking inventory of a new land they intended to explore, settle, develop and Christianize—in brief, to colonize. It is in their works that much of what Braudel called Europe's "own nature" is "most truly revealed." In differing ways it is made emphatically plain by each of these authors that the French objective in Acadia, in the words of Father Biard, was "to make a Garden out of the wilderness." Nor should this be read narrowly as simply meaning the evangelization of the people who lived in Acadia.[22]

In the revealing introduction to his rich and thoughtful *Relation* of 1616, Biard wrote: "For verily all of this region, though capable of the same prosperity as ours, nevertheless through Satan's malevolence, which reigns there, is a horrible wilderness, scarcely less miserable on account of the scarcity of bodily comforts than for that which renders man absolutely miserable, the complete lack of the ornaments and riches of the soul." The missionary continues, offering his scientific conviction that "neither the sun, nor malice of the soil, neither the air nor the water, neither the men nor their caprices, are to be blamed for this. We are all created by and dependent upon the same principles: We breathe under the same sky; the same constellations influence us; and I do not believe that the land, which produces trees as tall and beautiful as ours, will not produce as fine harvests, *if it be cultivated*." Wilderness the expanses of Acadia might be, but a garden it could become, if cultivated. For Father Biard and his contemporaries, "subjugating Satanic monsters" and establishing "the order and discipline of heaven upon earth,"[23] combined spiritual and worldly dimensions. Champlain, for whom the Devil and his agents were as real as for Biard, expressed the same objective in a more secular way when he told the local people he met in the region of the Penobscot River that the French "desired to settle in their country and show them how to cultivate it, in order that they might no longer live so miserable an existence as they are doing." The comment is made the more striking when we remember that Champlain knew that some of the inhabitants of Acadia did practise agriculture—though he never suggested that they "cultivated" the land.[24]

It is perhaps not too much to suggest that "cultivation" was a distinctly European concept. "For before everything else," Marc Lescarbot maintained, "one must set before oneself the tillage of the soil." At the first French settlement at Ste Croix gardens were sown and some wheat "came up very fine and ripened." The poor quality of the soil was one reason for the move across the Bay of Fundy to establish Port Royal, "where the soil was ample to produce the necessaries of life." But there was more to cultivation than the production of simple foodstuffs. For Lescarbot, at least, the powerful symbolism of planting a European garden in what had been a wilderness was manifest. "I have cause to rejoice," he wrote on his departure from Port Royal to return to France in July 1607, "that I was one of the party, and among the first tillers of this land. And herein I took the more pleasure in that I put before my eyes our ancient Father Noah, a great king, a great priest and a great prophet whose vocation was the plough and the vineyard; and the old Roman captain Serranus, who was found sowing his field when he was sent to lead the Roman army, and Quintus Cincinnatus, who, all crowned with dust, bareheaded and ungirt, was ploughing four acres of land when the herald of the Senate brought him the letters of dictatorship. . . . Inasmuch as I took pleasure in this work, God blessed my poor labour, and I had in my garden as good wheat as could be grown in France." While Lescarbot might be dismissed as suffering from an overdose of renaissance humanism, it seems more sensible to take him seriously. His florid rhetoric should be seen for what it really was: the ideology of what Alfred W. Crosby has called "ecological imperialism"—the biological expansion of Europe. What Lescarbot, and less literary Europeans, brought to bear on the Acadian landscape was the heavy freight of the European agricultural tradition with its long established distinction between garden and wilderness. In that tradition God's "garden of delight" contrasted with the "desolate wilderness" of Satan. Though the concept of "garden" varies widely, as Hugh Johnson notes in his *Principles of Gardening*, "control of nature by man" is the single common denominator.[25]

The transformation of the wilderness into a garden is a constant theme in the early writings about Acadia. Father Biard had brought European seeds with him when he arrived in 1611 and at St Saveur "in the middle of June, we planted some grains [wheat and barley], fruit, seeds, peas, beans and all kinds of garden plants." On Miscou Island (Shippegan Island), Denys discovered that although the soil was sandy herbs of all sorts as well as "Peaches, Nectarines, Clingstones" and what the French always called "the Vine"—grapes—could be grown. But, as so often is the case, it is Lescarbot who provides the most striking account of what gardening meant. At Port Royal, he "took pleasure in laying out and cultivating my gardens, in enclosing them to keep out the pigs, in making flower beds, staking out alleys, building summer houses, sowing wheat, rye, barley, oats, beans, peas and garden plants, and in watering them." European seeds, domestic animals— chickens and pigeons, too—fences—mine and thine.[26]

Of course before a garden could be planted, the land had to be cleared. Denys described that work—and its by-product: squared oak timber that could fill the holds of vessels that would otherwise have returned empty to France. If clearing the land did not produce enough space for the garden, then the sea could be tamed too. In the Minas basin, where the settlers apparently found cultivating the land too difficult, Dièreville recounted the construction of a remarkable piece of European technology. "Five or six rows of large logs are driven whole into the ground at the points where the Tide enters the Marsh, & between each row, other logs are laid, one on top of the other, & all the spaces between them are so carefully filled with well pounded clay, that the water can no longer get through. In the centre of this construction a Sluice is contrived in such a manner that the water on the Marshes flows out of its own accord, while that of the Sea is prevented from coming in." Thus the tidal marshes were dyked for cultivation.[27]

Pushing back the forest, holding back the water, fencing a garden in the wilderness. The rewards would be great—"better worth than the treasures of Atahulpa," Lescarbot claimed. Was the symbolism intentional? Atahulpa, the defeated Aztec ruler of Peru, offered his Spanish captors led by Francisco Pizarro a room full of gold and silver in return for his freedom. The Spaniards accepted the ransom and then garrotted the Inca. Hardly a scene from a garden of delights.[28]

The French in Acadia were certainly not the Spanish in Peru. Still the garden they planned was intended to produce a greater harvest than just sustenance for anticipated settlers. It was to be a garden for the civilization of the indigenous peoples. "In the course of time," Champlain observed on his initial meeting with the people he called Etechemins (Maliseet), "we hope to pacify them, and put an end to the wars which they wage against each other, in order that in the future we might derive service from them, and convert them to the Christian faith." The words were almost exactly those attributed to Columbus at his first sighting of the people of the "Indies": "they would be good servants . . . [and] would easily be made Christians." Even the most sympathetic observers of the Native peoples of Acadia were appalled by their apparent failure to make for themselves a better life, a failing which was often attributed to their unwillingness to plan for the future. For Father Biard, Christianity and husbandry obviously went hand in hand. Living the nomadic life of hunters, fishers and gatherers resulted in permanent material and spiritual backwardness. "For in truth, this people," he claimed, "who, through the progress and experience of centuries, ought to have come to some perfection in the arts, sciences and philosophy, is like a great field of stunted and ill-begotten wild plants . . . [they] ought to be already prepared for the completeness of the Holy Gospel . . . Yet behold [them] wretched and dispersed, given up to ravens, owls and infernal cuckoos, and to be the cursed prey of spiritual foxes, bears, boars and dragons." In Father Le Clercq's view the "wandering and vagabond life" had to be ended and a place "suitable for the cultivation of the soil" found so that he could "render the savages sedentary, settle them down, and civilize them among us." Though Lescarbot's outlook was more secular, he shared these sentiments completely and expressed them in verse:

Ce peuple n'est pas brutal, barbare, ni Sauvage,
Si vous n'appelez tels les hommes du vieil âge,
It est subtile, habile & plein de jugement,
Et n'en ay conu un manquer d'entendement,
Seulement il demande un père qui l'enseigne
A cultiver la terre, a façonner la vigne,
Et vivre par police, a être menager,
Et sous des fermes toicts ci-après herberger.

The *leit-motif* of this rhetoric is obvious: the images of the Christian garden and the satanic wilderness, summed up in the verse from the Book of Joel, quoted by Father Biard: "The Land is a Garden of Eden before them, and behind them a desolate wilderness."[29]

Yet it would be quite wrong to assume that these seventeenth-century French visitors to the New World were blind to the potential costs of gardening in the Acadian wilderness. Indeed, there is considerable evidence of nagging suspicions that the very abundance of nature provoked reckless exploitation. Denys witnessed an assault on a bird colony that is reminiscent of the profligacy of Cartier's crew among the birds at Funk Island in 1534. Denys's men "clubbed so great a number, as well of young as of their fathers and mothers . . . that we were unable to carry them all away." And Dièreville captured all too accurately the spirit of the uncontrolled hunt when he wrote that:

> . . . , Wild Geese
> And Cormorants, aroused in me
> The wish to war on them. . . .

He used the same militant language in his admiring account of the "Bloody Deeds" of the seal hunt, and also provided a sketch of another common pursuit: the theft of massive quantities of birds' eggs. "They collect all they can find," he remarked, "fill their canoes & take them away." Scenes like these presaged the fate of the Great Auk, the passenger-pigeon and many other species.[30]

These were the actions of men whose attitude towards the bounty of nature contrasted markedly with that of the indigenous inhabitants of North America. In Europe the slaughter of birds and animals was commonplace, indeed it was often encouraged by law. As Keith Thomas remarks in his study of *Man in the Natural World*—which is largely restricted to Great Britain—"It is easy to forget just how much human effort went into warring against species which competed with man for the earth's resources." Without succumbing to the temptation to romanticize the attitude of North American Native people towards their environment—they hunted, they fished, some practised slash and burn agriculture—there is no doubt that their sense of the natural world was based on a distinctive set of beliefs, a cosmology that placed them in nature rather than dominant over it. Animistic religion—"everything is animated," Father Le Clercq discovered— a simple technology, a relatively small population, and what Marshall Sahlins has termed "stone age economics," made "war" on nature unnecessary, even unacceptable. "They did not lack animals," Nicolas Denys noted, "which they killed only in proportion as they had need of them." By contrast, the Europeans who arrived in Acadia at the beginning of the seventeenth century belonged to a culture where, in Clarence Glacken's words, "roughly from the end of the fifteenth to the end of the seventeenth century one sees ideas of man as controllers of nature beginning to crystalize." Or, as Marc Lescarbot put it, articulating as he so often did the unstated assumptions of his fellow Frenchmen, "Man was placed in this world to command all that is here below."[31]

The distinction between the "wilderness" and the "garden," between "savagery" and "civilization," between "wandering about" and commanding "all that is here below," is more than a philosophical one, important as that is. It is also, both implicitly and explicitly, a question of ownership and possession. In what has been called "enlightenment anthropology"— though I think that places the development too late—the function of the term "savage" was to assert the existence of a state of nature where neither "heavy-plough agriculture nor monetarized exchange" were practised and from which, therefore, civil government was absent. Moreover, civil government, agriculture and commerce were assumed to exist only where land had been appropriated—where "possessive individualism" had taken root. Thus the wilderness was inhabited by nomadic savages, without agriculture or laws, where the land had never been appropriated. Consequently, when Europeans set about transforming the wilderness into a garden, they were engaged in taking possession of the land. "The ideology of agriculture and savagery," in the words of J.G.A. Pocock, "was formed to justify this expropriation."[32]

As European gardeners began slowly to transform the wilderness of Acadia so too, as was their intent, they began the re-making of its indigenous inhabitants. And once again, though they rarely expressed doubts about the ultimate value of the enterprise, some Europeans did recognize that a price was being exacted. First there was the puzzling evidence of population decline. In a letter to his superior in Paris in 1611, Father Biard wrote that the Micmac leader Membertou (who himself claimed to be old enough to remember Cartier's 1534 visit) had informed him that in his youth people were "as thickly planted there as the hairs upon his head." The priest continued, making a remarkably revealing comparison: "It is maintained that they have thus diminished since the French have begun to frequent their country; for, since they do nothing all summer but eat; and the result is that, adopting an entirely different custom and thus breeding new diseases, they pay for their indulgence during the autumn and winter by pleurisy, quinsy and dysentery which kills them off. During this year alone sixty have died at Cape de la Hève, which is the greater part of those who lived there; yet not one of all of M. de Poutrincourt's little colony has ever been sick, notwithstanding all the privations they have suffered; which has caused the Savages to apprehend that God protects and defends us as his favorite and well-beloved people."[33]

The reality, of course, was more complex than this assertion that God was on the side of the immunized. Though the French were unaware of it, Acadia, like the rest of the Americas, was a "virgin land" for European pathogens. Denys hinted at this when he wrote that "in old times . . . they [the Natives] were not subject to diseases, and knew nothing of fevers." Certainly they had not been exposed to the common European maladies— measles, chickenpox, influenza, tuberculosis and, worst of all, smallpox. (The "pox"—syphilis—Lescarbot believed was God's punishment of European men for their promiscuous sexual behaviour in the Indies.) The immune systems of the indigenous peoples of Acadia were unprepared for the introduction of these new diseases which were, consequently, lethal in their impact. Father Le Clercq, at the end of the century, reported that "the gaspesian nation . . . has been wholly destroyed . . . in three or four visitations" of unidentified "Maladies." Marc Lescarbot probably identified one important carrier of European infections when he stated that "the savages had no knowledge of [rats] before our coming; but in our time they have been beset by them, since from our fort they went over to their lodges."[34]

Disease, radical alterations in diet—the substitution of dried peas and beans, and hardtack for moosemeat and other country foods—and perhaps even the replacement of polygamy by monogamy with a consequent reduction in the birth rate, all contributed to population decline. Then there was the debilitating scourge of alcohol, another European import for which Native people had little, if any, tolerance. Just as they sometimes gorged themselves during "eat all" feasts, so they seemed to drink like undergraduates with the simple goal of getting drunk. Even discounting Father Le Clercq's pious outlook, his description of the impact of brandy on the Gaspesians was probably not exaggerated. The fur traders, he charged, "make them drunk quite on purpose, in order to deprive these poor barbarians of the use of reason." That meant quick profits for the merchants, debauchery, destruction, murder and, eventually, addiction for the Amerindians. Though less censorious, or less concerned, than the priest, Dièreville remarked that the Micmacs "drank Brandy with relish & less moderation than we do; they have a craving for it."[35]

Estimating population declines among Native peoples is at best controversial, at worst impossible. Nevertheless there seems no reason to doubt that Acadia, like the rest of the Americas, underwent substantial reduction in numbers of inhabitants as a result of European contact. Jacques Cartier and his successors, who fished and traded along the coasts of Acadia, likely introduced many of the influences that undermined the health of the local people. Therefore Pierre Biard's 1616 estimate of a population of about 3500 Micmacs is doubtless well below pre-contact numbers, as Membertou claimed. Since it has been estimated that neighbouring Maliseet, Pasamaquoddy and Abenaki communities experienced reductions ranging from 67 to 98 percent during the epidemics of 1616 and 1633 alone, Virginia Miller's calculation that the pre-contact Micmac population stood somewhere between 26 000 and 35 000 seems reasonable.[36] That was one of the costs of transforming the wilderness into a garden.

If the effects of disease and alcohol were apparent, though misunderstood, then another aspect of the civilizing process was more subtle. That process combined Christian proselytizing, which eroded traditional beliefs, with the fur trade, which undermined many aspects of the Native peoples' way of life. There is among contemporary historians of European-Amerindian relations a tendency to view the trading relationship, that was so central to the early years of contact, as almost benign, a relation between equals. Missionaries, politicians, and land-hungry settlers are credited with upsetting the balance that once existed between "Natives and newcomers" in the fur trade. There can be no doubt that recent scholarship has demonstrated that the Natives were certainly not passive participants in the trade.

Far from being naïve innocents who gave up valuable furs for a few baubles, they traded shrewdly and demanded good measure.[37]

Nevertheless, it is impossible to read seventeenth-century accounts of the trade and still accept the whole of this revisionist account. These were eyewitness testimonies to the devastating impact of alcohol on the Native traders and their families: murder of fellow Natives, maiming of women and abuse of children, the destruction of canoes and household goods. Beyond this, brandy, often adulterated with water, was used by Europeans "in order to abuse the savage women, who yield themselves readily during drunkenness to all kinds of indecency, although at other times . . . they would be more like to give a box on the ears rather than a kiss to whomsoever wished to engage them in evil, if they were in their right minds." The words come from the priest, Father Le Clercq, but the merchant, Nicolas Denys, concurred. That, too, was part of the fur trade.[38]

Moreover the trade cannot be separated from other aspects of contact that contributed to the weakening of Micmac culture. Fur traders carrying disease and trade goods, unintentionally, contributed to the decline of both traditional skills and indigenous religious belief. Nicolas Denys's discussion of Micmac burial customs illustrates this point neatly. Like other Native people the Micmacs buried many personal articles in graves so that the deceased would have use of them when they disembarked in the Land of the Dead. The French judged this practice both superstitious and wasteful— especially when the burial goods included thousands of pounds of valuable furs. They attempted to disabuse the Native of the efficacy of this practice by demonstrating that the goods did not leave the grave but rather remained in the ground, rotting. To this the Natives replied that it was the "souls" of these goods that accompanied the "souls" of the dead, not the material goods themselves. Despite this failure Denys was able to report that the practice was in decline. The reason is significant and it was only marginally the result of conversion to Christianity. As trade between the French and the Micmacs developed, European goods—metal pots, knives, axes, firearms—gradually replaced traditional utensils and weapons that had once been included in burial pits. The use of European commodities as burial goods proved prohibitively expensive. Denys wrote that "since they cannot obtain from us with such ease as they had in retaining robes of Marten, of Otter, of Beaver, [or] bows and arrows, and since they have realized that guns and other things were not found in their woods or their rivers, *they have become less devout*." Technological change brought religious change. It also led to dependence.[39]

No doubt the exchange of light, transportable copper pots for awkward, stationary wooden pots was a convenient, even revolutionary change in the lives of Micmacs. But convenience was purchased at a price, and the Native people knew it. Father Le Clercq was vastly amused when an old man told him that "the Beaver does everything to perfection. He makes us kettles, axes, swords, knives and gives us drink and food without the trouble of cultivating the ground." It was no laughing matter. If, at the outset of European contact the Native people of Acadia had adapted to the trade with Europeans rather successfully, they gradually lost ground, their role of middlemen undermined by overseas traders who came to stay. While Nicolas Denys deplored the destructive impact of itinerant traders and fishermen on the Native people, his only solution was to advocate European settlement and the enforcement of French authority. "Above all," he concluded his assessment of the changes that had taken place in Native society during this time, "I hope that God may inspire in those who have part in the government of the State, all the discretion which can lead them to the consummation of an enterprise as glorious for the King as it can be useful and advantageous to those who will take interest therein." In that scheme, when it eventually came to pass, the Micmacs and their neighbours found themselves on the margin.[40]

To these signs that the work of cultivation produced ugly, unanticipated side-effects must be added the evidence of near crop failure in the spiritual garden of Acadia. In 1613 a disgusted Father Biard reported meeting a St John River sagamore (Cacagous) who, despite being "baptized in Bayonne," France, remained a "shrewd and cunning" polygamist. "There is scarcely any change in them after baptism," he admitted. Their traditional "vices" had not been replaced by Christian "virtues." Even Membertou, often held up as the exemplary convert, had difficulty grasping the subtleties of the new religion. He surely revealed something more than a quick wit in an exchange which amused the Jesuit. Attempting to teach him the Pater Noster, Biard asked Membertou to repeat in his own language, "Give us this day our daily bread." The old sagamore replied: "If I did not ask him for anything but bread, I would be without moose-meat or fish." Near the end of the century, Father Le Clercq's reflections on the results of his Gaspé mission were no more optimistic. Only a small number of the people lived like Christians, most "fell back into the irregularities of a brutal and wild life." Such, the somewhat depressed Recollet missionary concluded, was the meagre harvest among "the most docile of all the Savages of New France . . . the most susceptible to the instruction of Christianity."[41]

It was not just these weeds—disease, alcohol, dependence, and spiritual backsliding—in the European garden in Acadia that occasionally led the gardeners to pause and reflect. Possibly there was a more basic question: was the wilderness truly the Devil's domain? The Northeastern Algonquian people were admittedly "superstitious," even "barbarian," but certainly not the "wild men" of mediaeval imaginings, indistinguishable from the beasts. If they enjoyed "neither faith, nor king, nor laws," living out "their unhappy Destiny," there was something distinctly noble about them too. Despite the steady, evangelical light that burned in Biard's soul he could not help wondering if the Micmac resistance to the proffered European garden of delights was not without foundation. "If we come to sum up the whole and compare their good and ill with ours," he mused briefly in the middle of his *Relation* of 1616, "I do not know but that they, in truth, have some reason to prefer (as they do) their own kind of happiness to ours, at least if we speak of the temporal happiness, which the rich and worldly seek in this life." Of course these doubts quickly passed as he turned to consider "the means available to aid these nations to their eternal salvation."

Marc Lescarbot, for whom classicism and Christianity seemed to have reached their apogee in the France of his day, and whose fervour for cultivating the wilderness was unlimited, found much to admire in the peoples of Acadia. They lived "after the ancient fashion, without display": uncompetitive, unimpressed by material goods, temperate, free of corruption and of lawyers! "They have not that ambition, which in these parts gnaws men's minds, and fills them with cares, bringing blinded men to the grave in the very flower of their age and sometimes to the shameful spectacle of a public death." Here surely was "the noble savage," a Frenchman without warts— "a European dream," as J.H. Elliott remarks of the Humanists' image of the New World, "which had little to do with American reality."[42]

There was yet another reason for self-doubts about the superiority of European ways over Amerindian ways; the Native people struggled to preserve their wilderness, refusing the supposed superiority of the garden. Even those who had become "philosophers and pretty good theologians," one missionary concluded, preferred "on the basis of foolish reasoning, the savage to the French life." And Father Le Clercq found that some of the people of Gaspesia stubbornly preferred their movable wigwams to stationary European houses. And that was not all. "Thou reproachest us, very inappropriately," their leader told a group of visiting Frenchmen, "that our country is a very little hell in contrast with France, which thou comparest to a terrestrial paradise, inasmuch as it yields thee, so thou sayest, every provision in abundance . . . I beg thee to believe, all miserable as we may seem in thine eyes, we consider ourselves nevertheless much happier than thou in this, that we are contented with the little that we have." Thus having demonstrated, three hundred years before its discovery by modern anthropology, that having only a few possessions is not the same as being poor, the Algonquian leader then posed a devastating question: "If France, as thou sayest, is a little terrestrial paradise, are thou sensible to leave it?" No reply is recorded.[43]

It is simple enough to imagine one. Even those who could describe as "truly noble" the aboriginal people of Acadia remained convinced that civilization meant cultivation. "In New France," Lescarbot proclaimed, "the golden age must be brought in again, the ancient crowns of ears of corn must be renewed, and the highest glory made that which the ancient Romans called *gloria adorea*, a glory of wheat, in order to invite everyone to till well his field, seeing that the land presents itself liberally to them that have none." The state of nature, a Hobbesian state of nature without laws or kings or religion would be tamed, "civilized," when men "formed commonwealths to live under certain laws, rule, and police." Here, in Braudel's phrase, Europe's "own nature" was revealed.[44]

Perhaps such thoughts as these filled the heads of the Frenchmen who, according to Micmac tradition, gathered to enjoy one of the "curious adventures" of Silmoodawa, an aboriginal hunter carried off to France "as a curiosity" by Champlain or some other "discoverer." On this occasion the Micmac was to give a command performance of hunting and curing techniques. The "savage" was placed in a ring with "a fat ox or deer . . . brought in from a beautiful park." (One definition of "paradise," the *OED* reports, is "an Oriental park or pleasure ground, especially one enclosing wild beasts for the chase.") The story, collected in 1870 by the Reverend Silas Tertius Rand, a Baptist missionary and amateur ethnologist, continues: "He shot the animal with a bow, bled him, skinned and dressed him, sliced the meat and spread it out on flakes to dry; he then cooked a portion and ate it, and in order to exhibit the whole process, and to take a mischievous revenge upon them for making an exhibition of him, he went into a corner of the yard and eased himself before them all."[45]

If, as Lescarbot's contemporaries believed, the wilderness could be made into a garden, then the unscripted denouement of Silmoodawa's performance revealed that a garden could also become a wilderness. Or was he merely acting out the Micmac version of Michel de Montaigne's often quoted remark about barbarians: we all call wilderness anything that is not *our* idea of a garden?

NOTES

1. Fernand Braudel, *The Perspective of the World* (London: William Collins and Son 1985), 387, 388.

2. Cecil Jane, ed., *The Journal of Christopher Columbus* (New York: Bonanza Books 1989), 191; Patricia Seed, "Taking Possession and Reading Texts: Establishing the Authority of Overseas Empires," *William and Mary Quarterly*, XLIX, 2, April 1992, 199.

3. Marc Lescarbot, *History of New France* (Toronto: The Champlain Society, 1914), III, 246. The theme of my lecture might have benefited had I been able to substantiate the claim, sometimes made, that "Acadie" is a corruption of "Arcadie"—an ideal, rural paradise. Unfortunately the claim, sometimes made on the basis of Verrazzano's 1524 voyage when he described the coast of present-day Virginia as "Arcadie," is unfounded. "Acadie" likely is derived from the Micmac word "Quoddy" or "Cadie," meaning a piece of land. The French version became "la Cadie" or "l'Acadie," even though the French sometimes thought of the area as a potential "Arcadie." See Andrew Hill Clark, *Acadia: The Geography of Early Nova Scotia* (Madison: University of Wisconsin Press 1968), 71.

4. J.G.A. Pocock, "Deconstructing Europe," *London Review of Books*, 19 December 1991, 6–10.

5. J.H. Elliott, *The Old World and the New, 1492–1650* (Cambridge: Cambridge University Press 1989), cited 10.

6. Alfred W. Crosby, Jr, *The Columbian Exchange: Biological and Cultural Consequences of 1492* (Westport, Conn.: Greenwood Press 1972), 67.

7. Tzvetan Todorov, *The Conquest of America* (New York: Harper Colophon 1985), 146.

8. Kirkpatrick Sale, *The Conquest of Paradise: Christopher Columbus and the Columbian Legacy* (New York: Knopf 1991), 129.

9. William Cronon, *Changes in the Land Indians: Colonists and Ecology in New England* (New York: Hill and Wang 1983), 12.

10. Leslie Upton, *Micmacs and Colonists: Indian–White Relations in the Maritimes, 1713–1867* (Vancouver: University of British Columbia Press 1979), 25.

11. Peter Mason, *Deconstructing America: Representation of the Other* (London: Routledge 1990), and Antonello Gerbi, *Nature in the New World* (Pittsburgh: Pittsburgh University Press 1985).

12. *The Works of Samuel de Champlain* (Toronto: The Champlain Society 1922), 1, 243.

13. Lescarbot, III, 484–85; Nicolas Denys, *Description and Natural History of the Coasts of North America (Acadia)* (Toronto: The Champlain Society 1908), 390, 393; Hugh Honour, *The New Golden Land: European Images of America from the Discovery to the Present Time* (New York: Random House 1975), 36–37.

14. Denys, 362–69; Le Clercq, *New Relation of Gaspesia* (Toronto: The Champlain Society 1910), 279.

15. Le Clercq, 275; Denys, 257–340; Champlain, 247, 368; Denys, 199.

16. Champlain, 327; for a discussion of the distribution of Native peoples, see Bruce J. Bourque, "Ethnicity in the Maritime Peninsula, 1600–1759," *Ethnohistory* (1989), 36: 257–84.

17. Sieur de Dièreville, *Relation of the Voyage to Port Royal in Acadia* (Toronto: The Champlain Society 1933), 130–41; Lescarbot, III, 54, 164, 205; Karen Anderson, *Chain Her by One Foot* (London: Routledge 1990).

18. Lescarbot, III, 200–2; Le Clercq, 243.

19. Le Clercq, 135–39; Denys, 420; Marc Lescarbot, *The Conversion of the Savages* in Reuben Gold Thwaites, ed., *The Jesuit Relations and Allied Documents* (New York: Pageant Books 1959), I, 101; *Jesuit Relations*, III, 83; Le Clercq, 265, 273.

20. Le Clercq, 243; Lescarbot, III, 333.

21. Lescarbot, III, 27, 113, 365; *Jesuit Relations*, III, 21; Todorov, *Conquest*, 27–33; Marshall Sahlins, *Islands of History* (Chicago: University of Chicago Press 1985), 10.

22. *Jesuit Relations*, III, 33–35.

23. *Jesuit Relations*, III, 33.

24. Champlain, 295.

25. Clarence J. Glacken, "Changing Ideas of the Habitable World," in William L. Thomas, ed., *Man's Role in Changing the Face of the Earth* (Chicago: University of Chicago

Press 1956), 70–92; Lescarbot, III, 241, 351, 363–64; Alfred W. Crosby, Jr, *Ecological Imperialism: The Biological Expansion of Europe, 900–1900* (Cambridge: Cambridge University Press 1986); A. Bartlett Giamatti, *The Earthly Paradise of the Renaissance Epic* (Princeton: Princeton University Press 1969); Hugh Johnson, *The Principles of Gardening* (London: Michael Beazley Publications 1979), 8.

26. *Jesuit Relations*, III, 63; Denys, 303; Lescarbot, I, xii.

27. Denys, 149–50; Dièreville, 94–95; see Andrew Hill Clark, *Acadia: The Geography of Early Nova Scotia* (Madison: University of Wisconsin Press 1986), 24–31.

28. Lescarbot, II, 317; John Hemming, *The Conquest of the Incas* (London: Penguin Books 1983), 77–88.

29. Champlain, 272; Jane, *Columbus*, 24; Le Clercq, 115; *Jesuit Relations*, III; Le Clercq, 205; Lescarbot, III, 487.

30. Denys, 156; Dièreville, 75–77, 102, 122–23.

31. William M. Denevan, "The Pristine Myth: The Landscape of the Americas in 1492," *Annals of the Association of American Geographers*, 82 (3), 1992, 369–85; Keith Thomas, *Man and the Natural World* (New York: Pantheon Books 1983), 274; Le Clercq, 331; Marshall Sahlins, *Stone Age Economics* (Chicago: Aldine Publishing Co. 1972); Denys, 403; Clarence J. Glacken, *Traces on the Rhodian Shore: Nature and Culture in Western Thought from Ancient Times until the End of the Eighteenth Century* (Berkeley: University of California Press 1967), 494; Lescarbot, III, 137. See also Richard White, "Native Americans and the Environment," in W.E. Swagerty, ed., *Scholars and the Indian Experience* (Bloomington: Indiana University Press 1984), 179–204.

32. Lescarbot, III, 94, 127; J.G.A. Pocock, "Tangata Whenua and Enlightenment Anthropology," *The New Zealand Journal of History*, 26, 1, April 1992,

35, 36, 41. Pocock bases much of his intricate argument on late seventeenth and eighteenth century sources, yet Marc Lescarbot's *History of New France*, first published in 1609, already articulates and assumes, though in a somewhat unsystematic way, a fairly full-blown version of the theory; see also John Locke's chapter "Of Property" in his *Essay Concerning the True Original Extent of Civil Government* (1640). Professor John Marshall has pointed to the importance of domestic animal imports as disease carriers by drawing my attention to Jured Diamond, "The Arrow of Disease," *Discover*, October 1992, 64–73.

33. Lescarbot, III, 254; *Jesuit Relations*, I, 177.

34. Denys, 415; Lescarbot, III, 163; Le Clercq, 151; Lescarbot, III, 227.

35. Le Clercq, 254–55; Dièreville, 77.

36. Dean R. Snow and Kim M. Lamphear, "European Contact and Indian Depopulation in the Northeast," *Ethnohistory* (1988), 35: 15–33; Virginia P. Miller, "Aboriginal Micmac Population: A Review of Evidence," *Ethnohistory* (1976), 23: 117–27, and "The Decline of Nova Scotia Micmac Population, A.D. 1600–1850," *Culture* (1982), 3: 107–20; John D. Daniels, "The Indian Population of North America in 1492," *William and Mary Quarterly*, XLIX, 2, April 1991, 298–320.

37. Bruce G. Trigger, *Natives and Newcomers* (Montreal: McGill Queen's Press 1985), 183–94.

38. Le Clercq, 255; Denys, 449–50.

39. Denys, 442.

40. Calvin Martin, "Four Lives of a Micmac Copper Pot," *Ethnohistory* (1975), 22: 111–33; Le Clercq, 277; Denys, 452. See also Wilson D. Wallis and Ruth S. Wallis, *The Micmac Indians of Eastern Canada* (Minneapolis: University of Minnesota Press 1945), and Bruce J. Bourque and Ruth Holmes Whitehead, "Tarrentines and the Introduction of European Trade Goods in the Gulf of Maine," *Ethnohistory* (1985), 32: 327–41.

41. *Jesuit Relations*, I, 166–67; Le Clercq, 193–94.

42. Denys, 437; *Jesuit Relations*, III, 135; Lescarbot, III, 189; Elliott, *The Old World*, 27.

43. Le Clercq, 125, 104.

44. Lescarbot, III, 229, 256–57.

45. Rev. Silas Tertius Rand, *Legends of the Micmacs* (London: Longmans, Green and Co., 1894), 279.

ABORIGINAL RESOURCE USE
IN THE NINETEENTH CENTURY
IN THE GREAT PLAINS OF
MODERN CANADA *

IRENE M. SPRY

o

The little that we know of pre-contact and early contact Indian life suggests that the peoples of the parklands and prairies usually enjoyed an abundant material basis for their lives. Vast herds of buffalo provided them with plenty of food, which was supplemented by other game, such as the millions of cabri (pronghorn antelope) that roamed the plains;[1] by wildfowl; by fish; by a rich variety of fruit in season; by root crops, such as Indian turnip; by wild rice; and by maple syrup. For clothing and coverings they used buffalo hides and robes and the hides and fur of other animals. Buffalo hides gave them shelter when spread on a framework of lodgepole pines to make mobile dwellings.

The pines also gave them a means of transportation when lashed together to form a *travois*. Other trees and shrubs supplied fuel, as did "buffalo chips" (dried dung) out on the treeless plains. For weapons, too, wood was put to work, as bows and spear shafts, along with flint and buffalo bones for spear and arrow tips, and buffalo sinews for bow strings. Buffalo hides and sinews were used for other types of cordage, while hides and bladders were fashioned into kettles and other receptacles, as were buffalo horns. These horns[2] also made tops for children to play with, and the great beasts' bones served as materials for implements.[3] Wild plants were the source of medicaments.

On the open prairies there was ample space for tribal assemblies and ceremonials, as well as the solitude needed for the vision quest. Shelter was

---

* Kerry Abel and Jean Friesen, eds., *Aboriginal Resource Use in Canada: Historical and Legal Aspects* (Winnipeg: University of Manitoba Press, 1991), 81–92.

sought, in the frigid winters, in wooded valleys and coulées. The air was pure, and water could be found by those who were knowledgeable about the country. Waste disposal was facilitated by the mobility of the camps and the organic, biodegradable character of most of what had to be disposed of; it was easily absorbed into the natural environment.

Certainly there must have been scarcity at times, and in specific localities when unusually severe or unusually mild weather made the buffalo detour from their usual seasonal haunts, or when fire or drought caused shortages; but statements made by more than one Native, as well as by early travellers, attest a primitive abundance. Chief Peguis told the Reverend William Cockran in 1831 that, "before the Whites came to trouble the ground, our River was full of fishes, our Creeks were full of Beaver; our plains covered with Buffaloes."[4] He may, of course, have been making a biased case, but more than one group gave the same testimony. The Ojibwa of the Rainy Lake area told the Palliser expedition, "our woods were wont to teem with animals, and our rivers and lakes to abound in fish."[5] Peter Erasmus reminisced of the 1860s that "the Country in those early years was overthrowing with animals and the lakes teeming with fish enough to satisfy any man's appetite."[6] Alexander Henry the Elder bore independent witness to this early abundance:

> The wild ox alone supplies them [the Indians] with every thing which they are accustomed to want. The hide of this animal, when dressed, furnishes soft clothing for the women; and, dressed with the hair on, it clothes the men. The flesh feeds them; the sinews afford them bow-strings; and even the paunch, as we have seen, provides them with that important utensil, the kettle. The amazing numbers of these animals prevent all fear of want; a fear which is incessantly present to the Indians of the north.[7]

The question that immediately emerges is: How was it that the Native population of the western interior of what is now Canada apparently did not expand in a Malthusian manner to put pressure on this plentiful material resource base? Estimates of the pre-contact and early contact plains population differ widely, but there does not seem to be evidence that there was any general tendency for numbers to increase in the early contact era in such a way as to jeopardize this primitive abundance.[8] Why not? I have found no answer to this question. Was it that the Indians' mobile life inhibited procreation? Or was it the result of social customs such as polygamy and periods of nursing that sometimes lasted as long as four years?[9] There can be no doubt that a roaming life is a hard life. Was there, perhaps, a high death rate?

The Indians' life was, indeed, a hard life, but a satisfying, diversified and challenging life. Periods of strenuous activity were followed by periods of leisure, which allowed ample time for ceremonials and the vision quest, sociability, dancing, music, games and the development of creative artistry in painting tipis, and making and adorning clothes and accoutrements. Traders and missionaries complained about the "indolence" of the Indians and Métis. A modern economist would say that they had a high leisure preference. Their way of life made it possible for them to satisfy that preference.

There was no soul-destroying daily routine drudgery. Securing food meant the exciting chase or buffalo drive, hunting other big game, wandering in the bush to pick berries or out on the prairie to dig roots. All these diversified activities—even snaring rabbits and prairie chickens—were enjoyable. Moreover, they required skill and a profound knowledge of the environment. Processing the wild harvest, too, called for considerable expertise.[10]

The mobile life imposed on Indian bands and on their cousins, the Métis, by the search for food was due to the necessity for moving with the migrating herds of wild cattle, as they followed the sequence of ripening grasses,[11] and moving about in search of other sources of food, as these became available, season by season.[12] In summer, congregating herds of buffalo out on the open prairie made possible great tribal gatherings, for sociability and ceremonials.[13] In winter, both buffalo and human beings had to seek shelter in coulées, on the wooded slopes of prairie "mountains," in valleys in the foothills, or in the fringes of the "strong woods."[14]

The Indians and the Métis loved this wandering life. It gave them a continual change of scene and the enjoyment of a variety of a lovely landscapes,[15] as a part of their normal life, not just in rare and expensive holidays, such as those taken by modern city dwellers. Moreover, getting a living was a zestful, community affair.[16] Hunting and gathering foodstuffs and raw materials, processing the products, and fashioning from them clothing and accoutrements were sociable and satisfying activities that gave outlets for skill, knowledge and creative ability.

Their mobile lifestyle made impossible any personal accumulation by Indians of material wealth, so it was on human quality, not on individual riches, that social esteem was based. Those distinguished for skill, courage, endurance and wisdom were outstanding. In particular, generosity was important in an economy based on sharing the work that had to be done and the proceeds of hunting and gathering.[17]

As Marshall Sahlins has demonstrated in his *Stone Age Economics*, such hunters and gatherers may well be considered to have constituted "The Original Affluent Society."[18] By no means a "consumer society," the peoples of the plains enjoyed what Kenneth Boulding has called "paleolithic bliss."[19] This economy could never have been described as a "joyless economy," the designation given to our own high consumption society by Tibor Scitovsky.[20] The Indians with whom Charles Mackenzie lived in the Missouri considered that the white man did "not know how to live." When told that "the Northern nations were very industrious" in trapping beaver, they replied: "We are no Slaves." They would not hunt beaver to satisfy the "avarice"[21] of whites.

Those Indians who took to trapping furbearing animals to trade with the white men for knives, kettles, guns and ammunition, textiles and blankets, tea, sugar and tobacco, to say nothing of "fire-water," eventually substituted a fur-trapping cycle for the seasonal food-quest cycle. This interruption to their usual pattern of a search for food meant that they were sometimes short of provisions, and had to beg the traders for what they needed for survival.[22] As A.J. Ray has shown, they became dependent on the white man's stockpiles of food instead of moving season by season to the sources of food supplies and leaving it to nature to provide a store of the food they required.

This increasing dependence on white traders, not only for trade goods, but also for food, had a second effect. The traders' open-ended demand for peltries resulted, in the period of cut-throat competition between the Hudson's Bay Company (HBC) and the North West Company (NWC), in the Indians' trapping-out areas formerly rich in fur-bearing animals.

This raises another unanswered question: Were Indians in pre-contact days conservers of the wild life on which they depended? Or were they heedlessly wasteful in the slaughter of game?

More than one white traveller described apparently wanton slaughter. Charles Mackenzie, for example, on the Missouri in 1804, wrote: "large parties who went daily in pursuit of buffaloes killed whole herds, but returned only with the tongues."[23] However, there seems to have been an ulterior object in this proceeding: the wolves gorged themselves on the buffalo carcasses and were then easily captured by the hunters.[24]

There are, in contrast, records of Indian aversion to excessive kills. Roe, in his exhaustive discussion of alleged Indian "wastefulness" in hunting, gives a number of instances, ranging from Groseilliers and Radisson onwards, of Indian restraint in harvesting wildlife.[25] Admittedly, when a herd of buffalo was driven into a pound on the plains, the entire herd was killed, but, as Roe indicates, citing the younger Henry, the Indians had a reason for this. Any animal that escaped might warn other herds.[26] Moreover, reminiscing of the 1870s, old "Kootenai Brown," who had lived and hunted with his wife's Métis relatives, asserted that, contrary to most generalizations, the Métis were not wantonly wasteful. Indeed, "it was a rule in all half-breed hunting camps that every part of every animal must be used unless it was diseased."[27]

By then, it had become apparent that the great herds were dwindling. White men, as well as Indians and Métis, were already engaged in ruthless slaughter of the wild cattle. In view of the desperate competition for the remaining buffalo, it was natural and, indeed, entirely rational, for the Indians to hunt unsparingly. Once the Indians' formerly jealously guarded hunting territories were opened to other tribes, to Métis and to white men, there was no longer any reason for restraint. If the Indians did not secure the buffalo, the huge beasts would fall prey to hide hunters and the robe trade.

With the coming of the whites' guns and horses, there had been important changes in the Indians' lifestyle, and in their relationship to the gifts of nature. The Indians could now "run" the buffalo herds, whereas before they had to depend on carefully stalking them or on developing a strategy for driving them into a pound or over a buffalo jump.

With horses, the ease, speed and range of travel widened. War parties could go further and faster, and horse stealing became a serious cause of inter-tribal warfare, which became more lethal. At the same time, owner-ship of horses meant new demands on the environment: pasture and sup-plies of water were necessary for them. Still more significant, horses, being mobile, were a type of material wealth that could be accumulated by indi-viduals, which eroded the old egalitarian structure of society.[28]

In addition, the Métis, using horses in their well-organized buffalo hunt, with its para-military discipline, penetrated Indian hunting grounds,[29] first from Red River and then from bases further and further west such as St. Albert[30] and Victoria (Pakan).[31]

Encroachment by intruders became more difficult to resist. When the North-West Mounted Police (NWMP) arrived, they forbade the use of force to keep other tribes, Métis and whites out of tribal territories.[32] Controlled, common property use of resources gave way to open access use by all cor-ners.[33] This resulted in over-use and progressive depletion of the buffalo and other game, as well as of other nature-given resources.

Meanwhile, the Métis population seems to have been growing rapidly. The total population of the Red River Settlement rose from 2751 in 1832[34] to 12 288 in 1870. Of this total, 11 228 had been born in Manitoba and the North-West Territories.[35] This increase was at least in part because the HBC was trying to send all freemen, including their Métis families and other Métis from upcountry areas and posts to the Red River Colony, but it was probably also attributable to a high birth rate. Whatever the reason, the drain on buffalo herds escalated. Alexander Ross recorded that, in 1820, 540 Red River carts went out from the Colony on the biannual hunt; by 1840 the total had risen to 1210.[36] As buffalo grew scarcer and scarcer in the Red River Valley, the Métis hunt travelled progressively further west. An increasing number of the hunters began to "winter over" at camps like those on Buffalo Lake (Alberta)[37] and Petite Ville on the South Saskatchewan.[38] Some of these winter camps later became permanent settlements. From them, as well as from missionary settlements (such as the Catholic mission at St. Albert[39] and the Methodist mission at Victoria, or Pakan)[40] and from HBC posts, hunting parties ranged the plains in search of buffalo. As the herds dwindled, the hunters had to go progressively further and further afield. Peter Erasmus records of the late 1860s:

> Ten years ago, on my first hunt, there had been a herd of more than three hundred animals less than ten miles from the Saskatchewan River. Now we had to travel more than thirty miles further south before we spotted buffalo and this was a herd of only fifteen ani-mals, whereas there had been small herds of from fifteen to fifty head all along our route from Saddle Lake crossing to near the Fort Saskatchewan ford.[41]

The demands of the fur trade on the wild cattle were very heavy. Pemmican was needed to supply the scattered posts with food, as well as the voyageurs who carried trade goods inland from Hudson Bay (and later from Red River) and the harvest of furs out to market. Besides beaver and other traditional furs, markets began to develop for buffalo tongues and buffalo robes. In these, the HBC carried on a modest trade, but the Missouri traders, with easy steamboat transportation down "the Great Muddy," offered a most demanding market. Indeed, in a recent study of a Métis winter camp at Buffalo Lake (Boss Hill), John Foster attributes the destruction of the buffalo herds on the western Canadian plains to the robe trade.[42] This became important when whiskey traders from Fort Benton began to tap Canadian sources of robes for the Missouri outlet.[43] The Benton traders also opened up a market for wolf skins. American "wolfers" invaded the Canadian plains, using strychnine poison.[44]

When it was discovered that buffalo hides could be used in the multiplying American factories for belting to connect steam engines to the machines they drove, hide hunters, armed with long-range, repeating rifles and travelling on the new transcontinental railroads, wreaked havoc among the herds.[45] They left the carcasses to rot, to the rage of the Indians,[46] and were so careless that they uselessly killed three animals for every one marketable hide.[47] Whether this affected the Canadian herd is a matter of disagreement. Recent writers believe that the western Canadian herd followed a circular migratory path north of the forty-ninth parallel,[48] but Charles MacInnes[49] and Roe[50] held that the Canadian herd migrated across the American border. If so, not only American hide hunters, but also American military policy may have had a serious effect on the Canadian buffalo population. American policy was to exterminate the wild cattle in order to force the Indians into submission.[51] Charles MacInnes states that the American army established a cordon of wolfers and Métis along the border, to keep the herds from moving north into Canadian territory, in order to compel Sitting Bull and his Sioux to return to the United States from their refuge in Canada,[52] where they had certainly put added pressure on the Canadian herds.

The ultimate fate of the buffalo had been long foreseen. As early as the 1850s, the Palliser expedition had reported uneasiness among some Indians, such as the Qu'Appelle Lakes Cree, about the future of the herds, and their desire to learn how to farm.[53] In fact, there was a long tradition of Indian agriculture on the plains, not only among the Mandans of the Missouri, but also among the Ojibwa.[54] Some traders, such as Alexander Henry the Younger, had encouraged Indian cultivation, supplying seeds and trading for their produce.[55] The HBC had grown grain and potatoes at its posts and raised cattle and horses. Missionaries had, since their arrival, "preached farming," and both Indians and Métis increasingly practised some cultivation and raised some domestic livestock. James Hector, in 1859, saw gardens where Mountain Stoneys grew turnips,[56] no doubt under the influence of the Reverend Robert T. Rundle. The Reverend J.A. Mackay, in 1873, in a journey along the Carlton Trail near the North Saskatchewan, found Indians growing potatoes, to supplement fishing and hunting.[57] Métis settlements, not only on the Red River and the Assiniboine,[58] but also on the South Saskatchewan,[59] the North Saskatchewan,[60] the Battle River[61] and elsewhere, also cultivated gardens and small fields, as well as rearing livestock.

For these agricultural initiatives the Native peoples simply picked out a desirable plot of land, built a house and stables on it and proceeded to farm.[62] Even in the Red River "Settlement Belt," such occupation and "improvement" of land, without any formal entitlement, was a well recognized and widespread procedure.[63] For example, when the NWMP reached the Cypress Hills in 1875, they found a thriving farm run by the Métis trader, Edward McKay.[64] He did not own any of the land he was using.[65]

In some cases, such land occupation, especially by white immigrants like Kenneth McKenzie, was the cause of Indian resentment.[66] The Métis, too, were angry when, as on the Assiniboine, white newcomers usurped land and timber they had long regarded as theirs.[67]

Timber, a necessity for building and heating, was a continuing bone of contention, from Lake of the Woods to the Rockies. On the Dawson Route, S.J. Dawson contended that "Her Majesty's subjects had a common right to the forest and the waterway."[68] He meant that there was open access to these resources by any who wished to use them. All that had to be paid for was the work of cutting the timber down and hauling it to where it was needed.[69] On the Roseau River (a tributary of the Red), lumbermen were cutting trees on the Indians' as yet unsurveyed reserve.[70] On the Assiniboine, Métis occupants objected to white men cutting the trees on which they traditionally relied for wood. The lands would be of little use if all the wood had gone.[71] Along the steamboat route, timber cut for fuel ate into supplies of wood for the local people.[72] In the course of negotiations for Treaty 7, Button Chief raised the problem of NWMP use of timber resources that the Indians considered to be theirs.[73]

The white solution to the problem of conflicting uses of nature-given resources was to establish private property rights in those resources and, where that was not possible, in the case of such "fugacious resources" as fish and game, to make rules and regulations to restrict their use. But this could not be done until the Indians had surrendered their claims to the use of the lands they lived in and the resources of those lands. It was in the negotiations for that surrender that the difference in the point of view of the Native peoples and the white newcomers about the use of nature-given resources became evident. When, in the Treaty 7 negotiations, the Indians asked to have outsiders excluded from hunting in their country, their request was refused, on the grounds that "the Commissioners could not agree to exclude the Crees and Half-breeds from the Blackfoot country: that they were the Great Mother's children as much as the Blackfeet and Bloods, and she did not wish to see any of them starve."[74]

They were also assured, in these and other treaty negotiations, that, until their lands were needed for public works or farms, Indians would be free, as before, to roam and hunt.[75] Reserves were to be set aside as a protection against white encroachment, to ensure that the Indians would always have land of their own that could never be taken from them.[76]

Whether the Indians realized that they were actually selling their lands outright to the Canadian government, or whether, as I am inclined to think, they believed that what they were surrendering was the exclusive right to use those lands and their resources, is not clear.[77] Some of the Indians do seem to have understood that they were in fact giving up their lands, notably Poundmaker, in the Treaty 6 negotiations. His cry, "This is our land! It isn't a piece of pemmican to be cut off and given in little pieces back to us. It is ours and we will take what we want,"[78] expressed the depth of his aversion to the treaty terms. He and his supporters were over-ruled. The women, too, understood what was happening. When the NWMP paraded with their band and the commissioners to the treaty-making tent, they fled into their lodges, crying, "We are losing our country."[79] The newcomers were, indeed, taking their country from them.

Whether or not they realized its full implications, Treaty 6 was accepted by Mistawasis (Big Child) and Ah-tuk-uk-koop (Star Blanket), because they were so anxious about the impending loss of the old way of life when the buffalo finally disappeared.[80] They hoped that, if they signed the treaty, their people might learn to farm. In the tribal council, Mistawasis summed up the agonizing issue: "I for one think that the Great White Queen Mother has offered us a way of life when the buffalo are no more."[81] Ah-tuk-uk-koop agreed:

> We have always lived and received our needs in clothing, shelter, and food from the countless multitudes of buffalo that have been with us since the earliest memory of our people. No one with open eyes and open minds can doubt that the buffalo will soon be a thing of the past. Will our people live as before when this comes to pass? No! They will die and become just a memory unless we find another way. For my part, I think that the Queen Mother has offered us a new way and I have faith in the things my brother Mista-wa-sis has told you.[82]

Surveyors of the Dominion Lands Branch of the Department of the Interior staked out the chequerboard of townships, ranges and sections, for disposition as Crown lands "for the purposes of the Dominion,"[83] to white farmers, railroaders and colonization companies. Timber and grazing permits were issued, mining lands alienated and regulations devised for the use of water.[84] The buffalo had gone; other game—even gophers—had grown scarce. Unbelievably, the Native peoples found that they might no longer roam over what had been the land with which the Manitou had endowed them. Lieutenant W.F. Butler, in his *Great Lone Land*, recorded the Indians' outraged response: "We who have dwelt on these prairies ever since the stars fell . . . do not put sticks over the land and say, 'Between these sticks this land is mine; you shall not come here or go there.'"[85] The homeland of the Indians and Métis had become the frontier of settlement and exploitation for the citizens of central Canada.

The Indians and Métis faced the desperate necessity of learning a new way of providing subsistence for themselves and their families. Their old way of life as hunters and gatherers, warriors and wilderness roamers was over. It was a sad transition to a sedentary life on reserves, scraping a meager living by cultivation and stock raising under the control of an Indian agent, a living eked out by grudging government rations. The glory and excitement of the old life had given way to dismal boredom; accustomed freedom and independence to subordination to the Indian Act and dependence on the Indian agent even for permission to sell what was produced on the reserve.[86] The nature-given resources, even of the reserves, seemed no longer to be the Indians' inheritance from a bounteous Great Spirit.

NOTES

1. Jim Gibson gives a total of from 30 to 50 million on the North American plains. "Three Tiny Prairie Parks Saved the Pronghorn," *Canadian Geographic*, 107, 6 (December 1987/January 1988): 59.

2. For a more detailed description of the uses made of the buffalo by the Indians, see Amelia M. Paget, *The People of the Plains* (Toronto: Ryerson Press, n.d.), chapter 5.

3. Isaac Cowie, *The Company of Adventurers* (Toronto: William Briggs, 1913), 260. See also, Irene Spry, ed., *The Papers of the Palliser Expedition, 1857–1860* (Toronto: The Champlain Society, 1968), 175.

4. John Foster, ed., "Missionaries, Mixed-Bloods and the Fur Trade: Four Letters of the Rev. William Cockran, Red River Settlement, 1830–1833," *Western Canadian Journal of Anthropology*, 3, 1 (1972): 103.

5. Spry, ed., *Palliser Expedition*, 77.

6. Peter Erasmus, *Buffalo Days and Nights* (Calgary: Glenbow-Alberta Institute, 1976), 185.

7. Alexander Henry the Elder, *Travels and Adventures in Canada and the Indian Territories* (Edmonton: Hurtig, 1969; reprinted for the third time from the first edition of 1809), 317–18.

8. It should, however, be noted that "an increase in Cree population forced the tribe into territories they had not previously inhabited," as David G. Mandelbaum states, citing an 1804 comment by Duncan Cameron, in *The Plains Cree*, Canadian Plains Studies, 9 (Regina: Canadian Plains Research Center, 1979), 40.

9. *Ibid.*, 142–43.

10. For example, Adrien Nelson, in a letter from Bad Throat River, Lake Winnipeg, March 18, 1887, described how Indian women harvested and processed wild rice. Discussing the difficulty of expanding production, he wrote: "No labour could be obtained understanding the process except that of the Indians" (Journals of the Senate of Canada, First Session of the Sixth Parliament, Appendix to Vol. 21, 1887, 25–28.

11. Bryan H.C. Gordon, *Of Men and Herds in Canadian Plains Prehistory* (Ottawa: National Museum of Man, Mercury Series, Archaeological Survey of Canada, Paper No. 84, 1979).

12. Arthur J. Ray, "Periodic Shortages, Native Welfare, and the Hudson's Bay Company, 1670–1930," in *The Subarctic Fur Trade: Native Social and Economic Adaptations*, edited by Shepard Krech III (Vancouver: University of British Columbia Press, 1984), 2–3.

13. Diamond Jenness, *The Indians of Canada* (Ottawa: Department of Mines, National Museum of Canada, Bulletin 65, 1932), 127 and 310.

14. *Ibid.*, 130. See also, Gordon, *Of Men and Herds*, 37, 50–51.

15. Edward Ahenakew, *Voices of the Plains Cree*, edited by Ruth M. Buck (Toronto: McClelland and Stewart, 1973), 88.

16. For an illuminating explanation of this characteristic of Indian life see Theodora Kroeber, *Ishi in Two Worlds: A Biography of the Last Wild Indian in North America* (Berkeley: University of California Press, 1964).

17. Ahenakew, *Voices of the Plains Cree*, 33.

18. Marshall David Sahlins, *Stone Age Economics* (Chicago: Aldine-Atherton, 1972), chapter 1. I am indebted to Professor A.J. Ray for this reference.

19. Dr. Boulding used this phrase in a recent lecture at Carleton University.

20. Tibor Scitovsky, *The Joyless Economy* (New York: Oxford University Press, 1976).

21. L.R. Masson, *Les Bourgeois de la Compagnie du Nord-Ouest*, 2 vols. (New York: Antiquarian Press Limited, 1960; reprinted from the original edition, Québec: A. Coté et Cie, 1880–1890), vol. 1, 331.

22. Ray, "Periodic Shortages."

23. Masson, *Les Bourgeois de la Compagnie*, vol. 1, 331.

24. *Ibid.*

25. Frank Gilbert Roe, *The North American Buffalo: A Critical Study of the Species in its Wild State*, 2nd ed. (Toronto: University of Toronto Press, 1970; 1st edition, 1951), 292. "The wild men [savages] kill not except for necessary use." See also pp. 654–57.

26. *Ibid.*, 632 and 648.

27. William Rodney, *Kootenai Brown: His Life and Times* 1839–1916 (Sidney, B.C.: Gray's Publishing, 1969), 104–5.

28. Frank Gilbert Roe, *The Indian and the Horse* (Norman: University of Oklahoma Press, 1955), part 2, 175–375.

29. W.L. Morton, *Manitoba: A History* (Toronto: University of Toronto Press, 1957), 78–79.

30. Victoria Calihoo, "Our Buffalo Hunts," *Alberta History*, 6, 1 (Winter 1960): 24–25.

31. R.G. Ironsides and E. Tomasky, "Development of Victoria Settlement," *Alberta History*, 19, 2 (Spring 1971): 21–22.

32. John Peter Turner, *The North-West Mounted Police, 1873–1893*, 2 vols. (Ottawa: King's Printer, 1950), vol. 1, 210.

33. Irene M. Spry, "The Tragedy of the Loss of the Commons in Western Canada," in *As Long as the Sun Shines and Water Flows*, edited by Ian Getty and Antoine S. Lussier (Vancouver: University of British Columbia Press, Nakoda Institute Occasional Paper No. 1, 1983), 203–28, revised and reprinted from "The Great Transformation: The Disappearance of the Commons in Western Canada" in *Man and Nature on the Prairies*, edited by Richard Allen (Regina: Canadian Plains Research Center, Canadian Plains Studies 6, 1976).

34. Provincial Archives of Manitoba, Red River Census, 1832.

35. Provincial Archives of Manitoba, Census of Manitoba, 1870, pp. 386–87. This total must have included the children of Selkirk and other white settlers, but most of the residents born in Manitoba and the North-West Territories were of mixed white and Indian descent.

36. Alexander Ross, *The Red River Settlement: Its Rise, Progress, and Present State* (Edmonton: Hurtig, 1872; reprinted from the original edition, London: Smith, Elder and Co., 1856), 246.

37. John Foster, "The Métis Hivernement Settlement at Buffalo Lake, 1872–1877," 3 vols. (Edmonton: April 1987, typescript).

38. Marcel Giraud, "Métis Settlement in the North-West Territories," *Saskatchewan History*, 7, 1 (Winter 1954): 5.

39. Calihoo, "Our Buffalo Hunts."

40. Ironsides and Tomasky, "Development of Victoria Settlement," 21–22.

41. Erasmus, *Buffalo Days and Nights*, 182.

42. Foster, "Métis Hivernement Settlement."

43. Foster, "Métis Hivernement Settlement"; and Paul F. Sharp, *Whoop-Up Country: The Canadian-American West 1865–1885*, 2nd ed. (Helena: Historical Society of Montana, 1960;

reprinted from Minneapolis: University of Minnesota Press, 1955).

44. *Ibid.*, 51; and Alexander Morris, *The Treaties of Canada with the Indians of Manitoba and the North-West Territories* (Toronto: Belfords, Clarke and Co., 1880), 273.

45. Ralph Andrist, *The Long Death, The Last Days of the Plains Indian* (London: Macmillan, 1964), 179.

46. *Ibid.*, 182.

47. *Ibid.*, 179–82.

48. Gordon, *Of Men and Herds*. For a bibliography of works on the North American buffalo see George W. Arthur, *A Buffalo Round-up: A Selected Bibliography* (Regina: Canadian Plains Research Center, 1985).

49. C.M. MacInnes, *In the Shadow of the Rockies* (London: Rivingtons, 1930), 146.

50. Roe, *North American Buffalo*, chapters 19 and 21.

51. Spry, "Tragedy of the Loss of the Commons," 209. The "indiscriminate slaughter" of the buffalo was, according to Ahenakew, encouraged in Canada. He knew that south of the border it had been a deliberate policy to subdue warlike tribes. Ahenakew, *Voices of the Plains Cree*, 106.

52. MacInnes, *Shadow of the Rockies*, 146.

53. Spry, ed., *Palliser Expedition*, 137.

54. D.W. Moodie, "Agriculture and the Fur Trade," in *Old Trails and New Directions: Papers of the Third North American Fur Trade Conference*, edited by Carol Judd and Arthur J. Ray (Toronto: University of Toronto Press, 1980), 282–83.

55. Elliott Coues, ed., *New Light on the Early History of the Greater Northwest* (New York: Francis P. Harper, 1897), 48, 82n, 439n, 448.

56. Spry, ed., *Palliser Expedition*, 434–35.

57. Rev. J.A. Mackay, "Journal," *Saskatchewan History*, 19, 2 (Spring 1966): 74–76.

58. Morton, *Manitoba*, 88, 152–53.

59. Diane Payment, *Batoche* (St. Boniface: Les Editions du Blé, 1983); and Marcel Giraud, *Les Métis Canadien* (St. Boniface: Les Editions du Blé, 1984; reprinted from Paris: Institut d'Ethnologie, 1945), part 6, chapter 3.

60. Ironsides and Tomasky, "Development of Victoria Settlement."

61. W.C. Wonders, "Far Corner of the Strange Empire: Central Alberta on the Eve of Homestead Settlement," *Great Plains Quarterly* (Spring 1983): 102–3.

62. H. Douglas Kemp, "Land Grants under the Manitoba Act, The Halfbreed Land Grant," Papers read before the Historical and Scientific Society of Manitoba, series 3, 9 (1954): 33–53.

63. P.R. Mailhot and D.N. Sprague, "Persistent Settlers: The Dispersal and Resettlement of the Red River Métis, 1870–85," *Canadian Ethnic Studies*, 17, 2 (1985): 1–30.

64. Senator F.W. Gershaw, "Edward McKay," *Canadian Cattlemen* (March 1956): 41; and W. Henry McKay, "The Story of Edward McKay," *Canadian Cattlemen*, 10, 2 (September 1947): 100–1, 105.

65. *Ibid.*, 77.

66. Morton, *Manitoba*, 115–16.

67. Joseph Royal to Lieutenant-Governor Archibald, 15 February, 1871, Provincial Archives of Manitoba, Archibald Papers, 193, 198.

68. W.E. Daugherty, *Treaty Research Report, Treaty No. 3* (Ottawa: Treaties and Historical Research Centre, Indian and Northern Affairs Canada, 1986) citing Department of Indian Affairs, Annual Report, 1874, pp. 15–16.

69. Spry, "Tragedy of the Loss of the Commons," 213–14.

70. Royal to Archibald, 15 February 1871, Archibald Papers, 193, 198.

71. Spry, "Tragedy of the Loss of the Commons," 214.

72. *Ibid.*

73. Morris, *Treaties*, 257.

74. *Ibid.*, 258.

75. *Ibid.*, 257.

76. *Ibid.*

77. Edward Ahenakew said of the Indians that "they could not realize what the signing over of their lands meant" (Ahenakew, *Voices of the Plains Cree*, 105). See also: W.E. Daugherty, *Treaty Research Report*, Treaty No. 3, 13 and 40; and *Report of Meetings between Indians of the North West Territory and the Governor General*, 16 November 1881.

78. Erasmus, *Buffalo Days and Nights*, 244.

79. Hugh A. Dempsey, ed., *William Parker: Mounted Policeman* (Calgary: Glenbow-Alberta Institute, 1973), 23.

80. Erasmus, *Buffalo Days and Nights*, 247–50.

81. *Ibid.* This, as far as I know, is the only account extant of the discussion in a tribal council about the problem of whether the terms of a treaty should be accepted.

82. *Ibid.*, 250.

83. Chester Martin, *"Dominion Lands" Policy* (Toronto: Macmillan of Canada, Canadian Frontiers of Settlement series, vol. 2, 1938).

84. See successive Dominion lands acts and Northwest Territories irrigation acts.

85. W.F. Butler, *The Great Lone Land: A Narrative of Travel and Adventure in the North-West of America* (London: Sampson, Low, Marston, Low and Searle, 1874), 272.

86. Ahenakew, *Voices of the Plains Cree*, 147.

INDUSTRIALIZATION AND THE SPREAD OF SETTLEMENT

○

N ot surprisingly, environmental historians associate the Industrial Revolution with the dramatically increased pressure that humans exerted on the rest of the environment during the nineteenth century. Less familiar is their conclusion that many contemporaries were well aware of the environmental degradation produced by this increasing pressure. The ecological impact of the Industrial Revolution may not have been fully understood at the time, but ignorance does not fully explain the attitudes and actions characteristic of the Great Transformation that produced modern Canada. In some cases, knowledge of environmental degradation was simply disregarded uncaringly while, in other cases, it was seen as a necessary price to be paid for "progress."

In the first reading in this section, George Altmeyer provides a framework for analysing the complex debate about nature that resulted from increasing urbanization, industrialization, and materialism. Altmeyer agrees that many writers of the time maintained the definition of nature as a monster that had to be mastered. However, he argues that Canadians also came to express quite positive views of nature by the end of the nineteenth century. Altmeyer's research shows that many of the negative consequences of modern culture and economy were immediately recognized and that a variety of alternative relationships between humans and nature in Canada were proposed to offset these consequences.

While Altmeyer focuses on ideas, Gilbert Allardyce examines one specific example of how, in the absence of a "higher sense of community" during the Industrial Revolution, neither ecological knowledge nor legislation prevented environmental degradation and, ultimately, the destruction of local societies. In describing the far-reaching effects of the pollution of New Brunswick rivers during the nineteenth century, Allardyce explains how a widespread fear of short-term economic loss resulted in a far more profound long-term loss. This chapter reminds us that the Industrial Revolution in Canada was not limited to major cities and large factories. Substantial population growth characterized many rural areas during the nineteenth century while increasingly powerful technologies were implemented in expanding rural industries. As a result, the environmental degradation of industrial Canada has been a rural as well as urban process.

The third and fourth selections in this section examine the emergence of the conservation movement in turn-of-the-century Canada. Peter Gillis and Thomas R. Roach analyse the birth of this movement within the forest industries, some of the leaders of which had become concerned about deforestation and the long-term prospects of the forest economy. Similarly, A.F.J. Artibise and G.A. Stelter discuss the vast and innovative work of the Canadian Commission of Conservation during the early twentieth century. This commission promoted applying scientific planning to nature rather than continuing the "doctrine of usefulness" that had justified resource exploitation without regard for the longer term. While these two articles emphasize the considerable ecological knowledge gained during the later nineteenth and early twentieth centuries, they also reveal the extent to which the conservation movement simply produced, in the words of Gillis and Roach, "lost initiatives."

The final reading in this section emphasizes the extent to which governments in Canada became "clients of the business community" in the development of natural resources during the industrial age. H.V. Nelles bases this argument on his extensive research concerning Ontario's support of those who sought to exploit the province's forests, mines, and rivers. Rather than responsibly representing the interests of all residents, the province used its official ownership of natural resources "for the purpose of helping capitalist enterprise." As a result, even Ontario Hydro has not represented the concept of public ownership but has instead become an example of state capitalism. Taken together with the other readings, Nelle's interpretation explains why human pressure on the rest of the Canadian environment continued to increase despite the "city beautiful" movement, the creation of urban gardens, and the new government regulations concerning natural resources.

THREE IDEAS OF NATURE
IN CANADA, 1893-1914 ◈

GEORGE ALTMEYER

o

The interaction between man and his natural environment is an integral part of the Canadian experience. Economically, Canada has been developed through the exploitation of a series of natural resources: cod, beaver, timber, and, most recently, mineral deposits. Certain geophysical characteristics of the country have served as the basis for both national and continental political models; an east-west waterway functioning as the underlying premise of the former, four north-south "barriers of nature, wide and irreclaimable wildernesses or manifold chains of mountains"[1] utilized as the rationale of the latter. In its rude beginning, Canadian writing—explorers' diaries, natural histories, guide books, immigration tracts and essays on hunting and fishing—centred upon the practical aspects of man's relationship with wilderness. In subsequent years a persistent theme of Canadian literature has been to discern what effect life in that wilderness has had on the collective national consciousness.[2] Likewise, Canadian painting, from Paul Kane to the Group of Seven and Emily Carr, has found its most enduring expression in the portrayal of Canada's natural heritage. When viewed in this perspective, it is with some consistency that Canada is identified by two wilderness symbols: the beaver and the maple leaf.

Yet, no matter how thoroughly one documents the significant role played by the natural milieu in Canada's economic, political, literary and artistic development, an important question remains: how have Canadians themselves perceived their relationship with Nature? According to the given interpretation, Canadians view Nature in a negative, even frightening manner. Based primarily on literary sources, this viewpoint depicts Nature as a hostile, terrifying monster, which threatens the very existence of those

◈ *Journal of Canadian Studies* 11 (Aug. 1976): 21–36. Reprinted with permission.

who dare intrude upon its domain. In a review which appeared in 1943, Northrop Frye first set forth the central thesis of this interpretation. After reading the selections in A.J.M. Smith's *Book of Canadian Poetry,* Frye somberly concluded that "Nature is consistently sinister and menacing in Canadian poetry";[3] that, in fact, "the outstanding achievement of Canadian poetry is in the evocation of stark terror"[4] in regard to Nature. Frye identifies the immediate source of this terror as the frightening loneliness of a huge and thinly settled country. But, as he explained in more detail elsewhere, at a more profound level, the "tone of deep terror in regard to Nature . . . is not a terror of the dangers or discomforts or even the mysteries of Nature, but a terror of the soul at something that these things manifest."[5] The reason for this deeper fear of Nature, Frye claims, is historical. Canada began as a group of small, outpost communities set amidst a menacing continent which could be penetrated, but, unlike the American example, could not be pushed back. The all-pervasive insecurity inherent in such isolation compelled Canadians to retain a psychological, as well as a political and economic connection with England. Forced always to cling to the mother country for security, Nature became, for Canadians, the evil antithesis of all they most cherished in English society: order, security and, above all, civilization. In short, Frye's thesis claims that, because Canadians did not make the psychological break with Europe through revolution, they could not face the harsh realities of North American Nature with the same positive attitude as the Americans.

Frye's conception of Nature as a reservoir of a "vast unconsciousness" of sinister intent, has coloured all subsequent attempts to investigate the theme of Nature in Canadian literature.[6] In her book, *Beyond the Land Itself,* Marcia B. Kline uses the idea of Nature as a malevolent force to explain the differences between Canadian and American attitudes toward Nature. Contrasting the romance novels of John Richardson and James Fenimore Cooper, the works of Susanna Moodie and the American Caroline Kirkland and various other nineteenth century poets and novelists, she finds that, unlike American literateurs who exhibit a positive attitude towards Nature, Canadian writers see Nature as "part of a world that is terrifying, hostile to human values and human endeavour, and inferior to civilization."[7] In a similar manner, Margaret Atwood, in advancing her thesis that Canadians have seen themselves primarily as victims, asserts in a chapter aptly entitled "Nature the Monster" that in Canadian literature Nature is "often dead and unanswering or activity hostile to man."[8] Following the accepted thesis, D.G. Jones, examining the theme of evil in Canadian literature, posits that the Canadian image of Nature is pregnant with the "threat of disorder, irrational passion and violence, the crude, the mortal, and the absurd."[9]

While this interpretation may be useful in examining literary works, it nonetheless obscures the immense complexity characteristic of the Canadian attitude towards Nature. Certainly, at the turn of the century, many Canadians, even in their literature, did not view Nature in the way these literary critics suggest. Indeed, as a reaction against certain distressing tendencies in their society, many Canadians wanted to get "back to nature," to better manage her resources and to use her as an instrument of religious expression. It is the intention of this essay to show that, from the mid-1890s to the First World War, one facet of the Canadian attitude towards Nature was positive and typically North American. This positive perception involved the ideas of Nature as a Benevolent Mother capable of soothing city-worn nerves and restoring health, of rejuvenating a physically deteriorating race and of teaching lessons no book learning could give; as a Limited Storehouse whose treasures must in the future be treated with greater respect; and as a Temple where one could again find and communicate with Deity.

o

It is commonplace to depict the Laurier years as a time of optimism, a period in Canadian history when the national future looked so bright as to merit the dictum that the twentieth century would belong to Canada. While this scenario is no doubt accurate for many aspects of Canadian life, it tends to conceal a certain uneasiness about what this new era of industrialization, urbanization and materialism meant for people on a personal level. This apprehension manifested itself in a number of ways: "The papers are filled," wrote the Women's editor of the *Canadian Magazine* in 1908, "with advertisements of tonics and nerve pills, the magazines learnedly discuss 'Worry: the Disease of the Age,' and the doctors who are canny enough to establish rest cures are millionaires in no time, while the lady who exploits a 'don't worry' religion is a benefactor to the race."[10] Others, more exotic in temperament, dabbled in various forms of Occultism and Spiritualism. In such an atmosphere it was not unusual for the major English-Canadian journal of the day to publish a series of five articles on "Worry: the Disease of the Age."[11] The author of these articles, a Dr. C.W. Saleeby, submitted that "worry is preeminently the disease of this age and of this civilization, and perhaps of the English-speaking race in particular."[12] Worry was the price for the advancement of civilization; each successive step intensified the type and tempo of the struggle for existence, culminating in the present society whose chief malady was stress. One of the most important causes for the anxious state of the Anglo-Saxon race, the doctor explained, was city life.

While Saleeby's social analysis no doubt appealed to many readers, his comment on city life came closest to identifying the source of this anxiety. By the early 1900's Canada was in the midst of a demographic revolution of enormous proportions. Comparison between the 1891 and 1911 censuses shows that Montreal and Toronto more than doubled in size, Vancouver and Winnipeg increased fivefold, while Calgary, Edmonton and Regina arose from nowhere.[13] During the decade 1901–1911, Canada's urban population increased by 62 percent and the rural population by only 17 percent. In the Maritime Provinces and in Ontario, the rural population actually decreased. In 1901, urban dwellers formed 38 percent of the total population; in 1911, this proportion had been increased to 45 percent.[14]

Canadian response to rapid urbanization was generally unfavourable.[15] A recurring motif in contemporary journals portrayed city life as artificial: the city was seen as a place of "stone and mortar," "of rattlin', roarin' streets," and of clanging telephones.[16] The artificiality of modern urban life created what one journalist called "jaded minds" wanting only to satisfy what another one called "jaded tastes."[17] In a poem titled "A Voice From the City" a Vancouver poet succinctly expressed the frustration and tension felt by many urban dwellers:

> I am tired of the shifting City,
> And the ceaseless cry of the streets
>
> Sing me a song of the free life
> When a man is a man again
> When the joy of life calls madly
> And the pain is a lesser pain.[18]

To find personal contentment, the Ottawa poet Archibald Lampman maintained that one had to escape from the horror of the city,

> Out of the heat of the usurer's hold,
>   From the horrible crash of the strong man's feet;
> Out of the shadow where pity is dying;
> Out of the clamour where beauty is lying,
>   Dead in the depth of the struggle for gold;
> Out of the din and the glare of the street.[19]

Paradoxically, "high-tuned" city life evoked in many people a sense of monotony, isolation and, above all, the feeling that the "artificial method of life we call civilization"[20] produced a basically unhealthy mode of living. In this age of anxiety who among the tense yet bored inhabitants of larger Canadian cities could resist the beckoning question put forth by a writer in *Rod and Gun*, "Do you want to rest a season from the Life Artificial and live the Life Natural?"[21] Who among them could doubt the wisdom of Adam Shortt's advice that Canadian social life could best be ameliorated through an "improvement in the whole physical setting of our social life, involving the relations of man and nature"?[22]

The thousands of urban Canadians who took to the out-of-doors at the turn of the century in a movement "back to nature" provided a positive response to this query.[23] As early as 1894, a Canadian journalist observed it to be "one of the characteristics of modern times" that, as the competition in all aspects of life becomes keener, people "seek recreation and restoration in a closer approach to nature than can be found in the busy street or crowded mart."[24] For much the same reasons, J.W. Dafoe, in 1899, took solace that: "In these days the country has been discovered anew. No fact of contemporary life is more significant or more hopeful than this return to nature, for breathing space, for those whose daily walk is the tumultuous city streets."[25] At its mildest, "back to nature" meant leisurely rides into the countryside astride a bicycle on Sunday afternoons, tramping through a marsh or hillside thicket to get the perfect "kodak" snapshot of some animal or bird,[26] or taking up the popular sport of birdwatching. Somewhat more strenuously, it meant hiking, camping, canoeing and alpine climbing.[27] Reflecting the general interest in Nature, at least ten journals—*Canadian Athletic* (Toronto, 1892), *Pastoral* (Toronto, 1901), *Rod and Gun* (Montreal, 1899), *Athletic Life* (Toronto, 1895), *Canadian Outdoor Life* (Toronto, 1907), *Outdoor Canada* (Toronto, 1905), *Western Canadian Sportsman* (Winnipeg, 1904), *Sports* (Halifax, 1908), *Canadian Sport* (Montreal, 1911) and *Canadian Alpine Journal* (Banff, 1907)—devoted exclusively or in part to out-of-door activities, began publication.[28] Moreover, the animal stories of Ernest Thompson Seton, Charles G.D. Roberts and W.A. Fraser, whose first books in this genre appeared in 1898, 1900 and 1902 respectively, ranked among the best read Canadian books.

In this awakening to the benefits of outdoor life, the countryside, which a half century before had been thought of as "an absolutely uninteresting wilderness, only fit for men and women of no mind,"[29] took on new and added significance. It became the haunt of that "Old Dame Nature, that great, placid, untroubled Mother of us all," who, as one canoeist wrote, was capable of taking

> . . . us quietly to her bosom,
> and, as a mother sooths and 'gentles'
> a tired and fretful child, had
> quietly and completely cleared away
> the mists and cobwebs from the
> mind, soothed the tired spirits,
> and induced in both mind and body
> a comprehensive and deep reaching
> peace and an unconcern for the
> things of the too busy world.[30]

For Lampman, Nature was the
> Mother of all things beautiful, blameless,
> Mother of hopes that her strength makes
>   tameless,
>   Where the voices of grief and of
>   battle are dumb,
>   And the whole world laughs with the
>   light of Her mirth.[31]

Yet, no matter if her voice be expressed as "the call of the wild," "the lure of the woods," "the lure of the wild," "the lure of the open," or any of a dozen other idioms, what Nature promised was always the same:

> Leave the city: it is soiling
> Leave your worry and your toiling,
> Seek the camp beside the river,
> Haunt of bear and home of beaver,
> It will cool the world's mad fever,
> Won't you come, won't you come?[32]

The conception of Nature as a healing mother rested on her purported ability to provide city dwellers with what they most lacked: health and relief from boredom. Her supporters did not question for a moment her ability to provide these conditions. "Health and strength go hand and hand beneath the trees," guaranteed a camping veteran in *Rod and Gun.*[33] "Almost anyone will tell you today," said another, "that the open air is the great remedial agent for badly strung nerves."[34] According to one writer, at a time when sanitariums are much in vogue, "a trip to the woods is the very best kind of sanitarium," one better than any doctor or institution.[35] Similarly, Nature was the home tonic prescribed for boredom. Instead of turning to alcohol, tobacco or silly fads for relief from urban monotony, L.O. Armstrong noted that "the right thinking turn to Mother Nature, and she cures them of boredom."[36] One of the chief benefits of alpine climbing, maintained the secretary of the newly-formed Canadian Alpine Club, was that "a new and unknown world is unfolded to dwellers in cities and places where life is either an eternal grind or an eternal show."[37] The lists of testimonials such as these literally fill the articles and speeches on outdoor activity at the turn and early part of the century. Again, it was Lampman who expressed most directly the therapeutic benefits derived from close contact with Nature:

> Are you broken with the din
>   Of the streets?
> Are you sickened of your thin
>   Hands and feet?
>
> Are you bowed and bended double
> With a weight of care and trouble,
> Are you spectral with a skin
> Like a sheet?
>
> Take your body and your soul
>   To the woods,
> To the tonic and control
>   Of its moods,
> Where the forest gleams and quivers,
> Where the only roads are rivers,
> And the trunk-line bears the whole
>   of your goods.[38]

When seen in this light, it is not as strange as it might seem today that Banff, Canada's first national park, was originally established to protect the hot spring geysers, or that the words "health resort" should appear prominently in the list of reasons for the establishment of provincial parks such as Algonquin (1894) and Quetico (1909).

The curative benefits ascribed to Nature were, of course, not limited to adults. J.E. Atkinson, publisher of the *Toronto Star*, after touring some of the poorer sections of Toronto during the terrible heat wave of '91, established The Star Fresh Air Fund.[39] The avowed purpose was to provide slum children with a dose of clean air at least for a few weeks in the summer. "Fresh Air!" declared the *Star* article that kicked off the drive, "what can those words mean to a child whose experience of pure atmosphere is limited to the breezes which creep about the dusty lanes or rise from the sun-heated pavements of the city?"[40] The *Montreal Star* soon followed Atkinson's lead and set up a similar fund.[41] For children of wealthier families, boys' camps became the vogue. Camp Temagami, or as it was affectionately known, "Cochrane's Camp," was probably the first summer camp in Canada devoted to boys. Set up by an Upper Canada College teacher who wanted to find a productive way to occupy his young charges during summer vacation, Cochrane's Camp offered camping, canoeing, swimming, all manner of sport and plain wholesome food.[42] At about the same time, Ernest Thompson Seton, the Toronto-based artist, naturalist and animal story writer, founded the Woodcraft Indian club for boys, an organization dedicated to tracking, camping, canoeing and woodcraft.[43] First proposed in a series of articles in *Ladies Home Journal*, hundreds of Woodcraft Indian groups soon sprang up all over the United States and Canada.[44]

The idea of Nature as a refuge from the ills of city living also underlay the development at this time of the cottage syndrome. While, at least in Ontario and Quebec, summer cottages date back to the mid-nineteenth century, it was not until the 1890s that the practice of spending a part of the summer in the woods came into wider practice.[45] In 1900, the *Canadian Magazine* pointed out: "The growth of the Canadian urban population has increased the number of people who are desirous of getting 'back to nature' for at least one month of the year. Hence, in the neighbourhood of each city there are one or more special districts where the summer cottage is in increasing evidence."[46] The Lake of the Woods region of Manitoba, the Georgian Bay and Muskoka Lakes region of Ontario, the Lower Lakes region of Montreal and certain beach areas around St. John and Halifax were listed as examples of cottage districts. Whether one lived in a tent, a modest cottage or a luxurious summer home,"[47] the custom of getting "back to Nature" for short and frequent holidays was becoming, in the words of J.W. Dafoe, "firmly established as a factor of city life."[48]

Some social critics, however, looked to Nature for more than mere relief from the anxiety, boredom and general unhealthfulness associated with urban living. Taking stock [of] the overall physical condition of Canadian manhood, they saw in Nature a way of rejuvenating a rapidly degenerating race. Again the cause of this malady was urban, industrial life. "One of the most serious problems that confront[s] the British Empire," wrote R. Tait McKenzie in 1907, "is the physical deterioration of the people in towns and cities." McKenzie attributed this deterioration to the increase in the number of factories and other industries incidental to the demands of trade. "These conditions," he warned, "are beginning to show even in Canada."[49]

While McKenzie, and others such as F.E. Dorchester, John Kelso and J.A. Cooper,[50] looked to athletics, physical culture and frugal dietary habits to stem the trend towards physical degeneracy, others looked to Nature. "Are we Anglo-Saxons degenerating?" asked *Rod and Gun* in 1904. "Is the

Englishman, the American, and the Canadian less hardy than his forefathers?" To dispel any doubt on this important question, the editorial suggested that canoeing and camping be made the "national pastimes." It urged every Canadian male to get into the woods and lakes at least once a year in order to prevent them from becoming "helplessly soft and luxurious."[51] Similarly, fear of the deleterious effects of urban living on the nation's youth led to the formation of Boy Scout packs in Canada. According to the movement's founder, Lieutenant-General Robert Baden-Powell, "scouting," which for Canadian boys meant the emulation of "the work and attributes of backwoodsmen, explorers and frontiersmen," was the best way to counter the trend towards physical deterioration.[52] Through outdoor activities such as "pioneering," "camping," "tracking" and "woodcraft, or knowledge of animals and Nature," Baden-Powell contended Canadian boys might prepare themselves physically and mentally to defend their empire in time of peril.[53]

The idea of Nature as a teacher of youth was not confined to scouting movements or summer camps. By 1910, chiefly through the efforts of Natural History and Field-Naturalist Societies, farm organization and the staff of the Central Experimental Farm,[54] nature study classes were introduced into the public schools of British Columbia (1900), Alberta (1908), Winnipeg (1903), Ontario (1904), and Nova Scotia (1901).[55] As part of the Froebelian doctrine of progressive education,[56] the central theme of these courses was "primarily and essentially the study of the out-of-doors."[57] Why was it important to study Nature? A member of the Ottawa Field-Naturalists' Club explained it this way:

> The foundation of all education is the training of the senses, but in this artificial and introspective age we are losing sight of this objective influence of nature, ignoring the plan by which the human race has been nourished and developed for untold generations.[58]

That modern society had atrophied or stunted the senses was an often expressed idea associated with nature study. As one Toronto teacher said, "Nature study is a method rather than a subject."[59] It was a way of sharpening blunted senses; it provided students, according to the editor of the St. John *Educational Review*, with "eyes to see."[60] Perhaps C.J. Atkinson of Toronto best articulated the meaning of the Nature Study movement when he said:

> ... the unnatural surrounding and conventionalities of city life dwarf the boy physically and mentally, and [so] that to have the boy at his best [we] must counteract the influence of man-made environment by getting him back to Nature.[61]

For all these reasons, then, the idea of Nature as a Benevolent Mother, acting as a refuge from the boring and unhealthy aspects of urban life, as a means of stiffening the backbone of a slacking race and as a teacher of natural values, appealed to many Canadians at the turn of the century. It would be a mistake, however, to see this positive attitude towards Nature as uniquely Canadian. As many studies have shown, interest in camping, hiking, birdwatching, nature study, wildlife photography, scouting and summer cottages was keen in the United States during these years.[62] Indeed, to put it into its proper perspective, the Canadian "back to nature" movement must be viewed in its North American context. This is not to say, however, there were not important motivational differences between the two movements. Many writers have identified as one of the main sources of the American desire for a closer relationship with Nature the "perceived" closing of the American frontier and all its attendant psychological consequences. This surely is not the case in Canada, where exactly at this time, the lands of New Ontario and the "last, best West" of the prairies were opening up. Instead, it seems likely that the impetus for the Canadian "back to nature" movement came from three sources: first, from a reaction against urban, industrial life; secondly, from the influence of the movement in the United States; and thirdly (and this is highly speculative), from a desire on the part of some eastern urban Canadians to share in some limited way with the national excitement accompanying the opening up of the Canadian West. Yet, whatever were the motivational differences between the United States and Canada in this regard, the general movement for closer contact with Nature was similar in substance in both countries. This point was not lost to the railroad company directors, resort operators and other interest groups, who promoted the notion that Canada was rapidly becoming "the natural playground of the world."

The potential of Canada as a tourist haven was not a new idea in the 1890's. It had been discussed at least as far back as the Confederation period. But with the shift in vacationing preference at the turn of the century from seaside resorts to woodland retreats, the idea took on new importance. "It is certain," predicted J.A. Cooper in a special issue of the *Canadian Magazine* in 1900, "that Canada shall become more and more the resort of the summer traveller, especially from the United States. Her thousands of lakes and rivers afford plenty of sport after pleasant excitement, her vast forest preserves are still well stocked with the finest game in the world, and the natural beauty of the many regions, which the prosaic hand of civilization has not touched, affords rest to the tired man or woman of the world."[63] In a series of articles which followed Cooper's introductory remarks, every region of Canada from Vancouver to Prince Edward Island was portrayed as a wonderful tourist area, each stressing its particular advantage as a natural retreat from the work-a-day, urbanized world.

Other interests also picked up the theme. Arthur O. Wheeler, president of the Canadian Alpine Club, described Canada's mountain ranges as "a great national playground" where those who were tied to desks and shut behind closed city walls might escape their "prison environment."[64] Other Alpine enthusiasts christened the Canadian Rockies as the "great international playground,"[65] as the "playground of the world,"[66] and, in a label used extensively in C.P.R. advertisements, as "50 Switzerlands in One." The founder of the Ontario Fish and Game Protective Association even maintained that, if Ontario could get proper hunting regulations, it would become the "Scotland of North America."[67]

The practical motif of Nature as a playground rested upon the willingness of Canadians to use their natural heritage as a means of economic development. In the latter part of the nineteenth century the entire concept of the use of natural resources was in transformation, the idea of Nature as a bottomless Horn of Plenty, which one could indiscriminately exploit, giving way to the more positive idea of Nature as a Limited Storehouse.

o

The Canadian Conservation Movement defies any simplistic analysis. On one level the movement to conserve Canada's natural resources was pragmatic, financially motivated and a continuation of previous policy; on another it was idealistic, devoid of monetary considerations and a break from traditional approaches. Two different philosophies, the "doctrine of utilization" and the "doctrine of unselfishness" underlay its two main impulses. Yet in defining the movement in this manner, a fundamental point must be made. These two aspects of the Canadian Conservation Movement were not mutually exclusive. They were not opposites separated by some unbridgeable divide. They did not represent in the Conservation Movement the "purist" and the "realist" positions. Rather, they were expressions of the same impulse on two distinct levels. On the first level this impulse took the form of wanting to use Nature's bounty in such a manner as to ensure that it could be exploited again in the future. Yet the feeling underlying even this most practical consideration was a sharp departure from previous assumptions.

The purpose of the economic policy of the Macdonald government was to create a national economy based on the exploitation of Canada's natural resources. This National Policy was predicated on the idea that Canada possessed these resources in unlimited quantity.[68] The philosophy of "usefulness" on which this economic strategy rested was clearly elucidated by Macdonald in a speech given on his return from a trip through Western Canada. Describing the Canadian Rockies, Macdonald observed:

> The mountains are rich in gold, and silver and all description of minerals, and clothed with some of the finest timber, an inexhaustible means of supplying the treeless expanse of prairies in the Northwest.[69]

As the historian R.C. Brown queries: "Could anyone in Macdonald's audience, anyone who knew John A., believe for a minute that the tapping was not about to begin ?"[70] A storehouse of unlimited natural wealth was there for the taking; the only real question was who should direct the operation. This problem quickly solved, a pillage of Canadian forests commenced. So great was the rate of cutting that, according to one critic, the only question remaining was whether "the idea of boundless wealth of woodland—of forest with exhaustless supplies of timber—would survive the forests themselves."[71]

Gradually in the 1890's, the idea of unlimited abundance came under reappraisal. The shift of attitude surfaced first in occasional articles appearing in popular journals on the danger of unregulated cutting to forests.[72] In these articles, and in many others like them in the following decade, the solution proposed was not of ending or even limited lumbering activity but of employing "scientific techniques," based on German models, to eliminate the wanton and largely unnecessary wasteful characteristics of contemporary forestry methods. This new outlook of forest resource management found a focal point in the Canadian Forestry Association.

Founded in 1900, the Canadian Forestry Association sought "to advocate and encourage judicious methods in dealing with our forests and woods" and "to awaken public interest to the sad results attending the wholesale destruction of the forest."[73] Through the pages of its official organ, *Rod and Gun*,[74] the C.F.A. expounded its position that in a commercial age it was good business to farm scientifically the nation's lumber wealth, rather than simply to work it as a mine until exhausted. Emphasizing that Canadian forests were in no immediate danger of depletion, the Association warned Canadians that they could not afford to repeat the mistakes made by American foresters. This hard-nosed, business attitude toward resource development dominated the C.F.A. first national convention in 1906. Presided over by Sir Wilfrid Laurier and addressed by such notable American conservationists as Gifford Pinchot, the C.F.A. convention of 1906 gave the Canadian Conservation Movement a legitimacy it had previously lacked and propelled the issue into public prominence. The convention led to regular annual meetings which provided the only national forum where resource professionals, the Government and conservationists could exchange views and ideas, the founding of schools of forestry at the University of Toronto in 1907 and at the University of New Brunswick in 1908, and the establishment of forest services by various provincial governments.[75]

The same philosophy of scientific utilization rather than sheer exploitation pervaded the work of the Canadian Commission of Conservation. Like the Washington Conference (1909) from which it emanated, the Canadian Commission preached the ideals of efficient resource management in the areas of forestry, lands, water, minerals and fuels and public health. In his opening address to the Commission, Clifford Sifton, its Chairman and chief spokesman, set the business oriented tone maintained throughout its twelve year history:

> I have heard the view expressed that what Canada needs is development and exploitation, not conservation. This view, however, is founded on erroneous conceptions which it must be our work to remove. If we attempt to stand in the way of development our efforts will assuredly be of no avail, either to stop development or to promote conservation. It will not, however, be hard to show that the best and most highly economic development and exploitation in the interests of the people can only take place by having regard to the principles of conservation.[76]

For Sifton, as for this part of the Conservation movement in general, no contradiction existed between development and conservation, the latter only being an aspect of the former. Conservation meant simply the sound business principle of planning ahead for tomorrow's needs. "Canadians," wrote one conservationist in 1910, "have lived for many years in a fool's paradise as to their natural resources."[77] Canadian businessmen, fully realizing the unprofitability of living in a fool's paradise, were quite willing to change their exploitative technique from one of unlimited "use" to the more gentle approach of scientific "utilization."

The practical considerations that led lumbermen to take a fresh look at their relationship with the forests prompted sportsmen to take renewed action to protect fish and game. In this new effort the idea of harvesting rather than wantonly killing wildlife became the sportsman's ideal.[78] Concern for the well-being of fish and game supplies was not new in Canada. For example, Upper Canada passed laws on salmon fishing in 1807 and deer hunting in 1827.[79] But season and limit regulations such as these, enacted in many parts of Canada over the next half century, were seldom enforced. In the early 1890's both the Royal Commission on Game and Fish and the Royal Commission of Forests and National Parks lamented the fantastic desecration of wildlife occurring in Canada.[80] The focal point of agitation for better and rigorously enforced hunting and fishing regulations was *Rod and Gun*. Used by sporting organizations in much the same way as C.F.A.,[81] *Rod and Gun* urged its readers to adopt a new and more responsible attitude towards wildlife. It advocated stricter enforcement of game and fish laws, carried news of Fish and Game Protection societies in all the provinces and even launched the League of Canadian Sportsmen in 1899.[82] The efforts of *Rod and Gun* and provincial sporting fraternities were not without result: specific Game Acts were secured in Prince Edward Island (1906), Nova Scotia (1912), New Brunswick (1909), British Columbia (1919), Manitoba, Saskatchewan and Alberta, while in Ontario and Quebec more stringent bounty and season laws were put on the books.

For the hunting and fishing sportsmen, as for the lumbermen, Nature did not in itself possess any intrinsic value. It was merely a storehouse of animate and inanimate wealth to be exploited for their own needs. For very pragmatic reasons their attitude towards Nature's storehouse had changed. Yet it would be a mistake to equate the Conservation Movement in Canada only with this practical aspect. For the Conservation Movement, involving as it did a complexity of elements, had a humanitarian side whose philosophy was not "utilization" but "unselfishness."

Two events, more than any others, symbolized for many North Americans the need for wildlife preservation. In a Cincinnati zoo, in 1911, the last passenger pigeon died—the sole survivor of a species which had once numbered in the billions.[83] Meanwhile, on the prairies, the last remnants of the once vast herds of buffaloes were rounded up and placed into protected areas. The main reason for this unbelievable pillage of Nature's creatures, held the naturalist C.W. Nash, echoing a current sentiment, was the greed of the so-called civilized whiteman. Warning that animal life in Canada was being depleted so rapidly that the next generation would know them only through a few skins in museum cases, Nash pleaded with his fellow Canadians to enact laws for the survival of the remaining wildlife.[84] Nash's call for wildlife conservation, like that of thousands of naturalists and nature lovers across the country, was not premised upon economic motives. Rather, it rested on the idea that Nature itself should be protected. This custodial attitude towards Nature embodied itself in what one naturalist called the "gospel of unselfishness."

"Conservation," contended the Dominion Entomologist C. Gordon Hewitt in 1911, "is nothing more than the gospel of unselfishness," a gospel whose most fundamental tenet is the "protection of Nature."[85] Fully recognizing that it was a pragmatic age in which he lived, Hewitt nonetheless posited that conservation contained an "aesthetic and ethical side" as well as a practical one.[86] He insisted that national well-being could not be equated with material progress alone:

> Nature is not ours to squander, to amass wealth at her expense, and
> enjoy a transient prosperity; it is ours to protect, and the protection
> of Nature is more or less the ensuring of a national happiness.[87]

The national happiness demanded the "use without waste, or with as little waste as possible" of Canada's natural resources.[88] Hewitt's doctrine of conservation was not in conflict with the doctrine of utilization expounded by Sifton. It merely added another dimension—the moral and aesthetic one.

The campaign to substitute animal photography for hunting is a good example of the naturalists' desire to inject moral considerations into the conservation debate. In a speech reprinted in *Rod and Gun*, Ernest Thompson Seton, who, like his fellow animal story writer Charles G.D. Roberts, had forsaken hunting on humanitarian grounds,[89] urged hunters to take up the morally and aesthetically superior sport of animal photography where the "weapon is the camera, not the rifle."[90] Seton's plea for a more humane method of hunting found advocates in many contemporary journals.[91] But probably the most vocal proponent of camera hunting was Bonnycastle Dale, who popularized the message in journals across Canada that the "noiseless, houndless, barrelless, merciful camera" was a more manly way of hunting.[92] For all its advocates, then, photography was seen as a way of conserving Nature by sublimating a destructive, wasteful impulse towards Nature with a more humane method of possessing her.

Of more immediate concern for naturalist conservationists was the establishment of bird and wildlife sanctuaries. The first governmental birdlife sanctuary in North America was set up by the Canadian Government in 1887 in Saskatchewan.[93] Although this particular sanctuary failed, it provided the impetus for greater efforts in bird protection. In 1904, Jack Miner established his first bird sanctuary in Kingsville, Ontario, beginning for him a life devoted to fowl preservation.[94] Encouraged by the Kingsville sanctuary, local Naturalists' Clubs in Ottawa and Vancouver secured legislation setting aside public parks in those cities as bird preserves.[95] The example of pioneering efforts such as these eventually led to greater action for wildlife protection by Federal and Provincial Governments.[96]

While naturalist conservationists often stressed the practical aspects of wildlife protection in soliciting aid for these projects, their primary concern was to protect Nature from the exploitative instincts of man. Lieut.-Colonel William Wood, an avid naturalist conservationist, expressed the essence of this concern when he defined a wildlife sanctuary as "a place where man is passive and the rest of Nature active."[97] His plan to set aside a section of Labrador as a massive fish and game preserve does not fit into the argument that the Canadian Conservation Movement was simply an extension of the National Policy. For Wood, Hewitt, Miner and countless other naturalist conservationists, Nature was more than a resource to be exploited. For them, it was important as well to protect Nature for moral and aesthetic reasons. The moral duty to preserve Nature for future generations, the aesthetic beauty inherent in Nature, even Colonel Wood's desire to conserve a part of Labrador as a unique "stage on which the prologue and living pageant of Evolution can be seen together from a single and panoramic point of view"[98]—all demanded the conservation of Nature for more than monetary reasons. In their desire to protect Nature for "higher reasons" the naturalist conservationists were akin in feeling to those, at the turn of the century, who looked to Nature for religious meaning.

o

The closing years of the nineteenth century were a portentous time in the religious development of Canada. The general religious atmosphere of the day might best be described as spiritual uncertainty. The reason for this uneasiness lay in the assault mounted by the Higher Criticism, the Darwinian hypothesis and the seemingly endless advances of science against the tenets of traditional beliefs. While for some this apprehension was swiftly quieted by disclaimers such as Sir John Dawson's assertion that "as applied to man, the theory of the struggle for existence and survival of the fittest . . . is nothing less than the basest and most horrible superstition,"[99] others sought spiritual reassurance in Nature.

On its simplest level the search for religious meaning through Nature took the form of seeing in the natural environment the hand of God. Although nature lovers of all descriptions found spiritual inspiration in contact with the out-of-doors, it was alpine climbers who expressed most clearly the idea that Nature was God's Temple. "Do you not hear the Gospel of Nature preached anew from these perfect hills?" asked one Western mountain climber. "Do you not . . . feel that God's pulpit is up there on the massive crags?"[100] It was in the spirit of the Gospel of Nature that the secretary of the Canadian Alpine Club urged Canadians to become mountain climbers so that they might stand "face to face with Infinitude" and learn spiritual truths which would be otherwise denied them.[101] She further declared that the "large spiritual vision" afforded in alpining was a more potent force in offsetting the materialism of the age than all the long-winded sermons put together.[102] Yet, however strong Miss Parker's faith might be in the spiritual value of mountain climbing, it was the Club's

President who put most bluntly the religious significance of alpining. "The one spot above all others where there is no place for an atheist," claimed Wheeler, "is on the summit of a mountain peak."[103]

On a more profound level, Canadian poets of the 1890's such as Charles G.D. Roberts, Bliss Carman and Archibald Lampman attempted to define more precisely the nature of the new relationship among man, Nature and God necessitated by Darwinian theory. The importance of Darwinian theory for understanding the way these poets looked at Nature can hardly be overemphasized, for evolutionary science at once struck down the long-standing barriers erected between man and the natural world by the teachings of the medieval Christian church. In the older Hebrew and Greek traditions, the natural world had been seen as a positive component of the order of things: for the Jews of the Old Testament, it manifested the power of the Deity and revealed His purpose; for the Greeks, it stimulated the mind and fed a love of beauty. According to the medieval church, however, man was primarily a spiritual being, inherently distinct from and superior to the non-spiritual world of Nature.[104] After the publication of Darwin's *The Origin of Species* in 1859, things were much different. Man was seen now not as a product of special creation, which, by definition, separated him from the rest of physical existence, but as a part of an evolutionary process common to all. In the post Darwinian world, man was not a foe of Nature but her off-spring.

Moreover, for Canadian poets, who in an earlier period may have indeed used sentimental romantic concepts such as the "picturesque," the "sublime," and "grandeur" to mask the stark reality of life in the wilderness, evolution provided the tool by which they could penetrate the overwhelming presence of Canadian Nature. According to Stevenson, evolution allowed them "a glimpse of unity pervading nature and the control directing her mysterious ways." It provided a standpoint from which they "might obtain a vision of life in which man's puny figure and Nature's brooding power assumed a conceivable proposition, both subordinate to a supernal plan."[105]

The terms most often used to describe the new relationship between man and Nature were "kinship" and "companionship." For Lampman, companionship with Nature demanded:

> Let us be much with Nature; not as they
> That labour without seeing, that employ
> Her unloved forces, blindly without joy;
> Nor those whose hands and crude delights obey
> The old brute passion to hunt down and slay;
> But rather as children of one common birth,
> Discerning in each natural fruit of earth
> Kinship and bond with this diviner clay.[106]

For Roberts, in a poem entitled "Kinship," the new bond with Nature commanded them:

> Back to the bewildering vision
>   And the borderland of birth;

Back into the looming wonder,
   The companionship of earth.[107]

Carman entitled one of his most important works *The Kinship of Nature*.[108]

The sense of kinship with the natural world extended to the "lower orders" of nature, that is, animal and plant life. In many of his poems Bliss Carman identified himself totally with the natural object he describes, resulting in poems portraying how a tree or flower might think or feel:

Between the roadside and the wood,
   Between the dawning and the dew,
A tiny flower before the sun,
   Ephemeral in time, I grew.[109]

The same technique of integration is employed in Charles G.D. Roberts' "realistic" animal stories which are told from the animal's point of view. In them we are asked to think and feel as a bear, fox and any other animal might, in a given situation. Similarly, Lampman, whom the president of the Ottawa Field-Naturalist Club called "in the truest sense of the word a naturalist,[110] felt so strongly the sense of kinship between man and the "lower orders" of Nature that he could not condone even the picking of wild flowers."[111]

If evolution provided man with a new and closer tie to the natural world, it also threatened to separate him from the traditional spiritual one. Lampman and Roberts, both sons of clergymen, sensitive to this tension, found it difficult to live within the religious boundaries of their youth.[112]

Roberts, whose "slightly heterodox religious convictions" prevented him from teaching a Sunday School class at his father's church,[113] directly challenged the traditional view of Deity in "O Solitary of the Austere Sky":

How small am I in thine August regard!
   Invisible,—and yet I know my worth!
When comes the hour to break this prisoning shard,
   And reunite with Him that breathed me forth,
Then shall this atom of the Eternal Soul
   Encompass thee in its benign control![114]

Likewise, Lampman, who had serious doubts about the validity of established faiths, described the feeling he received from city churches:

O Life! O Life! I kept saying,
   And the very word seemed sad.[115]

Yet even in rejecting traditional religion, neither Lampman nor Roberts, nor any other Canadian poet, embraced scientific materialism. Instead, they alleviated their spiritual anxiety by employing Nature as a medium for communing with Deity. Vague transcendentalism, based loosely on the teachings of Emerson and Thoreau, may be the best way to depict the religious position of Roberts, Lampman and Carman. That they came to hold these beliefs is understandable on three counts. First of all, as has been often noted, New England, the birthplace of the North American variant of transcendentalism, served during this period as a path for currents of thought into Canada.[116] Secondly, both Roberts and Carman proudly claimed family lineage (through the Bliss family) with Emerson.[117] And thirdly, as Georges Ross Roy points out,

> Emerson et l'école des transcendantalistes étaient originaires de la partie des Etats-Unis qui ressemble le plus aux régions d'ou venaient les poètes du Groupe de Soixante, c'est-à-dire des Provinces Maritimes, du Québec et de l'Ontario. . . . Ce fait est important, car les descriptions de la nature que les poètes canadiens trouvaient chez leurs ainés de l'autre côté de la frontière traitaient plus ou moins des mêmes phénomènes qu'eux mêmes voyaient et voulaient chanter; aussi, quant Emerson ou un autre de son école traite de l'hiver, c'est une réalité pour les Canadiens; quand Keats ou Wordsworth le font, il n'en est pas de même.[118]

The influence of Emerson's central principles that "behind nature, throughout nature, spirit is present," and that "spirit, that is, the Supreme Being, does not build up nature around us but puts it forth through us"[119] is readily observable in the works of Roberts and Lampman. For Roberts, the spirit present in Nature is named the "enigmatic Will,"[120] the "Control"[121] or simply the "force" underlying the cyclic movement of all life; while the idea that man is an element of a world soul is explicitly put forward in "Autochthon" and "O Solitary of the Austere Sky." For Lampman, the omnipresent spirit in Nature is alternately christened "energy," "force," and "spirit"; while in regard to man's connection with that spirit, Lampman boldly contends: "We know with the fullest intensity of sympathy that we are of one birth with everything about us, brethren to the trees, and kin to the very grass that now . . . flings the dew about our feet."[122] Finally, the later writing of Carman, according to his biographer, possesses:

> the Transcendental belief in the essential identity of man's soul with the Soul of the universe, the belief in man's consequent kinship with Nature, and . . . the reliance upon intuition as the means whereby man becomes aware in ecstatic moments of his mystical union with the Over-soul.[123]

It was, then, on this more sophisticated level that Canadian transcendental poets used the idea of Nature as a Temple.

○

The mid-1890s through the First World War were years of economic, political and social transformation in Canada. Beneath the buoyant optimism which accompanied this transition was a feeling of loss emanating from the realization that there was a price to be paid for the benefits accruing from a modern urban and industrial society. In this cognition many Canadians became aware that the serenity, robustness and simplicity of country living was the price exacted for the comforts and accruements of city life. They gradually understood that the practice of gross exploitation which, in the past, had characterized their use of natural resources was no longer tenable and they saw that, in an age of materialism and evolutionary science, traditional religions were inadequate for fulfilling their spiritual needs. In seeking solutions for each of these problems many Canadians, in a way unaccounted for by the literary explanation, turned to Nature, seeing her in a new, more positive light.

This paper has attempted to examine this positive attitude toward Nature. Through the inspection of three specific motifs, this positive attitude was found to be a protective reaction against the unsettling tendencies in modern society. The idea of Nature as a Benevolent Mother was a reaction against the effects of urban life. The idea of Nature as a Limited Storehouse was a result of the death of the myth of abundance. The idea of Nature as a Temple was an attempt to alleviate religious uncertainty. For each of these themes, Nature served as a medium through which one might deal with the complexities of a nation in transformation.

NOTES

1. Goldwin Smith, *Canada and the Canadian Question*, University of Toronto Press edition (Toronto, 1971), p. 4.

2. The titles of the two most recent thematic studies of Canadian literature are suggestive of this preoccupation: "Survival" and "Patterns of Isolation."

3. Northrop Frye, "Canada and Its Poetry," *Canadian Forum*, XXIII (Dec., 1943), p. 210.

4. *Ibid.*, p. 209.

5. Northrop Frye, "Conclusion," in Carl F. Klinck, ed., *Literary History of Canada* (Toronto, 1965), pp. 821–49.

6. A notable exception to the Fryean conception of Canadian Nature is found in John Moss' recently published work, *Patterns of Isolation in English Canadian Fiction* (Toronto, 1974). Moss rejects completely all anthropocentric conceptions of Canadian Nature. "Nowhere in our literature," he contends on page 111, "is adequate support to be found for these obtrusive assumptions. With few exceptions, Canadian writers have perceived nature to be amoral, impassive, indifferent. The landscape and its seasons have no ethics, no consciousness. Nature is neither willful nor benign, malevolent nor beneficent. Some of our writers respond to it with hostility, some with reverence, or hope, or fear, but the emotion is in their response—neither emotion nor conscious design is apparent in nature itself."

7. Marcia B. Kline, *Beyond the Land Itself: Views of Nature in Canada and the United States* (Cambridge, 1970), p. 25.

8. Margaret Atwood, *Survival: A Thematic Guide to Canadian Literature* (Toronto, 1972), p. 49.

9. D.G. Jones, *Butterfly on Rock: A Study of Themes and Images in Canadian Literature* (Toronto, 1970), p. 90.

10. Jean Graham, "Camping Out," *Canadian Magazine*, XXXI (July, 1908), p. 272.

11. C.W. Saleeby, "Worry—the Disease of the Age," *Canadian Magazine*, XXXIII (Dec., 1906), pp. 118–20; (Jan., 1907), pp. 225–30; (Feb., 1907), pp. 347–53; (March, 1907), pp. 452-7; (April, 1907), pp. 537–43.

12. *Ibid.* (Jan., 1907), p. 225.

13. From figures cited in Robert Craig Brown and Ramsay Cook, *Canada, 1896–1921: A Nation Transformed* (Toronto, 1974), pp. 98–9.

14. "The Back-To-The-Land Movement," *Conservation of Life*, 1 (Oct., 1914), p. 30.

15. Paul Rutherford, "Tomorrow's Metropolis: The Urban Reform Movement in Canada, 1880–1912," *Canadian Historical Association Papers, 1971*, p. 203.

16. C.A.B., "Camping Out," *Rod and Gun*, III (Aug., 1901), p. 19; F.W. Wallace, "The Lure of the Open," *Rod and Gun*, V (Oct. 1911), p. 518; F.W. Wallace, "The Lure of the Wild," *Rod and Gun*, XII (July, 1910), p. 178.

17. Julian Durham, "Summer on the Pacific Coast," *Canadian Magazine*, XV (May, 1900), p. 6; "The Rest Cure in a Canoe," *Rod and Gun*, XII (Oct., 1910), p. 619.

18. D.C. Ireland, "A Voice From the City," *Westward Ho! Magazine*, II (March, 1908), p. 52.

19. "Freedom," in D.C. Scott, ed., *The Poems of Archibald Lampman* (Toronto, 1905), p. 17.

20. C.W. Nash, "The Bass of Ontario," *Canadian Magazine*, XVII (Aug., 1901), p. 333.

21. "The Rest Cure in a Canoe," *op. cit.*, p. 619.

22. Adam Shortt, "Some Aspects of the Social Life of Canada," *Canadian Magazine*, XI (May, 1898), p. 8. For Shortt's personal attempt to break down the "artificialities between himself and nature" see: Adam Shortt, "Down the St. Lawrence on a Timber Raft," *Queen's Quarterly*, X (July, 1902), pp. 16–34.

23. The "back-to-nature" movement differed from the "back-to-the-land" movement. The former was the sentiment of urban Canadians to return to nature for short periods of time; the latter was part of the movement to have people live permanently in rural areas. Bliss

Carman: Going back to nature does not mean "going back to savagery nor to barbarism nor to any pestilential past; it only means opening the doors and the windows." (*The Making of Personality* [Boston, 1908], p. 315.) For "back-to-the-land" movement, see: John A. Cormie, "Back to the Land," *University Magazine*, XVII (1918), pp. 197–203; Canada, "The Back-to-the-Land Movement," *Conservation of Life*, I (Oct., 1914), pp. 30–1.

24. Thomas W. Gibson, "Algonquin National Park," *Canadian Magazine*, III (Sept., 1894), p. 543.

25. J.W. Dafoe, "A Day in the Laurentians," *Rod and Gun*, I (Aug., 1899), p. 51.

26. The trouble to which amateur photographers went to get "natural" pictures of wildlife at close range prompted a journalist in *Canadian Magazine* to satire. With tongue-in-cheek, three methods of concealment were listed: a bogus tree-trunk made of cheesecloth stretched over hoops and uprights, a fake cow constructed of muslin stretched over a framework of split bamboo and, especially applicable to bird photography, an open umbrella draped in dark muslin XXI [May, 1903], p. 94.

27. The Canadian Alpine Club was organized in Winnipeg in 1906.

28. *McKein's Directory of Canadian Publications* (1892, 1899, 1901, 1905, 1907, 1909, 1911, 1913). Of these journals, *Rod and Gun* was by far the most popular, its circulation reaching over 18,000 in 1913.

29. L.O. Armstrong, "Boredom and One of Its Antidotes," *Rod and Gun*, VI (Oct., 1904), p. 241.

30. "The Rest Cure in a Canoe," *op. cit.*, p. 623.

31. "Freedom," *op. cit.*, p. 17.

32. Donald Black, "The Call of the Wild," *Rod and Gun*, XII (Nov., 1910), p. 769. Women also responded to the call of the out-of-doors: "It is

almost as necessary for a woman to be an enthusiast for outdoor games as it is for her to be beautiful and well-dressed." ("As She Sees It," *Westward Ho! Magazine*, II [April, 1908], p. 57.)

33. "Camping Out," *op. cit.*, p. 19.

34. "Our Medicine Bay," *Rod and Gun*, VI (Oct., 1904), p. 249.

35. H.G. Wilson, "The Pleasures and Benefits of Camping," *Rod and Gun*, VII (Dec., 1905), pp. 721-2.

36. L.O. Armstrong, *op. cit.*, p. 241.

37. Elizabeth Parker, "Mountaineering in Canada," *University Magazine*, XI, p. 135.

38. "An Invitation to the Woods," in Arthur S. Bourinot, ed., *Archibald Lampman's Letters to Edward William Thompson* (Ottawa, 1956), pp. 59-60.

39. Ross Harkness, *J.E. Atkinson of the Star* (Toronto, 1963), pp. 70-1.

40. June 28, 1901, p. 3.

41. Paul Rutherford, *op. cit.*, p. 204.

42. "A Boys' Camp in Temagami," *Rod and Gun*, X (June, 1908), pp. 49-51; Roy I. Wolfe, "The Summer Resorts of Ontario in the Nineteenth Century," *Ontario History*, LIV (Sept., 1962), p. 159. Also see: C.B. Powler, "A Boys' Camp in the Laurentians," *Rod and Gun*, IX (July, 1907), pp. 168-72; Harold G. Salton, "A School Boy's Search for an Ideal Vacation," *Rod and Gun*, X (July, 1908), pp. 154-8.

43. Ernest Thompson Seton, *Trail of an Artist-Naturalist* (New York, 1940), pp. 374-85.

44. Fred Bodsworth, "The Backwoods Genius With the Magic Pen," *Maclean's Magazine*, LXXII (June 6, 1959), p. 40.

45. R.I. Wolfe, *op. cit.*, pp. 149-50, 157.

46. J.A. Cooper, "Canada and the Tourist," *Canadian Magazine*, XV (May, 1900), p. 4. Also see: "The Outdoor Life of Canada," *Canadian Pictorial*, IV (June, 1909), p. 1.

47. In Muskoka the term "camping" was expanded to include "picturesque wooden homes, large or small, ornamental or plain" as well as the traditional "bed or branches and a canvas roof." (Catherine Blindfield, "Muskoka Days and Doing," *Canadian Magazine*, V [Sept., 1898], pp. 486-7.)

48. J.W. Dafoe, *op. cit.*, p. 51.

49. R. Tait McKenzie, "The University and Physical Efficiency," *University Magazine*, VI (April, 1907), p. 168.

50. Both Kelso and Dorchester were advocates of using physical culture for putting Canadians back into shape. See: Frank C. Dorchester, "Physical Culture: A Nation's Need," *Rod and Gun*, XI (Sept., 1907), pp. 347-9. J.A. Cooper: "If Canadians are to be physically strong there are some reforms to be effected. They must eat less pastry, they must breathe more fresh air, they must encourage still more athletic sports and physical culture. . . ." (*Canadian Magazine*, CMXXII [April, 1904], p. 588.)

51. "A Word of Caution," *Rod and Gun*, VI (July, 1904), pp. 60-1. Also see: L.O. Armstrong, "Out of Doors," *Rod and Gun*, VI (June, 1904), p. 15.

52. Sir Robert Baden-Powell, *The Canadian Boy Scout* (Toronto, 1911), p. ix.

53. *Ibid., passim*. Baden-Powell's manual was a thinly disguised rewrite of Seton's Woodcraft Indians guide, *The Birch Bark Roll*, only with Seton's emulation of the Indian thrown out and Baden-Powell's militarianism inserted.

54. W. Lockhead, "Agencies for the Promotion of Nature-Study in Canada," *The Ottawa Naturalist*, XX (Dec., 1906), pp. 193-6.

55. Charles C. Phillips, *The Development of Education in Canada* (Toronto, 1957), p. 435; J.B. Wallis, "Nature Study in the Winnipeg Schools," *The Ottawa Naturalist*, XVIII (May, 1904), pp. 61-4; J.F. Power, "The Importance of Nature Study, With

Some Suggestions as to Methods," *The Ottawa Naturalist*, XXII (Nov., 1908), pp. 145–53; A.H. MacKay, "Nature Study in the Schools of Nova Scotia," *The Ottawa Naturalist*, XVIII (Feb., 1905), pp. 209–12.

56. C.C. Phillips, *op. cit.*, pp. 421–35.

57. Frank T. Shutt, "Nature Study and the Camera," *The Ottawa Naturalist*, XVIII (Nov., 1904), pp. 161–4. The Nature Study Movement was also heavily influenced by the desire to keep rural children on the farms. See: W.T. Macoun, "The Practical Aspect of Nature Study," *The Ottawa Naturalist*, XVII (Jan., 1904), pp. 181–4; J.W. Hotson, "Nature Study and Rural Education," *The Ottawa Naturalist*, XVII (March, 1904), pp. 221–4.

58. D.A. Campbell, "The Need of Nature Study," *The Ottawa Naturalist*, XVII (June, 1903), p. 61.

59. W. Scott, "What is Nature Study?" *The Ottawa Naturalist*, XVII (Nov., 1903), p. 148.

60. G.U. Hay, "It is the Spirit Which Gives It Effect," *The Ottawa Naturalist*, XVII (Nov., 1903), p. 148.

61. C.J. Atkinson, "Mother Nature and Her Boys," *The Ottawa Naturalist*, XIX (Feb., 1906), p. 215.

62. Russel B. Nye, "The American View of Nature," in *This Almost Chosen People* (East Lansing, 1966); John Higham, "The Reorientation of American Culture in the 1890's" in H. J. Weiss, *The Origins of Modern Consciousness* (Detroit, 1965); R. Nash, "The American Cult of the Primitive," *American Quarterly*, 18 (Fall, 1966), pp. 517–37; R. Nash, "The American Wilderness in Historical Perspective, *Forest History*, VI (Winter, 1963), pp. 3–13; Peter J. Schmitt, *Back to Nature: The Arcadian Myth in Urban America* (New York, 1969); Hans Huth, *Nature and the American: Three Centuries of Changing Attitudes* (Berkeley, 1957).

63. J.A. Cooper, "Canada and the Tourist," *op. cit.*, p. 4.

64. Arthur O. Wheeler, "Canada's Mountain Heritage," Address delivered before the Toronto Canadian Club (Dec. 20, 1909), p. 63.

65. J.W.A. Hickson, "Climbs in the Canadian Rockies," *The University Magazine*, IX (Oct., 1910), p. 438.

66. T.A. Langstaff, "The Canadian Mountain Regions as a National Assett," Address delivered before the Toronto Canadian Club (Oct. 13, 1910), p. 43.

67. A. Kelly Evan, "Fish and Game Protection in Ontario," *Rod and Gun* (Aug., 1905), p. 310.

68. The historical development of the Conservation Movement is discussed in: Thomas L. Burton, *Natural Resource Policy in Canada* (Toronto, 1972), pp. 23–46; F.J. Thorpe, "Historical Perspectives on the 'Resources for Tomorrow' Conference," *Resources for Tomorrow Conference, Background Papers*, I (1961), pp. 1–13; R.C. Brown, "The Doctrine of Usefulness: Natural Resource and National Park Policy in Canada, 1887–1914," in J.G. Nelson, ed., *Canadian Parks in Perspective* (Montreal, 1970), pp. 46–62; C. Roy Smith and David R. Witty, "Conservation, Resources and Environment," *Plan*, XI (1970), pp. 35–70, XI (1972), pp. 199–216.

69. Cited in Brown, *op, cit.*, p. 48.

70. *Ibid.*, p. 48.

71. E.J. Toker, "Our Forests in Danger," *Canadian Magazine*, I (July, 1893), p. 336.

72. *Ibid.*, pp. 336–40; Phillips Thompson, "Forestry—A Neglected Industry," *Canadian Magazine*, VIII (Nov., 1896), pp. 24–9.

73. "Constitution of the Canadian Forestry Association," *Rod and Gun*, I (April, 1900), p. 204. In these aims, the C.F.A. followed closely its sister organization in the United States,

the American Forestry Association, which had been established in 1875.

74. At the first meeting of the C.F.A., *Rod and Gun* was designated as the official organ of the Association. Thereafter, the magazine devoted a special section to forestry. See: *Rod and Gun*, II (March, 1900), p. 1.

75. F.J. Thorpe, *op. cit.*, p. 3.

76. Commission on Conservation, Canada, *First Annual Report, 1910* (Ottawa, 1910), p. 6.

77. *Ibid.*, p. 16.

78. William T. Hornaday, "The Ideals of Sportsmanship," *Rod and Gun*, X (March, 1909), p. 10. Adopted by North American Fish and Game Protective Association.

79. J.K. Reynolds, "One Hundred Years of Fish and Wildlife Management in Ontario," *Rod and Gun*, LXVIII (Jan.–Feb., 1967), p. 14.

80. C. Roy Smith and David R. Witty, *op. cit.* (1970), p. 58.

81. For example, *Rod and Gun* carried the news of almost all Forest and Fish and Game Associations across Canada. See: "Our Ninth Birthday," *Rod and Gun*, X (June, 1908), p. 3.

82. "League of Canadian Sportsmen," *Rod and Gun*, I (July, 1899), p. 1.

83. "The Last Wild Pigeon," *Rod and Gun*, XII (Sept., 1911), p. 429. Also see: C.W. Nash, "Passing of the Pigeons," *Canadian Magazine* (Feb., 1903), pp. 315–7.

84. C.W. Nash, *op. cit.*, p. 317.

85. C. Gordon Hewitt, "Conservation, or the Protection of Nature," *The Ottawa Naturalist*, XXIV (March, 1911), p. 221.

86. *Ibid.*, p. 210.

87. *Ibid.*, p. 209.

88. *Ibid.*, p. 221.

89. See: James Polk, *Wilderness Writers* (Toronto, 1972), pp. 45–6, 64–7.

90. Ernest Thompson Seton, "Hunting with the Camera," *Rod and Gun*, II (June, 1900), p. 259.

91. For example, F.B. Doud, "Still Hunting With a Camera," *Rod and Gun*, XI (Aug., 1909), pp. 213–5; John Innes, "Buffalo Hunting: Modern and Ancient," *Canadian Magazine*, XIX (May, 1902), pp. 9–17; H.M. Johnston, "Another Use for the Hand Camera," *Rod and Gun*, IV (Feb., 1903), pp. 324–5.

92. Bonnycastle Dale, "The Opening of the Season," *Westward Ho! Magazine*, I (Oct., 1907), p. 33. Dale published extensively on this theme in *Westward Ho!, Canadian Magazine* and *Rod and Gun*.

93. H.F. Lewis, "Wildlife Conservation Through the Century," *Rod and Gun* (Jan.–Feb., 1967), p. 12.

94. Harry McDougall, "Jack Miner's Bird Sanctuary," *Canadian Geographical Journal*, LXXXIII (Sept., 1971), p. 108.

95. Stanley Park in Vancouver and Rockcliffe Park in Ottawa. The establishment of a bird sanctuary in Rockcliffe Park was a result of an impassioned speech delivered by Hewitt to the Ottawa Field-Naturalist Club. See: "The Protection of Birds In and Around Ottawa," *The Ottawa Naturalist*, XXVII (March, 1914), pp. 161–71.

96. C. Gordon Hewitt, *The Conservation of the Wild Life of Canada* (New York, 1921), pp. 258–77, 300–9.

97. Lt.-Colonel William Wood, "Animal Sanctuaries in Labrador," *An Address Presented Before the Second Annual Meeting of the Commission of Conservation* (Quebec, 1911), p. 5. In the preface to the written publication of the address, Wood appealed to: "All to whom wild Nature is one of the greatest glories of the Earth, all who know its higher significance for civilized man today, and all who consequently prize it as an heirloom for posterity, . . . to help in keeping the

animal life of Labrador from being wantonly done to death."

98. *Ibid.*, p. 36.

99. Cited in W.E. Colin, *The White Savannahs* (Toronto, 1936), p. 8.

100. Julia Henshaw, "A Summer Holiday in the Rockies," *Canadian Magazine*, XX (Nov., 1902), pp. 3–4.

101. E. Parker, "The Alpine Club of Canada," *The Canadian Alpine Journal*, I (1907), p. 8.

102. E. Parker, "The Mountain Ideal," *Rod and Gun*, VIII (July, 1906), p. 146.

103. Arthur O. Wheeler, "Canada's Mountain Heritage," Address delivered before the Toronto Canadian Club (Dec. 20, 1909), p. 63.

104. Alec Lucas, "Nature Writers and the Animal Story," in Carl F. Klinck, ed., *Literary History of Canada* (Toronto, 1965), p. 364; Charles G.D. Roberts, *Kindred of the Wild* (Toronto, 1902), p. 13–4.

105. L. Stevenson, *Appraisals of Canadian Literature* (Toronto, 1924), pp. 78–9.

106. "On the Companionship With Nature," D.C. Scott, ed., *The Poems of Archibald Lampman* (Toronto, 1905), pp. 258–9.

107. "Kinship," in Charles G.D. Roberts, *Poems* (Boston, 1907), pp. 17–8.

108. *Kinship of Nature* (Boston, 1903).

109. "Wind-flower," cited in Odell Shepard, *Bliss Carman* (Toronto, 1923), p. 80. Shepard: "Carman identifies himself, so to speak, with the object, merging himself into it, seeming to pierce to the heart and inner nature of flower and tree and to become, as it were, a thinking tree, a feeling flower."

110. John Macoun, cited in A.S. Bourinot, *op. cit.*, p. 70.

111. Carl G. Connor, *Archibald Lampman: Canadian Poet of Nature* (New York, 1929), p. 149.

112. On Lampman, see: Barrie Davies, "Lampman and Religion," *Canadian Literature* (Spring, 1973), pp. 40–60.

113. E.M. Pomeroy, *Sir Charles G.D. Roberts: A Biography* (Toronto, 1943), p. 42.

114. Roberts, *op cit.*, p. 69.

115. "Life and Nature," in Scott, *op. cit.*, p. 138.

116. Pomeroy, *op. cit.*, p. xx.

117. Shepard, *op. cit.*, p. 114; Pomeroy, *op. cit.*, p. 98.

118. G.R. Roy, *Le Sentiment De La Nature Dans La Poésie Canadienne Anglaise, 1867–1918* (Paris, 1961), pp. 99–100.

119. Cited in Hans Huth, *op. cit.*, p. 88.

120. "Iminance," Roberts, *op. cit.*, p. 41.

121. "Origins," Roberts, *op. cit.*, p. 18.

122. Cited in Connor, *op. cit.*, p. 162.

123. Shepard, *op. cit.*, p. 115.

"THE VEXED QUESTION OF SAWDUST": RIVER POLLUTION IN NINETEENTH-CENTURY NEW BRUNSWICK◇

GILBERT ALLARDYCE

○

The lament over the polluted rivers of New Brunswick did not begin with our century. In a time when industrial chemicals and urban wastes foul our waters, it is nostalgic to imagine that things were very different before the coming of modern society. But the assault on the rivers and streams of New Brunswick is as old as the province itself, for the economic existence of the area was historically linked with the timber trade, and the timber trade was necessarily linked with running water. In the days before effective land transportation, rivers provided the only means of carrying great quantities of heavy logs to the sawmills and harbours. Beginning on the floods that started the "river drive" in the spring, the journey of lumber from provincial hinterlands to the timber markets of the North Atlantic progressed along a water route from rivers to mill ponds, and finally to the sea itself. Along the way was left the debris of the "drive" and the sawmill: sunken logs, bark, slabs, edgings, mill rubbish, and sawdust. Just as the moving water effectively carried the floating timber over long distances, it carried this debris as well, spreading it over entire river systems and into the harbours and bays on the seacoast. During the spring and summer months, the mills on every river and creek in New Brunswick droned with activity, releasing clouds of sawdust into the streams and dumping scraps and wastes that drove off the fish, endangered navigation, and littered vast stretches along the riverbanks and the Fundy shore.

Through most of the nineteenth century, government officials carried on a continuing struggle to clear the waterways and save the fishstocks.

◇ *Dalhousie Review* 52 (1972): 177–90.

With alternating kicks and caresses, they moved the millowners to dispose of their edgings and wastes. But sawdust was a more difficult problem. Of all the refuse of the sawmills, sawdust was the most troublesome to destroy. It was also the most dangerous to living things. Much like the toxic chemicals of today, sawdust was the stuff of death. Where it collected, the process of nature stopped. Writing in 1889, a Department of Fisheries official described the potential of the substance to spread its lethal effects through the levels of marine life:

> The ruinous effects of this sawdust scourge when deposited in the waters of the country are still greater than when cast upon the land. Its floatability at first gives it more widespread areas in which to work out its blasting influences, even passing down in some instances till it reaches the estuaries of streams and the small inlets and bays along the coasts of the sea and shores of lakes. Here it likewise kills the sources which give life and food for the smaller races of insects and other marine animals. . . . Settling here and there in its course down the streams, it forms a compact mass of pollution all along the bottoms and margins of the rivers and inlets, filling up the crevices on the gravel beds, and among stones, where aquatic life is invariably produced and fed. It becomes a fixed, imperishable foreign matter, and adheres to the beds of streams and other waters, and forms a long, continuous mantle of death. . . .[1]

The following pages present a case study of sawdust pollution in Alma Parish of Albert County, an area of darkest New Brunswick that has received little attention from modern historians. Perhaps this neglect results from the fact that, for the most part, the community that once existed there has itself come to an end. For in 1948, most of the region was expropriated to form Fundy National Park, and government bulldozers began the work of removing the traces of man from the area. In reality, however, they were completing a process which had begun long before. For Alma Parish was already a region of exhausted resources, shrunken population, and encroaching forests, an area that had been returning to wilderness since the closing decades of the last century. The bulldozers thus removed what a long period of economic decline had left behind. In the end Alma Parish had nothing left to sell except its scenery.

The beginning was very different. The things which today give Fundy Park its awe and beauty were the same things that made the first settlements in the area so difficult: the rugged hills, rocky terrain, rapid streams, and plunging waterfalls. It was a region particularly unsuited to farming, but for a time its forests and fishlife appeared inexhaustible. Protected from the ravages of fire damage by the damp air of the Bay of Fundy, towering stands of timber had grown uninterrupted for generations, and in the streams salmon and trout were plentiful. As far back as written records take us, what is now the Alma River was called the Salmon River—and with good reason. "The River had an abundance of salmon sporting in its sparkling waters," an Albert County pioneer recalled from one early visit in

1836, "and we used to catch all the fish we wanted in weirs and nets. . . . "[2] Out on the sea, the hard rock formations on the bottom that provided clear water up to Point Wolfe at the centre of the Parish shoreline turned thereafter into soft sandstone, resulting in the murky waters that attracted vast schools of shad toward their feeding grounds on the flats at the head of the bay. From a point just east of Cape Enragé, and stretching almost to the mouth of the Petitcodiac River, lay what was considered one of the best shad fisheries in the world.

In its early development, the economy of Alma Parish was in many ways a microcosm of the economy of New Brunswick itself. It was an economy of fish and timber, but where the provincial economy began to develop at least the rudiments of secondary industry during the nineteenth century, the economy of Alma Parish remained singularly concentrated on the exploitation of its two basic materials. Unfortunately, it was soon discovered that lumbering and fishing were not easily compatible, and that the vigorous exploitation of one resource would have its effects in the decline of the other. For the sawmills once located at the mouths of the Salmon and Point Wolfe Rivers developed during the nineteenth century into two of the largest timber operations on the Fundy coast; but timber meant sawdust, and in the end the mills became the major source of water pollution, not only of the river mouths themselves, but of the teeming shad fisheries at the head of the bay. What follows is the history of sawdust and fish in Alma Parish.

In 1850, the provincial government commissioned Moses H. Perley, a sometime government official and naturalist, to undertake a study of the fisheries of New Brunswick. Travelling up the Fundy Coast from Saint John, he discovered an "iron-bound shore," with few harbours and open spaces for fishing. Near Salmon River, however, at a spot known locally as Cannon Town Beach, Perley found the brush weirs of "the first regular shad fishery" on the coast. The weirs were worked as a cooperative enterprise, with fourteen local settlers taking an annual share of about eight barrels of shad. Out on the bay, the catch was abundant. Between July and August, the white sails of fishing boats could be seen clustered along the shad-infested stretch between the Petitcodiac and Grindstone Island. The waters indeed seemed procreant, but Perley was not optimistic. The catch of herring, he noted, was already falling away, and if precautions were not taken, the shad, he feared, would go the same way. The real crisis, however, was in the salmon streams along the shore.

All along the Fundy coast, Perley found sawmill dams blockading the rivers and preventing the passage of salmon toward their spawning grounds in the headwaters. Great quantities of sawdust were being dumped into streams, and mill rubbish clogged the river mouths and harbours. The rivers of Alma Parish were no exception. At Point Wolfe a lofty mill dam sealed tight the Point Wolfe River, and the salmon lay dormant in the pool below. It was essential, Perley observed, that the lumbermen learn to share the river with the fish. "The supply of logs decreases annually and after a time will cease altogether," he wrote of the busy lumber operation above the dam, "but if the salmon are preserved they will prove a source of wealth long after the sawmills are worn and useless."

At Salmon River, the mill dam was located at the head of the tide, and salmon were able to leap over into the pond above—but with little avail. "It was stated," Perley remarked after conversations with local residents, "that nearly all the salmon which passed were speared almost immediately after in the shallows above the mill pond."[3] The scenes he witnessed at Point Wolfe and Salmon River were repeated everywhere on his journey. In concluding his report, Perley gave bleak warnings of the effects of uncontrolled lumbering operations on the province's stock of salmon:

> The closing of the various rivers flowing into the Bay, and their tributaries, by mill dams; the injuries arising from sawdust and mill rubbish being cast into rivers and harbours; and the wholesale destruction of salmon on their spawning bed far up the rivers have been pointed out in this report. They are all evils that require an immediate check.

When, ten years later, another official toured some of the fisheries of the province, he found that Perley's warnings had gone unheeded, and that his forebodings of the decline of Atlantic salmon were proving accurate. "There is no doubt," the official wrote, "that the salmon are decreasing at a very rapid, and rapidly increasing rate." The problems of sawdust, dams, and mill refuse must be confronted at once, he argued, for further delay could make the existing trends irreversible: "every year adds tenfold to the difficulty of the task."[4]

New Brunswick, however, was timber country, and matters became worse before they got better. The lumber industry in the province was developing toward its peak in the late nineteenth century, and an estimated 500 000 000 board feet of lumber was moving each year through the sawmills or toward the seaports for export. Within the industry, as the virgin stands of timber fell away, there developed an inner direction toward larger operations and more aggressive enterprise, and the lumber barons of Alma Parish felt the urge as much as the others.

The mill at Point Wolfe passed through a succession of owners during the nineteenth century, but the growth of its operations remained constant. In 1831 twenty men were employed on the site; by 1874 the number of workers had increased to forty-eight, to sixty in 1889, and to over a hundred at the turn of the century. The output of lumber kept pace, increasing from 750 000 board feet in 1832 to an annual average of six million feet in 1889. In that year the businessman George Judson Vaughan purchased the mill, the fifth proprietor to control the operation since its beginning in 1825. Vaughan sustained the pace of his predecessors, turning out a million feet per month during the sawing season, and keeping three lumber schooners employed between Point Wolfe and Saint John—as well as two others making runs to the American markets.[5] More timber, of course, meant more sawdust; but it also meant more cost. Having achieved an output of six million feet a year, the mill, it appears from the scattered statistics available, was operating at the peak of its capacity, and it seems evident that the rule of diminishing returns was already beginning to take hold at Point Wolfe. Lumbering there was an increasingly expensive and venturesome business, and Vaughan would prove particularly resistant to regulations that inhibited the pace of his operations, or forced him into profitless investments in filtering devices or sawdust burners. His ambition was rather to expand his mill, hasten his workers, speed his cutting, and—in a very literal sense—let the chips fall where they may.

Developments at Point Wolfe were repeated at Salmon River—and on a larger scale. The mill at Point Wolfe had led the advance of the lumbering industry in the area, but in the 1870s the weight of timber output began to shift toward the larger river up the shore. In 1872, an American interest directed by the Talbot family of Machias, Maine, built a new sawmill on the riverbank a quarter-mile up from the bay. Such was the beginning of the Alma Lumber and Shipbuilding Company, an aggressive firm that sent cutting crews throughout the whole region drained by the Salmon River. Within a few years the firm was averaging over eight million feet of lumber a year, and kept one hundred eighty lumberjacks employed in the woods.[6]

Talbot's mill was to Alma what Vaughan's operation was to Point Wolfe. Both villages were company towns in the classic sense of that term, with the two mills employing the bulk of the work force, and providing the means of economic livelihood for the whole region. When the mills boomed, the villages surged with life and energy; when business went slack or the pace of production was slowed, men loitered without work, credit accounts weighed heavy at the company store, and the public mood turned sober. It all gave weight to the warnings of the millowners that government regulations on water pollution would mean economic ruin for themselves and unemployment for their workers. And it all made things more difficult in the matter that the Minister of Fisheries called "the vexed question of sawdust."

Government officials at Ottawa, however, had already committed themselves to the struggle for clean rivers—although the proper legislation was some time in coming. The earliest regulations had problems in legal language, with non-navigable streams (such as those in Alma Parish) escaping the jurisdiction of the statutes; and a subsequent act in 1873 (36 Vic, cap. 65) included a provision permitting individual millowners to receive specific exemption from the law if "it can be shown to the satisfaction of the Governor in Council that the public interest would not be injuriously affected thereby." In 1886, however, the government enacted legislation (49 Vic, cap. 36) which, though it continued the policy of exemptions, was recognized immediately as being decisive:

> No owner or tenant of any sawmill, or any workman therein or other person shall throw or cause to be thrown, or suffer or permit to be thrown, any sawdust, edgings, slabs, bark or rubbish of any description whatsoever, into any river, stream or other water any part of which is navigable, or which flows into any navigable water. . . .

With the words "or which flows into any navigable water," the new act took command over the entire water system of Canada. "I defy anyone," a member of parliament protested, "to find a river in this country which does not flow into navigable water, and by the very words of this clause you take possession of the rivers of this country, and you assume power to legislate upon them."[7]

If debate became heated on the question of jurisdiction, however, little was heard in opposition to the need for legislation. Somewhat as today, no one spoke in favour of pollution; men merely spoke against it in different ways. For some, the legislation was too little and too late; for others it was too much too soon. But while a minority cried ruin on both sides of the question, the majority refused to make a choice between timber and fish. Because of its paramount position in the Canadian economy, the timber industry, it was recognized, must necessarily be permitted to dominate the rivers of the nation, but lumbermen, Parliament decreed, must make sufficient accommodation with the fishing interests: the country needed both sawmills and fish.

Writing responsible legislation was one thing; enforcing it was another. In New Brunswick the new act suddenly called to account the sawmills located on the small streams entering into the Bay of Fundy, and in 1888 the Department of Fisheries determined to enforce the law in Alma Parish. It made little progress. The next spring, on April 27, 1889, Talbot's mill received an exemption from the act, permitting it to dump sawdust but enforcing the ban on rubbish; and the following year, on May 29, 1890, a similar exemption was authorized for George Vaughan's mill at Point Wolfe.[8]

The authorities at Ottawa, however, were not finished yet. In his report to Parliament in 1890, the Minister of Fisheries warned the lumbermen of the Dominion that the government had to balance the immediate interests of the mill owners against the long-term interests of fishing and navigation: the momentary power of one industry could not be permitted to compromise the future of another. His government, the Minister insisted, was not asking the owners to choose between profits and the public interest; rather it asked for modest investments in anti-pollution equipment that would profit the larger interests of lumbering and the public alike. Continued abuses, he warned, would in the end arouse the populace against politicians and lumbermen alike, forcing the government to take coercive action against the timber industry.[9]

In far away Alma Parish, however, the populace was concerned with more lively subjects than sawdust. During the last decade of the nineteenth century, when the conflict between the Minister of Fisheries and the local lumber barons reached its peak, the regional newspapers were absorbed in the feuds of the Temperance movement and the war on Demon Rum. It was not that men were unaware of the fact that sawdust was working its deadly ways in the waters of the region. "The principal cause of the decline in fishing is the immense quantities of sawdust that have been put into the streams," The Maple Leaf stated clearly on May 2, 1889, "and it is to be hoped that the law bearing on this evil will be rigorously enforced." It was rather that the populace of the lumbering villages could not connect the condition of their rivers with the immediate concerns of their own lives and occupations. Thus the Minister's prophecies of public wrath proved empty, and federal officials were left to carry the battle themselves. All the documents that have come down to us from the period indicate that the struggles over river pollution in Alma Parish were fought out over the heads of the public. Expressed in other terms, they were fought on a level at which the lumbermen could bring to bear all their financial influence and political connections.

In 1894, after long debate, the government began to remove the exemptions granted under the Act of 1886. Even before the blow fell on Alma Parish, however, tensions began to mount in the region. During the "log drive" in the spring, Frederick O. Talbot was accused of attempting to bribe a federal Fisheries Inspector, H.S. Miles, who reported receiving fifty dollars in a sealed envelope from Talbot's own hand.[10] Although the matter was dropped after Talbot assured the government that he intended the gift only as a "token of good will," the episode marked the beginning of a series of incidents in the remote area that would find their way to the desk of the Minister of Fisheries at Ottawa. The next one was not long in coming. On July 17, 1894, Inspector Miles received notification that the exemptions granted to both Talbot and Vaughan had been revoked. Talbot was "very much broken up," Miles informed his Minister on July 28; but by this time Talbot and Vaughan had informed acquaintances of their own, and political pressures began to weigh upon the authorities in Ottawa.

"I don't think the Government, which I have supported since the first, at the sacrifice of time and money, would tempt to injure me in this way did it fully realize the magnitude of the injury involved," Vaughan wrote to his Member of Parliament, Dr. R.C. Weldon, on July 20, 1894. And several days later, he outlined his protests—and his political connections—more fully to Inspector Miles:

> I received notice from the Ministry of Marine and Fisheries that I would have to take care of the sawdust by not letting it go into the water. I then immediately went to St. John and saw Mr. E. McLeod and Mr. Hazen, the members of St. John county, and they wrote to the Minister of Marine and Fisheries on my behalf and also to the Minister of Finance. And I also wrote to Doctor Weldon, and he replies that he has made out a strong case for me—setting forth how the mill was situated near the Bay and what a great loss it would be to me to shut down with the amount of logs I have on hand to cut, and that the lumber would be almost useless before I could erect a furnace to burn the sawdust and if I was stopped in my work it would ruin me and keep a large lot of men out of employment and would end in bankruptcy for me.[11]

Written appeals from all the parties mentioned found their way to the Minister of Fisheries, Charles Hibbert Tupper, and it seems likely that the Minister's Conservative colleague Dr. Weldon added some private pleas of his own: and with good cause. "I know," Vaughan's lawyer wrote to the Minister, "that . . . the withdrawal of the permission to dump sawdust will seriously injure Mr. Vaughan's prosecuting his work and I fear will imperil Mr. Weldon's election as it was largely owing to Mr. Vaughan's support that he was elected on the last occasion."[12]

On July 26, Tupper informed the lawyer of his reply: "I have looked carefully into this matter," the Minister wrote, "and I am glad to be able to inform you that as Mr. Vaughan has engaged to put a sawdust burner for next season, I have decided not to enforce the Act respecting the depositing of sawdust in the river in question until 1st May next." On August 7, Inspector Miles received word that the same privilege had been extended to the Talbot mill at Alma, but the message insisted again that the act would be consistently enforced as of the following May, when the government intended to remove all exemptions from the Sawdust Act. But the government had been brought to the knee once more, and the millowners found it easier the next time. The struggles of the summer of 1894 were not repeated the following year, and on May 6, 1896, one year after the deadline established by the Ministry, Inspector Miles admitted that "the sawdust regulation is not strictly enforced."[13]

Each year gained by the lumbermen, however, was one more lost for the fishing interests. The dam at Point Wolfe continued to obstruct the migration of salmon, and although a fishway had been constructed at Salmon River, sawdust drove the fish from the stream. "The fishways have been kept open and in repair," the local fisheries warden reported in 1889, "but it is doubtful if any salmon ever go through them."[14] Out on the Bay of Fundy, the years of delay took their toll as well. The catch of shad began to fail in the 1880s, and by the end of the decade it was apparent that the fish were rapidly deserting the head of the bay. In 1889, fishermen from Albert County landed twenty-five barrels of shad, compared to thirty barrels in 1888—but 3900 barrels had been taken in 1885![15] Accusations concerning overfishing and the injurious effect of brush weirs were circulated widely, but the Ministry of Fisheries placed the blame on sawdust pollution, and considered the mills at Point Wolfe and Salmon River to be especially responsible. "The two mills are so situated that their refuse is particularly injurious," a Ministry official wrote in 1894; "The shad ascending from the St. John River after spawning meet the floating refuse and offensive deposits immediately and appear to be deterred from further migration to their once favourite feeding grounds."[16] When the annual report on the once thriving fisheries of Albert County was forwarded to Ottawa in 1897, the text consisted of one sentence: "The fisheries of this county since the failure of the shad . . . are not important."[17]

The next year, in 1898, the government decided to try again. The mill at Salmon River had changed hands two years earlier, in July, 1896, when a firm headed by S.H. White of Sussex purchased the operation—but unfortunately for Ottawa, White proved as obstinate as Talbot. When a local official informed him that the Sawdust Act would be enforced, White dispatched a letter to the Minister of Fisheries, who was now the Liberal Sir Louis K.

Davies, that revealed all the spirit and swagger of the nineteenth-century timber barons:

> We have been informed by the fish warden of our town that after the first of May we will be required to take care of our own saw-dust, which hitherto has been put in the water. This is a matter that our attention was called to some two years ago, but was not enforced and we trust it is not the intention to be enforced now, as in our locality it is beyond all question unpracticable to do so. The fishing industry is nothing and can be made nothing, as the streams are very small, not navigable, and very rapid, there not being, or ever has been, any fishing industry in the vicinity, and to have this law enforced on the bayshore especially on the New Brunswick side would mean the shutting down of all the mills on the shore and an expense to each of from two to five thousand dollars. . . . The cost of such repairs to one mill would amount to more than all the fish on the shore for the last five years . . . as no doubt you are well aware this is the lumbering district of the southern part of New Brunswick. We trust that it is not intended to carry out this law in our vicinity, as it is beyond the shadow of a doubt that the lumber business and the fishing business are not at all in comparison.

A ministry official jotted a note on White's letter, informing Davies that the abuses at the Alma mill had caused widespread complaints, and assured the Minister that "it is untrue that these mills in most cases could not destroy their sawdust."[18] But White's argument had both logic and power: Alma Parish *was* a lumber district, and the lumbermen had a way of turning their economic influence into political advantage. When, for instance, a group of Westmorland County fishermen petitioned Davies in 1900 "to protect as much as possible what little remains of the once famous shad-fisheries of the Bay of Fundy," they specifically condemned White's exemption from the Sawdust Act: "While we think no exemptions should be made," their lawyer wrote on their behalf, "we specially complain of sawmills in Albert County at Salmon River where the deposited sawdust may be seen at low tide mixed with mud covering large extent of grounds."[19] Davies' reply to the lawyer, however, who happened to be a fellow Liberal, reveals the Ministry's fear of another confrontation with the lumber kings, especially in an election year. "I made a vain attempt a year ago," he wrote on January 22, 1900, "to put the law in force to prevent saw-dust being dumped into the streams, but there was nearly a revolution on the part of the millowners and their friends, and I would submit to you for your consideration whether just now it would be desirable to incur the enmity of all the millowners by adopting the suggestions contained in the petition."

Thus through the years at the turn of the century the Ministry vacillated between the quarreling sides, taking up the anguished cries of the fishing interest at one moment, and yielding to the pressures from the lumbermen at the next. "It appears difficult to decide what is the best course to pursue," a Fisheries Inspector admitted in 1898, "where the fishing interests are so small and the lumber so large. . . . "[20] In 1894 the Ministry had stated unequivocally that "the irritating effect of sawdust on the gills of shad has been scientifically proved"; but in 1900 the question was declared to be "under study," and officials parried the complaints of fishermen with appeals for patience and understanding:

> With respect to the escape of sawdust and mill rubbish into the rivers and bays of Albert County, I beg to say that as some experiments have been in progress under the superintendence of a qualified expert in order to decide beyond question the precise effect of floating sawdust and mill refuse on fish-life, the Department proposes to await the completion of the report on this subject before authorizing further action. The amount of harm done to fish-life has been much disputed.[21]

Some fishermen, however, had reached the end of patience and understanding. Their story is perhaps best reflected in the letters of one M.C. Anderson, a lone New Horton fisherman who had fished the bay for over thirty years. He remembered when it was once full of shad and herring, but in a series of crudely-written protests to the Ministry of Fisheries at the turn of the century, he told of his growing despair over the fouled waters and the empty fish barrels. "Instead of getting herring in the morning," he complained, "I have seen the nets full of mill trash that took till noon to pick out."[22] His letters are a mixture of protest and pleading, the reproaches of a little man against powerful interests and unconcerned authorities. With them, in the Public Archives at Ottawa, are filed other grievances and remonstrances against the abuses of the millowners. But particularly relevant is the case of Leonard Martin of Alma, who fished a weir on the shore at a spot still known as Cannon Town Beach, i.e., the same weir that Moses Perley described a half-century earlier as "the first regular shad fishery" on the coast.

The Cannon Town Weir, we have observed, was once a considerable enterprise, yielding around one hundred and twelve barrels of shad a year in the middle of the nineteenth century. Thereafter, however, it went the way of all fishing ventures in the region. A report in 1874 reveals that only sixty barrels had been taken that season.[23] And Martin's catch as well had been declining year by year. In 1908, a Fisheries Inspector investigating protests about sawdust pollution from White's mill reported that the weir— which he identified as the only fishing activity in the area—was earning about two hundred dollars per year. "Against the $200 worth of fish caught in the weir," he remarked, "the output of lumber in the same district . . . returns . . . $200,000."[24] Two years later, in 1910, Leonard Martin brought the history of the Cannon Town Weir to an end. "I have been fishing a weir here," he wrote to the Ministry of Fisheries on May 23, 1910, "but had to abandon it this year on account of the refuse that is dumped in the stream."

Thus ends the story of fishing and sawdust in Alma Parish. It must be admitted that it is a story of lumbermen without conscience, government officials without courage, and a population without concern. Certainly it was not knowledge or adequate legislation that was lacking; what was lacking was a higher sense of community, and a common recognition that even subordinate economic interests had a right in the environment of the region. Fishing, it is true, had always been a subordinate activity in the area, where the primacy of lumbering was established from the beginning. By the turn of the twentieth century, however, the sawmills had driven out even the most rudimentary fishing operations. Fish and timber were once equally abundant, but the exploitation of one natural resource drove out the other. In the history of the area, therefore, fishing can be considered as a missed opportunity, an activity incompatible with the unbridled growth of large lumber enterprises.

Having failed to find the balance between lumbering and fishing, the region in the end would have neither one. In 1893, a local newspaper observed that, with the forests of the area growing thin, an economic transformation was about to begin in Albert County. "As the lumber becomes exhausted," it explained, "farming will claim more attention. This our farmers are beginning to realize, and how to best utilize the extensive and valuable marshes as well as the well-watered uplands to the best interests of the present and future is the question to which they are giving attention."[25] The county, it appeared, would fall back upon its fertile land. But Alma Parish, we have already observed, had little fertile land to fall back upon. Its economy was concentrated upon its forests, and even before the turn of the new century, the area began to decline along with its timber.

NOTES

1. "Annual Report of the Department of Fisheries, 1889," *Sessional Papers*, vol. xxiii, no. 12, 1890, section 17, 17.

2. See the reminiscences of J.S. Dodge in *The Maple Leaf* (old weekly newspaper published at Albert, New Brunswick), July 2, 1891.

3. Perley, *Reports on the Sea and River Fisheries of New Brunswick* (Fredericton, 1852), 142. For the full text of Perley's findings in Alma Parish, see 139–42.

4. "Report on the Salmon Fisheries in Certain Rivers of New Brunswick: 1862," *Journal of the Legislative Assembly of New Brunswick*, 1863, Appendix 10, 1–19.

5. For the changing statistics on production at Point Wolfe, compare the figures in *Statement of Saw Mills and Mill Property in the Province of New Brunswick, 1831* (Saint John, 1831), 129, with the following sources: *Saint John Daily Telegraph*, September 3, 1874, *Our Dominion: St. John, Prominent Places and People* (Toronto, 1887), 79, and *The Maple Leaf*, October 19 and 30, 1893.

6. "Business done by the Alma Lumber and Shipbuilding Company" in the records of the Ministry of Marine and Fisheries, Public Archives of Canada: RG 23, Access 67/24, TR 66, no. 993, 1-3.

7. Guillaume Amyot, *Parliamentary Debates* (Commons), 1886, Vol. II, 956.

8. See the information contained in the folders marked "Sawdust from Alma Lumber and S.B. Co.'s Mills on the Salmon River" (RG 23, access 67-24,

TR 66, no. 993) and "Enforcement of Saw-dust Act, Point Wolfe River, Geo. J. Vaughan's Mill," Ministry of Marine and Fisheries at the Public Archives of Canada. The information here on the sawdust problem in Alma Parish is drawn largely from the correspondence contained in these folders.

9. "Annual Report of the Department of Fisheries, 1889," *Sessional Papers*, vol. xxiii, no. 12, 1890, section 17, 33–34.

10. See Miles' letter of September 10, 1894, to the Minister of Fisheries, in "Enforcement of Saw-dust Act, Point Wolfe River. . . ," no. 1642.

11. See Vaughan's letter of July 26, 1894, in "Enforcement of Saw-dust Act, Point Wolfe River. . . ," no. 1642-24.

12. See the letter of J. Gordon Forbes of Saint John, dated July 20, 1894, in "Enforcement of Saw-dust Act, Point Wolfe River. . . ," no. 1642-16.

13. Letter of May 6, 1896, "Enforcement of Saw-dust Act, Point Wolfe River. . . ," no. 1642-52.

14. *The Maple Leaf*, May 2, 1889.

15. "Annual Report of the Department of Fisheries, 1889, *Sessional Papers*, vol. xxiii, no. 12, 1890, section 17, 129.

16. See the letter of Edward E. Prince, July 4, 1894, in "Enforcement of Saw-

dust Act, Point Wolfe River. . . ," no. 1642-20.

17. "Annual Report of the Department of Fisheries, 1897," *Sessional Papers*, vol. xxxii, no. 9, 1898, section 11a, 1113.

18. See White's letter of May 2, 1898, in "Sawdust from Alma Lumber and S. B. Co.'s Mills on Salmon River," no. 993-35.

19. See the petition of forty-one Acadian fishermen to Davies, in the folder cited above, no. 993-41.

20. Letter of R.A. Chapman, May 21, 1898, "Sawdust from Alma Lumber and S.B. Co.'s Mills on the Salmon River," no. 993-37.

21. Compare the letters of the Acting Deputy Minister of Fisheries dated July 12, 1894 (PAC, RG 23, access 67/24, RT 90, no. 1580-3), and October 2, 1900 TR 66, no. 993-44).

22. Letter of November 26, 1900, in the folder last mentioned, no. 993-60.

23. *The Daily Telegraph* (Saint John), September 3, 1874.

24. Letter of R.A. Chapman, July 11, 1908, in "Sawdust from Alma Lumber and S.B. Co.'s Mills on the Salmon River," no. 993-76.

25. *The Maple Leaf*, December 21, 1893.

THE BEGINNINGS OF A MOVEMENT: THE MONTREAL CONGRESS AND ITS AFTERMATH, 1880—1896[*]

PETER GILLIS
THOMAS R. ROACH

○

The rise of the North American conservation movement and of forestry as an art, a science, and a political movement dates from the 1860s and the work of a Vermont naturalist. George Marsh's widely read and discussed work, *Man and Nature*, was one of a number of books that led North Americans to rethink their conception of society and its relationship with the natural environment. When John Astin Warder founded the American Forestry Association in 1875, the movement coalesced into a group of diverse correspondents scattered across North America. From its founding, the American Forestry Association had a small Canadian membership. The Canadians benefitted greatly from the suggestions and support they received from their correspondents in the United States. This led to what Paul Pross has termed a "ferment of ideas" in eastern Canada, which brought the issue of forest conservation to the notice of the public and the government. In Canada, the proponents of conservation came from three distinct sections of society, each with a unique approach to the concept.[1]

From Canada's fledgling scientific community, arborculturists and entomologists joined with members of the scientific farming movements to form organizations such as the Ontario Fruit Growers Association. From its foundation the Association was oriented toward practical and efficient resource management. Most of the members of this Association lived and worked in central and southwestern Ontario and were interested in improving the

[*] Reprinted from *Lost Initiatives: Canada's Forest Industries, Forest Policy, and Forest Conservation* (Westport, CT: Greenwood Press, 1986), 31–49.

agrarian environment which had suffered greatly by deforestation through the settlement process.

A second group comprised a number of lumbermen from eastern Ontario and Quebec who were concerned that the quality and quantity of the trees they were felling were declining yearly. Was the limit of the exploitable forest being reached? Should the trees, and the forest, be treated as if they were inexhaustable, or was there a better way? Was there a method of management that would not require operators to be forever moving farther and farther into the hinterland?

A third group, environmental preservationists, ably represented in the United States by John Muir and his followers, was present in Canada in small numbers. Coming mainly from the country's educated, largely urban elite, they became important later after their number had increased. Eventually representing a broad cross-section of Canada's new, reasonably affluent middle class, they were to provide the movement with a popular base. This group was active in supporting the establishment of Algonquin National Park by the Ontario government in 1893. As in the United States, Canada's preservationists were initially attracted by the idea of resource conservation but were eventually repelled by the practical, utilitarian nature of the forest conservation movement and consequently played only a small role in its organization and promotion.[2] For this reason, early leadership for the conservation movement in Canada was provided by the scientific farmers and the lumbermen. From these groups came influential men who pushed for the introduction of some elementary improvements in the way the forest resource was treated in Canada. Eventually they were successful in persuading the federal and provincial governments to take some rudimentary steps toward a more responsible and provident forest policy. In doing so, they left their mark not only on Canada but also on the whole North American conservation movement.

In Canada the concept of forest conservation had to be properly publicized in order to have much impact on public policy and general public opinion. The first publicity the movement received came from the Dominion and provincial government departments responsible for agricultural resources. In their annual reports these departments provided space which played educational and information-distribution roles in the decades before World War I. The reports had a noncritical, positive tone that limited their usefulness to any reform-minded movement. No government, no matter how sympathetic to the aims of the conservation movement, was going to publish critical material that might scare away potential settlers or upset the voting public. Through the years, this negative aspect of government assistance was experienced by many of the proponents of conservation. The movement therefore began to publish its own journals as well as use the public and trade press to its own advantage.

While some government departments regarded the resources for which they were responsible from a strictly exploitive viewpoint, others were more enlightened. In the Province of Ontario, it was the department responsible for agriculture and the arts that supported the work of the Fruit

Growers Association and published the reports of its annual meeting. Thus it was this department that first spread the ideas of the movement and became involved in forest conservation. Following this tradition, Ontario's Department of Agriculture and Arts hired the first of a number of official propagandists who advocated scientific forest management of woodlands.[3]

By no means were the members of the Ontario Fruit Growers Association all orchard owners; many were farmers whose main interest was the general advance of agriculture. In the 1870s a lack of extension services, chemical pesticides, fungicides, and fertilizers restricted the ability of farmers and fruit growers alike to react to pathogens and other difficulties encountered in the growing of crops. The Association first took on the task of collecting and disseminating information about the pests commonly found on Ontario farms. The approach of the scientists who prepared information for the Association was to look for ways to manipulate the environment of the crops and thus control pests by natural means. Publication of the results of their studies allowed members of the Association, and the public having access to the reports, to identify and tackle the problems they faced.

It is not surprising that the Fruit Growers quickly became interested in all aspects of "farming." The protection of their fields from wind damage or water erosion and the realization that many beneficial animals lived in wooded areas led to an interest in farm woodlots. From there it was but a short step to advocating the reforestation, by planting, of farms abandoned because the land was unsuitable for agriculture. They viewed with alarm the wastes of sand dunes left after the forest had been removed in such southwestern Ontario counties as Norfolk and Simcoe. The Fruit Growers saw the proper maintenance of woodlots in economic as well as environmental terms. The Association's reports carried articles discussing how a woodlot could be managed to yield income as well as provide any fuelwood and fencing material required by its owner. Much to the concern of these early environmentalists, many farmers were selling the woodlots for cash payments that were well below the real value of the logs.[4] From an interest in farm woodlots and their efficient exploitation, it was only a short step for the members of the Fruit Growers Association to become interested in the fate of Canada's forests. This concern resulted in an alliance in the late 1870s with several of the lumbermen of Quebec and the Ottawa valley. This alliance was tremendously important to the future of forestry in Canada, and without it, the conservation movement would have had very little impact on public opinion or policy.

The lumbermen, who found a common cause with the Fruit Growers, were dynamic and powerful men. They represented an industry that, by this date, had been recognized by government as essential to the country's prosperity. While some modern writers have characterized them as "rapacious buccaneers" who had already creamed off the best timber and now wished to play "forester among the stumps," they genuinely sought a more stable basis for the investments they had made. Viewed by the political ideology of the time as the instruments by which land was stripped of trees for settlement purposes, they now saw themselves as permanent features on

the country's economic landscape. These men were in the process of forming a powerful lobby to plead for studies of the limits of economic agriculture and the creation of a permanent forest dedicated solely to lumber
production.[5]

On the lumbermen's side of the conservation movement were a father
and son, James and William Little. James Little had gotten his start in the
trade by exploiting the pine stands along the Grand river in southwestern
Ontario. He exported quantities of lumber cut from the forests of the watershed during the early years of the Reciprocity Treaty. By 1860 he had
moved on to Georgian Bay where untouched stands of pine had been discovered. These stands were soon thinned by Little and other lumbermen,
and Little, by now in his late sixties, once again had to move on. In 1873, at
the age of seventy, he was in Montreal with his oldest son, William, over-
seeing the family's new limits and timber brokerage business, concentrated
in the St. Maurice district of Quebec. This lifetime experience of movement
to new forests and their subsequent abandonment once cut-over had a profound effect on James Little. At first, he blamed the Reciprocity Treaty for
stimulating overproduction, but further thought led him to see the problem
in a wider context. His correspondence with conservationists in the United
States, who were members of Dr. Warder's American Forestry Association,
helped to clarify his thinking.[6]

In 1872 and 1876, James Little published the first call from industry for
forest conservation in Canada. The two pamphlets warned that the timber
resources of Canada and the United States were being destroyed by fire and
over-cutting. He called for strict regulations, to be enforced by government,
requiring that the forest be managed on a sustained yield basis. His greatest
worry was that, once the forest of the eastern states had been depleted, the
United States would turn to Canada for its supply of logs. Based on his own
experience, he forecast that if this happened the forests of Ontario and
Quebec would be quickly devastated. As a start to forest management,
Little wanted to see forest fires controlled, minimum cutting diameters
established, and lands classified to keep settlers out of nonagricultural but
forested areas. With controls like these, he thought the forests would be safe
from overcutting even if a large growth in demand occurred.[7]

The pamphlets published by James Little received a mixed reception.
His ideas had a sympathetic hearing from lumbermen, even though many
disagreed with his hypothesis that the United States would become totally
dependent on Canada for its lumber requirements. His views were widely
published in the press of the day, but unfortunately many of the public
were lured into a false sense of security by the widely held belief that
Canada's forests stretched on and on forever. Fortunately, the active members in the Ontario Fruit Growers Association recognized James Little as a
kindred spirit. They too had observed the decimation of the forests that had
once grown on the uplands bordering, to the north, the farmlands of central
Ontario and on the sandy areas of the southwestern portion of the province.

Thus, by 1880, there was a group of informed people in Ontario and
Quebec who were interested in the welfare of the nation's forests. Within

the nascent conservation movement, James Little was the most publicly prominent man on the strength of the pamphlets he had published and distributed. The leaders of the Fruit Growers Association, however, had more political influence because of their relationship with the Ontario Department of Agriculture and the Arts and because they represented a discernible political interest. These people, particularly James Little, shared their opinions with the members of the American Forestry Association; together, they made up a network of correspondents numbering fewer than a hundred people. It therefore came as something of a surprise to both American and Canadian members of the American Forestry Association when, in late 1881, they received invitations from Cincinnati, Ohio, to take part in the formation of the American Forestry Congress by attending its inaugural meeting in April, 1882.[8]

The reasons for the sudden creation of the American Forestry Congress have never become completely clear. According to a young forester, Bernhard Fernow, who had recently moved to the United States, it was a purely municipal affair. Fernow, who was later to become the first professional forester to be hired by the United States government and the first Dean of the University of Toronto's School of Forestry, was convinced that local politicians planned to use the occasion to enhance their reputations within the city, perhaps by honouring a visiting German forester, Richard von Steuben. The organizers were sincere in their interest in the issue, however, and were probably pleasantly surprised at the broad general interest engendered by their meeting and at the resulting events.

In Canada, the American Forestry Congress attracted the immediate attention of the Fruit Growers, and, at their annual meeting in December 1881, they decided to ask the provincial government of Ontario to support a delegation to the gathering. This request was granted, and James Gills, P.C. Dempsey, and Thomas Beall, all farmers or orchardmen, joined Professor William Saunders, an entomologist at the University of Toronto's Ontario Agricultural College at Guelph, to form a delegation led by the Secretary of the Fruit Growers Association, D.W. Beadle. In Cincinnati, Ohio, they met three men who had travelled from Montreal at their own expense: James and William Little and A.T. Drummond, a Montreal financier, lawyer, and author of articles about Canadian forests and forestry. The Quebec men joined the Ontario delegation and named Beadle as their official spokesman, although James Little, because of his reputation as a lumberman advocating forest conservation, fulfilled the organizers' invitation to give the keynote address to the meeting.

The opening session of the Congress was not auspicious: only 250 people attended, scattering themselves amongst the seats for 2000 in Cincinnati's Music Hall, which had been hired for the occasion. The meeting picked up momentum, however, with its first public session when the hall was filled to overflowing and the audience was divided into sections according to the topics of the papers being read. The importance of the Canadian group was recognized when its members were given specific roles to play in the conference proceedings. James Little and D.W. Beadle joined the committee discussing the future of the Congress. Because this was the first time that so many of the correspondents had met, this committee was discussing, by implication, the future of the forest conservation movement in North America.[9]

Two major problems faced this committee. The first was how to maintain and build on the momentum given to the movement by the meeting, and the second was how to ensure a united effort. Either the Congress should become a part of Warder's American Forestry Association, which still had fewer than one hundred members, or Warder should surrender leadership to the new body. This problem was more than the committee could resolve, so it moved on to name the time and place of the next meeting of the Congress. Beadle proposed that, instead of waiting a full year, they should take advantage of the upcoming concurrent meetings of the American Association for the Advancement of Science and the Society for the Promotion of Agricultural Science scheduled for August, 1882, in Montreal. The committee agreed, and Beadle issued an invitation to the members of the Congress on behalf of the Canadian delegation. This invitation was enthusiastically accepted by those attending the Congress, and thus the initiative for action in the young movement passed to Canada.[10]

Because the next meeting of the Congress was to be held in Montreal, the hometown of the Little family, it was agreed that William Little would organize the meeting. On his return home, William started to work on the program and to promote the August meeting. As Fernow had noted, the Cincinnati gathering had included botanists, entomologists, and professors of agricultural science, but only a few woodlot owners or lumbermen.[11] The Littles decided that the Montreal meeting had to attract significant numbers of men from the leadership of the forest industries for it to be a success and gain political momentum for the movement in Canada.

It soon became apparent that this task was to be easier than William or James Little had expected. Many Quebec lumbermen were in the mood to organize and lobby. Their logging teams were reaching the northern limits of the pine along the shores of the headwater lakes of the Ottawa river. They knew their forests contained proportionally more spruce than did the forests of Ontario, and this was making it increasingly difficult for them to obtain the timber they required. A complicating factor was that the lumbermen found themselves coming into competition for forest lands with the powerful colonization movement backed by the Roman Catholic clergy: colons and lumbermen were vying for the remaining stands of pine. Another major source of anxiety for the holders of limits in Quebec arose from their lease contracts. Those in force in 1868 had been granted for twenty or twenty-one years, renewable annually, with the timber dues fixed for the lease period.[12] Such licences covered the great majority of accessible timberland. The lumbermen naturally supported the continuation of this policy since it gave considerable security of tenure. The provincial government was oblivious to the advantages such a system could have in timber management, and, by the 1880s, was worried that the fixed timber dues prevented it from quickly increasing government revenue from timber duties.

It wished to eliminate long-term fixed licences in favour of a system that would enable it to raise rates immediately as the value of timber increased. In the forefront of the battle on the lumbermen's side was the Quebec Limitholders' Association. It was not long before this organization realized that the meeting of the American Forestry Congress was a means by which it could meet with the public and present its own point of view on land classification and the proper tenure for forest management.[13]

The Quebec Limitholders' Association was only partially successful in its attempt to dominate the proceedings of the American Forestry Congress because of the integrity of the Littles and their ability to see the issues in the widest context. The Littles guided the meeting into a discussion of a more general programme of forest conservation rather than into the particular interests of the lumbermen while ensuring the proceedings maintained a practical bent.

The Littles were immeasurably assisted in their preparations when they were joined by Henri Gustave Joly, the Seigneur of Lotbinière, a gentleman who quickly became a leader of the movement. Elected to the Legislature of Canada some six years before Confederation, Joly had taken part in all the major debates of the intervening years. Consistent with his Protestant religion and European education, he was a Liberal in political affiliation and personal philosophy. He thus complemented the Littles' Tory inclinations and added a political balance to the Congress. Joly was also a major landowner and a very wealthy man—factors which gave him a considerable degree of independence in thought and action. Joly had wide interests. In the 1880s he was President or Vice President of six societies concerned with agriculture, forestry, and the advancement of industry, as well as the Royal Humane Society of British North America. He was president of a railway company; he had turned down an offer to become a federal Minister of Agriculture in the administration of Alexander Mackenzie (1873–1878); and briefly he had been the Premier of his province and was now the leader of the Opposition. Later in his career, he would join Sir Wilfrid Laurier's cabinet, would be granted a knighthood, and would become Lieutenant Governor of British Columbia. More germane to the meetings were perhaps Joly's experimentations with European forestry techniques on his own lands and, in 1875, his publishing of the first forest survey of the Dominion, which had been undertaken as a project funded by the federal government. In this publication, he had called for more conservative use of the forest resource. With his moderate liberal stance and his modern views on the utilization of natural resources, he was a favourite of many in Quebec's anglophone minority. It would have been difficult for William Little to have found a more experienced, tactful, and dignified personage to propose as chairman for the upcoming Congress.[14]

The Quebec Limitholders' Association promoted the meeting of the Congress within its membership and arranged for its most influential members to present their views to the public. Included among these were the Honourable George Bryson Sr., Franklin H. Bronson, William C. Edwards, John R. Booth, and Peter White, M.P. All these men were prominent in the forest industry of the Ottawa valley. White, who was from Pembroke, Ontario, sat as the Tory member for the federal riding of Renfrew North. His major political role in the House was as the unofficial spokesman of the lumber industry. Enjoying the confidence of the Ottawa valley lumbermen, White continued to play the part of spokesman for them at the meeting of the Congress. In this role, he was supported by George Bryson, the patriarch of a family deeply involved in a lumber business based in the Pontiac district on the opposite side of the Ottawa river from Pembroke.[15] The Quebec lumbermen were most concerned that the Congress have something to say about the problem of settlers encroaching on forest land and causing forest fires. The problem, primarily a local issue, could be approached only indirectly at a meeting that was to be attended by a wide variety of participants from all over North America. As events were to show, Joly adroitly handled this problem and, by doing so, avoided alienating the representatives of the forest industry.

With Joly available to handle the delicate negotiations with the lumber interests, William Little was free to tackle the difficult issue of organization. By now, the membership of the American Forestry Congress was larger than that of the Forestry Association, and it gave the appearance of being a continued success. The organizers of the Congress were all concerned that the efforts of the forest conservation movement not be divided between two organizations that might compete for attention. From their point of view, it was logical that Warder's American Forestry Association dissolve itself by joining the Congress. They hoped to achieve this objective by persuading Dr. Warder to agree to the merger. With this aim in view, a meeting was held with Warder when he arrived in Montreal the day before the Congress opened. Warder met B.E. Fernow, F.B. Hough, Chief of the Division of Forestry in the United States Department of Agriculture, and William and James Little. After much persuasion, Warder acquiesced to the arguments of Fernow and James Little and agreed that his association would merge with the Congress before the meeting opened.[16]

With this auspicious beginning, the Congress convened on 21 August 1882 in the office area of the Littles' company, which had been especially renovated and renamed "Forestry Hall" for the occasion. The opening session was dedicated to business, and its main purpose was to organize several committees that would make reports to the final session. The room was crowded. In addition to a great many well-known people from the Quebec and Ottawa valley lumber trade, there was an expanded official delegation from the Ontario Fruit Growers Association. The government of Quebec was officially represented by G.B. Cooper, C.E. Bell, Eugene Renault, and, most notably, Minister of Crown Lands Dr. W.W. Lynch, accompanied by two major officials from his department, E.E. Tache and A.J. Russell. Federal members of Parliament and members of the provincial legislature also attended; whatever empty spaces remained in the Hall were filled by Canadian and American members of the two organizations.[17]

Henri Joly was named chairman of the proceedings, and the first major item of business discussed was the damage done to the forests by fire.

Because this was the topic dearest to the hearts of the lumbermen in the room, Little and Joly expected it to be the one most difficult to handle in the context of an international gathering. The problem was how to allow the men most directly involved in the issue to have their say without their monopolizing the proceedings. Fortuitously, a committee struck at the Cincinnati meeting to study the problem of forest fires had failed to present a report, and this enabled Joly to make a motion from the chair that a new committee be formed to study the issue. This committee would be instructed to complete its work in time to present recommendations to the final business session of the meeting. If accepted, these recommendations were then to be presented as a petition to all the levels of government concerned. Those nominated to the committee to represent Canada included Joly, Peter White, George Bryson, Sr., William Little, and J.K. Ward, a Montreal-based lumberman. These men had direct economic and political interests in the topics to be discussed by the committee: settler encroachments and the problems of forest fires. Representing the American members were Dr. F.B. Hough, Professor C.S. Sargeant, Dr. C. Mohr, E.D. Becker, and B.E. Fernow—a much more academically oriented group that would end up following the lead of the Canadians.[18]

Other committees struck at the opening session gave those in attendance the feeling that the movement was off to a dynamic start. There was so much business to attend to that the third and final business session was postponed half a day. At this meeting, the first report presented was the much-awaited recommendations from the forest fire committee. The chairman of the committee, George Bryson, recommended that governments, on behalf of the public represented by the Congress, be urged to enact effective regulations to combat forest fires. Specifically, the proposals were that reserves of forestland unfit for agriculture be established, that brush burning be prohibited in certain months of the year when the danger of wildfire was high, and that some kind of police force be created to enforce regulations and to organize fire suppression activities when necessary. The cost of the policing force was to be borne by a tax on the industry. These recommendations, which were accepted unanimously by the assembled members, were to be of tremendous importance in the future. Not only were they to form the basis of legislation passed by several governments in Canada, but they also resulted in the movement's gaining the support of industry. The recommendations were exactly what the Quebec Lumbermen's Association wanted from the Congress and, by not alienating this group, the Littles and Joly secured the support of many influential men for the cause of forest conservation.[19]

At the conclusion of the Congress, James Little was appropriately singled out for praise by the assembly. He was given the honorific of "Nestor in American Forests," an allusion to the advisory role played by the Greek chieftain Nestor during the siege of Troy, as recorded by Homer in The Iliad. The Montreal press was quick to label the meeting of the Congress a success even though they looked at it from a narrow viewpoint as just one of the "Three Great Congresses" that had brought large numbers of people to the city. Bernhard Fernow, however, was less enthusiastic in his analysis of the gathering. He had been impressed with the Canadians he had met and had become friends with Henri Joly, a man whom he had come to admire, but Fernow considered that only a few of the papers he had listened to took a "scientific" approach to forestry. Also, there was too much interest in tree planting and arborculture for his taste and not enough discussion about commercial forest management. These were complaints he was to voice frequently about future Canadian forestry meetings.[20]

From a Canadian perspective, the events of the following years were to show that the meeting had been very successful. For a start, the Congress now had a membership of 184, 103 of whom were Canadians. A third of the Canadian members were prominent men in the lumber trade of Ontario and Quebec. At this stage in its development, the American Forestry Congress was very much a Canadian affair and appears to have had something meaningful to say to industry. The two most important positions on the executive council of the Congress were firmly in the hands of Canadians committed to the cause, Henri Joly and William Little. This represented a Canadian "coup" of sorts. It is a pity that this situation did not last longer than to the next meeting of the Congress. In 1883, Joly, Little, and a handful of Canadians attended the annual meeting held that year in Minneapolis, Minnesota. At this meeting, the Congress returned to being a totally "American" body, which eventually evolved into the present-day American Forestry Association. This turn of events indicates that the Montreal Congress was designed to serve uniquely Canadian political ends by its organizers. It was an effort by the small forest conservation movement in Canada to demonstrate that it could attract the interest of both the public and the forest industry. The Congress pushed the movement from an almost exclusive focus on the environmental issues of the effect of forests on climate and the role of deforestation in the creation of desert wastes to one of practical business concerns of forest fire protection, land classification, and forest reserves.

In retrospect, the view of the Quebec and Ottawa valley lumbermen that, if adequate fire protection were given to the forest, regeneration would occur naturally seems somewhat naive. It would have been much more fruitful for Canadian forestry if the environmentalists and the lumber interests could have found more common ground. Only one paper at the Congress discussed how rudimentary silviculture could be used to improve forest production and growth, and so, from another aspect, certainly foresters like Fernow found little to support at the proceedings. Nevertheless, an enduring partnership had been forged—one that is tremendously important to the understanding of public forestry policies in Canada for, as would become obvious over the next decades, it was only when the forest industry, or a substantial part of it, was willing to support conservation measures that progress was made. The alliance between the more traditional environmentalist or preservationist wing and the industry, formed in Montreal, was shaky at best, but it did continue in such mutually advantageous fields as watershed conservation and, until World War I, the environmentalists seemed largely content to let industry's concern over fire protection and forest preservation become the political rallying cry of the movement. These, in turn, fitted easily into the wider interest in resource planning and efficiency in utilization which occupied the North American conservation movement as a public issue after 1900. At first, however, Little and Joly sought more limited gains from the impetus created by the Montreal Congress. From this time on, even though the number varied, there would always be a section of the forest industry in Canada that was helpful and sympathetic to the cause. This support was to be vital to conservation in Canada because it helped ensure its survival in the tough times that lay ahead while ensuring the movement remained relevant to the problems faced by the industry.

From the point of view of its supporters, the immediate success or fail- ure of the Montreal meeting was gauged by governments' responses to the resolutions of the forest fire committee. Little and Joly had been given an initiative, and the question waiting to be answered was what they would do with it. Both were impressive men. Both had come out of the meeting with their reputations enhanced. As Bernhard Fernow noted, he would be sur- prised if "our Canadian friends do not in a short time eclipse their cousins over the line in this field of political economy." The young German was right when he noted that the conservation movement had finally moved into the battleground of politics, government administration, and practical economics.[21]

Once the meeting of the American Forestry Congress was over, William Little added the duties of corresponding secretary for the organization to his already heavy workload as a businessman. The Canadian members of the forest fire committee wanted him to begin lobbying for the adoption of their resolution by writing to the Dominion and provincial administrations of Canada. Quebec was the first to react to the policy proposals circulated by Little. This is not surprising considering that the Congress had met in Montreal and that it had been well attended by many politically important people from that province. In the legislative session of 1883, the province's Conservative government enacted laws that provided for the hiring of for- est rangers to patrol timber limits under the supervision of a special super- intendent. This system was entirely paid for by the limitholders concerned. More important, provincial Commissioner of Crown Lands Dr. W.W. Lynch, who had attended the meeting, was persuaded to establish the nation's first forest reserve. This reserve covered a large area east of the Ottawa river that was drained by many of the river's tributaries. This land was set aside solely for timber production; settlers were not allowed, in the future, to locate lots within its boundaries. Both of these measures were directly related to the resolutions generated by the Congress's forest fire committee.[22]

The lumbermen of Quebec expressed delight with these new government initiatives, attributing them to the direct influence of the Congress. From their point of view, the forest reserve effectively separated the settlers from the loggers. But the setting up of the reserve had a dire political consequence that was not foreseen by those who advocated it and welcomed its establishment. The creation of the reserve and the effective withdrawal of land from settlement incensed the supporters of the colonization movement. In their eyes, the reserve prevented their access to a large area of land suitable for settlement. In actual fact, settlement of such areas was ill-advised as most of the area was within the Canadian Shield. Politically, Lynch's action drew lines of division between the government and one wing of its traditional support, the Ultramontanists or "Castor" group whose members tended to combine French Canadian nationalism with religious conservatism. The Ultramontanists considered the welfare of the *colons* to be more important than that of the dues-paying, but largely English speaking, lumbermen. This division combined with other political events inside and outside of the province and became a factor in the ouster of the provincial Tories from power. One of the symbolic and ideological acts of the Parti National administration that replaced the Tories in 1886 was the cancellation of the forest reserve.[23]

The Ontario government was slower to act than its counterpart in Quebec City, but the measures it enacted were more enduring. The government's first response to the resolution of the Congress was made in 1883 when it hired a forestry publicist, a former journalist, Robert W. Phipps. Phipps filled a newly created position in the bureaucracy: Clerk of Forestry in the Department of Agriculture and the Arts. By implication this recognized the influence and importance of the Fruit Growers Association. The action also showed that the government of Ontario interpreted "forestry" as a term related to the more traditional idea of woodlot management and the reforestation of abandoned farm lands. This interpretation is confirmed by the fact that the Clerk had nothing to do with the office responsible for the disposal of timber limits and the collection of timber dues, which remained in the domain of the Commissioner of Crown Lands.[24] Phipps, conscious that he was the Clerk of Forestry in the Department of Agriculture and the Arts, issued an extensive series of publications discussing, among other things, the settlement and subsequent abandonment of lands unfit for farming and their suitability for reforestation. With reference to the management of the province's extensive forests, conservationists in Ontario would have to wait some years before their government took its first tentative steps in that direction. Phipps was to prove to be the first in a long line of civil servants who laboured under the government's conception that forestry was part and parcel of farm management.

Meaningful action by the Ontario government on the Congress's recommendations had to wait three years. Ontario Commissioner of Crown Lands Timothy Pardee had promised in his report of 1882 that he would give sympathetic consideration to the recommendations of the Congress on their receipt. In spite of this, the reaction of the Liberal government of the province when it heard from William Little was to order that they be studied further. Pardee accomplished this by giving them to a new employee in the Woods and Forests Branch of his department, Aubrey White. White's previous experience as a woods ranger and Crown Land Agent in the

Bracebridge area of the province did not seem to speed up his deliberations materially. The new clerk took his time, and it was not until March, 1885, that he presented his superior with a long memorandum.[25] In spite of this delay, White's proposals went no further than the original recommendations he had received thirty months previously. Essentially, he suggested that rangers be appointed to patrol the districts at risk during the fire season. The rangers would organize fire-fighting efforts and educate the public to the risks of being careless with fire while in the forests. The cost of the program was to be shared between the government and all limitholders. White's report was accepted, the companies were polled to nominate candidates for the positions, and thirty-seven men were hired during the summer of 1885. This legislation served as the basis of fire protection in Ontario for many years.[26]

The Dominion government took the smallest step in the wake of the Montreal Congress. In 1882, Canada had stretched "from sea to sea" for some eleven years. The federal government controlled the land and natural resources in the North-West Territories, including Manitoba and the future provinces of Saskatchewan and Alberta, as well as a strip of land, forty miles wide, following the route of the proposed transcontinental railway through British Columbia. It was probably the largest area of unalienated land controlled by one government on the continent. The Prime Minister of Canada, Sir John A. Macdonald, had received the petition from William Little in February, 1883, just before the speech from the throne opening the first session of the fifth Parliament. Macdonald was acutely conscious of the depletion of timber supplies in the Ottawa valley, but, since the natural resources in that area were under provincial jurisdiction, he was limited to action in the Canadian west.[27]

For this reason, while the provincial governments of Ontario and Quebec reacted to William Little's memorandum with increased awareness of the risk of forest fires to standing licenced timber, Macdonald made a different interpretation. Like the earlier government of Reform Prime Minister Alexander Mackenzie, which had initiated an early but ineffective tree-planting programme in 1876, he was worried that the lack of trees on the prairies was inhibiting their settlement. Instead of opting for legislation based on the recommendations from the Congress, Macdonald decided to initiate a study of the problem as he saw it. In a memorandum sent to the Privy Council in February, 1883, he noted that the Congress had agreed it was important, for the welfare of the Dominion, that steps be taken "not only for the protection of present forests but also for the planting of forest trees in an extensive area." In order to further this "desirable end," the memorandum recommended that "a competent person be employed to inquire into and report upon the whole subject," the desired result being concerted action on the part of both the Dominion and provincial governments. The memorandum ended by recommending Joseph H. Morgan of Anderdon, Ontario, for the job.[28]

The memorandum is significant because it reveals much about attitudes toward conservation within the Dominion government at the time. In terms of control over logging practices and the lumbermen, clearly the federal government was not prepared to go any further than had the provincial governments. This was a policy that was followed until control over natural resources was turned over to the provinces concerned in the 1930s. At the time of the memorandum, and until the turn of the century, the barrenness of Canada's prairies was a continuous worry to federal politicians who were convinced that this was the reason why they were not being settled.[29] At the root of this concern was that a major portion of the income of the Canadian Pacific Railway was supposed to come from servicing settlements along its right-of-way through the prairies. Nominally a private company completely independent of government, the Canadian Pacific Railway had actually been built with the aid of heavy cash subsidies as well as immense land grants from the federal government. In addition, there were close links between the management of the company and the leaders of both political parties in Ottawa. The railway thus had no difficulty in ensuring that its concern over a lack of customers on the long haul from Manitoba to British Columbia was shared with the Dominion government of the day.

This concern about settlers restricted the Dominion government's response to the resolution from the American Forestry Congress in a number of ways. In the lands of the Dominion-owned Railway Belt of British Columbia there was already a conflict between settlers and lumbermen. If reserves were created or if restrictions were placed on burning brush, the settlers would be angered, and their conflict with lumbermen would be intensified. Moreover, in 1882, the government had created the Timber, Mineral and Grazing Lands Office in the Department of the Interior. This office, copying the policy of Ontario, had set up a system of leased timber berths that required bids on top of "upset prices" as well as the payment of royalties for the volume of timber cut.[30] The office also supervised the leases and permits for the exploitation of other resources on federal lands in western Canada. The few small sawmills in Manitoba, British Columbia, and western Alberta already resented having to pay for logs which previously they had obtained for free, and they would accept very little additional regulation. In this respect, the appointment of Morgan in late February, 1883, was, in the opinion of the Prime Minister, exactly the right kind of political response. It had several precedents, and its objectives were limited so they would not conflict with established interest groups.

The criterion for choosing Morgan for the task of producing a report was simply that he was a faithful Tory. But, even though the Congress and the ideals of the conservation movement were completely new to him, he embarked on his task with enthusiasm. He read widely and made an exploratory trip to the West. In March, 1884, he presented Macdonald with a report he described as "preliminary," suggesting that a tree-planting programme on the prairies was feasible and desirable.[31] Government apathy toward the West, however, prevented Morgan's plans from being followed. Finally, in the spring and summer of 1885, the North-West Rebellion led by Louis Riel intervened, and Morgan's work lay forgotten.

After the rebellion had been put down and the railway had been completed to the Pacific in 1886, the issues investigated by Morgan surfaced once again. The need for prairie settlement was considered to be even more pressing, and Macdonald therefore turned once more to Morgan. In July, 1887, an Order in Council gave him the title of Forestry Commissioner, and he received virtually the same instructions that he had received four years earlier. In addition, he was to consider ways of "preserving and protecting the forests of the Dominion." It was a hint that for the first time the federal government was considering the issue in somewhat wider terms. Morgan presented yet another positive report on tree planting and on the need to protect the headwaters of rivers in the Rockies through fire prevention and forest reservation. On the strength of this, his appointment was continued through 1889. Then, in the spring of 1890, he once more made his way westward and was in northern Saskatchewan in July when he was informed that his services had been terminated! By bureaucratic oversight or, more likely due to friction between Morgan and his superior, Deputy Minister of the Department of the Interior A.M. Burgess,[32] funds for Morgan's work had been omitted from the department's estimates for the year. Disconsolate, Morgan paid his own expenses for his trip home to Amherstburg, Ontario. That he then had to spend several years petitioning the government for reimbursement for these expenses is a comment on the amount of real interest there was in his activities.[33]

The only result of Morgan's efforts, other than giving moral support to western tree plantings, was one change in the Dominion Lands Act. Passed in 1884, this amendment provided for the "preservation of forest trees on crests and slopes of the Rocky Mountains, and the proper maintenance, throughout the year, of the volume of water in the rivers and streams" having the slopes as their sources. This amendment deserves some discussion because effectively it was the Dominion government's first step toward the creation of the forest reserve system that, in turn, led to the first flowering of forestry in Canada. The amendment was a direct result of Macdonald's desire to do everything possible to encourage the settlement of the western lands. Southern Alberta and Saskatchewan had a very dry climate. In spite of this, the land appeared suitable for ranching and some agriculture as long as water supplies were maintained. A convenient source of water were the rivers and streams of the eastern slopes of the Rocky Mountains. The government was warned that the forests played an important role in the storage of water. Forest preservation thus figured prominently in plans for the development of these semiarid lands.[34] From this combination of forest preservation and land and general watershed conservation, federal forest policy was to grow.

Unfortunately, once these amendments to the Dominion Lands Act were in place, federal policy toward its forests languished. It was another decade before any number of reserves were named, and it took a change of governing party before anything significant was done to administer them. The boundaries of the initial Rocky Mountain reserve were established, on paper, and adjacent treed areas were added to it. The responsibility for the area was given to the Timber, Mineral and Grazing Lands Office, which was known by the semiofficial sobriquet "Timber and Grazing Branch." The Branch had one problem with the reserves—and this was that it had already leased considerable areas inside their boundaries. The leases for these timber berths were renewable annually in perpetuity as long as the lessor paid the ground rents and stumpage. Beyond ensuring that no further timber berths were let inside the boundaries of the reserved areas and some token attempts . . . to warn operators about the danger of fires, the Branch did absolutely nothing with the areas. It did not even try to halt the inevitable trespassing by the operators, the illegal squatting by settlers, or the wildfires that swept across the hills. Effectively, the government of Canada had hardly paid lipservice to the ideals of the early forest conservation movement.

Of the Dominion and six provincial governments governing in Canada in the last decades of the nineteenth century, only Ontario and Quebec had actively responded to the requests of the American Forestry Congress meeting of 1882. The gains in Quebec unfortunately did not last long. The Conservative party in that province retained power until the furor following the trial and execution of Louis Riel in 1885 split the party. In the provincial election of October, 1886, Honoré Mercier led the newly formed Parti National to power. The lumbermen of Quebec now found themselves with a government openly sympathetic to the emotional issues then sweeping through the province. In particular, this included fullhearted support of the colonization movement and its desire to have access to all of the unalienated lands of Quebec. Mercier championed the *colons'* cause and, after having the case of those on the forest reserve lands heard before the full Cabinet in early 1887, set out a policy for abolishing the provincial forest reserves. Mercier kept this promise in 1888, although he allowed the legislation establishing the fire patrols to stand and settled licence tenures for a period up to 1900.

The case prompting the Premier's action was an emotional battle in court between the Gilmour Lumber Company and a group of *colons* led by the activist priest Father Charles Paradis. The settlers, located in the Gatineau river valley, had challenged the action of the company when it had seized logs they had cut on their lots located within the boundaries of the forest reserve and began to harvest all standing timber as well. The legal case was fought, with the active support of the provincial government, all the way to Britain's Judicial Committee of the Privy Council, the highest court of appeal in the Empire. In 1889, this body upheld the case for the settlers.[35]

The defeat in Quebec coincided with difficult times for the Canadian lumber industry as a whole. During the late 1880s and early 1890s, the economic situation was depressed. The impetus of the conservation movement lay dormant as lumbermen sought to hedge against low profit margins by cutting costs and high-grading the remaining forests. Careless operating practices were compounded by forest fires. The effect of these and overcutting on the accessible forest of eastern Canada became more and more noticeable as cut-overs failed to regenerate in a satisfactory manner and soil erosion and flooding became rife. For all those who had participated in the Montreal Congress there came the increasing realization that there were real limits to the size of the exploitable forest. The Canadian leaders of the

Congress pointed to these effects and advocated ways to conserve the remaining forest but generally found politicians of all persuasions and at all levels of government uninterested in their agenda.

The one bright spot during this period was the establishment of Algonquin National Park by the government of Ontario. First proposed in 1885 and finally created in 1893, the rationale behind the park was to remove a large area of white pine forest from the threat of settlement. At the same time, the forest cover of the watersheds of several major tributaries of the Ottawa as well as Muskoka area rivers would be protected. A feature of the act setting aside the park was that the berths leased by the lumber companies were allowed to remain. Public opinion was brought to the side of the park, which was really a forest reserve, by some adroit publicity that touted it as a nature sanctuary and recreation area. In retrospect, the only people to suffer from the creation of Algonquin Park were a few trappers and pseudosettlers since the land was undeniably unsuitable for agricultural development. Many of these individuals quickly found lucrative employment as fishing and canoe trip guides for the groups of tourists who soon invaded the area.[36] The establishment of Algonquin National Park was emulated two years later by Quebec, when two more "national" parks, Laurentides and Mont Tremblant, were founded, shutting extensive areas off from settlement, setting up game preserves, and, like Algonquin, leaving the timber licences in place.[37]

By the 1890s, however, the preservationist's definition of a park was well understood in North America, and the dual role for the three national parks created by the governments of Ontario and Quebec was viewed with some scepticism. The scepticism grew to open criticism as large numbers of tourists overcame the isolation of the areas and saw for themselves the beauty of the forest and the horror of logging methods: This brought a new dimension to the forest conservation movement in Canada adding a stronger preservationist wing based largely in the rising educated urban elite of the major cities of the east. As the new century approached, pressure from this group resulted in a political reorientation in Ontario, and the conservation movement found itself once more with political power culminating in the founding of the Canadian Forestry Association and the hiring of professional foresters by various jurisdictions.

In retrospect, the fifteen years following the meeting of the American Forestry Congress in Montreal in August, 1882, were mixed ones for the nascent movement. On the negative side was the fact the movement showed it was affected by the state of the economy. When economic times were difficult, the forest industry lost interest in implementing conservation measures, concentrating instead on cutting operating costs. Down to the present, this attitude has prevailed with short-term economies winning over more risky and longer term advantages. In a way, it is as if a predominant part of the industry has never abandoned the nineteenth-century notion of the limitless forest. The loss of the nation's first forest reserve was also a setback because it demonstrated that conservation could be usurped by populist causes. That Ontario chose to treat conservation more as a publicity venture rather than implement new timber-management policies was also to cause difficulties in the future. By doing this, the government showed it considered that its definition of forestry had little to do with forest management in direct contrast to then already well-established European practice. It was a policy emulated many times over in Canada in following years.

On the positive side, the movement captured the attention and sympathy of many influential people, including Henri Joly, who, for the rest of his life, was to play a role of quiet leadership and provide an example of forest management on his estate that was effective precisely because it was not public. The years also witnessed the acceptance by two provinces of the recommendations of the forest fire committee of the Congress and a minimal start on a forestry policy by the Dominion government. In fact, it can be argued that the conservation movement achieved a success just by staying alive in the difficult years of the depression of the early 1890s. Some long-term accomplishments during this difficult period also can be identified. For instance, after Ontario created Algonquin National Park, it was much more difficult for governments to create a reserve restricted to the exploitive activities of one industrial group; the interests of the public had to be taken into consideration. From this period forward, forest reserves would be created at both the federal and provincial levels in Canada. Their intent would be to promote scientific forest management, and often attached to this activity, to realize such other goals as protection of game, water control, preservation of natural beauty, and promotion of the area for recreational purposes, all of which went beyond simple forest industry demands. Once the public saw logging at first hand, it lost some of its sentimental aura, and conservationists found themselves supported by a growing and diverse group stretching from outright environmental preservationists to modern businessmen concerned with efficient resource development. After the Congress, forest conservation had moved from being the interest of a few individuals into the storm and fury of politics and economics. The next fifteen years saw it evolve into a progressive reform movement that was to be actively courted by the major players on Canada's political scene.

NOTES

1. The origins of the early conservation movement are discussed in a number of works, notably: H. Cheer, ed., *Origins of American Conservation* (New York, 1966); Samuel P. Hays, *Conservation and the Gospel of Efficiency* (Cambridge, Mass., 1959); Roderick Nash, *Wilderness and the American Mind* (New Haven and London, 1967); John R. Ross, "Man over Nature: Origins of the Conservation Movement," *American Studies* 16, 1 (Spring 1975): 49–60. George Marsh is best recorded in D. Lowenthal, *George Perkins Marsh:* *Versatile Vermonter* (New York: 1958). The Canadian movement is mentioned in R.S. Lambert with Paul Pross, *Renewing Nature's Wealth* (Toronto, 1967), pp. 162 and 167. Interesting and controversial commentaries can be found in Gabriel Kolko, *The Triumph of Conservatism* (New York, 1963) and Anthony Scott, *Natural Resources: The Economics of Conservation* (Toronto, 1955 and Ottawa, 1983).

2. The urban and preservationist wing of the early Canadian conservation

movement is analyzed to some extent in H.V. Nelles, *Politics of Development* (Toronto, 1974), pp. 184–214, and Janet Foster, *Working for Wildlife: The Beginning of Preservation in Canada* (Toronto, 1978), chap. 3. The lumbermen's influence on the conservation movement is discussed in Peter Gillis, "The Ottawa Lumber Barons and the Conservation Movement, 1880–1914," *Journal of Canadian Studies* (February 1974): 14–31.

3. Lambert with Pross, *Renewing*, p. 162.

4. Ontario, Department of Agriculture and Arts, "Report of the Fruit Growers' Association of Ontario," *Annual Report, 1878–1883*, A.D.

5. See Gillis, "Ottawa Lumber Barons."

6. Little's career is discussed by P. Gillis, "James Little," *Dictionary of Canadian Biography*, vol. XI (Toronto and Quebec City, 1982), pp. 521–522, and Donald Mackay, *Heritage Lost: The Crisis in Canada's Forests* (Toronto, 1985), pp. 29–36.

7. James Little, *The Lumber Trade in the Ottawa Valley*, 3rd ed. (Ottawa, 1872). James Little, *The Timber Supply Question of the Dominion of Canada and the United States of America* (Montreal, 1876).

8. The Cincinnati meeting is discussed in Lambert with Pross, *Renewing*, pp. 162–163; Mackay, *Heritage Lost*, pp. 29–31; and, more fully, A.D. Rodgers, *Bernhard Eduard Fernow* (Princeton, 1950), pp. 31, 38–39.

9. Ibid.

10. Rogers, *Fernow*, pp. 38–39.

11. American Forestry Congress, Proceedings of the American Forestry Congress at its Sessions held at Cincinnati, Ohio, April 1882 and Montreal, Canada, August 1882 (Washington, D.C., 1883).

12. P. Gillis, "Ottawa Lumber Barons," p. 19; D. McCalla, "The Rise of Forestry" (unpublished research manuscript, Ontario Department of Lands and Forests, 1966), pp. 1–4; PAC, MG28 III 26, Bronsons and Weston Company Records, E.H. Bronson to Peter White, M.P., 21 June 1882.

13. Bruce W. Hodgins, Jamie Benidickson, and Peter Gillis, "The Ontario and Quebec Experiments in Forest Reserves, 1883–1930," *Journal of Forest History* 26, 1 (January 1982): 20–23. Hon. Ruggles Church, *Report of Argument Submitted to the Honourable the Executive Council for the Province of Quebec On Presentation of a Memorial Respecting the Vested Rights of Limitholders In Their Limits, March 16th 1880*. The contract issue was multidimensional and complex. Besides the question of whether or not stumpage and ground rents should be fixed for the life of any future contract issued by the Quebec government, there was a major problem over the terms of renewal. Contracts were nominally renewable annually for a stated number of years. Quebec lumbermen expected that, on expiry, a new contract would be issued to them for their limits following a mutual agreement over terms. Some politicians, on the other hand, considered the government had the right and duty to place the limit up for auction with open bids once the contract had expired. In contrast, timber berths in Ontario at this time were leased for as long as the operator worked them and were returned to the Crown or sold to other operators to rework for a different product until they were completely cut out.

14. H.G. Joly is a Canadian who has too long been neglected by biographers considering the excellence of his family papers (PAC, MG 27 II C2 M794). Some published sources include: J.K. Johnson, ed., *The Canadian Directory of Parliament* (Ottawa, 1968), p. 295; Brian Young, "Federalism in Quebec: The First Years after Confederation," in Bruce W. Hodgins, D. Wright and W.H. Heick, eds., *Federalism in Canada and Australia: The Early Years* (Waterloo, 1978), pp. 97–108; Mason Wade, *The French Canadians*, vol. 1 (Toronto, 1968), pp. 331–392.

15. P. Gillis, "Ottawa Lumber Barons," p. 20; and *Canadian Parliamentary Companion* (1887), p. 234.

16. Ontario Legislature, "Report of the Delegation appointed to Attend the American Forestry Congress Held in Montreal, Province of Quebec," *Sessional Paper No. 3* (1883), pp. 21–37.

17. Ibid.; Rodgers, *Fernow*; PAC, RG15 vol. 298, file 6241; *Montreal Gazette* 23 August 1882, p. 5.

18. Ibid.; and Ontario Legislature, "Report," pp. 34–36. See editions of *The Montreal Herald*, 21 August 1882 to 30 August 1882, and *Montreal Gazette*, 21 August 1882 to 23 August 1882.

19. Ibid.

20. Ibid.; Rodgers, *Fernow*, p. 39.

21. Rodgers, *Fernow*, p. 29.

22. PAC, MG28 IÏI 26, vol. 103, Bronsons and Weston Company to W.W. Lynch, Quebec Commissioner of Crown Lands; P. Gillis, "Ottawa Lumber Barons," p. 20; Province of Quebec, Legislature, *Sessional Paper No. 4* (1883–1884), p. viii; Bruce W. Hodgins, *Paradis of Temagami* (Cobalt, Ontario, 1976), pp. 13–24.

23. Quebec's colonization movement was made up of societies that were themselves the outgrowth of agricultural clubs devoted to farming improvement and dating from around 1869–70. Backed by some members of the clergy, the societies encouraged the movement of colonists into areas of Quebec until then untouched by settlement. This was promoted as an alternative to emigration to the northeastern United States, as a lure to those who had already left, as a means of extending French-Canadian influence northward and westward across northern Ontario and into Manitoba, and as a means of perpetuating the agrarian roots of French-Canadian culture and thus ensuring its survival. The movement started to settle people in the area of the Laurentian mountains from about 1875 on. Many of the lots chosen by the settlers of the northern forest were located on land already leased to lumbermen. The *colons*, under Quebec law, had the right to cut and sell the timber on this land as long as they paid Crown dues on the volume. Conflict with the limitholder resulted as soon as the settlers cleared land not only for the obvious reason of ownership of the logs, but also because the settlers were a source of wildfires. *Colons* habitually piled and burnt their brush and slash with little concern to the safety of the surrounding forest. The forest fires that resulted often got out of control, financially hurting the lumbermen. Due to these problems, at the time of the Montreal meeting, the Quebec lumbermen were already promoting the cause of forest reserves and land classification systems as well as organization of fire prevention and suppression efforts. For a summary of the motivations behind this movement, see: Jack Little, "La Patrie: Quebec's Repatriation Colony, 1875–1880," *Historical Papers* (Ottawa, 1977), pp. 66–85; G. Vattier, *Esquisse Historique de la Colonisation de la Province de Québec* (Paris, 1928).

24. Lambert with Pross, *Renewing*, pp. 164–165.

25. Ibid.

26. Ibid., p. 163; and Gillis, "Ottawa Lumber Barons," p. 20.

27. Ibid.; and PAC, RG15, Department of the Interior, vol. 298, file 62441.

28. Ibid.

29. PAC, RG15, Department of the Interior, vol. 317, file 72369. The treelessness of the prairies had worried successive Dominion governments since at least 1871. In this year, Great Britain's west coast colony of British Columbia had joined the Canadian Confederation. One of the terms of the union was that the Dominion government would guarantee the construction of a transcontinental railway. Settlement of the prairies would speed this construction as

well as lower its cost. To encourage settlement, the Liberal government of Alexander Mackenzie established a forestation program in 1876. Western settlers could file for a "Forest Tree Culture Claim" and obtain an extra 160 acres of land as long as they planted a proportion of their total holding with trees. Many settlers took advantage of this program and planted nursery stock obtained from Ontario only to see it die of winter-kill. By the mid-1880s, the word was rapidly spreading that trees could not be grown on the prairies. Farmers who tried soon came to be considered faddists and, according to a later report, were subjected to "local ridicule." Imported stock was used not only because Ontario was the only nearby source of young trees, but also settlers keen on tree planting generally came from eastern Canada or western Europe and looked to familiar trees for solace in their new land. See Norman M. Ross, *The Tree-Planting Division: Its History and Work*, Canada, Department of the Interior, Forestry Branch, 1923; and Peter Murphy, *History of Forest and Prairie Fire Control Policy in Alberta* (Edmonton, 1985), pp. 70–71. During speeches in the House of Commons, Macdonald referred to European experiments with tree nurseries as an example to be investigated for the west.

30. PAC, RG2, Records of the Privy Council, Order in Council no. 640, 23 May 1882. The head of the Branch was given the title "Chief Clerk." This title was retained until the Branch was disbanded in 1935. During all these years, the Branch successfully avoided employing pro-

fessional foresters to manage the lands it was responsible for. In fact, college graduates were a rarity among its employees, PAC, RG15, vol. 15, book 9, pp. 195–199, Saskatchewan and Alberta Resources Commission, memo: George W. Payton to J. Lorne Turner, 9 March 1934.

31. PAC, RG15, file 62441.

32. Ibid.; and Murphy, *Prairie Fire Control*, pp. 82–83. Burgess was convinced that Morgan's work was properly the responsibility of the Department of Agriculture and may also have been apprehensive over Forestry recommendations that would expose Tory patronage activities in giving away a large number of (up to 50) timber berths in western Canada without fees being charged.

33. PAC, RG15, vol. 311, file 69113.

34. Murphy, *Prairie Fire Control*, p. 132; PAC, RG15, vol. 311, file 69113 and vol. 630, file 235667, pt.2; Canada, *Statutes* 47 Vict, cap 25 and Senate, *Debates* (28 March 1884), pp. 358–364.

35. These events are recorded in Hodgins, *Paradis*, pp. 13–24. See Province of Quebec, "An Act Respecting Public Lands," *Statutes* (1887), pp. 51–52 Vict, cap 15.

36. Lambert with Pross, *Renewing*, pp. 165–168; and P. Gillis, "Ottawa Lumber Barons," p. 21.

37. Province of Quebec, *Statutes* (1894), 58 Vict, cap 22 and cap 23. One reason for establishing northern parks in Quebec was to try to save the caribou from extinction.

CONSERVATION PLANNING AND URBAN PLANNING: THE CANADIAN COMMISSION OF CONSERVATION IN HISTORICAL PERSPECTIVE ⬦

ALAN F.J. ARTIBISE
GILBERT A. STELTER

o

Conservation planning in Canada began on an organized basis shortly before World War I when a Commission of Conservation was established. Prior to this time, the predominant attitude in Canada in regard to resources was "the doctrine of usefulness," an attitude that had at its centre the rapid exploitation of the country's resources in the interests of creating a national economy in the recently confederated nation.[1] The establishment of the Commission of Conservation signalled the beginning of the end of unchecked and unplanned development. Between its establishment in 1909 and its dissolution in 1921, the Commission of Conservation was the main focus of Canadian planning activity. The termination of the Commission marked the onset of a long period of inactivity in both the conservation and urban planning fields; with only a few exceptions, major new initiatives were not taken in either area until near the end of World War II.

Significantly, during its existence, the Commission of Conservation took as its mandate the widest possible view of planning. Rather than limiting its purview to natural resources, the Commission broadened it in such a way that its work entered all areas of the human environment, including, most notably, the urban environment. The reason for this close interrela-

---

⬦ Roger Kain, ed., *Planning for Conservation* (New York: St. Martin's Press, 1981), 17–36.

tionship between urban and conservation planning was the particular pattern of Canadian development. The closing years of the nineteenth century had witnessed the rapid physical expansion of the country and the massive exploitation of natural resources. This expansion was aided by and reflected in the growth of Canadian urban centres. By the early 1900s, there was increasing concern in the country about the wasteful and destructive use of resources and the growing "evils" of urbanization. Both required attention and both received it from the Commission of Conservation, which combined conservation and urban planning in a way never again duplicated by any government or private agency.

PLANNING IN CANADA TO CIRCA 1900

Conservation planning and urban planning both passed through distinct phases prior to the establishment of the Conservation Commission in 1909. In terms of conservation planning, the period leading up to the early 1900s was characterized by development and exploitation based upon the concept of a relatively inexhaustible supply of resources. Whether the resource was fur, fish, timber, or land, the object of both government and private enterprise was unchecked use. There was, in short, no policy of conservation planning. Resources were to be utilized to promote rapid and sustained growth and to bolster the development of the country. That such growth and development would be prodigal and even wasteful of resources, if perceived at all, was to be regretted as an unfortunate byproduct of an essentially desirable process.[2] In contrast, urban planning passed through two phases prior to 1900. In an initial phase, imperial officials determined the form of colonial towns. Central direction was evident in the planning of early Louisbourg, Halifax, and Toronto. Even some commercial enterprises were planned communities, as in the case of the Canada Company towns of Guelph and Goderich.[3] A second phase was represented by the Victorian era, when *laissez-faire* thinking dominated the question of who should make the decisions which would shape urban communities. It would be a mistake, however, to assume that planning did not take place during this period. Rather, planning was carried out at a private level without regulation by municipal or provincial government. Many new towns founded by corporations in the late nineteenth century were built on the basis of plans drawn up by company officials, including Sudbury, Ontario, by the Canadian Pacific Railway Company, and Nanaimo, British Columbia, by coal barons in London.[4] In the larger cities, however, the results of the private decisions of thousands of individuals and corporations usually led to fragmented patterns of development.[5]

By 1900, then, both conservation and urban planning were poorly developed. The policies and programmes of various governments and of private individuals or corporations were unrelated and resource and urban development were largely unchecked. In the first decade of the twentieth century, however, both areas of planning underwent a dramatic transformation.

URBAN GROWTH AND CITY PLANNING

The surge of interest in both conservation and urban planning that occurred in the decades of the 1890s and the 1900s was a response to the innumerable problems that accompanied the unregulated development of the Victorian period. These problems became more acute and apparent because of rapid urban growth. Between 1881 and 1921, the proportion of Canadians living in urban places doubled from about twenty-five percent to almost fifty percent of the total population. The largest cities were the main recipients of this growth. In the forty years after 1881, Montreal grew by four and a half times to a total of 618 506, and Toronto by six times to 521 893. Even more dramatic was the sudden emergence of Winnipeg and Vancouver in the first decade of the twentieth century during which Winnipeg's size increased by more than three times and Vancouver's by almost four.[6] Several factors contributed to this rapid population growth. One was the enlargement of boundaries. In Toronto, a series of annexations took place in the 1880s, which added Yorkville, Rosedale, the Annex, and several other outlying areas to the city. Montreal also annexed several suburbs, including Hochelaga in the 1880s, and incorporated nine more municipalities before 1919. An orgy of suburban subdivision in every major city placed enormous financial and physical strain on the central city's ability to supply services. A second factor was migration to the cities from other Canadian urban centres, from rural areas, and particularly from abroad. Foreign immigration significantly altered the racial composition of every major city, but especially of places such as Winnipeg where the foreign-born constituted 55.9 percent of the population by 1911. In the eyes of many contemporary observers, rapid urban growth was creating problems of the kind usually found in European cities, for big cities seemed to breed disease, poverty, and crime. Slums had become more visible, and much of the working class was not properly housed.[7]

By 1900, "it was widely accepted that urban growth posed a serious menace to the future of the nation."[8] A host of reformers including newspapermen, politicians, businessmen, and academics cast about for solutions to the city's ills. Virtually no Canadian institution escaped the impact of these changes. Churches, mourning the passing of rural Canada, responded to the problems of urbanization with the formation of such organizations as the Social Service Council. Businessmen like Herbert Ames and Morley Wickett formed groups dedicated to putting the "machine" in honest hands.[9]

In terms of city planning, several concepts were developed, based on American and British experience. The most sweeping approach was the City Beautiful movement, which was exemplified in the Chicago Exposition in 1893, but whose roots went back at least to baroque planning. Supporters of this approach visualized a civic landscape of monumental public buildings, great diagonal boulevards, squares, and parks, and especially a magnificently designed civic centre. It was felt that these measures would lead to a miraculous disappearance of the pressing urban problems of slums, poverty and poor health. Another approach to urban planning was the

Garden City or New Town movement, which originated about the same time. It was led by a British planner, Ebenezer Howard, who advocated a retreat from big-city life to self-sufficient small towns surrounded by a green belt, with planned preserves for residential, cultural, commercial, and industrial uses. These planned communities were originally proposed by Howard for reasons of health and social advantage; he reacted against the overcrowded conditions of the industrial towns in Britain and advocated the growth of new self-contained settlements in the countryside where housing, jobs, and all the other necessities would be provided.

The Garden City approach to urban planning differed from the City Beautiful approach on the important question of the purpose of planning. While the City Beautiful advocates tended to emphasize urban aesthetics, Garden City planners stressed the health and housing of the residents. In several important respects, however, these two approaches had much in common. In both, planners would have a great deal of power (presumably with the support of government officials) in changing the existing urban structure or planning completely new towns. They both also stressed the segregation and sorting out of various urban functions—residential, commercial, industrial, and institutional. These common features emerged, as Jane Jacobs has pointed out, and became the planning orthodoxy in North America.[10]

During the first thirty years of the twentieth century, Canadians experimented with a variety of these planning approaches. The emphasis shifted successively from aesthetics and the large-scale plan to the regulation of suburban expansion, to providing housing for workers, to zoning in order to segregate functions and protect property values. Some of these approaches were advocated or practised at the same time as others, but a rough periodization based on the dominating theme in a particular time period is possible. From the 1890s to the beginning of World War I, the vision of the City Beautiful was in force. The professionals in town planning—architects, engineers, and surveyors—dreamed of coherent, unified streetscapes, of variations in street patterns, and of the grandeur of a city centre. Grandiose plans were drawn up for several cities, including Toronto in 1905 and 1909, Montreal in 1906, Winnipeg in 1913, Calgary in 1914, and Ottawa and Hull in 1915. Little came of these plans, usually because the public was horrified by the enormous costs involved in putting them into practice. By 1914, planners generally were denouncing the entire approach, arguing that beauty and aesthetics were not the top priority in solving urban problems.[11]

The City Beautiful idea was far from dead, however. The 1929 Bartholomew Plan for Vancouver incorporated some of its basic principles and several other examples can be cited.[12] Perhaps the most spectacular adoption of the concept in a Canadian city took place late in the 1930s in Prime Minister W.L. Mackenzie King's supervision of the redevelopment of Ottawa as federal capital. King personally hired a French planner, Jacques Gréber, whose views coincided with his own on introducing a sense of grandeur into Ottawa. Whether the Gréber Plan succeeded in this respect is debatable, but it certainly met Mackenzie King's needs. For example, after getting general agreement on the location of the War Memorial monument, King recorded in his diary: "I at once saw that I had my Champs Elysées, Arc de Triomphe and Place de la Concorde all at a single stroke."[13]

While the City Beautiful approach remained in existence, Garden City planning dominated the thinking of the professional planners and the public from 1914 to the mid-1920s.[14] The impact of the British New Towns movement in Canada was considerable. The diffusion of New Town planning principles and ideology into the Canadian setting involved a variety of channels, including the official influences of the Governors-General of Canada, notably Sir A.H.G. Grey, the Duke of Connaught and the Duke of Devonshire, and the writings of W.L. Mackenzie King.[15] But it was the Commission of Conservation and the work of its town planning adviser, Thomas Adams, that were the most important influences. Indeed, largely as a result of the work of the Commission, the concepts of resource conservation and urban planning were locked firmly together.

THE ESTABLISHMENT OF THE COMMISSION OF CONSERVATION

The Commission of Conservation was established as an advisory body to the Government of Canada in 1909, but its origins went back several years. The conservation movement in Canada, like its counterparts in the United States, had its birth in the 1890s. Early achievements of the movement included the new profession of forestry and the establishment of a few areas as parks for recreational uses.[16] But if there is a single event and date when the concern for conservation planning can be said to have been born in Canada, it was at the first Canadian Forestry Convention in 1906. This conference, called by Prime Minister Wilfrid Laurier, had as its guest speaker Gifford Pinchot, the apostle of conservation and scientific management in the United States.[17] The main concern of the delegates was with forestry, but the area of forest practices and management was sufficiently broad to lead to frequent discussion of general natural resource issues. The convention also led to regular annual meetings of the Canadian Forestry Association and these meetings were influential in focusing the attention of the Canadian government upon conservation issues at a time when the conservation movement was well underway in the United States. Most important, however, was the fact that the events of 1906 led directly to the sending of a Canadian delegation to the North American Conservation Conference, assembled at the call of President T. Roosevelt in February 1909. Delegates to the conference drew up a Declaration of Principles covering a wide range of natural resources, including forests, waters, land, minerals, and wildlife. Also included among the points in the Declaration was a call for each participating country to establish a commission of conservation.[18]

The Canadian government accepted this idea and in the spring of 1909 Prime Minister Laurier introduced in Parliament an Act to Establish a

Commission for the Conservation of Natural Resources. The Act provided for the creation of a body on which would sit *ex officio* the federal ministers of the agriculture, interior and mines departments and the members of each provincial government responsible for natural resources. There was also a third group of members that was to include at least one university professor from each province. The Commission was to meet once a year and report to the Governor-General-in-Council. The scope of the Commission was to be all questions related to the conservation and better utilization of the natural resources of Canada.[19]

From the outset, the Commission of Conservation was a unique body. It was not a part of the normal governmental administration of the federal government but was intended to be a completely non-partisan body with advisory and consultative powers; it had no administrative or executive powers.[20] In order to facilitate the immense task of gathering information on the natural resources of Canada and of advancing a sound policy for their development, the Commission's first chairman, Clifford Sifton, suggested that the thirty-two members be divided into a number of working committees.[21] Committees were established for each of the major resource areas—lands, forestry, fisheries, game and fur-bearing animals, public health, waters and water powers, and minerals. Another committee, publicity and cooperating organizations, was responsible for publicizing the Commission's activities and organizing public support for the conservation movement. Each year, the committees convened to present a summary of the year's work and to determine the topics of research for the coming year.

The work of the Commission in the twelve years of its existence was considerable and ranged over a wide field of subject matter. Valuable research work was done in each of the main committees and the Commission soon became a major research organization. It published almost 200 papers and studies.[22] Many of these studies were highly technical documents useful only to those closely associated with the subject area, such as *The Canadian Oyster, Animal Sanctuaries in Labrador, Fur Farming in Canada, Altitudes in Canada, Conservation of Coal in Canada, The Prevention of the Pollution of Canadian Surface Waters,* and *Forest Protection in Canada.* Other publications were much less technical and were designed to promote public interest. An example of these less technical works was the regularly published journal *Conservation of Life,* issued under the Commission's direction from August 1914. It contained articles of interest to those concerned with public health under such titles as "Disinfection of Shaving Brushes," "National Committee for Combatting Venereal Disease," and "Maternal Nursing of Children." As well, the Commission published annual reports from 1910 to 1919.[23]

In so wide a range of activities, the Commission was able to record a number of accomplishments. It was responsible for water power inventories; a more consolidated federal health service; the fostering of national parks and game preserves; the encouragement of agricultural and technical education; the development of safer practices in mining and the utilization of western coal; the production of studies of mineral and energy resources; the reduction of patronage in the granting of forest licences; and many other related activities.[24] Of special importance, however, was the Commission's committee on public health for it was this committee which forged a link between conservation and urban planning.

THE COMMITTEE OF HEALTH AND THE INFLUENCE OF THOMAS ADAMS

The Committee of Health had been established by the Conservation Commission to undertake an investigation of all matters of public health and its very existence indicated that the body was concerned with the conservation of both the physical and social resources of Canada. Indeed, the health committee soon expanded its role to include broad issues such as town planning. This wide-ranging concern for environmental health grew out of the interests of one of the first specialists appointed by the Commission, Charles Hodgetts. Hodgetts, a former Medical Health Officer in Ontario, joined the Commission in 1909 and until he left in 1915 was able to arouse support and recognition for the need to improve the urban environment. His view was that town planning was an inevitable part of the concern for better health standards. In 1911, for example, Hodgetts stated:

> I would say no government can justify its existence unless it carefully considers this important question [of town planning] and places upon the statute book a law with ample and adequate regulation for dealing with unsanitary houses of all classes in the community and for conferring power on the city, town, or village municipality whereby they may not only control, but in a measure direct, town and suburban planning.[25]

The concern of the Standing Committee on Public Health with urban planning was strengthened considerably when Thomas Adams was invited to join the Commission as Advisor on Town Planning in 1914. The invitation was apparently fostered by Adams' impressive performance at a National Planning Conference held in Philadelphia in 1911. Adams was a noted British planner who had early become acquainted with Patrick Geddes, Ebenezer Howard, and the Garden City movement. In 1900 he had become Secretary of the First Garden City Company at Letchworth and, in 1906, a town planning consultant. He was one of the founders of the British Town Planning Institute and had a solid reputation as a speaker and facilitator. At the time Adams joined the Canadian Commission of Conservation he was serving as an Inspector of the Local Government Board which was responsible for the administration of the British planning act passed in 1909.[26]

Together, the influence of Hodgetts and Adams was such that the Commission of Conservation became a major force in the development of Canadian urban planning.

> Conservation and urban improvement came to be seen as opposite sides of the same coin. Industrialization and rapid urban growth had reduced the city to an obscene and unhealthy excrescence,

whereas nature was clean and pure, the resort of fundamental virtues and non-materialistic values. The strength of the country had therefore to be made accessible to the urban workers, through parks and wilderness reserves, industrial villages, and garden cities. Population and industry had also to be decentralized, to clear the way for the task of rebuilding the existing cities. It all added up to an image of powerful emotional appeal imbued with Arcadian romanticism, and strongly influenced by British experiments in town-building and by Ebenezer Howard's Garden City concept. At the same time, of course, nature had to be protected from the continual overspilling of deprived urban humanity. Urban decentralization was therefore to proceed in an orderly and controlled manner and, for all its romanticism and utopian idealism, the Garden City concept was firmly rooted in a belief in efficiently planned urban systems.[27]

As a symbol of the Garden City idea and as Town Planning Advisor to the Commission of Conservation, Adams was influential in promoting the development of urban planning in several respects. The first was provincial legislation regulating suburban expansion. Although planning was a local matter, Adams tactfully and persistently pressed for provincial legislation. Most of the provinces eventually adopted acts closely modelled on the British Housing, Town and Country Planning Act of 1909, or that part of it that dealt with municipal control over land-use planning.[28] The necessity of controlling land likely to be developed was apparent to many observers, for the era was one of incredible suburban subdivision, far in excess of actual population increase.[29] The second area of influence concerned the "new town" aspect of the British movement. Adams was directly or indirectly involved in planning satellite towns, like Ojibway, an industrial suburb of Windsor, Ontario, and resource towns like Temiscaming, Quebec.[30] A number of other small resource towns planned during this period also reflected these general principles, including Kapuskasing, Iroquois Falls, and Arvida.[31]

A third area where the influence of Adams and the Commission of Conservation was felt was in education. One of the first steps taken by Adams following his arrival in Canada was the initiation of the journal *Conservation of Life*, published between 1914 and 1921. It was used by the Commission to encourage town planning along the lines of the British model. Adams was also a tireless lecturer; he presented innumerable speeches at Canadian universities and at municipal and regional conferences. He was also influential in the establishment of the Civic Improvement League for Canada in an attempt to stimulate citizen interest in urban planning. The League, inaugurated in 1916, was soon followed by the establishment of numerous similar organizations at the municipal level. And, in 1917, Adams completed a major book, *Rural Planning and Development: A Study of Rural Conditions and Problems in Canada*, which succeeded in attracting a good deal of national and international attention.[32] In this comprehensive analysis of Canadian development trends, Adams outlined the components which he considered necessary to maintain a healthy environment. By stressing the importance of considering social aspects within the planning process, Adams stressed that less value should be placed on economic gains than on social and environmental quality.

> National prosperity depends on the character, stability, freedom and efficiency of the human resources of a nation, rather than on the amounts of its exports or imports, or the gold it may have to its credit at a given time. . . . While the conservation of natural resources and the promotion of industries are important and the development of trade has possibilities of benefit, the conservation of life and ability in the individual workers is supreme.[33]

Adams' considerable education effort, however, proved ineffective in coming to grips with one of the central concerns of Garden City planning— the provision of housing for the working man and the poor. In fact, the suburban movement accentuated rather than alleviated the problem, for it led to further fragmentation of the city into rich and poor because only the more prosperous could take part in the move away from the congested urban cores. The question of whether government at any level would get involved in providing housing was one of the key issues of the period. Garden City advocates like Adams constantly pushed for intervention on the British model, but provincial governments made clear their reluctance to enter this field; all provincial planning legislation excluded the provisions of the 1909 British Act which concerned "The Housing of the Working Classes." The earliest housing schemes were thus privately initiated, combining philanthropy and investment, a practice popular in the United States. For example, Herbert Ames, a Montreal businessman, built a small group of model apartments but his initiative was not imitated to any great extent by his business compatriots.[34]

In spite of a lack of action by private enterprise, city authorities generally remained aloof, and when civic government did get involved, it proved to be extremely minimal. Experiments in Toronto in 1913 and 1920 are examples. In one case the city guaranteed the bonds of a limited-dividend scheme of a joint stock company. In the other, a housing commission was appointed with clear instructions not to lose any city money. Together these ventures built over 500 housing units, but this housing generally proved too expensive for low-income families.[35] More popular with city officials was the strategy of improving housing through codes and strict code enforcement. Regulations were designed to ensure proper sanitary conditions, to control the quality of tenement housing, and to check the spread of slums. Codes, unfortunately, did not provide more or better low-income housing; if anything, they increased the cost of housing and reduced the available supply.[36]

The major government intervention in housing came, surprisingly, from the federal government, even though housing was a provincial jurisdiction. Between 1918 and 1925 the federal government operated a scheme to lend money to the provinces to encourage new housing construction. Most of the provinces participated; in Ontario, more than one hundred municipalities took advantage of the measures. Thomas Adams and other reformers hoped that this move signalled a new direction in government policy, but federal officials soon made it clear that it was a temporary measure to relieve the severe postwar housing shortages, especially for returning servicemen, and to reduce the threat of social unrest.

The accession of Arthur Meighen to the office of Prime Minister in 1920 cast the dye for a retreat from federal involvement. Symbolic of the federal move away from responsibility in the area was the abolition of the Commission of Conservation in 1921. The loan scheme was finally abandoned in 1923–24 and the federal government was not to return to the housing field until the crisis of the Depression in the 1930s.[37]

As housing reform declined as a positive force in the early 1920s, the pendulum swung back to a business-oriented approach to planning. Efficiency became the practical goal of reform, with planning seen as a rational, scientific activity. Technical experts were brought in to provide technical solutions. The trend was away from large-scale comprehensive plans to zoning as a means of achieving efficiency. The segregation of land uses was established on a legal-administrative basis by provincial legislation during the interwar years, borrowing heavily from the United States Department of Commerce Standard Zoning Enabling Act.[38] The move to zoning was characterized by a close relationship between planners and the property industry.[39] In fact, political support for land-use restrictions through zoning was possible because it protected property values. Zoning became a good way of prohibiting the intrusion of industry and low-income tenements into the more prosperous neighbourhoods. A second justification of zoning was the protection of public health. An examination of some Canadian city zoning plans reveals, however, that this concern over public health was definitely secondary. In the Kitchener plan, for example, the city was zoned into four categories: industrial, commercial, institutional, and residential. Although no industrial uses were allowed in the areas fortunate enough to be zoned residential, residential uses were allowed in the industrial areas of the city. In other words, while it was deemed important to keep noisy and polluting industries out of existing residential areas for public health reasons, it was not seen as important to keep new residential construction—usually workers' housing—out of the industrial areas.[40]

The extent to which public authorities and planners influenced the shape of early twentieth-century cities has been the subject of research only recently. A case study of Calgary indicates that the direction of development was determined by geography and the decisions of the railway company and speculators, but only marginally by civic planning. Subdivision was not regulated by a zoning by-law until 1932. The civic corporation's control was largely negative; it could, for example, discourage residential development in certain areas by withholding utility extensions.[41] In Toronto, planning before 1936 was limited to the relatively minor function of improving traffic flow, while zoning was largely a neighbourhood-based concern to prevent nuisances and protect property values.[42] It was only in the new resource towns of the period that planners, governments, and corporations were able to put the most advanced planning ideas into practice without the difficulties inherent in working with an existing community infrastructure. Some pulp and paper towns in particular were completely preplanned; in the case of Temiscaming, Quebec, with federal government advice; in the case of Kapuskasing, Ontario, by provincial planners.[43]

THE DISSOLUTION OF THE
COMMISSION OF CONSERVATION

During the era from 1890 to the early 1920s, the Canadian public developed a growing planning consciousness and were exposed to a wide range of ideas in the related areas of conservation planning and urban planning. By the late 1920s, however, Canadian planning was floundering and it was to be some time before it even began to recover. There were many reasons for this crisis,[44] but the dissolution of the Commission of Conservation in 1921 signalled most clearly the end of an era in Canadian planning history.

There are several reasons that explain the dissolution of the Commission of Conservation. The members of the Commission were very able men, as were their staff, but the terms of reference under which they operated were very restrictive. The Conservation Commission had been designed as an advisory and research body that could not actually carry out their projects but had to depend on other federal government departments or other levels of government to finish what they started. These projects were not always carried out to the Commission's satisfaction; sometimes the project was too long in being completed and some projects were simply not carried out. As the years passed, however, the Commission, anxious to get the job done, often overstepped the limits of its jurisdiction. This kind of activity soon caused friction between the Commission's staff and the civil service bureaucracy, particularly the Department of the Interior. Under Sir Clifford Sifton, a powerful figure in Canadian public affairs, the Commission's prestige was protected. But in November 1918 Sifton resigned in a dispute over staff salaries and the federal cabinet began to consider the possibility of dissolution.[45]

The end of the Commission came in the spring session of Parliament in 1921 when a Bill was passed to repeal the Commission of Conservation Act. Prime Minister Meighen opened the debate. In the course of his remarks he was to present several arguments for ending the Commission. It was far too expensive, he stated, and it was duplicating work done by the regular departments of government and creating a good deal of ill-feeling within the civil service. Meighen also felt that it was logical that a Commission "could only be of a temporary character" and that such a body, devoid of ministerial responsibility, was "not consistent with our system of government." He also noted that the creation of a department of pensions and public health, the development of the forest service, mines department, and other government branches, had made most aspects of the work of the Commission of Conservation redundant. Few speakers supported the Commission and the Bill to dissolve the body was passed.[46]

The end of the Commission of Conservation did not, of course, herald an abrupt termination of planning activity in Canada. Indeed, though the life of the Commission was relatively short, it left a strong legacy that continued for many years to influence planning activity. Perhaps its most important achievement was in assuming the role of a national forum for the discussion and development of issues and ideas about resource policy and management. It stimulated argument and research into a whole range of problems associated with particular resources and it initiated national consideration of public health and town planning problems, leading to the establishment of a national health department and a national planning association. More significantly, through the work of Adams, it developed concepts of total resource use in the field of urban planning. In short, the Commission of Conservation did more than any other institution to draw attention to integrated resource development.

In the decades following the demise of the Commission, planning in both the conservation and urban areas, however, developed slowly. In the former, there was no examination of natural resources on the same scale again until the Reconstruction Conference of 1945, although problems of forest, water, soil, and wildlife resources were discussed during the 1920s and 1930s at conferences with limited frames of reference.[47] In general, though, there was little conservation planning during the period from 1921 to 1961; instead, these were years of intense and rapid resource exploitation. The period was, in a sense, a return to the "doctrine of usefulness" which had held sway in the years before 1900. The focus of conservation planning, such as it was, was on natural science. The social motivation that had been evident during the life of the Conservation Commission was modified by a concern for the conservation of physical resources more in the physical than in the economic sense: "the object was to refine techniques to improve conservation . . . in the physical sense. . . . Conservation, or resource development, became a means to an end, an instrument of economic policy."[48]

The emphasis on resources for development was not to shift until at least 1961 when a major conference, "Resources For Tomorrow," was convened. The papers and discussions published in the conference report indicated that concern was again shifting to include a concern for both social and economic aspects in conservation planning.[49] It was the beginning of a new conservation movement in Canada, but unlike the earlier one, it did not achieve quick recognition in the form of a government agency or department. The new conservation movement, however, did constitute a political force and eventually, in 1971, a federal Department of the Environment was created that brought together in a single ministry a host of agencies involved in the management of renewable resources and the natural environment. In the last decade, conservation planning has been evident in a growing body of environmental legislation at both provincial and federal levels and it promises to be a major force in the immediate decades ahead.[50]

Urban planning also had a checkered existence in the years following 1921. Problems began in the 1920s when public interest turned from urban-oriented issues to provincial and national concerns. Cities particularly dropped in priority during the Great Depression and World War II.[51] One Canadian planner succinctly characterized the period:

For us the economic depression of the thirties was a vacuum and a complete break with the past. . . . We had no public housing programs and none of the adventurous social experiments of the New Deal. . . . We withered on the stem. So in 1946 we almost literally started from scratch with no plans or planners, and we immediately hit a period of tremendous city growth.[52]

The federal government had returned to the housing field during the crisis of the 1930s and formalized its intervention with a new National Housing Act in 1944. A Crown Corporation, the Central Mortgage and Housing Corporation (CMHC), was established in 1945 to operate the Act. The number of new housing units financed under this scheme increased from almost 12 000 in 1946 to 65 000 in 1955. The long-term results of this federal intervention were twofold. CMHC's lending policies literally created a Canadian house-building industry which built thousands of these new homes, but little planning accompanied this rapid growth and cities sprawled into formless suburbs.[53] During the 1950s, CMHC was reoriented from its previous emphasis on suburban mortgage lending to a concern for the interior of cities through urban renewal by contributing fifty percent of the cost of acquiring and clearing land for low-rental housing. The first major project was Regent Park South in Toronto, followed by the Jean Mance project in Montreal and Mulgrove Park in Halifax. What began with the enthusiasm of reform, however, soon became isolated monuments, for the expected tide of urban renewal failed to gather strength, leaving low-income people segregated in public-housing ghettoes.[54]

The federal government's activities in the cities were paralleled by the institutionalization of local planning through the establishment of departments of planning in municipal governments. This trend tended to bring planning more directly under political control, at the expense of the older system of planning commissioners or boards, whose respectable members presumably had been above politics.[55] In searching for planners, both the CMHC and local departments recruited heavily in Britain. One result was that the "British takeover of planning in the 1940s was massive."[56] According to one critic, the consequences of this domination by British planners was a planning profession preoccupied with the physical details of land use and a relentless desire to centralize planning power at the expense of the public's involvement in the process.[57]

While it is extremely difficult to generalize about recent trends in urban planning, at least two divergent directions are apparent. One represents a reaction to the centralizing policies of the federal agencies and city planning departments, and was symbolized by the citizen-oriented fight for local control of the Trefann Court project in Toronto. The issue was simply whether people who are affected by planning could have a major voice in that planning.[58] The other direction involved planning at an entirely different scale—the regional level—which was initiated with the studies leading to the concept of the Toronto-centred region. Metro Toronto combined with several departments of the provincial government in planning a parkway belt to accommodate future transportation and industrial development for a large section of southern Ontario, focused on Toronto. Both the local and regional planning concerns reflect a renaissance of urban consciousness. Ironically, this renewal is taking place in cities which no longer have the financial or political independence to determine their own destinies.[59]

In general, then, both conservation and urban planning continued to develop, albeit haphazardly, in the years after 1921. But they developed along distinct and frequently unrelated lines. The interrelationship between conservation and urban planning, so evident during the era of the Commission of Conservation, was no longer present. This was the tragedy of Canadian planning. The Commission of Conservation had articulated and fostered an integrated view of resource planning and, for all their naïvete and failures, the advisers and members of the Commission had discovered the best possible approach to planning.[60] In the years after 1921, however, this approach was lost in a plethora of political, jurisdictional, and ideological disputes. At a time when the need for planning was greatest— during the crisis of the 1930s and the massive growth of the 1950s and 1960s—the response of Canadian planning was weak. If it is to succeed in the future, Canadian planning must learn from the successes and failures of the Commission of Conservation.

NOTES

1. Canada was confederated under the terms of the British North America Act which came into force on 1 July 1867. The doctrine of usefulness is discussed in Brown, R.C. (1969) The doctrine of usefulness: natural resource and national park policy in Canada, in Nelson, J.G. (ed.), *Canadian Parks in Perspective*. Montreal: Harvest House, pp. 46–62.

2. Burton, T.L. (1972) *Natural Resource Policy in Canada: Issues and Perspectives*. Toronto: McClelland and Stewart, p. 42 and *passim*. For an excellent discussion of the role of staples in Canadian development see Buckley, K. (1958) The role of staple industries in Canada's economic development. *Journal of Economic History*, 18 (4), pp. 439–50.

3. Some of the earliest urban planning in Canada is briefly covered in Reps, J.W. (1969) *Town Planning in Frontier America*. Princeton, NJ.: Princeton University Press. See also Hugo-Brunt, M. (1968) The origin of colonial settlements in the Maritimes, in Gertler, L.O. (ed.), *Planning the*

Canadian Environment. Montreal: Harvest House, pp. 42–83.

4. See Gidney, N. (1978) From coal to forest products: the changing resource base of Nanaimo, B.C. *Urban History Review*, 1, pp. 18–47; and Stelter, G.A. (1971) The origins of a company town: Sudbury in the nineteenth century. *Laurentian University Review*, 3, pp. 3–37. Numerous other examples could be cited, including Prince Rupert, B.C., planned in 1904 by a distinguished Boston firm of landscape architects for the Grand Trunk Pacific Railway Company. See Richardson, N.H. (1968) A tale of two cities, in Gertler, L.O. (ed.), *Planning the Canadian Environment*. Montreal: Harvest House, pp. 269–84.

5. See, for example, Doucet, M. (forthcoming) Speculation and the physical development of mid-nineteenth century Hamilton, and Ganton, Isobel (forthcoming) Land subdivision in Toronto, 1847–1883, in Stelter, G.A. and Artibise, A.F.J. (eds.), *Shaping the Canadian Urban*

Landscape: Essays on the City-Building Process, 1821–1921.

6. For detailed statistics on Canadian urban growth see Plunkett, T.J. *et al.* (1973) *Urban Population Growth and Municipal Organization,* Local Government Reference Paper No. 1. Kingston: Institute of Local Government, Queen's University; or Stone, L.O. (1967) *Urban Development in Canada.* Ottawa: Dominion Bureau of Statistics.

7. See, for example, Artibise, A.F.J. (1975) *Winnipeg: A Social History of Urban Growth, 1874–1914.* Montreal: McGill-Queen's University Press; and Copp, T. (1974) *The Anatomy of Poverty: The Condition of the Working Class in Montreal.* Toronto: McClelland and Stewart.

8. Rutherford, P. (1977) Tomorrow's metropolis: the urban reform movement in Canada, 1880–1920, in Stelter, G.A. and Artibise, A.F.J. (eds.), *The Canadian City: Essays in Urban History.* Toronto: McClelland and Stewart, p. 368.

9. For an excellent collection of reformers' writings see Rutherford, P. (ed.) (1974) *Saving the Canadian City: The First Phase, 1880–1920—An Anthology of Early Articles on Urban Reform.* Toronto: University of Toronto Press.

10. Jacobs, Jane (1961) *The Death and Life of Great American Cities.* New York: Random House.

11. For an example, see Thomas Adams' comments in Commission of Conservation (1916) *Seventh Annual Report.* Montreal, pp. 118–19, and in Town planning and the housing problem. *Canadian Club Addresses,* Montreal, 11 January 1915. For a general discussion see Van Nus, W. (1977) The fate of City Beautiful thought in Canada, 1893–1930, in Stelter, G.A. and Artibise, A.F.J. (eds.), *The Canadian City: Essays in Urban History,* 162–85.

12. Bartholomew, H. (1929) *A Plan for the City of Vancouver, B.C., Including Point Grey and South Vancouver and a General Plan of the Region.* Vancouver

Town Planning Commission. See also Gunton, T. (1979) The ideas and policies of the Canadian planning profession, 1909–1931, in Artibise, A.F.J. and Stelter, G.A. (eds.), *The Usable Urban Past: Politics and Planning in the Modern Canadian City.* Toronto: Macmillan, pp. 177–95.

13. Quoted in Tomovcik, V. (1977) The Greber Plan for Ottawa. Unpublished M.A. Thesis, University of Waterloo, p. 40.

14. Contemporary sources for this period of planning are particularly rich. These include the voluminous Commission of Conservation annual reports, 1910–19; the Commission's magazine, *Conservation of Life,* 1914–21; the Proceedings of the National Conference on City Planning, usually held in the United States, but held in Toronto in 1914; the dozens of speeches Thomas Adams and others gave to Canadian Clubs in Montreal, Ottawa, Toronto, Hamilton, Winnipeg and Vancouver, and published in annual volumes of Club *Addresses* by those respective clubs.

15. For a detailed discussion of the diffusion process see Saarinen, O. (1979) The influence of Thomas Adams and the British New Towns movement in the planning of Canadian resource communities, in Artibise, A.F.J. and Stelter, G.A. (eds.), *The Usable Urban Past: Politics and Planning in the Modern Canadian City.* Toronto: Macmillan, pp. 268–92.

16. Brown, R.C. and Cook, R. (1974) *Canada, 1896–1921: A Nation Transformed.* Toronto: McClelland and Stewart, p. 96.

17. Hays, S.P. (1959) *Conservation and the Gospel of Efficiency: The Progressive Conservation Movement, 1890–1920.* Cambridge: Harvard University Press.

18. Thorpe, F.J. (1961) Historical perspective on "Resources for Tomorrow" conference, in *Resources For Tomorrow: Conference Background Papers.* Ottawa: Queen's Printer, pp. 2–3.

19. Armstrong, A.H. (1968) Thomas Adams and the Commission of Conservation, in Gertler, L.O. (ed.), *Planning the Canadian Environment.* Montreal: Harvest House, p. 18.

20. Commission of Conservation (1910) *First Annual Report.* Ottawa, p. 2.

21. Sifton was a logical choice as chairman. He had been a prominent member of the Laurier Cabinet from 1896 to 1905 and had served as Minister of the Interior. In this position he had gained a thorough understanding of conservation issues. He had also attended the North American Conservation Conference and the National Conference on City Planning where he argued for a more systematic approach to conservation and town planning. See *Proceedings of the Sixth National Conference on City Planning, Toronto, May 25–27, 1914.* Boston, 1914, p. 136. See also Dafoe, J.W. (1931) *Clifford Sifton in Relation to his Times.* Toronto: Macmillan.

22. Lists of these publications can be found in the 1919 and 1920 *Canada Year Books.*

23. The best summary of the work of the Commission is Smith, C.R. and Witty, D. R. (1970, 1972) Conservation Resources and Environment: an exposition and critical evaluation of the Commission of Conservation, Canada. *Plan Canada,* 11 (1), pp. 55–71; 11 (3), pp. 199–216. A short overview is Renfrew, S. (1971) Commission of Conservation. *Douglas Library Notes,* 19 (3–4), pp. 17–26.

24. *Ibid.* See also Armstrong, A.H. (1968) Thomas Adams and the Commission of Conservation, in Gertler, L.O. (ed.), *Planning the Canadian Environment.* Montreal: Harvest House.

25. Commission of Conservation (1911) *Second Annual Report.* Montreal, p. 75.

26. Armstrong, A.H. (1968) Thomas Adams and the Commission of Conservation, in Gertler, L.O. (ed.), *Planning the Canadian Environment.* Montreal: Harvest House.

27. Smith, P.J. (1979) The principle of utility and the origins of planning legislation in Alberta, in Artibise, A.F.J. and Stelter, G.A. (eds.), *The Usable Urban Past: Politics and Planning in the Modern Canadian City.* Toronto: Macmillan, pp. 201–2.

28. Armstrong, A.H. (1968) Thomas Adams and the Commission of Conservation, in Gertler, L.O. (ed.), *Planning the Canadian Environment.* Montreal: Harvest House; and Saarinen, O. (1979) The influence of Thomas Adams and the British New Towns movement in the planning of resource communities, in Artibise, A.F.J. and Stelter, G.A. (eds.) *The Usable Urban Past: Politics and Planning in the Modern Canadian City.* Toronto: Macmillan. See also Wiesman, B. (1977) The development and nature of provincial planning legislation, 1912–1975. Unpublished paper presented to "Canada's Urban Past," The Canadian Urban History Conference, University of Guelph.

29. Adams, T. (1917) *Rural Planning and Development.* Ottawa: Commission of Conservation, pp. 224–5. This problem is also discussed in some detail in a western Canadian context in Artibise, A.F.J. (forthcoming) Boosterism and the development of prairie cities, 1870–1913, in Stelter, G.A. and Artibise, A.F.J. (eds.), *Shaping the Canadian Urban Landscape: Essays on the City-Building Process, 1821–1921,* and in Artibise, A.F.J. (1979) Continuity and change: elites and prairie urban development, 1914–1950, in Artibise, A.F.J. and Stelter, G.A. (eds.), *The Usable Urban Past: Politics and Planning in the Modern Canadian City.* Toronto: Macmillan, pp. 130–54.

30. Commission of Conservation (1919) *Tenth Annual Report.* Montreal, Appendix VII, pp. 109–11.

31. McCann, L. (1978) The changing internal structure of Canadian resource towns, *Plan Canada,* 18, pp. 46–59.

32. In addition to a constant round of Canadian Club speeches in major cities, Adams spoke at a variety of

other gatherings. Examples are included in *Report of the Urban and Rural Development Conference, Winnipeg, May 28–30, 1917.* Ottawa.

33. Adams, T. (1917) *Rural Planning and Development.* Ottawa: Commission of Conservation, p. 2.

34. Examples of speeches on this subject are The Housing Problem. *Canadian Club Addresses,* Montreal, 24 February 1919, pp. 180–6; and *Report of the Preliminary Conference of the Civic Improvement League for Canada.* Ottawa, 1918, pp. 11–17. See also Rutherford, P. (1972) Introduction, to Ames, Herbert Brown, *The City Below the Hill: A Sociological Study of a Portion of the City of Montreal.* Toronto: University of Toronto Press (reprint of 1897 edition).

35. Spragge, Shirley (1979) A conference of interests: housing reform in Toronto, 1900–1920, in Artibise, A.F.J. and Stelter, G.A. (eds.), *The Usable Urban Past: Politics and Planning in the Modern Canadian City.* Toronto: Macmillan, pp. 247–67.

36. Weaver, J.C. (1977) "Tomorrow's metropolis" revisited: a critical assessment of urban reform in Canada, 1890–1920, in Stelter, G.A. and Artibise, A.F.J. (eds.), *The Canadian City: Essays in Urban History.* Toronto: McClelland and Stewart, pp. 403–9.

37. Grauer, A.E. (1939) *Housing. A Study Prepared for the Royal Commission on Dominion-Provincial Relations.* Ottawa: King's Printer; Saywell, J.T. (1975) *Housing Canadians: Essays on the History of Residential Construction in Canada.* Ottawa: Economic Council of Canada.

38. Wiesman, B. (1977) The development and nature of provincial planning legislation, 1912–1975. Unpublished paper presented to "Canada's Urban Past," The Canadian Urban History Conference, University of Guelph.

39. Van Nus, W. (1979) Towards the City Efficient: the theory and practice of zoning, 1919–1939, in Artibise, A.F.J. and Stelter, G.A. (eds.), *The Usable Urban Past: Politics and Planning in the Modern Canadian City.* Toronto: Macmillan, pp. 226–46.

40. Gunton, T. (1979) The ideas and policies of the Canadian planning profession, 1909–1931, in *ibid.,* pp. 223–43.

41. Foran, M. (1979) Land development patterns in Calgary, 1884–1946, in *ibid.,* pp. 293–315.

42. Moore, P. (1979) Zoning and planning the Toronto experience, 1904–1970, in *ibid.,* pp. 316–41.

43. Stelter, G.A. and Artibise, A.F.J. (1978) Canadian resource towns in historical perspective. *Plan Canada,* 18, pp. 7–16.

44. Gunton, T. (1979) The ideas and policies of the Canadian planning profession, in Artibise, A.F.J. and Stelter, G.A. (eds.) *The Usable Urban Past: Politics and Planning in the Modern Canadian City.* Toronto: Macmillan, pp. 223–43.

45. Thorpe, F.J. (1961) Historical perspective on "Resources for Tomorrow" conference, in *Resources For Tomorrow: Conference Background Papers.* Ottawa: Queen's Printer; Armstrong, A.H. (1968) Thomas Adams and the Commission of Conservation, in Gertler, L.O. (ed.), *Planning the Canadian Environment.* Montreal: Harvest House.

46. Canadian House of Commons (1921) *Debates,* pp. 3958–71.

47. Thorpe, F.J. (1961) Historical perspective on "Resources for Tomorrow" conference, in *Resources For Tomorrow: Conference Background Papers.* Ottawa: Queen's Printer; Burton, T.L. (1972) *Natural Resource Policy in Canada: Issues and Perspectives.* Toronto: McClelland and Stewart.

48. Thorpe, F.J., *ibid.,* pp. 11–12.

49. *Resources For Tomorrow: Conference Background Papers,* 2 vols. Ottawa: Queen's Printer, 1961. See also Dakin, J. (1968) Resources for Tomorrow, the background papers, in Gertler, L.O. (ed.) *Planning the*

Canadian Environment. Montreal: Harvest House, pp. 119–36.

50. For an overview of the federal environment ministry and its concerns, see Environment Canada (1972) *Canada and the Human Environment*. Ottawa.

51. See, for example, Taylor, J. (1979) Relief from relief: the cities' answer to depression dependency. *Journal of Canadian Studies*, 14 (1), pp. 16–23.

52. Carver, H. (1960) Planning in Canada, *Planning 1960: Proceedings of the American Society of Planning Officials*. Chicago, 1960, p. 22. The history of urban planning since World War II has not been examined in detail but some useful guides are available. The most readable and full account is Humphrey Carver's humanistic autobiography, *Compassionate Landscape*. Toronto: University of Toronto Press, 1975. An outline of federal legislation as applied to housing and planning can be found in Bettinson, D. (1975) *The Politics of Canadian Urban Development*. Edmonton: University of Alberta Press, pp. 61–104. For an anti-establishment interpretation of recent events, see Clark, R. (1976) The crisis in Canadian city planning. *City Magazine*, 1 (8), pp. 17–24. Also useful are the historical sections of papers by Brahm Wiesman and Kenneth D. Cameron in Oberlander, H.P. (ed.) (1976) *Canada: An Urban Agenda*. Ottawa: Community Planning Press.

53. Carver, H. (1975) *Compassionate Landscape*. Toronto: University of Toronto Press, pp. 107–57; and Carver, H. (1962) *Cities in the Suburbs*. Toronto: University of Toronto Press.

54. For a detailed description of the reformist expectations and the administrative and political problems, see Rose, A. (1959) *Regent Park: A Study of Slum Clearance*. Toronto: University of Toronto Press; and Carver, H. (1975) *Compassionate Landscape*. Toronto: University of Toronto Press, pp. 134–48.

55. Gerecke, K. (1976) The history of Canadian city planning. *City Magazine*, 2 (3–4), pp. 14–15.

56. Adamson, A. (1973) Thirty years of the planning business. *Plan Canada*, 13, p. 7.

57. Clark, R. (1976) The crisis in Canadian city planning. *City Magazine*, 1 (8), p. 22.

58. The major study of this struggle, when it still promised to be successful, is Fraser, G. (1972) *Fighting Back: Urban Renewal in Trefann Court*. Toronto: Hakkert. It should be noted that a federal Ministry of State for Urban Affairs was created in 1971. Smaller than the Environment Ministry, it was established to design and coordinate urban-oriented policies and programmes administered by other departments and agencies. Significantly, the MSUA was ended in April 1979, and federal involvement in urban planning was again spread over a variety of government departments and agencies.

59. See, for example, Nowlan, D.M. (1978) Towards home rule for urban policy. *Journal of Canadian Studies*, 13, pp. 70–9.

60. Humphrey Carver, a noted Canadian planner, wrote in 1975 that "in retrospect, the creation of the Commission of Conservation appears as a brilliant flash of national insight, anticipating by more than sixty years the departments of environment set up by federal and provincial governments in the early 1970s." Carver, H. (1975) *Compassionate Landscape*. Toronto: University of Toronto Press, p. 32.

THE IMAGE OF
THE STATE◇

H.V. NELLES

o

As Ontario entered the twentieth century the old pre-industrial concept of crown ownership of natural resources was very much alive. Because the lumbermen had discovered a useful ally in the state, and because the forests rented to the lumbermen became a production source of revenue, the statist philosophy underlying the Crown Timber Act came to be applied in the regulation of waterpowers and mines as well. Thus, on the eve of intensive development, the province of Ontario exercised proprietary control over its three most important natural resources. The survival of this authority was ... no accident, but instead a conscious choice. Looking ahead, the concept of the positive state appeared also to have much to recommend it as the basis of regulating the industrial process.

Did this tradition make any difference in what followed? Did an interventionist public philosophy significantly alter the pattern of resource development in the province from the continental norm? After surveying the record the answer must be a qualified no, the qualification being the important exception of Hydro. If anything, the proprietary relationship made it easier for business to establish a firm grip upon the instruments of the state. In this Hydro was not an exception, for it was run by businessmen, for businessmen, in what was always referred to as a "businesslike" manner.

The first and consistently most important function of the state in the industrial process was promotion, and successive Ontario governments bent their wills to this task with commendable zeal. Was it not in the interest of the landlord that his property should be productively occupied?

◇ From *The Politics of Development: Forests, Mines and Hydro-electric Power in Ontario 1849–1941* (Toronto: Macmillan, 1974), 489–95.

Accordingly, bounties of one sort or another fell on demand like a warm spring rain; roads to resources were built or bonused as required; services were provided, opportunities advertised and skills imparted with an enthusiasm tempered only by the imperatives of economy. Reluctantly at first, and then more confidently, the province could even be induced to meet the challenge of hostile American commercial policies. From the outset it was readily understood that Ontario's natural resources would be exploited primarily for the American market. But who was to do battle to ensure that these products were exported in as close to their fully manufactured form as possible? The province at length took on this responsibility with a determination that varied directly with the pressure applied to it by its business clients and the rise and fall of the business cycle. Invariably, this "economic provincialism" met strong resistance in the form of the federal government which, throughout this period, tended to take a more conciliatory view of Canadian-American commercial differences. As far as help with getting on with the job was concerned, no developer could ask for a better, more attentive partner than the government of Ontario.

What then of the other side of the relationship, regulation? To what extent did the proprietary situation of the state impinge upon the development process? Here again the government proved to be more than understanding. The miners began by demanding that the state give up its proprietary pretensions entirely. They very quickly won for themselves a form of tenure more in keeping with the American pattern. As far as taxation was concerned, the miners eventually brought a stabilizing influence to bear upon the government after some dubious experiments with leases, royalties and even public ownership inspired by progressive enthusiasm and the Cobalt rush. Thereafter, mining proceeded within the lenient free enterprise, freebooting environment as elsewhere. Furthermore, the industry always seemed to be able to count upon its faithful advocate, the provincial government, to caution those improvident enough to tamper with a going concern. In mining it would seem that the regulated group experienced greater success in bringing the regulator under control than the other way around.

Something similar might be said of the pulp and paper industry's relations with the provincial government up to the Second World War. In principle, public ownership of the raw materials remained as the legal basis of the industry. However, in practice the superior legal position of the state in this landlord-tenant relationship was not used to assert any major public claim upon the resource development process. In fact, quite the reverse appeared to be the case: the position of the state facilitated the organization of a relatively small number of substantial production units. The terms and conditions of the concessions were adjusted to suit the needs of developers and the land parcelled out in such a way as to accommodate the financial requirements of expansion. When the entire industry collapsed during the Depression the governments of Ontario and Quebec readily permitted their industrial tenants free access to the coercive powers of the state in the interests of orderly reconstruction as that was perceived by the pulp and paper men themselves. Public ownership of the resource base did not necessarily imply a more systematic pursuit of conservation programs. The conservation movement, becalmed during the second decade of the century, and the fire-ravaged forests of northern Ontario during the 1930s bear witness to that. The effective demands upon the state and its forest resources were promotional and private throughout.

The rhetoric of free enterprise notwithstanding, business could not get along without the active co-operation of the state. From the exploration phase up through reorganization and concentration the state had to serve as an understanding accomplice. The values that guided government intervention in Ontario during the first half of this century have been basically those of its business clients. This, of course, was the normal state of affairs in a continental, advanced capitalist context. "Capitalist enterprise," it has been argued, ". . . *depends* to an ever greater extent on the bounties and direct support of the state, and can only preserve its 'private' character on the basis of such public help. State intervention in economic life in fact *means* intervention for the purpose of helping capitalist enterprise. In no field has the notion of the 'welfare state' had a more precise and apposite meaning than here: there are no more persistent and successful applicants for public assistance than the proud giants of the private enterprise system."[1] In Ontario a formal legal relationship between the state and its resource developers seemed, if anything, to facilitate such co-operative action.

Only in the case of hydro-electric power did public ownership of the resource provide a model for the subsequent development of the industry based upon it. In this Ontario did deviate significantly from the North American norm. But as has been suggested, retention of public rights in waterpowers, while a helpful contributing factor, was certainly not a sufficient condition for public ownership of the hydro-electric distribution and generation industry. Instead, the energy requirements of the provincial manufacturers, their fear of economic stagnation, and the metropolitan tensions of the provincial economy were far more important determinants of state intervention. Power was far too precious as an agent of industrial expansion to be left under the control of monopoly capital, Canadian or American. If the ordinary corporate instruments could not be relied upon to deliver this power on time at reasonable rates, then the state had a duty to step in and perform this function itself for the greater well-being of the economy. The strongest and most persistent demand for public ownership came from businessmen. Of course, the hydro-electric question split the financial sector of the business community from the merchants and manufacturers, and the brilliant political organization of the latter group at the municipal and the provincial level by a charismatic leader determined the outcome. The decentralized character of Canadian federalism prevented the former group from reversing this verdict at the federal level as so often happened in the United States.[2] This same alliance of interests sanctioned Sir Adam Beck's later drive towards a public monopoly.

Ontario Hydro never became the beachhead for an ongoing critique of industrial capitalism. Instead, the dangerous principles upon which it rested remained locked up within the confines of the [Hydro-Electric Power Commission of Ontario], and the commission was allowed to remove itself as far away from politics (but not the treasury) as possible. This, it was argued, was absolutely essential if the organization were to be run in accordance with proper, businesslike principles, a key phrase. Hydro entered politics only to escape from it. In this there was a double loss. In the first place the conditions of Hydro's birth and the character of its founder prevented the accommodation of this new responsibility of state to the parliamentary system of government. Eventually the contradictions of this independent, non-accountable status practically wrecked Hydro. But the crisis of the thirties led only to the replacement of bad men by good men; it did not alter the structural relationship of the commission to the executive of the Legislature. Since then the only thought that has been given to the question has been in the direction of moving Hydro even further from the political process. Secondly, Hydro was nationalized in such a way and then managed in such a manner as to debase the concept of *public* ownership and discourage the extension of the principle. Hydro was not to be the experiment with socialized industry that the power barons and James Mavor feared, but the venture in state capitalism that the merchants and manufacturers of the power legions knew it to be from the beginning. Public ownership is in itself a neutral phenomenon. Its origins, benefactors and behaviour determine its character. On close examination the much-discussed Toryism that Ontario Hydro is supposed to represent looks much like some varieties of American corporate liberalism.[3] It might as well have the same name.

After the Second World War the integration of business and the state proceeded much more quickly, under Conservative one-party government, across a much broader front and on an entirely different scale. The points of connection between business and the state multiplied as both bureaucratized their structures and professionalized their operations. This qualitatively different kind of fusion lies beyond the scope of this book and warrants study in its own right.

Perhaps no better representation of the changing scope and character of the state in Ontario can be found than the architecture at Queen's Park. The Parliament Building, compact, comprehensive, facing inward upon the Legislature at the centre, typifies the late nineteenth-century state. It could be nothing else but a government building, except perhaps a Presbyterian church. Nor was it modesty that led Oliver Mowat to exclaim upon seeing the structure in 1892, "We'll never fill it." Beck's squat little Hydro headquarters on University Avenue followed in 1916, looking like nothing so much as a bank, setting a pattern that repeated itself in the East Annex of the 1920s and the new Hydro building of the 1940s. With each step the centre of gravity shifts away from the Legislature. In the sixties government spread itself out over entire city blocks of concrete and steel. To this Hydro and Canada Square have replied with a massive concave mirror that, on a fine day, will reflect the surrounding corporate monuments, the bank towers downtown, the hotels and insurance companies nearby. The image on the outside is perhaps a fair reflection of the new state on the inside.

The habit of authority that survived from the nineteenth century did not greatly alter the pattern of resource development. It did, however, contribute to a reduction of government—despite an expansion of its activities—to a client of the business community. This need not have been so. The failure to bring the regulatory and service functions of the state into the framework of democratic accountability was the failure of parties and politicians to pursue the logic of responsible government into the industrial age.

NOTES

1. Ralph Miliband, *The State in Capitalist Society* (London, 1969), p. 78; see also, Gabriel Kolko, *The Triumph of Conservatism* (Chicago, 1963), pp. 279–305; James Weinstein, *The Corporate Ideal in the Liberal State, 1900–1918* (Boston, 1968), ix–xv; Martin J. Sklar, "Woodrow Wilson and the Political Economy of Modern United States Liberalism," in Ronald Rodash and Murray Rothbard, eds., *A New History of Leviathan: Essays on the Rise of the American Corporate State* (New York, 1972), pp. 7–65.

2. Christopher Armstrong and H.V. Nelles, "Private Property in Peril: Ontario Businessmen and the Federal System, 1898–1911," *Business History Review*, Vol. XLVII (1973), pp. 158–76.

THE QUESTION
OF WILDLIFE

o

T he importance of fishing and the fur trade in Canadian history has ensured that animals occupy a significant place in our history books. Even so, scholars are now beginning to further emphasize this importance and to develop it as a central theme of modern Canada. An increasing number of historians have come to share Farley Mowat's assessment of the value of studying the interactions of humans and wildlife:

> In 1984 I made what I think may be my most useful contribution—
> a book called *Sea of Slaughter*. It details five centuries of human
> destruction of life on the Atlantic seaboard. Its epilogue sums up
> what I believe to be the truth about the works of modern man—
> and the failure of life on earth.[1]

Appropriately, therefore, the first reading in this section comes from Mowat's *Sea of Slaughter*. It offers a detailed description of what happens in a culture where "economic progress depends on a never ending elaboration of ways and means to turn a profit from available raw resources."

While beaver and cod have perhaps been studied more than other animals in Canadian history, the wolf has also occupied a prominent place in the Canadian imagination. Alan MacEachern's study of predator policy in national parks reveals the paradoxes and contradictions in the official view regarding wolves and other animals, especially during the 1930s. He focuses on the anomalous position of wardens who were instructed to kill certain predators but also to patrol the parks to protect the same species from poachers. This contradiction reflected two competing views: that there were "good" and "bad" animals and that all animals were interdependent members of nature.

The significance of incompatible perceptions is also a key theme of I.D. Thompson's discussion of the failures of forest and wildlife management in Canada. These failures have resulted, at least in part, from a refusal to see forests as complex, dynamic systems in which the components cannot be isolated from their larger web of relationships. Thompson exposes how official preserves are usually far too small to ensure the biodiversity necessary in the ongoing renewal of ecosystems. Similarly, Thompson emphasizes the land-use conflicts that have resulted from the competing desires of those with single-purpose ambitions for the forest.

The challenge of developing policies appropriate to the integrated character of wildlife in the biosphere has recently become more complex with the emergence of the animal rights movement. As Rebecca Aird describes in the closing article of this section, the concept of animal welfare has a long history in which various groups and associations have tried to limit animal suffering. At the same time, animal rights activists who demand an "equality of consideration" for members of all species, can also point to similar demands dating back at least two thousand years. These two views share certain assumptions but they are fundamentally different, with the result that major conflicts have developed between their proponents as well as with indigenous peoples and environmentalists. As Aird's description of recent controversies illustrates, the subject of wildlife reveals the diverse relationships between nature and competing economies and cultures.

NOTES

1. Farley Mowat, *Rescue the Earth: Conversations with the Green Crusaders* (Toronto: McClelland & Stewart, 1990), 24.

DEATH ON ICE
(OLD STYLE) ◇

FARLEY MOWAT

○

Now it is to be told that the ships of Karlsefini coasted southward with Snorri and Bjarni and their people. They journeyed a long time until they came to a river which flowed into a pond and thence into the sea. They settled above the shore of the pond and remained there all that winter.

One morning after spring arrived, a great number of skin boats came rowing from the south. They were so numerous it looked as if charcoal had been scattered on the sea. The two parties came together and began to barter.

Some of the Norse cattle were near and the bull ran out of the woods and began to bellow. This terrified the Skraelings and they raced to their boats and rowed away. For three weeks nothing more was seen of them, then a great multitude was discovered coming from the south. Thereupon Karlsefini and his men took red shields and displayed them. The Skraelings sprang from their boats, and they met and fought together.

Freydis Ericsdottir came out of doors and seeing that Karlsefini and the men were fleeing she tried to join them but could not keep up since she was pregnant. Then she saw a dead man before her, naked sword beside him. Freydis snatched it up and as the Skraelings came close she let fall her shift and slapped her breasts with the naked blade. Seeing this the Skraelings were frightened and ran to their boats and rowed away.

It now seemed clear to Karlsefini and his people that though this was an attractive country their lives there would be filled with fear

◇ Farley Mowat, *Sea of Slaughter* (Toronto: McClelland & Stewart, 1984), 344–65.

and turmoil because of the Skraelings and so they decided to leave. They sailed north along the coast and surprised five Skraelings dressed in skin doublets asleep near the sea, and they put them to death.

This paraphrased and shortened version of an old Norse saga describes an event that took place about the year 1000 when a Norse expedition from Greenland tried to establish itself on the west coast of Newfoundland. The attempt failed because of conflict with a native people whom the Norse called *Skraelings*. For almost a thousand years thereafter, the identity of these people remained a mystery.

Now we know they were not Indians, as might have been expected, but an Eskimoan people of the so-called Dorset culture who had been drawn from the High Arctic to make their homes in the relatively temperate Gulf of St. Lawrence region for the same reason that had attracted many other northern animals such as the bowhead whale, beluga, walrus, and white bear—because it was a place that met their needs.

The Skraelings were seal hunters, and what brought them to the Gulf and held them there was the unimaginable multitude of seals that inhabited the neighbouring waters—and, in particular, the species known to us as the harp seal, with which their culture was inextricably entwined.

Skraelings lived and prospered on all the coasts of North America adjacent to the seas wherein the harp abounded. Around Baffin Bay basin, on both sides of Davis Strait, among the eastern islands of the Canadian Arctic archipelago, south along the Labrador, and into the Gulf of St. Lawrence at least as far as Cabot Strait, their places of habitation can still be found. The sites are easily identified by characteristic microlithic stone implements found in midden heaps, but especially by the composition of the middens themselves, which consist mainly of decayed organic material and bones of seals. Some middens, such as those at Englee, Port au Choix, and Cape Ray in Newfoundland, are so vast and their greasy black layers of long-decayed seal offal so thickly impregnated with seal bones that they convey the impression of titanic butchery. But that is an illusion due to the telescoping of time. These accumulations are the product of as many as eight or nine centuries of subsistence hunting by generation after generation of people for whom the harp seal was the staff of life.

o

The adult harp is of moderate size as seals go, averaging about 300 pounds in weight and five and a half feet in length, roughly midway between the little dotar and the massive horsehead. It is pre-eminently an ice seal, spending much of its life on or close to the broken floes of the drifting pack. A superb swimmer, it can dive to at least 600 feet and make long passages underwater, or under ice, remaining submerged for as long as half an hour.

The harp nation is composed of three distinct parts. One lives in the White and Barents Seas to the north of Europe, the second in the Greenland

Sea east of that great island, while the third and largest inhabits the waters of the northwest Atlantic. This tribe, the one with which we are most concerned, summers as far north as Hall Basin, within 400 miles of the North Pole, but whelps off northeast Newfoundland and in the Gulf of St. Lawrence. During the cycle of one annual migration its members must travel 5000 miles or more.

These western harps begin their autumnal migration a few weeks before the Arctic seas begin to congeal, streaming south in companies of thousands and tens of thousands to form an almost unbroken procession down the coast of Labrador—a procession that once was composed of several million individuals. By late November the leading companies have reached the Strait of Belle Isle, and here the river splits. The mightiest stream passes through the Strait and heads west along the north shore of the Gulf. Some conception of its magnitude can be gained from the observation of a French trader who watched the harps pass the northern tip of Newfoundland in the autumn of 1760. He reported that they filled the sea from shore to horizon for ten days and nights. At one time this stream flowed as far west as Isle aux Coudres, only a few score miles short of Quebec City, though what is left of it today seldom gets beyond the Saguenay.

From the Strait of Belle Isle, the other river seems to flow southeastward—and disappears. Some biologists believe it reaches the Grand Banks, where its members disperse and spend the winter, but there is no sure evidence for this. Perhaps the most likely explanation is that the swiftswimming seals loop around eastern Newfoundland and enter the Gulf through Cabot Strait. Thereafter, I suspect, they make their way northward up the west coast of Newfoundland where, once, they brought the gift of life to the Skraeling settlements that waited for them there.

But this is mostly speculation. It is a salutary thought that even in these days of electronic eyes and ears, and in seas full of working fishing vessels, the whereabouts of the mighty mass of the harp herds still remain essentially unknown from January through to the latter part of February.

During the winter months a titanic tongue of polar pack as much as 100 miles in width thrusts southward in the grip of the Labrador Current until, by mid-February, its offshoots are clogging the shores of northeastern Newfoundland and pushing through Belle Isle Strait to meet and mingle with winter ice born in the Gulf.

To the untutored human eye this world of grinding, shifting pans and floes, lifting, splintering, and rafting in the ocean swell, swept by blizzards, gales, and fog, has the aspect of a white and desolate desert, seemingly the very anathema of life. Yet it is in this realm of frozen chaos that, as February ends and March storms in, the teeming legions of the harp seal reappear.

Flying low over the pack on a rare sunny day in mid-February, one sees nothing but a glittering empty wasteland except, perhaps, that here and there in open leads one catches a glimpse of animation as pale sunlight gleams from the wet backs of a few porpoising seals. Several days later, a miracle seems to have taken place.

From a light plane cruising at 1500 feet on a late February day in 1968, I looked down upon an endless vista of ice that was clotted, clustered, and speckled with whelping seals in such quantity that the biologist flying with me could only shrug when I asked how many he thought there were.

Even with the help of aerial photography, scientists can only roughly estimate the number of individuals in a major harp seal whelping patch. The working figure generally used is 3000–4000 adults per square mile, mostly female, together with nearly as many pups, depending on how far advanced the whelping is. There is *no* way of counting the males, which are generally in the water or under it. To make things even more difficult, the area occupied by the patch can itself be only roughly estimated. Although the heart of the one we flew over that day seemed to be about twelve miles long and at least six wide, amorphous strings and tongues of seals spread outward from it in all directions like the pseudopods of some gigantic amoeba. Our estimate, which was little better than a guess, was that this patch perhaps held half-a-million seals.

Yet it was as nothing to the size of those that once existed.

In the spring of 1844, more than 100 Newfoundland sealing ships worked a whelping patch off the southeast coast of Labrador, the main portion of which was at least fifty miles long and twenty broad. At a most conservative estimate that one patch contained more than 5 000 000 seals. What is known for *certain* is that the sealers landed approximately 740 000 pelts, the vast majority of which were stripped from newborn pups.

o

Western harp seals whelp in two well-separated regions: on the ice fields drifting off northeastern Newfoundland, which area is known as the Front, and in the Gulf. There are generally two well-defined patches at the Front and two or more in the Gulf. At each patch, the males linger in frolicking companies in open leads or rest companionably on the edge of the pans, while the females disperse across the ice plain, each claiming her own space on which to bear and nurture her single pup.

A description of the newborn pup, or whitecoat as it is called, is probably superfluous since its image has appeared so often that there can be few people who are not now familiar with it. This big-eyed, cuddlesome creature has become the ultimate symbol for those who are convinced that man must put a check-rein on his ruinous abuse of animate creation and, as such, it is by no means badly chosen.

It remains a whitecoat for only about two weeks. Then it is left to fend for itself when its mother, who has fed it such generous quantities of creamy milk that the pup has not only more than tripled in weight but has acquired a. two-inch layer of fat, abandons it and goes off to mate with the attendant males. Now the soft, luxuriant white fur begins to shed. At this stage the pup is called a raggedy-jacket. In several days the moult is complete, leaving the youngster in a mottled coat of silvery-grey. Called a beater now, the pup makes its first venture into the water at the age of five to six weeks, soon teaches itself to swim, and begins learning how to make a living from the sea, meanwhile subsisting on its reserves of fat and protein.

As spring progresses, the adult seals, duty done and pleasure taken, form a second series of enormous aggregations, called moulting patches. For days and even weeks, the harp multitudes remain in close company, hauling out in black-and-silver multitudes to sun themselves, shed their coats, and, we can believe, socialize. This is the annual harp seal festival, celebrated at the end of the breeding year before a new cycle begins.

Toward the end of April, as the great ice tongue begins to dissolve under the influence of the spring sun, the festival ends and the adults begin the long journey back to Arctic seas. A month or two behind them come hordes of beaters, travelling individually and apparently with only an inner voice to guide them in their solitary passage to the ancestral summering grounds.

Basque whalers were probably the earliest Europeans to become aware of the existence of the harp nation of the west, having seen the migrating companies come pouring through Belle Isle Strait during those winters when the whalers were forced to harbour in the New World.

The first European *sealers* seem to have been the French colonists who began settling along the lower St. Lawrence River valley in the mid-seventeenth century. Initially, as we have seen, they preyed upon the horsehead, but as more settlers spread eastward down the shores of the great estuary, they began to encounter a different kind of seal, one that appeared in January in almost inconceivable numbers.

Since these silvery animals with their distinctive black caps and dark saddle patches shaped rather like harps never entered river mouths or hauled out on shore or off-lying rocks as did dotars and horseheads, the only way to hunt them seemed to be by gunning from small boats. The combination of ineffective muskets and ice-filled waters not only made this unproductive but exceedingly dangerous. Nevertheless, some considered it worth the risk since each of these seals was so thickly layered with fat that it could yield almost as much oil as a much larger horsehead. So they were highly prized by the colonists, who called them *loup-marin brasseur* in distinction to the original loup marin, or horsehead.

The incredible abundance but relative untouchability of the loup-marin brasseur must have caused much frustration until, at last, the French found a way to slaughter them en masse. During the first half of the seventeenth century, some adventurer exploring eastward into terra incognita along the north shore of the Gulf encountered those most accomplished of all sealers, the Inuit. In those times, Inuit wintered at least as far west as Anticosti Island, subsisting primarily on seals, of which the harp was their principal quarry. Having no guns, they took it by means of nets woven of sealskin thongs set across narrow runs between coastal islands.

The French were always quick to learn hunting skills from native peoples and, in short order, were making and setting sealing nets themselves. This net fishery soon became so financially rewarding that the authorities in Quebec and Paris were kept busy selling new seigneuries. By 1700 these stretched as far east as the Mingan Islands, and in every case the wording of the grants clearly indicates that a local monopoly of the seal fishery was the most valuable right embodied in them.

Expansion farther eastward was halted, not by any shortage of seals but because the French had roused the enmity of the Inuit by associating themselves and their interests with various Indian tribes. The hostility that followed had grown so intense and bloody that neither French *nor* Indians dared winter on the Gulf coast east of Mingan until early in the eighteenth century.

A way around this was found by coming at it from the other end. The region around the Strait of Belle Isle had for long been dominated by cod fishermen from France and, although there had been bloody clashes with the Inuit there as well, French wintering parties could hold their own by retreating at need into the security of wooden blockhouses defended by ships' cannon. So, in 1689, two seigneuries, principally engaged in sealing, were established to encompass the whole of the Labrador and Newfoundland coasts bordering the Strait.

By then the harp seal fishery had become so lucrative that the French rallied their Indian allies and began waging a successful war of extermination against the Inuit for control of the Côte du Nord. By 1720, a string of seigneuries stretched from Tadoussac all along the north shore right to Belle Isle, then north along Labrador's Atlantic coast as far as Hamilton Inlet. Additional sealing stations also sprang up along the west coast of Newfoundland at some of the very sites once occupied by the vanished Skraelings.

The nature of the fishery had altered and become more complex as the French grew increasingly familiar with their quarry's annual cycle. To the eastward of Anticosti there were now two sealing seasons: one in early winter when the herds came pouring through the Strait and headed west along the Côte du Nord, and a second during the spring after the adults began making their ways northward to the moulting patches. Nets had changed, too. Instead of relying solely on mesh nets to entangle and drown the seals, pound nets were also being used. These soon grew to such size and complexity that it required up to a dozen men to operate one. By raising and lowering door panels with winches operated from shore, it was possible to trap entire companies of migrating seals, which could then be killed at leisure.

By the mid-eighteenth century, hundreds of men from the settlements of New France were engaged in harp sealing and the colony was exporting as much as 500 tons of seal oil every year, a quantity requiring an annual kill of some 20 000 adult seals. There was so much pressure to expand this money-minting enterprise as rapidly as possible that one contemporary visitor to New France felt compelled to register a warning.

"It is questionable whether it would be in the interests of the Colony to multiply the seal fisheries . . . on the contrary it is logical to conclude that too great a number of the same would lead in a shorter space of time to the destruction of this species of animal. They only produce one cub a year; the fishing takes place in springtime which is the season of breeding, or in the autumn at which time the females are pregnant, and in consequence a large number could not be caught without destroying the species and risk-ing the exhaustion of this fishery."

Predictably, this opinion was ignored. In fact, the urge to kill as many seals as possible was being inflamed by the emergence of competition. Early in the eighteenth century, English settlers from eastern Newfoundland, who had been used to sailing their small craft to the north coast to engage in a summer fishery for cod and salmon, discovered what the French were up to on the *Petit Nord* (the Great Northern Peninsula of Newfoundland) and themselves began harp sealing. Soon they were establishing permanent set-tlements around Fogo and in Notre Dame Bay, from which they could seal in winter and fish cod and salmon in summer.

The English even added a new twist to the business. Having discovered that hordes of beaters and sub-adults, which they called bedlamers (a cor-ruption of *bêtes de la mer*), haunted the northern bays in spring for some weeks after the adults had departed, they took to swatching (gunning from small rowing craft) for them amongst the thinning floes.

Such was the success attending both swatching and netting that, as early as 1738, the few scattered inhabitants of Fogo Island alone were ship-ping oil and skins valued at £1200, the produce from more than 7000 seals killed each year. Now the die was truly cast. Having become aware of the money to be made from the harp fishery, the English hastened to make it uniquely, and bloodily, their own.

At this stage, French and English sealers alike had no conception of the true size of the harp nation and knew little enough about the creature itself. For a long time they did not even realize that bedlamers and beaters were of the harp species. And they knew nothing about what the seals did when out of sight of land. The drifting world of the ice fields seemed so hostile that they avoided exploration of it. As long as this heartland of the ice seals remained sacrosanct, human predation, massive as it seemed to those engaged in it, could occur only on the periphery where it had small effect upon the nation as a whole. But this was a situation that, given accidents of fate coupled with the nature of the human beast, could not endure for long.

o

Very early one spring near the middle of the eighteenth century (it may have been in 1743), a prolonged period of unseasonably warm weather accompanied by heavy rains prematurely weakened the great ice tongue that thrusts down the Labrador coast to provide the floating fields whereon the largest part of the harp nation bears its young. By the time the million or more gravid females reached the fields, the floes had become so shrunken, dispersed, and rotten that the seals could find no proper place to whelp. Yet their time was on them and so, in desperation, they hauled out on any ice that would bear their weight; and there they pupped, not in the usual gigantic patches but scattered like chaff across thousands of miles of disin-tegrating floes.

A day or two after the mass whelping had taken place, a nor'easter came howling over the region. Seas quickly built to mountainous size in the open ocean outside the pack and, rolling in under the floes, began heaving them into wild and vertiginous motion until they were crashing into and crushing each other. Numbers of new-born whitecoats, and not a few of their mothers, were crushed, and many of the remainder of the pups, unable to swim as yet, were swept away and drowned. Those that remained alive found themselves on isolated fragments of swiftly disintegrating floes, inexorably driven south by wind and current. In mid-March, this ice began piling up along the western coast of Bonavista Bay, freighted with tens of thousands of pups.

A handful of English fishermen had already established a permanent foothold on that rocky and reef-strewn shore in order to be on hand to hunt for adult harps in winter and beaters in the spring. They were dismayed when the bay filled up with ice until it stretched so far from shore they could no longer see open water. Unless and until it blew out to sea again, there could be no boat hunting. It must have been at this juncture that some daring fellow ventured out onto the grinding chaos, perhaps because he thought he saw some sign of life, and found a scattering of small white seals.

Within hours every able-bodied person was scrambling across the dangerously uncertain pack. Before the wind hauled southerly and the ice slackened and drove offshore, they had dragged the bloody sculps (skins with the fat attached) of thousands of young seals back to land where the thick layers of blubber were peeled away and consigned to the trypots, there to produce many barrels of high-grade train oil.

It is recorded that the Bonavista people did not even realize what manner of beast it was they were slaughtering until someone noticed a whitecoat being suckled by a mother harp and drew the obvious conclusion.

There have been a number of such "Whitecoat Springs," each of which became a milestone in the history of Newfoundland. In 1773, the whelping ice piled into Notre Dame Bay allowing fishermen there to slay 50 000 pups. In 1843, the pack jammed into Trinity and Conception Bays, enabling the landsmen to slaughter an estimated 80 000. But the most sanguine massacre of all took place in 1861, when 60 000 embayed whitecoats were killed in Hamilton Sound together with 150 000 more in Bonavista Bay. In 1872, even the townees of St. John's were able to swarm out on the ice beyond the harbour mouth and butcher nearly 100 000 pups.

The trouble with windfalls such as these was that they only happened at intervals of roughly twenty years. It was inevitable that, with the gleam of this white gold to light the way, Newfoundlanders should have gone looking for the mother lode.

At the time the search began, the fishermen knew only that the seals pupped somewhere on the illimitable waste of ice to the northward. Although they had no idea how distant the nurseries might be, as early as the 1770s some began probing the southern fringes of the vast ice fields in the open boats they normally used for the cod fishery. When these proved too awkward and too fragile to be forced in amongst floes or hauled across intervening pans, they developed light, clinker-built punts, which could be hauled over the ice by a two-man crew. These ice-skiffs were designed primarily for swatching beaters but, as time went by, the sealers took them farther and farther into the pack, thereby acquiring skill in the precarious business of ice navigation.

Finally, in 1789, a group of these ice hunters encountered a small whelping patch, which had drifted well to the south of where it should normally have been. During the next few days, the men of a fleet of ice-skiffs sculped 25 000 whitecoats and the drive to find what was already being referred to as the "main patch" received fresh impetus.

With the growth of experience, these tough and implacable seafarers had come to realize that the main patch could probably not be reached except with vessels strong enough to brave the pack and big enough to shelter crews from bitter temperatures and killing blizzards. So they developed the reinforced shallop, or bully-boat: a bluff-bowed, extremely strong little vessel of about forty tons, decked fore-and-aft, yawl-rigged, and capable of crowding a crew of a dozen sealers.

The bullies could stay out for a week or two, which was about as long as even these weather-hardened men could endure. However, although the bullies could be worked thirty or forty leagues into the loose ice fringing the central pack and could scavenge stray pockets of whitecoats that had been whelped outside the main patch, they could not reach Eldorado.

Bigger boats were built to look for it. By 1802, fifty-foot, fully-decked schooners, double-planked against the ice, were sailing north. Although the main patch continued to elude them, they made fortunes anyway. In the spring of 1804, 149 bullies and schooners sailed from the northern bays and, though they got few whitecoats, they swatched 73 000 beaters and old harps. The net fishery that year yielded an additional 40 000.

From its beginnings, the search for the main patch had been expensive in terms of lives and vessels lost. But in 1817 a ferocious storm of the kind that sometimes devastated the whelping patches brought desolation to many a northern outport. The sealers landed only 50 000 sculps that year and paid a fearful price. At least twenty-five vessels were crushed and lost in the pack, taking nearly 200 men to icy deaths.

Those who survived were not intimidated. Bigger and stronger vessels pressed ever deeper into the great ice tongue until, in 1819, they finally found what they were looking for. The ice that year was singularly open, and prevailing northeast winds had drifted the main patch to within 100 miles of the Newfoundland coast. Here it was discovered by sealers in a new kind of vessel: 100-ton ice-strengthened brigantines each carrying fifty to sixty men. This opening act in a drama of ongoing slaughter seems to have gone unrecorded. Thus the eyewitness report of a Professor J.B. Jukes, who in 1840 went to the main patch in the brigantine *Topaz*, will have to serve. I have abbreviated it somewhat.

> We passed through some loose ice on which the young seals were scattered, and nearly all hands went overboard, slaying, skinning and hauling. We then got into a lake of open water and sent out

five punts. [The men of] these joined those already on the ice, the crews dragging either the whole seals or their sculps to the punts which brought them on board. In this way, when it became too dark to do any more, we found we had got 300 seals on board and the deck was one great shambles.

When piled in a heap together, the young seals looked like so many lambs and when from out of the bloody and dirty mass of carcasses one poor wretch, still alive, would lift up its face and begin to flounder about, I could stand it no longer and, arming myself with a handspike, I proceeded to knock on the head and put out of their misery all in whom I saw signs of life . . . One of the men hooked up a young seal with his gaff. Its cries were precisely like those of a young child in the extremity of agony and distress, something between shrieks and convulsive sobbings . . . I saw one poor wretch skinned while yet alive, and the body writhing in blood after being stripped of its pelt . . . the vision of [another] writhing its snow-white woolly body with its head bathed in blood, through which it was vainly endeavouring to see and breathe, really haunted my dreams.

The next day, as soon as it was light, all hands went overboard on the ice and were employed in slaughtering young seals in all directions. The young seals lie dispersed, basking in the sun. Six or eight may sometimes be seen within a space of twenty yards square. The men, armed with a gaff and a hauling rope slung over their shoulders, whenever they find a seal, strike it a blow on the head. Having killed, or at least stunned all they see, they sculp them. Fastening the gaff in a bundle of sculps, they then haul it away over the ice to the vessel. Six pelts is reckoned a very heavy load to drag over the rough and broken ice, leaping from pan to pan, and they generally contrive to keep two or three together to assist at bad places or to pull those out who fall in the water.

I stayed on board to help the captain and cook hoist in the pelts as they were brought alongside. By twelve o'clock, we stood more than knee deep in warm seal-skins, all blood and fat. By night the decks were covered in many places the full height of the rail.

As the men came aboard they snatched a hasty moment to drink a bowl of tea or eat a piece of biscuit and butter; and as the sweat was dripping from their faces, and the hands and bodies were reeking with blood and fat, and they spread the butter with their thumbs and wiped their faces with their hands, they took both the liquids and solids mingled with blood. Still, there was a bustle and excitement that did not permit the fancy to dwell on the disagreeables, and after this hearty refreshment the men would hurry off in search of new victims: besides every pelt was worth a dollar!

During this time hundreds of old seals were popping up their heads in the leads and holes among the ice, anxiously looking for their young. Occasionally one would hurry across a pan in search of the snow-white darling she had left, and which she could no longer recognize in the bloody and broken carcass that alone remained of it. I fired at these old ones with my rifle from the deck but without success, as unless the ball hits them in the head, it is a great chance whether it touch any vital part.

That evening the sun set most gloriously across the bright expanse of snow, now stained with many a bloody spot and the ensanguined trail which marked the footsteps of the intruders.

Topaz returned from her voyage freighted to her marks with between 4000 and 5000 sculps. But the vessels that in 1819 first found the main patch brought back nearly 150 000 whitecoats, bringing the total landings for that "bumper year" to 280 000 harp seals, young and old! The fires that would consume the harp nation were now flaming high.

o

A digression must be made here to deal with a misconception that has been of great service to those responsible for the recent "management" of the seal herds: namely, that the number of seals *destroyed* has always been, and remains, essentially the same as the number of sculps *landed*. Even in the net fishery this assumption is untrue, since a very large percentage of netted seals are pregnant females, the death of each of which represents two lives lost.

As applied to the gun fishery, it is also false. Prior to the breeding season, when they are still fat but not fully buoyant, at least half the adult harp seals killed in open water will sink before they can be recovered. In addition, most of those hit are only wounded and will dive and not be seen again. Of those adults killed outright in the water *after* the breeding season, when the fat reserves of both sexes have largely been exhausted, as many as four out of five will sink and so be lost.

Beaters more than a month old are mostly hunted in open water and are seldom fat enough to float. The current recovery rate by hunters using modern rifles is probably no more than one of every six or seven hit. The rate of loss for bedlamers is lower than that for fully adult animals, because bedlamers suffer little fat depletion and so retain considerable buoyancy; nevertheless the sinking loss is heavy. It is also high in the eastern Canadian Arctic and west Greenland where, in the 1940s, native hunters annually landed as many as 20 000 harps killed in the water—but lost as many as seven out of every ten they shot. In recent years landings in these regions have ominously declined to about 7000 a year.

The gun kill of harp seals on the ice itself is equally wasteful. Seals shot at the ice edge, which is where the males congregate during the whelping season and where both sexes gather while moulting, *must* be killed outright if they are to be recovered. Even then, muscular spasms plunge a good many into the sea where the corpses sink into the depths. But instant kills are hard to achieve. Even such a staunch proponent of sealing as Newfoundlander Captain Abraham Kean, who went to the ice sixty-seven springs and is credited with landing more than a million seal sculps (a feat for which he was awarded the Order of the British Empire), admitted that his men had to kill at least three adult seals on ice for every one they recovered. Dr. Harry Lillie, who went to the Front ice in the late 1950s, reported that only one seal was recovered for every five shot by the Newfoundland sealers he accompanied. During April of 1968 I went to the Front in a Norwegian ship under charter to Canadian government scientists who were collecting specimens from the moulting patch. Their seals were shot for them by experienced Norwegian sealers, yet the recovery rate was only one of every five seals hit. There remains the loss entailed in the whitecoat slaughter; but this we shall examine in succeeding pages.

In the meantime, it should be clear enough that landings are *not* and never have been synonymous with killings—a fact to be born in mind as you read on.

o

After 1819, Newfoundland went mad for seals. Although still vigorous, the net and swatching fishery of the outport dwellers was overshadowed and almost lost to view in the frenzied efforts of merchants and ship-owners in St. John's, and a handful of major towns in Trinity and Conception Bays, to exploit the main patch. They went about it with a single-mindedness that only unadulterated greed can induce. New vessels began coming off the ways at such a rate that, by 1830, nearly 600 brigantines, barques, and schooners were together carrying nearly 14 000 Newfoundland sealers to the ice each spring—a number that probably represented most of the able-bodied men of the northern coasts.

What followed was unregenerate carnage with no quarter given. Considering that oil was the prime objective (whitecoat skins themselves were worth very little at this period), the sealers might, in their own best interests, have been expected to refrain from killing pups until these had attained their greatest weight of fat at between ten days and two weeks of age. They might also have been expected to spare the females, at least until they had borne their young and nursed them to "commercial maturity."

They did neither.

Urged furiously forward by his vessel's owner, every sealing Captain sought to be first to reach the main patch. The result was that the fleet sailed earlier and earlier each year, until it was arriving in the region where the patch was expected to form as much as two weeks *before* the females began to give birth. With nothing else to occupy them, the sealers waged war against adult harps as these clustered in the leads or hauled up on the floe edge. The indiscriminate slaughter that ensued resulted in the loss of uncounted tens of thousands of adult females and, not only of the pups they carried in their wombs, but of all the pups they might have produced during the remainder of their lives.

Females that did manage to whelp got no better treatment. Competition between ships' crews was so ferocious that men would be sent out on the ice to butcher pups only a day or two old rather than risk letting them fall into someone else's hands. To compensate for the loss of fat entailed by this barbaric (and idiotic) practice, the men would club or shoot all females they encountered, whether whelping, about to whelp, or nursing young.

"Never leave nothin' to the Devil" was the watchword of the individual sealer, whose own pitifully small returns were based on the lay or percentage system, and, therefore, on his ship obtaining the absolute maximum amount of fat. In consequence, each sealer did his best to ensure that the "devils" in the surrounding vessels would have to sail home "clean," or at least with only a poor "showing of fat" in their holds.

Yet another and equally destructive consequence of the ruthless rivalry was the system of "panning" sculps. Instead of encouraging each sealer to drag his own tow back to the ship after every "rally," captains divided their crews into battle groups whose task was to cover as much of the ice field as swiftly as possible. Some men in each group were to do the sculping, which they did almost on the run. Others gathered the steaming pelts from each area of slaughter, stacked them into a pile on some convenient floe, marked them with a company flag atop a bamboo pole, then hurried on. Such groups might travel miles during ten or twelve hours on the ice, leaving a glaring trail of blood to mark their passage from one pile of sculps on to the next.

Theoretically, the mother ship would push along as close as possible on the sealers' heels, bruising a passage through the floes or being towed through by her working crew, and picking up each pan of sculps as she came abreast of it. In practice, even latter-day steam-powered sealers, built as icebreakers, often found the task impossible. In 1897 five steam sealers at the main patch abandoned some 60 000 panned sculps they could not reach; while in 1904, the steamer *Erik* alone abandoned eighty-six pans that together held about 19 000 sculps. In the days of sail, sealing ships frequently lost half their pans, and it was not unusual for them to fail to pick up any if the men had been working distant ice when a storm came down. Such losses were considered no great matter. There were always lots more whitecoats waiting to be killed.

Not only pans were lost; ships were, too. Vessels were sunk when the ice set tight and crushed their hulls and, when they went down, they often took thousands of seal sculps with them. None of this was of any great consequence to the Captains of Industry who controlled and directed the seal hunt from their counting houses in Newfoundland towns and English cities. The profits being made were so enormous that such losses constituted no more than a negligible nuisance.

From 1819 to 1829, the annual average *landed* catch was just under 300 000 sculps; but when the unrecorded kill is calculated we find that the slaughter must have been destroying at least 500 000 seals a year. In 1830, some 558 vessels went to the Front, returning with 559 000 sculps. The following spring saw the landings rise to at least 686 000 (one authority gives the catch that year as 743 735). The smaller of these two figures indicates a real kill in excess of a million seals. The consuming fire of human greed was roaring now.

o

Harp seals have so far engrossed this chapter; but theirs was not the only seal nation in the world of floating ice. They shared that realm in evident amity with a larger species known to sealers as the hood—a name derived from an inflatable sac carried by each adult male on the front of his head.

If harps can be thought of as urbanites of the ice, living by preference in dense concentrations, then hoods constitute a kind of rural population. Usually their breeding patches are composed of dispersed and distinct families, each consisting of a male, female, and single pup. The patches are located by preference on the chaotic surface of old polar pack, which is much thicker and rougher than the relatively flat and fragile first-year ice that is the usual choice of the harp nation.

Hoods are monogamous in any given year, intensely territorial and fiercely protective of their young. Neither sex will flee an enemy. If a sealer approaches too closely, one or both adult hoods may go for him. Since a male hood can be more than eight feet long, weigh 800–900 pounds, is equipped with teeth a wolf might envy, and can hump his vast bulk over the ice about as fast as a man can run, he poses no mean threat. Nevertheless, hoods are no match for modern sealers, as Dr. Wilfred Grenfell tells us.

"[The hood] seal displays great strength, courage and affection in defending its young and I have seen a whole family die together. Four men with wooden seal bats did the killing, but not before the male had caught one club in his mouth and cleared his enemies off the pan by swinging it from side to side. This old seal was hoisted on board whole so as not to delay the steamer. He was apparently quite dead. As, however, he came over the rail the strap broke and he fell back into the sea. The cold water must have revived him, for I saw him return to the same pan of ice distinguished by the blood stains left by the recent battle. The edge of the pan was almost six feet above water, but he leapt clear up over the edge and landed almost on the spot where his family had met its tragic fate. The men immediately ran back and killed him with bullets. "

Until well into the nineteenth century, sealers took few hoods. The animals were too big and powerful to be held by nets and generally too tough to be killed in open water with the kind of firearms then available. Because they were so seldom taken, some biologists have concluded that they must have always been rare. They were, in fact, extremely abundant. Although never approaching the harp nation in terms of absolute numbers, the hood nation may not have been far inferior in terms of biomass—until the day when it became the companion in bloody misfortune to the harp.

Black days for the hoods began when Newfoundlanders started searching for whitecoat nurseries. Since these were usually embedded deep in the great ice-lobe that hung pendant off the southeast coast of Labrador and were protected by rugged barriers of old polar pack along the outer edges, wooden sealing vessels could only penetrate to the harp sanctuaries when wind and weather made the pack go slack. Consequently, they were often held at bay for days along the outer edge, and here they encountered the hood seal.

Hoods offered no small reward to killers with fortitude enough to tackle them. For one thing, their pups—called bluebacks—were clothed in lustrous blue-black fur above and silver-grey below, and unlike the whitecoat, whose fur would not remain "fast" when tanned by then-existing methods, that of the blueback would. The skin of a hood pup was therefore of considerable value. Furthermore, its sculp would produce twice as much oil as that of a whitecoat. And the parent hoods, both of whom could usually be killed along with their pup, together produced as much oil as several adult harps.

By as early as 1850, Newfoundland ship sealers were regularly and intensively hunting hoods to such effect that, during the later years of the nineteenth century, according to a study by Harold Horwood, as many as 30 percent of all sculps landed were from this species.

Hoods whelped on the Gulf floes, too, where easier ice conditions made them still more vulnerable to sealers. In the spring of 1862, schooner sealers from the Magdalens slaughtered 15 000–20 000 in a five-day period. A few years later the crew of a Newfoundland barquentine "log-loaded" their vessel with hoods during a voyage to the Gulf.

Mass industrial slaughter was particularly disastrous to the hood nation. When sealers savaged a harp whelping patch, most males and a goodly proportion of the females escaped alive and so could at least help to make good the loss of that year's pups. But when sealers assaulted a hood whelping patch, almost none of its occupants escaped destruction. That patch was wiped out for all time.

Despite the fact that hood seals are referred to in the current scientific literature as being "a comparatively rare species" . . . "few and scattered" . . . "much less numerous than harps, and have always been so," careful analysis of the history of sealing not only demonstrates that they were once exceedingly numerous, but also shows that their current rarity was brought about entirely by our slaughterous assault upon them.

o

The period between 1830 and 1860 is still nostalgically referred to in Newfoundland as the Great Days of Sealing. During those three decades, some 13 *million* seals were landed—out of perhaps twice that number killed. Indeed, they *were* great days for those who controlled the industry, and this monumental massacre provided the substance for many Newfoundland merchant dynasties that survive into our day.

Many changes in the nature of the hunt took place, none of them advantageous to the seals. For one, the previously ignored or, it may be, virtually unknown harp and hood whelping patches in the Gulf of St. Lawrence came under sustained attack from the ever-growing Newfoundland fleet.

For another, the skins of adult seals, particularly hoods, became extremely valuable as leather, a large part of which was used in the manufacture of industrial belting. The pelts of young hoods had always fetched a good price in the luxury clothing trade, but now a way was found to market some whitecoats, too, not by inventing a fur-fast tanning process but as a result of the gruesome discovery that the fur of just-born or unborn white-coats, called cats by the sealers, would remain fast on its own. Early in the 1850s, some Newfoundland entrepreneur shipped a consignment of cats to England. When muffs, stoles, and other female adornments were made out of them, the soft, white fur proved well-nigh irresistible to wealthy women. Such was the origin of the fashion-fur demand for whitecoats that became a multimillion-dollar business in recent times. However, until the post-World War II discovery by a Norwegian company of how to fix the fur of *all* white-coats, the market had to be satisfied for the most part with the fur of unborn pups. This, of course, led to a huge increase in the butchery of pregnant harps.

It is axiomatic that modern economic progress depends on a never-ending elaboration of ways and means to turn a profit from available raw resources. By the 1860s so much ingenuity had gone into "product development" of seals that the demand was outstripping the supply. Furs and skins were being sold for such diverse uses as ladies' jackets and blacksmiths' bellows, while seal fat was being used for a multitude of purposes ranging from locomotive lubricants to a substitute for olive oil. The industry was coining money and, although most of it stuck to the fingers of the merchant masters, some dribbled down to ordinary fishermen, a few of whom found themselves relatively wealthy, if briefly so. Dr. Grenfell tells of one liveyere who ran a net fishery in a remote bay on the Labrador at about this time.

"At one little settlement a trapper by the name of Jones became so rich through regular large catches of seals that he actually had a carriage and horses sent from Quebec, and a road made to drive them on; while he had a private musician hired from Canada for the whole winter to perform at his continuous feastings. I was called on awhile ago to help supply clothing to cover the nakedness of this man's grandchildren."

o

The destruction engulfing the ice seals was not confined to North America. Early in the 1700s, Scots and English whalers sailing west in European Arctic waters had discovered a gigantic population of whelping harps and hoods on the so-called West Ice of the Greenland Sea, in the vicinity of uninhabited Jan Mayen Island. So long as sufficient bowhead whales could be killed in these waters, the seals generally went unmolested; but, by the middle of the eighteenth century, the whale population to the east of Greenland had been so decimated that it was a lucky ship that could kill enough to make her voyage pay. It was at this juncture that the whalers began turning their attention to the hordes of hoods and harps on the West Ice and in Davis Strait.

As was the case with Newfoundlanders, they learned ice-sealing the hard way, but by the spring of 1768 a dozen British whaling ships each loaded about 2000 hood and harp seals at the West Ice. They were soon joined on that living oil field by Germans, Danes, Hollanders, and the inevitable Norwegians, and amongst them they were landing a quarter of a million sculps a year before the nineteenth century was well begun.

The massive devastation that engulfed the harp and hood nations off Newfoundland as the nineteenth century aged was matched by a similar orgy of destruction at the West Ice. In 1850, about 400 000 seals were landed from there, and in the following year the figure for Newfoundland and the West Ice combined passed the million mark.

Greed took its toll of men as well as seals at the West Ice. During the spring of 1854, the skipper of the British sealer *Orion* dispatched a rally of his men to kill what appeared to be a patch of hoods amongst a torment of upthrust ice. The patch resolved itself into the frozen corpses of seventy shipwrecked Danish sealers, keeping company with hundreds of blueback carcasses with which the doomed men had tried to construct a barricade against the killing edge of a polar gale.

As at the Newfoundland Front, mounting competition for skins and fat forced the ever-diminishing West Ice seals deeper and deeper into the protective pack until they were all but inaccessible, even to the most foolhardy skippers. Losses of ships and men soared, and the catch began going down. For a time, it looked as if the halcyon days of sealing were coming to an end.

It was the English who found a way out of this impasse. In 1857, the Hull whaler *Diana*, newly equipped with auxiliary steam power, challenged the West Ice and was able to return home "log-loaded with fat." She also rescued eighty men from two sailing sealers that had been beset and had sunk in the ice when the wind failed them. The point was made. Crude and inefficient as it was, *Diana*'s forty-horsepower engine, driving an awkward iron screw, was the technological key to mastery of the ice fields, and a flood of steam-auxiliary sailing vessels followed on her heels.

The first of the steam-auxiliaries to try their luck in Newfoundland waters were the British whaler/sealers *Camperdown* and *Polynia*, which made a trial voyage to the Front in 1862. They took only a few seals because ice conditions were so appallingly bad that some fifty sailing vessels were crushed and sunk. But the steamers were at least able to extricate themselves, and the lesson was not lost on the St. John's sealing tycoons. Another bad season in 1864, which saw twenty-six more Newfoundland sailing sealers crushed, drove it home.

Thereafter the steam-auxiliaries quickly took the lead, and as quickly proved their terrible effectiveness. During the spring of 1871, eighteen of them unloaded a quarter of a million sculps on St. John's greasy wharves, bringing Newfoundland's total landings that year to well above the half-million mark for a value of about $12 million in today's currency. Seals were by then second only to cod in the Newfoundland economy.

It was not uncommon for a steam sealer, with her superior speed and ability in ice, to make several trips to the Front during one spring season; loading whitecoats and adult harps on her first trip; bluebacks and harp and hood adults on a second; and moulting harps on a third and even fourth. The *Erik* once landed 40 000 seals from three such ventures.

Although the advent of steam enormously increased the efficiency of the massacre, it did not change its nature, as the Reverend Philip Tocque, writing in 1877, confirms: "The seal-fishery is a constant scene of bloodshed and slaughter. Here you behold a heap of seals which have only received a slight dart from the gaff, writhing, and crimsoning the ice with their blood, rolling from side to side in dying agony. There you see another lot, while the last spark of life is not yet extinguished, being stripped of their skins and fat, their startlings and heavings making the unpractised hand shrink with horror to touch them."

While the steamers ravaged the seal sanctuaries deep within the ice tongue at the Front and on the ice plains in the Gulf, the remaining sailing vessels scoured the outer reaches of the pack. Meantime, landsmen went swatching in inshore waters and made rallies into any whelping patches they might find; and the net fisheries killed as many as 80 000 adult harps each year, mostly during the southbound migration when the females were carrying young.

The all-embracing nature of the slaughter was awesome tribute to the genius of modern man as mass destroyer. It also bore awesome testimony to the vitality of the western ice-seal nations, which between 1871 and 1881 suffered decimation in excess of a million individuals each year *yet still managed to endure.*

They endured—but both nations were fast wasting away. Average landings declined by almost half between 1881 and 1891 and continued to decline until after the turn of the century when there was an improvement, from the point of view of the sealing industry, due to the determined application of that basic principle of exploitation whereby a diminution in supply is countered by ever more ruthless effort.

After 1900, the "catch-to-effort ratio" was much improved by the introduction of really large, full-powered, steel-hulled, icebreaking steamers on the one hand, and modern repeating rifles on the other. Assisted by wireless telegraphy, which enabled the sealing fleet to co-ordinate its assault, the Newfoundland fishery maintained landings averaging nearly 250 000 a year until World War I. By then, however, sealers had been living on capital for more than half a century. It could only have been a matter of a few more years before the industry collapsed, had not the war intervened.

By the time the Armistice was signed, most of the new steel sealers had been sunk by enemy action, and those auxiliary steamers that still remained afloat were so old as to hardly dare face the ice again. Furthermore, the price of seal oil, which had risen to outrageous heights during the war, now slumped below pre-war levels and soon, with the onset of the Great Depression, became only marginally profitable. Although sealing still continued, it was at a much lower level of intensity than it had known for a century. The eruption of World War II in 1939 virtually brought it to an end.

While that war raged in Europe and the North Atlantic, the seals had five whelping seasons in which to bear and rear their young in relative security. By 1945 females born at the war's beginning were themselves bearing pups, with the result that the western harp and hood nations were showing a modest increase for the first time in a hundred years.

War's end brought no revival of interest in commercial sealing in North America. By then all but two vessels of the Newfoundland sealing fleet were gone, and the island's capitalists preferred to concentrate their resources on rebuilding the Grand Banks fishing fleet.

Although the Great Sealing Game had rewarded with enormous wealth the handful of mercantile aristocrats who ruled the island, it had returned precious little to ordinary men, thousands of whom had perished along with the tens of millions of ice seals they had slain. Now, it seemed, the time had come for the dead to bury the dead; time for the great dying of men and seals to become no more than a memory of an earlier and darker time, when human rapacity had known no bounds.

RATIONALITY AND RATIONALIZATION IN CANADIAN NATIONAL PARKS PREDATOR POLICY*

ALAN MacEACHERN

o

I do not think we need to shoot them but I think it is unrealistic to
say you should not shoot them. I suspect that if I were living in one
of those areas and had a rifle I would be shooting them.
W.W. Mair, head of the Canadian Wildlife Service,
on the killing of predators in national parks, 1956

When Commissioner of the Canadian National Parks system James Harkin,
an ex-newspaperman, spoke on the value of sanctuaries at a 1919 wildlife
conference, it was with a keen sense of what would capture his audience's
imagination. Animals, he enthused, had an uncanny understanding of
where they were safe from hunters. Harkin was happy to report that game
flocked to national parks, knowing instinctively that "a sanctuary is a sanctuary." He told his listeners:

As you know, at certain periods of the year a good many of the
farmers in the West go out coyote hunting for the specific purpose
of reducing the numbers of this predatory animal. The farmers in
the vicinity of Buffalo Park came to the Department with a complaint that as soon as they started coyote hunting all the coyotes
made a bee line for the Park where they evidently knew they were

---

* Unpublished paper presented at the Canadian Historical Association Annual
Meeting, Calgary, 12 June 1994. Used with the permission of the author. The
author wishes to thank Thomas Dunlap, John Wadland, Ian McKay, George
Rawlyk, and Jeannie Prinsen for their reading of this essay. Thanks also to the
Social Sciences and Humanities Research Council of Canada and the School of
Graduate Studies at Queen's University for providing financial support during the
writing of this essay.

safe. There was no doubt about the facts of the case and the result was the Department itself had to go into coyote hunting with dogs and traps within the Park.[1]

The irony was lost on Harkin. Coyotes were predators and, as such, were uninvited guests in national parks. For such animals, a sanctuary was to be no sanctuary at all.

Predators are animals that hunt and kill other animals for food.[2] Historically, they have been whatever animals people have *considered* to be predators—in other words, animals whose feeding habits in some way compete with human interests. In 1886, the Canadian Ministry of the Interior sent W.F. Witcher to Banff to assess the land at the national park that had been recently established there. Included in his report is a "black list" of animals whose presence in the park was unwanted:

> Wolves, coyotes, foxes, lynxes, skunks, weasels, wild cats, porcupines and badgers should be destroyed. . . . The same may be said of eagles, falcons, owls, hawks and other inferior rapaces, if too numerous; including also piscivorous specimens, such as loons, mergansers, kingfishers and cormorants.[3]

There was no need for Witcher to defend his conclusions; his reasoning would be clear to anyone of his time, or even fifty years later. Wolves, coyotes, and the like threatened the animals, such as deer, beaver, and mountain sheep, that were regarded favourably within the parks, and they threatened the population of game and livestock living outside the parks. The larger predators, especially wolves and mountain lions, were especially feared because of their mythic history of preying on people. The eagles, falcons, and "inferior rapaces" attacked fish and songbirds as well as other birds whose feathers, wings, or entire bodies were valued in the turn-of-the-century hat trade.[4] These were the rational reasons to kill predators, but the irrational reasons were just as real. Predators were seen as cutting against the divine grain, usurping what was otherwise human's dominion, and doing so as if with malicious design (hence laughing hyenas, wily coyotes). Eradicating them was not merely a duty, it was a pleasure.[5]

The Canadian National Parks system's practice of killing predators was not unique. The first wolf bounties in North America were in Massachusetts Bay and Virginia in the 1630s.[6] Moreover, the vigilance of kills within the parks system paled in comparison to those outside its boundaries: when kills of coyotes in Canadian parks numbered in the hundreds in the 1920s, bounty was being paid on 100 000 nationwide.[7] Even today, the United States Animal Damage Control agency continues to kill upwards of 100 000 coyotes per year.[8] What makes the parks' record of interest is that national parks were created specifically as wildlife preserves. To spend decades devoting energy and resources to the killing of certain wildlife within them demanded comprehensive, formal, and continual justification. A study of National Parks Branch predator policy can therefore help our understanding of why we have hunted predators with such zeal.

Such a study may also shed light on why our attitudes toward predators are different today. Historian Thomas Dunlap credits the national parks systems of the United States[9] and Canada[10] with helping bring about this ideological change. In the interwar years, he suggests, parks administrators depended for wildlife policy on a small league of scientists, mostly mammalogists, who adopted the concepts of animal ecology to promote the protection of all species. Their defence of predators became park policy, and the parks helped transmit these ideas to North America at large. Dunlap argues that "the crucial element in the shift was the scientists' ability to use the cultural authority of science to define wilderness."[11]

I would argue that what Dunlap sees as a sweeping victory for rationalism is not nearly so clearcut. Science was less an ultimate objective arbitrator in the making of predator policy than it was a tactic, a language used to defend what were still quite human positions. As late as 1950, the victory of science was far from complete. First, when pressed, the parks staff continued to bow to the barstool biology of livestock owners and hunting groups. Second, scientism allowed parks staff to think of animals as units, permitting the continued killing of predators for questionable experimental reasons. Finally, regardless of how the official predator policy changed in Ottawa, within the parks themselves entrenched attitudes about predators remained.

At its creation in 1911, the Canadian National Parks Branch of the Department of the Interior seemed hardly the bureau to change or even question contemporary wildlife management philosophies or techniques. Its Animal Division consisted of three men, and was headed by Maxwell Graham, an Ontario farmer with an agricultural degree. National Parks Commissioner James Harkin's experience with parks consisted of terms as private secretary to Ministers of the Interior Clifford Sifton and Frank Oliver.[12] Harkin is considered the father of the Canadian National Parks system, and in *Working for Wildlife* Janet Foster applauds him as a man fifty years ahead of his time in his appreciation of wilderness.[13] It is a contention that deserves review. Many of the conservationist policies and statements attributed to him were written by his assistant, F.H.H. Williamson, or by Hoyes Lloyd, who as of 1918 was the supervisor of Wild Life Protection in Canada.[14] Although Harkin certainly had final authority within the Parks Branch, it is not at all clear what knowledge of wildlife conservation he brought to his job.

This is a significant question, especially in the early days of the Parks Branch when wildlife regulations were being designed for the first time. With very little support staff, Harkin relied a great deal on information he obtained from the American National Parks Service and from American sources in general. When his chief superintendent of Rocky Mountains Park, Howard Douglas, informed Harkin that ranchers near Waterton Lakes National Park had reported cattle being killed by wolves and mountain lions, noting that "something will have to be done in the way of destroying these brutes in the Park,"[15] Harkin responded by writing the superintendents of American parks for advice. Harkin seems to have been the sort of man who took seriously the advice given him by experts. Returning from a conference in New York, in 1921, he dropped Maxwell Graham a note: "Your attention is drawn to the claim made, and considered as justified, that a mountain lion, in country frequented by deer, kills on an average one deer per week."[16] This simple statistic immediately led to park policy that mountain lions were to be shot on sight. Within weeks two Waterton Lakes wardens reported killing an eight-foot cat.

Incredibly, the American policies Harkin was being fed, and which the Canadian National Parks Branch was adopting, relied on Canada's existence as an animal-rich frontier to the north. In at least one instance, the U.S. Biological Survey's Predator and Rodent Control agency defended its "local extermination" of large predators in the American West by maintaining that the targeted species would continue to thrive in Canada and Mexico.[17] Meanwhile, they were sending the Canadian Parks Branch their monthly newsletter with tips on the pros and cons of snares versus spring traps, strychnine versus potassium cyanide.

Even with such assistance, predator control in the Canadian parks was an unstructured enterprise in the 1910s and early 1920s. Generally, it seemed unnecessary to instruct wardens on the killing of predators: it was second nature to do so. Occasionally, a warden might buy hounds to hunt mountain lions, and could be expected to be reimbursed by the department for his trouble. If any animal was believed to be causing excessive damage, special attention might be paid to hunting it down, but generally the branch relied on their wardens' instinct to kill predators. In his autobiography, Jasper Park Warden Frank Camp recalls that "often a warden's ability and effectiveness was measured by the number of pelts he brought to town each month."[18] As Maxwell Graham informed Harkin,

> Only in the term of Rocky Mountains and Jasper parks was a record kept showing what may be termed the individual score of each warden. During last winter in Jasper Park, 183 coyotes were destroyed, 49 lynx, and 6 wolves, a grand total of 238 predatory animals. Of the coyotes among the above, Warden Biggs got top score 56, of which number he shot 28 and trapped 28. . . . Summarizing all of the above, it is clearly shown that we possess among our wardens some really good trappers and first class shots.[19]

Such numbers pale beside those registered for the entire Dominion. In the 1921–22 season, bounty was paid on over 30 000 coyotes and 3500 wolves, and by 1926–27 the number of coyotes killed was approaching 100 000.[20] The increase was probably due not to a predator population boom, but rather to a mix of sizable bounties and public fascination with these animals. A vast number of newspaper articles related everyday people's life-and-death struggles with wolves or mountain lions. Invariably, the stories would end with the discovery of a trapper's body ripped limb from limb,[21] or with a resourceful lad killing the brute with a hammer, a pipe, or (memorably) a cross-country ski.[22] The war on predators was fed not only by the self-interest of hunters and ranchers, but also by a universal horror and paranoia of animals that ate flesh.[23] The coverage of the incident at Vilna, north of Edmonton, in 1925, indicates perceived Canadian sentiment toward predators. The *Toronto Star* reported that a wolf pack had terrorized the town, forcing families to stay inside and bringing business to a standstill. Finally, the townspeople fought back. The menfolk gathered, "and after the singing of 'O Canada' and the shouting of an improvised yell, the refrain of which was: 'Wolves, wolves we'll eat you up,' the army of destruction set out" and killed seventeen wolves.[24] It was an inspiring story of Canadian frontier courage in the face of bullying nature, but it never happened. The Canadian press later reported that one bedraggled wolf had come to Vilna, and had been followed about by townspeople for its very novelty.[25] There had been no pack, no terrorizing, no hunt.

The National Parks Branch was not unaware of the increasingly emotional response to predators in the 1920s. The staff was constantly badgered by individuals asking to hunt predators in the parks.[26] On the other hand, parks staff were beginning to believe that predators contributed in positive ways to their habitat. Conservation officials on the prairies were finding that the decimation of the coyote population seemed to lead to rapid overpopulation of rabbits and gophers. In 1924, the American Society of Mammalogists called for an end to anti-predator propaganda, declaring that it was "advanced by arms and ammunition interests, and by others financially benefited, and mainly by persons only superficially acquainted with these animals, or by misinformed persons."[27] Yet scientists themselves were unsure just how predator–prey dynamics worked. They were beginning to sense that killing predators did no good, but they as yet had little proof. As the holders of cultural authority, though, scientists could express no doubt openly, especially in the face of opponents convinced by their own logic that all predators must be destroyed.[28]

In a perplexing environment of growing support both for predators and for their destruction, James Harkin—at the recommendation of Hoyes Lloyd—had the parks superintendents in 1924 review which animals they were killing and why. The reports differed little from Witcher's assessment in the 1880s. Wolves, coyotes, mountain lions, weasels, wolverines, crows, magpies, goshawks, sparrow hawks, and Cooper's hawks were being eradicated throughout the parks system. A few other species were killed on the initiative of superintendents: eagles at Waterton Lakes, owls at Revelstoke, blue herons at Buffalo Park.[29] These findings were generally expected, but the Parks Branch took the opportunity to draft a general policy statement on predators for the first time. Harkin, in a memo almost certainly written by Lloyd, directed his staff:

> In view of the fact that so many people are interested in seeing the various kinds of wildlife within the Canadian National Parks, even though in some instances some of these species of interest may be more or less injurious, it is felt that there should be a strict tightening up in the matter of killing birds and mammals because these are alleged to be predatory.[30]

Wolves, wolverines, coyotes, mountain lions, lynxes, goshawks, Cooper's hawks, great horned owls, crows, and magpies were to be the only predators killed (by gun or by trap), their skulls retained for supposedly scientific purposes. It is significant that Harkin explains the formulating of predator policy in terms of human, not environmental, need. Human interest was of paramount importance to the branch, and may also have been an easier explanation to offer the superintendents. Pronouncements on the merits of predators to the ecosystem might have proven contentious to men whose day-to-day life in the parks may have convinced them differently.

Predator policy evolving in Ottawa did not always successfully control the practices in the parks themselves. Following a conference with superintendents in 1928, Harkin decreed that wardens would no longer be given the proceeds from the sale of predator pelts they brought in, which had been considered a small perk to encourage the war on predators. Also, wardens were forbidden from trapping altogether.[31] The latter decision could be understood as a response to periodic reports that other animals, from dogs to grizzlies, had been caught in traps meant for coyotes, wolves, or cougars. However, as Harkin explained to his deputy minister W.W. Cory, there was more to it than that:

> It must be kept in mind that Wardens for years not only were encouraged to trap predators but were allowed to keep the skins. For a good many of our Wardens this meant quite a substantial financial return. Gradually we came to the conclusion that, in the first place, the system encouraged the Wardens to spend far too much time in trapping and too little on the more important duties of their position; and also that some of them at least were trapping numerous fur-bearers not on the predatory list. We felt that, in regard to some of our Wardens at all events, we were in the winter time virtually paying them a salary to carry on a general trapping business.[32]

Some wardens were maintaining full trap lines, catching marten, mink, otter, and beaver, whose furs were more valuable than the wolf's or the coyote's, and selling their pelts surreptitiously. If their trapping was discovered, they could blame the game deaths on the non-selectivity of traps.[33] It is impossible to tell how widespread such practices were—not surprisingly, the National Parks Branch kept the problem quiet—but it could quite easily have been common. The men hired as wardens were skilled with horses, knew their way in the wilds, and liked to live away from society. Thus, many who applied and were hired were ex-outfitters and trappers. Ultimately, national parks predator policy depended on the integrity of a small group of men responsible for huge tracts of land, working alone miles from their superintendents and light years from Ottawa. Commissioner Harkin's ban on trapping was the first admission that such a gulf existed.

The trapping ban did not signal a growing toleration of predator species. As Harkin assured an American seeking information on Canadian parks regulations, "Wildlife is given absolute protection with the further exception that war is waged on predatory animals to a reasonable extent in order that the safety of the remainder may be made more secure."[34] Wardens were expected to continue killing coyotes, wolves, and cougars— just their means of doing so were limited. In 1929, the Banff superintendent reported that only seventeen coyotes had been killed, down from fifty-four the year before. "I would say in the past," he wrote, "the Wardens have always secured the majority of Coyotes by the use of traps."[35] Other parks showed similar drops in this and subsequent years.

As the degree of control exerted on park predators lessened, the calls from ranchers, hunters, and politicians for a tougher predator policy grew. Newspapers carried stories of predators skulking in the mountains at night, wreaking havoc, and departing before dawn. Alberta fish and game associations began to lobby incessantly for an all-out assault on predators. A typical plea to the Parks Branch stated,

> Yesterday, Mr. Cecil R. Duncan, of Morley, Alberta, came into the office and was very much put out that that morning a Cougar had gotten into his flock of sheep, for the second time, and killed forty lambs, and did not eat any of them. We have left the matter too late and the Cougars are now coming out from the Park into the Foothills and have driven the game anywhere from twenty to fifty miles East of the Park. Honestly, it is a disgrace.[36]

Evident in such letters is a tenor of disgust that the animal life of Western Canada was being threatened by the whims of Eastern Canadian desk jockeys. The Banff newspaper *Crag and Canyon* grumbled that "the fat-heads in Ottawa pose as knowing more than the men who tramp the mountain trails during the winter time."[37] The Parks Branch staff and Eastern influence in general were viewed as predatory themselves.

Columnists and letter writers did not blame the wardens for their enforcement of park policy.[38] Perhaps they were aware that some of the wardens and even some of the superintendents agreed with them. A Jasper warden reported, "I am sick and disgusted looking at coyote kills, sheep and deer all over the country, but they don't do any harm at least, so they say down in Ottawa."[39] An acting superintendent confessed to his superiors, "I am more impressed every day that Ecologists and other 'gists' to the contrary[,] the policy of preventing Wardens from trapping coyote is causing a most serious, and in my opinion, shameful waste of our wildlife."[40] Such grumblings, like those of ranchers and hunters, might be dismissed as the complaints of men prevented from profiting financially from nature. But most opponents were undoubtedly disinterested, honestly believing that a faddish government agency was overturning a system that had allowed game and stock to prosper in the West and that had not exterminated any predators in doing so. It should be noted that because predators found some sanctuary within the parks, and were free to roam outside the parks' boundaries (and free, it is true, to be trapped, poisoned, or shot there, too), the national parks *were* affecting wildlife outside their borders.

There emerged within the Parks Branch two quite contrary methods of mollifying its opponents: proving that in fact the parks staff were continuing to kill predators at a respectable rate, and proving that predators were being allowed to live because they did little damage and could even be beneficial. Convinced that wardens were doing a sub-par job of killing predators once they could not profit from the furs, Commissioner Harkin initiated a system of monthly quotas for each warden. Superintendents were directed that every warden

> is to work in connection with the reduction of predators such hours and at such times as will best serve the purpose in view. . . . It is up to you and your staff to see that this coming winter there will be no legitimate ground for complaint in this connection. It is important that you impress upon each warden the necessity of his making a success of this predator work. His efficiency in the Service will be judged by what he accomplishes this winter.[41]

The branch even acquired the services of noted hunter E.R. "Cougar" Lee to hunt his namesakes in Jasper and Banff National Parks.[42] When Lee quit after several months, unable to kill enough cougars to make it worth his while, the Parks Branch used this case both as evidence that they were working to lower the predator population and that this population was in any case already quite small.

The other tactic was to gather evidence of the relative harmlessness or even benefit of predators. Hoyes Lloyd championed this view. The data he compiled for his memos to Harkin were regurgitated back to the inquiring public. But to call Lloyd's defence of predators a "tactic" is misleading. He, like many other North American biologists, had been greatly affected in the mid-1920s by the lessons learned in the Kaibab National Forest in Arizona. U.S. Biological Survey staff had cleansed this game reserve of all predators by 1920, and in subsequent years the deer population exploded. All foliage was soon picked clean, and by 1925 starvation wiped out much of the herd.[43] Lloyd referred constantly to the Kaibab debacle in the following years, stressing that any human action against a predator species affects the entire ecosystem in unpredictable ways. "It is a law of nature," he wrote, "that the destroyer is also the protector."[44]

In 1930, 1933, 1934, and 1935, Lloyd delivered lengthy reports to Harkin, judiciously outlining the criticisms of the predator policy from both within and outside the parks administration, emphasizing that there was never any proof that the predator numbers in the parks (or in the West in general) were at all "unnatural" or that game within the parks were being threatened. True, there were perhaps 25 wolves and 6000 coyotes in Jasper in 1933, but there were also 40 000 deer and 14 000 moose. Where was the evidence of carnage? "The records," he told Harkin, "show no reason to depart from the present policy."[45] Lloyd also ensured that the most up-to-date findings on predator–prey relations came to Harkin's attention, mixing data on the stomach content of coyotes (which suggested that they ate mostly rabbits, rodents, and carrion, not deer or sheep) with the pro-predator platitudes of noted naturalists.[46] An attempt to banish predators from national parks, Lloyd once wrote Harkin, meant "removing one interesting form of native life because it follows its life habit of preying on another form, which is, after all, the way of Nature. It is Nature, I take it, that we wish to preserve, not any particular part of Nature."[47] Lloyd never did convince the commissioner to adopt a more tolerant attitude toward predators,[48] but he supplied Harkin with ammunition to fight proponents of increased kills and in this way helped keep the policy stable despite the criticism of the early 1930s.

Change to the parks predator policy finally did occur in 1937, but not directly due to Lloyd's influence. Rather, the replacement of the retiring James Harkin by his longtime assistant F.H.H. Williamson signalled a period of sympathy for predator species. Just as Lloyd had been affected by the Kaibab National Forest in the 1920s, Williamson seems to have been influenced by what he was told had happened to the forests of New Zealand. According to the president of the New Zealand Native Bird Protection Society, the country's minister of tourism Sir Heaton Rhodes had introduced Austrian red deer to New Zealand in 1921. With no natural enemies, the deer thrived on the country's low, lush greenery, and by 1926 the government had been forced to institute a bounty on them; it paid for 28 hides the first year, and 23 500 by 1937.[49] Lloyd had brought the New Zealand case to the Parks Branch's attention in 1934,[50] but it was Williamson who followed it closely, writing New Zealand game officials only two weeks after becoming park director. He also continually used the episode as a cautionary tale to demonstrate the potential devastation that a "harmless" animal could wreak if unchecked by predators.

As soon as he became head of the National Parks Branch, Williamson made it clear that he considered its predator policy outdated. He told the director of Lands, Parks, and Forests, R.A. Gibson,

> Unfortunately, ever since the Parks were first established, we have given particular attention to the preservation of the so-called beneficial animals which comprise mostly the deer family. . . . I feel we made a mistake in allowing public opinion a few years ago to compel us to introduce lion dogs into Banff park to destroy Cougar. As you know Cougar were in the vicinity of Banff and there was a strong local public demand for the extermination of this predacious animal; a number were thus destroyed, and since then the Elk and Deer have become perfect nuisances around the townsite and we had to kill a number of the former a few months ago. Had we allowed the Cougar around the townsite the Elk herds would have become disperse, which is a proper and natural condition.[51]

In the future, national parks would have to use all available scientific proof to answer the criticisms hurled at it by outsiders, and demonstrate that it would be swayed only by evidence, not emotions. Returning a draft written by Lloyd to the Northern Alberta Fish & Game Association, Williamson noted, "This is too abrupt. I think we should discuss the whole situation. . . . We must present arguments of scientific men and give illustrations of detrimental effects of predator destruction on beneficial animals themselves."[52] Whereas Harkin had sought to answer all critics individually, Williamson's administration was more consistent, repeating, for instance, the morals of the New Zealand and Kaibab cases in letter after letter to Alberta fish and game clubs. Increasingly, the Parks Branch spoke in the language of animal ecology, defending its policies in terms of carrying capacities, population cycles, and the balance of nature.[53] By 1940, the philosophy within the Parks Branch on predator matters was the most outwardly coherent and consensual it had ever been.

The Parks Branch's use of science in the 1940s did not, despite Thomas Dunlap's assertions, lead immediately to the policy of protecting all species. Rather, science was used to justify the branch's role as the sole manager of predator policy: a park is a biological system and we cannot permit outsiders to tamper with one part of our system. The result was not a hands-off approach to wildlife. To fend off a constant stream of criticism (headed by W.C. Fisher of the Alberta Fish & Game Club and president of Ducks Unlimited's Canadian wing) against it for not eradicating all predators in the parks, the branch made clear that it was still implementing control when necessary. Even F.H.H. Williamson could tolerate the killing of a few predators if it would help the parks system defend its overall philosophy: in 1939, he permitted the snaring of wolves in Prince Albert National Park on the grounds that "it would seem desirable to allay public concern regarding wolf control in the Parks by such a method . . . ; otherwise the proponents of developing the Parks as meat ranches might take advantage of our inaction to further work on ignorant public opinion against our methods of wildlife management in the Parks."[54]

Perhaps Williamson was right, and the parks had to sacrifice a few predators to protect the rest. But the staff's deference to science made it ever easier to rationalize the sacrifice of a few predators. This is best exemplified by their "experiments" with the latest control technology—"coyote-getters"— in the late 1940s. Coyote-getters are hidden in bait and, when bit down on, shoot potassium cyanide into the animal's mouth, causing death immediately. Such speed was regarded as an advantage not because it was more humane, but because the animal did not wander off to die and thus the pelt was not wasted.[55] When first introduced to Canada, the devices were of questionable legality,[56] but the Parks Branch elected to try them out after complaints that wolves were abundant in Prince Albert National Park. After a series of tests, Canadian Wildlife Service biologist A.W.F. Banfield reported that the devices were not selective enough. "One fine specimen was taken at a mule deer kill," he noted. "It was a dog, six feet in length, weighing 92 pounds."[57] Nevertheless, two months later Banfield recommended that the coyote-getters be used in several parks where it was believed timber wolf control was necessary.[58] Parks Controller James Smart approved, even though he recognized that bait stations might be overly successful and wipe out too many animals. "I do not think," he wrote, "there needs to be any fear that the wolves would be completely exterminated as they are not entirely confined to the park area and are known to drift in from the North where no control measures are under way."[59] Perhaps some even escaped to find refuge outside the parks.

The scientization of national parks predator policy in the 1930s and 1940s had made the killing of predators both harder to justify and easier to tolerate. "We believe that our attitude and action in all such matters must be based on cool analysis of all pertinent, carefully-ascertained facts" contended biologist Harrison F. Lewis.[60] Thus, in 1948, the Canadian Wildlife Service tested the effectiveness of strychnine-laced bait dropped from airplanes in Wood Buffalo National Park. When asked at a federal–provincial wildlife conference whether these experiments were done to kill predators or to aid prey, Chief Mammalogist Banfield replied, "These experiments were strictly designed to kill predators and were purely experimental." Lewis added, "We have a sufficient stock of wolves so that we can experiment with them without danger of exterminating the species."[61] Such thinking very nearly did exterminate wolves in parts of Canada in the 1950s. Fears that wolves, some of which might be carrying rabies, were drifting southward from the Arctic in response to depleted caribou herds led to an extremely vigorous control program that Barry Holstun Lopez calls "the final act of the wolf war in North America."[62] The irony is that national parks may be said to bear some responsibility both for threatening and saving these predators. In the short term, the Parks Branch contributed to a mindset that considered animals as products of science, even permitting the use of parks as test sites for predator eradication. In the longer term, the Parks Branch articulated for many Canadians a belief that all parts of nature are interrelated and have an inherent right to exist.

The people most involved with the contradictions within the Canadian National Parks predator policy were the wardens who enforced it. Combining a lack of understanding of the scientific reasons why predators were useful, an unwillingness to follow the ever-changing whims of their Eastern bosses, and a stubborn resistance to new ideas, many wardens clearly overrode official procedure. In a 1946 report, A.W.F. Banfield wrote, "It was found that in the majority of the parks, carnivores from badgers to grizzly bears were looked upon with disfavour by the staff and every opportunity was seized to shoot them on sight."[63] The problem was considered so widespread that administrators were worried that initiating even the most limited of control programs would reinforce warden attitudes to predators.[64] Listening to an oral history series initiated by the warden service in 1984, one is struck by how killing wildlife was seen as just part of the job. Warden Herb Ashley tells a humorous anecdote of killing a grizzly and, laughing, ends, "There was [sic] lots of those kinds of stories." Henry Ness describes dynamiting fish for sport, and Bruce Mitchell wonders whether wardens were doing more poaching than anyone else.[65] Second-generation Jasper Park warden Frank Camp writes in his autobiography,

> In retrospect, there was such a contradiction in National Parks policy of game management during these years, yet the wardens treated it as a condition of their employment. One day we would be out killing elk, shooting wolves, poisoning small mammals and birds and the next day we were on patrol ensuring no one

entered the park with an unsealed firearm or caught fish in closed waters.[66]

The Canadian National Parks Branch was caught between a past that found predators antithetical to wildlife welfare and a future that recognized the right and need of all native wildlife to co-exist. Too often, parks staff attempted to accommodate both views. Unlike their superiors, the park wardens at least noted the contradiction.

NOTES

1. "Wildlife Sanctuaries" speech, 18 Feb. 1919, in RG84, vol. 35, file U.300, vol. 1, National Archives of Canada (henceforth NAC).

2. In *Predation* (New York: Chapman and Hall, 1984), Robert J. Taylor discusses four possible definitions of predation, and chooses this as the simplest (4). Eberhard Curio in *The Ethology of Predation* (Berlin: Springer-Verlag, 1976) suggests that predation is an imprecise term, and has generally been defined by what it is *not*—parasitism, browsing, carrion feeding, and so on (1).

3. W.F. Witcher to Hon. Thomas White, Minister of the Interior, 31 Dec. 1886, RG84, vol. 7, file R.200, NAC.

4. On North American attitudes to nature, see Roderick Nash, *Wilderness and the American Mind*, 3rd ed. (New Haven: Yale University Press, 1982). English and American attitudes to wildlife are discussed in Keith Thomas, *Man and the Natural World: Changing Attitudes in England 1500–1800* (Middlesex: Penguin, 1983), and Peter Matthiessen, *Wildlife in America*, 2nd ed. (New York: Viking Press, 1987). On the history of attitudes and policies toward predators, especially coyotes, see Thomas R. Dunlap, *Saving America's Wildlife* (Princeton: Princeton University Press, 1988).

5. Barry Holstun Lopez's remarkable *Of Wolves and Men* (New York: Charles Scribner's Sons, 1978) traces the centuries-long history of hatred people have had for the wolf.

6. Dunlap, *Saving America's Wildlife*, 5.

7. Dominion Bureau of Statistics figures, in RG84, vol. 157, file U.262, NAC. Even Gordon Hewitt, one of the most ardent conservationists in the country, could in his 1921 *The Conservation of the Wild Life in Canada* (New York: Charles Scribner's Sons), 193, suggest that "while the complete extermination of such predatory species is not possible, desirable, or necessary, a degree of control must be exercised to prevent such an increase in numbers as would affect the abundance of the non-predatory species."

8. See John G. Mitchell, "Uncle Sam's Undeclared War Against Wildlife," *Wildlife Conservation* 97, 1 (Jan./Feb. 1994): 30–42, 79. Animal Damage Control has recently announced it is changing its name to "Wildlife Services."

9. Thomas Dunlap, "Wildlife, Science, and the National Parks, 1920–1940," *Pacific Historical Review* (May 1990): 187–202.

10. Thomas Dunlap, "Ecology, Nature and Canadian National Parks Policy: Wolves, Elk, and Bison as a Case Study" in *To See Ourselves/To Save Ourselves: Ecology and Culture in Canada*, Proceedings of the Annual Conference of the Association for Canadian Studies, 31 May–1 June 1990 (Montreal: Association for Canadian Studies, 1991), 139–47.

11. Thomas Dunlap, "Wildlife, Science, and the National Parks," 201.

12. Janet Foster's *Working for Wildlife: The Beginning of Preservation in Canada* (Toronto: University of

Toronto Press, 1978) tells the stories of Harkin, Graham, and others, "a small group of remarkably dedicated civil servants who were able to turn their own goals of wildlife preservation into a declared government policy" (3). Though I question her estimation of Harkin, Foster's book is invaluable for an understanding of conservationists in Canada in the early twentieth century.

13. Ibid., 222.

14. There is a problem, of course, in attributing anything to anyone in a large bureaucracy such as the Canadian government. In this paper, I have given authorial credit to the person whose signature is at the bottom of a document, unless it is specifically mentioned that someone else has drafted the document.

15. Douglas to Harkin, 19 Dec. 1911, RG84, vol. 35, file U.300, vol. 1, NAC.

16. Harkin to Graham, 1 March 1921, RG84, vol. 157, file U.261, NAC.

17. Thomas Dunlap, *"Saving America's Wildlife,* 50. More research is needed in the U.S. Biological Survey's records to see how often Canada was utilized to justify American predator policy.

18. Frank Camp, *Roots in the Rockies* (n.p., 1993), 46.

19. Graham to Harkin, 3 Oct. 1917, RG84, vol. 120, file U.266, NAC.

20. Statistics are from information gathered by Harkin and sent to Ernest Thompson Seton, 30 June 1923, ibid., and to Paul G. Redington, Chief, U.S. Biological Survey, 23 Jan. 1930, RG84, vol. 157, file U.262, NAC.

21. For example, the alleged death of Ben Cochrane, 1922, which generated interest throughout North America until the trapper showed up alive; or the alleged deaths of three trappers in 1922, the story of which was carried in the *New York Times,* 28 Dec. 1922, as "Wolves Devour 3 Men in Northern Ontario" and followed up in the *Saskatoon*

Star, 8 Jan. 1923, as "Naturalists Laugh at Wolf Atrocity Yarn."

22. These and hundreds of similar wolf and cougar yarns can be found in RG84, vol. 120, file U.266 and vol. 157, file U.261, NAC.

23. The pictures newspapers used in wolf stories were either file photos or shots of hunters standing proudly beside their catch; pictures in deer stories were usually of a woman or child feeding the deer from their hands.

24. *Toronto Star,* 19 March 1925.

25. For example, *Montreal Gazette,* 31 March 1925.

26. R.S. Brown of Fort William, Ontario, offered to go anywhere to hunt predators. "There would nothing suit me better," he told Harkin, "than to devote my entire time to the extermination of these pests, as I would be carrying out my greatest ambition. The confidence I have and the freedom I would devine [sic], would be sublime." 15 Nov. 1924, RG84, vol. 36, file U.300, vol. 3, NAC.

27. Extract from July/Aug. 1924, *Parks and Recreation,* in RG84, vol. 36, file U.300, vol. 3, NAC.

28. I wish to thank Thomas Dunlap for pointing this out to me.

29. Reports are in RG84, vol. 7, file R.200 and vol. 36, file U.300, vol. 3, NAC.

30. Harkin to Superintendents, 30 Sept. 1924, RG84, vol. 36, file U.300, vol. 3, NAC.

31. The old policy is outlined in ibid., the revision in Harkin to Superintendents, 3 Oct. 1928, RG84, vol. 36, file U.300, vol. 4, NAC.

32. Harkin to Cory, 18 Jan. 1929, RG84, vol. 36, file U.300, vol. 5, NAC. Years later, Supervisor of Western National Parks James Wardle mentions in passing in a memo to Harkin that the Parks Branch had definite proof of two instances in which this had occurred. 22 Feb. 1935, RG84, vol. 37, file U.300, vol. 8, NAC.

33. Also, warden Frank Camp, whose father was a warden at Jasper early in the century, notes, "It was always suspected that some of the old time wardens in outlying areas travelled a fine line of honesty. It was easy enough to make a deal with a neighbouring trapper to overlook his activities for a cut of the action. Old marten trap sets were quite often found in the Park, far from where any poacher would dare to travel, but they were there for a reason," Camp, *Roots in the Rockies*, 40.

34. Harkin to W.B. Conger, Newcomb College, New Orleans, 24 Sept. 1929, RG84, vol. 36, file U.300, vol. 5, NAC.

35. Superintendent R.S. Stronach to Harkin, 15 Feb. 1929, RG84, vol. 7, file R.200, NAC.

36. Calgary Fish & Game Association to Harkin, 20 June 1936, RG84, vol. 37, file U.300, vol. 9, NAC. There are similar letters in this file from the Northern Alberta Game & Fish Protective League, the Waterton Lakes Rod & Gun Club, the Alberta Fish & Game Association, and S.H. Clark, Game Commissioner for the Alberta Department of Agriculture.

37. *Crag and Canyon*, 30 March 1934. This was a common refrain. In the *Crag and Canyon*, 23 Dec. 1932, the editor wrote, "An official is needed in Ottawa at the head of game conservation who is something besides a dreamer and a theorist. A man is needed who will make a study of the problem and will listen to advice from men who have lived in the mountains all their lives and who realize the present policy is entirely wrong." Similar editorials can be found in the *Toronto Star Weekly*, 28 Jan. 1933, and the *Edmonton Journal*, 27 Dec. 1935.

38. In fact, the *Crag and Canyon*, 23 Dec. 1932, saw the wardens as victims: "The trapping privileges of the wardens [to sell predators' pelts, apparently], so it has been said, led to jealousy on the part of a superintendent in one of the western parks. His chief guardian was making more money than he was and he concocted the scheme of taking the trapping from the wardens by advocating the policy of 'letting nature take its course.'" But in a response to this, a Parks Branch internal memo notes that when wardens were still permitted to sell predator pelts, they were averaging only 2.5 coyotes per man per year; if they were making what the newspaper called "good money" from the sale of pelts, it must have been from the sale of high-priced furbearers. ? to Harkin, 1 Feb. 1933, RG84, vol. 7, file B.300, vol. 3, NAC.

39. Warden F. Wells' report, 14 April 1932, RG84, vol. 157, file U.262, NAC.

40. Acting Superintendent of Jasper, Sgd. S.M. Rogers to Harkin, 16 Jan. 1932, RG84, vol. 148, file J.262, NAC.

41. Harkin to Superintendents, 17 Oct. 1933, RG84, vol. 37, file U.300, vol. 8, NAC.

42. In a note to Hoyes Lloyd at the time, Harkin wrote, "So far as cougar are concerned there is always need for action. There should be very definite instructions to hunt cougar at sight always. I have no fear of extinction of this animal." RG84, vol. 7, file B.300, vol. 4, NAC.

43. The story of the Kaibab is a staple in histories of ecology. A good study of its effect on conservationism of the day can be found in Susan Flader, *Thinking Like a Mountain: Aldo Leopold and the Evolution of an Ecological Attitude toward Deer, Wolves, and Forests* (Columbia: University of Missouri Press, 1974).

44. Lloyd in a draft of a policy statement to be sent from Harkin to superintendents, 31 Jan. 1925, RG84, vol. 36, file U.300, vol. 3, NAC. In *Discordant Harmonies: A New Ecology for the Twenty-First Century* (New York: Oxford University Press, 1990), Daniel Botkin offers a valuable critique of the simplistic lessons learned from the Kaibab. Essentially, he points out that deer and predator populations do not simply move up and down in relation to one another.

This ignores all other variables in their environment, and factors their "value" strictly by their absence or presence in the system.

45. Lloyd to Harkin, 16 Jan. 1933, RG84, vol. 7, file B.300, vol. 3, NAC.

46. Extract from Charles C. Sperry, U.S. Biological Survey, "Winter Food Habits of Coyotes: A Report of Progress, 1933," in Lloyd to Harkin, 25 Feb. 1935, RG84, vol. 37, file U.300, vol. 8, NAC.

47. Lloyd to Harkin, 10 Oct. 1930, RG84, vol. 36, file U.300, vol. 3, NAC.

48. Periodically, Harkin showed some testiness at Lloyd's insistence on drafting, for his signature, letters that Harkin would not have written. When, in a letter to the Banff superintendent, "Harkin" stated, "The view is held by the Department . . . that these predators are essential in forest areas such as Banff National Park," the real Harkin crossed out the note and scrawled, "Frankly, I think you are going too far in these statements." 11 Feb. 1935, RG84, vol. 7, file B.300, vol. 4, NAC.

49. Capt. E.V. Sanderson, President, New Zealand Native Bird Protection Society, to Williamson, 16 Jan. 1937, in a follow-up to correspondence between the two in 1934. RG84, vol. 156, file U.217, vol. 2, NAC. Sanderson's information was incorrect; deer were actually imported in the 1850s, and the government began to deal with them around 1900. See Graeme Caughley's *The Deer Wars* (Auckland: Heinemann, 1983). What is important here is that Williamson and Lloyd believed the information they were given.

50. Lloyd had read of it in an article by University of Manitoba professor V.W. Jackson in the April 1934 *Scientific Monthly*, and had Harkin (?) write to New Zealand for information.

51. Extracts from two drafts of a report, Williamson to Gibson, 21 and 27 July 1937, RG84, vol. 37, file U.300, vol. 9, NAC.

52. Williamson to Lloyd, 25 Nov. 1937, RG84, vol. 37, file U.300, vol. 10, NAC.

53. Thomas Dunlap, "Ecology, Nature, and Canadian National Park Policy," 144.

54. Williamson to Gibson, 9 Feb. 1939, RG84, vol. 157, file U.266, vol. 3, NAC.

55. C.P. Barager, "The Coyote-Getter," *Outdoor Canada* (May 1947) and Weldon B. Robinson, "The 'Humane Coyote-Getter' vs. The Steel Trap in Control of Predatory Animals," *Journal of Wildlife Management* 7, 2 (April 1943) are contemporary discussions of this new technology.

56. James Smart to individual Chief Provincial Game Wardens, 2 June 1947, notes that "the distribution or use of poison for killing wild animals is now generally prohibited," so coyote-getters are apparently a violation. Also, "the setting or use of spring-guns is prohibited by section 281 of the Criminal Code of Canada." RG84, vol. 83, file U.3.1, vol. 3, NAC.

57. Banfield to Harrison F. Lewis, 29 Nov. 1947, RG84, vol. 2134, file U.266, vol. 3, NAC.

58. Banfield to Lewis, 13 Feb. 1948, ibid.

59. Smart to R.A. Gibson, Director of the Lands and Development Services Branch, Dept. of Mines and Resources, 25 Sept. 1948, ibid. Smart had replaced Williamson in 1940.

60. Harrison F. Lewis to J.S. McDonald, General Tourist Agent, Passenger Traffic Department, CNR, 31 Dec. 1947, RG84, vol. 39, file U.300, vol. 17, NAC.

61. Lewis, in "Proceedings of the 13th Provincial–Dominion Wildlife Conference, 1–3 June 1949," 157, RG22, vol. 16, file 68, NAC.

62. Lopez, *Of Wolves and Men*, 194–95.

63. Banfield, "Report on Wildlife Conditions in the Mountain Parks, 1946," RG84, vol. 39, file U.300, vol. 16, NAC.

64. For example, H.N. Fisher writes Harrison Lewis: "I think that once

the wardens experience full freedom to shoot every wolf they see, the idea that predators are as much a part of wildlife as any other animal will be all the more difficult to get across, and many predators will continue to be shot after the authority is cancelled." 18 Sept. 1948, RG84, vol. 2134, file U.266, vol. 3, NAC.

65. Interviews, partial transcripts, and report by Maryalice Stewart, 1990-0205, ISN numbers, 159306 to 159320, Canadian Audio-Visual Archives.

66. Camp, *Roots in the Rockies*, 81. He also writes, "All wardens were encouraged to shoot, snare or poison all the wolves they could" (46).

THE MYTH OF INTEGRATED
WILDLIFE/FORESTRY
MANAGEMENT✧

I.D. THOMPSON

o

There is an implicit assumption by the general public in Canada that governments are fulfilling their role as guardians of our natural resources.
However, in the case of forested areas, consideration has seldom been given
to attributes other than the first crop of trees. The legacy of a desultory
approach to forest management is one of uncertainty about what we may
have lost. There is no doubt that governments now are committed to manage most forested lands and over the past decade an increased effort has
been mounted to produce a commercially valuable second (or third) forest.
Commitment to other forest "products," such as wildlife, has clearly not
kept pace. This may be changing, but at an achingly slow rate.

To manage a resource refers to an active process whereby nature is
"guided" to produce a desired result. A forest may be planted and tended, a
specific density of deer achieved through hunting restrictions and vegetation change or an eagle's nest protected from disturbance. All of these
involve techniques used within a planned context to derive benefits from
the land. Preservation may be seen as a passive action where an area is set
aside to protect a specific resource or a portion of an ecosystem.

Integrating management of the forest to benefit wildlife, recreation and
wood production refers to a co-ordinated programme whereby forest cutting proceeds in a planned manner to achieve goals relating to all of these
uses simultaneously. Although integrated resource goals are not mutually
exclusive, optimization of each is seldom possible. Removal of timber over
large areas is cheaper than logging several smaller sites because the latter
results in higher costs of road maintenance, increased hauling costs and lost

✧ *Queen's Quarterly* 94, 3 (Autumn 1987): 609–21.

travel time for loggers. However, to benefit wildlife and achieve recreational goals a diverse forest is preferable, including complete preservation of some extensive tracts of land. Logging large areas promotes monoculture and reduced diversity. To a logging company, cost is the quintessential issue, not other land uses. Here lies the root of recurring antagonism between industry and the promoters of other benefits from the forest. Governments have generally resolved these conflicts in favour of industry when the red flags of unemployment and export dollars were waved. However, growing public awareness that governments and industry have not always been good stewards of the land dictates that a closer scrutiny of management in forested areas is warranted.

FOREST MANAGEMENT

For more than one hundred fifty years, the forest industry has mined Canada's forests with a disregard for the composition of future forests, and with no concern for wildlife. Vast forests of white pine are gone from eastern Canada and less than three percent of virgin coastal forest remains in British Columbia.[1] Industry's position in regard to regenerating forests has been that as tenants (about seventy-five percent of forest lands are administered by the provinces) there is no point in spending money on planting because there is no assurance that money invested will be recovered. The provincial governments have argued that both industry and government should pay to regenerate forests because government cannot afford such a programme alone and industry will get most of the benefits. A plethora of committees and commissions since 1920 have all reached the same unheeded conclusions: forests are finite, timber is being wasted and there is a lack of funding for needed management. Of the funds generated by forestry operations (through taxes and payments to government by companies to cut trees), a miserable 2.5 cents of each dollar was put back into the forest by governments in 1950, and only five cents in 1978.[2] These self-interested and apathetic attitudes towards forest management were strongly influenced by the anachronistic perception that our forests were boundless. The Canadian logging industry (which was primarily foreign-owned) ignored the hard lessons from Europe and Asia where many countries—Lebanon, England and China, for example—had all but depleted their forests. As early as 1864, G.P. Marsh argued for conservation of forest lands[3] in the US, and together with I.P. Lapham[4] suggested that a forested land did more than supply lumber: trees purify the air, enrich soils, prevent erosion, and prevent vast fluctuations of the water table. However, the exploitive view of the forest prevailed, and in Canada this attitude has only recently begun to change. The result has been more than twenty-six million hectares of cut-over lands where no attention has been paid to the regenerating forests.[5]

A turning point in the political sense occurred between 1978 and 1980 with the publication of the Reed report on forest management in Canada (sponsored by the federal government[6]) and two forestry conferences, in Toronto in 1980 and Banff in 1981. Politicians were made keenly aware that wood shortages were on the horizon and that there was an urgent need to plan properly for future forests. Since that time there has been a quantum acceleration of forest management in the form of planting, tending, nursery capacity, genetic improvements, and (shudder) spray programmes. Costs have soared and in some provinces expenses for roads and regeneration far exceed funds accrued from forest companies. For example, in BC there was a net deficit to government of thirty-five million dollars for forest activities in 1984.[7] These costs are offset to a greater or lesser degree through federal-provincial agreement funds but in any case much of the cost of forest regeneration is now borne by the taxpayer.

OTHER FOREST PRODUCTS

Other forest uses—recreation, aesthetics, wildlife, and wilderness reserves have always taken a back seat in importance to logging. The value of our forests beyond use for pulpwood and two-by-fours is not widely recognized. In Reed's 1978 report[8], wildlife is dealt with in a single paragraph and in the federal document, *A Forest Sector Strategy for Canada* (1981),[9] no use for forest lands beyond fibre production is suggested.

Although wilderness reserves may be set aside and wildlife biologists control the number of deer or moose taken by hunters, more far-reaching consequences for wildlife result from the amount of habitat changed through logging practices. Each year 1.5 million hectares of forest lands are logged, and on virtually none of this land is the logging activity directed to benefit wildlife. This does not mean that the majority of wildlife species in Canada is about to become extinct. In fact many species, such as moose, deer, ruffed grouse, and white-throated sparrows, prefer younger or disturbed forests. But there is a cogent argument to be made for a holistic approach to management of forested lands, that is, to integrate forestry and wildlife management.

MULTIPLE-USE MANAGEMENT

Multiple resource forest management has been impeded by the self-interest and short-term profit motivation of forest companies, the lack of political will to force companies to consider other forest values, the failure of university forestry programmes to teach multiple use, the divided responsibility for forest resources among government departments in some provinces, scarce funding for research on forest wildlife species, failure by wildlife managers to provide tangible goals for habitat management, and a lack of recognition of principles of theoretical ecology and genetics in forest wildlife planning. Some of these situations have been corrected, some will never be changed and others are evolving slowly.

It is the architects of habitat change who should accept the burden of determining consequences of their actions. Usually industry is required to provide an environmental impact statement prior to governmental approval for a given action, but this is not always the case: in Ontario, for example, the timber industry has been exempt from requirements of the

Environmental Assessment Act by ministerial order for more than a decade. However, government itself has spent little money on long-term, large-scale research programmes to learn the basic ecology of wildlife species. In the scientific literature, there are precious few studies on how animals in the boreal forest respond to logging, and fewer still on the importance of mature and old-growth natural forest to species which live there. (As a forest grows to maturity, the rate that total wood volume is added to the trees declines. "Old-growth forest" refers to the post-mature period where the forest is beginning to open up and rejuvenate as trees die and are blown down.)

The major single limitation in any conservation argument is the unavailability of proof.[10] When wildlife biologists are asked to state the effects of logging on a particular species, they can only guess at the impact or extrapolate possible effects from American studies. This is remote from the preferred alternative of local knowledge. F.L. Bunnell has shown that, in the case of black-tailed deer, those in Oregon do not behave in a similar manner to the animals on Vancouver Island.[11] He warns that species of animals in Canada are often at the northern edge of their ranges, where habitat and weather conditions differ from areas further south, and animals may behave very differently.

Of animals trapped for their fur, lynx have been well studied in Alberta and marten have been researched in Ontario. But if a biologist were asked to predict densities of ermine, fox, otter, beaver, fisher, wolverine, or mink twenty years after logging relative to densities before logging, he or she could not answer. For better-studied species such as moose and wolves, considerable uncertainty exists about habitat preferences and how logging patterns may influence moose/wolf interactions. Forest song-birds are somewhat better understood, at least in terms of their habitat dependencies, but forest raptors (hawks and owls) are more secretive and knowledge of them is harder to gain. Basic ecology of most forest-dwelling wildlife remains unknown.

Fortunately, it is not a requirement of properly integrated forestry and wildlife management to know each species in minute detail. Wildlife research is expensive. Exclusive of salaries, a project over five years will cost from $100 000 to $3 000 000 depending on the species, need for aircraft support and the level of questions being asked. Americans are far ahead of Canadians in the development of sophisticated computer models to predict impacts of logging on "indicator" species and "featured" species. The concept involves management of specific areas for featured species, for which there is perhaps some economic importance, and management of broader areas for indicator species; if they are present in viable populations, usually less sensitive species are *de facto* considered. The indicator species approach includes a monitoring system enabling adaptive management to enhance or protect certain habitat features. Quantifiable goals can be set and achieved. This system is currently employed in US National Forest areas.[12] In Canada, there is only limited management of forests for game species, and habitat targets are not established. Given the lack of knowledge of most species, an approach using indicator species is at present of questionable value.

Land-use conflicts in Canada have polarized interest groups and resulted in a substantial loss of productive time and money in preparing suits, court arguments, publicity campaigns, and appeals. This has been true in all provinces, but particularly so in BC where Lyell Island, South Moresby, Stein River Valley, Nimpkish Island, Akamina, Kishinena, Stikine, and Meares Island (to name a few) have all been areas of confrontation between loggers and environmental and/or native groups. These conflicts are a symptom of a malaise in resource management in Canada which arises from conflicting attitudes about the forest: single use, multiple use, preservation. The problem could be corrected with legislation. However, it is the unification of attitude that should be sought.

The regeneration of logged forests is an optimization problem to a forester; compromising this goal to achieve other values means compromising professional abilities. Attitude is the key; wildlife production is an equally eminent goal. I.K. Fox has succinctly summarized needed changes in the decision-making process to enable multiple use of forests: no single aspect of resources from forested lands should have a preferred status; all government and non-government agencies should participate in land-use planning; and no single agency should unduly influence decisions.[13] What this suggests is that a utilitarian view of forests is archaic and elitist.

S.R. Kellert reported a survey of over 2300 urban and rural Americans who were asked the question, "Should cutting for lumber and paper be done in ways that help wildlife even if this means higher prices?" More than 76 percent agreed to a greater or lesser extent.[14] In Canada, a survey of 76 201 people reported that thirty percent hunt or go on specifically wildlife-related trips.[15] Clearly, people do want more from forested lands than the assurance of a continuing wood and paper supply, and the management process will have to acknowledge public priorities. Attitudinal change within management agencies towards viewing a forest as an ecosystem is occurring, albeit slowly. For example, most forestry schools now offer a range of multiple-use management and forest wildlife courses. This is a bottom-up response which is surely laudable. However, governments and industry must respond from the top down and begin to integrate long-term objectives for wildlife and preservation of forest ecosystems. A view of the forest as a multiple-use resource will eliminate current antagonism and enable a united approach to environmentally sound, publicly approved use of forest land.

Resource conservation reflects the quality of our personal lives and at the same time has far-reaching consequences for future generations. For John Livingston, "the fallacy of wildlife conservation is a flat denial of the [sensory options that are ever at hand and infinite in number, because our culture keeps us blinded to them]."[16] Values concerning wildlife do not exist outside our own minds and therefore deal with personal philosophies as, indeed, does wise use of our resources. In that sense, concern for integrated use of our forests is an altruistic moral and ethical attitude.

Shattering this altruism is the cold fact that if lands are to be managed for purposes in addition to timber exploitation there are going to be costs.

We need look no further than the South Moresby conflict. The resolution of this conflict was at a cost to the taxpayers of $108 million to commit the area to natural processes as a national park. (The federal money will compensate the BC government and logging companies for money lost by not logging.) But we cannot establish a national park every time controversy over a particular tract of land arises. Whatever rules are agreed upon must be applied fairly to the entire land base, not just some areas. Since virtually all forests have been assigned to companies, and logging plans drawn up for the next twenty years, withdrawal of areas or reductions in the amounts to be cut result in losses to those companies. Forecasts of increased demands for paper and our position in the global economy are major considerations in decisions on forest use. The process of forest management is not immutable, but change will result only through political will because governments must approve plans for logging and usually do so annually.

Multiple-use forestry means higher wood costs, fewer jobs or both. If Canadians want more than wood fibre from their forests, then those values become a cost of our life-style. An analogy can be drawn to the solution of the acid rain conundrum: we know acid rain is a problem which results from our industrialized, leisure-oriented life-style. Society must decide whether we are willing to tolerate dead lakes and forests, or if we will solve the problem by funding the needed pollution abatement equipment.

THE CASE FOR OLD-GROWTH FORESTS

The need to preserve some old-growth forests is a special case of forest and wildlife management. As a forest ages, it begins to break up. That is, older trees become susceptible to incessant insect and fungal attacks, die, and are blown over or burn. This stage is referred to as a "shifting mosaic steady-state,"[17] and in such a forest there is high diversity and structural complexity resulting from combinations of young and old trees, shrubs, increased areas for flowering plants, and a floor littered with decaying trunks and limbs. Old-growth forests support many more vertebrate, invertebrate and plant species than do even-aged, mature, species-depauperate forests. Old-growth forests are in a sense didactic in that we learn how forest processes develop and can examine the intricate interrelationships between the atmosphere, soils and plants that have evolved over hundreds of years. Further, plants in old-growth stands represent gene pools and as yet undiscovered storehouses of materials of potential benefit to mankind as sources of drugs, genetic variants for crops and seeds for future forests.

Typically, Canada lags behind much of the world in conservation of old-growth forests. Only three percent of our forested lands have assured protection, compared to nine percent in the US,[18] for example. Prior to the establishment of a park on South Moresby Island, the small amount of forest within Pacific Rim National Park was virtually the only old-growth rain forest in British Columbia under full protection.

Management of forests necessitates long-term planning. In Canada, 75 to one hundred years is needed for a second forest to grow to the stage where it is commercially valuable. In ideal forestry, a forest is cut using clear-cut methods (hundreds or thousands of hectares of even-aged forest cut over several months), regenerated by planting, tended to another even-aged stand, and logged again. This technocratic approach fails to consider possible value in old-growth or diverse forests. A forester seeking to maximize wood products sees an old-growth forest as a forest in decay, a veritable wasteland, and there are no plans in Canada to manage for old-growth forests. Indeed, there is no evidence that silviculture (the science of regeneration of forests) could mimic natural old-growth if it were a planned objective. Conservation of wild areas is presently the only method available to protect old forests.

Forests represent dynamic systems, products of a combination of circumstances and natural selection. A forest preserved from logging will not necessarily look the same a century later. A fire could sweep through South Moresby next year, for example. Old trees die and the forest changes constantly. In eastern Canada, most of an old-growth forest will eventually be killed by spruce budworm (a leaf-eating insect with severe outbreaks approximately every sixty years). Unless fire disrupts the process, a forest will eventually be dominated by balsam fir and perhaps aspen.[19] However, because fire plays almost an inevitable role, and in fact is desirable in maintenance of forest diversity, old-growth areas in eastern Canada should be large (100 000–500 000 hectares) rather than small (less than 100 000 hectares) so that neither fire nor budworm destroys an entire area at once.

Succession in preserved BC forests proceeds much more slowly because trees are substantially longer-lived than those elsewhere in Canada. Here too, the ultimate forest composition will be different from that of today: although the spectacular Douglas firs and red cedars are self-perpetuating on some sites, in most areas those forests will be replaced by the smaller western hemlock and silver fir. Fire can renew a Douglas fir forest.[20] Large areas rather than a number of small reserves are needed, but preservation of such large areas does not seem likely because few remain and those which do are highly valued for their timber.

A number of wildlife species need old-growth forest, or at least exist at higher densities in older forests. Most prominent among these in North America is the spotted owl whose existence is threatened because of logging in west coast forests. The fight to preserve this species is confounded by the rapid rate of logging older forests (in BC less than fifty years of cutting will eliminate all old-growth stands). Further, preserving individual stands results in a fragmented habitat pattern. These stands of habitats may be far apart so that young owls cannot disperse to re-colonize them.[21] Small isolated stands of habitat support other species of owls which either displace or prey upon spotted owls, resulting in reduced numbers of the latter species. The US Forest Service has developed a management plan for conservation of this species on federal lands; in Canada no such plan exists.

The spotted owl may be the best "indicator" species of degradation of western old-growth habitat. However, many other species also prefer the same habitat and our lack of knowledge as to how well they survive in younger regenerating forests precludes adequate management planning.

For example, studies in Ontario and Quebec have indicated the importance to moose of old-growth forest in late winter to escape deep snow and predators.[22] Further research is needed to determine the generality of these observations. Marten feed extensively on snowshoe hare in winter and prefer mature coniferous forest.[23] A combination of hare and mature trees occurs only in old-growth forest where openings have been created by fallen trees and allow the shrub growth needed by the hares for food. Much remains to be learned about wildlife and old-growth before these forests are gone, and time is rapidly running out.

THE NEED TO CONSIDER
BIOGEOGRAPHY AND GENETICS

Logging of forests and establishment of preserves result in the creation of habitat islands or fragments. These fragmented stands are surrounded by regenerating forest, and are often far from each other so that the exchange of wildlife or pollen grains is impossible. The theory of island biogeography, first espoused by R.H. MacArthur and E.O. Wilson,[24] seems to apply as well to these forest islands as it does to aquatic islands. MacArthur and Wilson noted that although islands make up seven percent of the earth's land area and contain less than ten percent of bird species, over ninety percent of known bird extinctions have occurred on islands. Small isolated populations of animals are particularly susceptible to extinction events caused by fire, poor weather, diseases, predation, and human interference which can affect the whole population at once. Isolation means little or no immigration from other areas to restock depleted populations, and results in local extinction.

Lack of immigration also has genetic consequences. Deleterious genes can accumulate through random genetic drift, and there can be a loss of genetic variation through inbreeding. Without immigration to counter these effects, a population may become extinct.[25] An instructive example of species loss comes from Mount Rainier National Park. In 1920, fifty species of mammals were recorded in the park but by 1976 only thirty-seven remained, including two new species.[26] This process is currently being assessed in Canada's national parks and preliminary results confirm the trend to local extinctions.

In the US, land managers must now consider minimum viable populations for many species such as spotted owls. This concept, unfortunately, refers to an estimate of the minimum number of breeding-age individuals of a particular species that is necessary to maintain a species in perpetuity. The minimum number translates to the minimum area of a particular habitat type needed, or that must be managed for that species. Many researchers believe that for most species a minimum viable population is fifty to one hundred individuals in the short term and five hundred over the long term.[27] In the case of grizzly bears which inhabit old-growth forests in the US northwest, concern about the loss of genetic variation in small populations has led to proposals to transport bears from one fragmented population to another.[28] This reflects a crisis stage in attempts to manage for both timber and wildlife.

The establishment of preserves must recognize these realities. There is no point in making a nature preserve if what you are trying to preserve becomes extinct. Particularly in the case of preservation of old-growth forest in Canada, the effects of fragmentation and genetics on the survival of species, which has to date been ignored, must become a consideration. Because forests are dynamic, we will have to learn to manage for old-growth forests.

THE TROPICAL CONNECTION AND A FAMILIAR PROBLEM

Many of our avian species migrate to South and Central America to spend the winter under more favourable weather conditions. Much of the tropical forested land has been logged and loss of forest habitat is proceeding so fast that more than two-thirds will be gone before the year 2000.[29] In Brazil alone, more than nine million hectares of forest is added each year to that being logged[30] as a short-term solution to a burgeoning foreign debt. Virtually none of the cut forests are replanted. Further, large areas are logged to permit the pasturing of beef cattle in what has been referred to as the "hamburgerization" of Central America, that is to grow the beef for fast-food restaurants in North America.[31] We can set management goals and establish preserves in Canada for our forest birds, but this will be for naught if tropical forests vanish.

Tropical forests are estimated to produce fifty percent of the earth's oxygen. Logging vast areas of these forests enhances the "greenhouse effect" which is a result of carbon dioxide and other pollutants in the atmosphere. This accumulation will produce a warmer, drier climate which will devastate already-arid regions in central North America.

All the conservation and wise-use arguments which apply to our forests are eminently applicable in South and Central America as well. Loss of these forests presents an international problem of considerable magnitude because of the wealth of diversity of plants and animals, many of which have only recently been seen for the first time and already are disappearing.

The World Resources Institute has published a three-volume report and claims that if all its recommendations are implemented there will be no need for further deforestation in the tropics.[32] One of the recommendations involves an expenditure of eleven billion dollars over five years. The cost of our life-style continues to mount.

CONCLUSION

The integration of forest and wildlife management on Canadian public lands is a laudable goal, but one which governments have not pursued with any rigour. The extent to which forests are managed for wildlife is equal to the extent that foresters have been willing to heed arguments of the biologists.

There are no laws, no focussed public opinion and no political will to set and achieve wildlife goals in the forest management process. To provide attention to resources other than timber, a societal commitment must be made to support multiple-use forest management. Only then will wildlife values and species preservation be perceived as integral to socio-economic decision-making, which applies now only to the primacy of the timber resource and profit margins of the forest industry.

Within the present framework of resource management, a number of changes are needed to nurture multiple-use forestry:

(1) Unanimity of purpose shown by the integration of provincial departments of resource management is a primary prerequisite to proper land management. Separation of foresters from wildlife biologists fosters adversarial relations through a lack of easy communication. (Some provinces, such as Ontario, have one department; others, such as Newfoundland, do not.)

(2) Provincial agencies must work to establish quantifiable wildlife goals, adopting such techniques as modelling with indicator species. These goals should be built within the contexts dictated by biogeography and genetics.

(3) There is a distinct and urgent need for ecological research on forest wildlife species, particularly those to be used as indicators. Co-ordination of provincial departments is needed to prevent duplication of research, given the limited funds available. This role should be an important component of a federal resource agency, which also should show leadership in the protection of important wildlife areas. The Canadian Wildlife Service is the logical agency to act in this regard, but since, under the ministership of Suzanne Blais-Grenier in 1984, all researchers on forestry-wildlife projects were fired, one wonders if it would willingly accept that role.

(4) An increase in the number of wildlife biologists (especially specialists on non-game species) is needed. At present in Ontario, for example, a district may have six or more foresters and only one biologist for the same land area.

(5) Increased preservation of old-growth forests is needed, and research into methods to manage second-growth forests to achieve diversity similar to natural old-growth is required.

(6) Public participation in land-planning processes is essential.

(7) The recommendations of the World Resources Institute regarding tropical forests should be adhered to.

All of this involves an assumption of future public preferences for forest management. Resource problems have generally developed in the US prior to their occurrence in Canada. Using that as an indicator, it is easy to foresee public opinion forcing legislation in Canada similar to the US National Forest Act which compels managers to determine and achieve wildlife and recreational targets. A change in attitude towards the multiple use of forests could obviate the need for such legislation here. Forest lands are a national heritage, owned by Canadians of every province. How these lands are managed can be readily dictated by society through the political system. However, Canadians should not assume land managers in government are protecting all land values equally, nor be persuaded by logging company propaganda that "wildlife loves them."

NOTES

1. E. Hoyt, "Paradise in Peril," *Equinox*, 19 (1985), pp. 23–42.

2. F.L.C. Reed and Associates, *Forest Management in Canada* (Forest Management Institute, Information Report FMR-X-102, 1978).

3. G.P. Marsh, *Man and Nature: On Physical Geography as Modified by Human Action* (New York: Scribner, 1864).

4. I.M. Lapham, *Report on the Disastrous Effects of the Destruction of Forest Trees Now Going On Rapidly in the State of Wisconsin* (Madison: Atwood and Rublee, State Printers, 1878).

5. H. Salwasser, "Integrating Wildlife into the Managed Forest," *Forestry Chronicle*, 61 (1985), pp. 146–49.

6. Reed.

7. C. Young, "The Last Stand," *Canadian Geographic*, 106 (1986), pp. 9–18.

8. Reed.

9. Canadian Forestry Service, *A Forest Sector Strategy for Canada* (Ottawa, 1981).

10. J.A. Livingston, *The Fallacy of Wildlife Conservation* (Toronto: McClelland and Stewart, 1981).

11. F.L. Bunnel, "Deer-Forest Relationships on Northern Vancouver Island," in O.C. Wallmo and J.W. Schoen, eds., *Sitka Black-Tailed Deer* (Washington: US Forest Service, Alaska Region Series No. R10–48, 1979), pp. 86–101.

12. J.W. Thomas, "Needs for and Approaches to Wildlife Habitat Assessment," *Transactions of the North American Wildlife Conference*, 47 (1982), pp. 35–46.

13. I.K. Fox, "Socially Optimal Allocation of Publicly Owned Resources among Competing Users," *Forestry Chronicle*, 61 (1985), pp. 140–42.

14. S.R. Kellert, "Social and Perceptual Factors in the Preservation of Animal Species," in B.C. Norton, ed., *The Preservation of Species* (Princeton: Princeton Univ. Press, 1986), pp. 50–73.

15. F.L. Filion, *The Importance of Wildlife to Canadians* (Ottawa: Environmental Canada, 1983).

16. Livingston.

17. F. Bormann and G. Likens, *Pattern and Process in a Forested Ecosystem*, (New York: Springer-Verlag, 1979).

18. J. Harrison, K. Miller and J. McNeely, "The World Coverage of Protected Areas: Development Goals and Environmental Needs," *Ambio*, II (1982), pp. 238–45.

19. R.J. Day and E.M. Harvey, "Forest Dynamics in the Boreal Ecosystem," in R.D. Whitney and K.M. McClain, eds., *Boreal Mixedwood Symposium* (Ottawa: Environment Canada, 1981), pp. 29–41.

20. J.F. Franklin and M.A. Hemstrom, "Aspects of Succession in the Coniferous Forest of the Pacific Northwest," in D.C. West, H.H. Shugart and D.B. Botkin, eds., *Forest Succession: Concepts and Application* (New York: Springer-Verlag, 1981), pp. 212–29.

21. D.S. Wilgrove, "Owls and Old-Growth," *Trends in Ecology and Evolution*, I (1986), pp. 113–14.

22. D.A. Welsh, K.P. Morrison, K. Oswald and E.R. Thomas, "Winter Utilization of Habitat by Moose in Relation to Forest Harvest," *Proceedings of the North American Moose Conference*, 16 (1980), pp. 398–428. A. Poliquin, B. Scherrer and R. Joyal, "Characteristics of Winter Browsing Areas of Moose in Western Quebec," *Proceedings of the North American Moose Conference*, 13 (1977), pp. 128–43.

23. I.D. Thompson and P.W. Colgan, "Numerical Responses by Marten to a Food Shortage in Northcentral Ontario," *Journal of Wildlife Management*, 51 (1987), pp. 824–35.

24. R.H. MacArthur and E.O. Wilson, *The Theory of Island Biogeography* (Princeton: Princeton Univ. Press, 1967).

25. D.S. Falconer, *Introduction to Quantitive Genetics* (New York: Longman, 1981).

26. L.D. Harris, *The Fractured Forest* (Chicago: Univ. of Chicago Press, 1984).

27. R. O'Toole, "National Forest Planning: Problems and Solutions," *Transactions of the North American Wildlife Conference*, 51 (1986), pp. 396–402.

28. F.W. Allendorf and C. Servheen, "Genetics and Conservation of Grizzly Bears," *Trends in Ecology and Evolution*, I (1986), pp. 88–89.

29. E. Salati and P.B. Vose, "Depletion of Tropical Rain Forests," *Ambio*, 12 (1983), pp. 67–71.

30. L. Sinclair, "International Task Force Plans to Reverse Tropical Deforestation," *Ambio*, 14 (1985), pp. 352–53.

31. N. Myers, "The Hamburger Connection: How Central America's Forests Become North America's Hamburgers," *Ambio*, 10 (1981), pp. 3–8.

32. Sinclair.

ANIMAL RIGHTS AND ENVIRONMENTALISM*

REBECCA AIRD

o

In recent years the animal welfare/animal rights movement has evolved into an increasingly powerful and complex phenomenon. This evolution is characterized by two interrelated developments: a growth in *active* concern for animal welfare, especially within the urban population of North America and Europe; and the effort to produce a consistent and rational philosophical foundation for animal rights.

As an institutionalized movement, animal welfare can be traced to the early 19th century beginnings of the Royal Society for the Prevention of Cruelty to Animals (RSPCA) in Britain. The movement's aim, based on an appeal to human compassion, was to minimize animal suffering. Traditionally, animal welfare groups have not been philosophically opposed to human use of animals. Rather they have worked to improve the conditions under which animals are used. Thus, they have often encouraged and assisted in the development of more humane methods for activities involving animals.

The animal rights philosophy, on the other hand, views human compassion as a fickle and inadequate basis for regulating the treatment of animals. At the extreme, it holds that any exploitative relationship is unacceptable.

Reasoned arguments against the exploitation of animals have arisen frequently throughout history. In the first century A.D., for example, the Greek author Plutarch spoke against eating meat, not only because of the sentience of nonhuman animals, but because he believed that killing animals to satisfy "nonessential appetites" led to progressive moral degeneracy. In the 18th century, the French philosopher Voltaire penned a

* Reprinted with permission of Pollution Probe. This article was originally published in *Probe Post* (Summer 1986): 20–25.

passionately argued rejection of Descartes' claim that animals are essentially machines without true sensitivity. It has commonly been held that the capacity of animals to suffer is deserving of consideration in human interactions with them. Without denying the influence of past arguments, over the last two decades particularly intensive attention has been devoted to the development of a more comprehensive, coherent philosophical framework for the concept of animal rights.

The cornerstone of the animal rights ideology is that nonhuman animals have interests (according to animal liberation philosopher Peter Singer, the capacity to suffer is a "prerequisite for having interests") and, therefore, have, or should be treated as if they have, rights. The definition of rights is, in itself, complex and controversial. Distinctions between rights as entitlements versus rights as claims, and natural rights (birthrights) versus special (conferred) rights, are relevant to the present issue, but these cannot be adequately explored here. The most straightforward conception is that animal rights include the right to life and—in appropriate context—liberty.

Singer argues for "equality of consideration" for members of other species and "an end to discrimination based on arbitrary characteristics," but he admits some ambiguity in applying this consideration. In its most extreme form, however, the philosophy holds that animal rights are/should be absolute. In other words, they should not be subject to human perceptions of the "merit" of an animal or species, nor human assessment of their degree of sentience. Similarly, the human benefits which are derived from use are not seen as particularly significant. The implications are sweeping. Virtually all interactions between humans and animals are brought into question.

Despite the distinct philosophical and legal implications of the concept of animal rights, at the level of state goals and actions it has become increasingly difficult to distinguish between animal welfare and animal rights groups. Partly due to the influence and public profile of animal rights supporters, some traditionally moderate animal welfare groups, such as the RSPCA and the Canadian Federation of Humane Societies, are becoming more "radical." This shift reflects a more youthful membership within these organizations and the membership growth and funding success of the more radical groups.

As this implies, the translation of animal rights from a generalized ideal into "real world" action involves some distortion, conflict and compromise. In principle, dogs, seals, pigs, and rats all deserve equal consideration. In practice, however, the motivation of many animal rights proponents derives from "gut reactions"—based on an animal's visual or behavioural appeal, and on subjective assessments of the legitimacy of a particular use—rather than from the application of a clear moral principle. Action is, therefore, not as consistent as the more philosophically oriented would probably like.

A look at the anti-sealing and anti-trapping movements will show how animal welfare, animal rights and environmental groups interpret and attempt to apply their philosophies, and the way in which these different groups handle conflict with sealers, trappers and aboriginal peoples. In turn, this helps to clarify some important aspects of the underlying philosophies and brings to light crucial differences between animal rights and environmentalism.

Some of the most widely read and cogently argued works on animal rights—including Singer's book *Animal Liberation*—focus much of their criticism on animal abuses in factory farming, medical experimentation and product testing. The rationale for this focus relates partly to the sheer scale of these activities and, therefore, the huge number of animals involved. Also, because farm and laboratory animals are now commonly raised under conditions of extreme sensory and social deprivation, their *entire lifespan* is seen to involve suffering at human hands. Singer, therefore, strongly castigates those who "take a stand about a remote issue (such as) bullfighting in Spain or the slaughter of baby seals in Canada while continuing to eat chickens that have spent their lives crammed in cages. . . . "

In spite of these arguments, however, protests against the abuses of domesticated and captive animals in agribusiness, research and industry have not garnered as much attention as protests against "remote" issues. The actions of such clandestine groups as the Animal Liberation Front tend to periodically draw attention to agricultural and experimental cruelty to animals, but in recent years the most well-coordinated and highest profile thrust of the animal welfare/animal rights movement has been the anti-sealing, and now the anti-trapping/anti-fur, campaigns.

In the process of winning their battle to end the harp seal pup hunt off Canada's East Coast, a number of groups garnered a high public profile. The Save the Seals Campaign and the efforts of the International Fund for Animal Welfare (IFAW) began to draw public attention to the issue in the mid-to-late 1960s. IFAW founder Brian Davies began his involvement with the sealing issue through the New Brunswick Humane Society, whose concern was to see that the hunt was conducted as humanely as possible. His own shift from this animal welfare concern to the animal rights camp is clearly reflected in the IFAW, which opposed the hunt on moral grounds.

Greenpeace brought widespread media attention to the issue in the mid-to-late 1970s. Greenpeace is generally known as an environmental organization. This designation implies a primary interest in preventing human damage to natural *systems*. Thus, in contrast to the animal welfare/animal rights movement, the concern lies with the integrity of the environment rather than with the well-being of individual organisms *per se*. Although the ultimate stimulus for environmentalism may be profoundly moral, the obvious rationale is, therefore, ecological. But despite its environmental classification, animal welfare/animal rights concerns have sometimes played as strong a role as ecological urgency in dictating Greenpeace's focus of action. In its anti-sealing campaign, Greenpeace initially emphasized the concern that the hunt was posing a threat of extinction to the North Atlantic harp seal population. The primary rationale was, in other words, an ecological one.

Although an understanding of the population dynamics of this species is by no means complete, the harp seal is one of the best researched species of marine animals. Studies in the 1960s which indicated that the North Atlantic population was declining led to the imposition of a number of protective measures by the Canadian government. Several years after the 1971 imposition of harvested quotas, studies began to indicate that the harp seal population was on the rise. More recent studies (for example, one in 1982 by the International Council for the Exploration of the Sea) indicate a high rate of successful reproduction. It appears that within four or five years of the 1971 introduction of the sealing quotas, the population began to increase and has continued to do so through the ensuing years.

Despite this evidence that the species was not endangered, Greenpeace did not withdraw from the battle. At a recent talk in Kingston, Ontario, Greenpeace Canada chairman Joyce McLean acknowledged that by the time their fears about population decline appeared unfounded, they were already committed to the anti-sealing campaign. Thus around 1977–78 Greenpeace was beginning to shift from an ecological to an animal welfare/animal rights focus. The argument that the hunt involved cruelty to animals for frivolous ends proved an even stronger public rallying force than ecological concerns.

Perceptions of the cruelty of the hunt varied widely. From the anti-sealing camp came accusations that seal pups were commonly being skinned alive in front of their mothers. On the other side, sealers and a number of veterinarians and biologists asserted that the killing method— the same as that traditionally used in abattoirs (a blow to the head followed by exsanguination [draining of the blood])—resulted in a quick death prior to skinning.

As the IFAW and reoriented Greenpeace campaigns were gaining strong momentum in the late 1970s, other groups clearly identified as animal rights organizations had also become involved in anti-sealing activities. These included Paul Watson's Sea Shepherd (founded in 1977 but particularly visible in the early 1980s), Cleveland Amory's Fund for Animals, and the Animal Protection Institute (API). These latter two groups circulated anti-sealing literature and undertook fundraising on the issue, but unlike Greenpeace, IFAW and Sea Shepherd were not involved in active protest on the ice.

Groups such as the API, Fund for Animals and others not directly involved in the anti-sealing campaign (including the Animal Defense League, Ark II, the Association for the Protection of Fur-bearing Animals, and the elusive Animal Liberation Front) are now rallying to the anti-trapping campaign. Most of these groups are either explicitly or implicitly animal rights proponents by virtue of their position that sealing and/or trapping, regardless of method, are *morally* indefensible.

Such groups, because they tend to base their public appeals on specific, attention grabbing issues such as anti-sealing, attract members and supporters who may not be fully cognizant of or committed to the concept of animal rights. Nonetheless, these organizations identify themselves with an animal rights philosophy which embraces all species and condemns all forms of exploitation by humans. This animal rights classification is rendered ambiguous, however, by the fact that many supporters, and even key organizers, such as Brian Davies, are not themselves committed to vegetarian diets and the avoidance of animal products in their personal lives.

The success of the anti-sealing campaign may be one reason for the high interest of many animal welfare/animal rights groups in the anti-trapping campaign. That the fur industry has been flagged as a key target by some of the major organizations is evidenced by such recent events as the launching of gorily graphic ad campaigns by Greenpeace and the RSPCA in Britain, the recent formation of the anti-trapping group called Lynx, and the October 1985 meeting of a coalition of groups (including the RSPCA, Greenpeace and a number of Belgian and Australian groups) in Brussels to coordinate strategy. In North America, groups engaged in or poised for anti-trapping activity include IFAW, the Animal Defense League, Fund for Animals, Association for the Protection of Fur-bearing Animals, and the Canadian Federation of Humane Societies.

Significantly, however, in October of last year, just as the anti-trapping campaign was moving into high gear in Europe, Greenpeace-U.K., one of the most active groups, officially announced its withdrawal from the fur-harvest protest and stopped its ad campaign. (It has, however, provided assistance and released ad rights to Lynx.) According to Greenpeace Canada's Joyce McLean, there were several reasons for the withdrawal. Greenpeace-U.K. was interested in developing the campaign on an international level, but a majority of the 10 voting member countries of Greenpeace International were opposed to this action, at least until further discussions were held with Indigenous Survival International (ISI), an aboriginal organization formed to support the native land-based cultures and economics of Canada, Alaska and Greenland. Some Greenpeace member nations also apparently expressed concern that the organization was straying too far from ecologically based concerns, such as those which motivated Greenpeace's nuclear protests, anti-whaling activity and pollution control work. According to McLean, there was also some dissension within Greenpeace-U.K. itself.

McLean asserts that Greenpeace Canada has not been actively developing the anti-trapping issue, partly because Canada would be significantly affected by the protest. From Greenpeace's perspective, the concern lies with the particular reluctance of many members to pursue an issue which would bring them into further conflict with aboriginal peoples. Although estimates vary, a recent survey by the federal Department of Indian Affairs indicates that about half of the more than 100 000 Canadians involved in trapping are aboriginal.

Indigenous peoples and communities are at centre stage in the campaign to counter the anti-trapping movement, because for them trapping is not only an important source of income and food but also the basis of a lifestyle that forms a crucial bridge with traditional culture. ISI holds that the cultural survival of indigenous peoples "is intimately linked to our continued ability to live in close harmony with the environment . . . and to harvest the natural and renewable resources thereof." George Erasmus, current

National Chief of the Assembly of First Nations, contends that "we are not fighting an issue, but rather for our way of life."

Indeed, although the Inuit do not hunt harp seal whitecoats (the North Atlantic harp seals whelp only off the East Coast), the European boycott and the subsequent collapse of the market for all seal products had a devastating impact on many northern Inuit communities. The government of the Northwest Territories estimated that the boycott resulted in 18 of 20 Inuit communities in the Arctic losing about 60 percent of their annual earnings. As a specific example, collective income from the hunt in the community of Igloolik, with a population of between 500 and 600 Inuit, dropped from $46 800 in 1982 to $5000 in 1983. The average annual income from sealskin sales in the NWT in the 10 years prior to the ban was $588 000. One year after, sales had fallen to $76 500. This represents a major blow to the long-embattled land-based economy of the Inuit people. While the informal or subsistence economy (food and other animal products for personal use and local trade) is still important in Inuit communities, the hunting, trapping and fishing activities that sustain it require some cash outlay. For this, many Inuit had depended on their sealing income.

While, on average, the economic impacts for Newfoundland sealers are not as stark, for many the income had provided a financial bridge into the fishing season. These sealers also lament the loss of autonomy accompanying that loss of self-garnered income. Socio-economic and renewable resource researcher Peter Usher admonishes the "urban environmentalist" who tells the Newfoundland sealers that they "should get jobs to replace their lost income, as though human well-being is totally and perfectly measurable by per capita income."

On the other hand, some animal rights groups, such as the Animal Protection Institute of America, have argued that sealers and trappers are actually victimized by being "forced" to do such "dirty work." Others, such as Brian Davies, see the cultural disruption as a price that must be paid to end a greater evil. In response to the impacts on native communities, many organizations, Greenpeace among them, have pointed out that the "harvesting" methods now used are not traditional and that, in any case, trapping is not a traditional activity. Native representatives, such as ISI's secretary-treasurer Dave Monture, label this a "museum" type perspective of native culture. He feels that if the ideological and practical respect for nature and the socio-cultural relationships which derive from a land-based economy are maintained, criticisms about the use of skidoos and guns are unwarranted.

As suggested above, however, some groups—most notably Greenpeace—have acknowledged difficulty in rationalizing the social and cultural implications for indigenous peoples of their campaigns. According to Erasmus, meetings held between aboriginal and Greenpeace representatives in mid-1985 revealed an obvious concern for the aboriginal position. And in his recent interview with CBC's Vicky Gabereau, Moore stated that Greenpeace is finding it difficult to sort out the issue and to develop a clear policy.

More insights into the anti-sealing and anti-trapping campaigns can be gained by looking at the significant differences in the styles used by the opposing sides. As suggested, those opposed to sealing and trapping have tended to make direct and powerful appeals to empathy, emotions and morality. In reaction, sealing and trapping proponents have taken a very different approach, though through hard won experience they are now remoulding their strategy.

Clearly, however, the manner in which the issue was dichotomized worked to the advantage of the "protesters." They deftly wielded their emotional weaponry and captured the high ground of moral rightness. The sealers and their supporters lost this ground by default and became bogged down in dreary and amoral (if not, in some eyes, immoral) "facts." Their labelling of the campaign as "mere emotionalism" was intended to be a criticism. Yet it soon became clear that the protesters, rather than being insulted by the label, willingly embraced it. Ecophilosopher and York University environmental studies professor John Livingston is not alone in expressing "enormous admiration for their (Greenpeace and IFAW) courage in taking on such controversial issues and not fearing to be called emotional." (Despite some reservations about animal rights philosophy, Livingston is supportive of the aims of the anti-sealing and anti-trapping campaigns.) In Europe at least, where the market really mattered, the moral/emotional appeal of the protesters won handily, and the European Economic Community (EEC) imposed a ban in October 1983 on imports of pelts from the harp and hooded seals less than one year old.

Although it began with much the same kind of "emotional" versus "rational" split, the nature of the anti-trapping debate is beginning to shift. Trappers' organizations—and especially aboriginal trappers, through such recently formed groups as the Aboriginal Trappers Federation (ATF) and ISI—have begun to play a more active role in the counter-protest, and they have begun to redress the imbalance in their arguments. The importance of sealing and trapping to the land-based culture and economy, and to local autonomy, now form part of the counter-protest's moral/emotional ammunition. Groups such as ISI have visited some of the most vocal anti-fur countries in Europe (including Britain and West Germany) and, within the last year, their efforts have begun to have an effect.

But it may not be only the socio-cultural concerns that have caused pause to groups such as Greenpeace. Environmental organizations, concerned primarily with the ecological devastation caused by urban-industrial activities, are confronted with important contradictions in opposing sealing and trapping. Based on renewable resources, these are the kinds of economic activities which, unlike much industrial development, are potentially ecologically sustainable. Aboriginal and other peoples with lifestyles closely tied to the land and wildlife argue that both their traditions and their economic interests ensure that they treat nature with respect, and that they are especially careful not to endanger the animal populations on which they depend. Moreover, aboriginal use of the land for hunting, fishing and trapping provides some (albeit inadequate) deterrence to other kinds of development which would be incompatible with wildlife. Many native leaders, including Steve Kakfwi, president of the Dene Nation, point to their commonality of interests with wildlife conservation organizations and appeal for greater cooperation rather than conflict.

With a growing understanding of the distinction between animal rights and environmentalism, the counter-protest being mounted by aboriginal and trappers' organizations is beginning to develop and reflects their underlying conservationist orientation. In recent years, considerable emphasis has been placed on trapper education, with trapping methods and principles of conservation forming major components of the courses. Through the government-funded Fur Institute of Canada, the development of more humane traps and trapping systems is being approached with renewed vigour. Further, the ISI has begun incorporating a clear conservationist approach.

The groups working to counter the anti-trapping movement are beginning to forge alliances with environmental/conservation organizations. While there is considerable diversity in the perspectives and motivations of these latter organizations, many are not opposed to such activities as hunting and trapping as long as the survival of the species is not in question. Here it should be noted that none of the species legally trapped in Canada is considered endangered by either the Committee on the Status of Endangered Wildlife in Canada or the Convention on International Trade in Endangered Species. (This is not to suggest that problems at the level of local populations don't sometimes arise.)

The World Wildlife Fund is one of the better known groups that accepts in principle the sustainable use of wild animals. Other environmental groups, such as the Yukon Conservation Society, the Sierra Club and Friends of the Earth, accept the rights of aboriginal peoples to hunt and trap, although here the question of "traditional" use may raise complications. Conservation organizations, such as the Canadian Wildlife Federation, whose membership includes a large proportion of hunters and anglers, are by definition supportive of sustainable "harvest" though competition between commercial and sport killing sometimes causes conflicts.

In contrast to these views, of course, animal rights groups feel that, short of a life-and-death situation, the taking of a wild animal by any person for any reason is unacceptable. A group such as Greenpeace, which Moore has described as "a spearhead of the environment *and* the animal rights movement" (emphasis added) is in the unenviable position of attempting to straddle the two philosophies.

The animal rights philosophy can be viewed as an extension of the humanistic belief in a moral obligation to improve the broader welfare while maintaining the paramountcy of respect for the individual. Indeed, many animal rights philosophers, including Peter Singer, hold that their position is merely the logical result of the historical expansion of human rights (i.e., the gradual increase in the sphere of human rights, to include all individuals regardless of sex, race, creed, age, etc.).

Ecologically based environmental and conservation groups, on the other hand, are motivated by an interest in the integrity of natural systems. Thus the locus of concern is primarily the population, the species and the ecosystem, rather than the individual. Many environmental organizations actually promote an economic and social reorientation toward modes of production based on local autonomy and renewable resources. Ultimately, of course, such a reorientation would respond to some of the concerns of animal welfare groups with respect to factory farming and industrial products testing. What conserver society advocates refer to as "human scale" may also correspond to "humane scale."

This potential notwithstanding, there is a clear divergence of opinions between the animal welfare/animal rights movements and the environmental movement on what characterizes an appropriate relationship between humans and nonhumans. Livingston, among others, has expressed the concern that to extend the concept of human rights to nonhuman animals is to draw nature even further within the net of humanly defined good and human control.

Nonetheless, the animal welfare/animal rights movement is demanding a conscious assessment of the legitimacy of human treatment of animals. It is making clear the need to evaluate the morality of many of our uses of animals.

Another lesson can be drawn from these issues. It appears that people are becoming less intimidated by the bluster of scientific "value free" rationality and are reclaiming the right to apply their own sense of moral rightness to socially important decisions. This would seem to indicate that a new synthesis is required in which rationality is characterized by a commitment to arrive at resolutions through open discussion in which all forms of input—emotional/intuitive/factual/and philosophical—are recognized as valid.

The animal rights debate also indicates the need for another kind of synthesis. Many cultures—including aboriginal societies in North America—have evolved a relationship with nature in which the use of animals is not incompatible with a deep and functionally relevant respect. The animal rights philosophy, regardless of intention, tends to reinforce the perception of humanity as separate from the rest of nature. On the other hand, because ecological environmentalism often phrases its concern in terms of direct appeals to human self-interest, it has arguably been remiss in fostering a respect for the intrinsic value of nonhuman nature.

In conclusion, perhaps it is somewhere in the blend of the various perceptions that the vision can be found to bring us to a more harmonious understanding of humanity's place in nature.

COMMON AND
UNCOMMON PROPERTY

o

W ho owns Canada? As the readings in this section indicate, each part of this question is problematic. Does "who" refer to individuals, groups, nations, institutions, the state, the continent, or some larger collectivity that goes beyond humans? Does "own" imply possession in the sense of private property, or perhaps stewardship, or even "belonging in common?" And how should "Canada" be defined? How, for example, can the concept of boundaries be applied to fish, flowing water, and the atmosphere?

The following articles illustrate the complexity of the question of property as well as the ways in which different answers have produced major environmental confrontations in Canada. M. Patricia Marchak attacks the idea that resources have been depleted in Canada because they have been seen as a "common property" for which no individual or group felt long-term responsibility. Instead, Marchak argues that privatization and the commercialization of nature is at the heart of resource depletion. Moreover, she emphasizes that the government is not in a position to manage resources as "commons" because it must constantly deal with the formidable pressure for revenue, employment, and other priorities that often work against long-term interests. After focusing on the case of the British Columbia fishery, Marchak proposes the development of a public management system "that begins with concern for the total environment, and assigns priority to conservation over private accumulation."

The need to view the environment in its totality is also at the heart of David A. Gauthier and J. David Henry's quite different proposal to establish government administration based on regions defined by ecological criteria. In their overview of the environmental history of the Prairies, Gauthier and Henry show how even a relatively small human population can produce "one of the most disturbed, ecologically simplified and over-exploited regions in the world." Like Marchak, these authors describe the ecological devastation that has resulted from a consumer, rather than an environmental, ethic. Their proposal to create administrative structures in keeping with ecoregions is designed to promote responsibility for resource use with the guiding principle of preserving the complexity and diversity of the biosphere.

The remaining readings in this section concern two of the most famous controversies in recent Canadian history. In both cases, international attention came to be focused on the question of the "commons" in British Columbia. In his description of the Columbia River Treaty, Larratt Higgins shows how power affects environmental definitions, concepts, and evaluations. The competing ideas of "Canadian resources" and "continental resources" illustrate how nature has been most affected by those with the most power.

As John Broadhead reminds us, this power is not absolute or unchangeable. While scholars now challenge the idea that small regions possess the biological diversity necessary to preserve the environment, the termination of logging represented an historically surprising victory for those who contested the view that trees are simply "money." The experience of the activists who fought to save South Moresby from devastation at the hands of logging companies suggests the central importance of philosophically reconnecting humans to nature. Broadhead stresses the extent to which "seeing" and "feeling" the ecosystem contributed to the increasing willingness to support the environment over the pursuit of short-term profits.

In her presentation concerning South Moresby to the British Columbia Supreme Court, Gwaganad of Haida Gwaii emphasized the inherent connections between nature and her people. The text of this presentation concludes this section. It provides a striking example of how the different concepts of common property in different cultures and economies problematize the question of who owns Canada.

WHAT HAPPENS WHEN COMMON PROPERTY BECOMES UNCOMMON?✧

M. PATRICIA MARCHAK

○

A popular American song of the 1940s expressed a general and uncontentious belief: the moon—and as well, it was believed, the air, the water, and the natural resources of the earth (though already with some notable exceptions)—belonged in common to everyone, and the best things in life were free.[1] Today not even the moon is uncontentious: property rights are extending into space just as they have extended over the whole of the earth.

Yet the term "common property" is widely used with reference to fish, and sometimes to standing timber. The central idea is that no one can unilaterally control the resource and no one can be excluded from access to and use of it. An argument has been advanced by scholars, governments, and private companies in British Columbia, as elsewhere, that because fish and trees are not privately owned, they are becoming depleted; ultimately no one has the management responsibilities for them.

This paper argues a contrary case. I contend that the argument is both logically flawed and factually false. With reference to the fishing and forest industries in British Columbia, the argument is entirely misplaced. What is signally missing when the depletion of the resources for these industries is blamed on their common property status is the central fact that the resources are potential commodities, and their excessive exploitation is directly connected to private commercial activities combined with state management. The literature sometimes confuses the state with the commons, and that confusion contributes to the ambiguity of the property status of resources used in commercial industries.

✧ *BC Studies* 80 (Winter 1988–89): 3–23.

PRIVATE, STATE, AND COMMON PROPERTY

As MacPherson argued, property is a right and a relationship, rather than a thing,[2] and the rights go beyond mere possession because they define socially enforceable claims. Property implies a power relationship between people, since the claims determine who may benefit and who may be excluded. Private property rights define the rights of individuals (which may be corporate bodies) to use and benefit from natural resources (among other things) and to exclude other citizens of a state or of foreign states from access and use. Private property has had a distinguished history of defence by political theorists. Locke[3] argued that men had the "natural right" to property, that property rights took precedence over civil law, and that the purpose of government was the preservation of that right (late seventeenth century). Bentham[4] (early nineteenth century), Mill[5] (mid-nineteenth century), and Green[6] (late nineteenth century) elaborated on this argument, defending private property as a natural right, as a necessary means of conserving the earth, and as a means of preserving liberty.

State property is of two kinds: the variety which is most like private property in that the state has the right to exclude members of the general public (commoners) from access and use, such as state offices and crown corporations; and the variety which is most like common property in that the general public has equal access and use rights, such as highways and public parks.[7]

Common property, in contemporary economic theory, is that category of things to which no one can make a property claim and, *ipso facto*, no one can be excluded from access or use. However, there are two other meanings to the term, and the economists' version is contested. Macpherson argues that common property remains a set of individual rights in the sense that each individual has the right of access. His is the positive interpretation of the same general maxim of non-exclusivity. In contrast, Ciriacy-Wantrup and Bishop[8] argue that the term refers to collective rights where the collectivity can exclude outsiders. Their usage is the more consistent with historical terminology.

The term initially derives from the area of pasture on large estates in Europe, especially England and Scotland, which all farmers attached to the estate could use, and to timber lands shared by a specific community. That usage is still in evidence in Japan as well as less industrialized countries.

In contemporary economic theory, common property, initially regarded as an archaic or primitive occurrence, is seen as a positive evil. The argument advanced by Hardin,[9] and with reference specifically to fisheries by Gordon,[10] Scott,[11] and Ostrom,[12] *inter alia*, is that "everybody's right is nobody's right." Hardin argues his case with reference particularly to two features of the commons: population and land. He argues that when the earth is regarded as a commons, over-population necessarily results and voluntary controls will not work precisely because each couple reckons their marginal utilities without reference to the collectivity. In the same fashion, he argues, the individual tenant farmer using a common pasturage will add cattle without reference to the land-carrying capacity until collectively all users will deplete the land. In his opinion, the *Enclosures Acts* in Britain came about because of the erosion of the land. Similarly, Crowe[13] refers to the "classic example" of the "tragedy of the commons" as the overgrazing and lack of care and fertilization of the pasturage in England, "so destructive that there developed in the late 17th century an enclosure movement" [*sic*].

In Canada, this argument has been adapted by governments, private companies, and Royal Commissioners to the fisheries. A recent Royal Commission in British Columbia assumed from the outset that the fisheries constituted a common property problem:

> Because of the common property nature of the fisheries and the need to constrain the total catch within biological limits, various groups that compete for the catch are preoccupied with their shares; this gives rise to the pervasive allocation problem, and is the source of "gear wars."[14]

In a study prepared for the Economic Council of Canada, Scott and Neher[15] begin with these words:

> Regulation and control spring up naturally when economic activity involves *common property*. When people can exploit a resource together, when they cannot enforce contracts against third parties, then the resource is prone to abuse.

This use of the term implies that property is a thing, rather than a social arrangement of rights. As soon as we recognize the social source of property rights, this use of the term "common" in association with "property" becomes a contradiction, for if property necessarily involves a socially enforced set of exclusive rights, then a situation wherein there are no enforceable rights involves no property.

An earlier and influential paper by Gordon[16] likewise argues that the fisheries have a common property nature, and maintains that overexploitation of natural resources tends to occur where they are "owned in common and exploited under conditions of individualistic competition." He concludes for the more general case that sole and private ownership is superior as a method of conservation. In this view, developed further by Scott,[17] common property does not provide any incentive to the individual fisher to conserve the resource. For each fisher, profit will depend on capture of the greatest number of fish regardless of the long-term effects, if fishers are primarily motivated by short-term profits. Because the fishers are competitive and the resource is owned in common, no fisher can benefit from conservation unilaterally practised; thus short-term profits would motivate competitive fishers.

Scott distinguishes between the short-run and long-run probabilities that might affect private and sole owners. If they engaged in the fishery for only a year, they would operate in precisely the same fashion as the independent fisher in a common resource is assumed to behave. But if the sole owner planned to stay in business over a longer period, he could be expected to seek means of conserving the resource. Among these means would be development of technologies to capture greater efficiencies, and integration of facilities and vessels. Thus, he argues, sole ownership leads to better conservation if it is a long-term investment. Again there is the assumption that multiple users with long-term investments are either unwilling or incapable of advancing the same objectives.

A similar argument has been advanced in the forest industry. The provincial state in Canada has formal jurisdiction over land and resources. In British Columbia, about 5 percent of forest land was given away to railway companies or sold outright early in the twentieth century. The remainder continued under state control, known as "crown property." This is sometimes equated with "common property," apparently with the meaning that no individual user (company) can unilaterally determine uses or sell the resource in its native state. The state allocates harvesting rights by licence to individuals (usually corporations), collecting a resource rent known as "stumpage" in return. The argument is that had land rights, rather than merely the harvesting rights, been privatized, the resource would have been conserved (replanted); since the state (being equated to the commons) held the property rights, the resource was not replenished.

THE HISTORICAL USAGE OF
THE TERM "COMMON PROPERTY"

Macpherson notwithstanding, and as noted above, it appears that when the term "common property" is used in reference to a situation where no one may be excluded and contracts against third parties cannot be enforced, it is a contradiction. For that set of things that are ubiquitous, such as air, or which no one has managed to corral, such as a view of the heavens, we do need a new term, and it does not help to say that for these there is a positive property right not to be excluded. The right is meaningless. Calling these things, and also calling resources under public management "common property," is historically inaccurate and misleading in an important way, because the terminology subtly implies but does not demonstrate the superiority of private ownership.

The historical usage of the term "common property" referred to definite property rights between co-owners, and these rights involved co-management responsibilities. There is a significant difference between a situation wherein all citizens of a common and delimited territory have equal access and use rights but may exclude non-residents, and one wherein no one at all may be excluded. The first is, or has been, typical of small hunting/fishing tribal groups in British Columbia and elsewhere. Indian bands, catching fish for local use or barter, did not deplete resources even where they fished the same rivers, streams, and sea coasts for many generations. Their situation was analogous to that of the farmers using the English commons as pasturage.

Anthropologists have stressed the co-management responsibilities of individuals engaged in common property use, and other scholars as well have suggested a contrary case to that of the economists using the term "common" pejoratively. Insisting on a more restricted usage of the term than that employed by fisheries economists, Ciriacy-Wantrup and Bishop[18] investigate the commons in economic history, concluding that: "In communal hunting and gathering societies, without markets on which to sell surpluses, emphasis on sharing among members of the group tended to discourage accumulation." Not all pre-market societies managed their resources well, and one should beware of romanticizing "indigenous management systems," which vary according to resource base, cultural habits, and homogeneity of the management group, but there is a fair body of evidence to indicate that many such groups did and still do co-manage a common property in the interests of conservation. Berkes,[19] for example, argues that the "tragedy" would occur only if three conditions were fulfilled:

> fishermen must be maximizing short-term individual gains over long-term community benefits, the rate of exploitation must exceed the natural rate of renewability of the resource, and the resource must be common property and freely open to any user (open-access).

He presents data on three groups of fishers in Canada (Cree Indians in the eastern subarctic, Nishga Indians in northern B.C., and Lake Erie fishers, the latter two of which are engaged in commercial fisheries, the first only in a subsistence fishery), arguing that the three conditions are not met for these. Community pressures inhibit entirely selfish behaviour, and community controls and/or government licensing delimit access and use. His conclusion suggests that, given the chance, co-users of a common property, with long-term commitments, act in the same fashion as sole owners are expected to act in Scott's argument.

Whether or not all communal groups have adequately managed natural resources, there is little doubt that Hardin's argument on the English pasturage is historically false. He cites a verse which is interesting because it actually refutes his argument:[20]

> They clap in gaol the man or woman
> Who steals the goose from off the common;
> But let the bigger knave go loose
> Who steals the common from the goose.

Ignoring the fact that the commons, according to this verse, was strictly regulated prior to the *Enclosures Acts*, he says of the *Acts* that, "Unjust though [they] were, they did put an end to the tragedy of the commons."

This classic example, while certainly a tragedy, was not caused by overgrazing the commons; it was caused by turning the commons into private property, in order to use it for sheep pasturage and for commercial crops destined for markets. There is no evidence that the commons were habitually over-grazed (or that geese were regularly stolen from them, for that matter). If the enclosures are called "movement," then the term should surely apply to the forced evictions rather than any social currents of reform. Barrington Moore goes so far as to suggest that the practices of the commons before they were privatized were important preconditions to the eventual development of democracy; where no commons existed in the feudal period, certain ideas failed to emerge.[21]

Despite considerable variation, the main idea connected with these arrangements stands out very clearly: every member of the community should have access to enough resources to be able to perform obligations to the community carrying on a collective struggle for survival.

Population increases do become a central issue in exerting pressure on the resource base, but not in connection with the tragedy of the commons. Markets may have provided the conditions for the growth of population, or the growth may have encouraged the increasing importance of markets (as far as I can determine, this remains an unsolved issue); in any event, the growing markets created means of survival outside the rural areas and simultaneously created a demand for agricultural produce to feed nonproducing populations. As these populations increased, their capacity to informally enforce co-management responsibilities decreased, not because they all over-grazed a commons, but rather because there was no co-management group and, in fact, no commons.

In summary, then, we need to make a distinction between common property (which is, in fact, communally managed property) and anything to which no claims may be enforced (which is therefore not property at all). These non-properties may be better understood if they are called "free goods." The distinction is not merely semantic. The current usage is historically inapt, and it leads to the placement of blame where it does not belong. This is particularly evident in the fisheries.

GOVERNMENT AS MANAGER

The argument about fish rests on their mobility. As then-Canadian Prime Minister Pierre Trudeau observed, in reference to the need for a Law of the Sea, it was essential "because fish swim." This suggests that fish fall into that category of things to which no enforceable claims exist. But in fact, everywhere there are enforceable claims on fish. The first claim is that of national governments, insistently made throughout the history of a commercial fishery and apparent in the 200-mile fisheries boundaries off coastal states.

Governments have become the custodians of natural resources within their territories, and in the case of fish, they have claimed rights beyond traditional land territories. Are governments to be viewed as the successors to communities sharing a commons, as some writers assume? I would argue that such cannot be assumed, because there are substantial differences between the two entities. The community sharing a commons had equal interest in that area, and all members needed the resources in both the short and long terms. Further, all members could, physically, impose sanctions on others because such communities were small. The participants in the commons were roughly equal in power, and no one party could impose restrictions on others. Finally, the resources in question were used directly for subsistence.

Governments, by contrast, are institutionally constructed so as to manage not one resource but many, not one use but many; and they are required to balance, negotiate, and make decisions about conflicting interests. Not all members of the population have an immediate interest in any resource, and the interests that exist have divergent and conflicting requirements. Members may not know one another, and certainly cannot impose effective sanctions in the form of social disappropriation or the like. Some participants are vastly more powerful than others, and the actions of the more powerful can and often do preclude action by others. And all of these conditions rest on a prior fact: the resources are no longer used primarily for subsistence. They are now potential commodities.

Governments in contemporary capitalist economies rest ultimately on the effective accumulation of private capital (and governments in non-capitalist economies rest on accumulation of capital by state-owned institutions). For any resource (and, in the case of fish, for the habitat as well), the issue is not simply how best to conserve a resource in perpetuity; it is how best to manage the resource so that, in the short as well as the long run, the greatest profits can be accumulated from its exploitation. This involves balancing and evaluating the relative claims of all potential users. In the case of fish, the users include commercial fishers, subsistence food-fishers (mainly native Indians), sports fishers, processing firms, other industries using or adjacent to the habitat, the tourist industry, and recreational users of the habitat.

These users have diverse interests. In British Columbia, the interests of the fishers and processors may be in conservation so that their industry survives in the long run, but even if that were true these users' interests have to be weighed against alternative uses of the habitat by the forestry and mining industries, and of the fish by sports fishers connected to the growing tourist industry. The forestry and mining industries generate vastly greater profits, provide more taxation funds for government, employ greater numbers of workers, bring in more export dollars, and pay greater rents (the rents in B.C. are much below regeneration costs for the forest, but there are no rents at all for fishing, and licence fees are not to be confused with rents, as discussed below).[22] In B.C., the anticipated profits from sale of hydropower, though never realized, were much greater than the returns on fish. As well, the damming or regulation of rivers such as the Nechako by specific industries such as Alcan affects water levels downstream, and again the argument in favour of such projects is that they generate more employment than the fisheries. Thus as a minimum restriction on good management of the fisheries, competing uses of the habitat inhibit conservation of fish as a government priority.

PARTICIPANTS IN THE FISHERY

The assumption that all participants in the fisheries industry itself have a long-term interest in conservation may be questioned as well. Those fishers who are permanently attached to the industry, and who have invested in vessels and gear, do have such an interest; this may be demonstrated both logically and empirically. Logically, their survival depends on continuing catches over a long run. Empirically, numerous B.C. fishers and their various organizations are on record in their concern for better conservation. Many fishing vessels are family enterprises, and parents teach children to fish in anticipation of the children inheriting the investment and carrying on the tradition.[23] Fishers for whom the investment is a short-term activity have no investment in the future and may be less concerned with conservation. A majority, however, are long-term participants, and for them "fishing is a way of life" rather than only an economic activity.[24]

But fishers are not the sole participants in the industry, and it is on this point that the typical arguments about fishers depleting the resource are most blind. Processing firms operate on the same general economic principles as any other companies. There is a general assumption that companies are always in business for the long run, but in fact there is plenty of evidence that for most industries this assumption is tenuous at best. Once a firm has passed the stage of small family enterprise, it becomes an investment for stockholders who need not, themselves, know anything about the business and have no cause to become involved in management of its affairs. Companies so owned engage in specific businesses as long as they are profitable for the investors. Investors have options in the fisheries as in other businesses. The objective is not to make profits from fish forever, but to make profits in one way or another. If fishing is profitable in the short run, then the investor will extract the profits as quickly as possible and move on to other industries; or the largest companies will buy out the smaller ones, gain a greater control of supplies and markets, and thereby increase the profits. In none of these actions is there an inherent logic that leads to conservation of the resource.

In British Columbia, the processors preceded the commercial fishers, establishing canneries and then seeking a labour force to catch the fish. Initially, this labour force was paid a daily wage and the vessels were company-owned. This is one of several ways that processors could obtain supplies. Two alternatives—variously employed elsewhere according to the resource, the availability of labour, cultural attitudes and history—are purchasing supplies from independent fishers or re-inventing technologies for capture that reduce the significance of migratory fish mobility. A privately owned fleet requires investment, maintenance, and labour costs, but guarantees the supplies even if the raw material cannot be corralled. Independent fishers pay their own way, and labour costs may be avoided, but if there are competitive processing companies the supplies are not guaranteed. In fact, over time another option emerged in British Columbia: the development of a fleet of independent fishers, owning their own boats, but working under service contracts or with start-up funds from companies. Since the companies declined in number very rapidly after the turn of the century, each company could obtain sufficient supplies at competitive costs without putting high investments in the fleet or the labour. In this fashion, the companies "owned" the fishers rather than the fish. This solution was similar to the indenture system adopted by the Hudson's Bay Company earlier, for the catching of fur-bearing animals.

Throughout the first half of the twentieth century on the west coast, larger companies bought out smaller ones or merged with equals.[25] In 1962, the largest company, B.C. Packers, became the target of a large food supplies conglomerate, Weston's, which had, through another subsidiary, the retail grocery chain Loblaws, long purchased canned salmon from B.C. Packers. The purchase was part of a general acquisitions policy for Weston's, increasing its control of food supplies for its retail outlets.[26] In 1969, B.C. Packers and the only other large processing company still in the business, Canadian Fish Company, owned by New England Fish of the United States, took over the assets of a third company, Anglo-British Columbia Packing Company. Finally, in 1980, the New England Fish Company, encountering financial problems at its head plant in the United States, sold its plant at Prince Rupert, B.C., to B.C. Packers. The only remaining independent processing firm of any size, and that much smaller than B.C. Packers, was the Prince Rupert Fishermen's Cooperative Association, which by 1982 was also experiencing severe financial problems.[27] Specific fisheries in somewhat varying market conditions have maintained smaller, more specialized processing firms from time to time,[28] but in the main salmon fishery B.C. Packers has a secure hold on raw fish supplies. In this situation, competition among fishers does not diminish the company's profits; on the contrary, it increases the vulnerability of any one fisher in what is very close to a monopsony supply situation.

There is no doubt that this arrangement has depleted the resource, just as the Hudson's Bay Company arrangement depleted the supplies of fur-bearing animals. But what has to be understood in this is that the resource, even if not "owned" until caught, is ultimately controlled by the raw fish market dominated by one firm and occupied, in total, by very few. Competition by fishers is a consequence of the structure of that market, so that blaming the competition for resource depletion is somewhat like blaming low-income wage earners for their poverty. Investors can move their capital elsewhere if the resource is depleted; few fishers have that option, and their investments in vessel and gear would become worthless without a durable supply of raw fish. Yet fishers have no management rights. They have only a private right in the form of a licence to fish, and since 1968 the state has granted that right to more participants than the fishery can sustain.

There are other participants in the fishery who are not so obvious but equally significant. These are banks which lend funds to both fishers, for the upgrading or purchase of vessels and gear, and processors. Banks have no immediate interest in conservation; on the contrary, they have a pronounced interest in obtaining quick returns on their loans. Their participation in the industry increased in the 1970s, a period which requires special attention in the saga of the B.C. fisheries.

THE ESCALATION OF COMPETITION, 1970s

In 1968, the Canadian government embarked on what is known as the "Davis Plan," ostensibly to diminish the pressure on the salmon resource of the west coast. The strategy was to limit the number of fishers, buy back vessels and retire others, and to limit fishers by selling transferable licences.

The number of fishers and vessels declined, but the size and capacity of remaining vessels increased, and licences, now private property consigning limited access rights, became marketable commodities. Since the exchange value of licences was captured by vessel owners who sold them rather than by the state, and the original cost bore no resemblance to the market value, it cannot be argued that licensing was a form of resource rent.

The government took on all responsibility for regulation, imposing catching times and places for the various types of vessel and gear. In these ways, an artificially induced competition was created, and each gear type struggled against the others for diminished fishing time. In such a struggle, the rational behaviour for individuals with long-term commitments to the industry is to upgrade their vessels and gear. Technological developments were adopted for improving information on fish movements, refrigerating fish for longer periods in vessel holds, and travelling longer distances on each trip. Fuel costs escalated, and those who invested in the new gear became indebted to banks and government agencies for loans that could only be paid off if they caught large quantities of fish every year. Individual fishers are on record as fearing the decline of the resource, but collectively they had no means of taking responsibility and were obliged to accept government regulation.

As chance had it, for several years in the mid-1970s, the salmon and herring runs were unusually heavy, and, simultaneously, a strong, though as it turned out short-term, market demand emerged in Japan for herring roe and salmon. The government not only relaxed its rules, it actively encouraged fishers to upgrade and increase the capacity of their vessels through loans and various incentives. This behaviour was clearly contrary to the intentions of the "Davis Plan" and to any serious conservationist policy.

The explanation for this contradictory behaviour is embedded in the nature of government in an industrialized country. As noted above, government is not a substitute for a small co-management unit. It is a collection of departments with an overall mandate to somehow balance the diverse and often conflicting interests of companies and individual citizens in its territory. In this case, the Department of Fisheries and Oceans was charged with the responsibility of conserving the resource; the Department of Northern and Native Affairs was charged with the responsibility for improving the lot of native fishers; the Department of Industry and Small Business was charged with the responsibility for helping the boat builders and fishers now defined as small businesses.[29] In this array of interests, the one interest which did not create immediate profits—conservation—was least salient.

Processing companies were primarily concerned with capturing fishers and increasing their catch in what turned out to be, though briefly, changed and much more competitive conditions for their own operations. New companies emerged, backed by investments from Japan, and cash buyers attempted to pre-empt the processing companies' supplies on the fishing grounds. Unionized shore-workers shared the concerns of their employers when raw fish failed to come through the processing facilities, and both the major union and the processors pressed the government to impose curbs on foreign investment.[30]

Banks, backed by government guarantees on loans to fishers, became major investors in the fleet during this period.[31] Once they became participants, government policies had to take their loans into account. A major conservationist policy would have diminished the likelihood of fishers paying their debts, and banks could be expected to offer resistance. By 1980, the unusual runs and the unusual market demand had diminished, and a renewed interest in conservation spurred the government to appoint a Royal Commission. The Commissioner, though assuring that the problem was the common property nature of the resource, called fishing "a privilege," and the recommendations involved royalties, quotas, new licensing restrictions, and other means by which the state, as manager of the resource, would tighten its management role over what had now become "state" and certainly was not "common" property. None of the recommendations would delimit the profits of the processing sector, and the "buyback" provisions would reduce the risks for the banking industry which by 1980 was experiencing a high rate of defaults on its loans. Only the fishers would suffer, and only the fishers were blamed for their competitive behaviour.

IMMOBILE PROPERTIES: COMPARISONS

Since the argument is that the mobility of fish is the reason for their "common property" status, and their property status, in turn, the cause of resource depletion, it is instructive to consider what has occurred in both non-mobile resource sectors and non-resource industries.

Consider first the status of trees.

Forest lands in British Columbia are largely under the jurisdiction of the provincial state, which licenses companies to cut trees for their mills. Most licences have over twenty years' duration, the argument being that companies require long-term security of supplies before they will invest in processing plants. The state has responsibility for re-forestation, silviculture, and management, though under the new regulations instituted in 1987, more of these responsibilities may be shifted to the companies. Throughout the history of this industry, the stumpage has been very low.

As with fish, this renewable resource was not renewed, and a lush softwood forest provided by nature has been depleted as companies cut and processed trees into lumber and pulp. The companies argue that had they privately owned the resource, they would have replanted it. But first, the evidence is far from overwhelming in favour of this proposition on the 5 percent of lands which have been privately owned; and second, the arrangement has been extremely profitable for the companies. They have paid a rent below the cost of replenishing the resource, taken little responsibility for management, and profited from extraction and sale of a relatively unsophisticated semi-processed material. In the economic downturn of the 1980s, with new technologies for pulping hardwoods elsewhere in place, several large American companies sold their properties and exited from British Columbia. Since the mills were now becoming obsolete, what in fact they sold were their timber-cutting rights. Obviously, if they can sell such rights, trees are not common property.

The forestry example raises two pertinent questions: what is the role of the state in a state-managed resource for which there are private harvesting companies, and why have private companies not replenished the resource when they had long-term harvesting rights?

The second question is probably easier to answer than the first: investments in the resource were not profitable in the short run, and the long run was just too long. Softwoods require between 50 and 100 years to grow to maturity; few investors are planning to reap benefits that far into the future. Investors in modern industry know that nothing remains constant in world markets, and valuable resources may have no value when technologies change, substitutes are developed, or cultural habits change. Indeed, investors promote some of the changes when they provide funds for technological development. In the forest industry, technological changes have made hardwoods viable sources of fairly high-grade pulp, and hardwoods, grown in less than ten years in some countries, are in plentiful supply.[32] In short, Scott's assumption that sole owners (in this case, owners of harvesting rights) with long-term commitments to an industry will seek to conserve the resource is demonstrably false: they are as likely as multiple owners to exploit it at high speed and without concern for long-term conservation.

In both the fisheries and forestry, the problem apparently is not ownership, but management. In both, the state has been charged with management yet the state, as presently constituted, has failed to provide that. This is not caused by a lack of professional expertise: in both industries there are government bureaucracies filled with technically qualified experts. It is a problem, rather, of social goals and priorities. Since governments reflect (if they do not actively respond to) the social priorities of their most powerful constituents, the fundamental problem is that these—private companies which use resources as commodities—are disinterested in conservation.

But even this conclusion needs to be further examined. Consider several other industries which are not connected in any direct fashion with natural resource extraction, and where governments do not have a custodial role: automobiles, electronics, textiles, steel, for example. Here we discover that there are repetitive cycles of diminishing profits, over-production, technological change, and geographical movement toward lower-wage or lower-taxation regions. Competition not infrequently leads to the demise of an industry in a particular form, though it then may lead to a restructured industry and greater profits for fewer participants. The turmoil of this process in such industries as these cannot be attributed to common property even in the economists' sense of that term. In each case, the problem of diminishing profits, excessive productive capacity, and economic downturns occurs in the context of private property rights and either market competition or the manipulation of markets to reduce the risks of competition for privileged contestants.

The conclusion one might reach in surveying the outcomes of this competition among private property holders is that short-term profits are normal objectives, and long-term interests are met not by conservation (whether of resources, plant, or labour) but by alertness to alternatives purchasable with fluid capital. Tying up capital in resource conservation would rarely make sense in a privatized world.

The basic problem as far as the state is concerned is that the interests of private capital, combined with the numerous and diverse demands for public capital, do not dictate conservationist measures either. And for fishers, the one group in the fisheries for whom long-term conservation really does make sense, management rights have been divorced from use of the resource; far from mismanaging a common property, fishers are not permitted to manage the fishery at all.

THE SEA-BED AS PROPERTY

To this point we have considered the sea, apart from a mention of the 200-mile limit for national sea-territory, as but the context for migratory fish and increasingly mobile fishers. Since the discovery of manganese nodules at great depths of international waters, mining companies, and nations that house them, have moved toward the privatization of the sea-bed. The arguments were not new in thrust: nations had already articulated the notion of property rights to ocean resources at the United Nations Law of the Sea Conferences in the late 1950s and early 1960s. But up to that time, the United States, in particular, was more concerned with shipping rights, the rights of oil companies to mine on continental shelfs, military rights, and, but far down the line of priorities, the rights of national fishers.

As late as 1970, the U.S. was still voting in favour of a United Nations General Assembly resolution designating mining sea-bed resources as "the common heritage of mankind" to be exploited "in accordance with an international regime to be created."[33] At that time it was still thought that both the manganese nodules (which contain rich mineral deposits) and oil were likely to be found within the continental shelf. Gradually it became apparent that this was not so, and the mining companies became very active in lobbying the American government to abandon its commitment to an international agency and "the common property" of the sea.

Marine scientists and environmentalists argued for open access for research and international authority over deep-sea resources, but such a stance was strongly opposed by countries interested in safeguarding their military research and applications. No guarantees for scientific freedom were contained in the U.S. Draft Seabed Treaty of 1970 or subsequent documents.[34]

As nations moved toward the 200-mile limit, the concerns of fisheries biologists, conservationists, negotiators concerned about habitat pollution and over-fishing, and internationalists concerned with a more just distribution of the world's resources were equally ignored or subjugated to the interests of private mining companies, oil companies, shipping companies, and the military establishments of dominant countries.[35] Fish ownership was a secondary concern: ownership of the sea-bed was the central issue. With so much of the world's sea-bed now "owned," the mobility of fish has much reduced importance. The scale of this "enclosures movement" is much greater than that of the English countryside in an earlier age, but its impact is similar. Far from being a common property, much of the sea and the fish that swim therein have been privatized.

FREE GOODS AND ECOLOGICAL LINKAGES

Air may be one of the few free goods still in existence, since no one has successfully advanced a claim on it, no group has ever co-managed it, no one can be excluded from access and use, and no state has laid claim to it, though for the first time in history there are small attempts by international agreement to reduce damage to it. There can be little doubt that air pollution is an ecological problem of immense proportions, but again, is this because no one has property rights or because the property rights elsewhere and commoditization of everything else, including fish and forests, lead incidentally to deterioration of free goods?

Consider the linkages between forestry and air pollution. Forests are evaluated in terms of numbers, girth, height, age, and species of trees because these affect the commercial values; the oxygen-generating capacities are ignored. The problem here is not that air is free but that private property owners elsewhere in the ecological system have been permitted to externalize costs and accumulate profits without reference to the environment.

Like trees, other resources have been transformed from free goods to common properties, thence to private or state plus private properties, and with the transition, their non-commercial characteristics have been ignored in the accounting of costs and benefits. As long as their uses are entirely commercial and designed for the accumulation of capital, there is no mechanism for conservation. Ultimately the only way such mechanisms could be effectively introduced would be to either rediscover the inherent responsibilities in co-management of genuine common (communal) properties, or devise a system of public responsibility superseding private property rights.

SUMMARY

This paper has argued that the depletion of fish stocks and forest resources cannot be blamed on their status as "common property." Property, it is contended, following Macpherson's argument, is a set of rights, socially determined and enforceable, and not to be confused with the things to which the rights pertain. Given this understanding but departing from Macpherson's argument on the positive rights to not be excluded, I have accepted the proposition that "common property" is a contradiction if it literally means that no one may be excluded and implies no common management responsibilities. This argument is contrary to that proposed by Hardin with reference to the common pasturage in England, and widely cited by way of justification for blaming B.C. fishermen for the depletion of salmon.

Historically and in some contemporary small-scale hunting societies, common property involves enforceable co-management rights among users of resources on which all members depend for their livelihood. The invocation of the term on the grounds that fish are mobile and therefore cannot be physically owned until captured inhibits recognition of the structure of an industry for which fish are not food supplies but commodities, and processing firms purchase them regardless of how many fishers are engaged in the capture. Once fishers themselves are licensed, fishing becomes a privileged activity and the ownership of a licence delimits the rights of non-licensed individuals to fish; so, again, on that ground, fish cannot be regarded as common property.

One of the confusions that arises in some of the literature on the fisheries (and occasionally on forestry) is that government, or the state, is confused with the commons. It is argued here that the state is not the inheritor of the commons and is institutionally structured such that it cannot manage resources as if they were the commons. The state must respond to numerous and diverse private interests, some of which are detrimental to resources such as fish habitat; it must be concerned with the greater profits, resource rents, taxes, and employment, for example, generated in other sectors that may impinge on resource conservation.

When we look at other industries, we discover much the same cycle of excessive investment, surplus production, technological change, and elimination of competitors. This occurs in the forest industry where rights to harvest are contractual and the resource is stationary; it occurs in non-resource industries where governments are not cast in custodial roles. In these sectors the same problems as are found in the fisheries occur in the context of privately owned property. It is suggested that these examples question the conventional wisdom about the long-term interests of private owners.

When we discover the fish habitat, we discover that much of it has been privatized and the property rights have been legally established under international law. Indeed, one might view the law of the sea as a contemporary enclosures movement.

Some resources may fall into a category here called free goods, to which no property rights apply. Air is the obvious example (there are few others remaining). Air is polluted, and it is argued here that the pollution does not occur because of its non-property status but because it is the context for private and commercial activities. The destruction of forests contributes to air pollution, and that destruction occurs through privatization of harvesting rights with no corresponding assignment of responsibility for sustaining the environment. In short, conservation of the earth, air, water, trees, and fish is impeded through privatization and transformation of nature into market commodities rather than because they are held in common.

If this argument is valid, then it follows that solutions to pollution and resource depletion are not to be found in further privatization. Needed instead is a system that builds in public responsibilities, specifies management obligations, and adjusts calculations of costs and benefits with reference to ecology.

Fishers in a commercial industry could not co-manage the resource precisely as did their ancestors in small communities. In some places, sufficiently isolated so that local communities could impose mutual restrictions, co-management is possible, as Berkes has demonstrated. But for most of the B.C. coast, fishers no longer inhabit specifically "fishing" communities; they reside in urban neighbourhoods and capture fish anywhere along the coast in high-powered, highly mobile vessels. Nonetheless, in the shock following the Pearse Report, fishers came very close to developing associations that could have been used for self-management purposes. The failure to assign them responsibility for management, while they were so organized and ready to accept it, was embedded in the general assumption that only government could perform this task. It was also contingent on the unacknowledged understanding that the present system involves a range of private interests beyond the fishers.

An alternative possibility would be to impose quotas not on fishers but on the processors. If they were disallowed excessive raw fish supplies, the capture fleet would decline and further capitalization of vessels would probably cease. Likewise, if banks were obliged to accept loan defaults and disallowed the option of making further loans to either processors or fishers, the fisheries would decline as an economic sector in the provincial economy. Yet a further possibility involves provision of incentives to fishers entering other occupations; the funding of fish farms is along this line. More punitive damages for polluters of the habitat would probably contribute to better conservation. But ultimately all of these methods are stopgap, punitive, or of dubious value. Missing in them is a positive move toward development of a management system that begins with concern for the total environment and assigns priority to conservation over private accumulation.

In the fisheries, but even more in the fields of energy, mineral extraction, and forestry, we have accepted a system of social priorities that puts profits, employment, and a particular kind of economic development first; the costs to the environment have been externalized. We are now at a point in world history when those externalized costs are being experienced in polluted waters, dead sea mammals, poisoned fish, and a damaged atmospheric environment. When conservation of our resources is not the priority, where private profits are paramount, where private interests in the commodization of resources dictate resource policies, then resources will be depleted. It is not because they are common property that they suffer tragedies but, on the contrary, because private property has superseded the commons.

NOTES

1. As noted by Charles Plourde, "Conservation of Extinguishable Species," *Natural Resources Journal* 15 (1975): 791–97.

2. C.B. Macpherson, "The Meaning of Property," in C.B. Macpherson (ed.), *Property: Mainstream and Critical Positions* (Toronto: University of Toronto Press, 1978), 1–14.

3. John Locke, "Two Treatises on Government: Second Treatise on Civil Government," in *Social Contract: Essays by Locke, Hume and Rousseau* (London: Oxford University Press, 1960).

4. Jeremy Bentham, "Principles of Morals and Legislation," in *The Utilitarians, An Introduction to the*

Principles of Morals and Legislation (New York: Doubleday, 1961).

5. John Stuart Mill, "Utilitarianism," and "On Liberty," in *The Utilitarians* (1961).

6. T.H. Greene, *The Principles of Political Obligation* (London: Longmans, 1955).

7. Macpherson, "The Meaning of Property."

8. S.V. Ciriacy-Wantrup and R.C. Bishop, "'Common Property' as a Concept in Natural Resource Policy," *Natural Resources Journal* 15(3) (1977): 713–27.

9. Garrett Hardin, "The Tragedy of the Commons," in Garrett Hardin and John Baden (eds.), *Managing the Commons* (San Francisco: W.H. Freeman, 1977); and "Denial and Disguise," *Science* 162 (1968): 1243–48, repr. in *Managing the Commons*, 45–52.

10. H. Scott Gordon, "The Economic Theory of a Common-Property Resource: The Fishery," *Journal of Political Economy* 62(2) (April 1954): 124–42.

11. Anthony Scott, "The Fishery: The Objectives of Sole Ownership," *Journal of Policy Economy* 63(2) (April 1955): 116–24; see also E.A. Keen, "Common Property in Fisheries: Is Sole Ownership an Option?" *Marine Policy* 7(3) (July 1983): 197–211.

12. Vincent Ostrom, "Alternative Approaches to the Organization of Public Proprietary Interests," *Natural Resources Journal* 15 (1975): 763–89.

13. Beryl L. Crowe, "The Tragedy of the Commons Revisited," in *Managing the Commons*, 53–65.

14. Peter H. Pearse, Commissioner, *Turning the Tide: A New Policy for Canada's Pacific Fisheries* (Vancouver: Minister of Supply and Services, 1982), 4.

15. Anthony Scott and Philip A. Neher, *The Public Regulation of Commercial Fisheries in Canada*, prepared for the Economic Council of Canada (Ottawa: Minister of Supply and Services, 1981).

16. Gordon, "The Economic Theory of a Common-Property Resource: The Fishery," 124–42.

17. Scott, "The Fishery: The Objectives of Sole Ownership," 116–24.

18. Ciriacy-Wantrup and Bishop, "'Common Property' as a Concept in Natural Resources Policy," 717.

19. F. Berkes, "A Critique of the 'Tragedy of the Commons' Paradigm," paper presented to the "Natural Management Systems" Symposium I-A18l, IXth International Congress of Anthropological and Ethnological Sciences, August 1982, Quebec City.

20. Hardin, "Denial and Disguise," 46.

21. Barrington Moore, *Social Origins of Dictatorship and Democracy* (Boston: Beacon Press, 1966), 497.

22. Comparative data on these industries are given in Patricia Marchak, "Uncommon Property," in Patricia Marchak, Neil Guppy, and John McMullan (eds.), *Uncommon Property: The Fishing and Fish Processing Industries in Canada* (Toronto: Methuen, 1987), 14.

23. Neil Guppy, "Labouring at Sea: Harvesting Uncommon Property," in *Uncommon Property*, 173–98. This is also evident in briefs to the Pearse Commission, 1982; Department of Fisheries and Oceans, "Summary of Minister's Advisory Council Meetings," Session II, 17–21 January 1983, Vancouver; and fishers' conferences in the years 1982–84.

24. Neil Guppy, "Labouring at Sea: Harvesting Common Property," 173–98; see also other chapters in *Uncommon Property*.

25. Alicja Muszynski, "Major Processors to 1940 and Early Labour Force: Historical Notes," in *Uncommon Property*, 46–65.

26. John McMullan, "State, Capital, and the B.C. Salmon Fishing Industry," in *Uncommon Property*, 122–23.

27. McMullan, ibid., 138–39; and Patricia Marchak, "Organization of Divided

Fishers," in *Uncommon Property*, 235–36.

28. Evelyn Pinkerton, "Competition Among B.C. Fish-Processing Firms," in *Uncommon Property*, 66–91.

29. John McMullan, "State, Capital, and Debt in the British Columbia Fishing Fleet, 1970–1982," in *Journal of Canadian Studies* 19(l) (Spring 1984): 65–88; and McMullan, "State, Capital, and the B.C. Salmon Fishing Industry," 107–52.

30. Trevor Proverbs, *Foreign Investment in the British Columbia Fish Processing Industry* (Vancouver: Economics and Statistical Services, Pacific Region, Department of Fisheries and Oceans, 1978); *Update*, 1980; *Update*, 1982.

31. McMullan, "State, Capital, and the B.C. Salmon Fishing Industry," 107–52.

32. *Hay-Roe's PaperTree Letter* (Vancouver, November 1985); see also, for background, Patricia Marchak, *Green Gold: The Forest Industry in British Columbia* (Vancouver: UBC Press, 1983); and, for updating, "Public Policy, Capital and Labour in the Forest Industry," in Rennie Warburton and David Coburn (eds.), *Workers, Capital, and the State in British Columbia, Selected Papers* (Vancouver: UBC Press, 1988), 177–200.

33. Ann L. Hollick, "Bureaucrats at Sea," in A. Hollick and R. Osgood (eds.), *New Era of Ocean Politics* (Baltimore: Johns Hopkins University Press, 1974), 1–74; Barry Buzan and Danford W. Middlemiss, "Canadian Foreign Policy and the Exploitation of the Seabed," in B. Johnson and M. Zacher (eds.), *Canadian Foreign Policy and the Law of the Sea* (Vancouver: UBC Press, 1977).

34. Hollick, "Bureaucrats at Sea," 26.

35. Barbara Johnson, "Canadian Foreign Policy and Fisheries," in *Canadian Foreign Policy and the Law of the Sea* (1977); Donald McRae, "Canada and the Law of the Sea: Some Multilateral and Bilateral Issues," in *Canadian Issues: Canada and the Sea* 3 (I) (1980): 161–74.

MISUNDERSTANDING
THE PRAIRIES◆

DAVID A. GAUTHIER
J. DAVID HENRY

○

Within one human lifetime, the prairies have passed from wilderness to become the most altered habitat in this country and one of the most disturbed, ecologically simplified and overexploited regions in the world.

Dr. Adrian Forsyth

Adrian Forsyth's incisive criticism is an indictment of the way we have treated the prairies over the past century. Successive waves of explorers and settlers, each eager to harvest the impressive productivity of a grasslands ecosystem, have eroded the natural processes that underlay the great fertility of the prairie landscapes. And this massive alternation of the prairies continues to this day.

To examine this transformation, we must first know what the Canadian prairies looked like at the time of the arrival of the first Europeans. In August 1691, Henry Kelsey was travelling overland north of the Touchwood Hills of present-day Saskatchewan. In his journal, he described the prairies in this manner: "Today we pitched to ye outermost edge of ye woods. This plain affords nothing but short round sticky grasses and buffalo and a great sort of a bear which is bigger than any white bear and is neither white nor black but silver-haired. . . . "

La Vérendrye explored southern Manitoba between 1783 and 1739, describing the long-grass prairie as follows: "it is all very level, without mountains, all fine hard wood with here and there groves of oak; . . . every-

◆ Reprinted from Monte Hummel, ed., *Endangered Spaces* (Toronto: Key Porter, 1989), 183–93.

where there are quantities of fruit trees, and all sorts of wild animals; the savage tribes are there very numerous, and always wandering.... " Later that summer in his journal, he states: "I found the water [in the Assiniboine River] very low, as there had been no rain all the summer. There are fine trees along the banks, and behind these a boundless stretch of prairies in which are multitude of buffalo and deer."

Edward Umfreville explored the prairies adjacent to the Saskatchewan River in 1790. He described the northern edge of the prairies:

> The fruits, which spontaneously shoot up, are not in such great variety in the wilderness of Canada, as in the country, I am speaking of.... Raspberries, strawberries, currants, cranberries, and an infinity of other kinds which I know not the names of, are to be found everywhere.... In the valleys and humid situations, the grass grows to a great height, which fattens our horses in a short time; but the buffalo usually makes choice of hilly, dry ground, to feed on, the blades of grass on which are small, short and tender. When a numerous herd of these animals stay any length of time in one place, the ground is absolutely barren there for the remainder of the season, the grass being ate off....

Thus, the early European explorers were deeply struck by the natural productivity of the Canadian prairies. The massive herds of bison, the scattered groupings of elk, the ubiquitous pronghorn antelope combined with the packs of prairie wolves and scattered plains grizzly bears left a lasting impression upon these early travellers. Despite the harshness of its climate, the rich prairie soils together with the abundant wild fruits and plentiful wildlife deepened their conviction that this was a land of great endemic productivity.

Unfortunately, the northern prairies has always been an ecosystem that can be easily impacted, and it took surprisingly few years and remarkably few Europeans to leave an indelible mark on these abundant wildlife populations. In his famous travel classic, *The Great Lone Land*, William Francis Butler described the Canadian prairies as he encountered them between 1870 and 1872:

> Around it, far into endless space, stretch immense plains of bare and scanty vegetation, plains seared with the tracks of countless buffalo which, until a few years ago, were wont to roam in vast herds between the Assiniboine and the Saskatchewan. Upon whatever side the eye turns when crossing these great expanses, the same wrecks of the monarch of the prairie lie thickly strewn over the surface. Hundreds of thousands of skeletons dot the short scant grass; and when fire has laid barer still the level surface, the bleached ribs and skulls of long-killed bison whiten far and near the dark burnt prairie.... There is not a sound in the air or on the earth; on every side lie spread the relics of the great fight waged by man against the brute creation; all is silent and deserted—the Indian and the buffalo gone, the settler yet to come.

This drastic alteration of the prairies was largely promoted by the leaders of the time. Removal of the bison provided a simultaneous solution to what was referred to as "The Indian Problem." In the United States, this unsanctioned policy of the U.S. Government was perhaps most baldly stated by General Philip Henry Sheridan of the U.S. Cavalry. In 1875 he stated: "The Buffalo Hunters have done more in the past two years to settle the vexed Indian Question than the entire regular army in the last thirty years. They are destroying the Indian's commissary. Send them powder and lead if you will, and let them kill, skin and sell until they have exterminated the buffalo!"

Farley Mowat in *Sea of Slaughter* points out that General Sheridan later told Congress it should strike a medal honouring the buffalo hunters, with the imprint of a dead buffalo on one side—and a dead Indian on the other.

Humans have been present on the Canadian prairies for the past 12 000 years. This amount of time—a fleeting moment in terms of geological time—has been marked by several successive waves of increasing exploitation across the North American grasslands. In the ancient "dog days" before they acquired horses, native hunters would have had little effect upon prairie wildlife populations. The low numbers of native hunters, their reliance on large, shifting big-game populations, their relative lack of mobility, and their lack of firearms meant a harsh, nomadic lifestyle. During the nesting season they hunted waterfowl, but the plains Indians were primarily bison hunters.

By the early 1700s, hunting efficiency and movements of plains tribes had become affected by the introduction northward of horses that had been brought into the southern plains by Spaniards. The expansion of the fur trade into the Canadian West also affected native lifestyles by providing voracious trading partners in the form of the competing Hudson's Bay and North West companies. The companies required substantial supplies of food to feed the men stationed at a growing number of posts. In turn, they provided native people with new tools, including firearms, that helped to reduce the harshness of their lives. It became readily apparent that the prairie and parkland regions, with their abundance of wildlife, could serve to meet that growing demand and that plains tribes and a growing Metis population could be used to obtain that food.

Beginning in the 1820s and over the next sixty years, organized bands of Metis hunters and settlers from the Red River colony set off each summer to hunt the large buffalo herds that lay to the west. The hides were sold for blankets, coats, and leather; the meat was turned into pemmican and dried meat, then sold to the fur companies. These organizations used the meat to support their fur transportation routes and trading posts located farther north.

It has been estimated that 100 000 to 300 000 plains bison may have been slaughtered annually to meet the food needs of the trading companies and Metis and Indian communities. But the numbers of plains bison so greatly exceeded those numbers that the slaughter for food was not regarded as a serious threat to the survival of the bison herds. The tragic story of the extinction of the plains bison really begins after 1830, when the buffalo-robe trade developed further and increased settlement eliminated the great herds in settled areas from Manitoba to Kansas. In addition, the early 1870s brought forth a process for making commercial leather from buffalo hides. Each year the buffalo hunters had to extend their range farther to harvest sufficient numbers of animals. Then in 1883 the Red River carts of the hide hunters returned home from the buffalo range with empty wagons, and the hunt was never again attempted.

In the incredibly short span of forty years, the plains bison became extinct in Manitoba. By the 1870s, remnant herds were found only in southern Alberta and southwestern Saskatchewan. These were soon to be killed by settlers and starving Indians. The plains Indians whose hunting lifestyle had been based largely on a single resource were reduced to extreme poverty and growing dependence on government assistance.

After the hide hunters quit, the bone pickers came. Buffalo bone commanded six to ten dollars per ton. The bones were ground up and used in refining sugar; horns were fashionable as buttons, combs, and knife handles; and hooves were salvaged and turned into glue. The bone-and-skull trade was over by the 1890s. And the great herds had vanished forever.

Bison had dominated the prairie landscape, but with their loss other wildlife also suffered. The plains-dwelling wolves and grizzly bears were eliminated with the loss of their prey. Elk and deer became overhunted as traders tried to replace their losses of bison with other animals. By the early 1880s the fur-trading era was over, but the ability of prairie wildlife to survive was to be strongly affected by even more significant impacts.

ESCALATING EXPLOITATION

Buffalo harvesting was only the first wave of exploitation initiated by Europeans to roll across the Canadian prairies. Since then, ranching, agriculture, and mining have successively swept the region. The formation of the Province of Manitoba in 1870 opened the region to agricultural settlement. Settlers moved into the region in large numbers, facilitated by the completion of the Canadian Pacific Railway in the 1880s.

Demands escalated on wildlife populations, as elk, moose, mule deer, and other animals were hunted for food, driving their numbers even lower. Corridors of agricultural development appeared along the main and spur rail lines. As land was cleared and planted, vegetative cover was altered significantly. White-tailed deer moved north from Minnesota into this new preferred habitat with no fear of competition from bison and elk. The greater prairie chicken also moved north into the prairie region of Manitoba and Saskatchewan, occupying the islands of untilled rocky habitat set in a growing sea of cultivated lands.

Between 1901 and 1913, two million more people settled on the prairies. In the same time period, cultivated land increased from 2 million to 25 million hectares. Wildlife habitat became severely modified. Pronghorn disappeared from Manitoba and were seriously reduced in Saskatchewan. To meet hunter demands, exotic upland game birds were introduced: ring-necked pheasant, gray partridge and chukar, and the wild turkey.

Waterfowl are one of the great natural resources of the prairies. The prairie pot-hole region has traditionally been productive habitat for waterfowl in the breeding season, with larger lakes and marshes used in the postbreeding period and migration. In the early days of agriculture, before farms became mechanized, waterfowl adapted to human impacts without substantial losses. With time, however, available habitat decreased, idle lands became cultivated, wetlands were drained, and farming practices were intensified. Lost wetland habitat has been placed at 1.21 million hectares.

The faunal complex of the prairies developed in an environment subject to overgrazing by bison, fire, and drought. With settlement by immigrants, the prairies underwent drastic changes. Cattle replaced bison as the dominant grazer on the prairies. Large prairie fires had maintained the prairie ecosystem by removing dense vegetation, recycling nutrients, and stopping aspen trees from spreading and multiplying. With fire suppression, aspen groves soon became established in the northern prairies, surrounded by developing grain fields and a road-and-rail system. The original stable condition of soil and grass—maintained by large grazers, fire, and periodic drought—had given way to an intensively managed, inherently unstable system, and widespread deterioration of the landscape ensued.

The net result has been that the Canadian prairies have become one of the most endangered natural habitats in Canada. Human efforts have been directed towards maximizing economic return. The natural productivity of the soil and precious water resources has been viewed as a bank in which the emphasis has been on withdrawals, not deposits.

Unfavourable global markets for certain agricultural produce (especially wheat), global subsidy wars, soil erosion and nutrient losses, massive debt loads for agricultural operators, and contradictory federal and provincial government resource policies have all led to significant social and economic problems for farm operators. Biological diversity has decreased, as only a few highly productive crop and pasture seeds strains are planted. Organic matter and biomass have been reduced by 50 percent since the first land was broken, a fact masked by the current heavy use of commercial fertilizers.

Increased mechanization in terms of larger tractors and equipment results in larger areas of land being ploughed. This equipment-oriented farming encourages the removal of shelterbelts, whose loss reduces snow accumulation and soil moisture. Native wildlife habitat has been reduced by agricultural encroachment, increased urbanization, industrialization, pollution, construction of roads, and overexploitation of remaining wildlife resources. More and more marginal lands are being converted to agricultural use, even though such lands are highly susceptible to soil erosion, salinization, and nutrient loss. The failure rate for farmers occupying these marginal lands has increased as small family operators are replaced by larger corporate agricultural interests.

Over the past seven hundred years on the Great Plains, there have been thirteen drought periods lasting five or more years, with an average duration of thirteen years and a cyclic recurrence of about twenty years. The

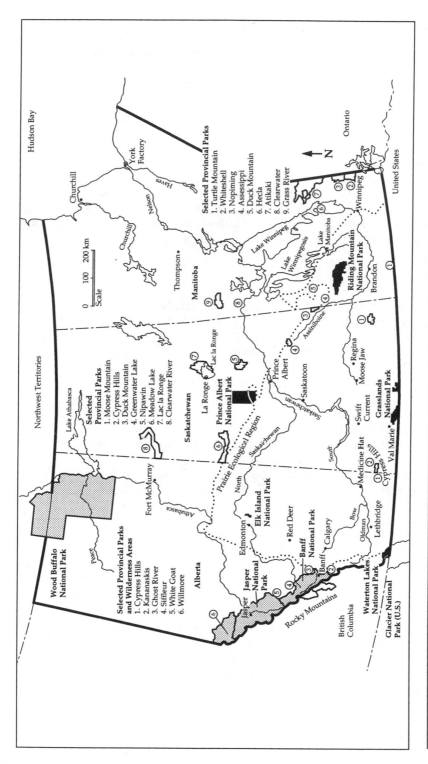

F I G U R E 1 *THE PRAIRIES: ALBERTA, SASKATCHEWAN, AND MANITOBA*

drought of the "Dirty Thirties" is well documented. However, the worst wheat drought during the past fifty years occurred in 1961. The 1980s has again seen a period of extended drought. Abnormally hot, dry conditions have resulted in destruction of agricultural crops and grazing pastures. Unseeded and even seeded soils are blowing away. Adding to the concerns about cyclic short-term drought are fears raised by long-term climatic changes caused by the "greenhouse effect": a trend to higher temperatures caused by increased accumulation in the atmosphere of gases generated by human activities. Studies of the effect of increasingly higher temperatures on the prairies all predict substantial adverse effects as a result of greater frequency and duration of droughts.

Today, the wildness of "prairie wool" has been succeeded by field after field of tidy furrows. It is a highly geometric, checkerboard landscape measured out by roads into sections and quarter-sections. It is indeed one of the most altered environments found on the face of our planet.

PRAIRIE PRODUCTIVITY

Where did the natural productivity of the northern prairies come from? How was it that this region could support an estimated 60 million buffalo, 30 million pronghorn, plus millions of deer, elk, and waterfowl? To understand this endemic productivity, we must begin by understanding what natural processes interact to cause it.

We should start by probing the fertility of grassland soils, a resource which is highly dependent upon the sedimentary geology of the region. As time passed, ancient seas alternately inundated and retreated over the area of the present plains, leaving sediments that, as a result of accumulated weight and uplifting pressure, hardened into layered sedimentary rock, often as much as 3000 metres in depth.

Approximately 150 million years ago the Cordilleran mountains to the west began to form, an event with monumental effects on the prairies. Without the sheltering effect of the Cordilleran ranges, the plains would not have become as warm or arid, and the grasslands would never have developed. The mountain-building process also caused rivers to flow easterly, carrying sediments from these mountains to be deposited in vast blankets over the plains. These deposits would alternately be scoured and redeposited by the action of huge continental icesheets that flowed and ebbed over the plains area, finally disappearing from the plains approximately 10 000 years ago.

The wasting away of blocks of ice entrapped in sediments created the pot-hole topography of the Canadian prairies. Today, this legacy from the last continental icesheet has left a maze of sloughs, teeming with insects and invertebrate aquatic life—a habitat responsible for more than 50 percent of all ducks born in North America. Prairie sloughs also attract red-winged and yellow-headed blackbirds, grebes, herons, bitterns, avocets, and willets as well as many different kinds of shorebirds. These prairie wetlands are also essential as resting areas and staging areas for the migration of many other waterfowl species which nest on the tundra farther north.

The meltwater channels created by the massive amount of water pouring off the wasting glaciers are also responsible for creating the deep river valleys that dissect the prairies. These river valleys offer wooded coulees and sheltered microhabitats, which become extremely important to wildlife, especially during the harsh prairie winter.

Wayne Lynch aptly describes in *Married to the Wind* the debt that prairie farmers owe the glaciers. As the glaciers melted, they:

> retreated in a northeasterly direction, forming a barrier to the normal drainage of the land, so that water was ponded between the glacier and the higher ground in the west. The ponded water formed glacial lakes that filled with sediments up to 6 metres thick. The flat, silt and clay bottoms of Rosetown, Indian Head, and Regina lakes were to become the prime wheat-growing areas of Saskatchewan. The glacial lakes of Saskatchewan and Manitoba tended to spread out and cover large areas. Lake Agassiz, which formed in the Manitoba Lowlands, was the largest of all the glacial lakes and was probably the largest lake of any type that the Earth has ever known. The lacustrian clays formed on the bottom of Lake Agassiz constitute the belt of heavy lands—the most fertile agricultural lands across Manitoba and into southeastern Saskatchewan.

PICKING UP THE PIECES

Agriculture, and to a lesser degree urbanization, have transformed more than 80 percent of the native prairie landscape. Some 90 percent of the rough fescue grassland in Canada has been ploughed, and much of the remaining 10 percent has been significantly modified by livestock grazing and haying.

Almost all of the tall-grass prairie is gone—one of the few sizeable plots remaining (about 10 hectares) is within the city limits of Winnipeg. A 1978–82 census indicated that only 18 percent of the once-abundant short-grass prairie remains in its native state, about 24 percent of the mixed grass prairie, and 25 percent of the aspen parkland. About 1.2 million hectares of wetland habitat in the prairie region have been converted to agricultural use—a loss of 40 percent of the original wetlands.

These losses are not just in quantity; they are losses in quality. The areas of tall-grass, parkland, mixed grass, and short-grass that go under the plough are usually the most fertile, productive areas. What remains in an undisturbed state are either the drier or the water-saturated sites, lands considered marginal for agriculture. Now, under increased economic pressure, even these marginal sites are under siege.

What can be done to pick up the pieces? Given the radical transformations which the Canadian prairies have seen during the last century, how should we proceed to protect what is left of the prairie natural heritage?

Part of the answer certainly rests in changing our attitudes. We must learn to think in terms of ecological concepts and evolutionary processes. For example, the prairie provinces were built on agriculture, and farming depends heavily upon genetic diversity. Native plant species are the prime source for new strains of domesticated forages and cereals. Native species are valuable for their adaptability to severe environmental conditions such as drought, and for their natural resistance to insect pests. Yet, commercial agriculture focusses the interest of most farmers on only a few highly productive strains: four varieties of wheat account for 75 percent of the Canadian wheat crop. We know very little about the values that prairie species may hold for future foods, forage crops, pharmaceutical, and other uses. A larger effort should be made to preserve prairie plant species *in situ*; that is, in representative, undisturbed ecological reserves with a mandate for preserving benchmark communities of the Canadian prairies.

Loss of habitat is the most critical issue facing prairie wildlife. The potential for species extinctions on the prairies is a matter of serious concern. Nine Canadian species are known to have been lost in the last two hundred years, several of these from the prairies. The swift fox and the black-footed ferret have been extirpated, and the passenger pigeon is extinct. Subspecies such as the plains wolf and the plains grizzly have also been lost. Today, the few remaining herds of buffalo found on the prairies are no longer free-roaming. Only two national parks in Canada (Wood Buffalo and Prince Albert) can claim to contain free-ranging buffalo.

Many more species are now on the brink. About one-quarter of the bird and mammal species designated on the 1988 list of the Committee on the Status of Endangered Wildlife in Canada are found in the prairie provinces. Most of these live in the grasslands or aspen parkland. The status of many other prairie species is unknown, but certainly more species will join the list if action is not taken soon to conserve much of the remaining native prairie wildlands.

Over the short term, our goals are clearly definable. Since 1986 the World Wildlife Fund has brought together scientists, resources managers, and leaders from the business community to focus on the ecological degradation that has taken place on the Canadian prairies. It has been an effort to apply the global objectives of the World Conservation Strategy—maintaining essential ecological processes, preserving genetic diversity, and ensuring sustainable utilization of species and ecosystems—to the grasslands region of Canada. The World Wildlife Fund's analysis concludes that the terrestrial and wetland ecosystems of the prairies are indeed endangered spaces. The Prairie Conservation Action Plan produced by the WWF outlines an urgent five-year blueprint, which, if carried out through co-operative endeavours by government, universities, environmental organizations, and the private sector, would accomplish much towards the ultimate goal of re-establishing the biological diversity of the Canadian prairies. Conservation goals of this plan are organized around six initiatives, and specific implementation on a region-by-region basis is derived from these conservation objectives. The six objectives are:

- Complete the inventories of the remaining native prairie parkland where necessary for conversation purposes;

- Protect at least one large, representative area in each of the five major prairie ecoregions;

- Establish a system of protected native prairie ecosystems across the three prairie provinces, including representative samples of each eco-region and habitat subregion;

- Prepare management and restoration plans for threatened ecosystems and habitats;

- Prepare and implement recovery and management plans for every prairie and parkland species designated nationally or provincially as vulnerable, threatened, endangered, or extirpated;

- Ensure that no additional species become threatened, endangered, or extirpated.

We fully endorse these objectives of the WWF's Wild West program, as outlined in the Prairie Conservation Action Plan. We cannot imagine conservation priorities that have a more pressing urgency to be achieved during the immediate future. However, we are convinced that over the long term a more fundamental reorganization of our economic enterprises and resource management must be undertaken if the natural productivity and biological diversity of the Canadian prairies is to be reclaimed.

A century and a half of land and water management on the prairies has resulted not in preservation, but in massive ecological degradation. We have departments of wildlife and agriculture, water agencies, and a seemingly endless list of administrative units ranging through municipal, provincial, and federal levels of government. These are "cells" of a larger honeycomb of human efforts intended to wisely manage our resources. But on what ecological basis were these management cells formed, and on what basis do they operate? Do they place high priority on maintaining ecological processes and preserving biological diversity? If they do, why have we lost so much of our natural heritage?

It is easy to understand why decision-makers would opt for goals that have immediate political payoffs but long-term costs. Yet, the past century of our misunderstanding of the prairies must be accounted for. Will the processes and institutions that led us to our current state of ecological degradation be the means to lead us out? We think not. Innovative and integrative approaches to resource management are required, approaches that put the highest priority on maintaining ecological processes and preserving biological diversity.

The prairies cannot continue to be arbitrarily administered as provincial or municipal units. The current organization of the federal and provincial bureaucracies must no longer be imposed on the ecology of the prairies. We must integrate our management using ecological principles. We must manage the remaining resources and surviving productivity of the prairies as functional ecological entities.

Imagine that we could redesign our government administration to reflect ecological processes. We might structure it according to ecoregions; for example, a department of fescue grasslands, a department of mixed-grass prairie. Each department would operate according to a similar set of priorities; for example, those of the World Conservation Strategy. All land, air, and water management—all utilization of resources—would be incorporated under these priorities.

This management model is not as fanciful as it seems. Yet a reorganization of priorities will happen in one of two ways. Either wise people will recognize the need to integrate our demands on the environment with the capability of the environment to sustain those demands, and consequently design creative means for the integration; or environmental disaster will compound upon environmental disaster until the costs of our action exceed even the short-term benefits and we will be forced to react, albeit too late to regain much of what we have lost. In essence, we can create for the future, or we can be forced to react to an increasingly impoverished environment.

The Prairie Conservation Action Plan of the World Wildlife Fund is a call for creative measures. But it is only a start. We must build on that initiative and numerous other ones, such as those related to interprovincial parks, the establishment of Grasslands National Park, the Alberta-Saskatchewan interprovincial parks, ecological-reserve and wilderness-area provincial legislation, acquisition and protection of critical wildlife habitat, the Prairie Farm Rehabilitation Administration initiative to reduce the overuse of marginal agricultural lands, and other water and soil conservation strategies. But despite these valuable initiatives, the larger arena of political decision-making does not adequately reflect the ecological processes that form the basis of much of the prairie economy. We must frame our entrepreneurial proposals, government policies, and decisions within a larger context of environmental ethics. We must all try to find moments in the hurried pace of our short lives on this planet to consider our legacy. As Rachel Carson states in *Silent Spring*: "Why should we tolerate a diet of weak poisons, a home in insipid surroundings, a circle of acquaintances who are not quite our enemies . . . Who would want to live in a world which is just not quite fatal?"

THE ALIENATION OF CANADIAN RESOURCES: THE CASE OF THE COLUMBIA RIVER TREATY*

LARRATT T. HIGGINS

o

Canada's presence on the international stage has been fading for the past fifteen years or so, especially in its dealings with the United States. During this period there has been also a noticeable decline in the power of the federal government in relation to the provinces. There is a connection between these two processes. The erosion of federal power in both respects stems in great part from a view, held widely in Ottawa, that the federal government is little more than an agent of the provinces on the one hand, and little more than a province of the United States on the other. A corollary of this view is that the government at Ottawa has no prerogative to exercise initiative or to take decisions in international negotiations concerning matters which come under provincial or divided jurisdiction. The result has been to reduce the federal government to something resembling a secretariat, whose function is but to implement decisions taken at other levels. The decline of Ottawa's power and influence in these terms can be seen clearly in its dealings with the United States and British Columbia in the Columbia River dispute.

The dispute was resolved finally on September 16, 1964, when the Columbia River Treaty of January 17, 1961, came into force.[1] Under the terms of the treaty, Canada undertook to build three storage dams in British Columbia at a cost then estimated at $410.6 million. In return Canada was to receive $274.8 million on the ratification date, with other payments totalling $70 million to follow.[2] The operation of these dams was to be

* Originally published in Ian Lumsden, ed., *Close the 49th Parallel: The Americanization of Canada* (Toronto: University of Toronto Press, 1970), 224–40. Reprinted with permission of University of Toronto Press Incorporated.

under international supervision by a Permanent Engineering Board consisting of two members designated by each country. The two American members are Washington officials; on the Canadian side one member represents Ottawa while the other is a British Columbia nominee. The Canadian operating entity is provincial—the BC Hydro and Power Authority.

After thirty years Canada might receive a small but undefined amount of electric energy. In exchange for other unspecified energy benefits which would accrue to a Canadian corporation, Canada is also required to make available, at its expense, some seventeen thousand acres of land in British Columbia for flooding by a dam to be built in the United States. The treaty can be terminated after sixty years upon ten years' written notice. Certain provisions relating to Canadian operation for flood control do not expire with the treaty.

The Columbia River Treaty, in its effect, is revolutionary.[3] The previous law and the institutions for administering the Columbia basin are swept away. In place of co-operation by national entities, the Canadian portion of the Columbia basin has been placed under international control, which is to be based upon the greatest good for the basin as a whole. The American portion of the basin remains under American control. This means that, in cases of conflict, Canadian operation must give way to the majority interest with no compensation for lost opportunity. In other words, the costs of co-operation are to be borne by Canada while the benefits will be reaped by the United States wherever a divergence of interest arises. The Columbia River Treaty is not for co-operative development and operation; it integrates the smaller but vital Canadian part of the basin into the whole.

One result of the Columbia River Treaty is that there are now two quite different sets of legal principles in force governing relations between Canada and the United States in water questions. The Columbia is governed by the continental resource concept of integrating Canadian resources into the economy of North America. This concept does not recognize the possibility of conflict in that all actions are dictated by the majority interest.

Other watersheds are still governed by the Boundary Waters Treaty of 1909,[4] which rests upon a premise of development of North America by separate national entities. The principle behind this treaty recognizes the possibility of conflict, and accordingly provides for its resolution. It provides also for international co-operation where both parties stand to gain without sacrificing more favourable alternatives. A set of rules and a mechanism were provided whereby disputes between Canada and the United States could be settled equitably within an agreed legal framework. The International Joint Commission was set up consisting of two national sections, each with three members headed by a chairman, as the machinery for resolving conflict between the two countries.

Two legal doctrines were embedded in the 1909 treaty. The first, and the more important, was the Harmon doctrine, which asserted that the upstream country has an unfettered right to "exclusive jurisdiction and control over the use and diversion . . . of waters on its own side of the line which in their natural channels would flow across the boundary or into boundary waters."[5] In addition, the downstream state is prevented from "construction . . . of any works in waters at a lower level than the boundary, the effect of which is to raise the natural level of the waters on the other side of the boundary"[6] without the approval of the International Joint Commission.

The Harmon doctrine favours the United States both vis-à-vis Mexico and the eastern parts of North America, which were of concern when the treaty was being negotiated.[7] However, in the western part of the continent, the doctrine favours Canada on most of the trans-boundary rivers of significant size and potential. The doctrine was asserted most recently by the United States in 1952. Canada sought permission on behalf of the Consolidated Mining and Smelting Company (Cominco) to construct the Waneta dam on the Pend d'Oreille River, a tributary of the Columbia which flows from the United States into Canada. The Waneta dam would raise the level of the river at the boundary by a matter of inches and thus cause slight flooding of two and a half acres of US territory. The United States reiterated its claim to upstream sovereignty in a manner designed to preserve its future freedom of action to divert the Pend d'Oreille. The Order of Approval issued by the International Joint Commission in July 1952 stressed: ". . . the right of the United States recognized in Article II of the Boundary Waters Treaty to construct such works as it may consider necessary or desirable for making most advantageous use reasonably practical on its own side of the international boundary by diversion for power purposes or otherwise." The order carried with it the concurrence of both countries, and consequently is a valid precedent.

The second doctrine embedded in the treaty is that of prior appropriation. This doctrine is not as explicitly stated in the treaty as is the Harmon doctrine, but it was asserted by the United States in a protocol to the treaty.[8]

Within the International Joint Commission, many of the words used were strong, and most of the positions taken were firm; but for the most part, the resulting actions provided harmonious and equitable lawful solutions. Canadian diplomats, who tend to assume that under no circumstances can Canada afford to offend Uncle Sam, were often made nervous by the proceedings. Nevertheless, in the process of sharp debate, much misunderstanding was cleared away, and an impressive body of precedent was created within the international law derived from the Boundary Waters Treaty.[9]

Part of the reason for the success of the International Joint Commission in the past undoubtedly was that, in most cases, the disputes were not international confrontations. Conflicts over problems such as the Great Lakes, the Niagara River, and the St Lawrence were for the most part between functional interests such as navigation, power, conservation, and riparian owners on both sides of the boundary. Canadian interests were not pitted against American interests, as such. For example, the Chicago diversion reduces the power potential of the Niagara and St Lawrence rivers in both countries. Conflicting interests within each country prevented each national section of the International Joint Commission from taking an extreme view, and tended to promote a greater reliance upon legal precedent than otherwise might have been the case.

Another reason for the original success of the International Joint Commission, at least from a Canadian point of view, was the willingness of the government to support a vigorous assertion of Canada's rights under the Boundary Waters Treaty. This included a sufficient delegation of authority to the Canadian Section. The United States has been hampered by a tendency to make the chairmanship of the American Section a political appointment, and thus in effect to relegate it to a somewhat less important status than that of its Canadian counterpart. Very often, this has worked to the advantage of Canada.

The initiative for joint development of the Columbia River basin had come originally from the United States when the US Army Corps of Engineers realized in 1943 that the full potential of the river within American borders could not be achieved without the provision of storage for flood flows in Canada, and for their release during the low-flow season. The Corps of Engineers was directed to make a new study of the American portion of the basin. In March 1944, at the request of the United States, the two governments referred the matter of co-operative development of the Columbia basin to the International Joint Commission.[10] The IJC set up the International Columbia River Engineering Board (ICREB) to investigate and report.

The United States had an early advantage because a great deal of work had been done already on the American side. Two of the largest dams in the world were generating power on the main stem of the Columbia at Bonneville and Grand Coulee. In Canada, on the other hand, little was known about the basin, and there were no developments on the Columbia. Topographical maps had to be prepared and streamflow records had to be accumulated for at least a decade in order to provide adequate information of the dimensions of water supply before engineering proposals could be made. Thus the American plans were formulated before the Canadian alternatives emerged.

The Corps of Engineers issued a comprehensive report on the American portion of the basin in 1949.[11] This report was important, not only for the detailed information it brought together, but also for a thesis it sought to establish according to which the benefits of storage decline over time.[12] This fallacy was never challenged at the official level by Canada, and ultimately it led to serious defects in the Columbia Treaty as it applied to Canada.

The final report of the ICREB was published in 1959. Long before the report was issued, the United States had begun to exert pressure on Canada through its early advantage in knowing its own requirements. Canada was able to resist these pressures, in part because they were blatantly premature and in part because the government of Canada was prepared to act upon the advice of the chairman of the Canadian Section, General A.G.L. McNaughton.

American pressures created two issues. One thrust came from the private sector. The Kaiser Aluminum Company approached the British Columbia government with a proposal to build a small dam at the outlet of Arrow Lakes on the main stem of the Columbia, a short distance upstream from Trail. The dam would yield $14 million annually to the United States corporation; Premier Bennett of British Columbia had agreed to accept an annual payment of $2 million with the dam to be built at Kaiser's expense.[13] The power generated in the United States during the low-flow season from released water was to be used to produce aluminum behind the American tariff to supply the market there in competition with Alcan's Kitimat project.[14]

The government of Canada intervened by passing the International River Improvements Act in 1955,[15] under which a federal licence is required for works which would "increase, decrease, or alter the flow of an international river." The policy of the Canadian government was set forth at the time by Jean Lesage, minister of northern affairs: "According to the Canadian constitution, works built on rivers in Canada having an effect outside the country fall under the jurisdiction of Parliament even if they are located in one province."[16] He went on to say that any projects, to be approved, must be compatible with optimum development of the resources by Canada, and that benefits from any downstream utilization must be commensurate with the resources made available.

The Kaiser deal had important implications. In the first place, it constituted recognition by downstream interests of the fact that storage dams in Canada would provide benefits in the United States, and also recognition that these should be shared. Although the transaction was between private interests and a provincial government, it provided a useful precedent. Second, the passing of the International River Improvements Act demonstrated the power of the federal government to impose its veto on a development with international implications, even though the resource was otherwise under provincial jurisdiction.

The other thrust of United States pressure on Canada was the proposal of the Corps of Engineers to build a dam near Libby, Montana, on the Kootenai River in the Columbia basin.[17] Because this dam would cause flooding into Canada for forty-two miles, putting over seventeen thousand acres under water of depths up to 150 feet, Canadian consent was needed under Article IV of the Boundary Waters Treaty. The Libby dam was suggested by the Corps of Engineers as early as 1948 and approved by Congress in 1950. The application was made to the IJC in 1951. Within the IJC, the Libby and Waneta applications were under consideration simultaneously.

In the face of the Libby application, the American action in reconfirming the right to divert the Pend d'Oreille in the Waneta order was a major blunder, for construction of the Libby dam, the key to United States control of the Columbia, required a repudiation of the Harmon doctrine. Moreover, while the Americans lacked firm plans to divert the Pend d'Oreille, the Canadians were developing their plans to divert the Kootenay to the Columbia. It happens that as the Kootenay River flows south in British Columbia, it passes within a mile of the headwaters of the Columbia, and at the same elevation. In fact, some of the waters of the Kootenay actually find their way into the Columbia via a shallow canal that joins the two rivers. It is therefore a simple matter to increase this diversion to the Columbia. The waters of the Kootenay could be put to good use in Canada, either to produce power on the Columbia (and perhaps the Fraser), or to provide water for irrigation on the prairies by diversion across the Rocky mountains.

Indeed, the Kootenay-Columbia diversion was required for Canada if best use was to be made of the huge reservoir to be built at Mica Creek. To add force to the Canadian position, the diversion plan was cheaper and more efficient than the Libby proposal. Moreover, there was no downstream interest in the United States that would suffer damage from the diversion: on the contrary, it would provide needed flood protection.

The plan to build the Libby dam was controversial, even in the United States, because of its poor economics, and also because many Americans suspected that it was merely empire building on the part of the Corps of Engineers. In Canada the federal government opposed the application on the advice of General McNaughton, who had conceived the Canadian plan of diverting the Kootenay to the Columbia on the basis of his experience in the area many years previously. Local interests in the Kootenay valley where the river re-enters Canada tended to support the United States application. Among these was Cominco, which expected to receive a windfall gain in the order of $3 million a year from the operation of upstream storage at Libby.[18]

Cominco's support of the US proposal undoubtedly was based on self-interest. The company's attitude probably would have been more in tune with Canadian policy objectives if it had been made plain that it would not reap any windfall gains from Libby; there was no reason why these should not have accrued to the province of British Columbia on payment of an equitable rental for Cominco equipment used. Apparently, however, Cominco feared that the Canadian diversion plan would reduce its power output; and in this case, the government should have ensured that these fears were dispelled. The Duncan Lake project was proposed primarily to compensate Cominco for the flows that would be diverted. It is not possible to document any part that may have been played by Cominco in Premier Bennett's subsequent decision to veto the Canadian diversion plan; but the influence could have been considerable.

The first application for the Libby dam was withdrawn by the United States on April 8, 1953, because of opposition by US railway interests; under the plan, there would be extensive flooding of track. Another reason, not stated publicly, was that the Americans entertained hopes that pressure from Cominco would cause the removal of McNaughton from the IJC. They were anxious to get rid of him after he had sprung the trap they set for themselves in the language of the Waneta order; the Waneta precedent, coming during the Libby proceedings, completely deprived them of a legal case. After the local opposition had been mollified, and after it had become evident that McNaughton would retain the confidence of the Canadian government, the Libby application was resubmitted on May 22, 1954. It was never disposed of by the International Joint Commission, but became a part of the political negotiations on the Columbia Treaty in which the IJC was not directly involved.

At one point, early in these political negotiations, the United States abandoned its demand for Libby and acceded to the Canadian diversion plan, which would provide the needed flood protection downstream in Idaho. Then the Bennett government, for its own political reasons, vetoed

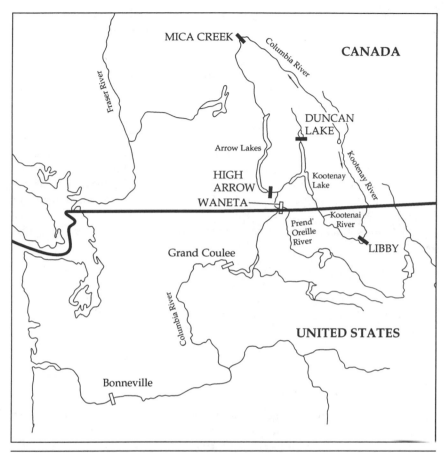

F I G U R E   1   *FLOOD PROTECTION*

the Canadian diversion plan, much to the astonishment of the Americans. It was this action and, incredibly, its acceptance by the government in Ottawa that transformed the development of the Columbia from a triumph of common sense and international co-operation into the wasteful disaster that has integrated the Canadian Columbia into the United States economy. There was no stand-by Canadian plan. Not only was the Libby proposal included in the Columbia Treaty, but the vested interest so created was reinforced by a clause which effectively prevents Canada from making a significant diversion.

When confronted with the British Columbia veto, the federal government could have broken off negotiations with the United States, or it could have given the Americans the option of continuing discussion within reduced terms of reference, excluding development on the Kootenay. There seems little doubt that the United States would have elected to continue the discussions because 80 percent of the power benefits, and virtually all of the flood protection could be achieved without the Kootenay; in any event, the Kootenay plan could have been implemented later as no options would be closed off. But the Canadians had permitted themselves to be convinced that the value of storage declines over time, and therefore concluded that any treaty was better than no treaty.[19]

Diefenbaker's decision to go ahead with the signing of the Columbia River Treaty on January 17, 1961, was undoubtedly made on the advice he received, although there is ample evidence to indicate that this advice should have been conflicting. In Ottawa McNaughton was bitterly opposed, and he seemed to have the support of External Affairs Minister Howard Green. There was no binding agreement with British Columbia: on the contrary, the storm warnings were flying. Bennett had expressed serious reservations about the draft treaty in letters to Donald Fleming, minister of finance.[20] He had also referred the whole matter of the feasibility of the Columbia and Peace rivers to the BC Energy Board for detailed study in December, 1960.

Diefenbaker described the decision curiously to the House of Commons the next day:

> May I say that in the signing of this tremendous treaty the course followed was one that gave emphasis to the importance of the occasion. The fact is that it was the last major official discharge of responsibility on the part of the President of the United States. That fact gives it emphasis. During the course of our stay there the Minister of Justice, myself, and several representatives from the two countries were entertained at luncheon at the White House, the last function of the kind that will take place during the presidency of Dwight D. Eisenhower.[21]

Like so many Canadian prime ministers before him and after, Diefenbaker seems to have been overawed by the experience.

The Columbia River Treaty was a disaster beyond the confines of the Columbia basin. In order to justify its action, the Diefenbaker government put forth a view of federal-provincial relations which was the antithesis of the position taken by Jean Lesage in 1955. Specifically, it claimed that the role of the federal government in any international dealings concerning matters under provincial jurisdiction was merely to satisfy the niceties of protocol in the international arena while acting as an agent of the province. In other words, it was an abdication by the government of Canada from its over-riding jurisdiction in external affairs. Such a view inevitably would destroy the credibility, relevance, and consequently the power of the Ottawa government.

In the two years that followed, the dispute between Ottawa and Victoria over the financing of the Columbia and whether to sell the power benefits added almost as much frustration to relations between Canada and the United States as did the Bomarc question. The news media were preoccupied with the Ottawa-Victoria squabble, and permitted it to steal the limelight from the important discussion which concerned the merits of the treaty.

Public discussion of the merits of the treaty was opened up when Diefenbaker abruptly retired General McNaughton as chairman of the Canadian Section, IJC, in April 1962 because of McNaughton's bitter opposition to the Columbia Treaty. As leader of the opposition, Lester Pearson took advantage of McNaughton's dismissal to create the impression that a government led by him would seek a renegotiation of the treaty to meet the objections of critics in Canada to the Libby project. As he fought his way to political power, Pearson intimated that before any decisions were taken there would be public hearings to ventilate the objections of the people in the affected areas, and to hear the recommendations of such critics as McNaughton.

During the election campaign of 1963, which brought Pearson to power, even George Cady, his Liberal candidate in the heart of the Columbia valley, was persuaded that Pearson intended to renegotiate the Columbia Treaty. Part of the confusion was due to a series of articles published in the Vancouver *Sun* under the byline of Jack Davis, MP. Davis was the author of the energy study for the Gordon Commission on Canada's Economic Prospects, and had been director of research for BC Electric. In Parliament Davis had been appointed chairman of the power study group of the Liberal opposition caucus, and he was widely regarded as the official Liberal spokesman on Columbia matters during the election.

His "Plan for Action on the Columbia" advocated immediate conclusion of an interim agreement on principle, under which early construction could start on Mica Creek. It was an ingenious proposal; it satisfied the political need for something to be done; it left open the option of whether to scrap the Columbia Treaty or modify it; and it would produce approximately 80 percent of the benefits to be had. It carried the support of most of the critics and during the election Pearson gave no indication that he did not support Davis.

It was a shock to those who had been taken in by the Davis election promise when the new prime minister quietly and promptly accepted the demands of both British Columbia and the United States for ratification of the Columbia Treaty. Pearson had proposed his protocol to the Treaty when he was in Washington to attend President Kennedy's dinner for Nobel prizewinners in April 1962, a year before the Liberals came to power.[22] The crucial action was taken within twenty-one days of Pearson's coming to power, and the intention to negotiate a protocol appeared in the communiqué of May 13, 1963, issued at the conclusion of his two-day meeting at Hyannis Port with President Kennedy. It was confirmed by an agreement signed with British Columbia on July 8.[23]

Pearson's betrayal had made Davis look silly. The new prime minister was brutally frank in putting his defeated candidate in Trail into the post-election picture. On July 23, 1963, he wrote to Cady: "While the financial and other terms embodied in the present draft treaty will be improved, the physical plan will not be altered to any great extent."

During this time Paul Martin, who had become minister of external affairs and had been put in charge of wrapping up the Columbia, was busy picking the brains of the critics, including General McNaughton. This was not, however, participatory democracy; Martin intended to convey the impression that the critics had been consulted in order to allay public fears, and to give the government time to prepare answers to the critical arguments.

These answers were pathetic. The government of Canada even went so far as to admit its own ignorance of what it was selling: "The actual benefits purchased [by the United States] are unknown."[24] The government of Canada was attempting to tell the Canadian people that the Americans were about to lay out $275 million for a package of unknown benefits! The Americans know what the benefits are worth, and so do the Canadian critics. A billion dollars is a modest estimate. It will cost Canada about $100 million to give the Columbia away,[25] to say nothing of the cost of losing the International Joint Commission as an effective means of protecting Canadian rights elsewhere.

During the debate in Parliament on the Boundary Waters Treaty, Sir Wilfrid Laurier described the merits of the arrangement incorporating the Harmon doctrine: "At the same time, we shall have the same power on our side, and if we choose to divert a stream that flows into your territory you shall have no right to complain, you shall not call upon us not to do what you do yourselves. The law shall be mutual."[26] Laurier's hopes were not justified. What had been done was described by D.S. Macdonald, parliamentary secretary to the minister of justice: "The governing law under the Boundary Waters Treaty as it applies to the Columbia is being set aside by agreement and an entirely new regime of law governing the river is created."[27] Under the old law, Canada could divert rivers subject to claims for damage. Under the new law, Canada's right to divert waters from the basin probably has been lost.

The Saskatchewan government was of the opinion that the Columbia River Treaty, if ratified, would foreclose the possibility of moving Columbia water to the Saskatchewan river, and it opposed ratification on these grounds. The language of the treaty supports the Saskatchewan contention. The government was unable to refute the argument, other than by unsupported denial based on a unique claim to higher wisdom on the part of Paul Martin.[28] The Pearson government, assured of support in the House from the Conservatives, paid no attention to Saskatchewan.[29] The Columbia Treaty was debated halfheartedly in Parliament between harangues on the flag debate. The Liberal party used a public flogging of the moribund British lion for public entertainment while it went about the flagitious business of selling out to Uncle Sam.

Pearson's protocol was a signal to the United States that Canadian water was for sale at distress prices. The reaction was swift. It came from the Ralph M. Parsons Company of California in a form described as a concept labelled somewhat pretentiously the North American Water and Power Alliance, complete with syncopated title—NAWAPA.[30] It was a scheme to divert vast amounts of Canada's water southward and eastward; as far as Mexico and the Great Lakes, with extensions to Labrador and the Gulf of Mexico. Mexico's share of this Canadian water would be slightly greater than Canada's, with almost two-thirds reserved for the United States.

The proposal was described by Trevor Lloyd, professor of geography at McGill, as "an exercise in sophomore civil engineering which has received far greater attention than it deserves."[31] General McNaughton minced no words in branding it as ". . . monstrous not only in terms of physical magnitude, but monstrous in another and more sinister sense in that the promoters would displace Canadian sovereignty, and substitute therefor a diabolical thesis that *all* waters of North America become a shared resource of which most will be drawn off for the benefit of the United States."[32]

The scheme is pure fantasy, but it has already become a factor in continental politics—not so much because it has been taken up by Senator Frank Moss of Utah, but rather because of the implied and open support it has received from high and influential quarters in Canada. As a result of this continentalist support from within Canada, Senator Moss undoubtedly was assisted in setting up in the US Senate his Special Subcommittee on Western Water Development. This was important because it provided a means of issuing NAWAPA propaganda at government expense and with the *imprimatur* of the Senate.

Three examples of utterances by continentalist-minded Canadians of some influence will serve to illustrate why Senator Moss has concluded that Canadian resources are ripe for picking:

1. The Merchant-Heeney Report[33] (whose Canadian author, Arnold Heeney, succeeded McNaughton as chairman of the Canadian Section, IJC) advocated a continental approach to energy to be negotiated behind closed doors.

2. A statement by the Western Canadian-American Assembly held at Harrison Hot Springs, BC, in August 1964 under the joint auspices of the University of British Columbia and Columbia University. The report is described as "aimed at presenting the consensus of opinion expressed during the discussions." This is an extract of the report: "Canada and the United States are moving in the direction of a new and significant policy for the development of energy resources, particularly water power, on a continental scale. Recent technological advances which have made the border increasingly irrelevant have brought about in both countries a willingness to consider an encouraging degree of integration . . . " The report went on to recommend that the IJC undertake long-range continental plans for water resources. Senator Moss later suggested that all of Canada's water be brought under international study.[34]

3. A statement on television during the 1965 election campaign by the Right Honourable Lester Pearson, Prime Minister of Canada:

   The United States is finding that water is one of its most valuable and is becoming one of its scarcest resources . . . the question of water resources . . . is a continental and international problem. We have to be careful not to alienate this resource without taking care of our own needs and we will be discussing this with the United States who are very anxious to work out arrangements by which some of our water resources are moved down south. This can be as important as exporting wheat or oil.

It was like an echo of a statement made by an American financier and NAWAPA supporter a few days before: "Every Canadian knows Canada needs exports. Water can be their most important export."[35]

NOTES

1. Departments of External Affairs and Northern Affairs and National Resources, *The Columbia River Treaty, Protocol, and Related Documents* (Ottawa, Feb. 1964), pp. 58–81. Referred to hereafter as *Documents*.

2. This arrangement was touted as giving Canada a "profit" of $52 million on the assumption that the funds received could be invested at $5\frac{1}{2}$ percent interest until they were needed to cover expenditures. However, operating costs were omitted, most of the money was invested in the United States at $4\frac{1}{4}$ percent, and the cost estimates took no account of inflation. *Documents*, p. 138.

3. For a detailed statement of this view, see *International Journal* (Canadian Institute of International Affairs)— Larratt Higgins, "The Columbia River Treaty: A Critical View," *International Journal*, Autumn 1961. See also C. Bourne, "Another View," *ibid.*, Spring 1962; A.G.L. McNaughton, "The Proposed Columbia River Treaty," *ibid.*, Spring 1963.

4. *Documents*, pp. 7–16.

5. *Ibid.*, p. 8, Article II.

6. *Ibid.*, p. 9, Article IV.

7. Prior to 1909, the United States had diverted the Allagash River in Maine into the Penobscot, thereby depriving a small Canadian lumbering operation of the water for log driving that was necessary for its survival. The diversion of Lake Michigan into the Mississippi basin is a similar assertion of the Harmon doctrine which continues to this day.

8. The following is an example of the doctrine in action. After the First World War the Canadian government wished to settle veterans on the Cawston benches in the valley of the Similkameen River (also in the

Columbia basin). The entire low season flow of the river had already been taken into use in the United States, and any diminution of this flow would probably give rise to a claim for damages under the provision in Article II. Canada therefore built a dam to capture unused flood flows to provide irrigation water for these lands.

9. L.M. Bloomfield and G.F. Fitzgerald, *Boundary Waters Problems of Canada and the United States: The International Joint Commission, 1912–1958* (Toronto, 1958).

10. *Documents*, p. 17.

11. United States 81st Congress, 2nd Session, House Document, 531.

12. This is a fallacy on any watershed where development is taking place. It is true that the benefits of additional increments of storage at any one time do decline, but the benefits derived from a given amount of storage increase over time as development proceeds. See J.V. Krutilla, *The Columbia River Treaty* (Baltimore, 1967), chap. 3.

13. *Electrical Digest*, Toronto, July 1955, pp. 34–50.

14. There was another private proposal by a syndicate of private power companies in the United States. They proposed to build the Mica Creek dam at a cost of $425 million, and turn it over to the province in return for timed releases, for a period of a hundred years. The economics of this proposal are considerably better than the Columbia Treaty arrangements, but Premier Bennett turned down the proposal.

15. RSC, 3–4 Elizabeth II, c. 47.

16. *Electrical Digest*, July 1955, p. 48.

17. The name of the portions of the river in Canada is Kootenay; in the United

States it is spelled Kootenai. The river flows south from Canada, past the source of the Columbia, into the United States. Then it loops to the northwest and flows back into Kootenay Lake in Canada. Thus Canada is alternately the upstream state and the downstream state on this river. The United States is first a downstream state, and then an upstream state.

18. Cominco seems not to have been concerned with the timing of releases from upstream storages, because it has been able to trade power to its satisfaction in a deal which is of enormous benefit to the Americans.

19. This was the view of Davie Fulton, Canada's chief negotiator. The Americans were never taken in by this fallacy; and they protected themselves against it in the terms of sale by inserting a clause which permits them to determine the real benefits for purposes of resale in the United States, while still retaining the decreasing benefits in dealing with Canada.

20. Premier Bennett wrote to Fleming on Jan. 13, 1961, regarding the Columbia: ". . . assuming of course that it is proved feasible from engineering and financial standpoints. I must tell you that British Columbia entertains serious doubts . . . " about the cost of energy delivered to Vancouver. The letter appears in the *House of Commons Debates*, Feb. 2, 1961, p. 1652.

21. *House of Commons Debates*, Jan. 18, 1961, p. 1159.

22. George Bain, "Liberal Ideas on River Treaty Not McNaughton's, Pearson Says," *Globe and Mail*, Toronto, April 30, 1962.

23. *Documents*, p. 100.

24. Departments of External Affairs and Northern Affairs and National Resources, *The Columbia River Treaty Protocol: A Presentation* (Ottawa, April 1964), p. 93.

25. *Financial Post*, May 28, 1966; Vancouver *Sun*, June 2, 1966; *Financial Times*, Montreal, Oct. 24, 1966.

26. *House of Commons Debates*, Session 1910–11, vol. I, p. 912.

27. D.S. Macdonald, MP for Toronto Rosedale, in a letter to the editor, *Globe and Mail*, Feb. 19, 1964.

28. House of Commons, 2nd Session, 26th Parliament, Standing Committee on External Affairs, *Minutes of Proceedings and Evidence*, no. 25, May 14, 1964, p. 1249.

29. Saskatchewan had not elected any Liberal members federally. During the hearings, the Liberals were returned provincially and apparently did not pursue the objections of the CCF to the Columbia Treaty.

30. Ralph M. Parsons Company, *NAWAPA Brochure* (Los Angeles and New York, 1965).

31. "A Water Resource Policy for Canada," *Canadian Geographical Journal*, July 1966.

32. "Canada's Water," an address to the Royal Society of Canada at Sherbrooke, Quebec, June 8, 1966, mimeo.

33. *Principles for Partnership* (Ottawa, June 1965).

34. *Congressional Record*, United States Senate, Sept. 1, 1965, p. 21788.

35. E. O'Toole, "Vast Diversion Plan is Pressed to Trap Canadian Rivers," *New York Times*, September 12, 1965.

THE ALL ALONE
STONE MANIFESTO *

JOHN BROADHEAD

o

An isolated islet in a distant archipelago, All Alone Stone is small as islands
go. On the largest maps it's just a speck near the bottom of Juan Perez
Sound, in the centre of the place called South Moresby. Yet up close, when
your hands are wet from jigging cod off its eastern shore, it's a substantial
chunk of rock, skirted in seaweeds, clad in moss, and capped by wind-blown
spruce trees. Crows with black beaks fly out on patrol. Oystercatchers with
red beaks bleep about in the rocks. An eagle perches in a snag, the breeze
ruffling its feathers, while another rides a thermal, watching.

An insignificant rock at first glance, yet magnificent to behold in
detail—in this, All Alone Stone is a symbol. Gwaii Haanas (South Moresby)
and Haida Gwaii (the Queen Charlotte Islands) were virtually unknown in
1974, not even shown on some national maps of the day. Yet, slowly but
surely, the islands came to occupy, then consume, the nation's attention. As
more people got closer for a better look or began to hear of them, an image
formed in the dominion's mind of a place of such startling beauty and—
well, differentness—that it could only be described in superlatives: isolated
and biologically unique; an evolutionary showcase containing more
endemic and disjunct kinds of plants, animals, and fish than anywhere else
in Canada; the most earthquake-active; the oldest forests; the largest colonies
of various seabirds and raptors; the highest energy coastline and the highest
average wind speeds; the most peculiar mosses, not to mention people.

The conflict over whether to log or to save South Moresby also lent
itself to superlatives. It was the hardest-fought wilderness-conservation
issue in Canada's history. Thousands of people in government, industry,
and public organizations participated in the debate. They came from labour

---

* Reprinted from Monte Hummel, ed., *Endangered Spaces* (Toronto: Key Porter,
1989), 50–62.

unions, political parties of every stripe, native nations, logging companies, the media, churches, airline companies, and human-rights organizations. They came from international and grass-roots environmental organizations. Celebrities and even heads of foreign states spoke in support of saving South Moresby.

It was also the most expensive campaign in conservation history. Its participants spent millions of dollars on countless meetings, legal proceedings, and lobbying efforts. The final pricetag for settling with British Columbia was $106 million. Because it involved the largest withdrawal ever from a B.C. Tree Farm Licence, it included $31 million in compensation to logging interests and $1 million to their displaced employees.

Clearly, South Moresby had shaken the national tree. A profound moral dilemma had crystallized in the Canadian conscience, and it could no longer be ignored. It was this: which is more important—the integrity of the earth and the spiritual recreation of future generations, or short-term legal responsibilities to corporations and their shareholders? More to the point, what kind of system is this that renders the two mutually exclusive?

The South Moresby story holds many such questions, not all of them easy, some yet unanswered. It is told here because there are similar struggles over environmental issues taking place elsewhere in Canada—offered in the spirit of an object lesson to those faced with the political obstacle course that conservation advocates usually encounter. It is hoped that they will find in the South Moresby story a reminder that, ultimately, every obstacle holds within it the clue to its own undoing. What's more, while the answer may not be easy, at least it's usually very simple.

DARE TO DREAM

It began in the fall of 1974. A logging company had applied for permission to move part of its operations to the south end of the archipelago, from Talunkwan to Burnaby Island. The company couldn't have been leaving behind an area more ecologically devastated or moving to one more pristine.

Talunkwan Island, at least the half that had been logged, was suffering severely from the effects of gravity. Watersheds that had once been stabilized by an interlocking web of living tree roots and had regulated the flow of rain-water for millions of incubating salmon eggs, were now collapsing. Rain-water tumbled over bare soils and bedrock, collecting in torrents, carrying mud, boulders, branches, and stumps downhill and into the streams— scouring out spawning beds or burying them under an impenetrable layer of rubble. The streams of Talunkwan Island had joined dozens of others on the Islands whose salmon families had come to spawn no more.

On Burnaby Island, an important food-gathering area called the Narrows, wildly rich in intertidal life, was designated to become a log dump. And while black bears were retreating into hibernation and salmon eggs incubated beneath clean stream gravels, lines were being drawn on maps for logging plans. There was something fundamentally offensive about the prospect of repeating Talunkwan's fate on Burnaby Island. It was time to stop and reassess the plan.

The Haida of Skidegate Village, whose ancestral homelands are for the most part in Gwaii Haanas, met on the Islands with the premier of British Columbia. They objected to the plan because their culture was rooted in this wilderness and sustained by it, physically and spiritually. As they would say for the next thirteen years: the fate of the land parallels the fate of our culture. If you proceed with this logging, then you are signalling your intention to destroy that which makes us distinct as a people.

And so a different line was drawn on a map, this one by a Haida (Guujaaw) and an itinerant kayaker (Thom Henley). It was called the South Moresby Wilderness Proposal. It was conveyed to the provincial government along with a petition from five hundred Island residents, which stated that all logging should be deferred pending an environmental review. Scientists had only started to discover some amazing natural features, and a closer examination was called for before committing the area to logging.

Reluctant to disturb the status quo, the government settled on a non-decision: some studies would begin, but so also would the logging. Only instead of on Burnaby Island, logging would be moved to Lyell Island, still within the proposed wilderness area. And so the battle line was drawn, the issue the same at the outset as it would be thirteen years later.

On one side were "the industrialists"—corporations with shareholders and a provincial government obliged by its own legislation to allow the logging. They asserted, in effect, that it was necessary that the area's unique ecological features be rendered into two-by-fours and cellulose fibres at the same time that they were being studied. They called it "Multiple Use" of the area's resources.

On the other side were "the preservationists"—at the outset a small ad hoc committee of Haida and other residents, who shared a different concept of responsibility. For them, "Multiple Use" meant singular abuse. They were motivated by a dream that, odd as it may sound, seemed to originate from the rocks, trees, and waters of the place itself. The dream was a good one. It was of a better world, of respectful relations and mutual benefits among two-leggeds, four-leggeds, no-leggeds, beaks, no beaks—the works.

Such a dream had a remarkable effect upon those who became its advocates. The Haida, having lived in the place for 10 000 years, had been the first to awaken to it. It was conveyed to a handful, and then to hundreds, then thousands of visitors who came to see for themselves, only to fall under its spell. It inspired the unshakable conviction that it was only a matter of time before the logging would end. Every time another tree fell, the dream and the conviction to achieve it only grew stronger.

THE HUNDREDTH MONKEY

In the annals of evolutionary biology, there's a fascinating (albeit controversial) story about a tribe of monkeys on the island of Koshima in the Japanese archipelago. Some researchers were feeding the monkeys with sweet potatoes, which they dumped on the ground before retreating to observe the monkeys' social interactions. The monkeys liked the potatoes well enough, but had an understandable distaste for the sand and dirt that coated them. Whether by accident or brainwave, one day a young female monkey was observed washing a potato in a stream before she ate it. Before long she was showing the technique to her mother, and then to her playmates, who in turn passed it on to their mothers.

It started with one, then two . . . a dozen, then fifty . . . until there were about a hundred monkeys washing their sweet potatoes—at which point something strange and fascinating happened. All of the monkeys over the whole island began to do it. They had adopted the behaviour as if by osmosis, regardless of whether they had seen it for themselves. Stranger still, all of the monkeys of the same genus on neighbouring islands, and even on the Chinese mainland, had also taken to washing their food.

The story is told here because something similar seems to have been at work in the movement to save South Moresby. It began with a place and a handful of people with a dream. A decade later, there were some three million people advocating the same idea. A ripple on a distant island had grown into a groundswell of international opinion.

As the monkey story illustrates, significant social change does not occur without a broadly shared experiential base. In the case of a wilderness proposal, a sufficient number of people must know the place and share a gut feeling for the values at stake, before the "critical mass" of opinion capable of precipitating political change can be attained. For the advocates of South Moresby, then, the situation called for a simple, two-pronged strategy: start talking and start bringing people to the place.

At the outset, credible scientific analysis was identified as one of the key components for building an effective case for preserving the area. In South Moresby, various agencies were lobbied successfully to conduct field studies, which confirmed that the natural history of the place showed a number of remarkable features. Where more research was required but agencies refused to provide it, funding for independent study was assembled locally. Qualified scientists were enlisted to conduct research on topics such as eagle-nesting densities, intertidal communities, and the effects of logging on salmon habitat. Over time, a body of information was assembled that was sufficient to argue the case for preservation on scientific merit alone. Not that that was enough.

Another ingredient that featured prominently in the South Moresby campaign was the use of images. It's not a simple matter to describe the impacts of logging on fish habitat, nor the effects that ripple out through associated ecosystems. So, photographers were coaxed to go into the field (most of them simply volunteered) to acquire images equal to the place and the issue. They returned with superlative photographs of wildlife and ancient ecosystems, and devastating shots of landslides and debris-choked salmon streams. It's no exaggeration to say that at least 100 000 photos were examined over the years, and then winnowed down into ever-improving slide shows for public presentation. Over time, an accompanying narrative was perfected to bring to life the interrelations between and within ecosystems, to convey a sense of being there and what the place is all about.

The show was taken on the road at every opportunity, presented to small-town naturalists' groups; to politicians, singly and in groups, from the municipal to the federal level; to assemblies of thousands in conference halls; and to impromptu audiences in railway cars. It was told in corporate boardrooms, high-school classrooms, and private living rooms. No audience was too small and no request for a show was denied.

Although the slide shows were received positively, another less transitory medium was needed to reach a much broader constituency, especially within those social circles that rarely attend slide shows in public auditoriums. The answer was *Islands at the Edge—Preserving the Queen Charlotte Islands Wilderness* (Douglas and McIntyre, 1984). In effect it was the slide show between covers, written by seven experts in the natural, cultural, and political history of the area. Careful attention was paid to assembling the most accurate information available, and to the highest design and production values possible. It had to be the kind of book that people would enjoy giving and receiving, that would linger on coffee tables in the living rooms and offices of opinion leaders in Canadian society. It had to invite the reader to browse for the sheer pleasure of looking at it, because once the intended audience got past the pictures and into the text, the message was surely a radical one. The book was released in time for Christmas 1984, and its promotional campaign resulted in nation-wide publicity for the issue, and a sellout of the first printing in three weeks.

The final ingredient in the Hundredth Monkey Syndrome was getting people into South Moresby to experience the place directly. It's one thing to sit comfortably in an auditorium or an armchair, but to go there is to arouse a sense of wonder that a hundred photographs can only hint at. Standing in the pitch-black forest while 30 000 seabirds return to their nesting colonies, crashing into the trees and tumbling to their burrows in the ground beneath your feet, you can begin to suspect the depths of your ignorance about the natural world. And cooking up a feed of abalone or halibut has a way of getting the place directly under your skin. Entering the bay at Ninstints Village—the intricately carved poles arrayed along the beach in front of the old Haida longhouses—is to be confronted with an idea of what it means to be human and in harmony with one of the earth's most dynamic and prolific places.

This not unpleasant task fell to a handful of adventure-tour operators. As wilderness explorers-turned-entrepreneurs, they delivered one of the more important elements in the South Moresby networking strategy. The tour experiences they offered were as special as the place. Haida and other experts in the area's natural and cultural history accompanied their tours as resource persons. Renowned artists and photographers led special workshop expeditions, resulting in many of the images that were later incorporated into slide shows and publications. The tour participants they sought were from a specialized market—writers, professionals, captains of industry, and senior politicians—and their intention to lobby their customers while providing a memorable holiday was explicit. Some operators even incorporated into their tour costs a surcharge, allotted to the environmental groups fighting to save the area. But the most effective lobby of all was the place itself, as illustrated by one commercial-tour operator's account.

He had taken a walk along a small salmon stream with one of his clients, a forester by profession, and had left him for a moment's peace in a mossy grove of sitka spruce. When the man failed to appear at the beach twenty minutes later, the tour operator retraced his steps, only to find him sitting on the same spot, deep in thought. All my life, the forester said, I've drawn lines on maps and consigned places like this to be logged . . . if I could have understood what I feel and see here now, I doubt that I could ever have done it.

Perhaps the forester was "the hundredth monkey," perhaps not. But while he sat there in the moss, something profound had been conveyed. Without his urban filters, without the alienating armour of glass and steel, concrete and technology—one man alone in an ancient ecosystem—he had encountered the archetype of wilderness, an overwhelming realization that we are a small part of a wondrous and formidable mystery.

It was an experience that has stirred the depths of man's religious imagination for millennia. It was something of inestimable personal value, something that should be cherished and protected for others to come to know, something unthinkable to destroy. And so it was that, whether or not visitors to South Moresby arrived as skeptics, they returned home convinced that there was only one good thing to do about such a place.

THE ART OF WAR

In 1974, the first South Moresby Wilderness advocates had no idea of the magnitude of effort ahead of them. They thought it might take them a year, unaware that it takes an average of about fifteen years to create a park in North America. They had yet to reckon with the depth of the institutional forces that would align against them.

At the time, the major players in the B.C. logging industry were engaged in an unprecedented consolidation of their control over the province's forests. The provincial government was enacting legislation and regulations to suit the industry's objectives. Tree Farm Licences had acquired an "evergreen" clause: they were automatically renewable, without resort to public review unless the Minister of Forests deemed it necessary—which he emphatically did not. When the industry encountered difficult market conditions, the province responded with a policy called "sympathetic administration," which meant that more trees were being cut, more habitat damaged, more forest land left unreplanted, and more wood left to rot, or to be burned or buried as "waste," than ever before.

And on every occasion that the Haida asserted their ownership rights in South Moresby, the spectre of "Land Claims" arose to haunt the status quo. Always the same response: "This is a *federal* issue . . . it has to be dealt with in the proper forum at the proper time . . . meanwhile, we must get on with our business."

Thus it was that, when logging operations were established on Lyell Island, the Crown committed the equivalent of a military offensive. Its intention was clear. The wilderness proposal and the world-view that it represented were anathema to "the industrialists," and reducing a Tree Farm Licence for a park was unthinkable. Yet for those who wanted to protect South Moresby, the prospect of Multiple Use abuse was equally repugnant. The time had come to talk fundamentals. It was the moral equivalent of war.

War, of course, is an ancient undertaking. And as long as you find yourself inexorably drawn into one, you would do well to study its history. In the fourth century B.C., for example, there lived in China a legendary general by the name of Sun Tzu, who was famous for having never lost a battle in hundreds of encounters. As the story goes, he retired at a venerable old age and wrote a concise account of the principles of his strategy called *The Art of War*, which is still considered a classic.

Although it's a long march from the Middle Kingdom to All Alone Stone, there are ideas in Sun Tzu's book that environmental advocates might wish to contemplate—ideas such as: never underestimate the importance of spies. It is essential that you understand your enemy—his plans, strengths, weaknesses, advantages, and limitations. Likewise, you must have an intimate knowledge of the terrain that you will operate in. As Sun Tzu is fond of repeating, "It will benefit you to meditate on this matter."

Another important principle is the unceasing cultivation of allies, which in many ways is how the lobby to end the logging grew to such proportions. The South Moresby Wilderness was endorsed by nearly a thousand agencies and organizations in Canada, the United States, and around the world, each of them more or less ready to respond at critical points in the campaign. Equally important, efforts to build personal networks of supporters paid off in the crucial final months of the campaign, with people in government and political-party machines prepared to advocate to their leaders that there was only one way to end the conflict.

The approach taken in seeking out supporters was single-minded: leave no stone unturned. Never presume that someone will be uninterested, because you never know where a new ally or opportunity is going to appear, and sometimes they appear where you least expect them. Often enough, the time and effort spent cultivating meaningful relations with one person will result in leads to new sources of support, whether financial, logistic, or political.

When the door to a new contact does open, make sure that you've done your homework, that you understand your audience and what their potential interest in your issue may be. When lobbying government or professional people, it's a rule of thumb that the higher up the ladder you go, the more valuable their time is and the more limited their attention span can be. So lay out your case concisely, remembering that a handful of explicit photos may save you hours of explanation. As a final preparation, rehearse the interview with a colleague or two, and reverse roles. It's a good way to examine your own assumptions and prepare yourself emotionally for those of your audience.

Above all, extend the courtesy of allowing your audience to arrive at their own moral judgments about the situation. They'll do that anyway, so the most valuable thing you can do is to listen and acknowledge their viewpoint. If you don't like what you hear, jumping to the defensive or otherwise reacting negatively will only make matters worse. Paying careful attention to what they say, on the other hand, will let them know that you respect them as people.

Then again, there are times when you are staring an adversary in the face, someone who seems dedicated to frustrating all efforts at reconciliation. Try as you may to keep to the high road, you can't help thinking that life would be better if that person simply wasn't around. In this case, you would do well to consider Sun Tzu's counsel that the act of attacking is the most risky business of all. Never engage the enemy in battle unless you are absolutely certain of the outcome. If you aren't, forget it. You will have conserved precious resources, risked nothing, and lost nothing.

But if you must attack, lead your adversary into his or her own weakness; and never forget that the wise course of action is to present no target until it's too late, or never at all. One of the more spectacular examples of this principle at work in South Moresby involved the resignations of two provincial cabinet ministers. It was January 1986, and the issue, featuring prominently in the media, had become a war of images. Some industry and government members had taken to attacking the credibility of park advocates. They were "wilderness fundamentalists," unwilling and unable to compromise their position. You might have thought that a band of Haida and quasi-religious confidence artists had perpetrated a grand sham on an unwitting public by exaggerating the values of South Moresby.

Credibility is a tenuous commodity, especially for politicians. Bearing Sun Tzu's counsel in mind, in this instance it was passed along to the media that an examination of the financial holdings of some government members might result in an interesting new angle on the issue. Reporters discovered that indeed, both the Minister of Forests and the Minister of Energy, Mines and Petroleum Resources held private investments in companies that stood to profit if logging continued. As members of the cabinet committee on land use, they were both making decisions to this effect.

The barrage of media criticism that led to their resignations caused irreparable damage to the credibility of the government and, by association, of other logging advocates. More important, when both ministers maintained that there was nothing morally wrong with holding such investments, they brought into focus the fundamental dilemma posed by South Moresby: their decisions would be the same regardless, because the government's legal obligations to permit the logging were paramount over the heritage values that the Haida and environmentalists sought to protect.

But for those less inclined to such a militaristic approach, there is a gentler strategy that is equally as important: you must cultivate an untiring sense of curiosity about those who are implicated in an issue with you. Until you understand the hopes and fears of your adversaries, they will remain your adversaries. For the art of successful negotiation requires that you understand what your adversaries value and need as people—and then give it to them—before you can get what you want. If what you are ultimately seeking is respect for your own values, and if what you value is a dream of respectful relations of mutual benefit, then the only way to achieve it is to grant it. Simple in theory, yet formidable in practice, but the biggest medicine of all.

PRIME TIME CRIME

The final act in the South Moresby story belongs to the Haida. In October 1985, the issue had reached a pivotal point. Provincial politicians had balked at Canada's proposal for a national park reserve, while pressure was mounting from the logging industry to issue new logging permits. The new cutting was planned for the south face of Lyell Island, which had been untouched by modern clearcuts.

B.C.'s Minister of Environment had travelled to the Islands, and in meetings with the Council of the Haida Nation and Hereditary Chiefs he pledged (on many handshakes) that no new logging would be permitted on South Lyell until the province had decided on Ottawa's proposal. Days later, the Minister of Forests issued the cutting permits.

In the face of such duplicity, the Haida Nation concluded that there was no other option for protecting their homeland but to blockade logging operations. The companies countered with a suit for damages against the Haida and asked for an interim injunction against the blockade. After four days of testimony by the Haida in B.C. Supreme Court chambers, the President of the Council of the Haida Nation concluded his argument against the injunction, saying:

> When our people speak to you, understand that we are a nation in every sense of the word; that we have for many years been trying to deal with our place in relation to Canadian society. We all feel somewhat insulted that people allege that we do not have a place in protecting our homelands, that land that our people love and feel deeply about.
>
> I ask you to hear what we say in a spirit of rightness and in a spirit of understanding. The Haida have worked to the best of our abilities to reconcile the differences between our people and yours . . . and to have people understand who we are as a self-respecting people and a people who are respectful of others. Our constitutional, legal, rightful place in our homeland is not being respected.

The judge, obviously struggling to overcome his personal inclination to grant that respect, ruled that the law he was sworn to uphold gave him no choice but to grant the injunction. Thus the blockaders would be liable for contempt-of-court charges if they continued—which they did.

The international media exposure that ensued propelled Haida Gwaii onto the world stage. Standing on a logging road, the Haida reminded us, in an uncommonly dignified way, that we all share responsibility for safe-guarding our natural heritage. Ears across the nation heard the Haida speak of a higher law, of respect for the integrity of the environment for its own sake and for the sake of future generations. Eyes around the world watched them being arrested.

On national television, a seventy-two-year-old Haida woman, arrested with an eagle feather in one hand and a Bible in the other, looked into the camera and said "Forgive them, Lord, for they know not what they do." An RCMP officer, obviously at odds with supervising the arrests, offered: "If I was free to say what I thought of politicians and the courts, I would, but I'm not, so I won't."

Coincidentally, in Ottawa, the prime minister was initiating sanctions against the apartheid government of South Africa—whose prime minister retorted that Canada wasn't exactly treating its own native people in an exemplary fashion. The remark apparently struck home, because as a way to end the conflict, the Minister of Indian Affairs made an unprecedented offer to side-step federal Land-Claims policy and sit down with the province in negotiations with the Haida.

The province declined; the arrests continued. In the end, seventy-two Haida were arrested and charged with criminal contempt of court. During the trial that followed, the Chief Justice of the B.C. Supreme Court mused that he was considering issuing a court order forbidding any Haida to travel to Lyell Island. Long-distance telephone circuits in Ottawa and Victoria began to feel the heat, as human-rights groups and newspaper edi-torials across the country cried foul. The Canadian parliament responded with a rare accomplishment, a unanimous resolution to end the confronta-tion and to respect the interests of the Haida in their homeland. It was one of the few positive exchanges between the Crown and native nations in the country's history. It also marked a shift in public attitudes towards aborigi-nal rights: a B.C. opinion poll revealed that a solid majority supported reso-lution of the Haida title issue.

That the conflict was ended and the logging stopped on July 11, 1987, is history. With this, it can be said that Canada acknowledged its dilemma. Induced, the federal government has agreed that the Islands will serve as a national model for "sustainable development," thus extending the sym-bolic role of this isolated archipelago in the evolution of Canada's environ-mental ethic.

Yet, a nagging question remains: Did the Crown really take its basic dilemma to heart? Or could the national park reserve actually be a political manoeuvre to avoid altogether the Haida and the aboriginal-rights issue that they represent?

The questions arise because, a year and a half later, the promises spo-ken by Canadian politicians to the Haida remain no more than words. On the contrary, government agencies are systematically deleting all acknowl-edgement of the Haida's aboriginal rights from official documents related to South Moresby. Also, negotiations to share responsibility for managing the proposed park reserve have been stalemated by a federal refusal to agree to anything more than a token role for the Haida.

The Haida have made it clear that until a framework for management that respects their interests and responsibilities is reached, there will be no South Moresby "park," and they will continue to manage Gwaii Haanas without Parks Canada. Much the same as the dispute over logging, this issue holds powerful ramifications for the task of completing parks systems in Canada. Many wilderness areas sought for preservation also involve aboriginal-title issues, so other native nations are watching with justifiable concern. If Canada cannot deliver on a unanimous resolution from its own parliament, then there is little hope for establishing the respect and goodwill required to negotiate protective regimes with native nations in other areas.

And so the South Moresby story ends, as it began, with a dilemma for Canada to ponder. The Haida have proposed a new model for parks in Canada—one that is inspired by the principle of respectful relations and mutual benefits between people of all origins and the natural world. The question is: Is Canada even capable of responding in kind, or will the Haida go on to show us how it's done on their own?

SPEAKING FOR THE
EARTH: THE HAIDA WAY*

GWAGANAD

○

Kilsli, Kilsligana, Kiljadgana, Taaxwilaas. Your Honour, chiefs, ladies held
in high esteem, friends. I thank you for this opportunity to speak today. I
was aware that I could get a lawyer, but I feel you lose if you go through
another person.

My first language is Haida. I feel through another person, a lawyer,
they also speak another language, and I would have lost what I hope to
help Kilsli understand and feel.

Since the beginning of time—I have been told this through our oral
stories—since the beginning of time the Haidas have been on the Queen
Charlotte Islands.

That was our place, given to us.

We were put on the islands as caretakers of this land.

Approximately two hundred years ago foreigners came to that land.
The Haida are very hospitable people. The people came. They were welcomed. We shared. They told us that perhaps there is a better way to live, a
different religion, education in schools. The Haida tried this way. The pot-
latches were outlawed. In many schools my father attended in Kokalitza,
the Haida language was not allowed to be spoken. He was punished if he
used his language. To this day, Watson Price, my father, understands every
word of the Haida language, but he doesn't speak it.

So the people came. We tried their way. Their language. Their education. Their way of worship. It is clear to me that they are not managing our
lands well. If this continues, there will be nothing left for my children and

---

* Judith Plant, ed., *Healing the Wounds: The Promise of Eco Feminism* (Philadelphia:
New Society Publishers, 1989), 76–79.

my grandchildren to come. I feel that the people governing us should give us a chance to manage the land the way we know how it should be.

It seems that the other cultures don't see trees. They see money. It's take and take and take from the earth. That's not the way it is in my mind.

On Lyell Island—I want to address Lyell Island and South Moresby, the injunction being served on us. I want to say why that concerns me. To me it is a home of our ancestors. As Lily stated, our ancestors are still there. It is my childhood. Every spring come March my father and mother would take me down to Burnaby Narrows. We stayed there till June. It's wonderful memories I had. I am thankful to my parents for bringing me up the traditional way. There was concern on the Indian agent's part that I missed too much school. But how can you tell them that I was at school?

Because of that upbringing, because I was brought down to Lyell Island area, Burnaby Narrows and living off the land—that's why I feel the way I do about my culture and the land.

In those early years the first lesson in my life that I remember is respect. I was taught to respect the land. I was taught to respect the food that comes from the land. I was taught that everything had a meaning. Every insect had a meaning and none of those things were to be held lightly. The food was never to be taken for granted. In gathering the food—the nearest I can translate—I can say to gather food is a spiritual experience for me.

We are a nation of people at risk today. They say that to make a culture the language is important. I am proud to say I speak my language, but not too many more people in my age do. So you can say in a sense, if this keeps up, the language is going fast. In the past the culture was in very much jeopardy when the potlatching was outlawed. We almost lost ourselves as a people. That culture has been revived in the past few years. There is pride in being a Haida, pride in being a native. The only thing we can hold onto to maintain that pride and dignity as a people is the land. It's from the land we get our energy. If this land such as Lyell Island is logged off as they want to log it off—and they will go on logging. We have watched this for many years. I have read records that our forefathers fought in 1913. It's been an ongoing fight. But no one is really hearing us. They said they wouldn't log Lyell Island at first and now I hear they are going to go ahead. So today I am here because pretty soon all we are going to be fighting for is stumps. When Frank Beban and his crew are through and there are stumps left on Lyell Island, they got a place to go. We, the Haida people, will be on the Island. I don't want my children and my future grandchildren to inherit stumps. They say, "Don't be concerned, we're planting trees again. Wait for the second growth. It will be just like before." I travel all around the Island a lot with my family. I see lots of things. This summer I got to see second growth and it pained me a great deal, because I kept hearing there is second growth coming. I saw twenty-year-old second growth around Salt Lagoon. They were planted so close that the trees couldn't grow big. They were small and there was no light getting into them. They couldn't grow. You could see and you could feel that they could not grow. Therefore, I don't feel too hopeful when I hear second growth.

I want to touch now on another very important area in my life as a good gatherer. It is my job, my purpose, to insure that I gather certain food for my husband and my children, and I want to share one part. It's called *gkow*. That's herring roe on kelp. In the spring the herring come and they spawn on kelp. For many years now I have been harvesting that and putting it away for the winter. But so far I haven't heard what—why is food gathering spiritual?

It's a spiritual thing that happens. It doesn't just happen every year. You can't take that for granted. We can't take that for granted because everything in the environment has to be perfect. The climate has to be perfect, the water temperature, the kelp have to be ready and the herring have to want to spawn.

But I want to share what goes on in my spiritual self, in my body, come February. And I feel it's an important point. That's what makes me as a Haida different from you, Kilsli. My body feels that it's time to spawn. It gets ready in February. I get a longing to be on the sea. I constantly watch the ocean surrounding the island where the herring spawn. My body is kind of on edge in anticipation.

Finally the day comes when it spawns. The water gets all milky around it. I know I am supposed to speak for myself, but I share this experience with all the friends, the lady friends, that we pick together this wonderful feeling on the day that it happens, the excitement, the relief that the herring did indeed come this year. And you don't quite feel complete until you are right out on the ocean with your hands in the water harvesting the kelp, the roe on kelp, and then your body feels right. That cycle is complete.

And it's not quite perfect until you eat your first batch of herring roe on kelp. I don't know how to say it well, but your body almost rejoices in that first feed. It feels right. If you listen to your body it tells you a lot of things. If you put something wrong in it, your body feels it. If you put something right in it, your body feels it. Your spiritual self feels it. In order to make me complete I need the right food from the land. I also need to prepare it myself. I have to harvest it myself. The same thing goes for fish, the fish that we gather for the winter. But I wanted to elaborate on the harvesting of kelp to give you an idea of how it feels as Haida to harvest food.

So I want to stress that it's the land that helps us maintain our culture. It is an important, important part of our culture. Without that land, I fear very much for the future of the Haida nation. Like I said before, I don't want my children to inherit stumps. I want my children and my grandchildren to grow up with pride and dignity as a member of the Haida nation. I fear that if we take that land, we may lose the dignity and the pride of being a Haida. Without that there is no—there is no way that I can see that we could carry on with pride and dignity. I feel very strongly—that's why I came down to express my concern for my children and grandchildren.

So today, if that injunction goes through and the logging continues— and there is a saying up there, they say, "Log it to the beach." Then what? What will be left and who will be left? We can't go anywhere else but the Island.

I study a lot about our brothers on the mainland, the North American Plains Indians in their history. They moved a lot because they were forced to. Some moved north, south, east, west, back up against the mountains and back again.

We as Haida people can't move anymore west. We can go over into the ocean is all. So when the logging is gone, is done, if it goes through and there is stumps left, the loggers will have gone and we will be there as we have been since the beginning of time. Left with very little to work with as a people.

Again I want to thank you, Kilsli, for this opportunity to speak and share my culture. Thank you very much.

RETHINKING ENVIRONMENTAL ASSESSMENT AND IMPACT

o

A s Michel F. Girard emphasizes in the opening article in this section, current analyses of the probable impact on the environment of various projects almost never take a historical perspective. In attempting to predict change, little effort has been made to benefit from an understanding of change in the past. Moreover, it is only recently that environmental-impact studies have begun drawing upon the expertise of those who actually live in the area under study. Rather than recognizing that residents have invaluable knowledge that cannot be acquired in distant laboratories, these studies are conventionally based on incomplete evidence gathered by "experts" whose familiarity with the setting under examination is environmentally and culturally limited.

In the Canadian context, the value of both a historical perspective and traditional indigenous knowledge in impact assessment is most apparent in the many environmental conflicts involving Native peoples. In his article on the Oka crisis of 1990, Girard addresses these issues by suggesting how this crisis might have been avoided if the official, superficial impact study had been replaced by an indigenously and historically informed environmental assessment. Girard describes how neither the environmental nor the cultural role played by the trees slated for removal to make way for a golf course was understood by the "experts" who advised the government authorities. The result was acceptance of a development proposal that was not defensible in terms of either humans or nature.

The Oka crisis is unusual in that violence has only rarely been associated with opposition to development projects in Canada. In fact, until quite recently, most projects simply proceeded without effective resistance. One of the best examples of the usual way in which such projects were undertaken is the construction of the Alaska Highway during World War II. In their contribution to this section, K.S. Coates and W.R. Morrison describe how Canada's dominant culture and economy imposed themselves on the vast territories of the Northwest. The war mentality added justification to the familiar reasons for environmental and cultural insensitivity. Without any advance warning, "an unprecedented assault" began on the land, "as strangers tore a path through the countryside." Coates and Morrison contrast the environmental ignorance of officials leading the assault with the sophisticated ecological knowledge of the Native peoples. Unfortunately for both nature and the aboriginal peoples, ignorance carried the day, with devastating results.

The concluding two readings explore the complex concept of traditional ecological knowledge and its implications for environmental assessment. The document prepared by the Dene Cultural Institute explains the emergence of a general appreciation of such knowledge within western science and offers examples of various approaches and their uses in recent environmental management strategies. Edward S. Rogers makes suggestions for future research by dividing his discussion into environmental and cultural considerations. In examining the question of land tenure in the case of the Subarctic Algonquians, Rogers admits that his own perspective has changed over the years in light of research on the relationship of Native peoples to land and its resources. This research includes considerable attention to the wisdom of elders and to the importance of understanding "the (sometimes extreme) cultural differences between peoples throughout the world."

THE OKA CRISIS FROM
AN ENVIRONMENTAL HISTORY
PERSPECTIVE, 1870–1990 ⋄

MICHEL F. GIRARD

o

Today, stories of environmental catastrophes or development projects opposed by local populations fill our newspapers and news broadcasts. According to the Decima polling firm, public concern for human and environmental health rose from the fifth rank in 1985 to the top of the public agenda in 1989, above other problems such as unemployment, government deficits, and the state of the economy.[1] Following publication of the Brundtland Report in 1987, the main stakeholders, from environmentalists and scientists to governments and business groups, seem to have found a common ground to discuss the difficult issue of how to promote environmental protection in growth-oriented market economies.[2]

Most agree that sustainable development can be achieved with a broader understanding of the world we live in. This begs the question of historians' possible contribution to help reach that goal. Can the study of the interrelationships between humans and their natural surroundings from a historical perspective offer useful information to decision-makers and populations facing difficult environmental choices? The following case study details how environmentalists and Aboriginals used historical information on the natural environment to counter a development project in the municipality of Oka (Quebec) before the crisis of July 1990.

⋄ Adapted and translated by Michel F. Girard from his article "L'aménagement de la forêt d'Oka à la lumière de l'écologie historique," *Journal of Canadian Studies/Revue d'études canadiennes* 27, 2 (Summer 1992): 5–21. Reprinted with permission.

ARE ENVIRONMENTAL IMPACT STUDIES ANTI-HISTORICAL?

One of the cornerstones of sustainable development is the proper environmental assessment of development projects before their implementation. In Canada, most industrial and public infrastructure development proposals must undergo some form of environmental assessment before gaining governmental approval.[3] In the province of Quebec, the Environmental Quality Act and Regulations define the scope and content of environmental assessments. For each project the impact study examines the geology, topography, soils, climate, hydrology, fauna, and flora surrounding the designated site, as well as the relevant laws regulating pollution standards. When the environmental impact is deemed significant, governments may propose alternative measures or may even refuse to authorize the project.[4] For mega-projects, such as those involving utilities, social impact studies may be added to assess how local populations may be affected.[5] If there is significant public concern, the Minister of the Environment can call for a public review of a project. The Bureau of Public Hearings on the Environment (Bureau d'audiences publiques sur l'environnement) can hold hearings and make recommendations to the Minister. In 1990, however, many projects were not being assessed through the bureau.

Current environmental impact studies and hearings ignore almost entirely ecological history and the history of the relationships between humans and their local areas. In Quebec, for example, the Department of the Environment employs ecologists, biologists, a sociologist, an anthropologist, an ethnologist, and an economist, but no historian.[6] Although some cooperation exists with the Department of Cultural Affairs to determine whether projects may have an impact on significant archeological sites, the research does not include the numerous primary and secondary materials available on the history of plants, animals, and forests, or review Aboriginal and post-contact land use.[7] This is also true elsewhere in Canada and the world. Among the 51 collaborators to the review *Environmental Conservation*, for example, one can find no historian.[8] This omission may explain why an article on deforestation in India (a phenomenon that dates back at least 2000 years) begins only in 1954.[9] In another article on forest degradation in the Himalaya area, the author commences his review of soil erosion with data obtained in 1960.[10] In a search through the articles published in *Environmental Assessment Review*, no environmental information prior to 1950 could be found."[11]

Recently, Great Britain took a different course. It broadened its review of some mega-projects to include short- and long-term risk analysis. Britain has also instituted a follow-up program to better predict the environmental, social, and technological impact of large-scale development. This approach, called total assessment, will integrate historical information such as species succession patterns and the history of land use.[12]

The evolution toward a more holistic approach is a step in the right direction. Indeed, many specialists admit that even today's best-financed and most sophisticated studies do not always predict significant environmental impacts.[13] This problem can also be found in social impact assessment studies. According to Patrick C. Jobes, the various specialists lack a basic knowledge of the history of the areas and peoples they are studying. Furthermore, many refuse to take historical information into consideration because it is largely qualitative and difficult to integrate into quantitative data.[14] As the following case study of Oka indicates, however, historical information can be used as a framework to analyze scientific data and put it into a proper perspective.

AN OVERVIEW OF RECENT EVENTS LEADING TO THE OKA CRISIS

In the spring of 1988, the Oka Golf Club, a 250-member private club, proposed to the Municipality of Oka the expansion of its golf course from nine to eighteen holes. The Municipality of Oka owns the golf course and part of the land required for its expansion. The existing nine-hole course is located west of the village, in a forest overlooking a cliff. The proposed expansion would require the cutting of 27 hectares (68 acres) of forested land. Following the proposed expansion, local developers hoped to build luxury condominium units in the remaining wooded area surrounding the golf course.

At that time, environmental protection law in Quebec excluded recreational development projects from mandatory environmental assessment studies.[15] In August 1988, however, the Oka Golf Club did hire a consulting firm specializing in the design and building of golf courses to undertake a study. Specialists looked at the soil surface and the forest cover only. Following their examination of the area the consultants estimated that the revenues generated from harvesting the trees at the site would be high enough to pay the costs of the expansion project. The consultants also claimed that the environmental impact would be negligible:

> We feel the land for the golf course expansion has excellent potential. The mature trees and sandy soil offer a superior site for dramatic and appealing golf holes. Construction of the golf course on this land will proceed without difficulty. The positive drainage of the soil, the lack of rock, and the usability of the soil will reduce construction costs and construction problems.[16]

The consultants' report convinced the Municipality of Oka to approve the expansion of the golf course. A few weeks later the municipality made a purchase offer to the owner of the remainder of the adjacent wooded area not yet owned by the municipality. Once it had obtained the additional land, it would offer a new long-term lease to the Oka Golf Club for property needed for the expansion.

This decision shocked local environmentalists, who formed a group to protect the remaining woodland. The Oka forest, one of the only remaining white pine forests in the province of Quebec, shelters some rare bird species such as the Pine Warbler, the Bald Eagle, and the Golden Eagle. Secluded in the woods is also a pond that feeds the birds and small mammals found in the forest. It is a perfect spot for bird-watching.[17]

The decision also angered the Mohawks of Kanesatake, who live west of the village. They have lived in the area for centuries and claim that they never signed any treaties surrendering their ancestral lands. They have formally negotiated land claims with the Federal Department of Indian Affairs since 1977, the forest being one of the territories in dispute. Among other things, the proposed golf expansion would completely isolate their cemetery, an ancient burial ground located in the woods beside the present golf course.[18]

A FRAGILE ENVIRONMENT

The decision to expand the golf course in the Oka forest startled the Kanesatake elders as well as some of the older residents of Oka. It also surprised those who know about the history of the area, because the forest protects the villagers of Oka from environmental catastrophe.

Before the square timber boom of the 1850s, old growth conifer forests, mostly white pine, covered the shores along the Ottawa River and the Lake of Two Mountains. The Sulpicians, a French religious order sent in the mid-seventeenth century to work to Christianize the Amerindians, received a concession of the land at Oka from the King of France in 1719.[19] By 1721, they had established the first farms at the Mission of the Lake of Two Mountains to teach the Indians how to grow European crops. Most soils were well suited for farming but the area west of the Oka village was not. There, a large sand bank about 30 metres high sat on a thick coat of clay, criss-crossed by a dozen small springs. As the water table lay only one metre below the surface of this giant sand dune, the dune was prone to shift.[20]

These sandy and unstable lands were called the "Grande commune" (Big Commons) and the "Petite commune" (Small Commons) by the Mohawks and the Oka villagers. It appears they were never cultivated but since the trees there were valuable and of easy access, many were felled in a short period of time. According to conversations with older people at Oka and some Mohawks from Kanesatake, the Small Commons and the eastern half of the Big Commons were deforested throughout the nineteenth century for timber and firewood. The western half of the Big Commons was harvested more selectively, since Amerindians found many plants there useful for medicinal and religious purposes. This would help explain why many mature trees can be found in that area of the Big Commons.[21]

While being harvested for trees, the eastern half of the Big Commons was also used for cattle and horse grazing. Mohawk farmers who lived along the Gabriel Road used the "Côte Croche" Road to get to the village.[22] According to old maps and to the testimony of Mohawk elders and long-time Oka residents, the Big Commons was once fenced. Access was controlled by means of Mohawk pay-tolls at specific entry points. Today, one can see remnants of the wooden fences around the Big Commons.

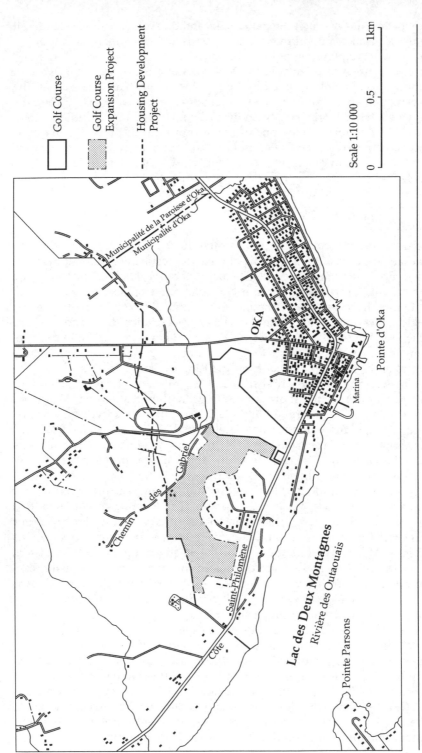

FIGURE 1 OKA FOREST

During the 1860s non-Amerindians were officially allowed to settle in the seigneury of the Lake of Two Mountains. Amerindians had to allow the new settlers in and were forced to give away some of the good farming land. Friction between the two groups led to Indian revolts in the 1870s and the burning of the church and presbytery. The disturbances, however, were soon suppressed.

In the 1870s the non-Amerindians' cattle and horses were allowed in the Commons. This probably accelerated the erosion that was already in progress. The substantial grazing of the thin coat of grass on the Commons uncovered the underlying sand, which began to slide down toward the village during the late 1870s and 1880s. Rain, spring runoff, and wind made matters worse. One night in 1886, for example, a huge sand slide 40 metres (100 feet) wide by 12 metres (40 feet) high descended on the western part of Oka.[23] During this period, spring runoffs created deep crevices along the Annunciation Road and carried the sand away. Like the familiar snowbanks of winter, sand covered fences one and a half metres (five feet) high. On the first street into the village, one house stood hidden by sand up to the second storey, and a cow was stranded neck-deep in sand in a nearby field. The sand completely destroyed the road network in the westerly part of the village.[24]

Following this disaster, the Sulpician order in Montreal hired an engineering firm to assess the damage and to recommend a course of action. The extent of the slide led the specialists to recommend that the village be moved a few kilometres east, by a bay at what is now Paul Sauvé Provincial Park. The area had been used by the Sulpicians in the 1720s as the first site for their mission.[25]

EUROPEAN SYLVICULTURAL METHODS

The Oka village priest, Joseph-Daniel Lefebvre (1829–1915), was not impressed by the engineers' report. He decided instead to reforest the whole sandy area west of the village. Born in Saint-Henri, a working-class neighbourhood in Montreal, Lefebvre had studied and prepared for the priesthood in France. Between 1858 and 1874, he was assigned to various positions in Sulpician seminaries throughout France.[26] During this long stay in France, Lefebvre undoubtedly saw some of the forests planted by state "bridge and road" engineers, who had begun a vast reforestation program in the 1830s. During the eighteenth century, England and many areas of western Europe faced ecological disaster as well as severe wood shortages as a result of deforestation.[27] Disasters and shortages are, it seems, the engines of change and of rational natural-resource management in the Western world. The French government took strong measures early in the nineteenth century to conserve the remaining forests and to protect watersheds.[28] The Forestry Code of 1827, for example, provided increased powers to the French state with respect to forestry and watershed reforestation. In Germany, universities funded by the state established new techniques and training programs for water, soil, and forest conservation.[29] It appears that the tree species and plantation methods chosen for Oka were borrowed from the sylvicultural practices popular in France at the time.

THE BEGINNINGS OF
REFORESTATION IN AMERICA

America was decades behind Europe in its recognition of the need for tree planting. In the United States, some hardwood trees were planted in New England during the nineteenth century. In her *Ecological Revolutions*, historian Carolyn Merchant states that, in the 1820s, the Massachusetts Society for Promoting Agriculture offered a prize for the planting of white oaks. In the same decade, Thomas G. Fessenden wrote extensively on tree planting and woodlot conservation. Tree planting became steadily more popular in New England during the second half of the nineteenth century, as a result of severe wood shortages in some areas.[30]

George Perkins Marsh, the father of modern American environmentalism, borrowed European ideas on how to manage natural resources efficiently. In 1865, he published *Man and Nature*, his classic study of contemporary environmental problems.[31] In the 1870s, the American Congress legislated the first national laws for the protection of the environment.[32] The American Forestry Association, founded in 1870, brought together businessmen, scientists, naturalists, and politicians worried about the deforestation of the continent. They sought laws to control tree harvesting, and promoted reforestation as a means to repair some of the damage done by unscrupulous lumbermen and settlers.[33] Many eastern Americans encouraged tree planting in the 1870s. In 1875, in Minnesota, for example, it is claimed that more than one million trees (mostly fruit and nut varieties) were planted by citizens during Arbor Day.[34] In 1878, Congress passed a law encouraging tree planting on private woodlots.[35] During the early 1880s, a dozen private companies from the Eastern United States offered a wide variety of tree seeds (mostly hardwood and fruit trees) through mailorder.[36] Only half a dozen softwood forests, however, had been planted by the early 1880s. Railway companies in the Eastern United States became the most active softwood tree planters, in order to safeguard their supply of railway ties.[37]

Canadians were also concerned about deforestation. In 1874, for example, Canon Provancher, founder and editor of *Le Naturaliste canadien* ("The Canadian Naturalist"), wrote an impassioned feature article on reforesting the Quebec countryside. The article, "Les arbres d'ornement et forestiers" ("Ornamental and Forest Trees"), describes the array of problems resulting from deforestation in agricultural areas: fewer predators of crop-damaging insects, deterioration of landscapes, and an overall deterioration in the fertility of the soils:

> Cette dénudation des campagnes, surtout dans les terrains montagneux, a produit les plus graves inconvénients en certains pays d'Europe, comme le dépouillement des collines du sol qui les recouvraient, pour entraîner dans les plaines, le gonflement subit des rivières pour causer des inondations, la soustraction de tout obstacle à l'impétuosité des vents qui balayent tout dans leur furie, etc.[38]

The following year, the federal government awakened to the impor-tance of forest conservation and asked Henri G. Joly de Lotbinière to pro-duce the first forest inventory for Canada.[39] By Joly de Lotbinière's own admission, the inventory was very limited in scope. Hard data on the size and state of the Canadian forest were non-existent. Born in France, Joly de Lotbinière emigrated to Quebec in order to make over the family seigneury.[40] Shortly after his arrival, he practised European forestry meth-ods on his woodlots and adapted them to Canadian climatic conditions. Every year, he planted hundreds of trees on his seigneury, recorded the results of his experiments, and travelled across the country to communicate his findings. His only experiment with softwood was undertaken in 1873: he planted about one hundred red pines in individual rows, one metre apart from each other.[41]

In the 1880s, Joly de Lotbinière became a leader in Canadian conserva-tion. In 1882, members of the American Forestry Congress and the American Forestry Association held a joint conference in Montreal. The meetings, presided over by Joly de Lotbinière, made front page news in the province's newspapers.[42] Of the 64 papers presented, about 20 dealt with reforestation. They indicate that some experiments with softwood planting were made before 1882 in the United States.[43] No Canadian reforestation experiment with softwood was discussed.

In a detailed paper on reforestation which he submitted to the Montreal Horticultural Society later that year, Joly de Lotbinière does not even men-tion softwood planting.[44] The biggest promoters of reforestation at the time were horticultural societies, and they limited themselves to encouraging the planting of fruit-bearing and maple trees. Reforestation of bald, abandoned, and marginal lands with softwood trees did not appear to be economically viable then, and governments refused to become involved in tree planting until the 1900s.

THE REFORESTATION AND PROTECTION OF THE OKA FOREST

A study of the history of reforestation in Canada shows that the Oka forest was the first large-scale reforestation project in Quebec and probably the second in Canada. The first was a small walnut plantation established in the 1870s in Simcoe County, Ontario.[45] The Oka forest is also one of the oldest softwood forests planted in North America. Father Lefebvre was therefore a pioneer in Quebec when he undertook the reforestation of the Oka sand dunes between 1886 and 1897. Most planting on the slopes was with white pine, while red pine and hemlock were planted on the flat surfaces. Most pines were planted in rows "à la française," not unlike the woodlots in France, while hemlock was planted randomly in the years 1915–20, after Lefebvre's death (about one-third of the reforested property, consisting mostly of hemlock trees, was targeted for the proposed golf course expan-sion in 1990).[46] Trees planted in rows were taken care of until 1946, but the hemlocks were left alone. In all, about 100 000 trees were planted.

The scale of Lefebvre's reforestation project was gigantic. At the time there were no tree nurseries operating in the province. In a "Chronique d'Oka" ("Oka Chronicle") published in *Le Canada* and *La Presse* in July 1918, Dr. J.K. Foran explained how these pines and hemlocks were obtained:

> Hommes, femmes, enfants, indiens algonquins, indiens iroquois, les gens d'Oka, et les paroissiens des campagnes [*sic*]. Ils allaient sur les montagnes, dans les savanes, au fonds des bois, sur les bords des lacs, déterrer des jeunes sapins et les transporter à Oka. Le séminaire donna deux centins et demi par sapin. Il fallait le trouver, le déraciner, le marquer sur le coté du nord pour qu'en le plantant de nouveau, l'arbre présenterait le même face au vent du nord [. . .] Sur le penchant des collines, on traça des lignes parallèles à distance de trois pieds. Sur les cent mille sapins ainsi plantés, plus de soixante seize mille enfonçaient leurs racines dans la terre sableuse [. . .].[47]

The logbooks of Father Lafontaine, a long-term friend of Lefebvre who recorded events at Oka, provide some corrections to Foran's account. According to one of Lafontaine's 27 logbooks, now preserved at the Saint Sulpice archives in Montreal, Monsieur Lefebvre supervised the planting of white pine, not fir, on the slopes. Also, it took about twenty years to plant the forest, not one year, as stated in Foran's article.[48] To our knowledge, Father Lafontaine's logbooks are the only primary written testimony describing the reforestation project. The parish presbytery was burned to the ground December 6, 1922, destroying all the plantation records.[49]

The tree planting in itself was far from easy. The sand dunes were unstable and strong winds often blew away saplings. Avila Bédard, a forest engineer at the Quebec Lands and Forests Department, wrote in 1910: "À Oka, l'abbé Lefebvre qui a dirigé et mené à bonne fin le reboisement des dunes, avait au préalable semé quelque cent poches d'agrains [*sic*] et étendu de la paille d'avoine, d'orge et de sarrasin, pour retenir les sables en place."[50] Even after all the saplings were planted, soils kept on moving, especially southwest of the actual golf course and along the banks of the Lake of Two Mountains, where the erosion process continues to this day. The lake and the village are 27 metres (90 feet) below the dunes, and the south and east banks have a slope of more than 15 percent in some areas.

Lafontaine's logbooks also reveal that, between 1886 and 1897, the Sulpicians spent about $1700, or about $155 per year, for finding and planting approximately 70 000 trees. That amount included wages and the price paid for the saplings. Another $876 was spent for the upkeep of the new forest, tree trimming, and the maintenance of damaged roads between 1897 and 1920. Since most of the work was done on a volunteer basis, this experiment in reforestation did not constitute a serious burden on the parish's finances.

One long-time resident of Oka who testified during forest expropriation hearings held by the municipality in 1947 stated that road upkeep was a constant concern of the Sulpicians. The following was taken from the expropriation commissioner's report:

Il [Lefebvre] avait travaillé lui-même à cette plantation dont le but, dit-il a été de remédier à de semblables désastres. Malgré cela, il soutient que les Messieurs de Saint-Sulpice tenaient là une équipe à l'année pour voir à l'entretien des talus et des chemins toujours exposés à des érosions causées par les pluies abondantes, car chaque fois qu'il y avait des coups de pluie, il se produisait de petites érosions.[51]

In effect, Father Lefebvre had to supervise important modifications to the village road network. First, he closed down the "Côte Croche" Road, the access road between the village of Oka and Gabriel Road, which repeated landslides had destroyed. A new road (now route #344), which ran parallel to the Lake of Two Mountains and reached the village of Saint-Placide to the west, replaced it. After another particularly large slide, the Annunciation Road became a huge ravine too. Lefebvre had it filled with tree branches, rocks, and earth to repair it.

According to Lafontaine's logbooks and the testimony of long-time local residents, the Oka Amerindians obtained most of the trees from forests to the north, transported them by canoe, and then planted them at Oka. Following the death of Father Lefebvre, the Amerindians also planted the hemlock forest west of the pine plantation. This area was forested before, but the original stands were deteriorating rapidly. Not keen on using rows, the Mohawks decided to plant the hemlocks randomly, which made the later task of identifying replanted lands more arduous. A study of the terrain made by the Quebec Ministry of the Environment in August 1989 confirms that the hemlocks date back about three-quarters of a century. Bédard's and Foran's articles indicate that approximately 30 000 hemlocks were planted. The cost of this operation remains unknown. It is interesting to note that today the hemlock forest is in much better shape than the pine forest. Scientific research on the site would help to explain this. It might also provide clues on how to increase success rates in future large-scale reforestation projects.

During the 1920s, major landslides finally stopped. The forest's root system retained the sandy soils. Tree branches caught the falling rain and this also reduced surface soil erosion. Pine needles accumulating on the ground contributed further to this process.[52]

The collective reforestation effort was a success as well as a symbol of the avant-garde spirit of environmental management of the village of Oka, the Sulpicians, and the Amerindians. During the period 1910–20, for example, the Quebec Department of Lands and Forests took note of the Oka experiment and used the same methods to stabilize sand dunes in Lachute, St-Jérôme, and Berthierville, where Quebec's first tree nursery was established. Efforts there also proved to be worth the cost, as the replanting stabilized the entire sandy area.[53] At the Laurentide Pulp and Paper Company in Grand-Mère, Québec, forest engineer Ellwood Wilson took notice as well and planted 23 million softwood trees on abandoned sandy lands purchased by his company between 1910 and 1929. Today, this mature forest is being harvested by the Stone-Consolidated Company.[54]

According to Lafontaine's logbooks, two Amerindians, under the Sulpicians' direction, selectively cut down those young trees that impinged on the growth of others. During planting, trees were placed in rows a metre apart. By the 1920s, about 80 percent of the saplings had been cut, to give space and light to the stronger trees. Today, the distance between trees planted in rows varies from about 4.5 to 5.5 metres (15 to 18 feet). The hemlock forest exhibits no signs of selective cutting, and the trees stand much closer to one another. However, only a fraction of what was planted remains today.

During the 1920s, the Sulpicians allowed some citizens to establish a small golf course on the last remaining public grazing site, by the old "Chemin de la Côte Croche." That small area had never been reforested. The golf course was quite rustic in appearance, and Oka residents won more than their fair share of games against outsiders, who were unused to playing golf among cows and grazing horses. The soil was very sandy, and the grass grew sparingly and only during wet summers. The so-called greens were made of gravel.[55] During the 1920s and 1930s, the "grass" was cut with a farmer's combine machine.[56]

In October 1936, the Sulpician order, then close to bankruptcy, had to sell most of the land on their seigneurie (including the Oka forest) to the Compagnie immobilière Belgo-Canadienné, owned by the Baron of Empain.[57] The Baron, who founded the Belgian Agricultural Institute in Canada, hoped to attract good Belgian farmers to Quebec and familiarize them with the agricultural techniques and the climatic conditions in Quebec. The Company hired two Belgian foresters to be responsible for the upkeep of the Oka forest. They adapted to Canadian conditions a European treatment of the white pine blister, a disease that was then attacking a significant proportion of the trees.[58] Following the Second World War, the Company sold the forest and agricultural lands of Oka. The Big Commons was sold in three parcels: the last grazing area and the golf course, occupying 15.5 hectares (38.9 acres); a parcel of "natural" forest, including the hemlock forest, of about 33 hectares (82.7 acres); and a third area of 21.2 hectares (53.1 acres), on which stood most of the white pines, for a total of roughly 69 hectares (175 acres).[59] Selling price was set at $40 000, but the numerous conditions added to the contract show that the owners were well aware of the fragility of the area. Restriction no. 8 in the contract, for example, specified not to build houses, buildings, or other constructions within one hundred feet on either side of the Annunciation Road.[60] As previously stated, this road marks the beginning of the western slope. Restrictions no. 10 and 11 stipulated:

#10 De respecter la beauté de l'ensemble de la grande Commune et de n'abattre, dans les pins plantés, aucun arbre de moins de 10 pouces à la souche sans avoir obtenu au préalable le consentement exprès et par écrit des vendeurs [...] quant aux autres arbres, les acquéreurs s'engagent à ne pas les couper s'ils sont d'un diamètre inférieur à 8 pouces [...] mais peuvent déroger pour fins de construction de routes ou de maisons [...] et doivent respecter la coutume établie d'utiliser partie de l'emplacement présentement vendu, comme terrain de golf ou de récréation [. . .] les acquéreurs n'auront pas le droit d'effectuer de coupes de bois sur le dit immeuble sans en verser le produit aux vendeurs [. . .] #11 Dans le cas où les acquéreurs enfreindraient l'une où l'autre des conditions prévues aux paragraphes huit et dix, les vendeurs [. . .] auront le droit de réclamer une indemnité de $15,000.00, sans préjudice à leurs recours.[61]

Unfortunately, the new owners of the lands in question did not worry about these restrictions. In December 1946, they submitted to the Municipality of Oka an ambitious plan for residential development in the forest. In the winter of 1946–47, the owners cut and sold 883 mature trees, totalling 202 839 board feet, 199 755 of which were white pine and 2905 hemlock.[62] A forest engineer hired the following year to determine the number of trees remaining in the planted forest estimated that of the 70 000 white pine planted between 1886 and 1918, about 18 percent remained in December 1947. Thinning operations and harvesting by the new owners were the two main causes of the change. As for the hemlock, fewer than 9 percent of the 30 000 planted were still standing by 1947.

TABLE   1   *FOREST ENGINEER ODILON BÉDARD'S SURVEY OF STANDING TREES IN THE EASTERN HALF OF THE OKA FOREST, 1947*

Number	Species
12 282	White pine
2 850	White spruce
2 271	Hemlock
2 107	Cedars
479	Firs
58	Larch
13	Red pines
10	Linden trees

Source: Report of Odilon Bédard, December 12, 1947, in *Jean-Louis Roux et al. vs La Corporation de la paroisse de l'Annonciation*, Comté des Deux Montagnes, #4488, Québec, Cour du banc du roi, vol. 1, 1951, p. 148.

The Oka Town Council and many citizens were concerned about further degradation of the forest. As a result, the Council took the necessary measures to purchase part of the forest and preserve the remaining trees. In April 1947, the Quebec Legislature adopted a special law allowing the Municipality of Oka to expropriate part of the forest on the Big Commons.[63] Following a referendum June 23, 1947, in which 110 citizens voted in favour of the proposed expropriation (80 voted against it), the municipality acquired the lands by borrowing $20 000.[64] It halted all proposed development on the Small Commons and the eastern half of the Big Commons. It then rented the golf course to local entrepreneurs, who established a public golf club.

Unfortunately, the history of the Oka forest does not end on this high note. As the American ecologist Raymond F. Dasmann said, the collective memory is quite short. The public rapidly forgets environmental catastrophes unless their effects are frequently felt.[65] In 1958, less than ten years after the expropriation, the owners of the western half of the Big Commons established a residential development called "Les jardins d'Oka" ("Oka Gardens"). More trees were destroyed in this area. In the 1970s, about thirty lots by the Lake of Two Mountains were sold. Trees were cut and houses were built, a clear invitation for more erosion. The public golf club became private, and many of its new members came from outside the Oka area. Trees were cut to enlarge the fairways, the course was fenced, and "no trespassing" signs were installed. Finally, in the spring of 1989, the club's executive committee unveiled its expansion project, which precipitated the Oka crisis the following summer.

The author, who lives near Oka, learned about the environmental history of the forest during research for a Master's thesis on the Quebec forest conservation movement at the turn of the twentieth century.[66] In July 1989, a historical dossier on the history of the forest was prepared and submitted to the Mohawks at Kanesatake and the environmentalists of Oka, who joined forces in opposing the proposed expansion of the golf course. The mayor of Oka and the media were also given documentation on the environmental history of the area. Historical information was repeatedly used by the media and by those opposed to the golf course expansion.

On August 4, 1989, the province of Quebec and the municipality agreed on a moratorium on all development on Mohawk disputed lands in the municipality. A negotiation process was established to accelerate resolution of the Mohawks' comprehensive claims.[67] But on March 3, 1990, the municipality unilaterally suspended the moratorium. On March 7, Mohawk Warriors established a symbolic barricade at Middle Road, near the golf course in the hemlock forest, in order to oppose surveying and tree harvesting. In May, the Mohawks decided to establish a new barricade, this time on the Mil Road, a dirt road rarely used nowadays, just beside the main route (#344), in order to get more media attention. Both the federal and provincial ministers responsible for Indian affairs received copies of the historical research and were informed of legal means available to them to impose a new moratorium. That month, the municipality asked for and obtained an injunction against the Mohawks, but the municipality was unable to dismantle the barricades. In early July, it won a second injunction from the Quebec Superior Court. On July 10, one day before the injunction expired, the municipality asked Quebec provincial police to force the re-opening of the dirt road.

The assault on July 11 ended with the death of one policeman and the creation of a series of barricades on roads entering the Big Commons. The Mercier Bridge, linking the town of Chateaugay to Montreal, was closed by the Mohawk Warriors of the Kanawake reserve. All across the country, barricades were set up on roads and railways by angry Native peoples. A local conflict over the future of a small forest escalated into a national crisis. In September 1990, after a 78-day siege, the Warriors at Kanesatake surren-

dered to the Canadian armed forces and barricades across the country went down. Mohawks had won the preservation of the forest threatened by the golf course expansion project: the federal government had purchased it from the Municipality of Oka for approximately $4 million. Negotiations for the transfer of these lands from the federal government to the band leaders at Kanesatake are currently under way. However, the eastern half of the Big Commons and all of the Small Commons remain municipal or private land. Mohawk Warriors have vowed that the fight will go on until all Commons land is given back to the Mohawk nation.

These events are undoubtedly changing the history of relations between non-Amerindians and the First Nations in Canada. But the Oka crisis also shows that a proper environmental assessment of the golf course expansion project, integrating historical information and information gained through public hearings with the scientific and cost-feasibility data, might have averted the confrontation.

Historical research can be a powerful instrument in the struggle to protect the environment, prevent ecological catastrophes, and achieve sustainable development. It is not limited to issues in Aboriginal history or the history of reforestation. The knowledge and skills of historians of technology, for example, can be of benefit in land-use planning. In Quebec, the Industrial Sites Decontamination Directorate is compiling historical information on hundreds of abandoned industrial sites, which could be used for other purposes once all possible contaminants are identified. In-depth historical research and analysis of private and municipal records would be useful to those conducting various inventories of contaminated sites across the country. Knowledge of environmental history is also essential in the fields of parks, shoreline, wildlife, and forest management. Combined with oral history, it could help decision-makers better understand the characteristics of the environment at a local level.

The idea of integrating history into development is not new. It follows the vision of the Annales school, which promoted a dynamic and total history. Back in 1922, French historian Lucien Febvre stressed that "le développement devait se faire en harmonie et en continuité avec le milieu géographique et humain. Ces pionniers croyaient que l'étude de l'histoire sur le terrain pouvait être bénéfique à la fois pour l'historien et la société."[68]

NOTES

1. *Decima Quarterly Reports*, Toronto, 1985–1989.

2. The World Commission on Environment and Development, *Our Common Future* (Oxford: Oxford University Press, 1987).

3. For an abstract or the history of the federal environmental assessment process, see Marie-Ann Bowden and Fred Curtis, "Federal EIA in Canada:

EARP as an Evolving Process, *Environmental Assessment Revie* [henceforth *EA Review*] 8 (1988 97–106; Canadian Environment Assessment Research Counc *Philosophy and Themes for Resear* Ottawa, 1986.

4. Quebec Environmental Quality A General Administrative Regulatic Q-2, R-9, Sections 2 and 3, adop in December 1980.

5. Charles P. Wolf has offered a useful definition of social impact studies: "A problem of estimating and appraising the condition of a society organized and changed by large-scale applications of high-technology." *EA Review* 4 (1984): 109.

6. Interviews with Yves Pagé, Director, and Abel Rodrigue, Sociologist, Environmental Assessment Directorate, Department of the Environment, Ste-Foy, Quebec, April 3, 1990.

7. Ibid.; Abel Rodrigue et F. Robert Boudreault, *Guide général des etudes d'impact sur l'environnement*, Québec: ministère de l'Environnement du Québec, juin 1987.

8. See the list contained in *Environmental Conservation* 16, 1 (January 1989): 1.

9. V.P. Singh and J.S. Singh, "Man and Forests: A Case Study from the Dry Tropics of India," *Environmental Conservation* 16, 2 (Summer 1989): 129–36.

10. Marcus Moench, "Forest Degradation and the Structure of Biomass Utilization in a Himalayan Foothills Village," *Environmental Conservation* 16, 2 (Summer 1989): 137–46.

11. *EA Review*, vols. 3–9, 1983–1989.

12. David Cope and Peter Hills, "Total Assessment: Myth or Reality?" in *The Role of Environmental Impact Assessment in the Planning Process* (London, 1988), 174–94.

13. Fikret Berkes, "The Intrinsic Difficulty of Predicting Impacts: Lessons from the James Bay Hydro Project," *EA Review* 8 (1988): 201–20.

14. Patrick C. Jobes, "Assessing Impact on Reservations: A Failure of Social Impact Research," *EA Review* 6 (1986): 385–94.

15. Quebec Environmental Quality Act, General Administrative Regulations, Section 2c. In December 1992, the government introduced sweeping changes to its Environmental Quality Act and Regulations. Under the new act, such projects would be subject to a mandatory environmental assessment.

16. Letter from Graham Cooke, President, Graham Cooke and Associates, Golf Course Architects, to Pierre Phaneuf, President, Expansion Committee, Oka Golf Club, August 12, 1988.

17. Letter from André Dion, Ornithologist, to the Regroupement pour la protection de l'environnement d'Oka, August 8, 1989.

18. Figure 1 shows where the swamp and the present golf course are located, as well as the proposed expansion project.

19. Acte de concession de la seigneurie de Saint-Sulpice, registered to the Greffe de Québéc, October 2, 1719.

20. Letter from Gilbert Prichonnet, Director, Department of Geology, Université du Québec à Montréal, to the Regroupement pour la protection de l'environnement d'Oka, August 9, 1989.

21. Interview with Jean-François Meilleur, spokesperson for the Regroupement pour la protection de l'environnement d'Oka, August 16, 1989.

22. Figure 1 shows the approximate location of these roads.

23. Testimony of M. Legault, in *Jean-Louis Roux el al. vs la Corporation de la paroisse de l'Annonciation*, Comté des Deux-Montagnes, #4488, Québec, Cour du banc du roi, vol. 1, 1951, p. 304.

24. Dr. J.K. Foran, "Chroniques d'Oka: l'histoire du bois de sapins," *Le Canada*, 10 juillet 1918, p. 2, and "L'histoire des bois de sapins," *La Press*, 10 juillet 1918.

25. René Marinier, p.s.s., *Une petite histoire d'Oka de sa fondation en 1721 à l'établissement de sa municipalité civile en 1875*, avril 1976, copy of a manuscript kept at the Oka Public Library, 1976, pp. 12–13; Dr. J.K. Foran, ibid.

26. Archives du Séminaire de Saint-Sulpice de Montréal, Circulaire de H. Garriguet, Supérieur de Saint-Sulpice, Paris, October 1, 1915.

27. W. Russell, *Man, Nature and History* (London, 1967), Introduction; CNRS, *Aspects de la recherche sur l'histoire des forêts françaises* (Paris: Editions du CNRS, 1980), 4–51; J.D. Chambers, "Enclosure and the Labor Supply in the Industrial Revolution," in *Europe and the Industrial Revolution*, ed. Sima Lieberman (London: Schenkman Publishing, 1972), 347–76; Robert G. Albion, *Forests and Sea Power: The Timber Problem of the Royal Navy, 1652–1862* (London, 1927); R.R. Mousnier et E. Labrousse, *Le XVIIIe siècle, l'époque des Lumières*, 6e ed. (Paris: Presses universitaires de France, 1985), 121–22; Paul Mantoux, "Coal and Iron," in *Europe and the Industrial Revolution* (London, 1972), 106–108.

28. Andrée Corvol, *L'homme aux bois: histoire des relations homme-forêt, XVIIe siècle, XXe siècle* (Paris: Fayard, 1986); Bernard Kalaora, *La forêt pacifiée. Les forestiers de l'École de Le Play, experts des sociétés pastorales* (Paris: Harmattan, 1986); Jacqueline Dumoulin, *La protection du sol forestier en Provence et en Dauphiné dans le Code de 1827* (Grenoble: CNRS UA, 1986).

29. Charles McClelland, *State, Society, and University in Germany, 1700–1914* (London: Cambridge University Press, 1984), 2–3.

30. Carolyn Merchant, *Ecological Revolutions: Nature, Gender and Science in New England* (Chapell Hill, NC: University of North Carolina Press, 1989), 228–30.

31. Michel F. Girard, "Conservation and the Gospel of Efficiency: un modèle de gestion de l'environnement venu d'Europe?" *Histoire sociale—Social History* 23, 45 (May 1990): 63–79; Henri Clepper, *Leaders of American Conservation* (1974), 217–18.

32. Carl H. Moneyhon, "Environmental Crisis and American Politics, 1860–1920," in *Historical Ecology*, ed. Lester J. Bilky (1980), 140–55.

33. Peter Gillis, *Lost Initiatives: Canada's Forest Industries, Forest Policies and Forest Conservation* (Toronto: Greenwood Press, 1986), chaps. 1, 2.

34. Henri Joly de Lotbinière, *The Returns of Forest Tree Culture: Paper Presented to the Montreal Horticultural and Fruit Growers' Association* (Toronto, 1882).

35. See W.W. Johnson, *A Practical Work on the Management of Trees for Forestry and Ornamental Planting. . .* (1884).

36. Ibid., 2–20.

37. Appendix to the *Report of Fruit Growers' Association: Forestry Report of Delegation appointed to attend the American Forestry Congress Held at Cincinnati [. . .] and Montreal [. . .], August 21 to 23, 1882* (Toronto, 1882), i–68.

38. *Trans.*: "This stripping of the countryside, especially in mountainous areas, provoked the most unfortunate difficulties in some European countries, like the erosion of the soils which covered the hills and tumbled down in the plains, the sudden swelling of rivers which caused flooding, the disappearance of any obstacles to stop powerful winds which sweep away everything in their fury, etc." Abbé Provancher, *Le Naturaliste canadien*, vol. 1 (1874), 287.

39. Donald Mackay, *Un patrimoine en péril: la crise des forêts canadiennes* (Québec: Les publications du Québec, 1986), 38–41.

40. Ibid., 38.

41. Henri G. Joly de Lotbinière, "Forest Tree Culture," in the Appendix to the *Report of Fruit Growers' Association . . .* , 109–14.

42. Gillis, *Lost Initiatives*, chap. 2.

43. Franklin B. Hough, "Tree Planting by Railroad Companies," in the Appendix to the *Report of Fruit Growers' Association . . .* , 116–18, and John A. Warder, "Tree Planting for the Railroads," in ibid., 119–21.

44. Joly de Lotbinière, *The Returns of Forest Tree Culture*.

45. See the Appendix to the *Report of Fruit Growers' Association*.

46. The Small Commons is east of the Annunciation Road. The Big Commons, west of the Annunciation

Road, encompasses all the land south of Gabriel Road.

47. *Trans.*: "Men, women, children, Algonquin Indians, Iroquois Indians, people from Oka and the country-side parishioners. [*sic*] They went in the mountains, in the valleys, in the woods, on the lakesides to uproot young saplings and transported them to Oka. The Seminary gave 2.5 cents for each tree. One had to find it, uproot it, mark its north side so when planted the tree would show the same side to the North. . . . On the slopes, parallel lines were traced three feet apart. From the one hundred thousand firs [*sic*] thus planted, more than seventy-six thousand dug their roots in the sandy soils.

48. Archives de Saint-Sulpice de Montréal, *Cahiers de l'abbé Lafontaine*, 257–63.

49. Marinier, *Une petite histoire d'Oka*.

50. *Trans.*: "At Oka, Father Lefebvre, who directed the reforestation of the dunes, had sowed about one hundred bags of grains and scattered oat, barley, and buckwheat straw to keep the sand from moving." Avila Bédard, "Les Dunes de Lachute," *Cahiers de la Société de géographique de Québec* 5, 1 (janvier-février 1911): 22.

51. *Trans.*: "He [Lefebvre] himself worked on this plantation with the goal of remediating such disasters. However, he states that the Messieurs of Saint-Sulpice kept a team there all year for the upkeep of the slopes and the roads, which were always exposed to erosion caused by abundant rain, because every time it rained, some erosion followed." Testimony of M. Legault, in *Jean-Louis Roux et al. . . .*, 304.

52. Testimony of Aimé Gagnon, agronomist at the Oka Agricultural Institute, specialist in soil sciences, in *Jean-Louis Roux et al. . . .*, 303.

53. *Rapport du Département des terres et forêts*, 1910, pp. 54–56, 96; 1921–22, pp. 28–29; Bédard, "Les Dunes de Lachute," 20–23.

54. Michel F. Girard, *La forêt dénaturée: les discours sur la conservation des forêts au Québec au tournant du XXe siècle*, Thèse de maîtrise, Université d'Ottawa, 1988, chap. 2.

55. "Rapport du Vice-président de la Commission des Services Publics," in *Jean-Louis Roux et al. . . .*, 217.

56. Interview with Mr. Roger Van De Hende, forest engineer employed at the time by the Compagnie Immobilière Belgo, March 29, 1990.

57. Bureau d'enregistrement district des Deux-Montagnes, *Acte de vente entre La Compagnie de Saint-Sulpice et la Compagnie immobilière Belgo*, 21 octobre 1936.

58. Interview with René Dourtre, forester from the Company, and Roger Van De Hende, administrator of the Company, August 16, 1989.

59. "Rapport du Vice-président de la régie des Services Publics," in *Jean-Louis Roux et al. . . .*, 191–92.

60. Bureau d'enregistrement district des Deux-Montagnes, *Acte de vente entre la Compagnie de Saint-Sulpice. . . .*

61. *Trans.*: #10, "To respect the beauty of the Big Commons and to refrain from cutting trees of a diameter of more than 10 inches at the stump in the planted forest without having obtained the written consent of the sellers. . . . As for the other trees, the purchasers will not cut them if they are less than 8 inches in diameter. . . . Notwithstanding house and road construction . . . they must respect the established custom to use part of the sold lands as a golf course or recreation area. . . . The purchasers will not harvest trees on the said lands without providing the profits to the sellers. . . . #11, If the purchasers violate any one of the conditions stipulated in paragraphs #8 or #10, the venders . . . will have the right to request compensation of the amount of $15,000.00 without prejudice." Bureau d'enregistrement du district des Deux-Montagnes, *Acte de vente par MM. Gerard Cinq-Mars et Gabriel Fauteux à MM. J. Harris*

Lauzon et Jean Louis Proulx, en date du 9 octobre 1946, No. 9912.

62. "Rapport du Vice-président de la régie des Services Publics," in *Jean-Louis Roux et al. . . .*, 220.

63. Quebec Statutes, Chapter 114, 11 George VI (1947).

64. Ibid., 187.

65. Raymond F. Dasmann, "Toward a Biosphere Consciousness," in *The Ends of the Earth: Perspectives on Modern Environmental History*, ed. Donald Worster (1988), 277–88.

66. See Girard, *La forêt dénaturée. . . .*

67. Caroline Montpetit, "Club d'Oka: les travaux suspendus pour 15 jours," *La Presse*, 4 août 1989, A5.

68. *Trans.*: "Development should be undertaken in harmony and in continuity with the geographic and human milieu. The early [research] pioneers believed that on-site historical study would be beneficial for both the historian and society." Lucien Febvre, *La Terre et l'évolution humaine* (1922; Paris: Éditions Albin Michel, 1970); see also Gaston Roupnel. *Histoire de la campagne française* (Paris: Éditions Bernard Grasset, 1932).

NATIVE PEOPLE AND
THE ALASKA HIGHWAY◇

K.S. COATES
W.R. MORRISON

○

Had the promoters of the Northwest defense projects paused to consider what effect they might have on the aboriginal people and the environment of the region, they would have painted a rosy picture. In the capitalist model of development, roads were the vanguard of progress. Native people had been held back from the benefits of progress by isolation; the road would bring good things to them, and make it possible for them to become better integrated into North American society. The region was rich in resources, which should be exploited for the advantage of all, and the Native people would benefit through jobs and the adoption of a more "civilized" way of life. As for the environment, it was there to be used—the trees to be cut down, the rivers to be bridged and dammed, the gravel and minerals to be taken from the ground, the game to be hunted for food and recreation. There were no conservationists among the projects' planners, and if there had been, they would have been ignored; as the cliché of that day put it, there was a war on, and what were a few trees and moose compared to the exigencies of continental defense?

No one, of course, asked the indigenous people of the Northwest what they thought about the Alaska Highway, or even told them in advance that it was coming. This was the way things had always been done. The Natives, whose ancestors had lived in the region for at least 8000 years, had been compelled to adapt to successive waves of fur traders, miners, and administrators, and were now forced to cope with another invasion of their homelands. They would also experience an unprecedented assault on their land, as strangers tore a path through the countryside, blocking rivers, spilling

◇ From *The Alaska Highway in WWII: The US Army of Occupation in Canada's Northwest* (Norman, OK: University of Oklahoma Press, 1992), 70–101.

oil, starting forest fires, shooting the wildlife, and generally attacking the fragile ecology of the sub-Arctic wilderness.

As outside scholars and the Native people themselves have shown, they are not and never have been the passive victims of such forces. They could adapt to change and in many cases make the best of it, seizing opportunities when they presented themselves. One option was simply to avoid the development corridor by moving elsewhere to continue working in the still-profitable fur-trading economy. Others, particularly women, took advantage of the employment possibilities the projects presented. Whichever option they chose, however, they all retained their deep attachment to the land, and continued to hunt, fish, and trap for sustenance. For many, the prewar pattern of a mixed economy remained intact, despite the many pressures put upon it.

The Native people of the Northwest had never been particularly averse to wage labor, though they had generally been unwilling to accept the limits and controls of the workplace—particularly on their time—for very long. Clifford Rogers, president of the White Pass and Yukon Railway, told Canadian journalist Gordon Sinclair that "the Indians were not a shiftless lot. They were strong, able and self-reliant, but the idea of working for a master made them turn up their snoots and drift into the bush."[1] But to the first contractors who arrived in the region in the spring of 1942, the Natives had a priceless asset—their knowledge of the terrain.

It was not surprising then that a number of contractors hired Native workers. Rogers, working with local people hired for their ability to manage Native workers, supervised the extension of the Whitehorse airport in 1941 as part of the Northwest Staging Route. His policy, unusual for that day, was that the Natives would receive the same pay as everyone else. To complaints that such a policy was "immoral, ridiculous, fantastic and all that stuff," Rogers replied, "Well, we won't have Jim Crow laws up here. If labor gets $7.50 and labor is Indian, then Indian gets $7.50." A more common view of Native labor was reflected in the suggestion that their wages be held in trust for them so that they would not misuse or squander their money.[2]

For Gordon Sinclair, the peripatetic Toronto journalist who had made a national reputation for his colorful stories from far-off places, such sober common sense was not enough. He had come to the Yukon looking for the facile stories that had made him famous, and the kind of Indians he wanted were primitive and picturesque. He padded his copy with lengthy commentaries on how they had to be educated to spend their money, a problem solved, he claimed, when the women were introduced to silk stockings, girdles, and hairdressers, and the children to ice cream. He also commented on their insistence on being paid weekly, a demand he attributed to their fear of dying while being owed money.[3] All of this was rubbish: the Native people of the Yukon had been commercially active for half a century, and were well versed in the nuances of the marketplace. The demand for weekly pay originated in the men's unwillingness to commit themselves to longer work terms, or was due to bad experiences with dishonest employers. Such shabby tales fed the public appetite for stories based on racist stereotypes of

Indians as credulous savages, wondering at the marvels of ice cream and fancy clothing.

Sinclair was not the only journalist who wrote this sort of thing, however; most reporters saw the Native people of the Northwest as primitives whose sayings were cute and naive. Don Menzies, a staff reporter for the *Edmonton Journal*, began a story about the aboriginal people around Dawson Creek with the following: "Indians who have spent all their lives in northern British Columbia think the white man must be crazy. All they can say is a disgusted "ugh ugh," added to the usual "ugh."[4] Don MacDougall, who wrote an interesting and fairly accurate series of articles on the Alaska Highway for the same paper, adopted a droll tone when talking about Native people:

> George Johnston, Thlinget [*sic*] Indian of the Teslin Bay band, thinks the Alaska highway is a fine idea. In 1933, George had a good year on his trap line and, with sudden affluence, decided on a purchase of an automobile. The car was shipped in by rail and water from the coast and landed at Teslin Bay almost before George realized that cars require roads if they are to be operated with any degree of success. A little thing like that didn't dismay the husky George. He took up his axe and cleared out three miles of road . . . operated the car up and down his private road, charging his Indian friends for pleasure rides . . . when it is not being used in chasing wolves along the ice of frozen lakes and streams.[5]

The tone adopted in the press when writing about the blacks who were assigned to work in the region was much the same. An article in the *Edmonton Journal* entitled "Negroes on Alaska Highway Sing and Chant as They Labor" was full of stereotypes:

> There are dark spots in the world coverage of the U.S. army today but they aren't ominous. They're the U.S. Army Negro Corps. . . . in London a big buck rolled his eyes over the scene and said "We sho' like it here." Now they've popped up on the Alaska highway adding their high tones to that already colorful project. . . . Light-hearted lads, heavy logs on their shoulders, come shuffling out of the brush to a red-hot vocalization of the "Chattanooga Choo-Choo."[6]

Examples of this sort could be quoted almost endlessly, but perhaps the prize might go to the writer who managed to combine black and Indian stereotypes in a single paragraph:

> One place an Indian coming down his old pack trail met a cat[erpillar tractor] coming up. Just as he came into view the Negro operator rolled his old white eyes, shoved in the clutch and three jack pines flew into the air and rolled over the bank. The savage left and tarried not in the leaving. When he finally reached the trading post he was only able to gasp, "Big black devil him come!"[7]

Sporadic employment did not, however, prepare the Native people for the invasion that began in the spring of 1942. Many of them knew nothing about the construction projects until surveyors, or in some cases bulldozers, arrived in their communities. Virginia Smarch of Teslin recalled that a Carcross man visited their community with news of the building of the highway—an army battalion was moving cross country from Carcross to Teslin. They believed him, but still had trouble comprehending the scale or purpose of the project. Then the troops arrived in Teslin; the fact that they were blacks, the first most local people had ever seen, only added to their confusion and surprise.[8] Some of the most isolated aboriginal populations in Canada were, almost overnight, placed in direct contact with an American or Canadian construction workforce. Places like Fort Nelson, Liard, Aishihik, Snag, Watson Lake, Ross River, Burwash, Dezdeash, and nearby Klukshu, where the Natives lived almost exclusively off country produce and the proceeds from the sale of furs, suddenly had sizable non-Native populations.

Many Native people were employed in the early stages of the defense projects, but there was never any serious consideration given to making use of them over the long term, though the Canadian government was not opposed in principle to the idea. Some were hired by the U.S. Army and the Public Roads Administration (PRA) for the initial surveys and locating work, and Native guides and wranglers were invaluable in determining a route for the pioneer road in the early months of 1942.[9] But such work only confirmed the perception that their skills were "Native"—that is, their knowledge of the land and their ability to live off it. Beyond that, the stereotypes which portrayed them as indolent and unreliable prevented any real effort to integrate them into the civilian work crews.

Nonetheless, the seasonal employment the projects brought to the Northwest was important to its Native people. In some areas, particularly northern Alberta, the upper Mackenzie River valley and the Whitehorse-Carcross region, they had long played an important role in the transportation industry. They worked as laborers on the riverboats, cut wood for sale, and helped load and unload the vessels. They were accustomed to seasonal employment, generally in the summer, when there was little hunting and trapping to be done. For several generations the Natives of the region had mixed a harvesting and a wage economy, and the Northwest defense projects continued this pattern. After the army of occupation arrived, Native workers were employed unloading and loading trains, barges, and trucks; continued to serve as guides and packers; and found additional occasional work around some of the camps. In other regions the situation was different; along the British Columbia portions of the Alaska Highway, where there had been little contact between the Native people and the wage economy, they were seldom employed on the defense projects. Non-Natives working in northern British Columbia reported almost no contact with the local indigenous population, in contrast to those who served in the western Yukon, or in the Athabasca-Fort Smith area of the Northwest Territories.

The military and civilian workers also created an instant market for Native handicrafts, and one in which demand quickly exceeded supply. One surveyor, working near Burwash Landing, noted that "Natives would make caribou coats, muklucks, moccasins, caps, etc. decorated with sequins with very reasonable prices as we went north. On the way back though, prices had gone way up. They learned fast."[10] J.E. Gibben, the Indian agent in the Yukon, tried to encourage Native women to cash in on the handicraft market, but with mixed results. He had trouble getting the necessary supplies, especially beads, and found the idea hampered by a generation gap: "It appears that most of the work is done by the older women and it seems difficult to interest the younger generation in their traditional handicraft." But there was money to be made: the women of Moosehide, just downriver from Dawson City, grossed over $1300 from the sale of one consignment of handicrafts to Whitehorse.[11]

The defense projects also created a number of openings for Natives in occupations not directly related to military work. The high wages paid in the construction camps drew dozens of non-Native workers from their jobs in the region, leaving openings in the retail, hotel, transportation, and mining sectors. This led some employers to consider (often for the first time) hiring Native labor as replacements. In the Dawson area, the Yukon Consolidated Gold Corporation, faced with a major labor shortage, hired indigenous workers from the area for the first time in its history. The Natives answered one of the company's concerns; they were not as mobile as non-Native workers and were not likely to go south to seek jobs with the construction companies. The company managers found that the Natives could easily handle the work given to them, but that they were "undependable." That is, they would not give up the traditional hunting part of their way of life for permanent wage labor. At the end of the war, J.E. Gibben observed, "I have endeavoured at all times to induce the Indians to become self-sustaining, but regret that I do not see much progress in this regard."[12]

Many of the workers who arrived in the Northwest in 1942 had never met or rarely seen Native people, and were willing to believe stories about them based on racial stereotypes and misconceptions. Nearly fifty years after the event, some of the workers described them as awe-struck by the white man's technology. Stories recounting Native surprise at everything from binoculars, photography, and doorknobs are commonplace: "We ran across some that had never seen a motor vehicle or been in a town. They came wandering into camp and were trying to open the door to the mess hall. I guess they hadn't seen a door handle and didn't know you had to turn it."[13]

One man who spent eighteen months working on the southern part of the highway reported only a single contact with the local Natives, which "occurred at the Beaton River Bridge. A group of 12–15 natives, 2–3 males on horseback with the women, children and dogs following on foot, stopped at the bridge. The males dismounted and approached the concrete structure. They felt the concrete, tapped it and evidently discussed the product. After a short while they mounted and continued on southward."[14]

In the short term, most of the Native people of the Northwest remained hunters and trappers. While time and a postwar slump in fur markets would later undermine the viability of this way of life, fur prices remained high throughout the war years, providing an alternative to wage labor on the construction projects.[15] The Canadian government recognized the importance of hunting and trapping in the lives of these people, particularly since the activities prevented the Natives from becoming a charge on the public purse.[16] The governments of British Columbia and the Yukon agreed with this view, and demonstrated flexibility in enforcing regulations on Natives who hunted back and forth across the territorial-provincial boundary.[17]

Arguably the worst effect of the invasion of workers was the diseases they brought with them. Native people across North America had always been vulnerable to "virgin soil epidemics"—imported diseases for which they had no natural immunity. Many times before 1940 isolated Native bands had been exposed to a new illness, often following the arrival of a stranger in their midst. The disease would usually spread rapidly, affecting particularly the elderly, the weak, and the very young; no one knew how many, since statistics were not kept, and medical care was limited or unavailable. Despite these waves of sickness, which had swept the region for over 100 years before the workers arrived, many Natives still had little immunity to their diseases, and the results of an invasion of newcomers were truly devastating.

J.F. Marchand, a doctor stationed at Teslin in the winter of 1942–43, noted that the community had in the space of less than a year suffered outbreaks of measles, dysentery, jaundice, whooping cough, mumps, and meningococcic meningitis.[18] David Johnson, a resident of Teslin working as a guide for an army survey crew, arrived home to find that the entire village was sealed off and his children were seriously ill. Ignoring the quarantine, he returned to his family and soon became sick himself.[19]

C.K. LeCapelain, Canadian liaison officer with the defense projects, painted a sad picture of the situation:

> The Indians of the Teslin and Lower Post bands until the advent of this new era have been almost completely isolated from contacts with white people and have had the least opportunity of creating an immunity to white people's diseases. Consequently they have been distressingly affected by the new contacts. No doubt a contributing factor has been the fact that to a considerable extent the adult males have abandoned their normal nomadic pursuits and have accepted work on various construction projects, both American and Canadian.
>
> The band of Teslin suffered epidemics of measles and whooping cough, which in some cases developed into pneumonia, last year, and now are plagued with an epidemic of meningitis and have suffered three deaths so far from the latter. The bands at Lower Post were devastated last spring with an epidemic of influenza which caused 15 deaths among a total population of about 150 of all ages. There is no doubt in my mind that if events are allowed to drift along at will, but what the Indian bands at Teslin and Lower Post will become completely decimated within the next four years. The problem is how to prevent this, or at least to ameliorate conditions as far as possible.[20]

At one point, 128 of the 135 residents of Teslin were sick with measles. St. Philip's Anglican Mission school and church were used as a hospital, and patients were cared for by army doctors and RCMP constables, and later by two nurses sent from Whitehorse. Bessie Johnston, a young Tlingit woman from the community, assisted with the care of her people, helping with the cooking and cleaning for sixty patients in the makeshift hospital while also caring for her parents at home. Having worked herself to exhaustion, Bessie herself caught measles, lapsed into a coma, and died within twenty-four hours.[21]

Because reporting was so spotty, it is hard to assess the full impact of the epidemics that swept the Northwest during the construction period. John Honigman, an anthropologist working among the Native people near Fort Nelson, reported that the diseases had not appeared there.[22] At Watson Lake, 300 miles to the north, a major influenza outbreak occurred in April 1942, affecting a large number of whites as well as many Indians.[23] Perhaps the previous length of contact between the races had something to do with the difference; in the Mackenzie valley, where aboriginal people had been in regular contact with non-Natives since the early nineteenth century, there were fewer major outbreaks of epidemic diseases. Even here, though, the arrival of thousands of outsiders brought illness and suffering. In October 1942, a government official at Fort Norman reported, "Fewer Indians were seen during this month but at month's end word from Willow Lake had it that they were all very sick with influenza."[24] Along the Canol route, particularly at the isolated trading post of Ross River, the arrival of U.S. troops touched off major outbreaks of diphtheria. A local Native woman who had had some training as a nurse tried to treat the ailment, but several parents, terrified by the illness, would not let her near their children. Those unattended died; most of the others lived.[25]

The medical officers serving with the U.S. Army in the Northwest, and to a lesser extent the civilian contractors, gave what medical assistance they could to the Native people. Their aid was welcomed, though there was a brief squabble when the Yukon Territorial Council debated barring American doctors from treating Canadian patients. It was the military doctors, for example, who imposed the quarantine on Teslin, and who tended the sick there. In 1943, Dr. Lucey of the U.S. Army cared for the sick during an influenza epidemic at Watson Lake. He provided the RCMP with sulfa drugs, aspirin, and a thermometer for visits to the bush camps, for there was illness there too. A constable reported from one camp:

> Most of the sick are up and around now but of course are extremely weak. Mrs. L _____ T _____ was found laying out on the snow and her husband, L _____ T _____ was persuaded to build a bunk of spruce logs and cover it with spruce boughs and cover her with blankets. Patrol remained at the camp until this was done. All are well supplied with food and cannot be suffering in any way for want of eatables.[26]

While the military and civilian doctors provided care freely to the indigenous population, one of their goals was to keep the epidemics from reaching the non-Native population, an effort that was largely successful. In 1943, the medical officer for the Whitehorse area reported that

> the health of troops and civilian employees within the Post area during the past year has continued to be satisfactory. There have not been any serious epidemics, nor have any of the diseases endemic among the local Indians affected our troops. On the contrary, several epidemics of communicable diseases appeared among the Indians which they had apparently never before experienced. This was attributed by an investigator of the USPHS [U.S. Public Health Service] to the influx of outside contacts (carriers), both civil and military.[27]

Though it is difficult to be precise, what figures are available show that the diseases brought in by the construction workers led to a serious, though short-term, demographic crisis among the Native people of the Northwest. In 1942 deaths outnumbered births by nineteen, and by fifteen in 1943, among the Natives of the Yukon. By 1947 the trend was reversed; in that year births outnumbered deaths by forty-nine, and in 1948 by thirty-nine. It is also likely that the enumerators missed many deaths due to disease, especially among infants, when they occurred in the bush, where many Native families had retreated in an attempt to escape the invasion and the illness that accompanied it.[28]

The presence of American doctors cast a light into some of the darker corners of the Canadian Northwest. Elizabeth Carswell, a Canadian nurse working in a U.S. medical dispensary in the Lower Post district, contrasted the work of the Americans among the Native people with the Canadian neglect of them:

> The work of the R.C.M.P. is greatly to be admired—but they get no support. They go to endless trouble tracking down a grapevine rumor of a sick Indian, unmindful of personal comfort or hazardous weather. But, although they are expected to care for illnesses found, they are allowed to keep no medicines on hand and each time an emergency arises are obliged to wait precious days until the necessary drugs are sent. This delay sometimes adds up to one more dead Indian. . . .
>
> Another case involved a 30-mile trip by dog team to tend a woman acutely ill of pneumonia. To feed the hungry mouths of some 12 Indians, we found in that cabin one can of milk, some macaroni, a few prunes, a little tea. The R.C.M.P.'s wire to Whitehorse for permission to transport the patient up the 300 miles of highway to the nearest hospital, after a three-day wait, brought a reply in this vein: "Symptoms you describe are those common to 'flu. Do not bring patient in unless condition becomes worse." The woman is living today because the American army furnished life-saving sulfadiozine and American contractors contributed good meat, fresh vegetables and milk for the whole family.[29]

Though disease and death were perhaps the most dramatic marks left on the Native people by the invasion, there was also much official concern that the contact between them and the invaders would be harmful to them and might also hamper the construction projects by introducing an element of disorder into the camps. For both reasons efforts were made to keep the races separate. Official orders declared off-limits "all houses, tents, buildings, or shelters owned, occupied, or used by Indians or mixed breeds regardless of the blood percentage," but such regulations were hard to enforce, particularly away from the major centers.[30]

The common ground for contact between the workers and the Native people was all too often alcohol. Until 1960, Canadian Indians were forbidden by law to possess or drink alcoholic beverages. This regulation, aimed at keeping Native people away from the worst features of white society, had the opposite effect. Natives looking for alcohol had to seek it out in the lowest levels of society, at the hands of bootleggers, or they could make homebrew.[31] There had always been a lively market in illegal liquor in the Northwest, but the influx of thousands of single, often hard-drinking men into the region changed the dynamics of alcohol consumption in the region.

In recognition of the unique conditions in the Yukon and Northwest Territories, liquor and beer were not as strictly rationed there as in the provinces during the war, though the distribution machinery proved inadequate for the influx of workers. Interminable lines at the liquor stores were a notable feature of wartime life in the region. Native people who wanted commercially manufactured liquor had to buy it from some non-Native person, and it generally came at a high price. The penalty for bootlegging or supplying liquor to registered Indians—a stiff fine and a prison sentence—was reflected in the price paid by the consumer. Much Native drinking took place at parties (often referred to in press accounts as "drinking parties") where the main purpose was for everyone to get as drunk as possible—just the sort of situation the government had passed laws to prevent. In such a setting the price of liquor was often sex rather than money—a pattern familiar enough in the North. John Honigman observed this pattern often, particularly among truck drivers, who had numerous contacts along the highway and the means of bringing in liquor from the South.[32]

The government was determined to check this situation, and to punish offenders of both races. To this end, it moved members of the RCMP from the territorial headquarters in Dawson to Whitehorse, and in 1944 moved the headquarters there as well. The increased number of police officers in the southern Yukon resulted in increased convictions, but did little to solve the problem (see table 1).

The arrival of the troops had increased the amount rather than the nature of interracial drinking. The authorities, particularly in the southern Yukon and the upper Mackenzie basin, tended to view the problem as an "Indian" one, and concentrated on trying to keep alcohol out of Native hands—a reflection of North American stereotypes of the aboriginal weakness for liquor—but without much success. The Native people who wanted to drink found willing suppliers in bootleggers and in men from the construction crews looking for money or sex in the Native camps.

TABLE 1 *NATIVE ALCOHOL-RELATED CONVICTIONS AND POLICE MANPOWER, SOUTHERN YUKON, 1940–49*

Year	Convictions	Police Force
1940	3	4
1941	9	4
1942	28	4
1943	27	15
1944	34	25
1945	51	25
1946	75	30
1947	82	27
1948	61	21
1949	55(32)✧	22

✧ Records to July 1949; 55 equals rate of convictions projected over the entire year.

Note: Convictions include those for supplying, possession, drunkenness, and breaches of Indian Act.

Source: NAC, RG 18, Whitehorse Police Court Register.

o

Despite the popular mythology of the Northwest defense projects, accepted by most Natives and non-Natives in the region, the highway and the other defense projects dramatically affected the Natives' world, but did not overturn it. There were of course some serious dislocations, particularly the suffering and death resulting from contagious diseases. But during the war, trapping and hunting remained the cornerstone of Native life throughout the region. When Natives took jobs for wages with the construction companies, they did so for periods that suited their seasonal way of life. The main impact of the projects on the hunting way of life was that the new roads made it easier to get to once inaccessible hunting and fishing sites. On the other hand, the disruption of construction work and hunting by work crews drove much of the game far from the roads, affecting traditional hunting patterns.

What really changed the lives of the Northwest's Native people were two postwar developments that had nothing to do with the construction projects. In 1947 the North American fur trade went into a prolonged slump that undermined the commercial viability of an industry that had been the cornerstone of the Native economy for over a century. Even more important was the advent of the Canadian welfare state. During and after the war the Canadian government abandoned its traditional laissez-faire policy towards its citizens—it was inhumane, and did not sell well at election time—and began to pour a cornucopia of benefits upon them, targeting Native people for special attention. The first gift was the Family Allowance, popularly called the baby bonus, a monthly grant given to all parents of children under the age of sixteen. But government cornucopias come with strings attached, and these severely altered the Natives' way of life in the Northwest. Native people in the Yukon and Northwest Territories got the baby bonus in kind rather than in cash, which gave the government the right to interfere in their purchasing habits. Though the original grant was only $5 to $8 per month, a family with eight children would get about $50, a sum not to be sneered at in a cash-poor subsistence economy. Other programs followed, many of them with conditions: compulsory education, pensions, housing projects, employment schemes, and relocation of Native people to residential reserves.

These programs really struck at the core of aboriginal life and forced fundamental, painful changes in the nature of Native society in the region. But because bulldozers are easier to comprehend than bureaucrats, especially distant ones, many Native people continue to regard the projects as the cause of the transformation of their way of life. Their place in the historical consciousness of the indigenous people of the Canadian Northwest was shown over thirty years later, when plans for pipelines across the North became the focus of aboriginal hostility.[33]

Years later, the two Canadian pipeline inquiries—the Berger Commission and the Lysyk Commission[34]—demonstrated the fear among the region's Native people of megaprojects imposed upon them from the outside. Several witnesses for the Berger Commission testified that the Alaska Highway and Canol Project had devastated their communities, and said that they opposed the pipeline on the grounds that it was likely to do the same thing.

The two commissions also focused on another vital aspect of northern construction—environmental impact. Even in the 1970s, little was known about the impact of heavy construction on the fragile sub-Arctic, a fact that highlights the even greater ignorance of the engineers who worked in the Northwest in the early 1940s. Then, the highway and pipeline builders had virtually no experience in dealing with muskeg and permafrost, nor had they much information on rainfall, ice movement, snow packs, soil types, and other basic geological and climatological information. The kind of environmental impact studies that were to become the norm in the 1970s were undreamed of in the early 1940s. There was no information available, for example, on how to contain oil spills in sub-Arctic conditions, nor any real sense of the impact such environmental disasters would have on the region—nor was there much concern when the spills occurred. Little thought was given to the effect of construction activities on fish and wildlife. The projects, in short, took place in a general state of ecological unconsciousness, in which planners knew little about the area they were "developing," and gave scant thought to the long-term environmental impact of their activities.

This ignorance and lack of concern are reflected in the historical documentation. It is difficult to assess precisely the damage wrought by the builders, since few scientists visited the Northwest during the war to record the ruin of creeks and rivers, the erosion of hillsides, the disturbance of wildlife migrations, and other damage to the environment. After the war the scientists did come, and the studies they conducted in the 1950s were to become the bedrock of knowledge about the sub-Arctic ecosystem. The engineers should not be held wholly to blame, since they were sent to a region they knew nothing about, and were ordered to do a difficult job with maximum speed; concern for their surroundings was not part of their mandate.

It is clear, however, that the massive construction projects did much harm to the Northwest's environment. Some of the most dramatic damage involved the regions where permafrost was found. Here, as elsewhere, the overburden was ripped off with bulldozers; when the season warmed, the permafrost melted and the roadway turned to thick mud. Land wounded in this fashion took decades to heal, and building roads and pipelines across it was a massive challenge. This problem and others were solved by trial and error, often by adopting or rediscovering techniques that had been pioneered during the gold rush forty years earlier. These experiments left even more scars across the land—scars regarded at the time as the inevitable results of progress and victory in war. And after all, where were the builders to go for advice? The Alaskans knew little more than the southerners, the Scandinavians were cut off by war, and to ask the Soviet Union—an ally, but still the hated bastion of communism—was unthinkable, even if the Soviets had had a reputation for being helpful.

Probably the most immediate and wide-ranging damage caused by the construction projects came from the many forest fires that swept the region during the war years. The occupying forces furnished a potent combination of incendiary elements: widespread cigarette smoking, notably among truck drivers, who often threw their butts and matches into the ditches as they drove; portable sawmills that produced large quantities of sawdust; poor storage of oil and gasoline products; heavy equipment, such as welding gear, that produced heat and sparks; poorly organized fire-fighting plans; and a general attitude that the forest was limitless and the task urgent. Clearing the highway right-of-way left large piles of slash along the routes—tinder ready to be touched off by smokers or a variety of other causes.[35] So many fires were started by carelessness that the U.S. Army launched a prevention campaign; a directive from the summer of 1943 prohibited "throwing of lighted material of any kind from motor vehicles." Efforts were also made to clear up slash piles and flammable wastes located near camps and maintenance yards.

Some of the fires started by the army of occupation were large enough to destroy thousands of acres of forest. When U.S. troops first arrived in the Fort Smith area, for example, a number of forest fires soon broke out, caused by soldiers setting smoky fires in an attempt to keep the mosquitoes at bay. Several of these fires combined to become a large, uncontrollable blaze, burning through moss and muskeg for months. The troops seemed indifferent to the damage they were causing; one man who was fighting a fire in June 1943 passed a small group of U.S. soldiers sitting around a small campfire. When he returned a few minutes later, the fire had gotten out of control and was 75 feet in diameter. A small group of volunteers fought hard to keep the fire from reaching the Roman Catholic mission near Fort Smith. After working for hours on a fire break, they found to their dismay that some of the Americans had left smudge fires burning behind them, rendering their efforts useless. Much of the mission property and hundreds of acres of timber were destroyed before the fire burned itself out. Official indifference appeared to favor a policy of "let[ting] the country burn, it's no good anyway, and with that attitude in view fire suppression is a hard job indeed."[36]

Rather uncharacteristically, the Canadians actually took the Americans to task on the subject of fires. Commenting after the war, R.A. Gibson, director of the Canadian Lands, Parks, and Forest Branch, wrote, "You will remember the difficulty which we had with the United States Army before we finally had a show down with the American authorities here. . . . All we asked the Americans was that they should put out the fires that they started."[37] The Americans responded by ordering their military personnel to put out fires they had started and to "co-operate to a reasonable extent in fighting fires in the country tributary to the highway."[38] As with so many aspects of the invasion, rumors about fire damage, some true, some wildly exaggerated, circulated in and outside the Northwest. In the fall of 1943, a story reached Ottawa that a series of deliberately set fires had destroyed huge stretches of timber around Kluane Lake. RCMP officers who patrolled the region reported the facts, which were that many small fires had indeed been started along the construction corridors, but that most had quickly been brought under control.[39]

Fire was not the only threat to the forests of the Northwest, for there was a tremendous demand for wood to be used for heating, building construction, bridges, telephone and telegraph poles, and temporary bridges. A number of sawmills were hastily set up near the main communities and construction camps to supply the demand. By the fall of 1943 there were about sixty cutters working in the forest, supplying at least fourteen sawmills in the region. The appetite of the construction projects for cordwood was tremendous; the RCAF operations at Whitehorse alone required 10 000 cords of wood, and at Watson Lake 8000 cords for the heating season, a combined total representing a pile 4 feet high, 4 feet wide, and more than 27 miles long. A Canadian official observed that "it does not take much of a mathematician to figure out the effects in denuding the country of timber over a period of years, and this is not half of the total requirements."[40]

Little could be done about the cutting of timber, since the original agreement that set the projects in motion had guaranteed the Americans free access to whatever natural resources they needed; Canadian officials, while recognizing this fact, nonetheless felt "we have a right to expect that conservation principles will not be violated."[41] Their objectives were minimal: they hoped that the military and civilian contractors would cut timber so as "not to impair the scenery or cause hazard to the stand any more than is absolutely necessary," but there was little they could do to make this wish a reality.[42] Towards the end of the war, many of the camps were converted from wood to oil-stove heat, with the result that thousands of cords of wood were abandoned near the camps. An estimate in August 1945 was that 8000 cords, cut into 16-foot lengths, remained in the bush, presenting a fire hazard. Local residents were urged to make use of this timber, but few did so.[43]

The matter of timber did raise the whole question of conservation in the Northwest, a region where the issue had never been given much thought. C.K. LeCapelain, the Canadian liaison officer, remarked that "up to the present moment there have been no conservation thoughts in the timber cutting regulations. These were concerned principally with collecting revenues and not with conservation." He thought that the war was not a good time to initiate conservation measures, since they would be difficult to enforce on the contractors, but he did recommend that a timber inspector be hired to survey timber use in the Northwest, particularly with a view to fire prevention. For the present, he recommended, "If we can adequately protect the scenic values and beauty spots along the Canadian Alaskan Military Highway from spoilation we should be satisfied for the present."[44]

The same attitude, that little could be done while the war was on, also prevailed on the subject of wildlife preservation. Areas along the highway and pipeline corridors, particularly near the camps, were often badly overhunted, and the noise and construction also drove animals from traditional habitats.[45] One result was that by the end of 1942, the Natives were reporting severe shortages of game in some areas. Observers differed on the actual size of the losses; some suggested that the stocks had not been depleted at all, but that the animals were avoiding the construction corridors; others, like Joe Jacquot, argued that in some areas the game was all but wiped out:

> With this influx of activity, game moved away from the highway. It was rare indeed if a Moose crossed the highway and if it did it would not hang around long. If it wasn't scared off by the noise it more than likely would be shot and many times left to rot. There was an attitude of "Don't give a damn," probably because of the war and the fact that the soldiers were constantly rotated and had very little recreation facilities. . . . Fishing holes and many spawning grounds in the rivers were dynamited and ruined never to be used again, by people who didn't give a damn. In many cases the fish weren't even picked up. It was a horrible waste. In our Trading Post we would not sell any ammunition to non-residents or people that we knew would waste the game.[46]

The Canadian government did not want to upset the pace of construction, or to annoy the Americans. The Canadian and Yukon policy was to permit the visiting U.S. forces to purchase residents' hunting licenses in the Territory, a privilege not granted to nonresident Americans in Alaska for another year. The policy was different in the Northwest Territories; there the game resources, which were much sparser than in the Yukon and Alaska, were reserved exclusively for the Native population.

There was a particular problem in the southwest corner of the Yukon, an area noted for its game, especially the Dall sheep. Hunting pressure, and the American decision to set aside a large section of southeast Alaska for a game preserve, convinced the Canadian government to establish a new game preserve west of the Alaska Highway and the Haines Road. The idea was proposed by C.K. LeCapelain in September 1942:

> Almost all along the highway the scenery is lovely and the views along some of the lakes for instance are beautiful but they can be duplicated in many other areas in Canada. That stretch of the road running from Bear Creek, a tributary of the Dezdeash River to the White River in southwestern Yukon offers something that you cannot get anywhere else in Canada; a view of the St. Elias Mountains containing the largest glaciers and highest mountain peaks in Canada. Therefore, I respectfully suggest that the areas . . . bounded on the east by the Alsek River, on the north by the Canadian-Alaskan Highway and White River and west and south by the Alaska Boundary be reserved for consideration as a National Park. This area is well-known for its big game including White Bighorn Sheep (Ovis Dalli), mountain goat, Osborne caribou, moose and grizzly bear.[47]

His advice was adopted, and the Kluane game preserve was established that same year. The local Native people, who were not consulted, found themselves barred from an area they had relied on for generations. Fortunately for them, however, the boundaries were not enforced at first, permitting a local guide, Eugene Jacquot, to continue taking hunting parties into the area. A year after the sanctuary had been designated, a police officer traveling through the area reported, "Most men in the various construction camps do not know they are in a game preserve," a statement that reveals the difficulty of enforcing regulations.[48] Signs identifying the game preserve were posted along the Haines Road and Alaska Highway, but the hunting restrictions remained difficult to police.[49] The move was nevertheless a preliminary step in the eventual creation of the Kluane National Park (later named a UNESCO World Heritage Site). An additional result was to deprive the local residents, particularly those from Burwash Landing, of a rich and valuable hunting area. In 1946 they petitioned the government for redress, but to no avail:

> It is not the Indians that are a threat to the game and fur trade of the country, but it is them that are punished. Before the whites came in this country, game and fur were abundant although the Indians were in much greater number than they are today. . . . Hunting and trapping are our only resources—the whites have a thousand ways of earning money for a living. . . . We have no objection to the development of the country, on the condition however that we be left free to live and develop ourselves also.[50]

In the first year of construction, most of the workers were too busy to hunt more than a short distance from the construction sites, areas the game avoided.[51] In 1943, however, most of the military and civilian workers were able to take several days off to go on extended hunting trips. Though regulations governed the possession and use of firearms, generally no one was around to enforce them, and there were reports of the wanton destruction of game. One man working on the Canol pipeline reported a number of incidents and claimed that "there are guns in every camp killing everything from the smallest to the largest. . . . The soldiers kill anything. What are your people going to do? Stand by and see your game destroyed? It hurt a lot of us to see these trusting animals killed."[52]

There were already three large game preserves in the Northwest Territories (out of the way of the projects), and there was much debate in Canadian official circles on the advisability of establishing others in the Northwest Territories and in the Yukon. LeCapelain, after an informal survey of game resources in northern British Columbia and the Yukon, wrote in 1942, "I seem to be coming to the point of recommending no sanctuaries or preserves in the Yukon, other than the possible National Park and probably a game sanctuary in northern British Columbia along the Liard River or rather in the mountains south of the Liard River to preserve the band of elk in that area."[53] But Kluane remained the only preserve set up during the war.

Wartime hunting eventually became part of the mythology of the Alaska Highway, along with the stories of millions of dollars' worth of wrecked and abandoned equipment. Numerous stories circulated based on the Americans' alleged desire to shoot anything that moved, using everything from heavy machine guns to pearl-handled revolvers. One long-time Whitehorse resident remembered that "the Americans shot everything in sight, from Whitehorse to Lake Laberge."[54] The Native people of the Northwest unanimously reported disruptions of the local game supplies. In contrast, Robert McCandless argues in his history of wildlife use in the Yukon that most reports of overhunting were exaggerated, and that disruptions were comparatively slight.[55]

The reality lies somewhere between official wartime assurances that hunting activity had slight impact and the folklore legends of Americans strafing moose and caribou from fighter planes, leaving hundreds of carcasses abandoned in the bush. The Americans did hunt—some with permission, others without—and were enthusiastic about the prospect of having fresh meat to eat. One Oregonian even proposed an organized game hunt to feed military and civilian workers.[56] One man who served as an officer with the 93rd Engineers (a black regiment) recollected how "we would shoot game when we could until the RCMP got on us. We were supposed to get a licence or something before we did it but they didn't really bother us. But eventually we scared all the game away from the road so we didn't get that much, but we did shoot caribou, mostly if we could see anything . . . not really that much."[57] There were also incidents of simple foolishness:

> I happened to be driving and [they said] "Jim, stop the car. There's a moose." I stopped and they jumped out and the two of them ran down to where that moose was supposed to go in. They got down there and they saw something move and they shot it. And the first

thing I knew they come running out and they said "Get out of here." I said, "Well, what about the moose?" "It wasn't a moose, it was a farmer's cow.". . . He came down and told our company commander. . . . So, we had to pay for the cow. But the farmer wanted to keep the cow. We say no. . . . So we went out and got the cow and brought it home and hung it out in the cooler.[58]

There were areas where overhunting did take place, particularly in the sheep-hunting areas of the southwest Yukon. It is true that game became scarce throughout the construction corridors, though it did return after the building was finished. Canadian officials at the time usually discounted the stories about American overhunting. C.K. LeCapelain, who knew as much about what was going on as any Canadian, acknowledged early in 1943 that there had been considerable unregulated hunting, but agreed with the B.C. Game Commission, which did "not feel such killing to be excessive."[59] In some cases the killing was for the protection of the workers, particularly in the summer of 1942, when bears became a nuisance around the highway camps:

We first noticed them hanging around our abandoned camps in the rear, which they found good pickings because of the garbage pits, which they raided. Not satisfied with this, they then started visiting our forward camps, particularly the small ones occupied by men at watering points and small guard detachments. Here they became quite bold, entering men's tents in search of food, ripping open barracks bags, and causing confusion generally. It has become so bad that Col. Ingall had finally, and reluctantly, given men permission to shoot bears that come into camp, as the only way of preventing someone from getting mangled. It seems a shame, they are such friendly harmless seeming animals. We have had to shoot a number already, and the score undoubtedly will grow, as they seem to be having their national convention at our expense.[60]

Only a small percentage of the army of occupation had the time, the equipment, the permission, or the bush skills to hunt in the region. A greater number, however, brought their fishing tackle north with them. Most of the construction camps were located near lakes or rivers, where lake trout, grayling, pike, and other species provided ample rewards for fishermen. In short order much of the water near the camps was overfished, resulting in a serious depletion of stocks and reducing the supply available to local residents who depended heavily on this resource.

The idea that the Northwest was bursting with exploitable natural resources attracted a number of would-be developers, people who hoped to cash in on the easier access to the wilderness. One American proposed hunting along the highway for the commercial market. A company from Saskatoon asked for commercial fishing licenses for the area; the owner planned to catch fish in lakes such as Teslin and Swan Lake, now accessible via the Alaska Highway, sell all he could to construction workers, and market the surplus in Canadian cities.[61] Yukon member of Parliament George Black opposed the project on the grounds that such commercial operations would soon exhaust the resource. Canadian government officials agreed, believing that the resource should be used by the Natives of the region. The RCMP in Whitehorse estimated that it had received nearly 100 inquiries about commercial fishing licenses in 1942–43, a sure sign of the high prices and the demand for fish. The police believed that the northern lakes were already being fished close to capacity and could not tolerate large-scale commercial operations. Inspector H.H. Cronkite of the Whitehorse detachment proposed tough new restrictions on commercial and private fishing, leaving only Native fishing rights intact.[62]

In fact, many of the region's lakes and rivers had not been fully exploited before the war, and when the highway workers went fishing, they were rewarded with large catches and many trophy fish, particularly in northern British Columbia and the southern Yukon. As a result, fishing trips rank among the happiest memories of many members of the army of occupation. Over time, however, the waters close to the highway suffered as a result of fishing pressure. Once-rich streams became much less productive, a matter of only passing concern to the transient workers, but a serious problem to the local people who depended on the resource. Eventually the fish stocks increased again, but much more slowly than in southern waters, where there was more food and where the fish reproduced and grew at a faster rate.

As well as the dramatic environmental problems, like forest fires and depletion of wildlife stock, there were hundreds of small incidents of injury to the environment. Although both the Canadian and U.S. governments were at pains to reassure the public that controls were in place, the projects were so vast and diverse that effective policing or pollution control was all but impossible. There were hundreds of incidents like the following: A man driving a fuel truck arrived at his destination to find that storage tanks were nonexistent. Having fulfilled his mission, and under orders to be back at the refinery at a certain time, he simply dumped the fuel on the ground and drove off. Similarly, bridge construction proceeded with little care for the fish in the rivers; careless work by bulldozers disrupted the riverbeds and spawning activities, and eradicated the fish life in some of the smaller streams. Joe Jacquot described how spilled oil harmed the environment in the 1950s; the same kind of thing happened during the war:

When the line was cut the fuel ran into pockets and disappeared. Some went into peat bogs that acted as a large sponge. When the spring breakup came and the spring run-off was in effect, fuel flowed not only into the lakes but into the streams. The migratory birds heading north at this time became unknown victims. The muskrat and beaver died. Some of those lakes still don't have rat houses on them. Up until about 4 years ago [1972] the people couldn't eat the fish in Swede Johnson Creek because they tasted of fuel oil.[63]

Some of the smaller companies were inexcusably careless with their effluent. One witness lodged a complaint in August 1943 against Foley Brothers' Camp on Kathleen Creek, claiming that "the toilet is built over the stream. Not thirty feet below this I have seen several taking out big catches of fish and eating them." She also claimed that a sawmill company was dumping large quantities of sawdust into Miller Creek. The police officers who investigated reported that the larger camps avoided such obvious problems, but that "smaller, disorganized units, of a temporary nature," were more likely to pollute the waters near their establishments.[64]

These events took place in a time of national crisis, and one in which the North American conservation movement, though active, was not yet the powerful political force it is today. Nevertheless, they did not pass without comment, and sometimes protest. The news accounts of highway and pipeline work, which often gave brief comments on environmental matters, raised serious questions about the impact of construction activity. Reports of overhunting, particularly in the picturesque southwest corner of the Yukon, resulted in a number of written protests, in which outsiders, even those with little direct knowledge of the region, expressed their concerns to the Canadian government.[65] In the fall of 1942, Ira Gabrielson, a member of the U.S. Fish and Wildlife Service, reported stories "that United States soldiers in Yukon kill large numbers of big game animals unlawfully, and take large numbers of fish with dynamite." He expressed the hope that Canadian agencies were taking "corrective measures" to "stop this destructive waste of wildlife."[66] The response to Gabrielson's inquiry reveals a great deal about Canadian attitudes to game in the area. Acknowledging that the Americans "varied their fare with a certain amount of wild meat," [R.A.] Gibson concluded:

> We have not been greatly worried about serious depletion of the game resources because not many of the men showed a disposition to wander very far away from the right-of-way of the road and some numerous stories were told of the unfortunate experiences of some who went hunting and got lost for days at a time. However, we must admit that we have not the full information we should have about the game situation in the country tributary to the road and we must take steps to remedy this situation.[67]

Gabrielson's inquiry bounced around the Canadian and American civil services for several months, leading to considerable discussion as to how the hunting activity might be regulated.[68]

Gabrielson continued his efforts to publicize the lack of protection for wildlife in the Northwest, expressing concern that the Porcupine caribou herd would be overhunted by Natives eager to capitalize on the market for meat in the area.[69] He was particularly anxious to warn Americans that Alaska was not "a land teeming with unlimited quantities of big game," and was worried that the new roads and airfields would open the region to an influx of population that would crowd out the wildlife. In public lectures and press releases, he argued for new game reserves and more game wardens. Most important, he argued:

In order to place the management of the wildlife resources on a permanent basis of self-perpetuation it will be necessary to change the concepts of the people of Alaska[,] and of most of the people who are going to Alaska, regarding the extent to which wildlife may be utilized. Only by successfully changing the popular viewpoint may we maintain Alaska as the source of the most valuable salmon fishery in the world, as the home of the greatest bird colonies in the country, and as the last reservoir of the great game herds to be found under the American flag.[70]

Gabrielson was supported in his campaign by P.J. Hoffmaster, the president of the International Association of Game, Fish, and Conservation Commissioners, who, alarmed by the construction of the Whitehorse oil refinery, asked R.A. Gibson for assurance that the refinery effluent would not damage the local wildlife. Gibson replied that "the subject will be kept under active observation and review" and that "the design and operation of this refinery will include all provisions necessary to avoid harmful pollution of the Lewes River."[71] Fortunately for Whitehorse, the refinery did not operate long enough for its effluent to become a serious problem.

These questions, particularly when raised by foreigners, tapped a vein of guilt in Canada. The national and regional governments had to face the fact that they knew next to nothing about the environment of the Northwest and that they were relying for what they did know on pioneering work done by the Geological Survey of Canada.[72] During the war, they began to make up for this neglect by taking advantage of the new transportation facilities to send a number of scientists into the region, where few had ventured before 1941.[73] In 1943, Dr. A.L. Rand of the National Museum of Canada conducted the first major survey of mammal and bird life along the Alaska Highway.[74] In the same year, Hugh Raup of Harvard University's Arnold Arboretum led a small team on a survey of soil and flora conditions along the highway, with particular attention to the prospects for gardening and agriculture.[75] In 1944 Rand and A.E. Porsild traveled into the Mackenzie Mountains, using the Canol Road to reach an area that had previously been inaccessible to scientists, and Dr. W.A. Clemens of the University of British Columbia conducted a biological survey of the province's northern waters on behalf of the British Columbia fisheries department, "with special reference to the new Canadian Alaska Highway."[76] The same year, Dr. C.H.D. Clarke of the Lands, Parks, and Forest Branch, with T.M. Shortt of the Royal Ontario Museum of Zoology, received permits to collect specimens of mammals and nonmigratory birds along the Alaska Highway and in Kluane National Park.[77]

Perhaps the most important result of this activity was that it forced a reassessment of one of the Northwest's most durable myths—that it contained limitless wildlife resources ready for exploitation. The scientific studies showed how fragile the region's ecosystem was, how vulnerable to damage and overharvesting. In the last years of the war and the postwar period, the ethic of conservation appeared in the Northwest, marked by the establishment of the Yukon Fish and Game Association, the banning of the commercial sale of wild meat in 1947, and other measures designed to bring northern wildlife practices into line with those of the rest of the continent. In this way—and with disregard for the needs and way of life of the Natives and other long-time residents—the frontier relationship between the people and the environment began to break down. Over the next decade the Canadian government accelerated the process, urging the Native people to move off the land, regulating hunting and fishing, and changing the relationship of people and the environment from one based on consumption to one based on recreational use and the conservation of dwindling game stocks.[78]

By 1945 the Canadian government was also reconsidering its policy towards the Native people of the Northwest. For decades it had believed that they were "best left as Indians," and did little to try to integrate them into the national economy and society. Just as northern wildlife practices were brought into line with national standards, so the government began to draw the Native people into a complex web of national programs, a process that began with the introduction of the Family Allowance in 1945 and accelerated rapidly thereafter. By the mid-1950s the Native people of the Canadian Northwest were being drawn into the provincial and territorial educational systems and encouraged to integrate as much as possible into Canadian society. The wartime projects did not initiate this process, which proved painful and difficult for many of the people it was supposed to benefit—the postwar welfare state and changed attitudes towards Natives did that—but the construction of highways and airfields made it much easier for the government to impose a new agenda upon its Native clients.[79]

The U.S. invasion of the Northwest had a dramatic effect on the two constants in the region: the ecology and the Native people. The people were ravaged by epidemics, displaced by construction activity, abused in some cases by outsiders, and forced to compete with them for dwindling resources. In some areas, notably northern British Columbia, the Natives avoided the construction areas and played only a small part in the wartime activities. In other places, especially the southern Yukon and the upper Mackenzie valley, some Native people found jobs, mostly casual and unskilled. Throughout the region the greater availability of alcohol, sexual relations with non-Natives . . . and increased involvement with the legal system (largely through the enforcement of discriminatory regulations on alcohol use) disrupted the equilibrium of Native life in a way unmatched since the Klondike gold rush. Much the same was true of the northern environment. Forest fires ravaged large areas, destroying timber and wildlife habitat. The outsiders damaged streams, polluted the land, and put severe pressure on fish and game stocks.

Native life and the environment on which it was based were severely strained by the arrival of tens of thousands of southerners. Although many of those who came to the region in 1942 did not stay long, the mark they left on the land and its people proved to be permanent. The challenges to Native life in the region, and the threat to the sub-Arctic environment, both of which hit new peaks during the war, would gather strength over the next decades. The disruptions of the war proved to be a beginning (in the Yukon, a second beginning), not an end of this process.

NOTES

1. *Edmonton Journal*, 12 July 1941.

2. National Archives of Canada (hereafter NAC).

3. *Edmonton Journal*, 12 July 1941.

4. "Indians Puzzled by Rush on Road," *Edmonton Journal*, 20 March 1942.

5. "Road 'Swell Idea,' Says North Indian," *Edmonton Journal*, 23 November 1942.

6. *Edmonton Journal*, 15 August 1942.

7. Knox. F. McCusker, "The Alaska Highway," *The Canadian Surveyor* 8 (July 1943).

8. Barbara Bardie and Ken Coates, "The Gravel Magnet" (television program produced for Northern Native Broadcasting Yukon, 1988).

9. NAC, RG 27, vol. 676, file 6-5-75-5-1, T.R.L. MacInnes to L.E. Drummond, 23 June 1943.

10. Questionnaire answered by Hampton Primeaux, Rayne, Louisiana, 1989.

11. NAC, RG 85, vol. 1872, file 550-2-1, J.E. Gibben to Mr. Gibson, 31 May 1946.

12. Ibid.

13. Questionnaire answered by A. Forgie, Edmonton, Alberta, 1989.

14. Questionnaire answered by Joe Garbus, Westhaven, Conn., 1989.

15. Robert G. McCandless, *Yukon Wildlife: A Social History* (Edmonton: University of Alberta Press, 1985).

16. This issue, particularly as it relates to the Yukon, is described in Ken Coates, "The Sinews of Their Lives: Aboriginal Resource Use and the Law in the Yukon Territory, 1894–1950," in K. Abel and J. Friesen, eds., *Aboriginal Resource Use and the Law* (forthcoming).

17. YTA, YRG 1, ser. 3, vol. 10, file 12-20C, R. Sampson to D.M. MacKay, 20 May 1944, G. Jeckell to R.A. Gibson, 20 July 1944.

18. John Marchand, "Tribal Epidemics in the Yukon," *Journal of the American Medical Association* 123 (1943): 1019–20. See also YTA, Anglican Church, Champagne file, S. Webb to Bishop, 9 July 1943.

19. Interview with Daniel Johnson, January 1988.

20. YTA, YRG 1, ser. 1, vol. 9, file 149B, pt. J, C.K. LeCapelain to R.A. Gibson, 17 July 1943.

21. *Northern Lights* (newsletter of the Anglican Diocese of Yukon) 32, no. 1 (February 1943): 2. Bessie Johnston received a citation from Dr. P.E. Moore, superintendent of medical services, Indian Affairs Department, for her work during the epidemic.

22. J. Honigman, letter to the editor, *Journal of the American Medical Association* 124 (1944): 386.

23. NAC, RG 85, vol. 1872, file 550-2-1, D.J. Martin to Constable, RCMP, Watson Lake, 19 April 1943.

24. NAC, RG 85, vol. 916, file 11032, J.P. Harvey to Secretary, Indian Affairs Branch, 31 October 1942.

25. Interview with Kitty Grant, January 1988.

26. NAC, RG 85, vol. 1872, file 550-2-1, Const. J.D. Waring to O.C., RCMP, Whitehorse, 21 April 1943.

27. NA, RG 338, NWSC, box 26, file 314.7, Organization Histories, Annual Report, Post Surgeon, Post of Whitehorse, 1943, 26.

28. See Ken Coates, "The Alaska Highway and the Indians of the Southern Yukon," and Julie Cruikshank, "The Gravel Magnet," in Kenneth Coates, ed., *The Alaska Highway: Papers of the 40th Anniversary Symposium* (Vancouver: UBC Press, 1985).

29. *Edmonton Journal*, 11 April 1944.

30. NA, RG 338, box 47, Field Memo Book, General Orders No. 50, 23 August 1943, Section III: Limits (such orders were occasionally extended to entire Indian settlements); ibid., NWSC, box 9, General

Orders, 1944, General Orders No. 50: Off-Limits, 14 September 1943 (relating to the community of Tanacross, Alaska).

31. NAC, RG 85, vol. 1872, file 550-2-1, Inspector W. Grennan to N.C.O. in Charge, RCMP, Selkirk, 20 October 1942.

32. John and I. Honigman, "Drinking in an Indian-White Community," *Quarterly Journal of Studies on Alcohol* 5 (March 1945): 575–619.

33. See Ken Coates and Judith Powell, *The Modern North* (Toronto: James Lorimer, 1989).

34. These were formally known as the Mackenzie Valley Pipeline Inquiry and the Alaska Highway Pipeline Inquiry, respectively.

35. NWSC, microfilm reel 16, United States Defense Construction Projects in Canada, Minutes of Meeting, c. 1944.

36. NAC, RG 36/7, vol. 1, file 3-3, W.J. Taylor to Dr. J.A. Urquhart, 23 July 1943.

37. NAC, RG 85, vol. 608, file 2614, R.A. Gibson to J.M. Wardle, 19 June 1946.

38. Ibid., R.A. Gibson to R.M. Brown, 22 July 1946.

39. YTA, YRG 1, ser. 1, vol. 69, file 21, RCMP Report: Forest Fires—Kluane Lake District, 5 October 1943; Jeckell to R.A. Gibson, 4 September 1943.

40. NAC, RG 85, vol. 944, file 12725A, Dave Wilson to George Black, 9 September 1943; ibid., vol. 1512, file 1000/200, pt. 1, C.K. LeCapelain to R.A. Gibson, 15 October 1943. A cord is 8 feet long, thus 18 000 cords are 144 000 feet or 27.43 miles long—an impressive pile.

41. YTA, YRG 1, ser. 1, vol. 6, file 466i, R.A. Gibson to C.K. LeCapelain, 10 March 1943.

42. Ibid., R.A. Gibson to C.K. LeCapelain, 22 March 1943.

43. YTA, YRG 1, ser. 8, file 466-3a, F.H.R. Jackson to R.A. Gibson, 6 August 1945.

44. YTA, YRG 1, ser. 1, vol. 6, file 466i, C.K. LeCapelain to R.A. Gibson, 1 April 1943.

45. YTA, YRG 1, ser. 1, vol. 6, file 466iii, George Black to Jeckell, 23 March 1942; ibid., ser. 3, vol. 10, pt. 2 of 2, file 12-20A, G.A. Jeckell to R.A. Gibson, 22 September 1942.

46. NAC, RG 126, vol. 37, Testimony by Joe Jacquot before the Berger Commission, 21 April 1976. Jacquot also spoke of rumors that fighter planes had shot caribou and moose in open areas. McCandless, *Yukon Wildlife*, argues for a limited loss of game. For the Native perspective, see "The Gravel Magnet."

47. YTA, YRG 1, ser. 1, vol. 6, file 4661, LeCapelain to R.A. Gibson, 1 September 1942.

48. YTA, YRG 1, ser. 3, vol. 10, file 12-20, RCMP Patrol—Kluane to Yukon-Alaska Border and Rtd., 30 November 1943.

49. Ibid., Jeckell to Cronkite, 24 December 1943, 5 January 1944, Harrison Lewis to Mr. Smart, 2 November 1945.

50. NAC, RG 84, vol. 1390, file 406-11, vol. 1-A, Indians of Burwash Landing to J.E. Gibben, 23 June 1946.

51. YTA, YRG 1, ser. 1, vol. 6, file 466i, LeCapelain to Gibson 1 September 1942.

52. NAC, RG 85, vol. 944, file 12743, pt. 2, J. A. Phillips to Mountie, 17 August 1944.

53. YTA, YRG 1, ser. 1, vol. 6, file 466i, LeCapelain to Gibson, 1 September 1942.

54. Interview with Charlie Taylor, Whitehorse, January 1988.

55. McCandless, *Yukon Wildlife*.

56. YTA, YRG 1, ser. 3, vol. 10, file 12-20B, pt. 2 of 3, L.A. Pierre to Prentiss Brown, 16 April 1943, C.K. LeCapelain to J.S. Bright, 12 June 1943.

57. Interview with Leslie H. (Bud) Schnurstein, May 1988.

58. Interview with Jim and Iris Sutton, June 1988. The incident described took place near Dawson Creek.

59. NAC, RG 85, vol. 944, file 12743, pt. 1, C.K. LeCapelain to R.A. Gibson, 3 January 1943.

60. YTA, Miscellaneous Manuscripts 37–38, Heath Twichell to "My Dear Ones," 3 June 1942.

61. YTA, YRG 1, ser. 3, vol. 17, pt. 2 of 2, file 28798, S.H. Rosen of Saskatoon Tannery Co. to George Black, 10 September 1943.

62. Ibid., Cronkite to O.C., "G" Division, 29 October 1943. The fact that the RCMP should concern itself with a matter so far from its jurisdiction shows how wide-ranging its influence over the lives of the Native people was.

63. NAC, RG 126, vol. 37, Testimony of Joe Jacquot before the Berger Commission.

64. YTA, YRG 1, ser. 3, vol. 17, pt. 2 of 2, Alleged Unlawful Pollution of Streams—Complaint of Mrs. D. Mackintosh, 20 August 1943.

65. YTA, YRG 1, ser. 3, vol. 10, file 12-20B, G.A. Jeckell to R.A. Gibson, 15 June 1943.

66. YTA, YRG 1, ser. 3, vol. 10, file 12-20A, pt. 2 of 2, Ira Gabrielson to Hoyes Lloyd, Supt. of Wildlife Protection, 31 October 1942.

67. NAC, RG 85, vol. 944, file 12743, pt. 1, R.A. Gibson to Ira Gabrielson, 15 January 1943.

68. YTA, YRG 1, ser. 3, vol. 10, file 12-20B, W.E. Crouch to R.A. Gibson, 3 February 1943.

69. Ibid., Gibson to Jeckell, 3 June 1943.

70. YTA, YRG 1, ser. 3, vol. 10, file 12-20, Advance Release AMS of Wednesday, 20 October 1943.

71. YTA, YRG 1, ser. 3, vol. 10, file 12-20B, pt. 2 of 3, Hoffmaster to Gibson, 23 August 1943, Gibson to Hoffmaster, 27 August 1943. See also NAC, RG 85, vol. 1160, file 331-2/200-1, G.E.B.S. to Mr. Gibson, 13 April 1943.

72. Morris Zaslow, *Reading the Rocks: The Story of the Geological Survey of Canada, 1842–1872* (Toronto: Macmillan, 1975).

73. YTA, YRG 1, ser. 3, vol. 10, file 12-20A, pt. 1 of 2, F.R. Butler to Jeckell, 9 March 1942.

74. YTA, YRG 1, ser. 3, vol. 10, file 12-20B, F.C. Lynch to R.A. Gibson, 8 June 1943, Memorandum by R.M. Anderson, 8 June 1943, Gibson to Jeckell, 10 June 1943.

75. NA, RG 30, vol. 187, file 003.12-Canada, H. Raup to W.E. Thorne, 24 September 1943.

76. YTA, YRG 1, ser. 3, vol. 14, file 241-5, R.A. Gibson to G.A. Jeckell, 18 May 1944; ibid., vol. 17, file 28798, pt. 2 of 2, D.H. Sutherland to Commissioner, RCMP, 28 March 1944.

77. YTA, YRG 1, ser. 3, vol. 14, file 241-5, R.A. Gibson to Jeckell, 31 May 1944.

78. McCandless, *Yukon Wildlife*, examines this process.

79. As this relates to the Yukon Territory, see Ken Coates, "Upsetting the Rhythms: The Federal Government and Native Communities in the Yukon Territory, 1945 to 1973," in Gurston Dacks and Ken Coates, eds., *Northern Communities: The Prospects for Empowerment* (Edmonton: Boreal Institute for Northern Studies, 1988).

TRADITIONAL ECOLOGICAL KNOWLEDGE AND ENVIRONMENTAL ASSESSMENT*

DENE CULTURAL INSTITUTE

o

For thousands of years, aboriginal peoples around the world have exploited the natural resources of their local environment in an ecologically sustainable manner. Only recently has this knowledge, built up over generations of careful observation and experience, begun to be recognized among the western scientific community as a valuable source of ecological information. Variously labelled as folk or ethno-ecology, traditional environmental/ecological knowledge, or customary law, a growing body of literature attests not only to the presence of a vast reservoir of information regarding plant and animal behaviour, but also to the existence of effective indigenous systems of self-management which rely upon a sophisticated data base to determine strategies for conserving natural resources.

The purpose of this paper is to provide an overview of traditional ecological knowledge (TEK) field of study. Also identified are some of the major methodological, environmental, political and socio-cultural issues arising from efforts to document TEK, and to integrate it with scientific environmental assessment and management. The information presented is drawn primarily from a literature search, although it is by no means exhaustive. It must be stressed that, of the limited attempts to date to integrate traditional knowledge into the environmental assessment and management processes, few results have been published in reports, and most efforts have not been subjected to a formal evaluation. Thus, many of the issues raised in this paper are based solely upon the personal opinions of a

* Reprinted with permission of the Canadian Environmental Assessment Research Council. This article originally appeared in the unpublished report "Traditional Ecological Knowledge and Environment Assessment" edited by Barry Sadler and Peter Boothnoyd (March 1993), 6–27.

limited number of persons interviewed during the course of the study. Although some general references are made to the work of international agencies and to specific research projects occurring outside of Canada, the primary focus of the review is northern Canada, which clearly stands at the forefront of research about traditional knowledge.

The paper begins with an overview of the development of western scientific interest in traditional ecological knowledge. Reference is made to the issues that have been addressed by individual scholars and a number of national and international organizations holding an interest in the subject. The second section explains the nature and transmission of traditional ecological knowledge and compares it to western science within the context of ecological observations and resource management. Section three examines the different methodological approaches that have been tried or are being tested in the documentation of traditional knowledge. Section four reviews several examples of efforts to integrate traditional knowledge into the environmental management and assessment processes. The paper concludes with a discussion of the key issues surrounding the subject, together with recommendations for future action to further the recognition of the value of traditional ecological knowledge to western science.

WESTERN SCIENTIFIC RECOGNITION OF TRADITIONAL ECOLOGICAL KNOWLEDGE

Natural scientists working in different parts of the world have often remarked on the ability of indigenous people to distinguish and name many of the plants and animals in their environment.[1] In many instances, a close correspondence has been found to exist between the categories of plants and animals named by aboriginal peoples and the scientific taxa. Much of this knowledge also appears to be clearly esoteric for many of the named species serve no obvious utilitarian purpose.

The systematic study of traditional ecological knowledge began in a series of studies eliciting and analyzing the terminologies by which people in different cultures classify the objects in their natural and social environments. The studies of classification systems have shown that all peoples recognize what they consider to be natural classes of animals and plants and that peoples in all cultures are as much concerned to bring classificatory order to their world as are western scientists.[2]

The results of these early anthropological studies served to enhance the recognition of traditional knowledge among some members of the scientific community. At the same time, increased political pressure to recognize the rights of aboriginal peoples (often within the context of land claims), coupled with a growing international awareness of the important role of traditional knowledge and self-management in achieving sustainable development, has resulted in a shift away from more esoteric studies to applied research. Emphasis in recent years has focussed on understanding the ecologically sound practices that contribute to sustainable resource use among indigenous peoples, and ways that this knowledge can be successfully integrated with western scientific resource management.

One of the catalysts to spark the international surge of interest in traditional knowledge was the 1980 *World Conservation Strategy* (WCS) developed by the International Union for the Conservation of Nature (IUCN), the United Nations Environmental Programme (UNEP), the United Nations Educational, Scientific and Cultural Organization (UNESCO), the World Wildlife Fund (WWF), and the Food and Agriculture Organization (FAO).[3] The document focussed worldwide attention on the global environmental crisis and provided a framework and practical guidance for the conservation actions necessary to ensure the sustainable utilization of the planet's species and ecosystems. Part of the means to achieve sustainable development, it suggested, is to recognize traditional knowledge as an important source of ecological information and to involve local people directly in the management of natural resources.

The recommendations of the *World Conservation Strategy* were further echoed in the publication of the World Commission on Environment and Development report, *Our Common Future (The Brundtland Report).*[4] The report called for the development of a science based on the priorities of local people and the creation of a technological base that blends both traditional and modern approaches to problem solving.

The recommendations of the *World Conservation Strategy* and *Our Common Future* are being incorporated into the Inuit Regional Conservation Strategy (IRCS) developed through the work of the Inuit Circumpolar Conference and its Environmental Commission. The IRCS represents the first attempt to apply the World Conservation Strategy on a regional basis (in an international sense) and the first attempt by an indigenous people to develop a conservation strategy that stresses the importance of traditional knowledge in resource management.[5]

Within Canada, research incorporating traditional knowledge was part of several milestone land use and occupancy studies in the Northwest Territories and Labrador during the late 1970s. The Inuit Land Use and Occupancy Project[6] and the Mackenzie Valley Pipeline Inquiry[7] documented information about the land use of the Inuit, and the Dene and Metis peoples respectively. A similar study entitled *Our Footprints are Everywhere* documented similar information for the Inuit of Labrador.[8] In addition to delimiting the present and past use and occupation of the land and marine environment, these studies demonstrated the important cultural significance of the land for Native people.

Since the late 1970s, research in the Canadian North has turned to understanding indigenous systems of self-regulation and conservation practices and to investigating the possibilities of indigenous self-management of fish and game resources.[9] Much of this interest has stemmed from the increasing conflict and competition between Native and non-Native interests in resource use, particularly hydro-electric power development in Northern Quebec.

Community-based research about traditional environmental knowledge has been carried out by a number of northern communities themselves. Among the Dene, the indigenous people of the western Canadian Subarctic, papers by DeLancey and T'Seleie describe the work done in Fort

Good Hope on a project to document the traditional knowledge of animal behaviour.[10] The Fort Resolution Oral History project included ecological knowledge in its study.[11] Traditional ecological knowledge has also been collected as part of land use planning studies, the work of language centres, and the Dene Mapping Project. Most recently, the Dene Cultural Institute has initiated a long-term research project to continue the work of documenting Dene traditional ecological knowledge.[12] The ultimate goal of this research project is to integrate this knowledge into the environmental assessment, management, and land use planning processes.

A number of governments are also beginning to recognize the value of traditional knowledge and appear to support its role in environmental management. For example, the Government of the Northwest Territories recently affirmed that decisions about resource management and development will reflect the traditional knowledge which can be found in Northern communities. In keeping with this policy, the territorial Department of Renewable Resources has identified one of its goals as "the maximum involvement of local residents and the maximum use of their knowledge in renewable resource programs."[13]

On the international scene, the themes of traditional knowledge and local resource management are increasingly being discussed through the work of various international agencies, such as the International Union for the Conservation of Nature and Natural Resources (IUCN), the International Union of Biological Sciences, UNESCO Man and Biosphere Programme, and the United Nations Environment Programme. In May 1988, the IUCN hosted an international conference in Costa Rica with the purpose of developing a set of guidelines for the documentation and use of traditional knowledge.[14] As well, the IUCN Commission on Ecology has an active Traditional Ecological Knowledge Working Group that publishes an occasional newsletter, *Tradition, Conservation and Development*. Outside of Canada, local self-management of terrestrial and marine resources has been described in India,[15] in New Guinea,[16] in Indonesia,[17] and in the south Pacific islands.[18] In South America, research initiatives have been undertaken on traditional agricultural systems.[19] To date, outside of Canada, there appear to have been few attempts paid to the application of traditional knowledge to environmental assessment.[20]

One of the most extensive bibliographies about traditional knowledge was compiled by Andrews.[21] Originally prepared for the Dene Nation, the political body representing the Dene, the bibliography references over 200 studies of indigenous peoples' traditional ecological knowledge and management systems.

THE NATURE AND TRANSMISSION OF TRADITIONAL ECOLOGICAL KNOWLEDGE

Traditional ecological knowledge is the body of knowledge or natural history built up by a group of people through generations of living in close contact with nature. It includes a system of classification, a set of empirical observations about the local ecology, and a system of self-management that governs hunting, trapping, and fishing. Ecological knowledge and the rules for sustainable resource management are accumulated over generations and passed on by word of mouth (often through stories) and by direct experience. The legitimacy and authority for traditional resource management are determined at the local level. Any deviation from these rules and understandings is met by social pressure as necessary.[22] Although the terms traditional knowledge and self-management are most often used in reference to aboriginal peoples, community-based knowledge and systems of self-management may also be found among other groups of resource users, such as outport fishermen and farmers.

THE NATURE AND INTERPRETATION OF ECOLOGICAL OBSERVATIONS

Within northern Canada and Alaska, research about indigenous knowledge of specific components of ecosystems has been carried out by a number of scholars. For example, studies have been conducted on the behaviour of moose, [23] beaver,[24] geese,[25] wolves,[26] and eiders,[27] on ethnobotany,[28] on the use of coastal and marine resources,[29] on Inuit bird taxonomy,[30] and on the use of arctic sea-ice resources.[31] Most of these studies attempt to compare specific elements of the indigenous knowledge system to parallel elements in the scientific system.

For the purpose of this paper, examples of the nature and extent of traditional ecological observations are discussed in reference to the works of Feit, Gunn et al., and Stephenson, who worked among the James Bay Cree of Northern Quebec, the Inuit of the western Canadian arctic, and the Nunamiut of northern Alaska respectively.[32]

Feit examined James Bay Cree knowledge of moose and beaver.[33] In the case of beaver, information about the composition of beaver colonies is continually collected by Waswanipi Cree hunters from signs around the sites, from the sizes and sexes of the beaver caught, and from information collected in the process of butchering beaver. Such knowledge is sought in order to determine how many beaver are present and how many may be taken. Similar patterns of monitoring occur for moose, although for a more dispersed population. The numbers of occupied moose yards, the size of yarding groups, the frequency with which females are accompanied by young, and the frequency of twin young are all noted and discussed by hunters.

In both cases, Feit remarks that the parameters monitored by the Cree are all ones which wildlife biologists have found to be important indicators of the condition of the game populations. These indicators are useful for management decisions concerning the sustainability of present harvests. Absolute numbers are not recorded, but trends in the basic parameters are noted and discussed by Waswanipi hunters.

Regarding the distribution and use of knowledge within a community, Feit explains that the monitoring of indicators and the type of information hunters use is not universally available within a local community. This knowledge is typically synthesized only by a limited number of people who generally are leaders in hunting activities. Cree hunting bosses are aided in their judgments of the significance of trends in the wildlife populations on their hunting lands by hearing from others on whether similar trends are occurring elsewhere. For knowledge of current trends to be meaningful, it is also necessary that hunting leaders know the history of the wildlife populations which they are observing. This permits the evaluation of the duration and intensity of the trends, as well as making it possible to relate different points in the development of the trends to specific changes in the environment or to the history of harvesting intensity.

Although hunters and scientists may apply the same ecological indicators in their respective management regimes, the level of information available to the aboriginal hunter differs from that available to the scientist. From their work among the Inuit of the western Canadian Arctic, Gunn et al. noted that scientists have the advantage of being able to draw upon the extensive ecological knowledge gathered in many parts of the world for comparison and, with the help of technology, can observe wildlife over large areas or beneath the ice and water.[34]

Aboriginal hunters, on the other hand, have a reservoir of ecological knowledge that has been accumulated over generations. For instance, the arctic ecosystem is characterized by annual variations in the abundance and distribution of wildlife—a single or two seasons' observations can be misleading. The observations of hunters can thus be a valuable guide to some of the longer-term changes in wildlife distribution and behaviour. Similarly, the extensive travel of hunters during winter months leads to observations of behaviour unparalleled by biologists whose winter observations of arctic wildlife are often lacking.

Gunn et al. suggest that the difference between the two knowledge systems lies not so much in the type of observation (quantitative versus qualitative), but in the organization of the observations and the physical recording of them, which for the scientist usually has to be sufficiently detailed to be repeatable or comparable.

> Inuit hunters rarely question observations related by others and do not always ascribe more importance to multiple than single observations: both these characteristics are vital in small social groups and in preparing a hunter for often rare contingencies. The same characteristics are, however, the antithesis of science.[35]

Similarly, biologist Robert Stephenson notes from his studies of wolves in northern Alaska that the Nunamiut are willing to attribute more importance to individual variation and to volition than are biologists.

> The Nunamiut . . . believe that some decisions wolves make are likely to be foolish, "inefficient," or ambiguous of interpretation. In contrast, it appears that biologists, and even more so the wildlife-oriented public, look for "adaptive" value in most details of animal behaviour. The wolves I observed did many things that Western

science normally refers to as anecdotal behaviour, but which the Nunamiut believed contained rather significant information.[36]

Stephenson submits that scientists may be reluctant to recognize these elements of volition, instinct and individual idiosyncrasy because they are difficult to quantify. Nevertheless, he stresses, biologists must recognize this side of wolf behaviour and understand that "wolf populations are not composed of identical individuals or packs guided in their every move by ironclad laws of nature."[37]

Stephenson affirms that his work among the Nunamiut forced him to recognize an important difference between the generalized knowledge of an animal obtained through reading, and a more specific working knowledge derived from field experience. His own generalized knowledge, he claims, had actually interfered with his ability to comprehend the behaviour he observed. One must guard against the tendency to gloss over exceptions in the search for general laws, he argues, for it may be that the anomalies observed represent potentially important aspects of animal behaviour.

INDIGENOUS AND STATE SYSTEMS OF WILDLIFE MANAGEMENT

Although the observations of scientists and aboriginal peoples may be similar, their explanations of how the ecosystem works are based on two different world views. Western science separates the natural and the physical world from the human world. Phenomena are explained in terms of a set of laws which are continually tested over time through the accumulation of more quantified data. The natural environment is viewed as something that can be readily manipulated by humans to serve their needs. Aboriginal cultures, on the other hand, perceive humans and nature as being inextricably linked. The system of beliefs and values of the indigenous society are their basis for explaining the natural and the physical world.

Two distinct epistemologies underlie the indigenous and the state systems of resource management. Usher has outlined the different characteristics of the state and the indigenous systems of resource management as follows:

> The state system rests on a common property concept in which the state assumes exclusive responsibility and capability for managing a resource equally accessible to all citizens. The state manages for certain levels of abundance on a technical basis, and then allocates shares of this abundance to users on an economic and political basis. The system and management problems are resolved in a technical . . . framework.

In contrast:

> The indigenous system rests on communal property arrangements, in which the local harvesting group is responsible for management by consensus. Management and harvesting are conceptually and

practically inseparable. Knowledge comes from the experience of every aspect of harvesting itself—travelling, searching, hunting, skinning, butchering and eating.[38]

HOW THE INDIGENOUS SYSTEM OF SELF-MANAGEMENT WORKS

What are the practices employed by aboriginal peoples that ensure the exploitation of ecological resources in an environmentally sustainable manner? The ability to use resources sustainably stems from a combination of two factors: (a) the possession of appropriate local ecological knowledge and suitable methods/technology to exploit resources, and (b) a philosophy and environmental ethic to keep exploitive abilities in check and to provide ground rules by which the relation among humans and animals may be regulated.

Conservation management strategies have been recorded by a number of researchers working in Canada and in other parts of the world. For example, studies by anthropologists Scott of goose hunting and Feit of beaver and moose hunting among the James Bay Cree showed that hunters follow a system of rotation and "resting" of hunting sites.[39] According to Feit, many Cree trappers divide their hunting area into three or four units. They trap only one unit at a time and rotate the land similar to fallowing in agriculture. Feit's investigation of the system revealed that the harvest from an area rested for two years or more was significantly greater than that from an area harvested with no rest.

Berkes discusses the importance of the trapline system in the regulation of the use of wildlife resources among the James Bay Cree.[40] As recognized by the government, a trapline is a registered beaver trapping area in which a Cree tallyman or family head has harvesting rights. As seen by the Cree people, a trapline is a traditional family hunting-trapping territory. Accordingly, any violations are dealt with by social pressures rather than by recourse to state law. Only those people who are family members of the tallyman or who have been given permission by him can trap beaver on a trapline. Other people passing through the area can take animals which they encounter. By mutual agreement, there is no permission requirement for such people, and they can harvest animals, especially fish and small game, for their immediate food needs. The workability of this land tenure system is helped by the fact that hunting and fishing are normally done on a subsistence basis.

Elsewhere in the world, Johannes explains how reef and lagoon tenure was an important marine conservation measure employed in Oceania.[41] The right to fish in a particular area was controlled by a clan, chief, or family, who thus regulated the exploitation of their own marine resources. Fishing rights were maintained from the beach to the seaward edge of the outer reefs. In some areas, where the fishermen sought tuna in offshore "holes," fishing tenure included deep waters beyond the reef. It was in the best interest of those who controlled a given area to harvest in moderation. By doing so they could maintain high sustained yields, all the benefits of which would accrue directly to them. Other conservation measures were related to religious beliefs or taboos. For example, the eating of certain species was forbidden to particular clans, castes, age groups, or to women.

THE LIMITATIONS OF THE INDIGENOUS SYSTEM

One of the major questions raised by scientists and wildlife managers regarding the indigenous system is whether or not self-regulating systems that existed in the past continue to function effectively today, given the very significant changes now occurring in the North.[42] Berkes and Feit discuss several examples in Northern Quebec where the indigenous system has broken down as a result of outside influences.[43]

One of the main causes for the breakdown of self-management systems may be attributed to the commercialization of the subsistence hunt.[44] Incentive to create surplus breaks down the self-limiting principle of a subsistence operation and, together with it, the customary laws that regulate hunter-prey relations. Both Johannes and Berkes equate the commercialization of subsistence fisheries in the south Pacific and Northern Quebec respectively with overfishing in these areas.[45]

Also, Feit provides a few examples of self-management breakdown, particularly in northern Canada.[46] This is perhaps not surprising given the constantly changing and unpredictable environment of the North. What conclusions may be drawn from the limited observations available? The history of self-management is neither a history of continual success nor a history of continual and cumulative failures. Rather it is a history of the efforts to adapt and maintain self-management to changing circumstances. Moreover, as Berkes remarks, in cases where the root cause of the perturbation is dealt with, customary law becomes operative once again and the system recovers.[47] In other cases, there may be a permanent change; the ground rules are redefined and the system adapts to change. Under these circumstances, it is possible that the adaptations may not come about smoothly or rapidly and as a result there may be social disruption, which may contribute to poor conservation practices during the period of adjustment.

Regardless of whether self-management systems remain viable today, they may not be able to deal effectively with all of the problems local wildlife managers presently face. As Feit points out, local wildlife-resource users are only rarely isolated from the impacts of the international economic system or of state policy-making with respect to wildlife and development.[48] National and international commercial interests, sport interests, [and] nonrenewable resource developments are all often beyond the direct influence of the practitioners of traditional self-management systems. Consequently, traditional forms of self-management must respond to these threats to wildlife resources and to environments by extending self-management to new forms which regulate the actions of individuals and agencies outside the local or regional groups.

Another threat to the indigenous system is that rules, once widely followed, are no longer being passed down to the younger generation.[49]

Through the process of acculturation, new authority figures (school teachers, outside experts etc.) begin to displace the elders, reducing the likelihood of compliance with previously held social norms. Additionally, students attending conventional schools have few opportunities to learn the traditional skills of living off the land from their elders. Nevertheless, as Osherenko points out, most anthropologists working in the North and Native people themselves confirm the continued vitality of aboriginal cultures, and note that social norms and practices are changing or evolving rather than dying.[50] Therefore, it must not be assumed that customary law is no longer protecting wildlife in the North.

THE LIMITATIONS OF THE STATE SYSTEM OF WILDLIFE MANAGEMENT

While the indigenous system of resource management may have its limitations, it must not be forgotten that state management also has its share of problems, particularly in the North. A major obstacle to effective scientific wildlife management practices in northern Canada is the lack of knowledge of the ecology available to wildlife managers. As Theberge states:

> The depth of ecological ignorance is relatively greater in the north than elsewhere in Canada. . . . For example, a large increase in the size of the Kaminuriak herd in 1982 cannot be interpreted. It may have been due to census error, or in-migration, or in part to significantly higher than normal survivorship of calves.[51]

A second obstacle is the scale of the environment with which scientists and managers have to deal.[52] This is simply too large and complex to allow an understanding of all the interrelationships between the different components. Hence, it is difficult to conduct experiments and to extrapolate the results. As a result of these shortcomings, the managerial response has often been to depend very heavily on assumptions to fill the gaps.[53]

The problem is enhanced by the often highly specialized education that scientists receive as opposed to a more interdisciplinary approach. As Riewe and Gamble point out, wildlife managers are usually well-trained in zoology, botany, ecology, statistics, and computer sciences, but they are inadequately trained in the social sciences, including anthropology, linguistics, psychology, and sociology.[54] When a southern-trained biologist accepts a northern position, he or she usually arrives without any cross-cultural experience and is replete with southern cultural myths of the North and Native peoples. As Riewe and Gamble observe, "all too often these southerners believe that traditional Native management of wildlife was based merely on the fact that their hunting technology was so crude that they were unable to over-exploit their environment."[55]

Another problem with the state system is that the nature of its operation is fundamentally ill-suited to aboriginal communities. As Osherenko points out:

> It often relies on cumbersome paper-work (licenses, harvest tickets, reports), which is impractical in communities based on individual

bag limits rather than community needs. It relies on seasonal limits and gear restrictions that are often at odds with subsistence needs. Ultimately, it enforces by fine, forfeiture, seizure, and even personal confinement, rather than by social pressure to conform to community standards. Understandably, compliance with governmental rules is generally low.[56]

However, she notes, there are some efforts on the part of public authorities to adapt the system to meet indigenous needs. For example, regulators try to match seasonal restrictions with users' seasonal needs. The Northwest Territories Department of Renewable Resources issues general hunting licenses annually to Natives (permitting them to hunt in any season for subsistence needs and to trap in accordance with season restrictions), and agencies in Northern Quebec do not impose regulations on Native users except in cases of conservation need, and then only after consultation. Although these adjustments solve some of the problems of dualism, they fail to give indigenous users a sense of ownership in the decision-making process and do not address the difficult issues that arise when state managers fear overexploitation of a species.

TOWARDS AN INTEGRATION OF THE TWO SYSTEMS

A pivotal question in the whole discussion of traditional knowledge is the role it should play in the environmental management process. A complementary question is whether or not the state and the indigenous systems of resource management should develop separately or whether an integrated approach is the desired goal. There appears to be agreements among most scientists, governments, and aboriginal peoples that integration of the two systems is necessary given the pluralistic nature of society, and the fact that the decisions and actions of one group, no matter how autonomous, invariably have implications for other groups.[57] Furthermore, information obtained when either system operates alone is often incomplete and can lead to inaccurate conclusions. Thus both sets of data are necessary to produce a full ecological picture.

Despite considerable discussion regarding the most effective and just means to integrate the two systems, no one to date has been able to describe what a truly integrated state/indigenous wildlife or environmental management arrangement would look like or what the best approach to attain this ideal would be. Mulvihill submits that it would be inappropriate to attempt to achieve complete integration of the two systems:

The indigenous system, for example, should not attempt to duplicate or reinforce bureaucratic top-down hierarchical structures— they are antithetical to its practices. Integration of the two systems need not necessarily dilute the essence of either system, nor should it invalidate the underlying principles of either one. To embrace some of the epistemology of the indigenous system would not automatically imply the death of science for the state system. Instead, it might only mean that the scientific method was itself subjected to the same kind of rigourous scrutiny that it inflicts upon the phenomena which it encounters.[58]

In northern Canada, the future development of both systems must be considered within the context of devolution. The devolution of powers to the regional or local level in the Northwest Territories, through such vehicles as Native claims settlements, transfer of powers from federal to territorial or local authorities, and the establishment of cooperative management boards, is currently in progress. Usher sees devolution taking two forms: the movement of authority and responsibility from a higher to a lower level within an established and intact framework, or the actual transfer of authority and responsibility from one system to another, which implies a transformation of the management paradigm.[59] In regard to resource management Usher states, "Devolution is a necessary but not sufficient condition for conservation. Self-management, in a context where the necessary self-regulating mechanisms can operate effectively, is also needed. How do we get there?"[60]

At present, co-management regimes represent the most widespread attempt to integrate the two systems.

A co-management regime is an institutional arrangement in which government agencies with jurisdiction over resources and user groups enter into an agreement covering a specific geographic region and spelling out: 1) a system of rights and obligations for those interested in the resource; 2) a collection of rules indicating actions that subjects are expected to take under various circumstances; and 3) procedures for making collective decisions affecting the interests of government actors, user organizations, and individual users.[61]

Seven wildlife co-management regimes have been created in the North American Arctic to solve problems caused by clashes between indigenous and state systems of wildlife management, and several others are in various stages of evolution.[62] These include the James Bay and Northern Quebec hunting, fishing, and trapping regime, the Alaskan whaling regime (Bering and Beaufort Seas; Alaskan whaling communities), the Beverly and Kaminuriak caribou management regime (central Canadian Arctic), the Inuvialuit wildlife harvesting and management regime (Inuvialuit Settlement Region within the NWT), the Beluga management regime (Northern Quebec), the Canadian Porcupine caribou herd management regime (northwestern Canada, Yukon and NWT), and the Pacific walrus regime (coastal areas of northwestern Alaska). These regimes vary in their structure and in the degree of power accorded the participating user groups.[63] Most of these co-management regimes have been in existence for less than ten years, and it is difficult to draw any firm conclusions regarding their degree of success or failure. From her evaluation of the Beverly-Kaminuriak Caribou Management Plan, the Northern Quebec Beluga

Management Plan and the Yukon-Kuskokwim Delta Goose Management Plan in Alaska, Osherenko concludes that co-management in these cases has at least produced improved communication and understanding between Native users and public authorities.[64] In addition, the cases suggest that co-management has changed hunting practices in the interests of protecting declining species.

Nevertheless, in spite of an obvious step forward in bringing the state and the indigenous systems together to help solve environmental problems, these boards have only an advisory capacity. The question remains to what extent these boards actually incorporate new innovative strategies to problem solving, as opposed to using traditional knowledge merely to provide data for a decentralized state system, which continues to adhere to the scientific paradigm and to do the managing. The question for the future is whether these boards will be adopted as a model for comprehensive wildlife management under land claims settlements. And if so, which management system will provide the framework and who will retain authority?

If the integration of traditional knowledge and science is the desirable goal, why are there not many more examples of it taking place today? There are several related responses to this question. First, the problem appears to be clearly linked to the question of political power. Co-management may be regarded as an incremental step towards self-management for aboriginal peoples.[65] Second, the present bureaucratic system is unable and or unwilling to respond effectively to the needs of small communities.[66] And third, like most other elite groups in societies worldwide, scientists (as professionals) erect boundaries to keep out threatening ideas that might jeopardize their superior status.[67] This general lack of support at the political, bureaucratic, and scientific level means that there is a chronic lack of sufficient funding over a long enough period of time to enable innovative resource management projects to survive.

METHODS USED TO DOCUMENT TRADITIONAL ECOLOGICAL KNOWLEDGE

THE ETHNOGRAPHIC METHOD

Fieldwork in the area of traditional knowledge for the most part follows standard ethnographic methods. Ethnography is the work of describing a culture. The goal of ethnography, as Malinowski put it, is to "grasp the native's point of view, his relation to life, to realize his vision of his world."[68] A fundamental principle of ethnographic research is that it is based on fieldwork: the research is conducted on the group's home ground.[69] Information may be collected through surveys, directed interviews, or open-ended interviews, in a variety of settings. Interviews may be conducted with one individual at a time or in a group setting, either in a community or in bush camps. The most appropriate setting is often the camp, rather than the permanent settlement, and especially at the time when hunting, fishing, and food gathering activities are actively underway.

Another field technique which may be used alone or in conjunction with interviews is participant observation, whereby the researcher participates directly in the daily life of the society under observation. This procedure allows the investigator to observe people's actions and conduct informal discussions in a more natural social setting.

DeLancey reports the value of a combined interview and participation approach used by local residents to gather data in the Fort Good Hope Traditional Knowledge study:

> The Fort Good Hope study successfully combined a straight questionnaire survey method with the more open-ended approach of ethnographic field research. In this approach of ethnographic field research, the community researcher is supplied with a set of open-ended questions which will help to focus discussion on the study goals. The researcher has to use his/her discretion to elicit more detailed responses, to keep the interviews on track and to determine when to draw an informant back to the topic. The researcher's own awareness of the cultural context and linguistic context is an invaluable asset to this process. However, the direct confirmation of data provided by the participant observation technique would strengthen the results.[70]

Feit also used a variety of techniques to document traditional knowledge about moose and moose management systems.[71] He talked to hunters about how to hunt moose, listened to descriptions of specific hunts, asked specific questions about words and expressions used in the Cree language when talking about moose, and participated in casual conversations.

In his study of Northern Quebec Inuit knowledge of eider ecology, Nakashima reports that hunters were interviewed individually or in small groups.[72] Geographic information, which dealt primarily with migration routes, feeding/flocking areas, nesting sites and northern wintering areas, was recorded on large-scale maps or on air photos. Other types of information, such as breeding and feeding ecology and behaviour, were tape-recorded for subsequent transcription. For the actual format of the interview, a rigid style involving formalized sets of questions was avoided because it tended to draw out only short, specific answers. It proved more fruitful, he stated, to open the interview with a simple request to "tell about eiders," because it prompted the Inuit to take the initiative, leading the discussion into topics that they themselves considered important and which otherwise might not have been addressed. He notes that it is important to realize that although interviews provide a certain degree of insight into the nature of Inuit knowledge, they are subject to the shortcomings inherent in imposing the information gathering techniques of one culture upon another. In order to arrive at a true understanding of Inuit knowledge, Nakashima claims, it must be the Inuit who decide upon the information to be gathered and its method of collection.

However, the open-ended interview approach does pose some problems. Unstructured interviewing can become very time consuming and in the long run expensive. Considerable effort must be devoted to sifting through data to find specific types of information. This issue is particularly important to consider when traditional knowledge is to be used in conjunction with scientific data for the purposes of wildlife management or environmental assessment.

COMMUNITY-BASED RESEARCH

Since the coming of the first European explorers and the early missionaries to northern Canada, Native peoples have been the subject of numerous studies seeking to describe various aspects of their ways of life. In more recent years, social scientists representing universities and other academic institutions, government agencies and industry have carried out a variety of research projects. Unfortunately, in many cases, the topics of investigation have had little relevance to the concerns of Native peoples, and more often than not, the results of the studies have not been communicated back to the people who have shared their knowledge. In an effort to alleviate this problem, a growing number of aboriginal groups around the world are now taking measures to acquire control over their own research. This community-based approach to research involves the active participation of communities in determining research priorities and the training of local researchers to carry out all phases of the research process. The fundamental goal is to build a community's capacity for generating knowledge to solve problems.[73]

Within northern Canada, at least two projects are presently taking this approach to research traditional environmental knowledge. The Dene Cultural Institute has mounted a multi-year study to continue the work of documenting the traditional ecological knowledge in all regions of Denendeh with the ultimate goal of applying it to environmental management.[74] One of the primary objectives in carrying out the research is to develop an innovative and appropriate methodology for regional scale, community-based research. On the Belcher Islands, NWT, the Hunters and Trappers Association of Sanikiluaq and researchers from the Boreal Institute, University of Alberta[75] and other universities are attempting to apply the adaptive management approach to a case study in resource management. Both projects are committed to training local residents to assume the various roles necessary to carry out a research project.

TECHNICAL DICTIONARIES

Another approach being used to document traditional ecological knowledge in the community of Marovo Lagoon in the western Solomon Islands is the preparation of a series of technical dictionaries embracing four of the five languages of the area.[76] While the main dictionary is in the dominant Marovo language on the topic Environment and Resources, the others are primarily plant dictionaries listing local names and uses including scientific names. Baines notes that one particular advantage of the technical dictionary approach is that results can be made available to the community quickly.

ECOLOGICAL KNOWLEDGE AND LAND USE STUDIES

In addition to the land use and occupancy studies mentioned earlier, the research department of the Makivik Corporation representing the Inuit of Northern Quebec, has been involved in an ecological knowledge and land use study for the past ten years. The purpose of this research project, which is now drawing to a close, was to provide a precise information base on past and present land use, and on the extensive knowledge hunters have to support their patterns of land use. According to Kemp, information was gathered by individual and group interviews.[77] These interviews resulted in the creation of individual hunter maps by species, season, and time period, and they also resulted in ecological maps for individual species supported by written descriptive notes and taped interviews. All of the information has been compiled on mapping computers according to special programs written to accommodate the data and to produce maps and descriptive texts in Inuktitut.

The research has been funded by the Makivik Corporation in order to ensure Inuit control over the use of the information. The data are presently being used by [the] Kativik School Board for the development of education programs and for the creation of local geographies. The information is also being incorporated into an extensive wildlife management policy and program for Northern Quebec.[78] It is designed to develop a comprehensive approach to management that includes the biology and ecology of resources for subsistence, non-consumptive, and, when warranted, commercial purposes. The objective is to determine a strategy for management that will enable Inuit to identify and maintain healthy wildlife populations, as well as to identify geographic areas or species populations in which problems now occur so that management solutions can be established.

Geographical Information Systems offer another possibility for managing traditional ecological knowledge data. Designed to store and to analyze geographically referenced data through the use of computerized mapping, a GIS could provide a valuable tool to aid in the resource management decision-making process. In the Baffin Island Region, the Environmental Technology Program of Arctic College has explored ways to develop a geographical information system which will incorporate traditional knowledge gathered by students and staff.[79]

THE ADAPTIVE MANAGEMENT APPROACH

Adaptive management is a new approach emerging in the resource sciences that provides a potential methodological framework for helping aboriginal peoples and scientific resource managers to work together to resolve environmental problems. It is an open-ended, systematic process that designs management activities and policies that are responsive to biological changes occurring within a system, based on both indigenous knowledge of ecological relationships and scientific processes of knowledge. It is a concept that has risen from fundamental questioning of conventional scientific approaches to the management of renewable resources, and recognition of the need to develop an alternative, pragmatic approach based on discovering how a "partially observed" system functions.[80] A basic assumption of adaptive management is that socio-economic dynamics are inherent in the utilization of resources and must be taken into consideration if resource management problems are to be alleviated.

Furthermore, adaptive resource scientists question the adequacy of the linear-reductionist mode of inquiry, as they claim there is no assurance that understanding how an ecological system functions at a given moment will provide insight into how it will function under changed circumstances in the future. The act of management itself alters relationships and causes unknown changes within an ecological system, so that systems under study may be changing faster than they can be scientifically understood.[81] The goal is to develop an understanding of the implications of specific management decisions and to explore the response patterns of systems in order to identify new policy instruments and options. Management, as a result, becomes a continual process of analyzing historical experience in relation to ecological theory and constraints and directing searches for productive and sustainable harvesting policies.

Adaptive management is a "learning by doing" process in which all management actions are treated as well-designed experiments that will produce short-term system responses and better information for long-term management decisions.[82] Adaptive management is system-specific and an open-ended process in which there are the following phases of activity:

1. dialogue to determine the goals of management and the boundaries of the problem;

2. field study and analysis to determine the biological relationships that relate to the goals of management;

3. design of alternative management actions in light of (2) above;

4. monitoring and assessment of management actions; and

5. evaluation including determination of likely impact of alternative management options.

Successful implementation of the adaptive management process is dependent on bringing all the actors involved in the management and utilization of a particular resource together, and creating an environment conducive to addressing long-term management concerns. Open communication is integral to guiding field studies, analysis, modelling and consequent judgement about the likely impact of alternative management methods.[83] Dialogue is initiated and continues through a series of structured workshops. The workshops are designed to, first, identify the range of ecological and social variables for consideration in the management of the resource, and, second, to determine through active discussion the alternative methods for management.

As mentioned above, the potential for applying the adaptive management approach to northern renewable resources management is presently being tested in the joint Boreal Institute/Belcher Islands community-based research project. The purpose of this case study is to combine traditional knowledge and scientific investigative techniques to design a management scheme to manage the reindeer and their range on the Belcher Islands.[84]

EXAMPLES OF THE APPLICATION OF TRADITIONAL ECOLOGICAL KNOWLEDGE TO ENVIRONMENTAL ASSESSMENT AND MANAGEMENT

ENVIRONMENTAL MONITORING

For a number of years Native communities have argued for a stronger role in monitoring the effects of energy development in the Canadian North. Everitt reviews two examples where traditional knowledge was incorporated into environmental monitoring programs—the Mackenzie Environmental Monitoring Program and post-construction monitoring by the Dene of the Norman Wells Oilfield expansion.[85] He concludes from examination of these two programs that Native people have an important role to play at all stages of environmental monitoring for energy developments. Everitt observes that, because they are present at all times, "they are the best people to identify priorities for monitoring, the best people to collect harvest statistics, and they are the best people to monitor for local effects."[86]

Everitt recommends that northern communities be given contracts to undertake surveillance and local effects monitoring for those energy development activities that have direct effects (e.g., seismic activity) on the land and its resources. Monitors, he contends, should be responsible to the community and not the development companies as is currently the case. Furthermore, the community should direct the programs, and although scientific expertise would have a role to play, traditional knowledge should also be regarded as an important source of information.

The role of Native groups in monitoring programs designed to determine the regional effects is less clear, Everitt argues. Many of the regional programs have been concerned with determining effects at the population level for important fish and wildlife species. Native groups, he maintains, are at no particular advantage or disadvantage when it comes to mounting these programs. He suggests that the conduct of programs to look at the regional impacts will likely remain in the domain of the scientific community. However, the role of the Native groups will be in setting the scope and priorities of these programs.

Elsewhere, a community environmental monitoring project is being developed as part of the Marovo Lagoon traditional ecological knowledge project in the Solomon Islands.[87] Part of the exercise is to train people in methods of handling information and making conclusions about seasonal trends and causes of these trends. While this is a modern intervention, traditional observations, ideas and approaches will be incorporated into the monitoring package. In summary, the idea is to build on traditional knowledge using appropriate modern interventions.

LAND USE PLANNING

Regional land use planning provides another forum for the integration of traditional knowledge. For example, the 1983 Land Use Planning Basis of Agreement for the Northwest Territories states that:

- plans must reflect regional residents' values and priorities,
- plans must provide for conservation and development of all land and water resources, including the offshore,
- planning should be done in the North by Northerners,
- public participation is essential,
- Native people have special interests and roles to play.[88]

A proposal for a land use plan for the Lancaster Sound region was prepared after two years of consultation with local communities, industries, special interest groups, and government departments and agencies. Traditional knowledge was used in the planning exercise to identify community concerns, and was combined with scientific information to document and map the natural resources and cultural features of the region.[89]

THE CANADIAN FEDERAL ENVIRONMENTAL ASSESSMENT AND REVIEW PROCESS (EARP)

Undoubtedly, the most successful attempt to incorporate traditional knowledge into the environmental assessment process in Canada was the Berger Inquiry in the late 1970s. This process provided an informal forum for Native people to express their concerns about the impacts of the proposed Mackenzie Valley Pipeline. Their opinions, based on traditional knowledge, received important consideration in the final decision-making process.[90] Since the Berger Inquiry, public consultation and review phases have remained the principal methods of including traditional knowledge in environmental assessment. Whether traditional knowledge and the views of aboriginal peoples continue to receive adequate recognition through this forum has been questioned in a number of recent discussion papers and workshops.

One issue of concern raised in the National Consultation Workshop on Federal Environmental Assessment Reform,[91] and also by a number of individuals consulted during the course of writing this paper, was the need for the acceptance of non-technical data provided by non-scientists as a credible source of information. Environmental experts selected as advisors for the EARP process are generally chosen according to their academic and professional qualifications. Most of the aboriginal persons who would be recognized as "experts" in their communities by virtue of their extensive knowledge and understanding about the local environment would not possess the necessary qualifications (based on "southern" standards) that would allow them to participate as technical experts under the current processes.

Another issue raised during workshop discussions and personal interviews was the unequal access of all interested persons to participation in a public review. In many cases, individuals or groups are prevented from full participation because of inadequate financial support, access to "expert" advice, time to analyze documents, and resources to organize participation. In the case of aboriginal peoples, language and cultural differences as well as geographic isolation may exacerbate these inequities. As a result, there may not be adequate opportunities for aboriginal peoples to make panel submissions which evaluate a problem from the perspective of traditional knowledge.

A number of EA panel reports (e.g., Eastern Arctic Offshore Drilling—South Davis Strait Project; Lancaster Sound Drilling) note the lack of available baseline data from government agencies responsible for biological research and management.[92] As has been reiterated throughout this paper, local residents harbour a vast reservoir of knowledge about the local ecosystem that could be utilized to advantage in this part of the environmental assessment process. Current observations about different ecological components, combined with knowledge of historical trends, could aid significantly in understanding the potential impacts of development projects.

Despite its shortcomings, there is evidence that the federal environmental assessment review process is moving towards the recognition of traditional knowledge. For example, the present environmental assessment review of military flying activities in Labrador and Quebec is attempting to involve Native people directly in providing environmental information for the Environmental Impact Statement. As well, the Federal Environmental Assessment Review Office (FEARO) recently hosted a workshop on how aboriginal and other rural communities apply traditional knowledge to resource sustainability. An important theme of the workshop will be how to communicate more effectively with communities that become involved in the environmental assessment process.

DISCUSSION AND CONCLUSION

That non-western cultures should have a profound understanding about the functioning of local ecosystems should come as no surprise. As Feit points out, "there is no reason not to expect that indigenous peoples, any less than people of European descent, would develop a realistic body of knowledge about an environment with which they intensively interact, or that they would use that knowledge to conserve or manage resources which they value."[93]

Only recently has the western scientific community begun to recognize the value of the vast reservoir of ecological knowledge held by the world's aboriginal peoples. This reticence on the part of scientists to accept traditional knowledge and the self-management of wildlife resources may be attributed in large part to their ethnocentric view of science. In this view, not only are those who do not subscribe to the scientists' definition of the problem held to be somehow lacking in their understanding of reality, but also where these scientists have few solid facts to support their assertions, they still expect non-scientists to accept their opinions as if they were statements of fact.[94] Indigenous knowledge systems and forms of self-management are often overlooked because they depend on social institutions and practices unfamiliar in western society, and are fundamentally different from forms of bureaucratic decision-making and highly specialized fields of responsibility which characterize state-mandated wildlife management systems.[95]

Despite the different epistemologies underpinning the two systems of knowledge and resource management, . . . both systems rest upon the foundation of empirical observation and deductive logic, and both seek to manage natural resources in an environmentally sustainable manner.

Much of the scepticism on the part of state resource managers towards the indigenous knowledge system stems from the belief that, while it may have been impressive in its earlier forms, it is being irreversibly eroded by assimilation of aboriginal peoples into western culture, and by the failure of elders to pass on the knowledge to younger generations. In addition, the fact that traditional knowledge is based upon oral tradition and is concerned not so much with actual statistics but more with ecological trends does not lend itself to science, which emphasizes rigour and precision.

It is undoubtedly true that some erosion of the indigenous knowledge system has taken place. However, both the research of social scientists and the claims of aboriginal peoples themselves demonstrate that major elements of the knowledge system, including self-management practices, continue to persist. In any event, the indigenous knowledge system should no more be judged for its worth according to a static image of the past than should the knowledge system of any other culture. . . . Furthermore, as Usher states, "that a body of law is referred to as customary does not mean it is necessarily antiquated or immutable. Our own legal system is always being modified and updated."[96]

Bearing this in mind, the challenge now facing both state wildlife managers and aboriginal peoples is how to design a system that recognizes the strengths and the limitations of both paradigms and is just in its distribution of authority. The first step towards achieving this goal requires that traditional knowledge be documented by aboriginal peoples themselves. It is only through documentation that its usefulness can become apparent and an improved understanding can be gained of the practices and conditions which lead to the breakdown and reestablishment of self-management systems. Secondly, the guidance of the elders and the cooperation of the youth must be sought in order to make customary law relevant again. For example, find out what customary law has to say about the use of airplanes and snowmobiles, and about intersettlement trade or commercial fishing. How would these laws be enforced?[97] Thirdly, government and the scientific community must work towards developing an environmental assessment and management process that is flexible enough to accommodate new ideas and methods, and which accepts science as only one method of seeking new knowledge and new interpretations of that knowledge. Finally, aboriginal peoples must be fully involved in the design and production of any future resource management schemes, and they must be recognized through their participation with equal authority and legal standing.

The most urgent problem currently facing traditional knowledge is its rapid disappearance with the passing away of the older generations. Unless efforts are made to salvage it quickly, not only will it mean the loss of an important part of the cultural history of humankind, but it may also mean the loss of an important source of information. This has the potential to enhance our understanding of species and ecosystems and offer us important new insights into the sustainable use of the earth's natural resources.

NOTES

1. J.M. Diamond, "Zoological Classification System of a Primitive People," *Science* 151 (1966): 1102–04; L. Irving, *Birds of Anaktuvuk Pass, Kobuk and Old Crow*, National Museum bulletin 217 (Washington, DC: United States National Museum, 1960); and L.L. Snyder, *Arctic Birds of Canada* (Toronto: University of Toronto Press, 1957).

2. R. Bulmer, "Which Came First, the Chicken or the Egg-Head?" in *Exchanges et communications*, vol. 2, ed. J. Pouillon and P. Maranda (The Hague: Mouton & Co, 1970), 1069–91; B. Berlin, "Folk Systematics in Relation to Biological Classification and Nomenclature," *Annual Review of Ecology and Systematics* 4 (1973): 259–71; and E. Hunn, *Cognitive Processes in Folk-ornithology: The Identification of Gulls*, working paper no. 42 (Berkeley: University of California Language–Behavior Research Laboratory, 1975).

3. *World Conservation Strategy* (Gland: Switzerland: IUCN, UNEP, WWF, 1980).

4. World Commission on Environment and Development, *Our Common Future* (Toronto: Oxford University Press, 1987).

5. N. Doubleday, *The Inuit Regional Conservation Strategy: Sustainable Development in the Circumpolar Region* (Ottawa: Inuit Circumpolar Conference, 1988).

6. M.M.R. Freeman, *Inuit Land Use and Occupancy Project*, 3 vols. (Ottawa: Indian and Northern Affairs, 1976).

7. R. Berger, *Northern Frontier, Northern Homeland: The Report of the Mackenzie Valley Pipeline Inquiry*, vol. 1 (Toronto: Lorimer, 1977).

8. C. Brice-Bennett, ed., *Our Footprints are Everywhere* (Nain, Labrador: Labrador Inuit Association, 1977).

9. F. Berkes, "Fishery Resource Use in a Subarctic Indian Community," *Human Ecology* 5, 4 (1977): 289–309, "An Investigation of Cree Indian Domestic Fisheries in Northern Quebec," *Arctic* 32, 1 (1979): 46–70; Berkes, "Waterfowl Management and Northern Native Peoples with Reference to Cree Hunters of James Bay," *Muskox* 20 (1982): 23–36; Berkes, "Quantifying the Harvest of Native Subsistence Fisheries" in *Resources and Dynamics of the Boreal Zone*, ed. R.W. Wein et al. (Ottawa: Association of Canadian Universities for Northern Studies, 1983); Berkes, "Fishermen and 'the Tragedy of the Commons,'" *Environmental Conservation* 12, 3 (1985): 199–206; H. Brody, *Maps and Dreams: Indians and the British Columbia Frontier* (Vancouver: Douglas and McIntyre, 1981); H.A. Feit, "Political Articulations of Hunters to the State: Means of Resisting Threats to Subsistence Production in the James Bay and Northern Quebec Agreement," *Etudes/Inuit/Studies* 3, 2

(1979): 37–52; Feit, "Legitimation and Autonomy in James Bay Cree Responses to Hydroelectric Development" in *Indigenous Peoples and the Nation State: Fourth World Politics in Canada, Australia and Norway*, ed. N. Dyck (St John's: Memorial University, Institute for Social and Economic Research, 1985), 27–66; Feit, "James Bay Cree Indian Management and Moral Considerations of Fur Bearers" in *Native People and Renewable Resource Management* (Edmonton: Alberta Society of Professional Biologists, 1986), 49–65; Feit, "Self-Management and State-Management: Forms of Knowing and Managing Northern Wildlife" in *Traditional Knowledge and Renewable Resource Management in Northern Regions*, ed. M.M.R. Freeman and L.N. Carbyn (Edmonton: Boreal Institute for Northern Studies, 1988), 72–91; and J.M. Beaulieu, "The Role and Importance of Inuit Knowledge for Wildlife Management and Conservation in the North" (MES thesis, York University, 1988).

10. D.J. DeLancey, "Proposed Research Design for the Documentation of Traditional Knowledge" (report prepared for the Dene Nation, 1987), and D. T'Seleie, "Baseline Data: Dene Knowledge of Behaviour Patterns in Moose, Caribou and Fish" (unpublished report, Fee-Yee Consulting Ltd., Fort Good Hope, NWT, 1985).

11. Fort Resolution Elders, *That's the Way We Lived* (Yellowknife: Northwest Territories Culture and Communication Outcrop, 1987).

12. Dene Cultural Institute, *Dene Traditional Environmental Knowledge Pilot* (Yellowknife, 1989).

13. Department of Renewable Resources, *Department Mandate and Goals for the 1989–90 Budget Year* (Yellowknife: Government of the Northwest Territories, 1988).

14. G. Baines, Chair, IUCN Traditional Ecological Knowledge Working Group, personal communication, 1989.

15. G. Madhav, "Social Restraints on Resource Utilization: The Indian Experience" in *Culture and Conservation: The Human Dimension in Environmental Planning*, ed. J.A. McNeely and D. Pitt (London: Croon Helm, 1985), 135–54.

16. N. Kwapena, "Traditional Conservation and Utilization of Wildlife in Papua New Guinea" in *Traditional Lifestyles, Conservation and Rural Development*, ed. J. Hanks (Gland, Switzerland: IUCN, 1984), 22–26.

17. N.V.C. Polunin, "Traditional Marine Practices in Indonesia and Their Bearing on Conservation" in *Culture and Conservation*, ed. McNeely and Pitt, 155–79.

18. R.E. Johannes, "Traditional Marine Conservation Methods in Oceania and Their Demise," *Annual Review of Ecology and Systematics* 9 (1978): 349–64.

19. Baines, personal communication.

20. Ibid.

21. T. Andrews, "Selected Bibliography of Native Resource Management Systems and Native Knowledge of the Environment" in *Traditional Knowledge and Renewable Resource Management*, ed. Freeman and Carbyn, 105–34.

22. G. Osherenko, *Sharing Power with Native Users: Co-management Regimes for Arctic Wildlife*, policy paper no. 5 (Ottawa: Canadian Arctic Resources Committee, 1988).

23. H.A. Feit, "The Ethno-ecology of the Waswanipi Cree: Or How Hunters Can Manage Their Resources" in *Cultural Ecology*, ed. B. Cox (Toronto: McClelland & Stewart, 1973), 115–25, and T'Seleie, "Baseline Data."

24. Feit, "Self-Management and State-Management."

25. C. Scott, "Production and Exchange Among Wemindji Cree: Egalitarian Ideology and Economic Base," *Culture* 11, 3 (1979): 51–64; Scott, "The Socio-Economic Significance of Waterfowl Among Canada's Aboriginal Cree: Native Use and Local Management"

in *The Value of Birds*, ed. A.W. Diamond and F.L. Filion (ICBP Technical Publication no. 6, 1987), 49–62.

26. R. Stephenson, "Nunamiut Eskimos, Wildlife Biologists and Wolves" in *Wolves of the World: Perspective of Behaviour Ecology and Conservation*, ed. F. Harrington and R.C. Paquet (Parkridge, NJ, 1982), 434–39.

27. D.J. Nakashima, *Inuit Knowledge of the Ecology of the Common Eider in Northern Quebec* (Montreal: Makivik Corporation, 1984).

28. A. Johnston, *Plants and the Blackfoot*, occasional paper no. 15 (Lethbridge: Lethbridge Historical Society, 1987).

29. D.W. Ellis and L. Swan, *Teachings of the Tides: Uses of Marine Invertebrates by the Manhousat People* (Nanaimo, BC: Theytus Books, 1981); D.W. Ellis and S. Wilson, *The Knowledge and Usage of Marine Invertebrates by the Skidegate Haida People of the Queen Charlotte Islands*, Monograph series no. 1 (Charlotte City, BC: Queen Charlotte Museum Society, 1981).

30. Irving, *Birds of Anaktuvuk Pass*; M.C. Johnson, "Inuit Folk-ornithology in the Povungnituk Region of Northern Quebec" (MA thesis, University of Toronto, 1987).

31. M. Breton, T.G. Smith, and B. Kemp, *Studying and Managing Arctic Seals and Whales: The Views of Scientists and Inuit on Biology and Behaviour of Arctic Seals and Whales, Harvesting Sea Mammals, Management and Conservation for the Future* (Ottawa: Minister of Supply and Services, 1984); M.M.R. Freeman, "Contemporary Inuit Exploitation of the Sea-ice Environment" in *Sikimuit: The People of the Sea Ice*, ed. A. Cooke and E. Van Astine (Ottawa: Canadian Arctic Resources Committee, 1984).

32. Feit, "Self-Management and State-Management"; A. Gunn, G. Arlooktoo, and D. Kaomayak, "The Contribution of Ecological Knowledge of Inuit to Wildlife Management in the Northwest Territories" in *Traditional Knowledge and Renewable Resource*

Management, ed. Freeman and Carbyn, 22–29; Stephenson, "Nunamiut Eskimos."

33. Feit, "Self-Management and State-Management."

34. Gunn et al., "Contribution of Ecological Knowledge."

35. Ibid., 25.

36. Stephenson, "Nunamiut Eskimos," 438.

37. Ibid., 439.

38. P.J. Usher, "Devolution of Power in the Northwest Territories: Implications for Wildlife" in *Native People and Renewable Resource Management* (Edmonton: Alberta Society of Professional Biologists, 1986), 71.

39. Scott, "Socio-economic Significance of Waterfowl"; H.A. Feit, "Waswanipi Realities and Adaptations: Resource Management and Cognitive Structure" (Ph.D. diss., McGill University, 1978).

40. F. Berkes, "The Role of Self-Regulation in Living Resource Management in the North" in *Proceedings*, ed. M.M.R. Freeman, 166–78.

41. Johannes, "Traditional Marine Conservation Methods."

42. Usher, "Devolution of Power"; Feit, "Self-Management and State-Management."

43. Berkes, "The Role of Self-Regulation"; Feit, "Self-Management and State-Management."

44. Berkes, "The Role of Self-Regulation"; Johannes, "Traditional Marine Conservation Methods."

45. Ibid.

46. Feit, "Self-Management and State-Management."

47. Berkes, "The Role of Self-Regulation."

48. Feit, "Self-Management and State-Management."

49. Osherenko, *Sharing Power with Native Users*.

50. Ibid.

51. J.B. Theberge, "Commentary: Conservation in the North—An Ecological Perspective," *Arctic* 34, 4 (1981): 281–85.

52. Beaulieu, "Role and Importance of Inuit Knowledge."

53. M.M.R. Freeman, "Appeal to Tradition: Different Perspectives on Arctic Wildlife Management" in *The Quest for Autonomy and Nationhood of Indigenous Peoples*, ed. J. Brosted et al. (Bergen: Universitetsforlaget, 1985), 265–81.

54. R. Riewe and L. Gamble, "Inuit and Wildlife Management Today" in *Traditional Knowledge and Renewable Resource Management*, ed. Freeman and Carbyn, 31–37.

55. Ibid., 32.

56. Osherenko, *Sharing Power with Native Users*, 7.

57. P. Mulvihill, "Integration of the State and Indigenous Systems of Wildlife Management: Problems and Possibilities" (unpublished paper, School of Urban and Regional Planning, Faculty of Environment Studies, University of Waterloo, 1988).

58. Ibid., 15.

59. Usher, "Devolution of Power."

60. Ibid., 78.

61. Osherenko, *Sharing Power with Native Users*, 13.

62. Ibid.

63. Papers that discuss specific examples of co-management include Osherenko, *Sharing Power with Native Users*; D.J. DeLancey and T.D. Andrews, "Denendeh (Western Arctic)" in *Community-based Resource Management in Canada: An Inventory of Research and Projects*, ed. F.G. Cohen and A.J. Hanson (Ottawa: Canadian Commission for UNESCO, Man and the Biosphere Program, 1988); Freeman, "Appeal to Tradition"; Gunn et al., "Contribution of Ecological Knowledge"; K. Lloyd, "Cooperative Management of Polar Bears on Northeast Baffin Island" in

Native People and Renewable Resource Management (Edmonton: Alberta Society for Professional Biologists, 1986), 108–16; Usher, "Devolution of Power"; and P. Cizek, "The Beverly and Kaminuriak Caribou Management Board: A Case Study of Aboriginal Participation in Resource Management" (MA thesis, University of Waterloo, 1988).

64. Osherenko, *Sharing Power with Native Users*.

65. Mulvihill, "Integration of the State and Indigenous Systems of Wildlife Management."

66. D. Marshall, "Native Resource Management at a Turning Point?" in *Native People and Renewable Resource Management* (Edmonton: Alberta Society for Professional Biologists, 1986), 23–28.

67. M.M.R. Freeman, "Renewable Resources, Economics and Native Communities" in ibid., 29–37.

68. B. Malinowski, *Argonauts of the Western Pacific* (New York: Dutton, 1922), 25.

69. M.H. Agar, *The Professional Stranger—An Informal Introduction to Ethnography* (New York: Academic Press, 1980).

70. DeLancey, *Proposed Research Design*, 19.

71. Feit, "Legitimation and Autonomy in James Bay Cree."

72. Nakashima, *Inuit Knowledge of the Ecology of the Common Eider*.

73. Social Sciences and Humanities Research Council of Canada (SSHRC), *Community-based Research: Report of the SSHRC Task Force on Native Issues* (Ottawa: SSHRC, 1983).

74. Dene Cultural Institute, *Dene Traditional Environmental Knowledge*.

75. M.M.R. Freeman, "Traditional Knowledge and Adaptive Management: A Northern Canadian Case Study and Action Plan" (proposal submitted jointly by the Weasel's Hunters and Trappers Association, Sanikiluaq, NWT, and the Boreal

Institute for Northern Studies, University of Alberta, 1988).

76. Baines, personal communication, 1989.

77. W. Kemp, "Makivik Research Department and Development of Inuit-based Research and Scientific Education" in *Education, Research, Information Systems and the North*, ed. W.P. Adams (Ottawa: Association of Canadian Universities for Northern Studies, 1987), 39–42.

78. P. Jacobs, "Towards a Network of Knowing and of Planning in Northern Canada" in *Knowing the North: Reflections on Tradition, Technology and Science*, ed. W.C. Wonders (Edmonton: Boreal Institute for Northern Studies, 1988), 51–60.

79. B. Rigby, chair, Environmental Technology Program, Arctic College, personal communication, 1989.

80. M. MacDonald, "Traditional Knowledge, Adaptive Management and Advances in Scientific Understanding" in *Traditional Knowledge and Renewable Resource Management*, ed. Freeman and Carbyn, 65–71.

81. C. Holling et al., *Adaptive Environmental Assessment and Management* (Toronto: Wiley, 1978).

82. Cited in MacDonald, "Traditional Knowledge."

83. Holling et al., *Adaptive Environmental Assessment*.

84. Freeman, "Traditional Knowledge and Adaptive Management."

85. R.R. Everitt, "Native Roles in Monitoring of Energy Developments" in *Native People and Renewable Resource Management*.

86. Ibid., 46.

87. Baines, personal communication, 1989.

88. I. Robertson, "The Contribution of Land Use Planning to Oil and Gas Development in the Northwest Territories" in *Proceedings: Northern Hydrocarbon Development in the Nineties—A Global Perspective*, ed. F.T. Frankling (Ottawa: Carleton University Geotechnical Science Laboratories, 1989), 38.

89. Lancaster Sound Regional Land Use Planning Commission, *The Lancaster Sound Proposed Regional Land Use Plan* (1989).

90. Berger, *Northern Frontier*.

91. Federal Environmental Assessment Review Office, *The National Consultation Workshop on Federal Environmental Assessment Reform: Report on Proceedings* (Ottawa: Ministry of Supply and Services Canada, 1988).

92. Federal Environmental Assessment Review Office, *Report of the Environmental Assessment Panel: Eastern Arctic Offshore Drilling—South Davis Strait Project* (Ottawa: Ministry of Supply and Services Canada, 1978); Federal Environmental Assessment Review Office, *Report of the Environmental Assessment Panel: Lancaster Sound Drilling* (Ottawa: Ministry of Supply and Services Canada, 1979).

93. Feit, "Self-Management and State-Management," 76.

94. Freeman, "Renewable Resources."

95. Feit, "Self-Management and State-Management."

96. P.J. Usher, "Sustenance or Recreation? The Future of Native Wildlife Harvesting in Northern Canada" in *Proceedings*, ed. Freeman, 68.

97. Usher, "Devolution of Power."

ECOLOGY, CULTURE, AND THE SUBARCTIC ALGONQUIANS ✧

EDWARD S. ROGERS [1]

o

For centuries land and water have been subjects of controversy. Wars have been fought and innumerable lives lost to wrest control of some part of the globe from others. The struggle continues.

From a European point of view, what the land could produce through the sweat of one's brow (i.e., tilling the soil), or what lay hidden under the earth's mantle (i.e., was accessible through mining) was of utmost importance. At times, furs and timbers for ships were equally valuable. From an Indian point of view, the spiritual significance of the land or "mother earth" was of major importance. Within the universe, all life was one. This was not the viewpoint of Europeans, who believed that God created the universe for the exclusive use of humans. Nevertheless, Indians used the food, raiment, and shelter that "mother earth" provided.

Throughout the world, indigenous peoples are now seeking control of land and resources which were acquired by Europeans by various means over the past 500 years. Indigenous people believe they have a right to manage and preserve the land for their descendants, and to obtain compensation in the form of money, self-government, or other considerations for having lost their rights to aliens. Canadian Indians, Métis, and Inuit are now taking their claims to court. Examples of this litigation include the Baker Lake Inuit of the Northwest Territories, the Nishka of British Columbia, the Timagami Ojibwa in Ontario, the Lubicon Cree in Alberta, and the James Bay Cree in Québec. The "battlefields" of former times, such as Hannah Bay, Henley House, Mica Bay, and Batoche no longer exist. Often, with little knowledge of native people, their land, or their history, the

✧ *Anthropologica* 28, 1–2 (1986): 203–16.

press, environmentalists, politicians, and anthropologists come to the "rescue" only to muddy the waters of an already confused situation over Indian "title" to land.

From an ethnological perspective, "land tenure" is a complex issue. This is especially true because each culture has its own distinctive view of its relationship to the land. Indians of the eastern Subarctic in Canada represent one example of this complex relationship. Although ethnological interpretations of Subarctic Algonquian land tenure have varied over time, three phases can be identified. These three phases, as designated by Tanner, are termed the "classic," "postclassic," and "neoclassic" viewpoints.[2] . . .

Beginning in the early decades of the twentieth century, scholars such as Frank G. Speck, A. Irving Hallowell, and John M. Cooper began to examine how Algonquian-speaking Indians in the eastern Subarctic of North America dealt with land and its resources (the "classic period" described by Tanner). On the basis of what these investigators thought they had been told, they concluded that a form of individual or family land tenure (i.e., not communal) existed among Subarctic Algonquians. As early as 1915, Speck called this the "family hunting territory."[3] He and his colleagues concluded that the "family hunting territory" system of land tenure had existed from "time immemorial."

Soon, other scholars proposed that the European fur trade had been responsible for the origin of the family hunting territory among Subarctic Algonquians (the "postclassic period" described by Tanner). Diamond Jenness was one of the first to question the arguments advanced by Speck and others that family hunting territories existed amongst Subarctic Algonquians in precontact times. Jenness ascribed this form of land use to European intervention, specifically the fur trade.[4] Eleanor Leacock concurred, and carried the argument forward.[5] Other scholars made further refinements, specifying additional factors or events to account for the emergence of the "family hunting territory" which followed the arrival of European traders in the eastern Subarctic.[6]

By the late 1950s or early 1960s, I assumed that the issue of land tenure among Subarctic Algonquians had been resolved once and for all, and that "hunting territories" came into existence after the arrival of Europeans.

This assumption was challenged by investigators such as Toby Morantz and Harvey Feit, who began to undermine my conviction. The reevaluation of my thinking was further hastened when I listened to papers presented in an all-day session organized by Toby Morantz and José Mailhot for the Canadian Ethnology Society meetings at the University of Toronto, May 9–12, 1985. Scholars who spoke in this session convinced me that after several decades of my previous viewpoint, it was time to reexamine the complex topic of Subarctic Algonquian land tenure and resource use.

In spite of the extensive literature on the land occupied by the original inhabitants of North America, we still know very little about Indian relationships to land and its resources, especially in the Subarctic. Fortunately, there are scholars who continue to labor very hard at understanding the wisdom of Indian elders and the remarks of traders and other Europeans preserved in archives.

The thoughts expressed at the symposium noted above represent a third [neoclassic] phase in the ever-evolving view of land tenure among Subarctic Algonquians. As a rule, present scholars are not concerned with *when* hunting territories arose (i.e., whether they arose before or after the arrival of Europeans) or how the land-use system was adapted to ensure the survival of Subarctic Algonquians in their varied environments. Rather, current scholars emphasize how Subarctic Algonquians managed the resources provided by the lands they occupied. Critical attention is given to "conservation," the concept of "ownership" of the land and/or resources, and to "trespass" on "my/our land." However, these topics were not neglected by the scholars who first dealt with land tenure among Subarctic Indian people as a whole.

FUTURE RESEARCH

Stimulated by the Canadian Ethnology Society symposium, I began to rethink "land tenure" as practiced by Subarctic Algonquians. Future research may clarify issues that I believe have not been adequately dealt with, including environmental and socio-cultural considerations, and European and Métis contacts with Indians. Though a new generation of scholars has made great strides in probing the complexities of relationships between Subarctic Algonquians and the environment where they have made their living for millennia, further lines of inquiry may help resolve some of the varied opinions expressed in the published literature to date. A fuller understanding of Indian/land relationships within the eastern Subarctic will be gained only by examining all relevant data.

Finally, what are the ethical implications inherent in research on land tenure among the native peoples of Canada? This topic has become emotionally charged, to say the least. Indian land claims being debated in the courts pit scholar against scholar.

ENVIRONMENTAL CONSIDERATIONS

To understand better how Indians were able to survive the harsh conditions of the eastern Subarctic, various aspects of the environment must be examined in considerable detail. The subarctic environment was not merely a static backdrop against which one viewed the "noble savage." It was forever changing, and Indians had to be constantly alert and adaptive. Aspects of the environment are not presented here in any order of importance; to individual Indians, perhaps all aspects were equally vital.

1. *Climatic changes* no doubt affected the availability of certain species upon which Subarctic Algonquians depended at times, as for example changes that occurred during the Little Ice Age circa 1500–1750. Was this deterioration in climatic conditions responsible for the reduction in moose and caribou in the central Subarctic? What happens when snow accumulation is too deep for the survival of moose and caribou? Subarctic Algonquians had to devise new subsistence strategies if they

were to survive, and these may have affected land tenure. There were also climatic alterations of lesser amplitude, including years when little snowfall meant that beaver lodges were easily discovered, but that moose and caribou escaped even the fleetest hunters because they were not impeded by deep snow.[7] There were also years when the situation was reversed, and caribou were easily hunted.[8] Sometimes the land was flooded in the spring, drowning many muskrats and curtailing the production of wild rice.[9] What happened in 1816, the year without a summer?[10] Subarctic hunters must have had mechanisms for dealing with these events. What modifications in land use did they make to cope with serious climatic events?

Although the role of fire in human life has been studied, little attention has been paid to the effects of forest fires on Subarctic Algonquians beyond the work of Feit for the Waswanipi area.[11] What were the adjustments of Algonquian hunters when vast areas were destroyed and the intensity of fires was so great that not even a mosquito survived? Where did the hunters and their families go, and with whom? We might begin in Ontario, where fire maps have been prepared since 1920, and could be correlated with the registered trapline maps which were first plotted in 1947.[12] Combining these maps might yield insights about the effect of fire on Indian lands. This might lead to further field investigations which could try to unravel the social implications of fire. It is also important to note that the "fire rotation period" for the boreal forest is approximately sixty to one hundred years.[13]

2. *Game cycles*[14] are another variable to which mere lip service has been paid when examining resource use and land tenure among Subarctic Algonquians. Hare fluctuate in numbers from practically none[15] to a great abundance[16] every seven to ten years. The grouse population also rises and falls every so many years,[17] and ruffed grouse periodically undergo drastic fluctuations in numbers.[18] Geese fluctuate randomly. Some summers, many goose eggs fail to hatch due to adverse nesting conditions on the Arctic islands and/or the slaughter of adults to the south in the fall and winter. In the past, game hunters supplied the American market with immense quantities of geese. An age class of fish may be destroyed due to adverse conditions on spawning grounds.[19] What happened when many or all of the species upon which the Indians depended crashed at the same time? Is this what happened at the turn of the century (1899–1900), when there was "nothing to eat"?[20] What did Indians do when only a few food species were available and were not located in the same general area?

3. *The spatial distribution of resources* varied throughout the eastern Subarctic. Many plant, fish, bird, and animal species occurred widely, but there were other species, some of which were important to the Indians which inhabited restricted locales throughout the year. Among these spatially-restricted resources were berry patches, groves of maple trees, stands of wild rice, sturgeon, and lake trout.

Another form of restricted distribution occurred seasonally among certain species. For several weeks once or sometimes twice each year, these species assembled in certain areas in greater numbers than usual. Examples of this were caribou crossing the Severn River in the spring,[21] whitefish during the fall spawning runs,[22] suckers during the spring,[23] and millions of waterfowl, principally geese, which were found in the marshes bordering James and Hudson Bays in the spring and fall. These features of the landscape have rarely been mapped, and never over time. Given such distribution patterns, all of the resources upon which Subarctic Algonquians depended did not exist in every hunting territory. How did people accommodate these variable conditions?

4. *The production of trade items* which were desired by traders was certainly significant. Some of these items included waterfowl quills, castorum, sturgeon roe, swan feathers, caribou hides and meat, hare hides, and wild rice. Other resources, especially furs, were in even greater demand. Beaver provided both food and fur, as did hare and caribou when their skins were in demand. However, a lack of coterminous distribution, either continuously or periodically, of one or more fur-bearing species with food animals often caused problems for fur trappers.[24] How did Indian hunters solve this problem, especially when desired fur bearers such as marten were located far away from adequate food supplies of fish, hare, or caribou?

5. *Resource productivity* increases westward within the North American Subarctic from the Labrador Peninsula to Alaska. What effect did this have in the past and what effect does it now have on the concept of land tenure among subarctic hunter-gatherers? Territoriality is believed to be more efficient when food is sufficiently abundant and predictable in space and time. When reverse conditions prevail, non-territorial behavior may be more efficient.[25] If this is the case, why have Athapaskan-speaking Indians in the western Subarctic of North America rarely been reported as having territorial boundaries such as those found among the Algonquian-speaking Montagnais of the eastern Subarctic?

6. *The size of fish* was significant in the Subarctic. In the past, certain species of fish might have grown much larger than is generally the case at present. These species include lake trout, sturgeon, and whitefish. A recent example of a lake trout from Lake Athabasca, Saskatchewan tipped the scales at 102 pounds, while a sturgeon caught in Lake of the Woods in Ontario weighed 234 pounds,[26] and a sturgeon taken at Batchawana Island in Lake Superior in 1922 weighed 310 pounds. There are also lake whitefish weighing twenty pounds or more in the Great Lakes. One whitefish caught off Isle Royale, Lake Superior about 1819 weighed forty-two pounds.[27] A sturgeon weighing 650 pounds was recently found in Lake Washington in the United States. Although obviously not found everywhere in the Subarctic, these large fish

would have rivaled other species as a food resource wherever they occurred, and might have altered the subsistence strategy of Subarctic Indians.

CULTURAL CONSIDERATIONS

Indians in the eastern Subarctic had beliefs and behavior patterns which affected territoriality in one way or another. A few of these are mentioned below.

7. *Demographic patterns* among Subarctic Algonquians have been given little attention to date. Although some notice has been paid to both population size and the number of square miles allocated to each man, woman, and child, we must also consider the ratio of males to females born to each family, as there was sometimes a preponderance of one sex. Family size ranged from childless couples to polygynous families consisting of several dozen members.[28] How were offspring distributed across the landscape to ensure the continued survival of the population? What were the adoption, marriage, and residence patterns of Subarctic Algonquians, and what role did these customs play in land tenure? Abandoned orphans and ostracized adults must also be taken into account when examining land tenure. Detailed genealogies should be collected in the field wherever possible, and then traced back through time by means of archival sources.

8. *The technology of Subarctic Algonquians* and what they acquired from traders must be considered when examining land tenure. What artifacts were both indigenous to subarctic peoples and lacking in the Old World? What did Indian trappers acquire from traders? What was the quality of trade goods, and what quantities were exchanged? No doubt these two factors changed over time. Although the steel trap and the gun must always be kept in mind, these are not the only items that affected land use in the Subarctic.

9. *Sociopolitical organization* and the varied terminology used for different social units among Subarctic Algonquians must be clarified, especially where this behavior relates to territorial boundaries. What was an aboriginal "band" in the eastern Subarctic? Certainly it was not the same thing as the "trading post band" or the later "government/treaty band" or "settlement." Speck, for example, was never clear as to what he meant by the term "band." What is the difference between "communal property," "common property," "individual property," "personal property," and "private property"? How many families must work together to be considered "communal" as opposed to "atomistic"?

How did the Subarctic Algonquians themselves define or view various sociopolitical units ranging from the largest to the smallest? When does one leave one's "own land" and enter that of a *stranger* (usually a territory where the inhabitants were to be feared)? What is trespass? Is stepping over the "boundary" of one's next door neighbor the same thing as crossing a faraway line, beyond which live "strangers"? In short, where and how do we—and Subarctic Algonquians—draw boundaries?

10. *The influence of religious beliefs and behavior patterns* on land-use practices and the relationships of Subarctic Algonquians to their environment have been studied, but much more work needs to be done. Formerly, when a member of a Subarctic Algonquian group died, his or her group refrained from taking any more fur animals that season.[29] In some instances, the group moved to another area. All resources for home consumption were considered free goods which were available to all wherever they were found. But where was the boundary for the concept of free goods from the viewpoint of the individual Indian? Does the fear of witchcraft promote small hunting groups, regardless of environmental conditions? If this were the case, then hunting-territory size in the Subarctic would not be regulated by the productivity of the land. Finally, were certain areas in the Subarctic taboo to exploitation for spiritual reasons, or did they remain unused for practical reasons?

THE EUROPEAN AND THE INDIAN

Traders, missionaries, government agents, and other Western Europeans came to North America from Britain, Scotland, the Orkney Islands, France, Scandinavia, and elsewhere. All had distinctive ethnic backgrounds, and all were motivated by different religious convictions. Each group dealt with Indians in various ways, including with respect to land use. Because they were literate and left written records in numerous archives, many Western European immigrants have been accepted as authorities on Indians.

But what of the veracity, objectivity, and cross-cultural perspectives of these recorders? With few exceptions,[30] their accounts have yet to be critically examined with such points in mind. What did a trader mean when he recorded in his journal that such and such Indians had returned to their "hunting lands" or "hunting grounds"?

Western Europeans have been imbued with a concept of "Indian hunting grounds" through presentations of the concept of "manifest destiny" by historians and novelists. This concept of Indian land use was meant to contrast with that of European farming communities, where limited plots of land became important after the break-up of the commons, and individualization became the way to succeed.

11. *The role of traders* was significant in that they sometimes tried to influence the way Subarctic Algonquians used the land. For example, traders told Indians where to trap in any given year, and what size hunting group to use in a particular territory. They also promoted conservation measures among the Indians.[31]

12. *The role of missionaries* had less impact than that of traders, but missionaries hoped that Subarctic Algonquians would become more sedentary. In that case, it would be easier to oversee their religious practices.

13. *The role of the government and perhaps anthropologists* (such as Frank G. Speck) in promoting a particular concept of land ownership among Subarctic Algonquians has no doubt been significant. What was the impact of federal legislation such as the Migratory Birds Act, or provincial legislation and regulations such as game laws, on Indians who formerly knew only their own customs? What was the role of men such as Jack Grew and Hugh Conn in the implementation of registered traplines which took place in the 1940s?

LAND CLAIMS: AN ETHICAL ISSUE

"ARE EXPERT WITNESSES WHORES?"[32]

14. *Ethnocentric viewpoints* have often appeared in many studies of Indian land tenure to date. If the concept of Indian land tenure existed at all in the minds of non-Indian scholars, it tended to be modeled after Western European concepts. Do we believe what we want to believe? The answer is often yes. Thus, we must always be on guard, especially in this age of litigation over Indian land claims.

Both comprehensive claims (i.e., regarding land) and specific claims (i.e., regarding treaty obligations, hunting and fishing rights, etc.) are now before the courts or in preparation for adjudication. More and more "expert witnesses" are being called upon by plaintiffs (usually Indians) and defendants (usually the federal or provincial governments) to testify on behalf of clients. Although academics have traditionally debated their views through the medium of publication in scholarly journals, the issues are no longer the innocent disagreements that once occurred in these journals, although they may at times be equally vitriolic. Claims made by native people for what they believe to be past wrongs, and the millions of dollars sought in compensation for such wrongs, are also under scrutiny. The historical and academic validity or evidence for the conclusions drawn by Indians are being tested in the courts. Accordingly, expert witnesses called upon to testify in court are under oath "to tell the truth."

But what is "the truth" regarding land tenure among Subarctic Algonquians and others? As we have seen, anthropologists have held varying views over time about the antiquity of hunting territories. Which one of the three views on Subarctic Algonquian land tenure does an expert witness advocate? First, there was the "classic" view where scholars argued that family hunting territories existed in precontact times. This was followed by the "postclassic" view which argued that family hunting territories arose after the arrival of Europeans, primarily as a result of the fur trade. Finally, there is the modified view which might be termed "neoclassic.". . . Scholars have recently focused on how Indians now use the land. In so doing, they imply (if not categorically state) that systems of game management and use which are today associated with family hunting territories have considerable antiquity. Does this viewpoint support precontact land tenure, as argued in the "classic period"? Through an examination of archival documents, other scholars suggest that family hunting territories existed earlier than was previously thought.

Canadian courts sometimes base their rulings on aboriginal rights on particular dates relating to Indian legislature, such as the Royal Proclamation of 1763 and the Robinson Superior-Huron treaties of 1850. Thus, expert witnesses must do meticulous homework. At the same time, they are likely to be caught in the cross-fire of the conflicting opinions of other anthropologists. Finally, the narrowly confined views of the legal profession ensure that most members of this field will have little or no understanding of the (sometimes extreme) cultural differences between peoples throughout the world.

NOTES

1. I wish to thank Dr Toby Morantz for inviting me to prepare this discussion, and for her generous help in completing the manuscript. I also wish to thank my wife, Dr Mary Black-Rogers, for her critical reading of this work, and Mrs Shirlee Anne Smith of the Hudson's Bay Company Archives for her continued interest and invaluable assistance over many years.

2. Adrian Tanner, "The New Hunting Territory Debate: An Introduction to Some Unresolved Issues," *Anthropologica* 28, 1–2 (1986).

3. Frank G. Speck, "The Family Hunting Band as the Basis of Algonkian Social Organization," *American Anthropologist* 17 (1915): 289–305, and *Family Hunting Territories and Social Life of Various Algonkian Bands of the Ottawa Valley*, Canadian Geological Survey Memoir no. 70, Anthropological Series no. 8 (Ottawa: Canadian Geological Survey, 1915), 1–10.

4. Diamond Jenness, *The Ojibwa Indians of Parry Island, Their Social and Religious Life*, National Museum of Canada Bulletin no. 78, Anthropological Series no. 17 (Ottawa: Department of Mines, 1935).

5. Eleanor B. Leacock, *The Montagnais "Hunting Territory" and the Fur Trade*, American Anthropological Association Memoir no. 78 (Menasha, WI: American Anthropological Association, 1954).

6. Edward S. Rogers, *The Hunting Group—Hunting Territory Complex among the Mistassini Indians*, National Museum of Canada Bulletin no. 195, Anthropological Series no. 63 (Ottawa: Department of Northern Affairs and National Resources, 1963), and Rolf Knight, "A Re-examination of Hunting, Trapping and Territoriality Among the Northeastern Algonkian Indians" in *Man, Culture and Animals*, ed. A. Leeds and A.P. Vayda, American Association for the Advancement of Science Publication no. 78 (Washington, DC: American Association for the Advancement of Science, 1965), 27–42.

7. Many of the citations from trading post journals are quoted from notes taken by E.S. Rogers which were not always exact copies. Some of these notes are mere summaries of the information in the document. February 1791 (letter from Cat Lake): "there is so little snow they can kill no deer" (Provincial Archives of Manitoba/Hudson's Bay Company Archives, Osnaburgh House Journals B.155/a/5:fo. 15); December 1743: "not being able to kill deer for want of more snow on the ground" (Moose Post Journals, B.135/a/14:fo. 20d); February 1744: "a very hard starving winter with them all, there not being snow enough, and consequently no deer to be caught" (ibid., B.135/a/14:fo. 26). November 1762: "partridges plentiful but not snow enough yet to try a partridge net" (Severn Post Journals, B.198/a/4:fo. 16).

8. 1820–21: "All of the above Indians did well in winter. Snow was deep on the ground and they killed several deer" (Mistassini Post Reports on District, B.133/e/2:fo. 3).

9. June 1847: "they all complain that there are no muskrats to be found [;] all have frozen in their holes during the winter by the water being so low" (Trout Lake Post Journals, B.220/a/10:fo. 18 and 20d and B.220/a/11:fo. 2a and 3d); September 1827: "the extreme height of water prevents them from being able to find any muskrats to kill" (ibid., B.220/a/5:fo. 2d).

10. A.J.W. Catchpole, "Evidence from Hudson Bay Region of Severe Cold in the Summer of 1816" in *Climatic Change in Canada* 5, Syllogeus no. 55, ed. C.R. Harrington (Ottawa: National Museum of Natural Sciences, 1985), 121–46.

11. Harvey Feit, "Mistassini Hunters of the Boreal Forest: Ecosystem Dynamics and Multiple Subsistence Patterns" (Masters thesis, McGill University, 1969).

12. Ontario Department of Lands and Forests (now the Ministry of Natural Resources of Ontario).

13. Ross W. Wein and David A. MacLean, "An Overview of Fire in Northern Ecosystems" in *The Role of Fire in Northern Circumpolar Ecosystems*, ed. R.W. Wein and D.A. MacLean (Toronto: John Wiley and Sons, 1983), 1–15.

14. See Charles Elton, the "father" of the study of animal population dynamics: *Voles, Mice and Lemmings* (Oxford: Clarendon Press, 1942).

15. February 1780 (letter from Fort Severn): "rabbits are exceedingly scarce" (Severn Post Journals, B.198/a/24:fo. 22); December 1847: "no rabbits to be found no where, which is the complaint all over" (Trout Lake Post Journals, B.220/a/10:fo. 34d and 35d and B.220/a/11:fo. 12); December 1848: "no rabbits to be got" (ibid., B.220/a/12:fo. 17d and B.220/a/13:fo. 22); January 1849: "they are starving for want of rabbits which is the call all over this season"

(ibid., B.220/a/13:fo.24d); December 1849: "no rabbits to be found all over the country on this quarter" (ibid., B.220/a/15:fo. 18d); March 1850: "complains of starving for want of rabbits, which is the case all over the country on this quarter" (ibid., B.220/a/34:fo. 22d); December 1880: "rabbits are scarce this year" (ibid., B.220/a/43:fo. 74); March 1888: "no rabbits no place all around"(ibid., B.220/a/44:fo. 70d); December 1890: "rabbits are reported to be very scarce" (Osnaburgh House Journals, B.155/a/90:fo. 4d).

16. February 1820: "rabbits and partridges are plentiful" (Rupert House Correspondence Books, B.186/b/3:fo. 16).

17. November 1762: "partridges plentiful" (Severn Post Journals, B.198/a/4:fo. 16); April 1767: "there has been caught by the nets above 9,000 partridge since December last" (ibid., B.198/a/8:fo. 28d); November 1779: "partridges very scarce" (ibid., B.198/a/24:fo. 12d); February 1780: "partridges are exceeding scarce" (ibid., B.198/a/24:fo. 22); December 1847: "no partridges" (Trout Lake Post Journals, B.220/a/11:fo. 12).

18. W. Earl Godfrey, *The Birds of Canada*, National Museums of Canada Bulletin no. 203, Biological Series no. 73 (Ottawa: National Museum of Man, 1966), 110.

19. November 1844: "the Indians all complain of the same, they cannot take fish as usual all around the neighbourhood of this lake" (Trout Lake Post Journals, B.220/a/6:fo. 24); March 1888: "no fish to be got—going to be a pretty hard spring all around this lake" (ibid., B.220/a/44:fo. 70d).

20. April 1899: "country provisions have failed in all directions" (Rupert House Journals, B.186/a/107:fo. 47).

21. April 1762: "news of the deers' crossing above" (Severn Post Journals, B.198/a/3:fo. 25); April 1769: "Home Natives to await passing of deer to southward[;] as usual in the spring season deer plentiful within three days to northward" (ibid., B.198/a/11:fo. 23); June 1773: "deer crossing in many thousands

twenty miles up this River going northwards" (ibid., B.198/a/17:fo. 43); May 1775: "numbers of deer crossing river to southward about four miles above Factory" (ibid., B.198/a/19:fo. 35d); June 1778: "no deer lately crossed owing to the cool weather that has kept the insects immobile[,] not infesting the animals and causing them to move about" (ibid., B.198/a/22:fo. 40); June 1781: "they say few or no deer have crossed" (ibid., B.198/a/6:fo. 35d); April 1786: "deer arrive about river about 30 miles up. . . . Indians saw six deer crossing river to northward about half mile above" (ibid., B.198/a/33:fo. 28d).

22. Edward S. Rogers and Mary B. Black, "Subsistence Strategy in the Fish and Hare Period, Northern Ontario: The Weagamow Ojibwa, 1880–1920," *Journal of Anthropological Research* 32, 1 (1976):1–43.

23. March 1818: "the Indians are getting plenty of suckers from the weir" (B.125/a/1:fo. 9).

24. March 1827: "where they turned back they saw marten tracks but had nothing to live upon" (Trout Lake Post Journals, B.220/a/4:fo. 16); December 1847: "no rabbits this season, which will be much against the fur this season, and no partridges also" (ibid., B.220/a/11:fo. 12).

25. Robert David Sack, *Human Territoriality: Its Theory and History*, Cambridge Studies in Historical Geography (Cambridge: Cambridge University Press, 1986), 32.

26. William Beverley Scott and E.J. Crossman, *Freshwater Fishes of Canada*, Fisheries Research Board of Canada Bulletin no. 184 (Ottawa: Fisheries Research Board of Canada, 1973), 223, 86.

27. Ibid., 272.

28. For example, Captain Utchechauk in 1795: "the father of 23 children, 16 of which is sons" (Osnaburgh House Journals, B.155/a/10:fo. 25d).

29. April 1830: "one of them unfortunately has lost his father and the other his wife which losses according to their custom prevents them from hunting furs this winter" (Mistassini Post Journals, B.133/a/15:fo. 38d).

30. Mary Black-Rogers, "Varieties of 'Starving': Semantics and Survival in the Subarctic Fur Trade, 1750–1850," *Ethnohistory* 33, 4 (1986): 353–83, and José Mailhot, "Beyond Everyone's Horizon Stand the Naskapi," ibid.: 384–418.

31. December 1844: "for I am very much averse to an Indian interfering with anothers lands in these things" (Fort George Post Journals, B.77/a/19:fo. 17d).

32. J. Morgan Kousser, "Are Expert Witnesses Whores? Reflections on Objectivity in Scholarship and Expert Witnessing," *The Public Historian* 6 (Winter 1984): 5–19, and Donald J. Bourgeois, "The Role of the Historian in the Litigation Process," *Canadian Historical Review* 67, 2 (1986):195–205.

FURTHER READING

○

THEORY AND METHOD IN ENVIRONMENTAL HISTORY

"A Round Table: Environmental History." *Journal of American History* 76, 4 (March 1990): 1087–147.

Bird, E.A.R. "The Social Construction of Nature: Theoretical Approaches to the History of Environmental Problems." *Environmental Review* 11, 4 (Winter 1987): 255–64.

Cayley, David. *The Age of Ecology: The Environment on CBC Radio's Ideas.* Toronto: Lorimer, 1991.

Inglis, Julian T., ed. *Traditional Ecological Knowledge: Concepts and Cases.* Ottawa: IDRC, 1993.

Leibhardt, Barbara. "Interpretation and Causal Analysis: Theories in Environmental History." *Environmental Review* 12 (Spring 1988): 23–36.

Leiss, William. *The Domination of Nature.* Montreal: McGill-Queen's University Press, 1994.

Loewen, Candace. "From Human Neglect to Planetary Survival: New Approaches to the Appraisal of Environmental Records." *Archivaria* 33 (Winter 1991–92): 87–103.

Merchant, Carolyn. "The Realm of Social Relations: Production, Reproduction, and Gender in Environmental Transformations." In *The Earth as Transformed by Human Action.* Ed. B.L. Turner. New York: Cambridge University Press, 1990.

———. "The Theoretical Structure of Ecological Revolutions." *Environmental Review* 11 (Winter 1987): 251–74.

Mailhot, José. *Traditional Ecological Knowledge: The Diversity of Knowledge Systems and Their Study.* Montreal: Great Whale Public Review Support Office, 1993.

Nash, Roderick. "The State of Environmental History." In *The State of American History.* Ed. Herbert J. Bass. Chicago: Quadrangle Books, 1970.

Opie, John. "Environmental History: Pitfalls and Opportunities." *Environmental Review* 7 (1983): 8–16.

Sadler, Barry, and Peter Boothroyd, eds. *Traditional Ecological Knowledge and Environmental Assessment.* Manuscript Report. Hull, PQ: Canadian Environmental Assessment Research Council, March 1993.

Scarce, Rik. *Eco-Warriors: Understanding the Radical Environmental Movement.* Chicago: Noble Press, 1990.

White, Richard. "American Environmental History: The Development of a New Historical Field." *Pacific Historical Review* 54 (Aug. 1985): 297–335.

————. "Native Americans and the Environment." In *Scholars and the Indian Experience*. Ed. W.R. Swagerty. Bloomington: Indiana University Press, 1984.

Worster, Donald. "History as Natural History: An Essay on Theory and Method." *Pacific Historical Review* 53 (1984): 1–19.

SELECTED NON-CANADIAN WORKS

Adams, Carol J. *The Sexual Politics of Meat*. New York: Continuum, 1990.

Bailes, Kendall E., ed. *Environmental History: Critical Issues in Comparative Perspective*. Lanham, MD: University Press of America, 1985.

Berman, Morris. *Coming to Our Senses: Body and Spirit in the Hidden History of the West*. New York: Simon and Schuster, 1989.

Bilskey, Lester J., ed. *Historical Ecology: Essays on Environmental and Social Change*. Port Washington, NY: Kennikat Press, 1980.

Breeze, Lawrence E. *The British Experience with River Pollution, 1865–1876*. New York: P. Lang, 1993.

Bromwell, Anna. *Ecology in the Twentieth Century: A History*. New Haven, CT: Yale University Press, 1993.

Cadoret, A., ed. *Protection de la nature: Histoire et idéologie de la nature à l'environnement*. Paris: Éditions l'Hormatton, 1985.

Cronon, William. *Changes in the Land: Indians, Colonists, and the Ecology of New England*. New York: Hill and Wang, 1983.

————. *Nature's Metropolis: Chicago and the Great West*. New York: W.W. Norton, 1991.

Crosby, Alfred. *Ecological Imperialism: The Biological Expansion of Europe, 900–1900*. Cambridge: Cambridge University Press, 1986.

————. *Germs, Seeds, and Animals: Studies in Ecological History*. Armante, NY: M.E. Sharpe, 1994.

Crumley, Carole L., ed. *Historical Ecology: Cultural Knowledge and Changing Landscapes*. Seattle: University of Washington Press, 1993.

Deléage, Jean-Paul. *Histoire de l'écologie: une science de l'homme et de la nature*. Paris: La Découverte, 1991.

Diamond, Irene, and Gloria Orenstein, eds. *Reweaving the World: The Emergence of Ecofeminism*. San Francisco: Sierra Club Books, 1990.

Drouin, Jean-Marc. *Réinventer la Nature: l'écologie et son histoire*. Paris: Desclée de Brouwer, 1991.

Dunlap, Thomas R. *Saving America's Wildlife*. Princeton, NJ: Princeton University Press, 1988.

Elbers, Joan A. *Changing Wilderness Values, 1930–1980: An Annotated Bibliography*. New York: Greenwood Press, 1991.

Flader, Susan L. *Thinking Like a Mountain: Aldo Leopold and the Evolution of an Ecological Attitude toward Deer, Wolves, and Forests*. Columbia: University of Missouri Press, 1974.

Gaard, Greta, ed. *Ecofeminism: Women, Animals, Nature*. Philadelphia: Temple University Press, 1993.

Galley, Frank B. *A History of the Ecosystem Concept in Ecology: More than a Sum of the Parts*. New Haven, CT: Yale University Press, 1993.

Hays, Samuel P. *Beauty, Health and Permanence: Environmental Politics in the United States, 1955–1985*. New York: Cambridge University Press, 1987.

————. *Conservation and the Gospel of Efficiency: The Progressive Conservation Movement, 1890–1920*. Cambridge: Harvard University Press, 1959.

Jacobson, Judith E., and John Firor, eds. *Human Impact on the Environment*. Boulder, CO: Westview Press, 1992.

Lewis, Martin W. *Green Delusions: An Environmentalist Critique of Radical Environmentalism*. Durham, NC: Duke University Press, 1992.

Mannion, Antoinette M. *Global Environmental Change: A Natural and Cultural Environmental History*. New York: Wiley and Sons, 1991.

Mackenzie, Suzanne. *Visible Histories: Women and Environments in a Post-War British City*. Montreal: McGill-Queen's University Press, 1989.

Martin, Calvin. *Keepers of the Game: Indian-Animal Relationships in the Fur Trade*. Berkeley: University of California Press, 1978.

McEvoy, Arthur F. *The Fisherman's Problem: Ecology and Law in the California Fisheries, 1850–1980*. New York: Cambridge University Press, 1986.

Merchant, Carolyn. *The Death of Nature: Women, Ecology, and the Scientific Revolution*. New York: Harper and Row, 1989.

————. *Ecological Revolutions: Nature, Gender, and Science in New England*. Chapel Hill: University of North Carolina Press, 1989.

————, ed. *Problems in American Environmental History*. Lexington, MA: D.C. Heath, 1993.

————. *Radical Ecology: The Search for a Livable World*. New York: Routledge, 1992.

Mighetto, Lisa. *Wild Animals and American Environmental Ethics*. Tucson: University of Arizona Press, 1991.

Nash, Roderick. *The Rights of Nature: A History of Environmental Ethics*. Madison: University of Wisconsin Press, 1989.

————. *Wilderness and the American Mind*. New Haven, CT: Yale University Press, 1968.

Pepper, David. *The Roots of Modern Environmentalism*. London: Croom Helm, 1984.

Plant, Judith, ed. *Healing the Wounds: The Promise of Ecofeminism*. Philadelphia: New Society Publishers, 1989.

Ponting, Clive. *A Green History of the World: The Environment and the Collapse of Great Civilizations*. New York: St Martin's Press, 1992.

Primavesi, Anne. *From Apocalypse to Genesis: Ecology, Feminism and Christianity*. Minneapolis: Fortress Press, 1991.

Pyne, Stephen. *Fire in America: A Cultural History of Wildland and Rural Fire.* Princeton, NJ: Princeton University Press, 1982.

Scarpino, Philip V. *Great River: An Environmental History of the Upper Mississippi, 1890–1950.* Columbia: University of Missouri Press, 1985.

Seager, Joni. *Earth Follies: Coming to Feminist Terms with the Global Environmental Crisis.* New York: Routledge, 1993.

Simmons, I.G. *Changing the Face of the Earth: Culture, Environment, History.* New York: Blackwell, 1989.

———. *Environmental History: A Concise Introduction.* Oxford: Blackwell, 1993.

Thomas, Keith. *Man and the Natural World: A History of the Modern Sensibility.* New York: Pantheon Books, 1983.

Tober, James A. *Who Owns the Wildlife? The Political Conservation of Nineteenth Century America.* Westport, CT: Greenwood Press, 1981.

Vecsey, Christopher, and Robert W. Venables, eds. *American Indian Environments: Ecological Issues in Native American History.* Syracuse, NY: Syracuse University Press, 1980.

Weiner, Douglas. *Models of Nature: Conservation and Cultural Revolution in Soviet Russia.* Bloomington: Indiana University Press, 1988.

White, Richard. *Land Use, Environment, and Social Change: The Shaping of Island County, Washington.* Seattle: University of Washington Press, 1980.

———. *The Roots of Dependency: Subsistence, Environment and Social Change among the Choctaws, Pawnees, and Navahos.* Lincoln: University of Nebraska Press, 1983.

Worster, Donald, ed. *The Ends of the Earth: Perspectives on Modern Environmental History.* New York: Cambridge University Press, 1988.

———. *Nature's Economy: A History of Ecological Ideas.* 2nd ed. New York: Cambridge University Press, 1994.

———. *Rivers of Empire: Water, Aridity and the Growth of the American West.* New York: Pantheon, 1985.

———. *Under Western Skies: Nature and the History of the American West.* New York: Oxford University Press, 1992.

GENERAL CANADIAN WORKS

Abel, Kerry, and Jean Friesen, eds. *Aboriginal Resource Use in Canada: Historical and Legal Aspects.* Winnipeg: University of Manitoba Press, 1991.

Bartlett, Richard H. *Aboriginal Water Rights in Canada: A Study of Aboriginal Title to Water and Indian Water Rights.* Calgary: Canadian Institute of Resources Law, 1988.

Beavis, Mary Ann, ed. *Environmental Stewardship: History, Theory and Practice: Workshop Proceedings, March 11–23, 1994.* Occasional Paper 32. Winnipeg: Institute of Urban Studies, 1994.

Bella, Leslie. *Parks for Profit.* Montreal: Harvest House, 1987.

Cook, Ramsay. "Landscape Painting and National Sentiment in Canada." *Historical Reflections* 1, 2 (1974): 263–83.

Cox, Bruce, ed. *Cultural Ecology: Readings on the Canadian Indians and Eskimos.* Toronto: McClelland & Stewart, 1973.

Dagg, Anne Innis. *Canadian Wildlife and Man.* Toronto: McClelland & Stewart, 1974.

Franks, C.E.S. "White Water Canoeing: An Aspect of Canadian Socio-Economic History." *Queen's Quarterly* 82, 2 (Summer 1975): 175–88.

Gossage, Peter. *Water in Canadian History: An Overview.* Inquiry on Federal Water Policy. Research paper no. 11. Ottawa: Environment Canada, 1985.

Harris, Cole. "The Myth of the Land in Canadian Nationalism." In *Nationalism in Canada.* Ed. Peter Russell. Toronto: McGraw-Hill, 1966.

Innis, Harold A. *The Cod Fisheries: The History of an International Economy.* Toronto: University of Toronto Press, 1954.

———. *The Fur Trade in Canada: An Introduction to Canadian Economic History.* New Haven: Yale University Press, 1930.

Judd, Richard W. "Policy and Ecology in Forest History." *Acadiensis* 23, 1 (Autumn 1993): 188–93.

Kline, Marcia B. *Beyond the Land Itself: Views of Nature in Canada and the United States.* Cambridge: Harvard University Press, 1970.

Lambert, R.S., with P. Pross. *Renewing Nature's Wealth: A Centennial History of the Public Management of Lands, Forests and Wildlife in Ontario, 1763–1967.* Toronto: Ontario Department of Lands and Forests, 1967.

Lothian, W.F. *A History of Canada's National Parks.* 4 vols. Ottawa: Parks Canada, 1976– .

Morantz, Toby. "Historical Perspectives on Family Hunting Territories in Eastern James Bay." *Anthropologica* 18, 1–2 (1986): 65–91.

Matthews, John. "Literature and Environment: Inheritance and Adaptation— The Canadian Experience." In *Commonwealth Literature: Unity and Diversity in a Common Culture.* Ed. John Press. London: Heinemann Educational Books, 1964.

Mies, Maria, and Vandana Shiva. *Ecofeminism.* Halifax: Fernwood Publications, 1993.

Miller, D.H., and J.O. Steffen. *The Frontier: Comparative Studies.* Norman: University of Oklahoma Press, 1977.

Mowat, Farley. *Sea of Slaughter.* Toronto: McClelland & Stewart, 1984.

Murphy, Peter. *History of Forest and Prairie Fire Control Policy in Alberta.* Edmonton: Alberta Energy and Natural Resources, 1985.

Nelson, J.G., ed. *Canadian Parks in Perspective.* Montreal: Harvest House, 1970.

Spry, Irene M. "The Tragedy of the Loss of the Commons in Western Canada." In *As Long as the Sun Shines and Water Flows.* Ed. Ian Getty and Antoine S. Lussier. Nakoda Institute occasional paper no. 1. Vancouver: University of British Columbia Press, 1983.

Taylor, C. James. *Negotiating the Past: the Making of Canada's National Historic Parks and Sites.* Montreal: McGill-Queen's University Press, 1990.

Thorpe, F.J. *Resources for Tomorrow Conference: Background Papers.* Ottawa: Queen's Printer, 1961.

Turner, Robert D., and William Rees. "A Comparative Study of Parks Policy in Canada and the United States." *Nature Canada* 2, 1 (Jan.–March 1973): 31–36.

Lorimer, Rowland, Michael M'Gonigle, Jean-Pierre Reveret, and Sally Ross, eds. *To See Ourselves/To Save Ourselves: Ecology and Culture in Canada.* Proceedings of the Annual Conference of the Association for Canadian Studies, 31 May–1 June 1990. Montreal: ACS, 1991.

Wynn, Graeme. "New Views of the Great Forest." *The Canadian Geographer* 34, 2 (1990): 175–85.

Zaslow, Morris. *Reading the Rocks: The Story of the Geological Survey of Canada, 1842–1972.* Ottawa: Macmillan, 1975.

BEFORE THE LATE-NINETEENTH CENTURY

Berger, Carl. *Science, God and Nature in Victorian Canada.* Toronto: University of Toronto Press, 1982.

Clermont, Norman. "Le contrat avec les animaux: Bestiaire sélectif des Indiens nomades du Québec au moment du contact." *Recherches amérindiennes au Québec* 10, 1–2 (1980): 91–109.

Crowley, Terry. "Heredity and Environmentalism in the History of French Colonialization." *Acadiensis* 19, 1 (Fall 1989): 169–79.

Dickason, Olive Patricia. "'For Every Plant There is a Use': The Botanical World of Mexica and Iroquoians." In *Aboriginal Resource Use in Canada: Historical and Legal Aspects.* Ed. Kerry Abel and Jean Friesen. Winnipeg: University of Manitoba Press, 1991.

Hammond, Lorne. "Marketing Wildlife: The Hudson's Bay Company and the Pacific Northwest, 1821–1849." *Forest and Conservation History* 37 (Jan. 1993): 14–25.

Jasen, Patricia. "Romanticism, Modernity, and the Evolution of Tourism on the Niagara Frontier, 1790–1850." *Canadian Historical Review* 72, 3 (Sept. 1991): 283–318.

McLaren, John P.S. "The Tribulations of Antoine Ratté: A Case Study of the Environmental Regulation of the Canadian Lumbering Industry in the Nineteenth Century." *University of New Brunswick Law Journal* (1984): 203–60.

Pielou, E.C. *After the Ice Age: The Return of Life to Glaciated North America.* Chicago: University of Chicago Press, 1991.

Ray, Arthur J. "Some Conservation Schemes of the Hudson's Bay Company, 1821–1850: An Examination of the Problems of Resource Management in the Fur Trade." *Journal of Historical Geography* 1, 1 (Jan. 1975): 49–68.

Rothenberg, Diane. "Erosion of Power: An Economic Basis for the Selective Conservatism of Seneca Women in the Nineteenth Century." *Western Canadian Journal of Anthropology* 6, 3 (1976): 106–22.

Smith, Allan. "Farms, Forests and Cities: The Image of the Land and the Rise of the Metropolis in Ontario, 1860–1914." In *Old Ontario: Essays in Honour of J.M.S. Careless.* Ed. David Keane and Colin Read. Toronto: Dundurn Press, 1990.

Theberge, Elaine. "The Untrodden Earth: Early Nature Writing in Canada." *Canadian Geographer* 3, 2 (1974): 30–36.

Wolfe, Roy I. "The Summer Resorts of Ontario in the Nineteenth Century." *Ontario History* 54 (Sept. 1962): 149–60.

Wynn, Graeme. *Timber Colony: A Historical Geography of Early Nineteenth Century New Brunswick.* Toronto: University of Toronto Press, 1981.

Zeller, Suzanne. *Inventing Canada: Early Victorian Science and the Idea of a Transcontinental Nation.* Toronto: University of Toronto Press, 1987.

LATE NINETEENTH TO MID-TWENTIETH CENTURY

Benidickson, Jamie. "Private Rights and Public Purposes in the Lakes, Rivers, and Streams of Ontario, 1870–1930." In *Essays in the History of Canadian Law.* Vol. 2. Ed. David Flaherty. Toronto: Published for the Osgoode Society by University of Toronto Press, 1983.

Brown, Robert Craig. "The Doctrine of Usefulness: Natural Resource and National Park Policy in Canada, 1887–1914." In *Canadian Parks in Perspective.* Ed. J.G. Nelson. Montreal: Harvest House, 1970.

Burgar, R.J. "Forest Land-Use Evolution in Ontario's Upper Great Lakes Basin." In *The Great Lakes Forest: An Environmental and Social History.* Ed. Susan L. Flader. Minneapolis: University of Minnesota Press, 1983.

Coates, Ken. "The Sinews of Their Lives: Native Access to Resources in the Yukon, 1890 to 1950." In *Aboriginal Resource Use in Canada: Historical and Legal Aspects.* Ed. Kerry Abel and Jean Friesen. Winnipeg: University of Manitoba Press, 1991.

Dewar, C. "Technology and the Pastoral Ideal in Frederick Philip Grove." *Journal of Canadian Studies* 8, 1 (1973): 28–32.

Dunlap, Thomas R. "Ecology, Nature, and Canadian National Park Policy: Wolves, Elk, and Bison as a Case Study." In *To See Ourselves/To Save Ourselves: Ecology and Culture in Canada.* Ed. Rowland Lorimer, Michael M'Gonigle, Jean-Pierre Reveret, and Sally Ross. Proceedings of the Annual Conference of the Association for Canadian Studies, 31 May–1 June 1990. Montreal: ACS, 1991.

Ferguson, Barry. *Athabasca Oil Sands: Northern Resource Exploitation, 1875–1951.* Edmonton: Alberta Culture/Canadian Plains Research Center, 1985.

Foster, Janet. *Working for Wildlife: The Beginning of Preservation in Canada.* Toronto: University of Toronto Press, 1978.

Gammel, Irene. *Sexualizing Power in Naturalism: Theodore Dreiser and Frederick Philip Grove.* Calgary: University of Calgary Press, 1994.

Gertler, L.O., ed. *Planning the Canadian Environment.* Montreal: Harvest House, 1968.

Gillis, Peter, and Thomas R. Roach. *Lost Initiatives: Canada's Forest Industries, Forest Policy and Forest Conservation.* Westport, CT: Greenwood Press, 1986.

Gillis, R.P. "The Ottawa Lumber Barons and the Conservation Movement, 1880–1914." *Journal of Canadian Studies* 9 (Feb. 1974): 14–31.

———. "Rivers of Sawdust: The Battle Over Industrial Pollution in Canada, 1865–1903." *Journal of Canadian Studies* 21, 1 (Spring 1986): 84–103.

Girard, Michel. *L'écologisme retrouvé: Essor et déclin de la Commission de la Conservation du Canada*. Ottawa: Les Presses de l'Université d'Ottawa, 1994.

Hansen, Lise C. "Treaty Fishing Rights and the Development of Fisheries Legislation in Ontario: A Primer." *Native Studies Review* 7, 1 (1991): 1–21.

Hodgins, B.W., and J. Benidickson. "Resource Management Conflict in the Temagami Forest, 1898–1914." Canadian Historical Association *Historical Papers* (1978): 148–75.

Hodgins, B.W., J. Benidickson, and R.P. Gillis. "The Ontario and Quebec Experiments with Forest Reserves, 1883–1930." *Journal of Forest History* 26, 1 (Jan. 1982): 20–33.

Hubbard, Jennifer. "The Commission of Conservation and the Canadian Atlantic Fisheries." *Scientia Canadensis* 34 (Spring 1988): 22–52.

Linteau, Paul-André. "The Development and Beautification of an Industrial City: Maisonneuve, 1883–1918." In *Shaping the Urban Landscape: Aspects of the Canadian City-Building Process*. Ed. Gilbert A. Stelter and Alan F.J. Artibise. Ottawa: Carleton University Press, 1982.

Nedelsky, Jennifer. "Judicial Conservatism in an Age of Innovation: Comparative Perspectives on Canadian Nuisance Law, 1880–1930." In *Essays in the History of Canadian Law*. Vol. 1. Ed. David H. Flaherty. Toronto: Osgoode Society, 1981.

Nelles, H.V. *The Politics of Development: Forests, Mines and Hydro-Electric Development in Ontario, 1849–1941*. Toronto: University of Toronto Press, 1974.

Ray, Arthur. *The Canadian Fur Trade in the Industrial Age*. Toronto: University of Toronto Press, 1990.

Rees, R. "Images of the Prairie: Landscape Painting and Perception in the Western Interior of Canada." *Canadian Geographer* 20, 3 (1974): 259–78.

Sandberg, L. Anders. "Forest Policy in Nova Scotia: The Big Lease, Cape Breton Island, 1899–1960," *Acadiensis* 20, 2 (Spring 1991): 105–24.

Scace, R.C. "Western Canadian Antecedents to Northern Conservation Reserves." *Contact: Journal of Urban and Environmental Affairs* 8, 4 (1976): 3–29.

Simpson, Michael. "Thomas Adams in Canada, 1914–1930." *Urban History Review* 11, 2 (Oct. 1982): 1–16.

Smith, C. Ray, and David R. Witty. "Conservation, Resources and Environment: An Explanation and Critical Evaluation of the Commission of Conservation." *Plan Canada* 11, 1 (1970): 55–71.

Taylor, C.J. "Legislating Nature: The National Parks Act of 1930." In *To See Ourselves/To Save Ourselves: Ecology and Culture in Canada*. Ed. Rowland Lorimer, Michael M'Gonigle, Jean-Pierre Reveret, and Sally Ross. Proceedings of the Annual Conference of the Association for Canadian Studies, 31 May–1 June 1990. Montreal: ACS, 1991.

Van Nus, Walter. "The Fate of City Beautiful Thought in Canada, 1893–1930." In *The Canadian City*. Ed. Gilbert A. Stelter and Alan F.J. Artibise. Ottawa: Carleton University Press, 1984.

Waiser, W.A. *The Field Naturalist: John Macoun, The Geological Survey and Natural Sciences*. Toronto: University of Toronto Press, 1989.

RECENT CANADIAN ENVIRONMENTAL HISTORY

Berkes, Fikret. "Cooperation from the Perspective of Human Ecology." In *Common Property Resources: Ecology and Community-Based Sustainable Development*. London: Belhaven Press, 1989.

———. "The Intrinsic Difficulty of Predicting Impacts: Lessons from the James Bay Hydro Project." *Environmental Impact Assessment Review* 8, 3 (Jan. 1988): 201–20.

Bowden, Marie-Ann, and Fred Curtis. "Federal EIA in Canada: EARP as an Evolving Process." *Environmental Impact Assessment Review* 8, 1 (March 1988): 97–106.

Buchanan, Carrie. "Garbage Blues: Communities are Singing Them Nowadays." *Canadian Geographic* 108, 1 (1988): 30–39.

Carroll, John E. *Acid Rain: An Issue in Canadian-American Relations*. Toronto: C.D. Howe Institute, 1982.

———. *Environmental Diplomacy: An Examination and a Perspective of Canadian-United States Transboundary Environmental Regulations*. Ann Arbor: University of Michigan Press, 1983.

Cox, Bruce, ed. *Cultural Ecology: Readings on the Canadian Indians and Eskimos*. Toronto: McClelland & Stewart, 1973.

Creighton, Wilfrid. *Forestkeeping: A History of the Department of Lands and Forests in Nova Scotia, 1926–1969*. Halifax: Nova Scotia Department of Lands and Forests, 1988.

F.L.C. Reed and Associates. *Forest Management in Canada (Case Studies)*. Vol. 2. Ottawa: Forest Management Institute, 1978.

Franks, C.E.S. "White Water Canoeing: An Aspect of Canadian Socio-Economic History." *Queen's Quarterly* 82, 2 (Summer 1975): 175–88.

Freeman, Milton M.R. "Appeal to Tradition: Different Perspectives on Arctic Wildlife Management." In *Native Power: The Quest for Autonomy and Nationhood of Indigenous Peoples*. Ed. Jens Brosted et al. Bergen: Universitetsforlaget As, 1985.

———. "An Ecological Perspective on Man-Environment Research in the Hudson and James Bay Region." *Naturaliste canadien* 109 (1982): 955–63.

———, and Ludwig N. Carbyn, eds. *Traditional Knowledge and Renewable Resource Management in Northern Regions*. Edmonton: Boreal Institute for Northern Studies, 1988.

Friedman, James M., and Michael S. McMahon. *The Silent Alliance: Canadian Support for Acid Rain Controls in the United States and the Campaign for Additional Electricity Exports*. Chicago: Regnery Gateway, 1984.

Gagnon, Luc. *Échec des écologists? Bilan des décennies 70 et 80*. Laval, PQ: Éditions du Méridien, 1993.

Hocking, Brian. "Non-Central Governments and International Environmental Politics: Canada, the United States and Acid Rain." *British Journal of Canadian Studies* 6, 1 (1991): 172–202.

Hodgins, B.W., and J. Benidickson. *The Temagami Experience: Recreation, Resources and Aboriginal Rights in the Northern Ontario Wilderness*. Toronto: University of Toronto Press, 1989.

Hodgins, Bruce W., and M. Hobbs, eds. *Nastawgan: The Canadian North by Canoe and Snowshoe*. Toronto: Betelgeuse Books, 1985.

Hodgins, Bruce W., et al., eds. *Co-existence? Studies in Ontario-First Nations Relations*. Peterborough, ON: Trent University, 1992.

Hood, George N. *Against the Flow: Rafferty-Almeda and the Politics of the Environment*. Saskatoon: Fifth House Publishers, 1994.

Howard, Ross. *Poisons in Public: Case Studies of Environmental Pollution in Canada*. Toronto: Lorimer, 1980.

Hummel, Monte, ed. *Endangered Spaces*. Toronto: Key Porter Books, 1989.

Johnson, Murray. "And No Fish Swam: Acid Rain in Canada." *Queen's Quarterly* 88, 3 (Autumn 1981): 420–28.

Kershaw, Peter, ed. *Northern Environmental Disturbances*. Edmonton: Boreal Institute for Northern Studies, 1988.

Kidd, Joanna. "Pollution Problems in the '80s: How They Differ from those of the 1960s and 1970s." *Probe Post* 7 (Oct. 1984): 12–14.

Killan, Gerald. *Protected Places: A History of Ontario's Provincial Parks System*. Toronto: Dundurn Press, 1993.

Leiss, William. *Risk and Responsibility*. Montreal: McGill-Queen's University Press, 1994.

Munton, Don. "Conflict Over Common Property: Canada-U.S. Environmental Issues. " In *Canada Among Nations: A World of Conflict 1987*. Ed. Maureen Appel Molot and Brian W. Tomlin. Toronto: Lorimer, 1988.

———. "Dependence and Interdependence in Transboundary Environmental Relations." *International Journal* 36, 1 (1980–81): 139–84.

Nemetz, Peter N., ed. *Emerging Issues in Forest Policy*. Vancouver: University of British Columbia Press, 1992.

Ommer, Rosemary. "One Hundred Years of Fishery Crisis in Newfoundland." *Acadiensis* 26, 2 (Spring 1994): 5–20.

Prades, José A., Robert Tessier, and Jean-Guy Vaillancourt, eds. *Instituer le développement durable: Éthique de l'écodécision et sociologie de l'environnement*. Montreal: Fides, 1994.

———, eds. *Gestion de l'environnement: Éthique et société*. Montréal: Fides, 1994.

Prades, José A., Jean-Guy Vaillancourt, and Robert Tessier, eds. *Environnement et Développement: Questions Éthiques et problèmes socio-politiques*. Montreal: Fides, 1994.

Rabe, Barry. "Beyond the NIMBY Syndrome in Hazardous Waste Facility Siting: The Albertan Breakthrough and the Prospects for Cooperation in Canada and the United States." *Governance* 4 (April 1991): 184–206.

Ristoratore, Mario. "Siting Toxic Waste Disposal Facilities in Canada and the United States: Problems and Prospects." *Policy Studies Journal* 14, 1 (Sept. 1985): 140–48.

Sandberg, L. Anders, ed. *Trouble in the Woods: Forest Policy and Social Conflict in Nova Scotia and New Brunswick*. Fredericton: Acadiensis Press, 1992.

Scace, Robert C. *Banff: A Cultural and Historical Study of Land U[se] in a National Park Community*. Calgary: University of Calga[ry]

Steel, Brent S., and Dennis L. Soden. "Acid Rain in Canad[a] States: Attitudes of Citizens, Environmental Activists, [...] *Social Science Journal* 26, 1 (1989): 27–44.

Swainson, Neil A. *Conflict over the Columbia: The Canadia[n] Historic Treaty*. Montreal: McGill-Queen's University Pres[s]

Waldram, James B. *As Long as the Rivers Run: Hydroelectri[c] Native Communities in Western Canada*. Winnipeg: Univ[...] Press, 1988.

Wall, G., and J.S. Marsh, eds. *Recreational Land Use: Perspective[s] Canada*. Ottawa: Carleton University Press, 1982.

Wright, Henry A. *Fire Ecology: United States and Southern [...] John Wiley and Sons, 1982.

Date Due

RECENT CANADIAN ENVIRONMENTAL HISTORY

Berkes, Fikret. "Cooperation from the Perspective of Human Ecology." In *Common Property Resources: Ecology and Community-Based Sustainable Development*. London: Belhaven Press, 1989.

———. "The Intrinsic Difficulty of Predicting Impacts: Lessons from the James Bay Hydro Project." *Environmental Impact Assessment Review* 8, 3 (Jan. 1988): 201–20.

Bowden, Marie-Ann, and Fred Curtis. "Federal EIA in Canada: EARP as an Evolving Process." *Environmental Impact Assessment Review* 8, 1 (March 1988): 97–106.

Buchanan, Carrie. "Garbage Blues: Communities are Singing Them Nowadays." *Canadian Geographic* 108, 1 (1988): 30–39.

Carroll, John E. *Acid Rain: An Issue in Canadian-American Relations*. Toronto: C.D. Howe Institute, 1982.

———. *Environmental Diplomacy: An Examination and a Perspective of Canadian-United States Transboundary Environmental Regulations*. Ann Arbor: University of Michigan Press, 1983.

Cox, Bruce, ed. *Cultural Ecology: Readings on the Canadian Indians and Eskimos*. Toronto: McClelland & Stewart, 1973.

Creighton, Wilfrid. *Forestkeeping: A History of the Department of Lands and Forests in Nova Scotia, 1926–1969*. Halifax: Nova Scotia Department of Lands and Forests, 1988.

F.L.C. Reed and Associates. *Forest Management in Canada (Case Studies)*. Vol. 2. Ottawa: Forest Management Institute, 1978.

Franks, C.E.S. "White Water Canoeing: An Aspect of Canadian Socio-Economic History." *Queen's Quarterly* 82, 2 (Summer 1975): 175–88.

Freeman, Milton M.R. "Appeal to Tradition: Different Perspectives on Arctic Wildlife Management." In *Native Power: The Quest for Autonomy and Nationhood of Indigenous Peoples*. Ed. Jens Brosted et al. Bergen: Universitetsforlaget As, 1985.

———. "An Ecological Perspective on Man-Environment Research in the Hudson and James Bay Region." *Naturaliste canadien* 109 (1982): 955–63.

———, and Ludwig N. Carbyn, eds. *Traditional Knowledge and Renewable Resource Management in Northern Regions*. Edmonton: Boreal Institute for Northern Studies, 1988.

Friedman, James M., and Michael S. McMahon. *The Silent Alliance: Canadian Support for Acid Rain Controls in the United States and the Campaign for Additional Electricity Exports*. Chicago: Regnery Gateway, 1984.

Gagnon, Luc. *Échec des écologists? Bilan des décennies 70 et 80*. Laval, PQ: Éditions du Méridien, 1993.

Hocking, Brian. "Non-Central Governments and International Environmental Politics: Canada, the United States and Acid Rain." *British Journal of Canadian Studies* 6, 1 (1991): 172–202.

Hodgins, B.W., and J. Benidickson. *The Temagami Experience: Recreation, Resources and Aboriginal Rights in the Northern Ontario Wilderness*. Toronto: University of Toronto Press, 1989.

Hodgins, Bruce W., and M. Hobbs, eds. *Nastawgan: The Canadian North by Canoe and Snowshoe*. Toronto: Betelgeuse Books, 1985.

Hodgins, Bruce W., et al., eds. *Co-existence? Studies in Ontario-First Nations Relations*. Peterborough, ON: Trent University, 1992.

Hood, George N. *Against the Flow: Rafferty-Almeda and the Politics of the Environment*. Saskatoon: Fifth House Publishers, 1994.

Howard, Ross. *Poisons in Public: Case Studies of Environmental Pollution in Canada*. Toronto: Lorimer, 1980.

Hummel, Monte, ed. *Endangered Spaces*. Toronto: Key Porter Books, 1989.

Johnson, Murray. "And No Fish Swam: Acid Rain in Canada." *Queen's Quarterly* 88, 3 (Autumn 1981): 420–28.

Kershaw, Peter, ed. *Northern Environmental Disturbances*. Edmonton: Boreal Institute for Northern Studies, 1988.

Kidd, Joanna. "Pollution Problems in the '80s: How They Differ from those of the 1960s and 1970s." *Probe Post* 7 (Oct. 1984): 12–14.

Killan, Gerald. *Protected Places: A History of Ontario's Provincial Parks System*. Toronto: Dundurn Press, 1993.

Leiss, William. *Risk and Responsibility*. Montreal: McGill-Queen's University Press, 1994.

Munton, Don. "Conflict Over Common Property: Canada-U.S. Environmental Issues. " In *Canada Among Nations: A World of Conflict 1987*. Ed. Maureen Appel Molot and Brian W. Tomlin. Toronto: Lorimer, 1988.

———. "Dependence and Interdependence in Transboundary Environmental Relations." *International Journal* 36, 1 (1980–81): 139–84.

Nemetz, Peter N., ed. *Emerging Issues in Forest Policy*. Vancouver: University of British Columbia Press, 1992.

Ommer, Rosemary. "One Hundred Years of Fishery Crisis in Newfoundland." *Acadiensis* 26, 2 (Spring 1994): 5–20.

Prades, José A., Robert Tessier, and Jean-Guy Vaillancourt, eds. *Instituer le développement durable: Éthique de l'écodécision et sociologie de l'environnement*. Montreal: Fides, 1994.

———, eds. *Gestion de l'environnement: Éthique et société*. Montréal: Fides, 1994.

Prades, José A., Jean-Guy Vaillancourt, and Robert Tessier, eds. *Environnement et Développement: Questions Éthiques et problèmes socio-politiques*. Montreal: Fides, 1994.

Rabe, Barry. "Beyond the NIMBY Syndrome in Hazardous Waste Facility Siting: The Albertan Breakthrough and the Prospects for Cooperation in Canada and the United States." *Governance* 4 (April 1991): 184–206.

Ristoratore, Mario. "Siting Toxic Waste Disposal Facilities in Canada and the United States: Problems and Prospects." *Policy Studies Journal* 14, 1 (Sept. 1985): 140–48.

Sandberg, L. Anders, ed. *Trouble in the Woods: Forest Policy and Social Conflict in Nova Scotia and New Brunswick*. Fredericton: Acadiensis Press, 1992.

Scace, Robert C. *Banff: A Cultural and Historical Study of Land Use and Management in a National Park Community*. Calgary: University of Calgary Press, 1968.

Steel, Brent S., and Dennis L. Soden. "Acid Rain in Canada and the United States: Attitudes of Citizens, Environmental Activists, and Legislators." *Social Science Journal* 26, 1 (1989): 27–44.

Swainson, Neil A. *Conflict over the Columbia: The Canadian Background to an Historic Treaty*. Montreal: McGill-Queen's University Press, 1979.

Waldram, James B. *As Long as the Rivers Run: Hydroelectric Development and Native Communities in Western Canada*. Winnipeg: University of Manitoba Press, 1988.

Wall, G., and J.S. Marsh, eds. *Recreational Land Use: Perspectives on Its Evolution in Canada*. Ottawa: Carleton University Press, 1982.

Wright, Henry A. *Fire Ecology: United States and Southern Canada*. New York: John Wiley and Sons, 1982.